JUSTICE
59 Carter Lane
London EC4V 5AQ

Restorative Justice

The International Library of Essays in Law and Legal Theory
Second Series
Series Editor: Tom D. Campbell

Titles in the Series:

Freedom of Speech, Volumes I and II
Larry Alexander

Law and Legal Interpretation
Fernando Atria and D. Neil MacCormick

Privacy
Eric Barendt

Comparative Legal Cultures
John Bell

Contract Law, Volumes I and II
Brian Bix

Corporate Law
William W. Bratton

Law and Democracy
Tom Campbell and Adrienne Stone

Legal Positivism
Tom D. Campbell

Administrative Law
Peter Cane

International Trade Law
Ronald A. Cass and Michael S. Knoll

**Sociological Perspectives on Law,
Volumes I and II**
Roger Cotterrell

Intellectual Property
Peter Drahos

Cyberlaw
Brian Fitzgerald

Family, State and Law, Volumes I and II
Michael D. Freeman

Natural Law
Robert P. George

**The Creation and Interpretation of
Commercial Law**
Clayton P. Gillette

Competition Law
Rosa Greaves

Chinese Law and Legal Theory
Perry Keller

Constitutional Law
Ian D. Loveland

Human Rights
Robert McCorquodale

Anti-Discrimination Law
Christopher McCrudden

Medical Law and Ethics
Sheila McLean

Mediation
Carrie Menkel-Meadow

Environmental Law
Peter S. Menell

Criminal Law
Thomas Morawetz

Law and Language
Thomas Morawetz

Law and Anthropology
Martha Mundy

Gender and Justice
Ngaire Naffine

Seminal Issues in Mental Health Law
Jill Peay

Law and Economics
Eric A. Posner

Japanese Law
J. Mark Ramseyer

Restorative Justice
Declan Roche

Constitutional Theory
Wojciech Sadurski

Justice
Wojciech Sadurski

The Rule of Law
Frederick Schauer

Regulation
Colin Scott

War Crimes Law, Volumes I and II
Gerry Simpson

Restitution
Lionel D. Smith

Freedom of Information
Robert G. Vaughn

Tort Law
Ernest J. Weinrib

Rights
Robin West

Restorative Justice

Edited by

Declan Roche

London School of Economics and Political Science, UK

ASHGATE
DARTMOUTH

Published by
Dartmouth Publishing Company
Ashgate Publishing Limited
Gower House
Croft Road
Aldershot
Hants GU11 3HR
England

Ashgate Publishing Company
Suite 420
101 Cherry Street
Burlington, VT 05401-4405
USA

Ashgate website: http://www.ashgate.com

British Library Cataloguing in Publication Data
Restorative Justice. – (International library of essays in
  law and legal theory. Second series)
  1. Restorative justice
  I. Roche, Declan
  364.6'8

Library of Congress Cataloging-in-Publication Data
Restorative justice / edited by Declan Roche.
        p. cm. — (The international library of essays in law and legal theory. Second series)
    Includes bibliographical references.
    ISBN 0-7546-2348-3 (alk. paper)
      1. Restorative justice. I. Roche, Declan. II. Series.

K5103.R47 2003
364.6'8—dc22

2003066447

ISBN 0 7546 2348 3

Printed in Great Britain by The Cromwell Press, Trowbridge, Wiltshire

Contents

PART IV   RACE AND GENDER PERSPECTIVES

PART V   SOCIAL JUSTICE PERSPECTIVES

Acknowledgements

The editor and publishers wish to thank the following for permission to use copyright material.

Australian Academic Press Pty. Ltd for the essays: Allison Morris and Gabrielle M. Maxwell (1993), 'Juvenile Justice in New Zealand: A New Paradigm', *Australian and New Zealand Journal of Criminology*, **26**, pp. 72–90; Chris Cunneen (1997), 'Community Conferencing and the Fiction of Indigenous Control', *Australian and New Zealand Journal of Criminology*, **30**, pp. 292–311.

Blackwell Publishing for the essays: Lucia Zedner (1994), 'Reparation and Retribution: Are They Reconcilable?', *Modern Law Review*, **57**, pp. 228–50. Copyright © 1994 Modern Law Review; Barbara Hudson (1998), 'Restorative Justice: The Challenge of Sexual and Racial Violence', *Journal of Law and Society*, **25**, pp. 237–56. Copyright © 1998 Blackwell Publishers; Kader Asmal (2000), 'Truth, Reconciliation and Justice: The South African Experience in Perspective', *Modern Law Review*, **63**, pp. 1–24. Copyright © 2000 Modern Law Review.

Elsevier Ltd for the essay: Richard L. Abel (1981), 'Conservative Conflict and the Reproduction of Capitalism: The Role of Informal Justice', *International Journal of the Sociology of Law*, **9**, pp. 245–67. Copyright © 1981 Academic Press Inc. (London) Ltd.

Emory Law Journal for the essay: Jennifer Gerarda Brown (1994), 'The Use of Mediation to Resolve Criminal Cases: A Procedural Critique', *Emory Law Journal*, **43**, pp. 1247–1309.

Oxford University Press for the essays: John Braithwaite and Stephen Mugford (1994), 'Conditions of Successful Reintegration Ceremonies: Dealing with Juvenile Offenders', *British Journal of Criminology*, **34**, pp. 139–71; Nils Christie (1977), 'Conflicts as Property', *British Journal of Criminology*, **17**, pp. 1–15; Andrew Ashworth (2002), 'Responsibilities, Rights and Restorative Justice', *British Journal of Criminology*, **42**, pp. 578–95; Harry Blagg (1997), 'A Just Measure of Shame? Aboriginal Youth and Conferencing in Australia', *British Journal of Criminology*, **37**, pp. 481–501.

Prison Fellowship International for the essay: Daniel W. Van Ness (1993), 'New Wine and Old Wineskins: Four Challenges of Restorative Justice', *Criminal Law Forum*, **4**, pp. 251–76. Copyright © 1993 Prison Fellowship.

Sage Publications, Inc. for the essay: Sharon Levrant, Francis T. Cullen, Betsy Fulton and John F. Wozniak (1999), 'Reconsidering Restorative Justice: The Corruption of Benevolence Revisited?', *Crime and Delinquency*, **45**, pp. 3–27. Copyright © 1999 Sage Publications, Inc.

Preface to the Second Series

The first series of the International Library of Essays in Law and Legal Theory has established itself as a major research resource with fifty-eight volumes of the most significant theoretical essays in contemporary legal studies. Each volume contains essays of central theoretical importance in its subject area and the series as a whole makes available an extensive range of valuable material of considerable interest to those involved in research, teaching and the study of law.

The rapid growth of theoretically interesting scholarly work in law has created a demand for a second series which includes more recent publications of note and earlier essays to which renewed attention is being given. It also affords the opportunity to extend the areas of law covered in the first series.

The new series follows the successful pattern of reproducing entire essays with the original page numbers as an aid to comprehensive research and accurate referencing. Editors have selected not only the most influential essays but also those which they consider to be of greatest continuing importance. The objective of the second series is to enlarge the scope of the library, include significant recent work and reflect a variety of editorial perspectives.

Each volume is edited by an expert in the specific area who makes the selection on the basis of the quality, influence and significance of the essays, taking care to include essays which are not readily available. Each volume contains a substantial introduction explaining the context and significance of the essays selected.

I am most grateful for the care which volume editors have taken in carrying out the complex task of selecting and presenting essays which meet the exacting criteria set for the series.

TOM CAMPBELL
Series Editor
Centre for Applied Philosophy and Public Ethics
Charles Sturt University

Introduction

In 1995 the South African Parliament passed legislation creating the Truth and Reconciliation Commission.[1] Over the following three years, the Commission toured the country, collecting testimony from victims of human rights violations, hearing individual amnesty applications, and compiling recommendations for addressing the aftermath of apartheid. According to the Commission's Chairperson, Desmond Tutu (1999), the decision to deal with the past in this way was not just the result of a political compromise between the new and the old rulers: by rejecting mass prosecutions in favour of a truth commission South Africa had chosen a restorative form of justice. Since then, the influence of restorative justice has also been felt in the less turbulent surroundings of the English criminal justice system: juvenile offenders are diverted from court to restorative justice-inspired youth offender panels; the English Court of Appeal has given its encouragement to the concept in dealing with adult offenders,[2] and David Blunkett, the Home Secretary, has announced that restorative justice principles are to guide a new set of criminal justice reforms ('Blunkett', 2003). Meanwhile, on the other side of the world, restorative justice programmes, bringing together victims and offenders, exist in every Australian state and territory; and in New Zealand, the site of the first nationwide restorative justice programme for juvenile offenders, increasing numbers of adult offenders are referred to restorative justice conferences. Elsewhere, in the United States, restorative justice programmes have appeared across the country, from Texas in the south to Vermont in the north, and across the border in Canada, the same concept, already supported at all levels of government, is promoted further through the holding of an annual 'Restorative Justice Week'.

As a conception of justice, restorative justice is a relevant newcomer. But notwithstanding the fact that it was virtually unheard of only 15 years ago, discussion of restorative justice has become ubiquitous in criminal justice debates, and 'restorative justice' programmes and practices can now be found in countless countries around the world. This flurry of activity has been accompanied, and partly inspired, by a large and growing literature, with books, articles, edited collections and reports by governments and NGOs all devoted to the topic. This volume presents a collection of some of the most important essays relating to restorative justice. Some warrant inclusion for their influence on the development of restorative justice thinking and practice, others for the disquieting concerns they raise about this new phenomenon, and yet others for their imaginative ideas about how restorative justice might develop. The best ones do a little of each.

First, a few words about how this collection is organized. The essays that follow are organized around a number of themes. The first of the five Parts comprises a selection of the essays and authors that were important in first articulating the origins, nature and promise of restorative justice. The essays in the subsequent Parts elaborate, and in some instances respond to, concerns about the ideas articulated in Part I. These concerns relate to whether restorative justice achieves its own goals (Part II, 'Restorative Perspectives'), whether restorative justice meets the demands of conventional criminal justice, such as consistency and proportionality in sentencing (Part III, 'Juridical Perspectives'), the quality of justice provided to different groups (Part IV, 'Race and Gender Perspectives'), and the extent to which restorative justice addresses the forms of disadvantage and inequality underlying criminal offending (Part V, 'Social Justice Perspectives').

Restorative Justice: Origins, Nature and Promises

To their critics, modern criminal justice systems are characterized by their impersonal, professional and bureaucratic nature. Or, as restorative justice supporters put it, they have neglected the personal dimension of crime. The restorative justice movement has resurrected the idea that crime, in the words of Howard Zehr and Harry Mika, 'is fundamentally a violation of people and interpersonal relationships' (Chapter 4, this volume, p. 77). For restorative justice supporters, the chief way of recognizing the personal dimension of crime is to involve victims, offenders and their respective families and friends in the process of dealing with its aftermath. When asked to explain and justify the participation of ordinary citizens, supporters often refer to Nils Christie's celebrated essay, 'Conflicts as Property' (see Chapter 2), in which he argues that criminal justice professionals have stolen conflicts from local communities, their rightful owners. Among supporters, Christie's polemical claim has been elevated to the status of an article of faith, his closing words something of a creed: 'Let us re-establish the credibility of encounters between critical human beings: low-paid, highly regarded, but with no extra power – outside the weight of their good ideas. That is as it ought to be' (p. 50).

The precise extent of victims' and offenders' involvement in restorative justice processes varies considerably. In some processes – such as in the South African Truth and Reconciliation Commission – their involvement is limited to the opportunity to share their experiences, but more commonly it also encompasses the additional power to participate in decisions about an offender's fate. Indeed, an early popular definition defined restorative justice as a process that brings together all the parties affected by an incident of wrongdoing to decide how to deal with the aftermath of the incident.[3] But regardless of the exact model, all restorative justice processes, supporters say, allow the personal dimension of crime to be acknowledged. They accomplish this by giving victims the opportunity to ask offenders questions and relate stories about the harm they have suffered. As Iris Young puts it, storytelling can be an important bridge 'between the mute experience of being wrong and political arguments about justice' (Young, 2000, p. 72). Offenders and their families are also given an opportunity to explain what happened, and the background to criminal acts. Restorative justice supporters hope that this communicative encounter will break down victims' and offenders' stereotypes of each other: offenders find it difficult to deny or justify to themselves the harm they have caused, and victims commonly discover that offenders are less fearsome than they had imagined.

But, of course, there is no guarantee that any informal process will be restorative. On the contrary, informal justice is frequently cruel, oppressive and sometimes violent. Aboriginal practices of payback spearing and banishment (Findlay, 2000), the forms of charivari, or rough music, once practised throughout Europe (Thompson, 1988), the American tradition of vigilantism (including the resilient practice of lynching) (Walker, 1980), South African township street committees and people's courts, and paramilitary punishment violence in Republican and Loyalist areas of Northern Ireland all illustrate the stigmatizing and brutal side of informal justice (McEvoy and Mika, 2002). Most of these processes lack two features that must be present for informal justice to be restorative: victims and offenders must both be given a say, and the focus of people's deliberations must be on repairing the harm suffered by victims and reintegrating offenders into their communities. (Though restorative justice supporters agree that reparation and reintegration are key elements of restorative justice, there is debate about what these things imply in practice. For some advocates, reparation and reintegration cannot occur unless the meetings include a sequence of apology, forgiveness and, finally, reconciliation. Others argue that acts of apology and forgiveness are pointless if coerced.)

Much of the experimentation within restorative justice has occurred in the field of juvenile justice, where programmes that allow offenders to escape formal conviction are consistent with the tradition of treating offenders leniently on account of their youthfulness and immaturity. However, restorative justice activity is not confined to juvenile justice. It is seen as having relevance across the spectrum of criminal offences, from relatively minor crimes through to the sorts of state crimes and crimes against humanity addressed by the South African TRC. In many of these programmes, participation is an alternative to formal prosecution, but in others it is part of formal sentencing or an adjunct to it. Restorative justice is also seen as having relevance to the resolution of conduct which is harmful but not necessarily criminal. In several countries restorative justice ideas have influenced policies and practices dealing with child welfare and school discipline, as well as those dealing with neighbourhood disputes.

At first, many of these developments occurred more or less in isolation from each other. Victims and offenders sat in family group conferences in New Zealand and in sentencing circles in Canada, while in the United States they sat in mediation sessions in some places and appeared before community sentencing panels in others. One of the main accomplishments of restorative justice scholars has been to carry ideas and learning from one place to another. This collection includes contributions from some of the most influential writers, including John Braithwaite, Kathy Daly, Howard Zehr, Dan Van Ness, Allison Morris and Gabrielle Maxwell.[4] Likewise, practitioners, including some reform-minded police officers and judges, have played a key role in the growth of restorative justice, touring the world speaking about their experiences and training individuals in how to establish programmes and convene meetings.[5] The restorative justice movement has also benefited from the concurrent growth in information technology; countless websites are devoted to the promotion and discussion of restorative justice.[6] Restorative justice, like the alternative dispute resolution movement in civil law (see Freeman, 1995), further benefits from a wide political audience, with liberals attracted to its compassionate and humanistic philosophy and conservatives attracted to the emphases on offender accountability, delivering justice to victims and devolving responsibility for dealing with crime to local communities. It also has the support of many non-government organizations and institutions, foremost among which are faith-based groups with a tradition in social activism, such as the Quakers, Mennonites and Prisoners Fellowship.

For all the sharing and propagation that has taken place, some areas of restorative justice activity have remained separate from others. In particular, the restorative justice movement has mainly been concerned with processes for dealing with street crime, such as mediation and conferencing, and has tended to overlook restorative justice processes used to deal with state crime, notably the South African Truth and Reconciliation Commission. This, however, is starting to change as a growing number of authors draw connections between these developments (see, for example, Llewellyn and Howse, 1999; Minow, 1998).

Restorative Perspectives

Many lofty claims are made for meetings between victims and offenders: that victims will feel better for confronting their offenders and having them make amends, that offenders will begin to understand the harmful consequences of their actions and will be reintegrated into law-abiding communities, and even that communities will be brought closer together through the process of exercising responsibility for dealing with crime. Furthermore, many supporters hold the firm conviction that meetings cannot fail to achieve these goals. However, the history of penal reform reminds us that good intentions do not guarantee progressive reforms, providing many examples of reformers' benign ideals resulting in repressive controls (see Ashworth, Chapter 9, this volume, p. 191). Even the modern prison – the contemporary embodiment of repressive criminal justice – was the creation of humane reformers in the latter part of the eighteenth and the early nineteenth centuries. In Chapter 6 Sharon Levrant and her co-authors offer other examples, reminding us that theories of determinate sentencing, now invoked by campaigners for severe sentences (offenders must receive their 'just deserts'), started life in the 1970s as a progressive project designed to eliminate the excesses of rehabilitation (itself another benevolent project) (p. 111).

So, does restorative justice work in the manner that its supporters claim? The essays in Part II scrutinize these claims. Take, for example, the question of voluntariness. As Dan Van Ness explains in Chapter 7, restorative justice advocates emphasize that participation in meetings must be voluntary (p. 161). Offenders and victims should be able to exercise the right to choose not to participate in a restorative process and, once in a restorative process, they must be able to freely negotiate to ensure that they are not dealt with unfairly. But these assumptions are problematic in several respects. For a start, any communicative process favours the smooth talkers over the tongue-tied; terrified victims and inarticulate young offenders alike are at the mercy of more confident and assertive participants. Studies based on observations of conferences, and subsequent interviews with participants, such as those by Richard Young and Carolyn Hoyle in England, Larry Sherman and Heather Strang in Australia and Alison Morris and Gabrielle Maxwell in New Zealand, draw our attention to the tendency of professionals to dominate citizens' deliberations (Hoyle and Young, 2000; Sherman *et al.*, 1998; Morris and Maxwell, Chapter 3, this volume). This collection includes one such essay, by Richard Young and Benjamin Goold, based on their study of conferencing by the Thames Valley police, conducted under the traditional English police power to caution offenders (see Chapter 8).

The relationship of restorative justice to punishment is another subject of keen debate. Many restorative justice supporters express opposition not to just imprisonment, but to the very concept of punishment itself. According to them, when offenders participate in a restorative justice meeting, they are not undergoing a form of punishment but something altogether different. A smaller group of writers, including Kathy Daly (Chapter 5) and Anthony Duff (2001, 2003), while sympathetic to restorative justice, question this characterization. They argue that restorative justice provides not an alternative to punishment, but an alternative form of punishment. In Chapter 5 of this volume, Kathy Daly supports this argument with references to South Australian conferences, where she observed participants pursue multiple aims, including administering punishment, seeking compensation and encouraging rehabilitation (p. 89).

Though the expression 'restorative justice' is new, the ideas behind it are not. In fact, according to its supporters, the restorative justice movement revives an ancient and universal approach to justice. As John Braithwaite puts it, 'restorative justice has been the dominant model of criminal justice throughout most of human history for all the world's peoples' (Braithwaite, 1999, p. 2). Kathy Daly suggests that such claims present a highly nostalgic and romantic view of the history of punishment practices. She argues that these views of history, just like the presentation of restorative justice as an alternative to punishment, may be intended less as accurate statements than as rhetorical claims designed to serve a particular purpose: 'advocates are trying to move an idea into the political and policy arena, and this may necessitate having to utilize a simple contrast of the good and the bad justice, along with an origin myth of how it all came to be' (p. 93).

I previously suggested some reasons for the popularity of restorative justice. A further reason is the universally appealing promise to rehabilitate offenders. Drawing on the theories developed in his popular book, *Crime, Shame and Reintegration*, John Braithwaite (with Stephen Mugford) argues that restorative justice ceremonies have the potential to rehabilitate offenders by allowing the simultaneous expression of disapproval for offenders' actions, and continued support for the offender as a person (Braithwaite and Mugford, 1994, p. 142). But Sharon Levrant *et al.* (Chapter 6) caution against thinking that this model will work for all offenders. Research on behavioural change shows that, in order to be effective, rehabilitation strategies must be tailored to the risks, needs and circumstances of individual offenders. In the context of restorative justice, this warning suggests that restorative justice meetings may be appropriate for some offenders, and some types of offences, but not all. Rigorously designed recidivism studies of restorative justice programmes remain rare, but those to date suggest that meetings can reduce re-offending rates for some types of crime, notably those where there is a direct victim who has suffered serious harm (Sherman *et al.*, 2000). When thinking about the potential of restorative justice to reduce re-offending, several authors (for example, Johnstone, 2002) draw attention to the inherent limits of what can be accomplished in a two-hour meeting. If meetings with victims are to aid persistent offenders' rehabilitation, it is important that when meetings identify problems (such as drug addiction, or educational problems), convenors are able to refer offenders to effective programmes to address these problems.

Juridical Perspectives

Whereas the essays in Part II provide a mainly internal critique of restorative justice, the essays in Part III subject restorative justice to an external critique: to what extent does restorative justice satisfy the requirements of a modern criminal justice system? For example, as Andrew Ashworth points out in Chapter 9, when judges sentence offenders they attempt to select a sentence that is both proportionate to the harm caused and consistent with sentences imposed in similar previous circumstances. To what extent are the principles of proportionality and consistency respected when an offender and victim privately negotiate about how the offender will make amends for the harm caused? Ashworth also queries how a decision-making process comprising parties personally affected by an incident can be squared with an offender's right to have decisions made by an impartial decision-maker (an element of the right to a fair trial). A related set of concerns relate to the apparent exclusion of the state from restorative justice meetings. In an ideal world, according to most restorative justice supporters, the state would play only a minor role in restorative justice programmes, simply assisting citizens in making decisions by providing them with information. This alarms many writers, who point out that in modern societies the state's assumption of responsibility for criminal justice provides a valuable guard against vigilantism and mob rule.

As Andrew Ashworth rightly observes, criticisms of this sort tend to leave restorative justice supporters baffled, as they possess an almost blind faith in restorative justice. But a number of thoughtful writers – some supporters, some critics – have now begun to consider whether the demands of a modern criminal justice system could be juggled with the informality and creativity of restorative justice meetings. One option is to keep restorative justice completely separate from the criminal justice system. This is the approach favoured by Jennifer Brown (Chapter 10) who says that mediation should be decoupled from the established criminal justice system and provided simply as a therapeutic device for interested victims and offenders.

Most writers, however, suggest a different approach in which there is some form of partnership or mutual exchange (or what Richard Delgado, in Chapter 11, calls 'merging and borrowing') between restorative justice and conventional justice, in which restorative justice becomes part of the conventional criminal justice system, or in which meetings adhere to some of the principles and requirements of conventional criminal justice. The essays in Part III contain suggestions for how this could happen. In Chapter 12 Lucia Zedner suggests that restorative justice meetings could be opened to the public, in order to partly satisfy the need for public accountability (p. 302), while Andrew Ashworth considers the sorts of limit that could be used to constrain the agreements reached in restorative justice meetings (p. 186; also Cavadino and Dignan, 1997; Roche, 2003). As restorative justice continues to grow, the question of its relationship to formal justice promises to be one of the most pressing issues reformers will face (see Braithwaite, 2001; Duff, 2001, 2003; Roche, 2003; von Hirsch *et al.*, 2003; Cavadino and Dignan, 1997).

Race and Gender Perspectives

When family group conferencing was introduced in New Zealand in 1989, many writers were quick to claim that these restorative justice reforms revived traditional Maori methods of conflict resolution. Now, as I have mentioned, writers are wont to make the even more ambitious claim that restorative justice represents the justice not only of the Maori, but of *all* indigenous peoples. The subtext of such claims – sometimes the plain text – is that restorative justice may provide the solution to the overrepresentation of indigenous minorities within criminal justice systems, that, in essence, restorative justice and indigenous laws and customs make a neat fit. The essays by Harry Blagg and Chris Cunneen (Chapters 13 and 14) show that, unsurprisingly, the relationships between restorative justice and indigenous justice, and restorative justice programmes and indigenous communities are much more complicated than these sweeping claims suggest.

Looking first at New Zealand family group conferencing, it considerably distorts Maori justice to suggest that family group conferencing replicates Maori justice. The New Zealand reforms incorporated many of the features of traditional Maori justice, but also contain elements quite alien to Maori practices (Maxwell and Morris, 1993, p. 4). It is similarly problematic to suggest a close fit between restorative justice and the practices of other indigenous cultures.

For example, as Harry Blagg explains, ceremony in Australian aboriginal culture, 'involves an emphasis not on place as much as on movement, the ritual passages along the "song lines" and dreaming tracks, replenishing their links with kin groups, sacred sites and "country", settling for a time on traditional campsites and camp fires' (p. 321). Blagg further suggests that the tendency to oversimplify and misrepresent the complexity and diversity of indigenous life is a common technique for containing and appropriating unfamiliar cultures (p. 314). In response to these criticisms, some restorative justice supporters concede that restorative justice programmes do not replicate indigenous methods of justice, but contend that they nevertheless provide a format which is flexible enough to accommodate rituals and procedures that are culturally meaningful to participants, whether they be European, African or Aboriginal (Braithwaite, 1997, p. 504).

Chris Cunneen draws attention to other factors, such as communicative difficulties, which may make conferencing poorly suited to Aboriginal offenders. Many people, especially young people with limited education and confidence, find it difficult to communicate with strangers in unfamiliar surroundings, but Aborigines are susceptible to an additional difficulty. Australian linguists and anthropologists observe 'the very common Aboriginal conversation pattern of agreeing with whatever is being asked, even if the speaker does not understand the question' (Eades, 1994, p. 244). This pattern has been described as a 'strategy of accommodation (that Aboriginal people have developed) to protect themselves in their interaction with Anglo-Australians. Aborigines have found that the easiest method to deal with white people is to agree with whatever it is that the Anglo-Australians want and then to continue on with their own business' (Liberman, 1981, pp. 248–49). There is also an unfortunate irony in the identification of restorative justice with indigenous justice, given the exclusion of indigenous offenders from some restorative justice programmes. Ethnic minorities are less likely to benefit in the exercise of police discretion than other ethnic groups, and Chris Cunneen argues that 'this central feature in the relationship between Indigenous young people and juvenile justice system' is pertinent to restorative justice programmes, pointing to low referral rates of Aborigines to programmes in Western and South Australia (p. 340).

Another of the supposed virtues of restorative justice is its compatibility with the ethics of care articulated by Carol Gilligan (1993) and other feminist writers. As with the claims about the indigenous pedigree of restorative justice, these claims are highly problematic. In particular, many writers express concerns about the appropriateness of restorative justice for dealing with domestic violence against women. Two of the assumptions underpinning restorative justice are that victims will be able to negotiate a satisfactory response to acts of violence and that, in restorative justice meetings, community norms will be invoked to express disapproval for offending acts. Both assumptions are questioned in relation to family violence. In relation to the first, Stephen Hooper and Ruth Busch argue that a woman's experiences of victimization 'have in all likelihood led her to renounce or adapt her needs in an attempt to avoid repetitions of past violence' (Chapter 15, this volume, p. 360). With regard to the second assumption, scepticism surrounds any intervention that relies on the mobilization of community norms when those norms may not necessarily condemn the use of violence by men against their wives or partners. Hooper and Busch point out that even mediators themselves may not be immune from 'minimising, trivialising and victim-blaming attitudes' (p. 362). In essence, the concern about domestic violence, as Barbara Hudson puts it in Chapter 16 (p. 394), is that restorative processes could reproduce and reinforce the imbalance of power of the crime relationship.

Restorative justice supporters have not been silent on these issues. John Braithwaite and Kathy Daly respond that conferences do have a valuable role to play in responding to domestic violence. (They do not suggest, though, that restorative justice provides a comprehensive solution, also advocating imprisonment as a last option for recalcitrant offenders.) They acknowledge that misogynistic voices may be heard in conferences, but argue that a conference provides a valuable opportunity to challenge these attitudes by requiring men to listen to women and their male allies (Braithwaite and Daly, 1994, p. 208).[7] This is one of the many claims that bring the role of the 'community' in restorative justice into focus. All versions of restorative justice, as Hudson puts it, 'envisage some sort of "community" representation – to arbitrate, to mobilize resources, to express disapproval, to readmit' (p. 400). Conference organizers face a difficult task in attempting to find family members, friends and other people who can play these multiple roles in restorative justice meetings.

Social Justice Perspectives

Many of the criticisms of restorative justice criticize programmes on their own terms (for example, do victims feel better for meeting their offenders?), or on those of the conventional criminal justice system (for example, are the outcomes agreed in restorative justice meetings proportionate to the harm done by an offender?). However, there is a third, more fundamental, basis on which restorative justice programmes are criticized. Criminal law – and law generally – works by individualizing responsibility and ignoring the social context in which individuals commit crime. Individuals are assumed to be equally free and rational, whereas in reality a disproportionate share of street crime offenders come from populations afflicted by mental illness, poverty and poor education (Zedner, Chapter 12, this volume, p. 307). Restorative justice, critics argue, shares this shortcoming, concentrating on individual disputes while blocking out the larger picture (Pavlich, 1996). These concerns are not new; they were also expressed with regard to experiments with informal justice in the 1970s and 1980s. Critics then suggested that informal justice may be worse than conventional criminal justice. For a start, informal programmes widen nets of social control, drawing into them those people who previously may have remained outside and subjecting others to more intensive treatment than they would have otherwise received. As Richard Abel puts it in Chapter 17, 'if informal institutions render law more accessible to the disadvantaged, they also render the disadvantaged more accessible to the state, and the latter consequence may be more significant' (p. 420). Informal programmes were also criticized for their tendency to quell the disharmony that may otherwise ferment into revolutionary movements. As Abel again puts it, 'informal institutions neutralize conflict by responding to grievances in ways that inhibit their transformation into serious challenges to the domination of state and capital' (1982, p. 280).

Such critiques, though useful for drawing attention to the limitations of informal justice, have also been criticized for their tendency to adopt an overly 'top-down', conspiratorial view of how and why informal justice programmes are established, neglecting the considerable demand in local communities for such programmes. Moreover, the restorative justice movement shows signs of attempting to move beyond the limits of traditional criminal justice (whether formal or informal). South Africa provides two examples of how restorative justice might play this broader role. One of these is the South African Truth and Reconciliation Commission. This volume includes one of the many essays written on the topic. In Chapter 18 Kader Asmal, the South African Minister for Education, explains the country's choice of approach to dealing with the perpetrators of crime during the apartheid era:

> It seems less important to me, personally and as a Minister of State, to see P.W. Botha behind bars than to see his ideological followers stalled in their quest to perpetuate his socio-economic legacies. In a system that killed far more infants through malnutrition and the unavailability of water than it killed adults with bullets and bombs, the drama to be had from placing militarists on trial might easily overshadow the equally real atrocity of the system itself. (p. 446)

Notwithstanding Asmal's claims, one of the chief criticisms of the SATRC was that it gave too much attention to the abstract concepts of healing and reconciliation and too little to improving the abysmal living conditions in South African townships. But in recent years, independently of the SATRC, many townships throughout South Africa have established community governance programmes influenced by restorative justice principles. These community peace programmes respond to particular grievances (in a fashion similar to some community restorative justice programmes) but also help develop community-building initiatives (such as funding the purchase of equipment for local preschools) (Roche, 2002). Many accounts of restorative justice emphasize its usefulness as a device for shaming offenders, and its resonance with indigenous methods of justice, but Clifford Shearing (Chapter 20), one of the architects of South Africa's community peace programmes, sees its potential and origins in a different light. The roots of restorative justice, he argues, are within the world of business, and its future-oriented, problem-solving approach to security and governance. He argues that, whilst the advocates of restorative justice do not tend to draw attention to its compatibility with the use of a risk-logic, the logic of restorative justice in fact fits easily with that of risk (p. 481).

John Braithwaite, one of the most prolific restorative justice authors, also makes suggestions for how restorative justice principles could be employed to lessen social injustice. In 'Youth Development Circles' (Chapter 19) he proposes translating the idea of restorative justice meetings from the criminal justice arena into that of educational development: 'The main difference is that the circle would be a permanent feature of the young person's life rather than an ad hoc group assembled to deal with a criminal offense' (p. 458). Circles would comprise core members – including parents, siblings, a buddy – who attended every circle, as well as casual members – including current teachers and girlfriends, professionals and people affected by the young person's actions. Braithwaite argues that this approach could be used to help tackle the whole range of problems young people encounter – including drug abuse, mental illness and unemployment – in the transition from school to work. Imaginative ideas such as this point a direction for restorative justice to transcend the traditional limits of criminal justice interventions.

Conclusion

This collection of essays only scrapes the surface of the available literature on restorative justice. What it attempts to do, however, is provide a selection which is representative of some of the best and most thought-provoking writing on restorative justice. Some of these essays have already been influential on the development of restorative justice practice; others, by raising, and attempting to address, important concerns, are likely to become so.

Notes

1   The Promotion of National Unity and Reconciliation Act (1995).
2   2003-04-14 *Regina* v. *Collins* (David) Judgement, 18 March 2003.
3   This definition comes from Marshall (1996, p. 37). This definition emerged when a restorative justice supporter, Paul McCold, brought together experts to see if they could, through an iterative process, reach consensus about the meaning of restorative justice. Ultimately this process did not produce consensus but it was agreed that Tony Marshall's definition offered the most acceptable working definition.
4   Had space permitted there are a number of other influential individuals whose work could have been included, including Gordon Bazemore, Gale Burford, Paul McCold, Mark Umbreit, Lode Walgrave and Elmar Weitekamp.
5   Prominent practitioners include John McDonald, Fred McElrea, David Moore, Terry O'Connell, Charles Pollard, Kay Pranis, Annie Roberts and Barry Stuart.
6   A good place to start when doing Internet research on restorative justice is http://www. restorativejustice.org/ which contains an excellent range of materials, as well as links to many other websites.
7   There is some tentative empirical support for these claims, from programmes in Newfoundland and the Navajo nation. See Burford and Pennell (1995) and Coker (1999).

References

Abel, Richard (1982), 'The Contradictions of Informal Justice', in Richard Abel (ed.), *The Politics of Informal Justice: Volume I, The American Experience*, New York: Academic Press.
'Blunkett Launches Meet-the-Victim Scheme' (2003), *The Guardian*, 22 July.
Braithwaite, John (1997), 'Conferencing and Plurality: Reply to Blagg', *British Journal of Criminology*, **37**(4), pp. 502–506.
Braithwaite, John (1999), 'Restorative Justice: Assessing Optimistic and Pessimistic Accounts', in Michael Tonry (ed.), *Crime and Punishment: A Review of Research*, Chicago: University of Chicago Press.
Braithwaite, John (2001), *Restorative Justice and Responsive Regulation*, Oxford: Oxford University Press.
Braithwaite, John and Daly, Kathleen (1994), 'Masculinities, Violence and Communitarian Control', in Tim Newburn and Elizabeth Stanko (eds), *Just Boys Doing Business*, London and New York: Routledge.
Braithwaite, John and Mugford, Stephen (1994), 'Conditions of Successful Reintegration Ceremonies: Dealing with Juvenile Offenders', *British Journal of Criminology*, **34**(2), pp. 139–71.
Burford, Gale and Pennell, Joan (1995), *Family Group Decision Making: New Roles for 'Old' Partners in Resolving Family Violence: Implementation Report Summary*, St John's, NF: Memorial University of Newfoundland, School of Social Work.
Cavadino, Michael and Dignan, James (1997), 'Reparation, Retribution and Rights', *International Review of Victimology*, **4**, pp. 233–53.
Coker, Donna (1999), 'Enhancing Autonomy for Battered Women: Lessons from Navajo Peacemaking', *UCLA Law Review*, **47**(1), pp. 1–111.
Dignan, James (1997), 'Reparation, Retribution and Rights', *International Review of Victimology*, **4**, pp. 233–53.
Duff, R.A. (2001), *Punishment, Communication, and Community*, New York: Oxford University Press.
Duff, R.A. (2003), 'Probation, Punishment and Restorative Justice: Should Altruism be Engaged in Punishment?', *The Howard Journal*, **42**(2), pp. 181–97.

Eades, Diana (1994), 'A Case of Communicative Clash: Aboriginal English and the Legal System', in John Gibbons (ed.), *Language and the Law*, New York: Longman.

Findlay, Mark (2000), 'Decolonising Restoration and Justice in Transitional Cultures', in Heather Strang and John Braithwaite (eds), *Restorative Justice: Philosophy to Practice*, Aldershot: Ashgate.

Freeman, Michael (ed.) (1995), 'Introduction', *Alternative Dispute Resolution*, Aldershot: Ashgate.

Gilligan, Carol (1993), *In a Different Voice: Psychological Theory and Women's Development*, Cambridge, MA: Harvard University Press.

Hoyle, Carolyn and Young, Richard (2002), *Proceed with Caution: An Evaluation of the Thames Valley Police Initiative in Restorative Cautioning*, York: York Publishing Services/Rowntree Foundation.

Johnstone, Gerry (2002), *Restorative Justice: Ideas, Values, Debates*, Cullompton: Willan Publishing.

Liberman, Kenneth (1981), 'Understanding Aborigines in Australian Courts of Law', *Human Organization*, **40**, pp. 247–55.

Llewellyn, Jennifer and Howse, Robert (1999), 'Institutions for Restorative Justice: The South African Truth and Reconciliation Commission', *University of Toronto Law Journal*, **49**, pp. 355–88.

McEvoy, Kieran and Mika, Harry (2002), 'Restorative Justice and the Critique of Informalism in Northern Ireland', *British Journal of Criminology*, **42**(3), pp. 534–62.

Marshall, Tony (1996), 'The Evolution of Restorative Justice in Britain', *European Journal on Criminal Policy*, **4**(4), pp. 21–43.

Maxwell, Gabrielle and Morris, Allison (1993), *Family, Victims and Culture: Youth Justice in New Zealand*, Wellington: Social Policy Agency and Institute of Criminology, Victoria University of Wellington.

Minow, Martha (1998), *Between Vengeance and Forgiveness: Facing History after Genocide and Mass Violence*, Boston, MA: Beacon Press.

Pavlich, George (1996), 'The Power of Community Mediation: Government and Formation of Self-Identity', *Law and Society Review*, **30**(4), pp. 707–33.

Roche, Declan (2002), 'Restorative Justice and the Regulatory State in South African Townships', *British Journal of Criminology*, **42**(3), pp. 514–33.

Roche, Declan (2003), *Accountability in Restorative Justice*, Oxford: Oxford University Press.

Roche, Declan (2003), 'Gluttons for Restorative Justice', *Economy and Society*, **32**(4), pp. 630–44.

Sherman, Lawrence, Strang, Heather, Barnes, Geoffrey, Braithwaite, John, Inkpen, Nova and Teh, Min-Mee (1998), *Experiments in Restorative Policing: A Progress Report on the Canberra Reintegrative Shaming Experiments (RISE)*, Canberra: Australian National University/Australian Federal Police.

Sherman, Lawrence, Strang, Heather and Woods, Dan (2002), *Recidivism Patterns in the Canberra Reintegrative Shaming Experiments (RISE)*, Canberra: http://www.aic.gov.au/rjustice/rise/recidivism/index.html.

Thompson, E.P. (1988), *Customs in Common*, London: Penguin Books.

Tutu, Desmond (1999), *No Future without Forgiveness*, London: Rider Books.

von Hirsch, Andrew, Ashworth, Andrew and Shearing, Clifford (2003). 'Specifying Aims and Limits for Restorative Justice: A "Making Amends" Model', in Andrew von Hirsch, Julian Robert, Anthony Bottoms, Kent Roach and Maria Schiff (eds), *Restorative Justice and Criminal Justice: Competing or Reconcilable Paradigms?*, Oxford: Hart Publishing.

Walker, Samuel (1980), *Popular Justice: A History of American Criminal Justice*, New York: Oxford University Press.

Young, Iris M. (2000), *Inclusion and Democracy*, Oxford: Oxford University Press.

Part I
Restorative Justice: Origins, Nature and Promises

[1]

CONDITIONS OF SUCCESSFUL REINTEGRATION CEREMONIES

Dealing with Juvenile Offenders

JOHN BRAITHWAITE and STEPHEN MUGFORD*

Shifting criminal justice practices away from stigmatization and toward reintegration is no small challenge. The innovation of community conferences in New Zealand and Australia has two structural features that are conducive to reintegrative shaming: (a) selection of the people who respect and care most about the offender as conference participants (conducing to reintegration); and (b) confrontation with victims (conducing to shaming). Observation of some failures and successes of these conferences in reintegrating both offenders and victims is used to hypothesize 14 conditions of successful reintegration ceremonies.

The spectre of failure haunts modern criminology and penology. Deep down many feel what some say openly—that 'nothing works': that despite decades of study and debate, we are no nearer deterrence than we ever were and/or that more 'humane' forms of treatment are mere masquerades concealing a descent into Kafaesque bureaucracy where offenders suffer a slow and silent suffocation of the soul. Worse still, we fear that even when something does work, it is seen to do so only in the eyes of certain professionals, while 'outside' the system ordinary citizens are left without a role or voice in the criminal justice process.

This paper takes a different view. Rejecting the pessimism that pervades discussions about crime and punishment, it offers an optimistic view of at least one area—the punishment of juvenile offenders. It argues that it is possible to develop practices that 'work'—both in the sense of reducing recidivism and reintegrating offenders into a wider web of community ties and support and, at the same time, in giving victims a 'voice' in a fashion that is both satisfying and also socially productive. Further, it links a theory (reintegrative shaming) and a practice (the reintegration ceremony) which explain how to understand and how to implement this success.

While there are elements that are quite distinctive about both the theory and practice of reintegrative shaming, there is also a great deal in common with the theory and practice of 'making amends' (Wright 1982); restorative justice (Cragg 1992; Galaway and Hudson 1990; Zehr 1990); reconciliation (Dignan 1992; Marshall 1985; Umbreit 1985); peacemaking (Pepinsky and Quinney 1991); redress (de Haan 1990) and feminist abolitionism (Meima 1990). We differ from abolitionists, however, in believing that it is right to shame certain kinds of conduct as criminal in certain contexts.

The rest of the paper has two sections. The second section outlines some fieldwork

* Division of Philosophy and Law, The Research School of Social Sciences, The Australian National University.
We would like to thank John McDonald, Gabrielle Maxwell, David Moore, Jane Mugford, Terry O'Connell, and Clifford Shearing for the stimulation and critique they provided in developing the ideas in this paper.

JOHN BRAITHWAITE AND STEPHEN MUGFORD

which we have undertaken to examine such ceremonies, makes a relatively brief series of arguments which connect the theory of reintegrative shaming to the seminal paper by Garfinkel on degradation ceremonies and outlines how the latter must be transformed to cover reintegration ceremonies. The major point of this section is a specification of the conditions for successful reintegration ceremonies. The third and longer section follows the logic of such ceremonies, illustrating each point with material derived from the fieldwork and offering comments about policy and implementation.

Background to the Argument: Reintegrative Shaming in Theory and Practice

The theory of reintegrative shaming (Braithwaite 1989, 1993) has been offered as a way of achieving two major aims. First, to recast criminological findings in a more coherent and productive fashion. Secondly, to offer a practical basis for a principled reform of criminal justice practices. Central to the endeavour is an understanding of the relationship between crime and social control which argues for the shaming of criminal *acts* and the subsequent reintegration of deviant *actors* once suitable redress and apology have been made. It is argued that societies that have low rates of common types of crime (such as Japan) rely more upon this type of social control, working hard at reforming the deviant through reconstructing his or her social ties. Conversely, high crime societies (such as the US) rely upon stigmatization, thus doing little to prevent cycles of re-offending.

This theory has clear practical implications and people involved in various reform programmes have drawn on it in various ways—sometimes as an inspiration for reform blueprints (see e.g., Howard and Purches 1992; Mugford and Mugford 1991, 1992; O'Connell and Moore 1992), often as a way to articulate what they are trying to achieve and give it a sharper focus. Some, such as the New Zealand Maoris, have comprehended and applied the principles of the theory for hundreds of years (Hazlehurst 1985). Where we have heard of or been involved in programmes, we have sought to carry out some limited fieldwork which would help us to understand both what is practically possible and how we might refine our ideas.

This paper utilizes such ongoing fieldwork, specifically observations of community conferences for 23 juvenile offenders in Auckland, New Zealand, and Wagga Wagga, Australia. In New Zealand, these conferences are called family group conferences. While there are differences between the approaches adopted in the two cities, both involve diverting young offenders from court and keeping them out of exclusionary juvenile institutions. Both programmes subscribe to the philosophy of reintegrative shaming as outlined above. Shame and shaming is commonly used in both programmes to describe what is going on; reintegration is commonly used in Wagga, while healing is more commonly used in Auckland for this aspect of the process. The approach in both cities involves assembling in a room the offender and supporters of the offender (usually the nuclear family, often aunts, uncles, grandparents, sometimes neighbours, counsellors, even a teacher or football coach) along with the victim of the crime (and supporters of the victim, usually from their nuclear family) under the supervision of a co-ordinator—a police sergeant in Wagga, a youth justice co-ordinator from the Department of Social Welfare in Auckland. Auckland conferences usually only have single offenders, but can have multiple victims in the room. Wagga conferences often bring together multiple offenders who were involved jointly in the same offences with

CONDITIONS OF SUCCESSFUL REINTEGRATION CEREMONIES

multiple victims. In the conferences we observed, the number of people in the room ranged from five to 30. More systematic data from New Zealand puts the average attendance at nine (Maxwell and Morris 1993: 74). At both sites, the offender(s) plays an important role in describing the nature of the offence(s). The psychological, social, and economic consequences of the offence—for victims, offenders, and others—are elicited in discussions guided by the co-ordinator. Disapproval, often emotional disapproval, is usually communicated by victims, and often by victim supporters and family members of the offender. At the same time, the professional who co-ordinates the conference strives to bring out support for and forgiveness towards the offender from participants in the conference.

A striking common feature of both locations is that the formal properties of the cautioning conference have come to take on a ceremonial or ritual character, based partly upon 'common sense', itself expanded and tempered by experiences of what does and does not seem to work well. With varying degrees of accomplishment, co-ordinators have developed procedures designed to ensure that the potential for shaming and reintegration of offenders is realized in practice. In so doing, they have effectively invented the reintegration ceremony, even if that is not what they would always call it. In this ceremony, identities are in a social crucible. The vision that an offender holds of himself as a 'tough guy' or that victims have of him as a 'mindless hooligan' are challenged, altered, and recreated (for example, as a 'good lad who has strayed into bad ways').

Viewing these events as a reintegration ceremony recalls the seminal contribution of Harold Garfinkel (1956) on 'Conditions of Successful Degradation Ceremonies'. Perhaps the same kind of social structures and socio-psychological processes he analyses in that paper are at work here, but in different combination and directed to different ends? Posing the problem that way has been a productive way for us to organize our views of reintegration ceremonies and so we choose to use the Garfinkel approach as a way of outlining this rather different set of events.

By degradation ceremonies, Garfinkel meant communicative work that names an actor as an 'outsider', that transforms an individual's total identity into an identity 'lower in the group's scheme of social types' (1956: 420). Most criminal trials are good examples of status degradation ceremonies and this view of them became a central idea in the sociology of deviance, especially among labelling theorists (see Becker 1963; Schur 1973). For Erikson (1962: 311), for example, this communicative work constitutes 'a sharp rite of transition at once moving him out of his normal position in society and transferring him into a distinctive deviant role'. Moreover, Erikson continues, an '. . . important feature of these ceremonies in our culture is that they are almost irreversible' (1962: 311).

Such a view, however, is simplistic, exaggerated, and overly deterministic (Braithwaite 1989). Most people who go into mental hospitals come out of them; many alcoholics give up drinking; most marijuana users stop being users at some point in their lives, usually permanently; most kids labelled as delinquents never go to jail as adults. Labelling theorists did useful empirical work, but their work was myopic, exclusively focused on 'front-end' processes that certify deviance. Above all, they envisaged individuals as having 'total identities'. We suggest that by employing instead the notion of multiple identities one can recast the interest in transformation ceremonies, asking questions as much about ceremonies to decertify deviance as to certify it.

JOHN BRAITHWAITE AND STEPHEN MUGFORD

While degradation ceremonies are about the sequence disapproval–degradation–exclusion, reintegration ceremonies are about the sequence disapproval–non-degradation–inclusion. In a reintegration ceremony, disapproval of a bad act is communicated while sustaining the identity of the actor as good. Shame is transmitted within a continuum of respect for the wrongdoer. Repair work is directed at ensuring that a deviant identity (one of the actor's multiple identities) does not become a master status trait that overwhelms other identities. Communicative work is directed at sustaining identities like daughter, student, promising footballer, in preference to creating 'master' identities like delinquent.

Considerable analytic and policy implications follow this refocusing from degradation to reintegration. Indeed, we suggest that the implication is a redesign of everything about contemporary criminal justice systems and everything about the labelling theory critique of those institutions. To achieve this, however, it is necessary to show where one must transcend earlier accounts. As a first step, we juxtapose in Table 1 Garfinkel's conditions of successful degradation ceremonies with our own conditions of successful ceremonies of reintegration. These latter were condensed from our observations and cast in a form that allows comparison and contrast. Eight of the conditions we specify for reintegration ceremonies involve presenting a deliberate twist on Garfinkel's conditions. The other six are based on observations and discussions and, we feel, address some of the theoretical neglects of the ethnomethodological tradition.

Reintegration Ceremonies in Practice

In this section, we outline each of the 14 conditions identified in Table 1. For each one, we provide a detailed discussion, drawing on our field work observations.

(1) The event, but not the perpetrator, is removed from the realm of its everyday character and is defined as irresponsible, wrong, a crime

Courtroom ceremonies tend to degradation rather than reintegration—that is, they remove both event *and* perpetrator from the everyday domain in just the way suggested by Garfinkel. This is because the production-line technocracy and discourse of legalism makes it easy for the offender to sustain psychological barriers against shame for acts that the court defines as wrongful. It is hard for a person who we do not know or respect, who speaks a strange legal language, who forces us into a relationship of feigned respect by making us stand when she walks into the room, to touch our soul. Thus event and perpetrator remain united. One casts out both or neither. So the denunciation of the judge may degrade the offender, but the process is so incomprehensible, such a blur, that all the judge usually accomplishes is some authoritative outcasting.

In contrast to formal courtrooms, community conferences in New Zealand and Wagga are held in less formal spaces. Conference co-ordinators purposively assemble actors with the best chance of persuading the offender of the irresponsibility of a criminal act. Close kin are prime candidates for commanding the respect that enables such persuasion, but with homeless or abused children the challenge is to discover who

142

CONDITIONS OF SUCCESSFUL REINTEGRATION CEREMONIES

TABLE 1

Conditions of successful degradation ceremonies	Conditions of successful reintegration ceremonies
1. Both event and perpetrator must be removed from the realm of their everyday character and be made to stand as 'out of the ordinary'.	1. The event, *but not the perpetrator*, is removed from the realm of its everyday character and is defined as irresponsible, wrong, a crime.
2. Both event and perpetrator must be placed within a scheme of preferences that shows the following properties: (a) The preferences must not be for event A over event B, but for event of *type* A over event of *type* B. The same typing must be accomplished for the perpetrator. Event and perpetrator must be defined as instances of a uniformity and must be treated as a uniformity throughout the work of the denunciation. (b) The witnesses must appreciate the characteristics of the typed person and event by referring the type to a dialectical counterpart. Ideally, the witnesses should not be able to contemplate the features of the denounced person without reference to the counter-conception, as the profanity of an occurrence or a desire or a character trait, for example, is clarified by the references it bears to its opposite, the sacred.	2. Event and perpetrator must be uncoupled rather than defined as instances of a profane uniformity. The self of the perpetrator is sustained as sacred rather than profane. This is accomplished by comprehending: (a) how essentially good people have a pluralistic self that accounts for their occasional lapse into profane acts; and (b) that the profane act of a perpetrator occurs in a social context for which many actors may bear some shared responsibility. Collective as well as individual shame must be brought into the open and confronted.
3. The denouncer must so identify himself to the witnesses that during the denunciation they regard him not as a private but as a publicly known person.	3. Co-ordinators must identify themselves with all private parties—perpetrators, their families, victims, witnesses—as well as being identified with the public interest in upholding the law.
4. The denouncer must make the dignity of the supra-personal values of the tribe salient and accessible to view, and his denunciation must be delivered in their name.	4. Denunciation must be both by and in the name of victims and in the name of supra-personal values enshrined in the law.
5. The denouncer must arrange to be invested with the right to speak in the name of these ultimate values. The success of the denunciation will be undermined if, for his authority to denounce, the denouncer invokes the personal interests that he may have acquired by virtue of the wrong done to him or someone else.	5. Non-authoritative actors (victims, offenders, offenders' families) must be empowered with process control. The power of actors normally authorized to issue denunciations on behalf of the public interest (e.g., judges) must be decentred.
6. The denouncer must get himself so defined by the witnesses that they locate him as a supporter of these values.	6. The perpetrator must be so defined by all the participants (particularly by the perpetrator himself) that he is located as a supporter of both the supra-personal values enshrined in the law and the private interests of victims.
7. Not only must the denouncer fix his distance from the person being denounced, but the witnesses must be made to exprience their distance from him also.	7. Distance between each participant and the other participants must be closed; empathy among all participants must be enhanced; opportunities must be provided for perpetrators and victims to show (unexpected) generosity toward each other.
8. Finally, the denounced person must be ritually separated from a place in the legitimate order, i.e., he must be defined as standing at a place opposed to it. He must be placed 'outside', he must be made 'strange'.	8. The separation of the denounced person must be terminated by rituals of inclusion that place him, even physically, inside rather than outside.
	9. The separation of the victim, any fear or shame of victims, must be terminated by rituals of reintegration.
	10. Means must be supplied to intervene against power imbalances that inhibit either shaming or reintegration, or both.
	11. Ceremony design must be flexible and culturally plural, so that participants exercise their process control constrained by only very broad procedural requirements.
	12. Reintegration agreements must be followed through to ensure that they are enacted.
	13. When a single reintegration ceremony fails, ceremony after ceremony must be scheduled, never giving up, until success is achieved.
	14. The ceremony must be justified by a politically resonant discourse.

JOHN BRAITHWAITE AND STEPHEN MUGFORD

the child does respect.[1] Perhaps there is an uncle who he feels sticks up for him, a football coach he admires, a grandmother he adores. The uncle, the football coach, and the grandmother must then be urged to attend. Normally, they are flattered to be told that they have been nominated as one of the few human beings this young person still respects. So they come. They come when the appeal to them is 'to support and help the young person to take responsibility for what they have done'. Thus the setting and the ceremonial character seek to 'hold' the offender while allowing separation from the offence.

Victims play a crucial role in this, for they are in a unique position to communicate the irresponsibility of the *act*. Much delinquency is casual and thoughtless (O'Connor and Sweetapple 1988: 117–18). The offenders who thought all they had done was to take 50 dollars from the house of a faceless person find that person is a vulnerable elderly woman who did without something significant because of the loss of the money. They learn that as a result of the break-in she now feels insecure in her own home, as does her next door neighbour. Both have invested in new security locks and are afraid to go out in the street alone because they have come to view the neighbourhood as a dangerous place. Collateral damage from victimization is normal rather than exceptional and co-ordinators become expert at drawing it out of victims and victim supporters. Techniques of neutralization (Sykes and Matza 1957) that may originally have been employed, such as '. . . I am unemployed and poor while the householder is employed and rich' are seriously challenged when confronted by the elderly victim. Sometimes this shocks the offender. Other times it does not. Many of the worst offenders have developed a capacity to cut themselves off from the shame for exploiting other human beings. They deploy a variety of barriers against feeling responsibility. But what does not affect the offender directly may affect those who have come to support her. The shaft of shame fired by the victim in the direction of the offender might go right over the offender's head, yet it might pierce like a spear through the heart of the offender's mother, sitting behind him. It is very common for offenders' mothers to start to sob when victims describe their suffering or loss. So while display of the victim's suffering may fail to hit its intended mark, the anguish of the offender's mother during the ceremony may succeed in bringing home to the offender the need to confront rather than deny an act of irresponsibility.

Indeed, in our observations mothers often seize the ceremony of the occasion to make eloquent and moving speeches that they have long wanted to make to their child:

I imagine life as a family living in a valley and the children gradually start to venture out from the family house in the valley. Eventually they have to climb up the mountain to get out of the valley. That mountain is adolescence. At the top of the mountain is a job. When they have that they can walk gently down the other side of the mountain into life. But there's another way they can go. They can decide not to climb the path up the mountain but to wander in the easier paths out into the valley. But those paths, while they are easier, lead to greater and greater

[1] A common cynicism when we have spoken to American audiences about these ideas has been that it sounds like a good idea for sweet, sheep-loving New Zealanders, with their intact families, but that it could never work in the face of the family disintegration of American slums. This is an odd perspective, given the empirical reality in New Zealand that Youth Aid Officers saw 'poor family support/background' as the most important factor *in favour of* opting for referral of a case to a family group conference rather than some other disposition (Maxwell and Morris 1993: 60–1). Moreover, in practice, 14 per cent of young people processed in family group conferences do not live with their families, compared to 4 per cent of those processed by informal police diversion (Maxwell and Morris 1993: 64, 66).

CONDITIONS OF SUCCESSFUL REINTEGRATION CEREMONIES

darkness. I'm concerned that my little boy took one of those paths and I'm losing him into the darkness.

Co-ordinators work at bringing out collateral damage. Parents are asked: 'How did this episode affect the family?' Offenders are asked: 'How did mum and dad feel about it?' Typically, the offender will admit that their kin were 'pretty upset'. In Wagga, the co-ordinator then routinely asks why and in a large proportion of cases, young people will say something to the effect that the parents care about them or love them. This is the main chance the reintegrative co-ordinator is looking for. Once this is uttered, the co-ordinator returns to this again and again as a theme of what is being learnt from the conference. In the wrap-up, he will reaffirm that 'Jim has learned that his mum and dad care a lot, that his Uncle Bob wants to help . . .' This is not to deny that this strategy of reintegration can be mismanaged:

Co-ordinator: 'James, why are your parents upset?'

James: [Silence]

Co-ordinator: 'Do you think it's because they care about you?'

James: 'Don't know.'

Another way this path to reintegration can be derailed is when the parents indulge in outcasting attacks on their child. Co-ordinators sometimes manage this problem by intervening to divert stigmatization before it gets into full swing:

Mother: 'He used to be a good boy until then.'

Co-ordinator interrupts: 'And he still is a good boy. No one here thinks we're dealing with a bad kid. He's a good kid who made a mistake and I hope he knows now that that's what we all think of him.'

Even when serious stigmatic attacks are launched, the communal character of the encounter creates the possibility of reintegrative amelioration. The worst stigmatic attack we observed arose when the mother of a 14-year-old girl arrived at the conference. She told the co-ordinator that she was unhappy to be here. Then when she saw her daughter, who preceded her to the conference, she said: 'I'll kill you, you little bitch.' A few minutes into the conference, the mother jumped up from her seat, shouting: 'This is a load of rubbish.' Then pointing angrily at her shaking daughter, she said: 'She should be punished.' Then she stormed out. These events might have created a degradation sub-ceremony of great magnitude. Instead, the other participants in the room were transformed by it and developed a quite different direction. Victim supporters who had arrived at the conference very angry at the offender were now sorry for her and wanted to help. They learnt she was a street kid and their anger turned against a mother who could abandon her daughter like this. This dramatic example highlights two common processes seen in the conferences—the alteration of perspectives and the generation of social support. We believe these processes occur for two reasons:

1. the more serious the delinquency of the young offender, the more likely it is to come out that she has had to endure some rather terrible life circumstances. Rather than rely on stereotypes they see the offender as a whole person (a point we return to later); *and*

JOHN BRAITHWAITE AND STEPHEN MUGFORD

2. participants at the conference have been invited on the basis of their capacity to
    be supportive to either the offender or the victim. Being supportive people placed
    in a social context where supportive behaviour is expected and socially approved,
    they often react to stigmatic attacks with gestures of reintegration.

Even as they use stigmatic terms, ordinary citizens understand the concept of
communicating contempt for the deed simultaneously with respect for the young
person. An adult member of the Maori community caused tears to trickle down the
cheeks of a huge, tough 15-year-old with the following speech:

Stealing cars. You've got no brains, boy . . . But I've got respect for you. I've got a soft spot for
you. I've been to see you play football. I went because I care about you. You're a brilliant
footballer, boy. That shows you have the ability to knuckle down and apply yourself to
something more sensible than stealing cars . . . We're not giving up on you.

*(2) Event and perpetrator must be uncoupled rather than defined as instances of a profane
uniformity. The self of the perpetrator is sustained as sacred rather than profane. This is
accomplished by comprehending: (a) how essentially good people have a pluralistic self that
accounts for their occasional lapse into profane acts; and (b) that the profane act of a perpetrator
occurs in a social context for which many actors may bear some shared responsibility. Collective as
well as individual shame must be brought out into the open and confronted*

In speaking of degradation ceremonies, Garfinkel (1956: 422) says: 'Any sense of
accident, coincidence, indeterminism, chance or momentary occurrence must not
merely be minimised. Ideally, such measures should be inconceivable; at least they
should be made false.' There must be no escape, no loophole. Rather, degradation
insists upon fitting an identity of total deviant with a single, coherent set of motives into
a black and white scheme of things. In contrast, a condition of successful reintegration
ceremonies is that they leave open multiple interpretations of responsibility while
refusing to allow the offender to deny personal responsibility entirely. In degradation
ceremonies, the suppression of a range of motives and the insistence upon one account
of responsibility allow the criminal to maintain (at least in her own eyes) an identity for
herself as 'criminal as victim', to dwell on the irresponsibility of others or of
circumstances. When the crime is constructed as the bad act of a good person,
uncoupling event and perpetrator, a well-rounded discussion of the multiple account-
abilities for the crime does not threaten the ceremony as an exercise in community
disapproval. The strategy is to focus on problem rather than person, and on the group
finding solutions to the problem. The family, particularly in the New Zealand model, is
held accountable for coming up with a plan of action, which is then ratified by the
whole group. The collective shame and collective responsibility of the family need not
detract from individual responsibility for the crime nor from community responsibilities, such as to provide rewarding employment and schooling for young people. Yet
the collective assumption of responsibility moves the ceremony beyond a permanent
preoccupation with the responsibility of the individual that might stall at the point of
stigmatization and the adoption of a delinquent identity. The practical task of
designing a plan of action is a way of putting the shame behind the offender, of moving
from a shaming phase to a reintegration phase. Agreement on the action plan can be an

CONDITIONS OF SUCCESSFUL REINTEGRATION CEREMONIES

even more ceremonial decertification of the deviance of the offender through institutionalizing a signing ceremony where offender, family, and police put their signatures side by side on the agreement. In signing such an agreement, the responsible, reintegrated self of the offender distances itself from the shamed behaviour. The sacredness of the self is sustained through its own attack upon and transcendence of the profane act. Similarly, the collectivity of the family acknowledges its shame and takes collective responsibility for problem solving in a way that transcends its collective shame.

(3) Co-ordinators must identify themselves with all private parties—perpetrators, their families, victims, witnesses—as well as being identified with the public interest in upholding the law

Garfinkel's third condition of successful degradation ceremonies is that the denouncer must claim more than a private role but must communicate degradation in the name of an [imaginary, unified, and static] public. This condition is explicitly incorporated into Western criminal law, wherein the police and the judge in a criminal trial are legally defined as fiduciaries of public rather than private interests. In community conferences, this totalizing fiction is put aside. Co-ordinators have responsibilities to, and identify with, a plurality of interests. Reintegration and consensus on an agreement is quite unlikely unless the co-ordinator identifies with and respects all the interests in the room. Outside interests will put the agreement at risk unless the co-ordinator also speaks up on behalf of any public interest beyond the set of private interests assembled for the conference. This sounds demanding, perhaps even impossible. How can so many interests be juggled and a workable outcome reached? Our answer is simple—in practice consensus is reached more than 90 per cent of the time at both research sites and in most of these cases the consensus is implemented (Maxwell and Morris 1993: 121).[2]

(4) Denunciation must be both by and in the name of victims and in the name of supra-personal values enshrined in the law

For Garfinkel, degradation ceremonies are enacted in the name of the supra-personal values of the tribe. We have seen that successful reintegration requires confronting the private hurts and losses from the crime as well. A key condition for the success of reintegration ceremonies is to get the victim to turn up. Where victims are institutions (like schools), this means getting victim representatives to turn up (e.g., the principal, elected student representatives). Blagg (1986) has discussed the greater problems of making reparation meaningful with impersonal victims. Victim or victim representative attendance has been nearly universally achieved in Wagga, but in New Zealand the success rate has been under 50 per cent (Maxwell and Morris 1993: 75), though there is reason to suspect that the latter disappointing statistic has been improving in more recent times in New Zealand.[3] Some will be surprised at the near-universal

[2] See, however, the discussion of professionally manipulated consensus under point (5) and in the conclusion to this article.

[3] The main reason for non-attendance for victims in New Zealand was simply their not being invited, followed by being invited at a time unsuitable to them (Maxwell and Morris 1993: 79), a result of poor understanding of the philosophy of the reform by conference co-ordinators, heavy workload, and practical difficulties, such as the police failing to pass on the victim's address. Only 6 per cent of victims said they did not want to meet the offender (Morris *et al.*, in press).

JOHN BRAITHWAITE AND STEPHEN MUGFORD

success in Wagga and the recent higher success in New Zealand in getting victims along to conferences. But when the co-ordinator issues a combined appeal to private interest, public virtue (playing your part in getting this young person back on track) and citizen empowerment, the appeal is rather persuasive. In the words of Senior Sergeant Terry O'Connell—the key actor in adopting and developing the programme at Wagga—the key is to 'make the victim feel important and they will come'. And important they are: in New Zealand victims can effectively veto any agreement reached at the conference, but only if they actually attend and listen to the arguments. Even in conventional dyadic victim–offender reconciliation programmes in a non-communitarian society such as the United States, victim interest in participation is quite high (Weitekamp 1989: 82; Galaway 1985: 626; Galaway and Hudson 1975: 359; Novack *et al.* 1980; Galaway *et al.* 1980). Some of this may be sheer curiosity to meet the person who 'did it'.

When the victim and victim supporters turn up, of course, there remains the possibility that private hurts and losses will not be fully communicated to the offender. Sometimes the victim says that they suffered no real loss. For example, at one conference we attended, the victim said that the car stolen for a joy ride was found as soon as he noticed it to be missing and he could detect no damage. Here the co-ordinator must reiterate the public interest in being able to assume that one can park a car somewhere without constant worry that it might be stolen. Pointing out that '. . . it was a lucky thing for you and Mr X [the victim] on this occasion' reinforces responsibility in the absence of specific private harm. Furthermore, in stressing the public as well as the private view of a crime, if the absence of private harm means that there is no direct compensation to be paid or worked for, conferences will usually agree to some community service work for the offender. Often there will be both private compensation and community work, signifying both the private and the public harm. The gesture of restoration to both community and victim, even if it is modest in comparison to the enormity of the crime, enables the offender to seize back pride and reassume a law-respecting, other-respecting, and self-respecting identity.

(5) Non-authoritative actors (victims, offenders, offenders' families) must be empowered with process control. The power of actors normally authorized to issue denunciations on behalf of the public interest (e.g., judges) must be decentred

Degradation ceremonies for Garfinkel are about privileging authoritative actors with the right to denounce the profane on behalf of the tribe. Judges, for example, silence the denunciations of victims or pleas for mercy from relatives. Their role in the courtroom is simply as evidentiary fodder for the legal digestive system. They must stick to the facts and suppress their opinions. Consequently, they often emerge from the experience deeply dissatisfied with their day in court. For victims and their supporters, this often means they scream ineffectively for more blood. But it makes no difference when the system responds to such people by giving them more and more blood, because the blood-lust is not the source of the problem; it is an unfocused cry from disempowered citizens who have been denied a voice.

Reintegration ceremonies have a [dimly recognized] political value because, when well managed, they deliver victim satisfaction that the courts can never deliver. In

CONDITIONS OF SUCCESSFUL REINTEGRATION CEREMONIES

Wagga, a standard question to the victims is: 'What do you want out of this meeting here today?' The responses are in sharp contrast to the cries for 'more punishment' heard on the steps of more conventional courts. Offered empowerment in the way we have suggested, victims commonly say that they do not want the offender punished; they do not want vengeance; they want the young offender to learn from his mistake and get his life back in order. Very often they say they want compensation for their loss. Even here, however, it is suprising how often victims waive just claims for compensation out of consideration for the need for an indigent teenager to be unencumbered in making a fresh start.

Clifford Shearing attended two of the Wagga conferences with us. Struck by the readiness of victims not to insist on compensation claims but to press instead for signs of remorse and willingness to reform, Shearing said, '. . . they all wanted to win the battle for his [the offender's] soul[4] rather than his money'.

How can we make sense of outcomes that are so at odds with preconceptions of vengeful victims? In fact, even in traditional stigmatic punishment systems, victims are not as vengeful as popular preconceptions suggest (Weitekamp 1989: 83–4; Heinze and Kerstetter 1981; Shapland, Willmore, and Duff 1985; Kigin and Novack 1980; Youth Justice Coalition 1990: 52–4). Citizens seem extremely punitive and supportive of degradation ceremonies when asked their views in public opinion surveys. Distance, a stereotyped offender, and a simplification of evil conduce to public support for degradation ceremonies. But the closer people get to the complexities of particular cases, the less punitive they get (Ashworth 1986: 118; Doob and Roberts 1983, 1988). As we noted earlier, the reality of the meeting between victim, offender, and others tends to undermine stereotyping. Instead, immediacy, a particular known offender and a complex grasp of all the situational pressures at work conduce to public support for reintegration.

Some reconciliations at family group conferences are quite remarkable. The most extraordinary case we know of involved a young man guilty of aggravated assault with a firearm on a woman who ran a lotto shop. The offender locked the woman at gunpoint in the back of her shop while he robbed her of over $1,000. When the time for the conference came, she was mad, after blood. Yet after considerable discussion, part of the plan of action, fully agreed to by the victim, involved the victim housing the offender while he did some community work for her family! This is not an isolated case, although it involves the most dramatic shift of which we became aware. Occasionally, victims make job offers to unemployed offenders at conferences.

Unresolved fury and victim dissatisfaction is, of course, the stuff of unsuccessful reintegration ceremonies. An important recent New Zealand evaluation shows that failure as a result of such dissatisfaction remains (Maxwell and Morris 1993: 119). In fact over a third of victims who attended conferences said they felt worse after the conference, a result of insufficient attention to victim reintegration (see point (9) below).

It is not only victims who can benefit from the empowerment that arises from having cases dealt with in this non-traditional setting. Offenders and offenders' families are also very much empowered when community conferences work well. Maxwell and Morris (1993: 110) found that New Zealand conferences work better at empowering

---

[4] An allusion to Rose (1990) and his discussion of 'governing the soul'.

JOHN BRAITHWAITE AND STEPHEN MUGFORD

parents than offenders.[5] This is probably true in Wagga as well, though the Wagga approach rejects the Auckland tendency to give the arresting police officer the first opportunity to explain the incident of concern. Instead, the young person, rather than police or parents, are always given the first opportunity to describe in their own words what has brought them to the conference. We see this Wagga practice of temporally privileging the accounts of the young persons as a desirable way of seeking to empower them in the dialogue. For all parties, success is predicated upon a significant degree of agency. On the other hand, when agency is denied the ceremonies fail. Then there is the pretence of empowerment, with families and offenders being manipulated into agreements that are developed by the police or youth justice co-ordinators, an outcome that is not uncommon (Maxwell and Morris 1993: 112). There can be little real experience of shame when apology and remedial measures are forced on the offender and his family rather than initiated by them. Empowerment is crucial to reintegration, while manipulation makes instead for degradation.

(6) The perpetrator must be so defined by all the participants (particularly by the perpetrator himself) that he is located as a supporter of both the supra-personal values enshrined in the law and the private interests of victims

This condition of successful reintegration is accomplished by having the offender's responsible self disassociate itself from the irresponsible self. Apology is the standard device for accomplishing this, as Goffman pointed out:

An apology is a gesture through which an individual splits himself into two parts, the part that is guilty of an offence and the part that disassociates itself from the delict and affirms a belief in the offended rule (1971: 113).

At all the conferences we attended, the offenders offered an apology.[6] Often they agreed to follow up with a letter of apology or a visit to apologize again to the victim and other members of the family. Often there was also apology to parents, teachers, even the police. A common feature of successful reintegration ceremonies can be a rallying of the support of loved ones behind the disassociation of self created by a genuine apology. After one moving and tearful statement by a Maori offender in Auckland, for example, elders offered congratulatory speeches on the fine apology he had given to his parents.

The verbal apology can be accompanied by physical acts. The most common physical accompaniment to apology is the handshake. Female victims sometimes hug young offenders, an especially moving gesture when it reaches across a racial divide. In Maori conferences,[7] kissing on the cheek, nose pressing and hugging occur among

---

[5] This is not to downplay the wonderful successes with offender empowerment that can and do occur within the New Zealand process: 'I felt safe because my whanau [extended family] were there with me. I would have felt like stink if I had to face it on my own. My auntie explained it so I understood. It was good that she allowed me to take a role' (young person quoted in Maxwell and Morris 1993: 78).

[6] In this regard, we were somewhat surprised by Maxwell and Morris's (1993: 93) finding that an apology was formally recorded as offered in only 70 per cent of their sample of conferences. We wondered if all of the more informal means of apology including backstage apology) were counted in this result.

[7] With Samoan conferences, it is common for offenders to apologize on their knees, a degrading form of apology in Western eyes, but perhaps not so when the cultural context is to elevate the offender quickly, embracing his restored identity. That is, for the Samoan, the kneeling may represent part of a reintegrative sequence rather than signifying degradation.

CONDITIONS OF SUCCESSFUL REINTEGRATION CEREMONIES

various of the participants (even visiting sociologists!). Ritual bodily contact is not the only form of physical act to accompany apology. Other common acts include the handing over of compensation or the offer of a beverage. In a recreation of the theme that commensalism celebrates solidarity, successful ceremonies have ended with victim and offender families arranging to have dinner together after the conference.

Despite the manifestly successful effect of apology, it is not something encouraged by court rooms. Criminal trials tend to leave criminal identities untouched by attacks from responsible, law-abiding, or caring identities. Indeed, degradation tends to harden them. It is not a major challenge in identity management for a tough guy to sustain this identity during a criminal trial. The challenge is more difficult in an open dialogue among the different parties assembled for a community conference. Usually, there are some things that the police know about the offender's conduct that his parents do not know and there are vulnerabilities the parents know that the police do not. The traditional criminal process enables the offender to sustain different kinds of stories and even different identities with parents and police. Conferences can expose these multiple selves to the partitioned audiences for which these selves are differentially displayed. Out of one conference, Wagga parents learned that their teenage son had punched a 14-year-old girl in the face; then the police learned that the boy had beaten his mother before, once with a broom; then everyone learned that he had also hit other girls. There are some lies that the offender can live in the eyes of the police; others in the eyes of his parents; but many of them cannot stand in the face of a dialogue among all three that also enjoins victims.

All this is not to deny that apology, even the sincerest apology, can be secured without challenging a delinquent identity that remains dominant over a law-abiding identity. In one case, a 14-year-old girl acknowledged that the effect of stealing a cheque from the mail-box of an elderly woman had been 'awful' for the victim and she apologized with feeling. But when it came to the action plan, she was intransigently against the idea of returning to school: 'No. I don't like school.' Even a modest proposition from the group for community service work of 20 hours over four weeks was bitterly resisted: 'It's too much time. I want to be a normal street kid and if you're a street kid you need time to be on the street. That would take up too much of my time.' Nothing was going to interrupt her career path as a street kid! This is a familiar theme in literature on identity maintenance from writers associated with labelling and similar perspectives. There comes a point where a change which seems both possible and advantageous in the immediate context is resisted because of the degree of commitment to a path and the consequent 'side bets' (Becker 1960) that an individual has made in following that path.

Interestingly, however, our empirical observations match the general case we made earlier: namely, that while such commitment to deviance is possible, it is also rare. The norm is strongly towards the reversibility rather than irreversibility of the deviant identity and, as in the case just described, in contrast to the labelling claim, irreversibility seems more connected to the individual commitment to an identity (agency) than to structural features that prevent reversion. No doubt, the matter of commitment is not exhausted by these brief comments. We might suppose that as adults get older, deviant identities might become more encrusted and harder to change (and hence shaming and reintegration less relevant). For some people such a process probably occurs. But as data on the relationship between age and deviance shows

JOHN BRAITHWAITE AND STEPHEN MUGFORD

(Hirschi and Gottfredson 1983; Youth Justice Coalition 1990: 22–3) reversion from deviant to mainstream identities is the norm with progressing age. Thus the idea that shaming and reintegration ceremonies are valuable only for the young is not well founded. Indeed, preliminary qualitative evidence indicates that it may be extremely valuable for individuals well into middle age.[8]

(7) Distance between each participant and the other participants must be closed; empathy among all participants must be enhanced; opportunities must be provided for perpetrators and victims to show (unexpected) generosity toward each other

At the start of conferences, victims and offenders, victim supporters, and offender supporters tend to work hard at avoiding eye contact. By contrast, at the end of a successful reintegration ceremony, participants are looking each other in the eye. Reintegration ceremonies succeed when one side makes an early gesture of self-blame or self-deprecation. In one case, an offender wrote a long letter of apology to the victim before the conference was convened. At another conference, a mix-up by the police resulted in the victim being advised of the wrong date for the conference. Despite this, she came within 15 minutes of a 'phone call at 6 p.m. in the middle of preparing for dinner guests'. The conference co-ordinator said that she agreed to drop everything to come 'if it would help the boys'. 'What do you think of that?' said the co-ordinator. 'She's a nice lady', said one of the offenders. 'And I bet you were frightened to go out from your own house after this', added the mother of another offender.

In many cases, the offender's family does not wait for their offspring to come under attack from the victim. They pre-emptively launch the attack themselves in terms so strong that the victim can be moved to enjoin that the family '[Not] be too hard on the boy. We all make mistakes.' Self-deprecating gestures from either side can facilitate reintegration, which is powerfully facilitated by exchanges such as:

Victim: 'It was partly my fault. I shouldn't have left it unlocked.'

Offender: 'No that's not your fault. You shouldn't have to lock it. We're the only ones who should be blamed.'

A common strategy of all parties for seeking to elicit empathy from others is to refer to how they may suffer these problems themselves in another phase of their own life cycle. Offender's uncle to offender: 'In a few years you will be a father and have to growl at your boys.' Co-ordinator to victims: 'You were once parents of teenagers yourselves.'

[8] In Australia, we have been experimenting with reintegrative conferences with white-collar crime, cases that illustrate the problem of victim shame. A recent case has involved action by the Trade Practices Commission against a number of Australia's largest insurance companies in what have been the biggest consumer protection cases in Australian history. The victims were Aborigines in remote communities who were sold (generally) useless insurance and investment policies as a result of a variety of shocking misrepresentations, even the misrepresentation that the Aborigine would be sent to jail if he did not sign the policy. Victims sometimes escaped through the back door when the government man in the white shirt arrived to interview them, fearing that *they* had done something wrong. Many shook and cried throughout their interviews. They felt shame at losing the little money their families had. The apologies issued by company chief executives at highly publicized press conferences were about communicating the message that it was the company who had to face 'the same job' (as Aborigines put it). Moreover, full compensation with 15 per cent compound interest would acquit the shame victims felt as providers. In addition, insurance company top management were required to attend negotiation conferences at Wujal Wujal, where they faced their victims, apologized to them and lived the life conditions of their victims, sleeping on mattresses on concrete floors, eating tinned food, during several days of negotiation. For more details on this and other cases of corporate shaming praxis, see Fisse and Braithwaite (1993) and Braithwaite (1992).

CONDITIONS OF SUCCESSFUL REINTEGRATION CEREMONIES

One case we attended involved a father and son who had a stormy relationship. A Maori elder counselled the father that he should put his arm around his boy more often, advice the father conceded that he needed to take. The father was a harsh and tough man, once a famous rugby forward with a reputation as an enforcer. The attempt of a Maori police officer to elicit empathy in these difficult circumstances was both innovative and effective, since tears began to stream down the face of the young offender, who up to this point had managed the impression of being a young tough:

Policeman: 'Look what you have done to your father and mother. If your father hit you, you'd stay hit. You wouldn't be getting up. But he hasn't.' [Offender gasps, his chest heaving with unnatural struggling for air]. 'I was always angry and bitter at my father. He was a hard man.'

Uncle interjects: 'Yes, he'd hit you first, then ask questions afterwards.'

Policeman continues: 'Then he died. Then I realised how I loved and missed the old bastard. Don't wait till your father dies, Mark.'

At this point the mother buried her head in her lap with quiet sobbing. Then the father and then the son cried, by which point all in the room had tears in our eyes. How impressive an accomplishment this was—eliciting such empathy for a father about whom it was clearly difficult to say anything laudatory. Taken out of context, it does not seem a very positive thing to say about a father that he has refrained from ironing out his son. But for a son who himself was enmeshed in the culture of rugby and who knew his father's history of ironing out a great number of other human beings, the tribute was deeply moving.

(8) The separation of denounced persons must be terminated by rituals of inclusion that place them, even physically, inside rather than outside

Already we have mentioned a number of rituals of inclusion: apology and its acceptance, handshaking, the putting of signatures side by side on an agreement, and so on. In a traditional Samoan context, this is taken further. Following an assault, the Matai, or head of the extended family unit of the offender, will kneel on a mat outside the house of the victim family until he is invited in and forgiven. Sometimes that will take days. There may be something to learn from the Samoans here on the conditions of successful reintegration ceremonies, namely the provision of a spatio-temporal dimension to the imperative for reintegration. For how long should I continue to avoid eye contact with this person who still kneels in front of me? When do I conclude it by embracing him in forgiveness? The sheer physicality of his remorse makes ignoring him indefinitely a rather limited third option. The ceremony is driven by a spatial imperative. Indeed, most successful ceremonies in our own society specify place (e.g., a church, a presentation dais) and a time when it is appropriate and fitting to carry out that ceremony. Moreover, in moving individuals through space and time, those movements are not haphazard—they fit the messages of transformation or reaffirmation that the ceremony seeks to convey.

In Wagga, the spatial arrangement that is employed to convey both the unity of the community and yet the tension between victim and offender, is a horseshoe seating arrangement. At one end of the horseshoe sits the offender(s) with her family(ies) sitting in the row behind. At the other end sits the victim(s) with his family(ies) sitting

JOHN BRAITHWAITE AND STEPHÉN MUGFORD

in the row behind him. The horseshoe symbolizes the tension of the meeting, part of one community but at widely separated points on this matter. Moreover, movements within the space can and do occur, such as when people cross the central space to shake hands at certain moments. These are culturally contingent matters; offending boys are commonly made to sit on the floor during Polynesian conferences, a temporary obeisance that seems culturally appropriate to them rather than debasing. Sometimes they are asked to come out and stand at the front for their formal apology, after which they return to their seat in a circle. In each of these, the physical space is used constructively to convey important messages. And, as we shall see later, the separation of the overall space into front and backstage areas also has its uses.

The symbolic meanings signified by space rarely surface in the discursive consciousness of the participants (or so we presume) but the successful use of space is not predicated upon that level of reflection. In all probability, more still could be done with the symbolic use of space in such ceremonies—one could take this even further by placing offenders alone in the centre of the horseshoe for the first stage of the conference, though one might worry about this intimidating them into silence. These are matters that require more detailed exploration, but note here merely that there is a fine line between artifice and artificiality.

The temporal dimension of the ceremony is also important. The phases in a successful ceremony are clearly visible in the way that participants comport themselves and a 'winding down' is often discernible. Indeed, the phased structure is not dissimilar to that described by Bales (1950) in his work on interaction process analysis. As Bales argued there, the social group that has formed to handle a particular risk (in this case for the ceremony) comes to develop a bounded process of its own, marking its phases with different styles of comportment and mood. Although breaks in the meeting are rarely used in Wagga,[9] one could conceivably have a coffee break once there had been good progress toward a settlement during which the protagonists could physically mix; after the break, offender families could come back side by side with their children to present their plan of action. Certainly, such activities are used to mark the end of the formal ceremony and handle transitions back to the 'outside world' and at such moments drinking together, whether coffee or—as might be appropriate in other contexts, alcohol—serves to mark that transition (Gusfield 1987; cf. also Bott 1987; Hazan 1987).

It is also important to note here that the physical act of handing over money as compensation or a bunch of flowers (as happened in one case) creates a strong imperative for an apology–forgiveness interaction sequence. Most English-speaking people find it normal to cancel grudges at the moment of a physical act of compensating wrongdoing by uttering the word 'sorry'. Faced with such an utterance, only unusual victims resist the imperative to return a word of forgiveness, to 'let bygones by bygones', or at least to show acceptance, thanks, or understanding.

Regrettably the common legal processes of a gesellschaft society sanitize such physical moments out of transactions. They are, in the Weberian sense, 'disenchanted'. With the loss of that enchantment they lose also powerful opportunities for transformations of self and context. Rational actor models of the world notwithstanding, successful

---

[9] In New Zealand, it is usual to have a break in the proceedings during which the offender's family meets on its own to prepare a plan of action.

CONDITIONS OF SUCCESSFUL REINTEGRATION CEREMONIES

practice of justice is not merely a technical-rational action. When restitution is reduced to 'the cheque is in the mail' (likely put there by the clerk of the court) matters of deep moral concern have been reduced to mere money, to the ubiquitous question 'how much?' (Simmel 1978). In contrast, successful reintegration ceremonies put reintegrative physicality back into the process. In so doing they transcend the merely rational to speak to vital concerns of human conscience.

(9) The separation of the victim, any fear or shame experienced by victims, must be terminated by rituals of reintegration

The objective of reintegrating offenders is advanced by reintegrating victims; the objective of reintegrating victims is advanced by reintegrating offenders.[10] Victims are invisible in Garfinkel's model, but our thesis is that effective reintegration ceremonies are victim-centred, a centrality described under conditions (3), (4), and (5). Victims often suffer from bypassed shame (Scheff and Retzinger 1991) and bypassed fear. The girl who is sexually assaulted by a young man often feels that the incident says something about the respect in which she is held by males. She feels devalued to have been treated with such disrespect (Murphy and Hampton 1989). One way to rehabilitate her self-respect is a ceremonial show of community respect for her. Apology from the man who disrespected her is the most powerful way of resuscitating this self-esteem and community shaming of the disrespecting behaviour is also powerful affirmation of the respect for her as a person.

Victims often continue to be afraid after a crime and at an apparently irrational level. When a break-in causes a victim to feel insecure in her home, it is good for this fear to be openly expressed. For one thing, there is practical advice the police are usually able to give that can leave the victim both safer and feeling more assured of being safe.

In one Wagga conference involving teenage lads who inflicted a terrifying assault on a much younger boy and girl, the boys offered to come around to the home of the victim family to apologize more formally to all members of the family. The young girl looked afraid and said that she did not want them coming near her home. So it was decided they would apologize in writing. But from that point on in the conference, the cautioning sergeant highlighted the fact that there was no particular meaning to the choice of these two children as victims. It was a one-off incident that could have happened to anyone. At the end of the conference, the sergeant ushered the offenders and their supporters out, asking the victim family to stay behind. Then he asked the children if they now felt assured that these boys would not come after them again. He asked them what they thought of the boys and they said that the conference had put it all behind them now. They felt more sorry for the boys than afraid of them. The mother said later that she had come to see them as frightened little boys. This interpretation

---

[10] In practice, the Wagga process has been more oriented from the outset to reintegrating victims than the New Zealand process. Many New Zealand co-ordinators, interpreting literally a clause in the New Zealand Children, Young Persons and Their Families Act, have been reluctant to allow victim supporters to attend the conference. There has been a lot of learning in New Zealand on this question, but in some parts there is still a fear of the vindictiveness of victims and, more particularly, of victim supporters. If victims are to be reintegrated, however, caring supporters are a necessary ingredient. Our strongest criticism of the New Zealand reform effort has been the half-hearted commitment to victim reintegration in many quarters.

JOHN BRAITHWAITE AND STEPHEN MUGFORD

was confirmed by a minister of religion who met with the family immediately after the conference.

Note here the importance of two smaller backstage conferences after the formal conference—a further instance of the significance of space referred to earlier. Backstage conferences can do some reintegrative work for both offenders and victims that cannot be accomplished front stage. Every conference we have attended broke up into some important little backstage meetings after the main conference. At times, the reintegrative work that happened after the conference was more significant than that transacted within it. A boy who maintained a defiant demeanour throughout the conference shed a tear when his uncle put his arm around him after the conference (his identity as nephew allows him to cry, but not the identity he must maintain in the face of his mates). A mother confesses that she does not believe she can get her daughter to attend the agreed community work and another uncle volunteers to 'make sure she gets there'. Backstage intimacy can allow some masks to be removed that actors feel impelled to sustain during the conference proper. A practical implication is not to rush the exit from the theatre.

(10) Means must be supplied to intervene against power imbalances that inhibit either shaming or reintegration, or both

Of the various criticisms we have heard raised about the ceremonial process that we are describing in this paper, one of the most common concerns the imbalance of power in society and the way that this must spill over into, and hence structure in negative ways, the reintegration process. How, they ask, can this process disassociate itself from wider matters of class, race, patriarchy, and age stratification? If such disassociation does not occur, how can the ceremony act other than to reproduce that same patterning of ageism, class, race, and patriarchy? The risk is obvious. The ethnomethodologists of the 1960s, among whom Garfinkel is counted, were rightly condemned by the marxists of the 1970s (Taylor, Walton, and Young 1973) for inattentiveness to issues of power. By using Garfinkel's work as a starting point might we not fall into the same trap, blithely praising a ceremony whose deeper realities are much darker than we sense? Are the ceremonies of reintegration we are discussing capable of intervening against power imbalances in any serious way?

Our answer to this falls into several parts, and these parts relate to what we have seen in our observational work.

First, in no sense is intervention to deal with individual offences the most important thing we can do to respond constructively to the crime problem: attacking deeper structures of inequality is more important (Polk 1992; Braithwaite 1991, 1993). But let us not underestimate how important a basis of inequality criminal justice oppression is to (say) Aboriginal Australians. The structure of laws and the daily routines of the police and the courts contribute mightily to that oppression. Thus, to alter the police-court process is an important step, even if it is not a sufficient step. Indeed the very history of the Antipodean conferences we are discussing here begins with Maori frustration with the way the Western state disempowered them through the criminal justice system (Report of the Ministerial Advisory Committee 1986). These reforms 'came from below' and were explicitly understood by Maori protagonists to introduce

CONDITIONS OF SUCCESSFUL REINTEGRATION CEREMONIES

communitarian reintegrative features into a system that lacked them and which stigmatized their young people in destructive ways. In this sense, if in no other, we advocate the reintegration ceremonies because they are valuable in the eyes of most of those who are involved in them.[11]

Our second point is more theoretical. At the core of the criticism about power imbalances undermining the ceremony is a failure to think through the precise nature of the ceremony. The current of mainstream sociology that has dealt with ritual and ceremony has principally been conservative and functionally oriented (Cheal 1988). As a result, the tendency has been to emphasize static, system-integrative, and totalizing aspects of rituals over dynamic aspects, multiple identities, and social change. But that shortcoming is a feature of the theory, not the ceremony. If commentators associate conservatism with ceremony for this reason, they do so out of habit rather than evidence. There are dynamic features to these ceremonies which emphasize agency and social freedom (within obvious bounds) not merely totalizing conformity. No doubt, there are meanings which ceremonies permit and others they do not and no doubt some of those privilegings and silencings may be problematic. But we dispute that they can be 'read off' in advance.

Third and last, the criticism implies that anyone who pursues the course we describe here is utopian—class, race, and patriarchy are so ingrained in 'the system', it can be said that the system can never transcend them. Perhaps. But our view is quite different. We see that the existing 'system'—which is not particularly systematic in that it lacks unity, coherence, and direction—is racked with problems arising from differences in power which we can identify as 'class, race, and patriarchy'. But we go on to argue that if so, this identifies the places where we need to work relentlessly for change. Moreover, we suggest that our observations of such ceremonies indicate that while power imbalances remain ineradicably within what we describe, they also provide a greater space in which people can be agents than the existing processes. More voices are heard, saying more things than in conventional courts and that is a positive thing. Concrete examples may help to make the point.

It is an empirical question whether powerful outside voices are likely to be raised in a conference or a court against a father who dominates his daughter. Here we observe that the condition of the successful reintegration ceremony is that the co-ordinator act on this fact of domination by asking the daughter *who she would like* to be there to stick up for her against her father.

The philosophy of the New Zealand reforms (Children, Young Persons and Their Families Act 1989) is that when families are in deep trouble, a social worker from the state is not likely to be the best person to straighten out their problems (Maxwell and Morris 1993). However big a mess the family is in, the best hope for solving the problem of families resides within the families themselves and their immediate communities of intimate support. What the state can do is empower families with resources: offer to pay to bring Auntie Edna from another city for the conference (as they do in New Zealand), offer to pay for a smorgasbord of life skills, job training, remedial education, anger control courses, but with *the power of choice from that*

---

[11] In New Zealand, 53 per cent of the offenders processed through family group conferences are Maori (Maxwell and Morris 1993: 69). On Maori perceptions of the value of the reforms, see n. 13 below.

JOHN BRAITHWAITE AND STEPHEN MUGFORD

smorgasbord resting entirely with the young offender and her support group.[12] Processes like this do offer a redress of power imbalances centred upon race, albeit not completely. In New Zealand, where the Maori community contribute half the cases processed by the New Zealand juvenile justice system, conferences offer an important redress in a criminal justice system that is otherwise not a peripheral but a central source of their disempowerment. The same point can be made about racial minorities in all the English-speaking countries. It is a small blow against black oppression when the white father of the victim of a brutal assault offers to go with the family of the Aboriginal offender to argue the reversal of a decision to expel him from school because of the assault. Conferences will never usher in revolutionary changes; they do, however, give little people chances to strike little blows against oppression.

The possibilities for improving the position of women within criminal justice processes also seem to us to be quite promising. This is illustrated by the Wagga case mentioned earlier of the mother who was being beaten by her son. Court-based criminal justice systematically obscures the fact that in Australia we have a massive problem of son–mother violence. Domestic violence is constructed in the literature as spouse abuse because mothers keep the problems with their sons submerged, blaming themselves, refusing to complain against their own children. If the Wagga case discussed earlier had gone to court, it is most unlikely that the assault on the girl would have led on to a discussion of the wider problem of the assault on the mother and other females. The family group conference approach enabled community confrontation of this 15-year-old boy with the problem of his violence at an early enough age for such a confrontation to make a difference. But most mothers and sisters are unlikely to co-operate in a stigmatic or punitive vilification of their young son or brother. Ceremonies must be perceived as reintegrative, directed not only at getting the boy to take responsibility for his actions but also at supporting and helping him, before most mothers and sisters will break the silence.

We could add that the economic prospects of offenders, which are often very dim, are not always neglected in these conferences. While this is not a widespread feature, sometimes the unemployed are helped to find jobs; sometimes the homeless are found homes; often the school dropouts are assisted in getting back to school or into some alternative kind of technical training or educational development. Clearly there are many more important fronts on which to struggle for a more just economic system than through family group conferences, but these conferences are at worst not deepening the problems that the young offenders face.

In short, while the reintegration ceremonies we write of here do not overcome inequalities, they can be and are sensitive to them and do what they can to allow for and/or redress some of those inequalities. In so doing, they create spaces for agency and voice; they return conflicts that are 'stolen' by state professionals to ordinary citizens (Christie 1977). This, we think, is a progressive move. The structural feature of successful conferences that we hypothesize to be most critical here is proactive empowerment of the most vulnerable participants—offenders and victims—with the choice of caring advocates, who may be more powerful than themselves, to exercise countervailing power against whoever they see as their oppressors.

---

[12] With the weak welfare states that exist in both Australia and New Zealand, the range of such choices effectively available to young people, in most localities but particularly in rural localities, is very poor (Maxwell and Morris 1993: 180).

CONDITIONS OF SUCCESSFUL REINTEGRATION CEREMONIES

(11) Ceremony design must be flexible and culturally plural, so that participants exercise their process control constrained by only very broad procedural requirements

We should be pluralist enough to see that a good process for Maoris will not necessarily be a good process for Europeans, or even for some Maoris who say they don't believe in 'too much shit about the Maori way' (Maxwell and Morris 1993: 126).[13] At the same time, we should not be so culturally relativist as to reject the possibility of Europeans learning something worthwhile from Maori practice. Family group conferences are essentially a Maori idea, but the idea has been very favourably received by white communities in New Zealand and Australia, Australian Aboriginal communities, and Pacific Islander communities living in New Zealand. The reason is the flexibility built into the approach. Because Samoan participants have genuine process control, they can choose to encourage kneeling in front of the victim. Maori communities can choose to break the tension during proceedings by singing a song, something Westerners would find a rather odd thing to do on such an occasion. Maori conferences often signify the sacredness of the public interests involved (conditions 3 and 4) by opening and closing the conference with a (reintegrative) prayer.

Every conference we have attended has been completely different from every other conference. Indeed, flexibility and participant control of the process are the reasons why this strategy can succeed in a multicultural metropolis like Auckland. This is not a communitarian strategy for the nineteenth century village, but for the twenty-first century city. Flexible process, participant control—these are keys to delivering the legal pluralism necessary for the metropolis. Another key is that this is an individual-centred communitarianism, giving it a practical edge for constructing community in an individualistic society. The authors of this paper choose not to attend Neighbourhood Watch meetings, because the appeal of community obligation is not sufficient to motivate our participation. In contrast, if one of us were asked to attend a family group conference on the basis that either a victim or an offender from our neighbourhood or family had nominated us as a person who could lend support, we would go. We would be flattered to have been nominated by the individual. This is what we mean by the practical appeal of individual-centred communitarianism. Helping an individual is more motivating to citizens than abstractions such as 'contributing to making your neighbourhood safer'.

While the reintegrative strategy is firmly grounded in the theory of legal pluralism, certain basic procedural rules cannot be trumped. The most important of these is that if the offender denies committing the alleged offences, she has the right to terminate the

[13] While it is easy to find Maoris who resist the notion that there is a lot of point in turning back the clock to a pre-European society and others who see family group conferences as a corruption and debasement of Maori traditions by the Western justice system, we suspect the predominant Maori reaction is as expressed by the Maori researchers on the Maxwell and Morris project in the following quote—accepting the need for mutual accommodation between Maori and Western justice systems, especially when victims and offenders come from different cultures:

'We feel that the Act for the most part is an excellent piece of legislation which promises exciting possibilities for the future. When the processes outlined in the Act were observed, Maori families were indeed empowered and able to take an active part in decisions concerning their young people. It is not difficult to see the beneficial influences that the Act may eventually exert on wider Maori, Polynesian and Pakeha society. Maori society could gain immensely from legislation that acknowledges and strengthens the hapu and tribal structures and their place in decisions regarding the wellbeing of young people and [from legislation] that provides them with an opportunity to contribute to any reparation and to support those offended against. The same scenario would apply to Pacific Island peoples. Pakeha society would also benefit from a process which acknowledges the family and gives redress to victims' (Maxwell and Morris 1993: 187).

conference, demanding that the facts be tried in a court of law. She does not have to plead guilty. The conference can proceed only if she chooses 'not to deny' charges made by the police. Some of the more informal ground rules that co-ordinators enforce, such as 'no name calling' and 'no badgering of the young person' have the effect of tipping the balance against degrading discourse in favour of reintegrative dialogue. What such basic procedural rules do is constitute a generally acceptable framework within which a plurality of dialogic forms can flourish (see Habermas 1986).

Given a commitment to flexibility and participant empowerment, one central concern is the prospect of standardization and routinization. It would be easy for ceremonies to be converted into Foucauldian 'discipline', extending the net of state control. Disturbing signs of this as a future trend can be discerned, for example in the near-automatic tendency of some state officials at New Zealand conferences to suggest a curfew as part of the plan of action. Families can and do argue against their children being put on a rigid curfew, suggesting that a degree of participant control of the process is prevailing against pressures for standardized response, but the routinization of the suggestion without apparent consideration of case details implies a standardizing tendency. Similarly, after a training conference for co-ordinators in Wagga that we attended with Clifford Shearing and Jane Mugford, they expressed concern to us that some of the contributions to the training by local social workers and psychologists undercut the shifts away from stigmatization and toward community empowerment. The tendency there was to speak and reason in abstract categories such as 'problem youth' in a way that, taken seriously, would erode the agency and voice of participants in favour of the imposition of control by 'experts'.

These tendencies notwithstanding, our view is that, at present, the family group conferences do not extend the net of state control (see also Moore 1992), but rather extend the net of community control, partly at the expense of state control, partly at the expense of doing something about problems that were previously ignored (such as mother-bashing by sons).[14] Conferences can be used by communities to co-opt state power (formalism harnessed to empower informalism) (Braithwaite and Daly, in press); or they can be used by state authorities to expand their net of coercion by capturing informal community control (as in the net-widening critique). The contingent potential for both these developments and for the re-emergence of professionalized routinization need to be kept in mind in planning the expansion of such programmes.

(12) Reintegration agreements must be followed through to ensure that they are enacted

In the early days of the family group conferences in both New Zealand and Wagga, there was poor follow-up to ensure that agreements reached at the conference were implemented. Now more systematic procedures are in place in New Zealand to ensure, for example, that where monetary compensation is involved, victims do receive it. For a sample of 203 family group conferences held in 1990, Maxwell and Morris (1993: 102) found that in 59 per cent of cases agreements were completely implemented within three to four months and partly completed in a further 28 per cent of cases, leaving only

---

[14] Maxwell and Morris's (1993: 176) New Zealand data support this interpretation. They find that the result of the New Zealand reforms is fewer children going to court, fewer receiving custodial penalties, but more children whose delinquency was previously ignored altogether or discharged by the court experiencing moderate interventions such as formal apology, compensation, and community service decided through family group conferences or police diversion.

CONDITIONS OF SUCCESSFUL REINTEGRATION CEREMONIES

13 per cent of cases in which the tasks were largely uncompleted in this time frame—a very good result. At Wagga, young offenders and their families are invited to at least one follow-up workshop to close out the process. Families have an opportunity to swap notes at the workshop on the difficulties they have faced in implementing their plan of action. The Wagga police also see a reintegrative rationale for the workshop in helping families to overcome their shame by working with other families in the same situation. It is possible that this interpretation is right, as illustrated by the following passage from our fieldwork notes:

Of the three offenders [in this particular case] George was the one who seemed totally unmoved by what the victim and his family said at the conference. George's mother got together with mothers of George's friends who had also been in trouble, to talk about their problems. One of the mothers said that her boy had been sexually assaulted and that was one thing that upset him. Later George's mother said to George that he has not had it so tough as John, who had been sexually assaulted. George said nothing. Later, he called his mother back, broke down and said he had been sexually assaulted too (by the same person, we assume). George's mother now dates the assault as marking the time since which George had been getting into trouble. Her social construction of George is no longer as a boy who went bad. Now it is of a boy who was good, who went through a bad time as a result of a sexual assault, and who is now coming to terms with what happened to him and is coming out of it—a 'good boy' again.

Implementation of agreements from family group conferences is more effective than with court ordered compensation largely because the compensation is a collective obligation entered into by voluntary collective agreement.[15] Moreover, the co-ordinator will often secure the nomination of a relative who will be responsible for ensuring that the offender complies with the terms of the agreement. Dr Gabrielle Maxwell has made the same point about completion of community work orders: 'The community work projects that work are the ones the family comes up with itself.'

(13) When a single reintegration ceremony fails, ceremony after ceremony must be scheduled, never giving up, until success is achieved

Traditional criminal justice processes paint themselves into a corner because of two imperatives: the desire to give kids another chance; notwithstanding this, the desire to signal that 'the system is tough and next time you will not be so lucky'. These two imperatives intersect with the empirical reality that young offenders offend a lot during their years of peak offending. Most will come through this peak period within two or three years if the criminal justice system does not make things worse by degradation ceremonies (such as institutionalization). The two imperatives and the empirical pattern of offending intersect to cause the criminal justice system to do exactly what its

[15] As an aside, it is worth noting here the implications for the justice model which provides a critique of family group conferences as inferior to courts. Courts, according to this critique, provide singular, consistent justice, in contrast to the plural, inconsistent justice of conferences. It is an interesting empirical question whether in practice, as opposed to theory, courts do deliver more just sanctioning when compensation, fines, and community service ordered by the court are defied in the majority of cases. It is not inconceivable that even though there is greater inequity in the sanctions ordered by group conferences, in the sanctions actually implemented there is greater equity for the group conference than for the court process.

JOHN BRAITHWAITE AND STEPHEN MUGFORD

practitioners know is the worst thing to do, that is, set up a self-defeating chain of events:

Conviction 1:   'Take this as a warning.'
Conviction 2:   'I'll give you a second chance. But this is your last chance.'
Conviction 3:   'With regret, I must say that you have already been given your last chance.'

The policy in New Zealand is to avoid this slippery slope. While some cases in the juvenile justice system continue to slide down it, most do not and since 1988 the rate of institutionalization of young offenders has dropped by more than half (Maxwell and Morris 1993: 176), possibly by 75 per cent (McDonald and Ireland 1990: 16). Now, most detected offences are judged not to warrant the cost of convening a family group conference, and informal warnings to juveniles on the spot or at the police station remain the predominant response for very minor offences (Maxwell and Morris 1993: 53). Taking no action beyond a formal letter of warning from the police is also common (Maxwell and Morris 1993: 59). Visits by the police to the offender's home to arrange informally for reparation and apology to the victim occur in a quarter of non-arrest cases (Maxwell and Morris 1993: 53). Only if these steps are insufficient is a full conference arranged.

In addition to these informal pre-conference measures, some New Zealand young offenders have been through six or seven formal conferences for different offences. The New Zealand Police Association, which strongly supports the family group conference strategy for most offenders, has reservations about repeated use of the approach on 'hardened' offenders. They illustrated the problem with examples such as this:

Ngaruawahia reports that a 16 year old youth had a Family Group Conference on 26 June 1990 for three offences, another on 10 July for six offences, another on 20 July 1990 for two offences, Youth Court hearing on 24 July 1990, another Family Group Conference on 14 February 1991 for two offences. The youth committed suicide at Weymouth Boys Home in April 1991 (New Zealand Police Association 1991: 19).

Of course, such a case seems a 'failure'. But what kind of failure is it? We can think of three ways of categorizing it: (a) a failure of the family group conference; (b) the likely failure of any approach with the most difficult cases; or (c) the failure of giving up on the family group conference in favour of the court-institutionalization route. The implication of the passage is that this is a failure of type (a), but we suspect that it is better understood as type (b) and/or (c).

Of course, it would be naïve to expect that a one- or two-hour conference can normally turn around the problems of a lifetime. In any case, the theory of the conference is not really that what is said at the conference will change lives in an instant and irreversible way—a conference is a social activity, not a genie from a bottle. Rather the hope for the conference is that it will be a catalyst for community problem solving. Viewed in this way, when there is re-offending after a conference, it is to some extent the community that has failed. The failure of the conference was in not catalysing the right sort of community support for the offender. If the failure is not inherent to the conference process, but is a failure in the community catalysis of the intervention, then one conference after another, each time seeking to catalyse community support in a different way, or with different invitees, makes sense.

CONDITIONS OF SUCCESSFUL REINTEGRATION CEREMONIES

To achieve a successful reintegration ceremony, then, it is necessary that co-ordinators must never give up, that they act as if there is always a reason for the failure of the last intervention *other than* the irretrievable badness of the offender. Even if the offender dies before the community succeeds in preventing his offending, by trying again and again with reintegrative approaches, the co-ordinator believes that she has at least refrained from accelerating his criminal career path during the time he lived. The typical criminal career is a useful touchstone, here. Knowing the pattern typical of some offenders, it is *dis*abling to conceive success in terms of stopping offending. At the same time, it is *en*abling to define success as a downward shift in the slope of a criminal career path and failure as allowing an upward shift. Unless the offences are extreme,[16] it is always better to keep plugging away with a strategy that neither succeeds nor fails than to escalate to one that fails. At least the former does no harm.

Is there a practical way of implementing the attitude of never giving up? Below is an example of how the police might react to the first eight detected offences of a career criminal under a reintegrative strategy.

First offence: Boy warned by the police on the street for a minor offence. 'If I catch you at this again, I'll be in touch with your parents about it.'

Second offence: Same type of minor offence on the street results in a formal letter of warning and a visit to the family home to discuss the warning.

Third offence: Family group conference. Still a fairly minor offence, so no elaborate follow-up or detailed plan of action, just the reintegrative shaming of the offender and calling on the offender and the family to take responsibility for the problem in their own way. For the over-whelming majority of such minor offenders, this is the last the juvenile justice system will see of them, so any more detailed intervention is wasteful overkill.

Fourth offence: Second family group conference. More rigorous conference. What did the participants do, or fail to do, after the last conference? More detailed plan of action to respond to this analysis of the problem. Designation of offender supporters to monitor and report on implementation. Follow-up by co-ordinator to report back to participants on implementation. Modest quantum of community work.

Fifth offence: Third family group conference. Escalation of shaming of offender: 'You gave undertakings to your family at the last conference that you have broken in the most thoughtless way. You breached the trust your parents put in you with that agreement.' Redesign the plan of action. This time, secure a more solemn oath to the parents. Follow through. More community work.

Sixth offence: Fourth family group conference. New invitees. The smorgasbord of intervention options that the family group can choose (life skills or work skills courses, remedial education, church-run programmes, anger control courses, regular meetings with the school counsellor,

---

[16] There will be rare cases where the offender is so dangerous that escalation to institutionalization is inevitable and necessary. We have no dispute with such a course of action in those cases.

outward bound, drug rehabilitation programmes, etc.) is put before them in a different way. 'We chose the wrong option before. That was our mistake. But we believe in the caring side of you that your family sees so often, so eventually you will find with them the right option to assist you to consider the hurt you cause to victims like Mrs Smith and to consider your own future.' Keep up the shaming, this time focused on the particular circumstances of Mrs Smith. Work for Mrs Smith.

Seventh offence: Fifth family group conference. Try again basic strategy of fourth conference with a different victim, different participants, and a different way of presenting the smorgasbord of intervention options.

Eighth offence: Sixth family group conference. Change tack. Eventually come back to the fact that the offender is still responsible for this particular criminal act, but lead off with collective self-blame: 'As a group, your parents, your sister, grandfather and aunt, your teacher, Mrs Brown, who has such a soft spot for you, and me as the co-ordinator of this conference, we all feel responsible that we have let you down. We haven't listened to you well enough to come up with the right ways to help you. We need you to tell us where we have gone wrong.' Various other options can follow, such as one family member after another coming along prepared to give a speech on the mistakes they have made in the course of the saga. A search could be initiated by the family to find some new participants in the conference to add fresh perspectives, even asking another couple to become 'god-parents'. An option on the co-ordinator's side could be to bring in a consultant professional of some sort with new ideas to participate in the conference.

Obviously, it gets very difficult to keep coming up with new angles, to keep projecting faith in the essential goodness of the offender, to persist with the never-give-up ideology. The relentless optimism that successful reintegration enjoins may eventually surrender in the face of a natural human pessimism. We saw one stigmatizing conference for an offender (his fourth) which exemplified this surrender. During this encounter, the exasperated co-ordinator described the offender as a 'Yahoo'. Before inviting the offender to give his side of the story, he turned to the family and asked them what they thought was wrong with the boy. He said: 'The responsibility is the parents, not ours. I don't care. The Department doesn't care. We can just send it on to court.' The Youth Advocate said that she saw the key question as being whether 'his friends were bad or he was the bad one'. She supported the interpretation of the police that escalation to institutionalization was the track the boy was heading down. The police, the co-ordinator and the youth advocate had given up and everything they said gave the impression that they had given up on him. Even when the boy apologized, the co-ordinator evinced utter cynicism when he retorted dismissively, 'That's what you said last time.' This was a fully fledged degradation ceremony rather than an attempt at reintegration.

Pessimism is a natural human reaction to repeated misfortune and eventually the most determined commitment to 'never giving up on the offender' may succumb to it.

CONDITIONS OF SUCCESSFUL REINTEGRATION CEREMONIES

But a tenacious commitment to the ideology of never giving up will allow co-ordinators to cling to it for the fourth conference after the failure of the third. A slightly more tenacious commitment allows optimism to survive the fifth conference into the sixth. At each stage, more and more offenders drop off never to return, their criminal careers coming to an end without being inflicted with degradation ceremonies. Very few offenders indeed will make it through to a sixth conference. If we can hold out with optimism until then, the criminal justice system will have been transformed to a 99 per cent reintegrative institution. That can hardly be a bad outcome.

True disciples of reintegration, including ourselves, take the injunction to never give up on offenders to the absolute extreme. Even when a criminal career has continued to the point of the offender being the most powerful organized criminal in the country, the best hope for dealing with him is conceived as persuading him to convert his illegitimate capital into a legitimate business, giving his children a better future, a more respectable future, than the shame of his criminal empire. Going further still, as we have illustrated earlier (see n. 8 above), we think even the top management of certain Australian insurance companies are best negotiated with reintegratively! In the extraordinary cases where offenders are such a danger to the community that incarceration is defensible, we should not give up on pushing for reintegration, even though the degradation ceremony of confinement makes this maximally difficult.

(14) The ceremony must be justified by a politically resonant discourse

Shaming and reintegration are terms that we think have merit (that we will not defend here) in the discourse of criminological theory. These days, they have surprising currency among the police and community of Wagga. But in New Zealand, the terms that have more currency are, respectively, young offenders and their families 'taking responsibility' and 'healing'. The discourse of responsibility and healing may have more popular political appeal than that of shame and reintegration, as evidenced by the wide political support it has attracted in New Zealand and the growing support throughout Australia (Interim Report of the Select Committee on the Juvenile Justice System 1992; Tate 1992).

Much more crucial to this political and media support has been the marketing of this reintegration strategy as victim-centred and family-centred. It is a progressive reform that calls the hand of conservative politicians. They are forever claiming that victims are the forgotten people of the criminal justice system and bemoaning the declining importance of the family in contemporary society. Here is a reform that empowers victims and at the same time values and empowers families. Such a reform puts conservatives in a vulnerable position when they seek to oppose it.

Moreover, conservatives have also found in Australia and New Zealand that they cannot count on their allegedly 'natural allies' in law and order campaigns, the police. The Australian and New Zealand Police Federation carried a resolution at its 1991 conference supporting the New Zealand juvenile justice reforms. In New Zealand, 91 per cent of the time, police report that they are satisfied with the outcomes of the conferences in which they participate, a higher level than for youth justice co-ordinators (86 per cent), parents (85 per cent), offenders (84 per cent) and victims (48 per cent) (Morris and Maxwell 1992). Perhaps this should not surprise us. The approach appeals to the common sense of police. On balance, it cuts their paperwork

165

JOHN BRAITHWAITE AND STEPHEN MUGFORD

and economizes on criminal justice system resources; they often feel empowered by the capacity the conference gives them to make practical suggestions to the family on what might be done about the problem (an opportunity they are rarely given by courts); they like to treat victims with the decency that they believe courts deny them (in particular, they like to see victims actually getting compensation); and they find that the programme builds goodwill toward the police in communities that are empowered through the process. Most critically, they find participation in community conferences more interesting, challenging, and satisfying work than typing up charges and sitting around in courthouses for cases that are rushed through in a matter of minutes. This is by no means a universal police reaction. But we can certainly say that the strongest support for these reintegrative programmes in Australia has come from the police. While New Zealand reform was Maori-driven, the Australian reform is being police-driven.

Finally, the political appeal of the process is that it can be advocated in the discourse of fiscal restraint. In New Zealand, one of the most conservative governments in the Western world liked a reform that helped the budget deficit by allowing them to sell most of the institutions for juvenile offenders in the country. We were told that the Department of Social Welfare alone estimated that in 1991, they saved $6 million as a result of the reform. In this area of criminal justice, youth justice co-ordinators not only do the job more effectively than judges in court, they are cheaper than judges. By the same token, youth justice advocates are cheaper than prosecutors and public defenders. At all levels of the criminal justice system there are savings—not always massive savings, but rarely trivial.[17]

At the same time, reintegration ceremonies offer an attractive political package for a reforming politician. Presented properly, it can satisfy the otherwise incompatible imperatives of keeping the police and the finance ministry happy at the same time. It can even put the victims movement and liberally minded criminal justice reformers—who so often seem diametrically opposed—together on the same platform of support.

Conclusion

A useful way of thinking about ceremonies for dealing with rule breakers is in terms of the ratio of stigmatic to reintegrative meanings during the ceremony. When that ratio is high, we have a degradation ceremony; when low, a reintegration ceremony. There are few, if any, actors who are perfectly faithful to the theory of reintegrative shaming during such ceremonies. Typically, messages are mixed, as with the Maori participant quoted above: 'You've got no brains, boy (stigmatization) . . . But I've got respect for you (reintegration) . . .' There are many actors like this one who communicate shame while also sustaining a high ratio of reintegrative to stigmatizing meanings. The subtleties in the ways shaming and reintegration are mixed by practical human communicators are myriad. We noted one police sergeant who addressed male offenders by their names whenever he was engaging them in responsibility talk, but

---

[17] Against this view, economists might say that we should cost the (considerable) time involved in the attendance of victims and supporters, for example. If we calculated these costs, perhaps there would be no savings. But why should we make a negative entry for victims in the economic calculus when the fact is that the reform increases utility for victims? To enter the costs would make sense only if we could value the benefits. And if we did that, then no doubt the system we describe would again show a better balance sheet.

CONDITIONS OF SUCCESSFUL REINTEGRATION CEREMONIES

who called them 'mate' whenever he switched to reintegrative talk. When we pointed out this observation and asked him whether he was aware of the pattern, the sergeant told us it was a conscious communication strategy.

In Giddens's (1984) terms, many actors have practical but not discursive consciousness of the idea of reintegration; some actors, like this sergeant, have both. A feasible objective is to increase the proportion of actors who are conscious of the virtues of reintegration. This is not best achieved by lectures from theoretical criminology texts, but from telling stories (Shearing and Ericson 1991) and simple homilies such as that of one police constable: 'Just because we sometimes do stupid things; that does not mean we are a stupid person.' It could be that if there is a key principle of successful reintegration ceremonies, it is that there should not be too many principles. Training of co-ordinators should be kept simple, leaving them wide discretion to implement flexibly a few broad principles.

Stigma cannot be rooted out of confrontations between people who are angry and affronted by acts of rule breaking. But the ratio of stigmatization to reintegration can be shifted substantially by story-based training methods that focus on a few core principles—empower the victim, respect and support the offender while condemning his act, engage the offender's supporters. Just by having a process that is more victim-centred, problem-centred, and community-oriented, rather than centred on the offender and his pathologies, we institute a logic that produces less stigmatization and more reintegration. Obversely, the offender-centred logic of the courtroom or the psychiatrist's couch institutionalizes stigmatization.

One of the inevitable problems is that the stigmatizing, disempowering professional knowledges of the court and consultancy rooms penetrate the reintegration ceremony. Most depressingly, this was observed in New Zealand with the role of certain youth advocates, private lawyers contracted by the state to watch out for the rights of young offenders during conferences. Sometimes they 'earn their fee' by taking charge, telling the family what sort of action plan will satisfy the police and the courts. Or worse, we see 'the practice of law as a confidence game' (Blumberg 1967) where advocate, co-ordinator and police conspire to settle a practical deal among the professionals, then sell that deal to the conference participants, a deal that in at least one case seemed to us a sell-out of both the offender and the victim.

We commented earlier about the observations made by Clifford Shearing and Jane Mugford after a Wagga training session. Their point was that the reform process must create a new knowledge, a citizen knowledge, otherwise the old professional knowledges would colonize the spaces in the programme. We agree—hence the importance of the simple principles outlined above and the importance of the central involvement of local police–citizen consultative committees and other community groups in guiding reform. At the same time, however, we think the professional knowledges also include the seeds of their own reform. Reintegrative concepts have a major place in psychological and particularly social work discourse. These can be brought to the fore through reforms such as we are seeing in New Zealand and Wagga. While the youth advocates were criticized by a number of people we spoke to in New Zealand for importing professional control into family group conferences, some of these critics also pointed out how many advocates had changed their legalistic habits to accommodate the communitarian ideology of the conferences. Finally, there can be no doubt that these reforms are part of wider changes in police knowledges in Australia and New Zealand—away

JOHN BRAITHWAITE AND STEPHEN MUGFORD

from 'lock-'em-up' law enforcement and toward community policing. None the less, at the crucial middle management levels, the old punitive knowledges of policing continue to predominate and must be confronted by reasoned cases based on the success of alternative practices. Reformers can't lock professional knowledges out of the process. Hence, reformers must be engaged with police education, counter-colonizing that area with reintegrative ideas.[18]

There are no criminal justice utopias to be found, just better and worse directions to head in.[19] The New Zealand Maori have shown a direction for making reintegration ceremonies work in multicultural metropolises such as Auckland, a city that faces deeper problems of recession, homelessness, and gang violence than many cities in Western Europe. Implementation of these ideas by the white New Zealand authorities has been riddled with imperfection—re-professionalization, patriarchy, ritualistic proceduralism that loses sight of objectives, and inappropriate net-widening. The important thing, however, is that the general direction of change is away from these pathologies; it is deprofessionalizing, empowering of women, oriented to flexible community problem-solving and, for the most part, narrowing nets of state control (Maxwell and Morris 1993: 25, 134, 136, but see 128, 176; on net-narrowing at Wagga see Moore 1992; O'Connell 1992). Most critically, it shows that the conditions of successful reintegration ceremonies that criminologists identify when in high theory mode can be given practical content for implementation by police and citizens.

As both Max Scheler and Garfinkel point out: 'There is no society that does not provide in the very features of its organisation the conditions sufficient for inducing shame.' (Garfinkel 1956: 420). The question is what sort of balance societies will have between degradation ceremonies as a 'secular form of communion' and reintegration ceremonies as a rather different communion. Garfinkel showed that there was a practical programme of communication tactics that will get the work of status degradation done. We hope to have shown that equally there is a practical programme of communication tactics that can accomplish reintegration.

REFERENCES

ASHWORTH, A. (1986), 'Punishment and Compensation: Victims, Offenders and the State', *Oxford Journal of Legal Studies*, 6: 86–122.

BALES, R. (1950), *Interaction Process Analysis*. Cambridge: Addison Wesley.

BECKER, H. S. (1960), 'Notes on the concept of commitment', *American Journal of Sociology*, 66: 32–40.

—— (1963), *Outsiders: Studies in the Sociology of Deviance*. New York: Free Press.

BLUMBERG, A. S. (1967), 'The Practice of Law as a Confidence Game: Organizational Cooptation of a Profession', *Law and Society Review*, 1: 15–39.

---

[18] Something the senior author has been actively engaged with since 1986 as a member of the NSW Police Education Advisory Council.

[19] There is no persuasive evidence that the reforms we have described actually work in reducing delinquency. That would require random allocation experiments. We can say that official statistics do not support the conclusion that they are failing. Crime rates in Wagga Wagga seem to have fallen since the juvenile justice reforms were introduced. In New Zealand, juvenile crime rates were falling slightly before the Children, Young Persons and Their Families Act 1989 was passed, and continued to fall slightly after its introduction (Maxwell and Morris 1993: 45).

CONDITIONS OF SUCCESSFUL REINTEGRATION CEREMONIES

BLAGG, H. (1985), 'Reparation and Justice for Juveniles: The Corby Experience', *British Journal of Criminology*, 25: 267–79.

BOTT, E. (1987), 'The Kava Ceremonial as a Dream Structure', in M. Douglas, ed., *Constructive Drinking: Perspectives on Drinking from Anthropology*. Cambridge: Cambridge University Press, pp. 182–204.

BRAITHWAITE, J. (1989), *Crime, Shame and Reintegration*. Cambridge: Cambridge University Press.

—— (1991), 'Poverty, Power, White-Collar Crime and the Paradoxes of Criminological Theory', *Australian and New Zealand Journal of Criminology*, 24: 40–58.

—— (1992), 'Corporate Crime and Republican Criminological Praxis', Paper to Queens University Conference on Corporate Ethics, Law and the State, Kingston.

—— (1993), 'Inequality and Republican Criminology', in John Hagan and Ruth Peterson, eds, *Crime and Inequality*. Palo Alto: Stanford University Press.

BRAITHWAITE, J., and DALY, K. (in press), 'Masculinities, Violence and Communitarian Control', in T. Newburn and B. Stanko, eds, *Just Boys Doing Business? Men, Masculinity and Crime*. London: Routledge.

CHEAL, D. (1988), 'The Postmodern Origins of Ritual', *Journal for the Theory of Social Behaviour*, 18: 269–90.

CHRISTIE, N. (1977), 'Conflict as Property', *British Journal of Criminology*, 17: 1–26.

CRAGG, W. (1992), *The Practice of Punishment: Towards a Theory of Restorative Justice*. London: Routledge.

DE HAAN, W. (1990), *The Politics of Redress: Crime, Punishment and Penal Abolition*. London: Unwin Hyman.

DIGNAN, J. (1992), 'Repairing the Damage: Can Reparation Work in the Service of Diversion?', *British Journal of Criminology*, 32: 453–72.

DOOB, A., and ROBERTS, J. (1983), *Sentencing: An Analysis of the Public's View of Sentencing. A Report to the Department of Justice, Canada*. Department of Justice: Canada.

—— (1988), 'Public Attitudes towards Sentencing in Canada', in N. Walker and M. Hough, eds, *Public Attitudes to Sentencing*. Aldershot: Gower.

ERIKSON, K. T. (1962), 'Notes on the Sociology of Deviance', *Social Problems*, 9: 307–14.

FISSE, B., and BRAITHWAITE, J. (1993), *Corporations, Crime and Accountability*. Sydney: Cambridge University Press.

GALAWAY, B. (1985), 'Victim-Participation in the Penal Corrective process', *Victimology*, 10: 617–30.

GALAWAY, B., and HUDSON, J. (1975), 'Issues in the Correctional Implementation of Restitution to Victims of Crime', in J. Hudson and B. Galaway, eds, *Considering the Victim*. Springfield, IL: Charles C. Thomas.

—— (1990), *Criminal Justice, Restitution and Reconciliation*. Monsey, NY: Criminal Justice Press.

GALAWAY, B., HENZEL, M., RAMSEY, G., and WANYAMA, B. (1980), 'Victims and Delinquents in the Tulsa Juvenile Court', *Federal Probation*, 44: 42–8.

GARFINKEL, H. (1956), 'Conditions of Successful Degradation Ceremonies', *American Journal of Sociology*, 61: 420–4.

GIDDENS, A. (1984), *The Constitution of Society*. Berkeley, CA: University of California Press.

GOFFMAN, E. (1971), *Relations in Public*. New York: Basic Books.

GUSFIELD, J. R. (1987), 'Passage to Play: Rituals of Drink in American Society', in M. Douglas, ed., *Constructive Drinking: Perspectives on Drinking from Anthropology*. Cambridge: Cambridge University Press, pp. 73–90.

HABERMAS, J. (1986), 'Law as Medium and Law as Institution', in Gunther Teubner, ed., *Dilemmas of Law in the Welfare State*. Berlin: Walter de Gruyter.

HAZAN, H. (1987), 'Holding Time Still with Cups of Tea', in M. Douglas, ed., *Constructive Drinking: Perspectives on Drinking from Anthropology*. Cambridge: Cambridge University Press, pp. 205–19.

HAZLEHURST, K. (1985), 'Community Care/Community Responsibility: Community Participation in Criminal Justice Administration in New Zealand', in K. Hazlehurst, ed., *Justice Programs for Aboriginal and Other Indigenous Communities*. Canberra: Australian Institute of Criminology.

HEINZ, A., and KERSTETTER, W. (1981), 'Pretrial Settlement Conference: Evaluation of a Reform in Plea Bargaining', in B. Galaway and J. Hudson, eds, *Perspectives on Crime Victims*. St. Louis, MO: Mosby.

HIRSCHI, T., and GOTTFREDSON, M. (1983), 'Age and the Explanation of Crime', *American Journal of Sociology*, 89: 552–84.

HOWARD, B., and PURCHES, L. (1992), 'A Discussion of the Police Family Group Conferences and the Follow-Up Program (Stage 2) in the Wagga Wagga Juvenile Cautioning Process', *Rural Society*, 2: 20–3.

Interim Report of the Select Committee on the Juvenile Justice System (1992). Adelaide: Parliament of South Australia.

KIGIN, R., and NOVACK, S. (1980), 'A Rural Restitution Program for Juvenile Offenders and Victims', in J. Hudson and B. Galaway, eds, *Victims, Offenders and Alternative Sanctions*. Lexington, MA: Lexington Books.

MARSHALL, T. F. (1985), *Alternatives to Criminal Courts*. Aldershot: Gower.

MAXWELL, G. M., and MORRIS, A. (1993), *Family Victims and Culture: Youth Justice in ·New Zealand*. Wellington: Institute of Criminology, Victoria University of Wellington.

McDONALD, J., and IRELAND, S. (1990), *Can It be Done Another Way?* Sydney: New South Wales Police Service.

MEIMA, M. (1990), 'Sexual Violence, Criminal Law and Abolitionism', in B. Rolston and M. Tomlinson, eds, *Gender, Sexuality and Social Control*. Bristol: European Group for the Study of Deviance and Social Control.

MOORE, D. B. (1992), 'Facing the Consequences. Conferences and Juvenile Justice', *National Conference on Juvenile Justice*. Canberra: Australian Institute of Criminology.

MORRIS, A., and MAXWELL, G. (1992), 'Juvenile Justice in New Zealand: A New Paradigm', *Australian and New Zealand Journal of Criminology*, 26: 72–90.

MORRIS, A., MAXWELL, G., and ROBERTSON, J. P. (in press), 'Giving Victims a Voice: A New Zealand Experiment', *Howard Journal of Criminology*.

MUGFORD, J., and MUGFORD, S. (1991), 'Shame and Reintegration in the Punishment and Deterrence of Spouse Abuse'. Paper presented to the American Society of Criminology Conference, San Francisco, 20 November.

—— (1992), 'Policing Domestic Violence), in P. Moir and H. Eijckman, eds, *Policing Australia: Old Issues, New Perspectives*. Melbourne: MacMillan, pp. 321–83.

MURPHY, J. G., and HAMPTON, J. (1989), *Forgiveness and Mercy*. New York: Cambridge.

New Zealand Police Association (1991), Submission to the Review of the Children, Young Persons and their Families Act 1989. Wellington: New Zealand Police Association.

NOVACK, S., GALAWAY, B., and HUDSON, J. (1980), 'Victim and Offender Perceptions of the Fairness of Restitution and Community-Service Sanctions', in J. Hudson and B. Galaway, eds, *Victims, Offenders and Alternative Sanctions*. Lexington, MA: Lexington Books.

CONDITIONS OF SUCCESSFUL REINTEGRATION CEREMONIES

O'CONNELL, T. (1992), 'It May Be the Way to Go', *National Conference on Juvenile Justice*. Canberra: Australian Institute of Criminology.

O'CONNELL, T. and MOORE, D. (1992), 'Wagga Juvenile Cautioning Process: The General Applicability of Family Group Conferences for Juvenile Offenders and their Victims', *Rural Society*, 2: 16–19.

O'CONNOR, I., and SWEETAPPLE, P. (1988), *Children in Justice*. Sydney: Longman-Cheshire.

PEPINSKY, H. E., and QUINNEY, R. (eds) (1991) *Criminology as Peacemaking*. Bloomington: Indiana University Press.

POLK, K. (1992), 'Jobs not Jails: A New Agenda for Youth', *National Conference on Juvenile Justice*. Canberra: Australian Institute of Criminology.

Report of the Ministerial Advisory Committee on a Maori Perspective for the Department of Social Welfare (1986), *Puao-Te-Ata-Tu* (day break). Wellington, New Zealand: Department of Social Welfare.

ROSE, N. (1990), *Governing the Soul: Shaping the Private Self*. London: Routledge and Kegan Paul.

SCHEFF, T. J., and RETZINGER, S. M. (1991), *Emotions and Violence: Shame and Rage in Destructive Conflicts*. Lexington, MA: Lexington Books.

SCHUR, E. M. (1973), *Radical Non-Intervention: Rethinking the Delinquency Problem*. Englewood Cliffs, NJ: Prentice-Hall.

SHAPLAND, J., WILLMORE, J., and DUFF, P. (1985), *Victims in the Criminal Justice System*, Cambridge Studies in Criminology. Brookfield, VT: Gower.

SHEARING, C. D., and ERICSON, R. V. (1991), 'Towards a Figurative Conception of Action', *British Journal of Sociology*, 42: 481–506.

SIMMEL, G. (1978), *The Philosophy of Money*. London: Routledge.

SYKES, G., and MATZA, D. (1957), 'Techniques of Neutralization: A Theory of Delinquency', *American Sociological Review*, 22: 664–70.

TATE, SENATOR M. (1992), Opening Address, *National Conference on Juvenile Justice*. Canberra: Australian Institute of Criminology.

TAYLOR, I., WALTON, P., and YOUNG, J. (1973), *The New Criminology: For a Social Theory of Deviance*. London: Routledge and Kegan Paul.

UMBREIT, M. (1985), *Crime and Reconciliation: Creative Options for Victims and Offenders*. Nashville, TN: Abigton Press.

WEITEKAMP, E. (1989), Restitution: A New Paradigm of Criminal Justice or a New Way to Widen the System of Social Control? Unpublished Ph.D dissertation, University of Pennsylvania.

WRIGHT, M. (1982), *Making Good: Prisons, Punishment and Beyond*. London: Hutchinson.

Youth Justice Coalition (1990), *Kids in Justice: A Blueprint for the 90s*. Sydney: Law Foundation of New South Wales.

ZEHR, H. (1990), *Changing Lenses: A New Focus for Criminal Justice*. Scottdale, PA: Herald Press.

[2]

CONFLICTS AS PROPERTY*

Nils Christie (*Oslo*) †

Abstract

Conflicts are seen as important elements in society. Highly industrialised societies do not have too much internal conflict, they have too little. We have to organise social systems so that conflicts are both nurtured and made visible and also see to it that professionals do not monopolise the handling of them. Victims of crime have in particular lost their rights to participate. A court procedure that restores the participants' rights to their own conflicts is outlined.

Introduction

Maybe we should not have any criminology. Maybe we should rather abolish institutes, not open them. Maybe the social consequences of criminology are more dubious than we like to think.

I think they are. And I think this relates to my topic—conflicts as property. My suspicion is that criminology to some extent has amplified a process where conflicts have been taken away from the parties directly involved and thereby have either disappeared or become other people's property. In both cases a deplorable outcome. Conflicts ought to be used, not only left in erosion. And they ought to be used, and become useful, for those originally involved in the conflict. Conflicts *might* hurt individuals as well as social systems. That is what we learn in school. That is why we have officials. Without them, private vengeance and vendettas will blossom. We have learned this so solidly that we have lost track of the other side of the coin: our industrialised large-scale society is not one with too many internal conflicts. It is one with too little. Conflicts might kill, but too little of them might paralyse. I will

* Foundation Lecture of the Centre for Criminological Studies, University of Sheffield, delivered March 31, 1976. Valuable comments on preliminary drafts of the manuscript were received from Vigdis Christie, Tove Stang Dahl and Annika Snare.
† Professor of Criminology, University of Oslo.

NILS CHRISTIE

use this occasion to give a sketch of this situation. It cannot be more than a sketch. This paper represents the beginning of the development of some ideas, not the polished end-product.

On Happenings and Non-Happenings

Let us take our point of departure far away. Let us move to Tanzania. Let us approach our problem from the sunny hillside of the Arusha province. Here, inside a relatively large house in a very small village, a sort of happening took place. The house was overcrowded. Most grown-ups from the village and several from adjoining ones were there. It was a happy happening, fast talking, jokes, smiles, eager attention, not a sentence was to be lost. It was circus, it was drama. It was a court case.

The conflict this time was between a man and a woman. They had been engaged. He had invested a lot in the relationship through a long period, until she broke it off. Now he wanted it back. Gold and silver and money were easily decided on, but what about utilities already worn, and what about general expenses?

The outcome is of no interest in our context. But the framework for conflict solution is. Five elements ought to be particularly mentioned:

1. The parties, the former lovers, were in *the centre* of the room and in the centre of everyone's attention. They talked often and were eagerly listened to.

2. Close to them were relatives and friends who also took part. But they did not *take over*.

3. There was also participation from the general audience with short questions, information, or jokes.

4. The judges, three local party secretaries, were extremely inactive. They were obviously ignorant with regard to village matters. All the other people in the room were experts. They were experts on norms as well as actions. And they crystallised norms and clarified what had happened through participation in the procedure.

5. No reporters attended. They were all there.

My personal knowledge when it comes to British courts is limited indeed. I have some vague memories of juvenile courts where I counted some 15 or 20 persons present, mostly social workers using the room for preparatory work or small conferences A child or a young person must have attended, but except for the judge, or maybe it was the clerk, nobody seemed to pay any particular attention. The child or young person was most probably utterly confused as to who was who and for what, a fact confirmed in a small study by Peter Scott (1959). In the United States of America, Martha Baum (1968) has made similar observations. Recently, Bottoms and McClean (1976) have added another important observation: " There is one truth which is seldom revealed in the literature of the law or in studies of the administration of criminal justice. It is a truth which was made evident to all those involved in this research project as they sat through the cases which made up our sample. The truth is that, for the most part, the business of the criminal courts is dull, commonplace, ordinary and after a while downright tedious ".

But let me keep quiet about your system, and instead concentrate on my

CONFLICTS AS PROPERTY

own. And let me assure you: what goes on is no happening. It is all a nega-
tion of the Tanzanian case. What is striking in nearly all the Scandinavian
cases is the greyness, the dullness, and the lack of any important audience.
Courts are not central elements in the daily life of our citizens, but peripheral
in four major ways:—

1. They are situated in the administrative centres of the towns, outside the
territories of ordinary people.

2. Within these centres they are often centralised within one or two large
buildings of considerable complexity. Lawyers often complain that they need
months to find their way within these buildings It does not demand much
fantasy to imagine the situation of parties or public when they are trapped
within these structures. A comparative study of court architecture might
become equally relevant for the sociology of law as Oscar Newman's (1972)
study of defensible space is for criminology. But even without any study, I
feel it safe to say that both physical situation and architectural design are
strong indicators that courts in Scandinavia belong to the administrators of
law.

3. This impression is strengthened when you enter the courtroom itself—
if you are lucky enough to find your way to it. Here again, the periphery of
the parties is the striking observation. The parties are represented, and it is
these representatives and the judge or judges who express the little activity
that is activated within these rooms. Honoré Daumier's famous drawings
from the courts are as representative for Scandinavia as they are for France.

There are variations. In the small cities, or in the countryside, the courts
are more easily reached than in the larger towns. And at the very lowest end
of the court system—the so-called arbitration boards—the parties are sometimes less heavily represented through experts in law. But the symbol of the
whole system is the Supreme Court where the directly involved parties do not
even attend their own court cases.

4. I have not yet made any distinction between civil and criminal conflicts. But it was not by chance that the Tanzania case was a civil one. Full
participation in your own conflict presupposes elements of civil law. The key
element in a criminal proceeding is that the proceeding is converted from
something between the concrete parties into a conflict between one of the
parties and the state. So, in a modern criminal trial, two important things
have happened. First, the parties are being *represented*. Secondly, the one
party that is represented by the state, namely the victim, is so thoroughly
represented that she or he for most of the proceedings is pushed completely
out of the arena, reduced to the triggerer-off of the whole thing. She or he is
a sort of double loser; first, *vis-à-vis* the offender, but secondly and often in a
more crippling manner by being denied rights to full participation in what
might have been one of the more important ritual encounters in life. The
victim has lost the case to the state.

Professional Thieves

As we all know, there are many honourable as well as dishonourable reasons
behind this development. The honourable ones have to do with the state's

3

NILS CHRISTIE

need for conflict reduction and certainly also its wishes for the protection of the victim. It is rather obvious. So is also the less honourable temptation for the state, or Emperor, or whoever is in power, to use the criminal case for personal gain. Offenders might pay for their sins. Authorities have in time past shown considerable willingness, in representing the victim, to act as receivers of the money or other property from the offender. Those days are gone; the crime control system is not run for profit. And yet they are not gone. There are, in all banality, many interests at stake here, most of them related to professionalisation.

Lawyers are particularly good at stealing conflicts. They are trained for it. They are trained to prevent and solve conflicts. They are socialised into a sub-culture with a surprisingly high agreement concerning interpretation of norms, and regarding what sort of information can be accepted as relevant in each case. Many among us have, as laymen, experienced the sad moments of truth when our lawyers tell us that our best arguments in our fight against our neighbour are without any legal relevance whatsoever and that we for God's sake ought to keep quiet about them in court. Instead they pick out arguments we might find irrelevant or even wrong to use. My favourite example took place just after the war. One of my country's absolutely top defenders told with pride how he had just rescued a poor client. The client had collaborated with the Germans. The prosecutor claimed that the client had been one of the key people in the organisation of the Nazi movement. He had been one of the master-minds behind it all. The defender, however, saved his client. He saved him by pointing out to the jury how weak, how lacking in ability, how obviously deficient his client was, socially as well as organisationally. His client could simply not have been one of the organisers among the collaborators; he was without talents. And he won his case. His client got a very minor sentence as a very minor figure. The defender ended his story by telling me—with some indignation—that neither the accused, nor his wife, had ever thanked him, they had not even talked to him afterwards.

Conflicts become the property of lawyers. But lawyers don't hide that it is conflicts they handle. And the organisational framework of the courts underlines this point. The opposing parties, the judge, the ban against privileged communication within the court system, the lack of encouragement for specialisation—specialists cannot be internally controlled—it all underlines that this is an organisation for the handling of conflicts. *Treatment personnel* are in another position. They are more interested in *converting the image of the case from one of conflict into one of non-conflict.* The basic model of healers is not one of opposing parties, but one where one party has to be helped in the direction of one generally accepted goal—the preservation or restoration of health. They are not trained into a system where it is important that parties can control each other. There is, in the ideal case, nothing to control, because there is only one goal. Specialisation is encouraged. It increases the amount of available knowledge, and the loss of internal control is of no relevance. A conflict perspective creates unpleasant doubts with regard to the healer's suitability for the job. A non-conflict perspective is a precondition for defining crime as a legitimate target for treatment.

CONFLICTS AS PROPERTY

One way of reducing attention to the conflict is reduced attention given to the victim. Another is concentrated attention given to those attributes in the criminal's background which the healer is particularly trained to handle. Biological defects are perfect. So also are personality defects when they are established far back in time—far away from the recent conflict. And so are also the whole row of explanatory variables that criminology might offer. We have, in criminology, to a large extent functioned as an auxiliary science for the professionals within the crime control system. We have focused on the offender, made her or him into an object for study, manipulation and control. We have added to all those forces that have reduced the victim to a nonentity and the offender to a thing. And this critique is perhaps not only relevant for the old criminology, but also for the new criminology. While the old one explained crime from personal defects or social handicaps, the new criminology explains crime as the result of broad economic conflicts. The old criminology loses the conflicts, the new one converts them from interpersonal conflicts to class conflicts. And they are. They are class conflicts— also. But, by stressing this, the conflicts are again taken away from the directly involved parties. So, as a preliminary statement: Criminal conflicts have either become *other people's property*—primarily the property of lawyers—or it has been in other people's interests to *define conflicts away*.

Structural Thieves

But there is more to it than professional manipulation of conflicts. Changes in the basic social structure have worked in the same way.

What I particularly have in mind are *two types of segmentation* easily observed in highly industrialised societies. First, there is the question of segmentation *in space*. We function each day, as migrants moving between sets of people which do not need to have any link—except through the mover. Often, therefore, we know our work-mates only as work-mates, neighbours only as neighbours, fellow cross-country skiers only as fellow cross-country skiers. We get to know them as *roles*, not as total persons. This situation is accentuated by the extreme degree of division of labour we accept to live with. Only experts can evaluate each other according to individual—personal—competence. Outside the speciality we have to fall back on a general evaluation of the supposed importance of the work. Except between specialists, we cannot evaluate how good anybody is in his work, only how good, in the sense of important, the role is. Through all this, we get limited possibilities for understanding other people's behaviour. Their behaviour will also get limited relevance for us. Role-players are more easily exchanged than persons.

The second type of segmentation has to do with what I would like to call our re-establishment of caste-society. I am not saying class-society, even though there are obvious tendencies also in that direction. In my framework, however, I find the elements of caste even more important. What I have in mind is the segregation based on biological attributes such as sex, colour, physical handicaps or the number of winters that have passed since birth. Age is particularly important. It is an attribute nearly perfectly synchronised to a modern complex industrialised society. It is a continuous variable where

NILS CHRISTIE

we can introduce as many intervals as we might need. We can split the population in two: children and adults. But we also can split it in ten: babies, pre-school children, school-children, teenagers, older youth, adults, pre-pensioned, pensioned, old people, the senile. And most important: the cutting points can be moved up and down according to social needs. The concept " teenager " was particularly suitable 10 years ago. It would not have caught on if social realities had not been in accordance with the word. Today the concept is not often used in my country. The condition of youth is not over at 19. Young people have to wait even longer before they are allowed to enter the work force. The caste of those outside the work force has been extended far into the twenties. At the same time departure from the work force—if you ever were admitted, if you were not kept completely out because of race or sex-attributes—is brought forward into the early sixties in a person's life. In my tiny country of four million inhabitants, we have 800,000 persons segregated within the educational system. Increased scarcity of work has immediately led authorities to increase the capacity of educational incarceration. Another 600,000 are pensioners.

Segmentation according to space and according to caste attributes has several consequences. First and foremost it leads into a *depersonalisation* of social life. Individuals are to a smaller extent linked to each other in close social networks where they are confronted with *all* the significant roles of the significant others. This creates a situation with limited amounts of information with regard to each other. We do know less about other people, and get limited possibilities both for understanding and for prediction of their behaviour. If a conflict is created, we are less able to cope with this situation. Not only are professionals there, able and willing to take the conflict away, but we are also more willing to give it away.

Secondly, segmentation leads to destruction of certain conflicts even before they get going. The depersonalisation and mobility within industrial society melt away some essential conditions for living conflicts; those between parties that mean a lot to each other. What I have particularly in mind is crime against other people's honour, libel or defamation of character. All the Scandinavian countries have had a dramatic decrease in this form of crime. In my interpretation, this is not because honour has become more respected, but because there is less honour to respect. The various forms of segmentation mean that human beings are inter-related in ways where they simply mean less to each other. When they are hurt, they are only hurt partially. And if they are troubled, they can easily move away. And after all, who cares? Nobody knows me. In my evaluation, the decrease in the crimes of infamy and libel is one of the most interesting and sad symptoms of dangerous developments within modern industrialised societies. The decrease here is clearly related to social conditions that lead to increase in other forms of crime brought to the attention of the authorities. It is an important goal for crime prevention to re-create social conditions which lead to an increase in the number of crimes against other people's honour.

A third consequence of segmentation according to space and age is that certain conflicts are made completely invisible, and thereby don't get any

6

decent solution whatsoever. I have here in mind conflicts at the two extremes of a continuum. On the one extreme we have the over-privatised ones, those taking place against individuals captured within one of the segments. Wife beating or child battering represent examples. The more isolated a segment is, the more the weakest among parties is alone, open for abuse. Inghe and Riemer (1943) made the classical study many years ago of a related phenomenon in their book on incest. Their major point was that the social isolation of certain categories of proletarised Swedish farm-workers was the necessary condition for this type of crime. Poverty meant that the parties within the nuclear family became completely dependent on each other. Isolation meant that the weakest parties within the family had no external network where they could appeal for help. The physical strength of the husband got an undue importance. At the other extreme we have crimes done by large economic organisations against individuals too weak and ignorant to be able even to realise they have been victimised. In both cases the goal for crime prevention might be to re-create social conditions which make the conflicts visible and thereafter manageable.

Conflicts as Property

Conflicts are taken away, given away, melt away, or are made invisible. Does it matter, does it really matter?

Most of us would probably agree that we ought to protect the invisible victims just mentioned. Many would also nod approvingly to ideas saying that states, or Governments, or other authorities ought to stop stealing fines, and instead let the poor victim receive this money. I at least would approve such an arragement. But I will not go into that problem area here and now. Material compensation is not what I have in mind with the formulation " conflicts as property ". It is the *conflict itself* that represents the most interesting property taken away, not the goods originally taken away from the victim, or given back to him. In our types of society, conflicts are more scarce than property. And they are immensely more valuable.

They are valuable in several ways. Let me start at the societal level, since here I have already presented the necessary fragments of analysis that might allow us to see what the problem is. Highly industrialised societies face major problems in organising their members in ways such that a decent quota take part in any activity at all. Segmentation according to age and sex can be seen as shrewd methods for segregation. Participation is such a scarcity that insiders create monopolies against outsiders, particularly with regard to work. In this perspective, it will easily be seen that conflicts represent a *potential for activity, for participation*. Modern criminal control systems represent one of the many cases of lost opportunities for involving citizens in tasks that are of immediate importance to them. Ours is a society of task-monopolists.

The victim is a particularly heavy loser in this situation. Not only has he suffered, lost materially or become hurt, physically or otherwise. And not only does the state take the compensation. But above all he has lost participation in his own case. It is the Crown that comes into the spotlight, not the victim. It is the Crown that describes the losses, not the victim. It is the Crown

NILS CHRISTIE

that appears in the newspaper, very seldom the victim. It is the Crown that gets a chance to talk to the offender, and neither the Crown nor the offender are particularly interested in carrying on that conversation. The prosecutor is fed-up long since. The victim would not have been. He might have been scared to death, panic-stricken, or furious. But he would not have been un-involved. It would have been one of the important days in his life. Something that belonged to him has been taken away from that victim.[1]

But the big loser is us—to the extent that society is us. This loss is first and foremost a loss in *opportunities for norm-clarification*. It is a loss of pedagogical possibilities. It is a loss of opportunities for a continuous discussion of what represents the law of the land. How wrong was the thief, how right was the victim? Lawyers are, as we saw, trained into agreement on what is relevant in a case. But that means a trained incapacity in letting the parties decide what *they* think is relevant. It means that it is difficult to stage what we might call a political debate in the court. When the victim is small and the offender big—in size or power—how blameworthy then is the crime? And what about the opposite case, the small thief and the big house-owner? If the offender is well educated, ought he then to suffer more. or maybe less, for his sins? Or if he is black, or if he is young, or if the other party is an insurance company, or if his wife has just left him, or if his factory will break down if he has to go to jail, or if his daughter will lose her fiancé, or if he was drunk, or if he was sad, or if he was mad? There is no end to it. And maybe there ought to be none. Maybe Barotse law as described by Max Gluckman (1967) is a better instrument for norm-clarification, allowing the conflicting parties to bring in the whole chain of old complaints and arguments each time. Maybe decisions on relevance and on the weight of what is found relevant ought to be taken away from legal scholars, the chief ideologists of crime control systems, and brought back for free decisions in the court-rooms.

A further general loss—both for the victim and for society in general—has to do with anxiety-level and misconceptions. It is again the possibilities for personalised encounters I have in mind. The victim is so totally out of the case that he has no chance, ever, to come to know the offender. We leave him outside, angry, maybe humiliated through a cross-examination in court, without any human contact with the offender. He has no alternative. He will need all the classical stereotypes around " the criminal " to get a grasp on the whole thing. He has a need for understanding, but is instead a non-person in a Kafka play. Of course, he will go away more frightened than ever, more in need than ever of an explanation of criminals as non-human.

The offender represents a more complicated case. Not much introspection is needed to see that direct victim-participation might be experienced as painful indeed. Most of us would shy away from a confrontation of this character. That is the first reaction. But the second one is slightly more posi-tive. Human beings have reasons for their actions. If the situation is staged so that reasons can be given (reasons as the parties see them, not only the selection lawyers have decided to classify as relevant), in such a case maybe the situation would not be all that humiliating. And, particularly, if the situa-

---

[1] For a preliminary report on victim dissatisfaction, see Vennard (1976).

tion was staged in such a manner that the central question was not meting out guilt, but a thorough discussion of what could be done to undo the deed, then the situation might change. And this is exactly what ought to happen when the victim is re-introduced in the case. Serious attention will centre on the victim's losses. That leads to a natural attention as to how they can be softened. It leads into a discussion of restitution. The offender gets a possibility to change his position from being a listener to a discussion—often a highly unintelligible one—of how much pain he ought to receive, into a participant in a discussion of how he could make it good again. The offender has lost the opportunity to explain himself to a person whose evaluation of him might have mattered. He has thereby also lost one of the most important possibilities for being forgiven. Compared to the humiliations in an ordinary court—vividly described by Pat Carlen (1976) in a recent issue of the *British Journal of Criminology*—this is not obviously any bad deal for the criminal.

But let me add that I think we should do it quite independently of his wishes. It is not health-control we are discussing. It is crime control. If criminals are shocked by the initial thought of close confrontation with the victim, preferably a confrontation in the very local neighbourhood of one of the parties, what then? I know from recent conversations on these matters that most people sentenced are shocked. After all, they prefer distance from the victim, from neighbours, from listeners and maybe also from their own court case through the vocabulary and the behavioural science experts who might happen to be present. They are perfectly willing to give away their property right to the conflict. So the question is more: are *we* willing to let them give it away? Are we willing to give them this easy way out? [2]

Let me be quite explicit on one point: I am not suggesting these ideas out of any particular interest in the treatment or improvement of criminals. I am not basing my reasoning on a belief that a more personalised meeting between offender and victim would lead to reduced recidivism. Maybe it would. I think it would. As it is now, the offender has lost the opportunity for participation in a personal confrontation of a very serious nature. He has lost the opportunity to receive a type of blame that it would be very difficult to neutralise. However, I would have suggested these arrangements even if it was absolutely certain they had no effects on recidivism, maybe even if they had a negative effect. I would have done that because of the other, more general gains. And let me also add—it is not much to lose. As we all know today, at least nearly all, we have not been able to invent any cure for crime. Except for execution, castration or incarceration for life, no measure has a proven minimum of efficiency compared to any other measure. We might as well react to crime according to what closely involved parties find is just and in accordance with general values in society.

With this last statement, as with most of the others I have made, I raise many more problems than I answer. Statements on criminal politics, particularly from those with the burden of responsibility, are usually filled with

[2] I tend to take the same position with regard to a criminal's property right to his own conflict as John Locke on property rights to one's own life—one has no right to give it away (*cf.* C. B. MacPherson (1962)).

NILS CHRISTIE

answers. It is questions we need. The gravity of our topic makes us much too pedantic and thereby useless as paradigm-changers.

A Victim-Oriented Court

There is clearly a model of neighbourhood courts behind my reasoning. But it is one with some peculiar features, and it is only these I will discuss in what follows.

First and foremost; it is a *victim-oriented* organisation. Not in its initial stage, though. The first stage will be a traditional one where it is established whether it is true that the law has been broken, and whether it was this particular person who broke it.

Then comes the second stage, which in these courts would be of the utmost importance. That would be the stage where the victim's situation was considered, where every detail regarding what had happened—legally relevant or not—was brought to the court's attention. Particularly important here would be detailed consideration regarding what could be done for him, first and foremost by the offender, secondly by the local neighbourhood, thirdly by the state. Could the harm be compensated, the window repaired, the lock replaced, the wall painted, the loss of time because the car was stolen given back through garden work or washing of the car ten Sundays in a row? Or maybe, when this discussion started, the damage was not so important as it looked in documents written to impress insurance companies? Could physical suffering become slightly less painful by any action from the offender, during days, months or years? But, in addition, had the community exhausted all resources that might have offered help? Was it absolutely certain that the local hospital could not do anything? What about a helping hand from the janitor twice a day if the offender took over the cleaning of the basement every Saturday? None of these ideas is unknown or untried, particularly not in England. But we need an organisation for the systematic application of them.

Only after this stage was passed, and it ought to take hours, maybe days, to pass it, only then would come the time for an eventual decision on punishment. Punishment, then, becomes that suffering which the judge found necessary to apply *in addition to* those unintended constructive sufferings the offender would go through in his restitutive actions *vis-à-vis* the victim. Maybe nothing could be done or nothing would be done. But neighbourhoods might find it intolerable that nothing happened. Local courts out of tune with local values are not local courts. That is just the trouble with them, seen from the liberal reformer's point of view.

A fourth stage has to be added. That is the stage for service to the offender. His general social and personal situation is by now well-known to the court. The discussion of his possibilities for restoring the victim's situation cannot be carried out without at the same time giving information about the offender's situation. This might have exposed needs for social, educational, medical or religious action—not to prevent further crime, but because needs ought to be met. Courts are public arenas, needs are made visible. But it is important that this stage comes *after* sentencing. Otherwise we get a re-emergence of

CONFLICTS AS PROPERTY

the whole array of so-called " special measures "—compulsory treatments—very often only euphemisms for indeterminate imprisonment.

Through these four stages, these courts would represent a blend of elements from civil and criminal courts, but with a strong emphasis on the civil side.

A Lay-Oriented Court

The second major peculiarity with the court model I have in mind is that it will be one with an extreme degree of lay-orientation. This is essential when conflicts are seen as property that ought to be shared. It is with conflicts as with so many good things: they are in no unlimited supply. Conflicts can be cared for, protected, nurtured. But there are limits. If some are given more access in the disposal of conflicts, others are getting less. It is as simple as that.

Specialisation in conflict solution is the major enemy; specialisation that in due—or undue—time leads to professionalisation. That is when the specialists get sufficient power to claim that they have acquired special gifts, mostly through education, gifts so powerful that it is obvious that they can only be handled by the certified craftsman.

With a clarification of the enemy, we are also able to specify the goal; let us reduce specialisation and particularly our dependence on the professionals within the crime control system to the utmost.

The ideal is clear; it ought to be a court of equals representing themselves. When they are able to find a solution between themselves, no judges are needed. When they are not, the judges ought also to be their equals.

Maybe the judge would be the easiest to replace, if we made a serious attempt to bring our present courts nearer to this model of lay orientation. We have lay judges already, in principle. But that is a far cry from realities. What we have, both in England and in my own country, is a sort of specialised non-specialist. First, they are used *again and again*. Secondly, some are even *trained*, given special courses or sent on excursions to foreign countries to learn about how to behave as a lay judge. Thirdly, most of them do also represent an extremely *biased sample* of the population with regard to sex, age, education, income, class [3] and personal experience as criminals. With real lay judges, I conceive of a system where nobody was given the right to take part in conflict solution more than a few times, and then had to wait until all other community members had had the same experience.

Should lawyers be admitted to court? We had an old law in Norway that forbids them to enter the rural districts. Maybe they should be admitted in stage one where it is decided if the man is guilty. I am not sure. Experts are as cancer to any lay body. It is exactly as Ivan Illich describes for the educational system in general. Each time you increase the length of compulsory education in a society, each time you also decrease the same population's trust in what they have learned and understood quite by themselves.

Behaviour experts represent the same dilemma. Is there a place for them in this model? Ought there to be any place? In stage 1, decisions on facts, certainly not. In stage 3, decisions on eventual punishment, certainly not. It is too obvious to waste words on. We have the painful row of mistakes from

[3] For the most recent documentation, see Baldwin (1976).

NILS CHRISTIE

Lombroso, through the movement for social defence and up to recent attempts to dispose of supposedly dangerous people through predictions of who they are and when they are not dangerous any more. Let these ideas die, without further comments.

The real problem has to do with the service function of behaviour experts. Social scientists can be perceived as functional answers to a segmented society. Most of us have lost the physical possibility to experience the totality, both on the social system level and on the personality level. Psychologists can be seen as historians for the individual; sociologists have much of the same function for the social system. Social workers are oil in the machinery, a sort of security counsel. Can we function without them, would the victim and the offender be worse off?

Maybe. But it would be immensely difficult to get such a court to function if they were all there. Our theme is social conflict. Who is not at least made slightly uneasy in the handling of her or his own social conflicts if we get to know that there is an expert on this very matter at the same table? I have no clear answer, only strong feelings behind a vague conclusion: let us have as few behaviour experts as we dare to. And if we have any, let us for God's sake not have any that specialise in crime and conflict resolution. Let us have generalised experts with a solid base outside the crime control system. And a last point with relevance for both behaviour experts and lawyers: if we find them unavoidable in certain cases or at certain stages, let us try to get across to them the problems they create for broad social participation. Let us try to get them to perceive themselves as resource-persons, answering when asked, but not domineering, not in the centre. They might help to stage conflicts, not take them over.

Rolling Stones

There are hundreds of blocks against getting such a system to operate within our western culture. Let me only mention three major ones. They are:
  1. There is a lack of neighbourhoods.
  2. There are too few victims.
  3. There are too many professionals around.

With lack of neighbourhoods I have in mind the very same phenomenon I described as a consequence of industrialised living; segmentation according to space and age. Much of our trouble stems from killed neighbourhoods or killed local communities. How can we then thrust towards neighbourhoods a task that presupposes they are highly alive? I have no really good arguments, only two weak ones. First, it is not quite that bad. The death is not complete. Secondly, one of the major ideas behind the formulation 'Conflicts as Property' is that it is neighbourhood-property. It is not private. It belongs to the system. It is intended as a vitaliser for neighbourhoods. The more fainting the neighbourhood is, the more we need neighbourhood courts as one of the many functions any social system needs for not dying through lack of challenge.

Equally bad is the lack of victims. Here I have particularly in mind the lack of personal victims. The problem behind this is again the large units in

CONFLICTS AS PROPERTY

industrialised society. Woolworth or British Rail are not good victims. But again I will say: there is not a complete lack of personal victims, and their needs ought to get priority. But we should not forget the large organisations. They, or their boards, would certainly prefer not to have to appear as victims in 5000 neighbourhood courts all over the country. But maybe they ought to be compelled to appear. If the complaint is serious enough to bring the offender into the ranks of the criminal, then the victim ought to appear. A related problem has to do with insurance companies—the industrialised alternative to friendship or kinship. Again we have a case where the crutches deteriorate the condition. Insurance takes the consequences of crime away. We will therefore have to take insurance away. Or rather: we will have to keep the possibilities for compensation through the insurance companies back until in the procedure I have described it has been proved behond all possible doubt that there are no other alternatives left—particularly that the offender has no possibilities whatsoever. Such a solution will create more paper-work, less predictability, more aggression from customers. And the solution will not necessarily be seen as good from the perspective of the policy-holder. But it will help to protect conflicts as social fuel.

None of these troubles can, however, compete with the third and last I will comment on: the abundance of professionals. We know it all from our own personal biographies or personal observations. And in addition we get it confirmed from all sorts of social science research: the educational system of any society is not necessarily synchronised with any needs for the product of this system. Once upon a time we thought there was a direct causal relation from the number of highly educated persons in a country to the Gross National Product. Today we suspect the relationship to go the other way, if we are at all willing to use GNP as a meaningful indicator. We also know that most educational systems are extremely class-biased. We know that most academic people have had profitable investments in our education, that we fight for the same for our children, and that we also often have vested interests in making our part of the educational system even bigger. More schools for more lawyers, social workers, sociologists, criminologists. While I am *talking* deprofessionalisation, we are increasing the capacity to be able to fill up the whole world with them.

There is no solid base for optimism. On the other hand insights about the situation, and goal formulation, is a pre-condition for action. Of course, the crime control system is not the domineering one in our type of society. But it has some importance. And occurrences here are unusually well suited as pedagogical illustrations of general trends in society. There is also some room for manoeuvre. And when we hit the limits, or are hit by them, this collision represents in itself a renewed argument for more broadly conceived changes.

Another source for hope: ideas formulated here are not quite so isolated or in dissonance with the mainstream of thinking when we leave our crime control area and enter other institutions. I have already mentioned Ivan Illich with his attempts to get learning away from the teachers and back to active human beings. Compulsory learning, compulsory medication and compulsory consummation of conflict solutions have interesting similarities.

NILS CHRISTIE

When Ivan Illich and Paulo Freire are listened to, and my impression is that they increasingly are, the crime control system will also become more easily influenced.

Another, but related, major shift in paradigm is about to happen within the whole field of technology. Partly, it is the lessons from the third world that now are more easily seen, partly it is the experience from the ecology debate. The globe is obviously suffering from what we, through our technique, are doing to her. Social systems in the third world are equally obviously suffering. So the suspicion starts. Maybe the first world can't take all this technology either. Maybe some of the old social thinkers were not so dumb after all. Maybe social systems can be perceived as biological ones. And maybe there are certain types of large-scale technology that kill social systems, as they kill globes. Schumacher (1973) with his book *Small is Beautiful* and the related Institute for Intermediate Technology come in here. So do also the numerous attempts, particularly by several outstanding Institutes for Peace Research, to show the dangers in the concept of Gross National Product, and replace it with indicators that take care of dignity, equity and justice. The perspective developed in Johan Galtung's research group on World Indicators might prove extremely useful also within our own field of crime control.

There is also a political phenomenon opening vistas. At least in Scandinavia social democrats and related groupings have considerable power, but are without an explicated ideology regarding the goals for a reconstructed society. This vacuum is being felt by many, and creates a willingness to accept and even expect considerable institutional experimentation.

Then to my very last point: what about the universities in this picture? What about the new Centre in Sheffield? The answer has probably to be the old one: universities have to re-emphasise the old tasks of understanding and of criticising. But the task of training professionals ought to be looked into with renewed scepticism. Let us re-establish the credibility of encounters between critical human beings: low-paid, highly regarded, but with no extra power—outside the weight of their good ideas. That is as it ought to be.

REFERENCES

BALDWIN, J (1976) "The Social Composition of the Magistracy" *Brit. J Criminol.*, **16,** 171–174.

BAUM, M. AND WHEELER, S. (1968). "Becoming an inmate," Ch. 7, pp. 153–187, in Wheeler, S. (ed.), *Controlling Delinquents*. New York: Wiley.

BOTTOMS, A. E. AND McCLEAN, J. D. (1976). *Defendants in the Criminal Process*. London: Routledge and Kegan Paul.

CARLEN, P. (1976). "The Staging of Magistrates' Justice." *Brit. J. Criminol.*, **16,** 48–55.

GLUCKMAN, M. (1967). *The Judicial Process among the Barotse of Northern Rhodesia* Manchester University Press.

KINBERG, O., INGHE, G., AND RIEMER, S. (1943). *Incest-Problemet i Sverige*. Sth.

CONFLICTS AS PROPERTY

MacPherson, C. B. (1962). *The Political Theory of Possessive Individualism: Hobbes to Locke.* London: Oxford University Press.

Newman, O. (1972). *Defensible Space: People and Design in the Violent City.* London: Architectural Press.

Schumacher, E. F. (1973). *Small is Beautiful: A Study of Economics as if People Mattered.* London: Blond and Briggs.

Scott, P. D. (1959). "Juvenile Courts: the Juvenile's Point of View." *Brit. J. Delinq.*, **9,** 200–210.

Vennard, J. (1976). "Justice and Recompense for Victims of Crime." *New Society*, **36,** 378–380.

[3]

JUVENILE JUSTICE IN NEW ZEALAND:
A NEW PARADIGM

Allison Morris* and Gabrielle M Maxwell†

This study describes the system of juvenile justice adopted in New Zealand under the Children, Young Persons and Their Families Act 1989. The Act sets out objectives and principles which stress a number of innovative features including the integration of a western and an indigenous approach; the empowerment of families and young people; the involvement of victims; and group consensus decision-making. The principal mechanism for achieving these objectives is the Family Group Conference which replaces or supplements the Youth Court as the principal decision-making forum in most of the more serious cases. Police involvement in decision-making is also increased by a greater emphasis on diversion and by their role in reaching agreements in the Family Group Conference. Research data are presented which enable an evaluation of the extent to which the Act is meeting its objectives. The tensions in the system are discussed: particularly the issue of victim involvement versus an offender focus and the conflict between accountability and welfare.

The objectives and principles underlying youth justice in New Zealand

The Children, Young Persons and Their Families Act 1989 is probably unprecedented in the English speaking world in setting out in statutory form not only its objects but also a comprehensive set of general principles which govern both State intervention with the lives of children and young persons and the management of youth justice. Furthermore, there is no doubt that some of these objectives and principles are unique. The objects aim to:

- Promote the well-being of children, young people and their families and family groups by providing services which are appropriate to their needs, accessible, and culturally sensitive.
- Assist families and kinship groups in caring for their children and young people.
- Provide protection for children and young people.
- Enable young offenders to be made accountable.
- Enhance the development of children and young people.
- Deal with issues in a culturally appropriate manner.

A series of general principles emphasise the need to:

- Involve family, *whanau, hapu and iwi*[1] in decisions.
- Strengthen and maintain child/family relationships.
- Consider both the welfare of the child and family stability.
- Consider the wishes of the child or young person.
- Obtain the support of the child and the family for outcomes.
- Work in a time frame appropriate to the age of the child or young person.

Specific principles governing the Youth Justice sections of the Act emphasise that:

*Dr Allison Morris, Lecturer, Institute of Criminology, University of Cambridge, England.
†Dr Gabrielle M Maxwell, Research Fellow, Institute of Criminology, Victoria University of Wellington, New Zealand.

- Criminal proceedings should not be used if there is an alternative means of dealing with the matter.
- Criminal proceedings must not be used for welfare purposes.
- Young people should be kept in the community.
- Age is mitigating factor.
- Sanctions should be the least restrictive possible and should promote the development of the child in the family.
- Due regard should be given to the interests of the victim.
- The child or young person should be protected during proceedings.

To some extent these objects and principles reflect current trends (and tensions) in juvenile and criminal justice practice: disillusionment with aspects of a welfare approach, the separation of welfare and justice issues, the endorsement of certain principles of "just desserts" (that is, proportionality, determinacy and equity of outcomes), an emphasis on accountability and responsibility, the protection of children's and young persons' rights, a preference for diversion from formal procedures, deinstitutionalisation and community based penalties, a shift in resources from state agencies to the voluntary and private sector, and the use of least restrictive alternatives. More generally, the New Zealand system attempts to move some way towards a justice approach without abandoning the desire to achieve positive outcomes for young people who offend.

However, the new system also reflects certain innovatory strategies: the rights and needs of indigenous people have been taken into account; families are central to all the decision-making processes involving their children; young persons themselves have a say in how their offending should be responded to; victims are given a role in negotiations over possible penalties for juvenile offenders; and the model of decision-making advocated is by group consensus. These strategies are achieved partly through changes in police and court processes and practice but mainly through a new decision-making forum, the Family Group Conference (FGC), which enables mediation between victims and offenders, negotiation about the appropriate penalty between the enforcement agency and the family, and the involvement of the family and the young person in decision-making at a venue and using a procedure of their own choice and sensitive to their culture. Before describing in more detail how the Act's objects and principles are translated into a practical reality, we will first elaborate these various innovatory strategies.

Integration of Indigenous and Western Approaches

Marshall (1985:46-7) identifies features of strategies for dispute settlement in small scale societies which differentiate them from criminal justice arrangements in modern urbanised and industrialised societies. First, the emphasis is on consensus and involves the whole community rather than a single individual making the decision for the parties; second, the desired outcome is reconciliation and a settlement acceptable to all parties rather than the isolation and punishment of the offender; third, the concern is not to apportion blame but to examine the wider reasons for the wrong (an implicit assumption here is that there is often wrong on both sides); and fourth, there is less concern with whether or not there has actually been a breach of the law and more concern with the restoration of harmony.

These features were all apparent in the methods of dispute resolution which existed in New Zealand prior to colonisation. The early settlers believed that the indigenous Maori people, who had arrived in New Zealand from the Pacific Polynesian Islands before the European colonisation of 150 years ago, had no "law"

74   A MORRIS and G M MAXWELL   (1993) 26 ANZJ Crim

because they saw no written legal rules, police, prisons or the like; instead they described what they saw as "primitive and barbaric customs" (Jackson, M, 1991). But it is clear that Maori did not live in a lawless society. There were rules by which they lived and which covered all aspects of Maori life.

Tikanga i nga hara, for example, translates broadly into the law of wrongdoing in which there were clear concepts of right and wrong. The law, however, was based on notions that responsibility was collective rather than individual and that redress was due not just to any victim but also to the victim's family. Understanding why an individual had offended was also linked to this notion of collective responsibility. The reasons were felt to lie not in the individual but in a lack of balance in the offender's social and family environment. The causes of this imbalance, therefore, had to be addressed in a collective way and, in particular, the imbalance between the offender and the victim's family had to be restored through mediation.

Maori had also created *runanga i nga tura* which translates broadly into a council of law or court. These were headed by *Tohunga i nga ture,* experts in law, but also contained kaumatua or kuia (elders), a representative from the offender's family and a representative from the victim's family. This group sorted out the wrongdoing and restored the balance. For example, they might have ordered the transfer of the offender's goods to the victim or work by the offender for the victim.

Colonialism, however, all but destroyed indigenous systems of justice in all parts of the British Empire and New Zealand was no exception (Jackson, 1998; Pratt, 1991). The culture and values of the Maori were not allowed to exist alongside the culture and values of the colonisers. Dismantling these and the subsequent enforced assimilation to "the British way of life" was what Pratt (1991) ironically calls the "gift of civilisation". To be "one people" required one set of laws and since the colonisers had the power (first through weapons and later through increased numbers), it was their law which dominated. Indeed, removing Maori law was a powerful mechanism for destabilising the foundations of Maori society.

The new legislation, on the other hand, stresses the provision of services which are culturally sensitive and a process which is culturally appropriate. Hence it seeks to re-introduce elements of indigenous responses to dealing with offenders. This is partly a reflection of the resurgence of Maori culture and values over the last 15 years but it is also a recognition of the fact that the New Zealand population is made up of a number of different ethnic groups. Numerically, the most significant are the Pakeha (persons of European origin): more than 80% of the juvenile population. Maori make up around 12% and Pacific Island Polynesians, who have immigrated more recently than the Maori, make up 4%. It is estimated that by the year 2020, 1 in 4 of the New Zealand population will be of Polynesian descent including both New Zealand Maori and other Pacific Island Polynesians (Interdepartmental Committee on Population Policy Guidelines, 1990).

Although Maori and Pacific Island Polynesians make up together only a small part of the New Zealand population, they are over-represented in various indices of social and economic deprivation: higher infant mortality rates, lower life expectancy rates, higher unemployment rates and lower incomes than the dominant (Pakeha) group (Ministerial Advisory Committee on a Maori Perspective for the Department of Social Welfare, 1988). Maori are also over-represented in the population of known offenders, including juvenile offenders (Maxwell and Morris, 1990). Thus, according to current police statistics (1988), 37% of known offenders are described as Maori; amongst the known juvenile offender population, 43% are described as Maori (although it is not clear whether the same criteria are being used in police statistics as in population statistics). The new procedures recognise the over-representation of Maori among juvenile offenders and respond to it by attempting to incorporate traditional, extended family decision-making methods in the resolution of conflict.

The role of whanau is important in both Maori (and Polynesian) child-rearing and decision-making. It is not unusual, for example, for Maori children to live from time to time with different relatives within their whanau. This occurs in part because the child is considered not simply the child of the birth parents but also of the whanau, hapu and iwi. Bringing up children, therefore, and hence dealing with their delinquencies, is a communal responsibility. Moreover, in pre-colonial times most decisions, whatever their nature, were customarily made by the whanau, hapu or iwi depending on the importance and nature of the decision. Hence the involvement of whanau, hapu and iwi is directly recognised within the legislative framework in both discussions and decisions about appropriate solutions to juvenile offending.

The re-assertion of traditional Maori cultural values is of symbolic as well as of practical importance. As a result of colonisation, decisions on such matters as social welfare and criminal justice have been made for Maori and with little consultation with Maori. Thus traditional Maori structures have been weakened. The 1989 Act seeks, therefore, to empower Maoridom. It seeks to involve Maori directly in decisions about their young people and thus to acknowledge their identity as tangata whenua (the people of the land). Such an emphasis has implications for other cultural groups in New Zealand and has the potential for the validation of a variety of cultural practices.

However, it would be a mistake to describe the new system as the rejection of a Western criminal justice system in favour of the adoption of an indigenous method of resolution (and certainly the advocates of a Maori indigenous model would reject such a depiction). A distinction must be drawn between a system which attempts to re-establish the indigenous model of pre-European times and a system of justice which is culturally appropriate. The new New Zealand system is an attempt to establish the latter, not to replicate the former. As such, it seeks to incorporate many of the features apparent in whanau decision-making processes and seen in meetings on marae today, but is also contains elements quite alien to indigenous models (for example, the presence of representatives of the State) and other principles which, to our mind, are equally important: the empowerment of families, offenders and victims. Although families and victims had a recognised role in the resolution of disputes in traditional Maori society, their part in the new system is not necessarily identical. We will refer briefly in the final section of this article to the extent to which youth justice processes in New Zealand can be viewed as culturally appropriate.

Empowerment of the Family

A recurrent theme in conventional criminological literature is that deficiencies in the family lie at the root of juvenile crime (see Rutter and Giller, 1983 for a review) and so traditionally the State has acted to usurp the rights of families in situations of alleged abuse and neglect and the responsibilities of families whose children have committed offences. The exception is when the State has recognised family responsibility in a negative sense by holding the family accountable for their children's misdemeanours (as, for example, in the provision in England to fine parents whose children commit offences). Indeed, despite rhetoric about the importance of families, families have often in practice been undermined by the ways in which juvenile justice systems have tended to operate: by exclusion.

The idea of a partnership between the State and families in resolving issues which affect their children is a novel one. Thus, in contrast with most systems of juvenile justice, it is intended in the new system that responsibility be given to families, whanau, hapu, iwi and family groups to respond to their child's offending. The underlying intention is to empower families to deal with offending themselves and to restrict the power of professionals, in particular the power of social services. Thus, except for minor and inconsequential offending which is usually dealt with by the police by means of a warning, families are given the opportunity to formulate a plan. This plan must be considered by the judge should the case be referred to a court but the intention is to resolve matters informally through negotiation in the FGC with both the police and the victim(s) and hence a court appearance is avoided. The family itself, therefore, has become a key agency in diverting young people from formal proceedings. We will refer briefly in the final section of this article to the extent to which families have participated in new youth justice processes.

Empowerment of Offenders

To speak of the empowerment of offenders in conventional criminal justice systems is a contradiction in terms. Offenders do not participate much in court proceedings, a situation well depicted in Carlen's (1976) description of them as "dummy players". The "game" takes place all around them for the benefit of "repeat players" (Galanter, 1974) such as judges, prosecutors, defence counsel and the like, while they watch passively and uninvolved. They take on the status of objects or "dependants" and participate little (Ericson and Baranek, 1982; O'Connor and Sweetapple, 1988).

One method of meeting these concerns is through the introduction of mediation. The use of mediation developed rapidly in the USA in the 1970s-80s and has expanded to other countries since (Wright and Galaway, 1989; Marshall and Merry, 1990). The intention is not to make decisions for people, but to help them make their own decisions. As a practice, it has been used in a range of situations: for example, industrial disputes and arguments between landlords and tenants. More recently, it has been extended to include resolution between victims and offenders through the introduction of reparation schemes and restitution or compensation. In England, for example, in some circumstances, offenders who are cautioned are asked to make reparation and there are a number of mediation schemes in which offenders and their victims meet together to discuss such issues as reparation or where a group of offenders and a group of victims discuss more general issues of offending behaviour (see Marshall and Walpole, 1985; Davis et al., 1987 and Marshall and Merry, 1990, for more information).

Mediation also addresses a further concern which arises from practice in traditional criminal justice systems: the absence of any direct contact between the victim and the offender. Mediation, by bringing offenders and victims together, enables offenders to understand the consequences of their actions from the perspective of the victim, to accept responsibility for them and to actively make a commitment to some reparation. Thus, young people can feel a part of (rather than apart from) the proceedings. Indeed, in theory, offenders are empowered by the opportunity to take responsibility for their lives. It is these premises which underlie the new system of youth justice in New Zealand and in the FGC they are given force. We will refer briefly in the final section of this article to the extent to which young persons have participated in the new youth justice processes.

Empowerment of Victims

Traditionally, the criminal justice system has given only a minimal role to victims. Indeed, in part, one of its functions has been to protect offenders from the vengeance of victims. However, increasingly, criminal justice systems are giving more weight to the needs and wishes of victims. There are a number of reasons for this shift in emphasis: in particular, acceptance of the failure of criminal justice systems to reform and/or deter offenders and, consequently, the need to substitute alternative justifications for intervention; and the emergence of pressure groups from a range of political backgrounds (from the women's movement to "law and order" proponents) which have begun to highlight victims' concerns.

Thus, in most jurisdictions in recent years, there have been a number of significant changes in the provision of services for victims. In New Zealand, the Victim of Offences Act 1987 recognised the legitimacy of concerns for victims and provided for taking "victim impact statements" which could be used in evidence in court proceedings. There has also been an increase in the number of agencies providing support services, improvements in court procedures and the introduction of reparation as a sentence (see Hutton and Young, 1989, for a description). In that review, Hutton and Young comment that, at that time, there had been little concerted effort to set up, and no indication of official support for, reconciliation meetings between victims and offenders or to provide a forum in which victims could participate in the sentencing process or, at least, have their views taken into account. The new youth justice system introduces both of these provisions.

It should be noted here, however, that giving victims a greater voice and role fits too with many indigenous systems of justice. There, as we outlined in brief earlier, the victim is central rather than peripheral to the proceedings and the objective is not simply to punish the offender but to restore community balance. Traditionally, for example, Maori were concerned not only with atonement for the offence and restitution to the victim, but also with the individual offender's potential for reintegration within the whanau, hapu and iwi.

The main argument used in favour of increasing victims' representations about how offenders should be dealt with (through the presence of victims or their representatives at hearings, consultation with victims about appropriate outcomes, the introduction of victim impact statements and the like) is that they possess the information required to reach a "just" outcome. To do otherwise, it is argued, retains an imbalance in favour of offenders, for those making decisions about offenders can be influenced by information about their situation, for example, the impact of a particular outcome on them or their families.

There are other arguments in favour of victim involvement. Koehler (1988), for example, argues that, by providing victims with information and facilitating their participation in the process, the system will increase victim satisfaction, enhance the prospects of reconciliation and "peace-making" and provide a more effective mens of restitution and reparation. It is this participation which empowers. Counter-arguments are that the involvement of victims introduces subjectivity and emotion into what should be an objective and rational task, that outcomes will inevitably, therefore, become more punitive, and that disparities in outcomes will increase depending on the whims or idiosyncrasies of victims. Rock (1985) also draws our attention to some potential pitfalls for victims — in particular, the time consumed by meeting with minor offenders for minimal return and the pain caused by meeting with serious offenders. We will refer briefly in the final section of this article to the extent to which victims have become involved in youth justice processes and whether or not they feel "better" as a result.

Group Consensus Decision-making

The particular adaptation of whanau decision-making chosen in the new procedure not only involves face-to-face contact between the juvenile offender (and his or her family and whanau) and the victim(s) (or their representatives), but has been modified by introducing representatives from the police and social welfare services and providing for legal representation in the more serious cases.

However, the model of decision-making promoted is quite different both from traditional courtroom decision-making practices and from traditional diversionary procedures. The conventional approach can be characterised as both "linear" and "professional". A "linear" approach is when one person or group of people (for example, a judge or magistrates) makes the decision for others (for example, the young person and the family). A "professional" approach assumes that the decision-maker has certain qualities or training which ensure that the decision is "right" (for that young person and family) and hence that it is appropriate for the decisions to be (en)forced on the offender.

In contrast, the Children, Young Persons and their Families Act 1989 involves a group approach to decision-making which allows all the participants in a particular forum to contribute to the process and to work towards the determination of an outcome. A "facilitator" is provided whose role is that of a mediator who negotiates between parties with potentially different views, for example, between the family and the victim or between the family and the police. The aim is to move away from the adversarial and confrontational procedures apparent in courtrooms towards outcomes shaped by the families themselves and agreed to by all the participants, including the victims. We will refer briefly in the final section of this article to the extent to which participants in FGCs have been able to reach agreements about how to respond to juvenile offending.

Conflicting and contradictory objectives

Like most systems of juvenile justice, the New Zealand system has multiple goals and some of these are in conflict: for example, stressing the accountability of the young person may conflict with the emphasis given to the enhancement of the development of children and young persons, and giving due regard to the interests of the victim may also conflict with the emphasis placed on the enhancement of the development of children and young persons. We will refer briefly in the final section of this article to how these conflicts are resolved (or not as the case may be) in practice.

A description of the youth justice system in New Zealand

The age of criminal responsibility in New Zealand is 10 although published police statistics present data on offending below that age. However, children under the age of 14 cannot be prosecuted except for the offences of murder and manslaughter. In other cases where such children's offending causes concern, they may be dealt with by warning, police diversion or a Family Group Conference. Alternatively, they can be referred to the Department of Social Welfare as in need of care and protection. This replaces the former system by which such children could only come to court by way of a complaint brought against their parents after, at least in theory, a referral to what was known as a Children's Board. This was an informal meeting between the parent, child, a representative of the police, Department of Social Welfare and Department of Maori Affairs and various appointed representatives of the community at which it was discussed whether or not complaint proceedings should be brought, or whether or not a warning or some other informal action would suffice. The emphasis was on dealing with such children without recourse to court and on providing appropriate support to the families. The Children's Boards, however, were not generally effective in achieving these goals. They are now primarily to be met by the care and protection procedures of the new Act, though in certain circumstances children under 14 can be dealt with under the youth justice procedures.

A young person who commits offences beyond the age of 16 is dealt with in the same manner as an adult, that is, in the District Court or, if the offence is serious, in the High Court. The very serious offences of murder and manslaughter by any juvenile aged 10 years or over are automatically dealt with in the High Court. The Youth Court can transfer other serious offences (for example, arson and aggravated robbery) to the High Court. There is also provision in other cases for the Youth Court to transfer matters to the District Court depending primarily on the seriousness and circumstances of the offence. Such cases are rare and the vast majority of juvenile offending by young persons is now dealt with under the procedures described below.

These procedures reflect marked changes from the previous system. Then juveniles aged 14-16 who were arrested by the police were referred directly to the court (as is, in fact, still the case). However, before a prosecution in the Children and Young Persons Court of a young person who had not been arrested could take place, the police were required to consult with a social worker from the Department of Social Welfare. The primary intention of this requirement to consult was to explore whether or not the matter could be resolved informally and so reduce the number of young persons processed in court. The procedure was ineffective, however. This decision, whether or not to prosecute, had almost invariably already been made by the police. Indeed, arresting young persons was used in some areas as a way of avoiding the consultation process and of ensuring that the case was dealt with in court. The consultation process, therefore, did not act as a filter to prosecution; rather, at least in some areas, it was used to enable prosecution rather than diversion.

Figure 1 provides a diagrammatic description of the possible pathways through the new system. Now, the police have three main options when juvenile offenders are detected: they may warn or divert the juvenile, they may refer the juvenile for a FGC or they may arrest the juvenile provided he or she is over 13 years old and certain criteria are met or if the offence is murder or manslaughter. Most juveniles are warned or diverted. The next largest category are those dealt with at a FGC. Only a majority of juvenile offenders are arrested but almost all juveniles arrested are referred to the Youth Court (very few are subsequently released without charge) and they are then later referred by the court for a FGC. These matters will return then from the FGC to the court with recommendations. Any referrals by the police directly for a FGC and unresolved by the FGC or any case where a FGC recommends a court order may also be referred to the Youth Court by way of a summons. The Youth Court has the option of adopting the recommendations of the FGC and discharging the matter or of making a court order, although such a course of action is unusual when the FGC has agreed that this is not necessary. The roles of each agency are explained further in the following text.

80   A MORRIS and G M MAXWELL   (1993) 26 ANZJ Crim

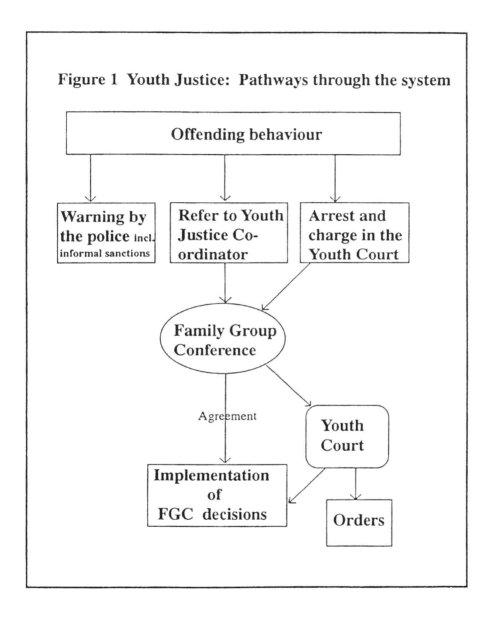

Figure 1 Youth Justice: Pathways through the system

Police

The intention underlying the Children, Young Persons and their Families Act 1989 is to encourage the police to adopt low key responses to juvenile offending wherever possible. Thus juvenile offenders cannot now be arrested unless certain tightly drawn conditions are met. The most important of these are that the arrest is necessary to ensure the juvenile's appearance in court, to prevent the commission of further offences, or to prevent the loss or destruction of evidence or interference with witnesses. Our research findings suggest that only 10% of juvenile offenders were arrested in 1990; this contrasts with conservative police estimates in 1984 of 29% (Maxwell and Morris, 1991).

Also, as in most jurisdictions now, it is expected that minor and first offenders will be diverted from prosecution by means of an immediate (street) warning. Where further action is thought necessary, the police can refer juveniles to the police Youth Aid Section (a specialist unit dealing only with juveniles) for follow-up — for example, a warning in the presence of the parents. The Youth Aid Section may also require an apology to the victim and give the child or young person an additional sanction (for example, some community work). During 1990, the first calendar year of operation of the 1989 Act, 74% of juvenile offenders were warned or diverted by the police. This contrasts with a figure of 55% for 1984 (Maxwell and Morris, 1991).

Youth Justice Coordinator

Where Youth Aid Sections feel that action beyond those they normally arrange themselves is required, they must now refer the juvenile to the Youth Justice Coordinator (YJC) in their area. It is his or her responsibility to negotiate with the police to divert juveniles from court unless prosecution is required in the public interest because the offence is serious or because of previous offending. The YJC also receives Youth Court referrals and referrals from other agencies, for example, the Ministry of Transport and social services. The YJC plays a similar negotiating role with other agencies.

The Youth Justice Coordinators come from a range of backgrounds — for example, social services, probation, and the prison system. Many are Maori. They are appointed by and are officers within the Department of Social Welfare (DSW). We will describe their role shortly.

The Family Group Conference

The Family Group Conferences lie at the heart of the new procedures: both as another means of avoiding prosecution and also as a means of determining how young persons who commit offences should be dealt with. It is mandatory for an FGC to be held to consider the case whenever criminal proceedings are contemplated (non arrest cases) or brought (arrest cases).

Where a young person is not arrested but is referred to the police Youth Aid Section, an FGC must be held before a prosecution can be brought. The FGC has responsibility to formulate a plan for the juvenile or to make such recommendations as it sees fit (including prosecution). The range of possibilities here include community work, reparation or an apology, but are limited only by the imagination of the parties.

Similarly, where a young person is arrested and brought before the court for alleged offending (other than murder, manslaughter or a traffic offence not punishable by imprisonment), the court must adjourn the matter to enable an FGC to be held if there has not been a denial or there has been a finding of guilt. The

FGC then has responsibility again to formulate a plan for the juvenile or to make such recommendations as it sees fit. The court in dealing with the case must have regard to this plan or these recommendations.

The FGC is made up of the young person, his or her advocate if one has been arranged, members of the family and whoever they invite, the victim(s) or his or her representative, the police, the social worker if one has been involved with the family and the YJC. The family and those it invites are entitled to deliberate in private during the FGC should they wish or can ask for the meeting to be adjourned to enable discussions to continue elsewhere. FGCs can take place in the Department of Social Welfare, in the family's home, on *marae* (meeting houses) or wherever the family wish.

The jurisdiction of the FGC is limited to the disposition of cases where the young person has not denied the alleged offences or has already been found guilty. The intended focus of the FGC outcome is the young person's offending and matters related directly to the circumstances of that offending. The Act clearly states that criminal proceedings should not be used to intervene in the life of the young person on welfare grounds and this objective has been interpreted to imply that FGCs themselves should primarily focus on issues of accountability rather than welfare. Welfare issues should only be addressed as voluntary additions to offence-based sanctions, or separately in care and protection proceedings. In the latter case, the YJC should refer the case to the Care and Protection Coordinator.

The YJC has the following duties in relation to the FGC:

- to ensure that everyone present is adequately informed about what happened and that the young person does not deny the information in the summary of facts;
- to ensure that information on the impact of the offence on any victims is given to the FGC;
- to provide families, whanau, hapu, iwi and family groups with the information they need for the FGC;
- to hand over decision-making power to the family;
- to support the family decisions made in the FGC; and
- to facilitate access to any resources that the family may need to carry out the decisions.

The plans and decisions are binding when they have been agreed to by an FGC, and, when it is relevant, accepted by the court. Where a young person fails to complete what the FGC has decided, the FGC may be reconvened to discuss that failure. At this stage, a new plan is formulated. At any stage, plans can include a recommendation for prosecution in court.

In order to ensure that the process works swiftly, the legislation has set time limits within which FGCs must be held. Where a young person is in custody, an FGC must be held within 7 days; where the court requests an FGC to be held, it must take place within 14 days; and where the YJC receives notification of an intended prosecution of a young person who has not been arrested or a child aged 10 to 13 is alleged to be in need of care and protection by reason of offending, the FGC must be held within 21 days of that notification. These time frames stem from an awareness that young people already work within much shorter time frames than adults and that responses to offending tend to have more "meaning" when applied relatively quickly.

Youth Court

A court process is reserved for a minority of young offenders. The Youth Court has been created as a branch of the District Court to deal with youth justice issues only. It replaces the Children and Young Persons Court which dealt with care and protection as well as control and youth justice issues. Its establishment underlines the importance of the principle that the offending of young persons should be premised on criminal justice not welfare principles; that is, on notions of accountability and responsibility for actions, due process, legal representation, requiring judges to give reasons for certain decisions, and imposing sanctions which are proportionate to the gravity of the offence.

The Youth Court is closed to the public to preserve the confidentiality of its proceedings. It operates an appointments' system in an attempt both to prevent young people associating with each other at court and to reduce the amount of time families are kept waiting. The court always appoints a youth advocate (a barrister or solicitor) to represent the young person where the young person does not already have a legal representative. The court may also appoint a lay advocate to support the young person in any proceedings in the Youth Court. Lay advocates are individuals of standing within the young person's culture and it is their responsibility to ensure awareness of cultural matters.

Where cases are referred to the Youth Court, the possible outcomes are as follows in order of severity: transfer to the District (adult) Court; supervision with residence; supervision with activity; community work; supervision; fine, reparation, restitution, or forfeiture; to come up if called upon within 12 months (a type of conditional discharge); admonition; discharge from proceedings; and police withdrawal of the information. In addition, it is possible to order the disqualification of a driver involved in a traffic offence.

Transfer to the District Court can only take place where certain conditions are met: the juvenile must be at least 15 years of age; the offence must be purely indictable, or the offence must be punishable by imprisonment for a term exceeding three months and the young person elects trial by jury; the nature or circumstances of the offence must be such that if the young person was an adult he or she would be sentenced to custody; and the court must be satisfied that any order of a non-custodial nature would be inadequate. A supervision with residence order may last for up to 9 months and is made up of 3 months in the custody of the Department of Social Welfare (this is reduced to 2 months if the young person does commit further offences during the custodial placement) and 6 months under the supervision of a social worker. Supervision with activity involves an order of up to 3 months' structured supervised activity followed by up to 3 months' supervision. Community work is for a minimum of 20 and a maximum of 200 hours and has to be completed within 12 months. Supervision is limited to a maximum of 6 months.

Thus orders are for a determinate period of time and plans must be prepared for the court detailing how the order is to be implemented, including the nature of any programme to be provided. Orders other than supervision with residence can be administered by any person or organisation so nominated. This enables cultural or tribal authorities to work directly with young people who offend. Resources are available for the development of such programmes (although it cannot yet be said a full and adequate range of community programmes has been developed). The person or organisation nominated is also required to report to the Youth Court at the expiry of the order on the effectiveness of the order, the young person's response to it and any other matter considered relevant.

The intention of the legislation is to allow families to influence outcomes. Thus the Youth Court cannot make a disposition unless a FGC has been held and it must take into account the plan and recommendations put forward by the FGC.

Evaluating the Act

We outlined at the beginning of this article the objects and principles underlying the Children, Young Persons and their Families Act 1989 and our primary purpose in writing this article is to introduce readers to the innovatory features of the 1989 Act. However, for the past 18 months we have been involved in a research project evaluating the translation of these objectives and principles into practice in five areas of New Zealand. This final section presents, in brief form only, some data on the extent to which these objectives and principles have been met (for a fuller account, see Maxwell and Morris, 1992).

We refer first in this section to those objectives which are dominant trends in current juvenile justice policy in most jurisdictions — diversion, enhancing the well being of juveniles who offend, holding juvenile offenders accountable for their offences and protecting juveniles' rights. Then we turn to the innovatory features in the New Zealand system — participation by young persons and their families, victims' involvement, consensus decision-making and cultural appropriateness. Finally we comment on the way in which potentially contradictory and conflicting objectives have been resolved in practice.

Diversion

There is no doubt that diversion from both courts and institutions were primary aims of the new Act. Both have been achieved. We referred earlier to national data on arrests and on warnings and diversion by the police. Our research data confirm these general trends. Only 10% of our sample of juvenile offenders appeared in the Youth Court, only about half of these were subject to any type of court order and less than a fifth of these were subject to any kind of residential or custodial order. This means that, overall, only 5% of the juveniles in our sample were subject to court orders and less than 2% were subject to residential or custodial orders.

On the other hand, if we treat FGC outcomes as diversionary outcomes (in the sense that they avoid a court appearance), it is clear that they were not limited by tariff considerations and often seemed moderately severe to the researchers. Nominal dispositions, for example, were rarely made in contrast to the position prior to the Act (in 1988, more than a third of the dispositions made by the judges in the Children and Young Persons Court could be described in this way). Of course, the dispositions resulting from FGCs are "agreed" to by the families and young persons involved. Whether or not this agreement was "real", "coerced" or "constructed" by the professionals is open to debate. Analysis of our observational data reveals examples of each.

Enhancing the wellbeing of juveniles who offend

The starting point in the new New Zealand system is to separate youth justice and care and protection issues: separate co-ordinators, separate procedures and separate courts. Young persons' needs and behaviour are not so easily separable, however, and an emphasis on one can mean the neglect of the other. It is perhaps self evident, therefore, that if outcomes stress accountability they can only enhance the young person's development in an indirect sense (by accepting responsibility for his or her actions). The legislation precludes referral into the youth justice system on welfare grounds, yet seems to expect or encourage discussion within the FGC of welfare issues at the same time that it expects or encourages resolutions to be determined by accountability. Thus contradictory expectations exist side by side. Suffice to say here that in our experience welfare issues were, not surprisingly, a secondary consideration. Certainly, we observed cases in which the needs of families and young persons were ignored at FGCs and where no "welfare" type follow-up was provided.

The legislation also encouraged the strengthening and support of families. If what was envisaged was the provision of resources to families in need of social services and the like, this did not occur; as we have just stated, we observed situations in which families were clearly asking for but not receiving help. We also observed, however, situations in which families were strengthened and supported by the involvement of their whanau or extended family; and on occasion services were provided within iwi. This happened in the main without sufficient state funding. Overall, in our view, the provision of adequate and accessible services to the young people in our sample was poor.

Holding juvenile offenders accountable for their offences

Most juveniles referred to FGCs or to the Youth Court agreed to perform tasks which seemed likely to making them accountable for their actions. What we have called "active penalties" (that is, community work, financial penalties, reparation and the like) were agreed to by 83% of those involved in non-court referred FGCs and by 89% of those involved in court referred FGCs. If we add "apologies" to this, the figures become 95% and 94% respectively. Nominal dispositions, as we stated earlier, were rare, as were solely welfare-oriented outcomes. More importantly, the vast majority of FGC plans were completed either fully — 58%, or in part — 29%.

However, on occasion, we observed FGCs in which young persons were not made accountable for their actions. Particularly with respect to those under 14 and possibly with respect to some girls, minor offenders and first offenders, and the question could be raised of whether or not the FGC referral might have been motivated by a desire to intervene where the perceived problem was one of a "welfare" or "parenting" nature. We also observed such long delays in the Youth Court before cases were finalised that any accountability must have had a fairly remote connection with the original act.

Protecting juvenile offenders' rights

With respect to the protection of juveniles' rights, we are concerned about breaches of statutory safeguards by front line police officers and, indeed, about their continuing resistance to these safeguards. We are concerned about the failure of some youth advocates to adequately advise their clients (or even to attend court-ordered FGCs). Pressures, both explicit and implicit, appear to be placed on young people to admit their guilt (as Wundersitz et al, 1991 found in their research in South Australia) and the costs of denying the offence seemed considerable both in terms of long delays and the resulting anxiety. Broadly speaking, we do not feel that practice yet meets expectations in this area.

Participation by young persons and their families

One of the major failings of the new system must be its failure to engage young people in the decision-making process. Only about a third felt involved in the FGC process and less than a fifth (16%) felt that they had been a party to the decision at the FGC. The level of perceived involvement in the court process was even lower. In this respect the objectives of the Act are not being met. There are a number of possible reasons for this continued lack of involvement by young persons. It may be that both families and professionals do not allow them to become involved; or it may be that the young persons themselves do not feel able to become involved. Many jurisdictions have tried in a range of different ways to increase the involvement of young people in the decision-making process and all that we can record here is that they have been no more successful than attempts in New Zealand. Indeed, arguably, even these very low figures for young persons' involvement in the New Zealand system reflect some progress. It may be that we have to accept that many young people have very little to say, at least in the presence of adults who are unknown to them, and that, therefore, we cannot expect them to participate more actively, whatever the forum. Many families do not encourage, or even actively discourage, the participation of young people in decisions about their own future. The problem may, thus, lie not in the system's response to young persons, but in the expectations of the wider society.

The involvement of parents in FGCs, on the other hand, was considerable. In contrast to young persons, more than two-thirds of the parents said that they felt involved in the decision-making process and about two-thirds also felt they had been a party to the decision. Thus holding parents responsible for their children's offending has been given a new and constructive (in both senses) meaning.

Victims' involvement

Victims simply by their presence participate more in this system than traditionally. However, only around a half of the FGCs in our sample had victims or victims' representatives present. Also, an unexpectedly high proportion of victims (around a third) said that they felt worse as a result of attending the FGC and an unexpectedly low number of victims (about a half overall) said that they were satisfied with the outcomes. In part, these views may be due to the inadequate preparation of victims (and other participants) about what to expect at the FGC and unrealistic expectations about likely or "appropriate" outcomes, especially with respect to reparation. Arguably this could be remedied through better briefing. But such views also raise a more fundamental issue: the extent to which victims' interests can be addressed in a forum set up primarily to divert young people from the court. Victims' pressure groups have long been suspicious of programmes which they feel "use" victims for the benefit of the offender. There must be some basis for this with respect to the current organisation of FGCs. Such a criticism could be met by clarifying the objectives of FGCs and by meeting specific victims' needs in a different way — for example, through improved procedures for compensation and through the provision of adequate support both within FGCs and more generally.

Consensus decision-making

Agreed outcomes should satisfy participants more than enforced outcomes and most FGC outcomes are "agreed" outcomes: 95% in our sample and 84% nationally (Maxwell and Robertson, 1991). Thus in these terms, participants at FGCs should be highly satisfied. The fact that this was not so in all respects raises two main points. First, victims were the least satisfied with the outcome and yet those victims who were present were supposedly parties to an "agreed" outcome. In some sense, then, it appears that victim agreement is being coerced.

Secondly, the most satisfied group were the police: 91%; the comparable figures for YJCs, parents and young persons were lower though similar to each other: 86%,

85% and 84% respectively. Victim satisfaction, in contrast, was only 48% and this finding undermines notions of participatory decision-making involving victims. Also, as we commented above, it is difficult to know whether families and young persons "truly" agreed or felt "truly" satisfied. The qualitative data from the research would suggest that, on many occasions they did, but that on other occasions they felt coerced to agree to decisions in essence made by the professionals.

Cultural appropriateness

As we outlined earlier, the New Zealand system attempted to create a youth justice system which was culturally appropriate. There are a range of ways in which this might be determined: participation by whanau (whanau participated in well over a half of cases involving Maori), the venue of FGCs (marae were rarely used) and participants' depiction of the process as culturally appropriate (views varied on this). A key issue here is the extent to which Western systems of criminal justice can accommodate elements of an indigenous approach. To be effectively responsive to indigenous needs, there probably has to be a different process, a different type of spirit and underlying philosophy and, potentially, different outcomes from those traditionally available in criminal justice contexts. In each of these respects, the practice showed both limitations and successes.

The FGC is an attempt to give a prominent place to a different and culturally appropriate process, but that process often failed to respond to the spirit of Maori or to enable outcomes to be reached which were in accordance with Maori philosophies and values. At times, FGCs can and do transcend tokenism and embody a Maori *kaupapa* (Maori protocol including language, customs and values). But not often. Also, money for iwi services and iwi authorities has not yet been allocated in sufficient amounts for a truly cultural approach to be taken.

The Youth Court in particular found it difficult, perhaps impossible, to accommodate Maori process and etiquette. We observed a number of situations where whanau wanted to be involved in the resolution of cases affecting their kin and yet providing time for receiving their submissions and, more importantly, giving real weight to them seemed problematic to the court. And there has been only a limited tolerance of the notion that the outcome should stress the restoration of social imbalance by the reintegration of the offender into the social group which will collectively redress the issue of reparation to the offender.

In short, our view, and that of many of the Maori and Pacific Island participants, is that the process (and hence spirit and outcomes) remained Pakeha and unresponsive to cultural differences. However, it is also our view, and that of many of the Maori and Pacific Island participants, that there is at least the potential for FGCs to be more able to cope with cultural diversity than other types of tribunals. This is best summed up in the words of the Maori researchers involved in the project:

> We feel that the Act for the most part is an excellent piece of legislation which promises exciting possibilities for the future. When the processes outlined in the act were observed, Maori families were indeed empowered and able to take an active part in decisions concerning their young people. It is not difficult to see the beneficial influences that the Act may eventually exert on wider Maori, Polynesian and Pakeha society. Maori society could gain immensely from legislation that acknowledges and strengthens the hapu and tribal structures and their place in decisions regarding the wellbeing of young people and [from legislation] that provides them with an opportunity to contribute to any reparation and to support those offended against. The same scenario would apply to Pacific Island peoples.

Pakeha society would also benefit from a process which acknowledges the family and gives redress to victims.

Resolving conflicting and contradictory objectives

There are two main areas of considerable potential conflict in the New Zealand system: reconciling offenders' needs and victims' interests, and enhancing offenders' wellbeing while maintaining tariff considerations and accountability. The primary arena for meeting offenders' needs is the FGC; this demonstrates both welfare and diversion goals. It is also the primary arena for protecting victims' interests; this reflects the goal of mediation and possibly crime control. Research suggests that when reparation and diversion are sought within the one forum then the victim almost invariably loses out. For example, Marshall and Merry (1990) argue that whatever aims are subscribed to in practice, in reality diversion becomes the over-riding objective and all other goals become subordinate to it. Thus the offenders' interests are promoted and the victims' neglected. It is our view that this has occurred in the New Zealand system of youth justice too. Tension has been created by expecting diverse interests to be met in a single forum without one or the other being compromised. Practical steps could be taken which might at least alleviate the imbalance in favour of offenders to some extent, but the fundamental difficulty may not be able to be eradicated.

Much the same point can be made with respect to attempting to make offenders accountable while enhancing their wellbeing. The way in which this conflict is resolved in the New Zealand youth justice system is primarily to stress accountability at the expense of welfare. By far the majority of FGC and court outcomes reflect responses to the young person's offence(s) rather than his or her needs. To the extent that this is what the legislature intended to be the primary focus of FGCs, it can thus be concluded that the system is working well. However, it is not clear from the Act that such a view is justified; there is no explicit or implicit ordering of objectives.

The tension between these two objectives — wellbeing and accountability — is increased when at the same time the victims' interests are also to be met. Inevitably and almost invariably in practice one objective is subsumed by the other. There are also potential tensions between increasing victims' rights to determine process (for example, allowing victims rather than families to determine the time and venue of an FGC) and victims' rights to determine outcomes (victims' demands may conflict not only with offenders' wellbeing but also with tariff considerations such as proportionality). Better briefing of all parties about the process and possible outcomes might alleviate, at least in part, some of these tensions. But again, the conflict is likely to remain.

What much of this discussion highlights is that at times the various purposes of the FGC are incompatible. This inevitably impacts on practice. One option would be to establish priorities among the principles and objectives. Alternatively, the balance among the various tensions can be left to find a resolution in each specific case — as indeed the court arrives at an individualised resolution of a variety of potentially conflicting factors when deciding upon a sentence.

Conclusion

There is much that is positive and novel about the New Zealand system of youth justice. It has succeeded in diverting the majority of young offenders from criminal courts and reliance on the use of institutions has been much reduced. Families participate in the processes of decision-making and are taking responsibility for their young people in most instances. Extended families are also becoming involved in the continuing care of their kin and as an alternative to foster care and institutions. Greater acknowledgement is being given to the customs of different cultural groups and the adoption in some instances of alternative methods of resolution through the use of traditional processes has occurred.

The new system has not, however, avoided all the difficulties which inevitably arise when attempting to reconcile conflicting objectives; it was unrealistic to expect that it would. And there are three areas of considerable concern to us: professionals taking over and thereby both distorting and destroying the FGC process; families being susceptible to this by being denied necessary information on both the process and the possibilities; and the lack of resources and support services which can undermine family decisions (for a fuller discussion, see Maxwell and Morris, 1992). However, it is early days. The approach is new and potentially radical. We must wait and see.

Acknowledgements

The research results reported here come from a study (Maxwell and Morris, 1992) conducted under the direction of Dr W Young and with the aid of a grant from the New Zealand Department of Social Welfare. A number of researchers were involved in the study including Jeremy Robertson, Maire Leadbeater, Gary Macfarlane-Nathan, Talosaga Manu, Teresea Olsen, Jennifer Bradshaw, Nicola Walsh and Rowena Morgan. Our thanks to all those who assisted with the project including staff of the Department of Social Welfare, the NZ Police, the Youth Court and youth advocates. In particular, we acknowledge our debt to those young people, families and victims who answered our questions.

NOTES
[1] The nearest literal translation of these Maori words is extended family, clan and tribe. But the words carry additional meaning relating to the way Maori society functions and the role these basic kinship units play in social organisation.

REFERENCES
Carlen, Patricia (1976) *Magistrates' Justice*, Martin Robertson, London.
Davis, G, Boncherat, J, Watson, D, and Thatcher, A (1987) *A Preliminary Study of Victim Offender Mediation and Reparation Schemes in England and Wales*, Research and Planning unit paper 42, Home Office, London.
Ericson, K V and Baranek P M (1982) *The Ordering of Justice: A Study of Accused Persons as Dependants in the Criminal Process*, University of Toronto Press, Toronto.
Galanter, M (1974) The Architecture of the Legal System. *Law and Society Review*, 9, 95.
Hutton, Neil and Young, Warren (1989) "The Provision of Assistance for Victims of Crime in New Zealand", Unpublished paper, Institute of Criminology, Victoria University of Wellington, Wellington.
Interdepartmental Committee on Population Policy Guidelines 1990, *Report of the Committee*, Department of Statistics, Wellington.
Jackson, Moana (1988) *The Maori and the Criminal Justice System, Part II*, Department of Justice, Wellington.
Jackson, Moana (1991) "Criminal Justice for Maori", unpublished address to students, Department of Criminology, Victoria University of Wellington, Wellington.
Koehler, M (1988) The Role of the Victim at Sentencing and in Key Correctional Decisions. In: New Initiatives in Sentencing and Corrections: Responding to Victim and Community Interests in the Context of Reparative Justice, Unpublished address at a conference, Ottawa.

Marshall, T (1985) *Alternatives to Criminal Courts*, Gower, Aldershot.

Marshall, T and Walpole, M (1985) *Bringing People Together: Mediation and Reparation Projects in Great Britain*, Research and Planning unit paper 33, Home Office, London.

Marshall, T F and Merry, S (1990) *Crime and Accountability: Victim/offender Mediation in Practice*, HMSO, London.

Maxwell, Gabrielle M and Morris, Allison (1991) "Juvenile Crime and the Children, Young Persons and Their Families Act 1989", Gabrielle M Maxwell (ed) *An Appraisal of the First Year of the Children, Young Persons and Their Families Act 1989*, Office of the Commissioner for Children, Wellington.

Maxwell, Gabrielle M and Morris, Allison (1992) "Families, Victims and Culture: Youth Justice in New Zealand" (in press), Social Policy Agency and Institute of Criminology, Wellington.

Maxwell, Gabrielle M and Robertson, Jeremy P (1991) "Statistics on the First Year", Gabrielle M, Maxwell (ed) *An Appraisal of the First Year of the Children, Young Persons and Their Families Act 1989*, Office of the Commissioner for Children, Wellington.

Ministerial Advisory Committee on a Maori Perspective for the Department of Social Welfare (1988) *Puao-te-ata-tu: (daybreak)*, The Report of the Ministerial Advisory Committee on a Maori Perspective for the Department of Social Welfare, Department of Social Welfare, Wellington.

New Zealand *Police Digest of Statistics* (1989) NZ Police, Wellington.

O'Connor, Ian and Sweetapple, Pamela (1988) *Children in Justice*, Longman, Cheshire.

Pratt, John (1991) "Citizenship, Colonisation and Criminal Justice", *International Journal of Sociology of Law*, 19, 293-319.

Rock, P (1985) in Marshall, T *Alternatives to Criminal Courts*, Gower Aldershot.

Rutter, M and Giller, H (1983) *Juvenile Delinquency: Trends and Perspectives*, Penguin, Harmondsworth.

Wright, M and Galaway, B (1989) *Mediation and Criminal Justice: Victims, Offenders and Community*, Sage, London.

Wundersitz, Joy, Naffine, N, and Gale, F (1991) "The Production of Guilt in the Juvenile Justice System: the Pressures to Plead", *The Howard Journal*, 30(3): 192.

[4]

FUNDAMENTAL CONCEPTS OF RESTORATIVE JUSTICE

HOWARD ZEHR[a] and HARRY MIKA[b]

[a] *Eastern Mennonite University, VA,*
[b] *Central Michigan University, MI*

As restorative justice programs continue to be widely adopted, the number of definitions of restorative justice has increased significantly. Oddly enough, some of the programs defined as restorative do not appear to contain some of the essential elements originally associated with restorative justice. In an effort to clarify what constitutes restorative justice, this article provides a fundamental definition of restorative justice. While the definition seeks to be as inclusive as possible, it also provides some basic principles against which programs might be measured to determine their restorative nature and potential.

KEY WORDS: Restorative justice, corrections, healing, punishment, criminology, crime prevention

INTRODUCTION

A working definition of restorative justice, such as the one we propose, is the product of a great deal of input and deliberation of practitioners and other professionals, who in their own work are attempting to clarify the basic values and indices of restorative justice practice. We are indebted for this breadth of experience and reflection, and the spirit in which we have been engaged. The limitations of our proposal should in no way reflect poorly upon the advice we have been given.

The definition is, as it were, a single side of a coin. Here, we have articulated the component parts of restorative justice practice. Elsewhere, these elements will need to yield measures of restorative practice—a restorative justice yardstick—that are so integral to evaluating justice practice, and improving program design.

The definition is couched within several parameters. First, it is unlikely that any restorative justice practice will incorporate all of the following elements. Further, the critical mass of these elements that would absolutely distinguish between retributive and restorative justice practice seem very hard to specify. Second, we suspect these elements are not static, but are rather dynamic in response to changing needs, changing relationships, and cultural values. Third, this definition is surely a product of largely U.S. experiences in justice programs, most of which have their genesis in community-based practice and initiatives. From time to time, what is now captioned as "restorative justice" has selectively incorporated innovations in community corrections, informal justice, community service, alternative sentencing, community mediation, victim-offender reconciliation, and the like.

A final parameter concerns the lexicon of restorative justice, itself a matter for contemplative critique. From time to time and place to place, the use of certain language forms becomes a barrier to shared meanings and understanding. For example, the terminology "victim" suggests to some dependence, resignation, and lack of capacity and competence, the very antithesis of support and advocacy by those who bear the harms of crime. The preference might be to refer to such persons as the "bereaved" and "traumatized." For some, the concept of "offender"—where it might include persons who break the criminal law—is itself a mechanism for denying the political nature of those behaviors that are intended as antistate actions. "Combatants," "political prisoners," and/or "prisoners of war" are felt to be more accurate representations. Similarly, the terms "offender" and "crime" presuppose that the actions and reactions of those oppressed politically and economically merit punitive intervention, and the conditions that beget such actions or "crimes" in the first place will not be subject to scrutiny. The idea of "community" is notoriously difficult to define, and at its worst, may conjure up romantic ideas of a place or a people that do not appear to have much basis in reality. "Restoration," it is said, may be impossibly ambitious for some bereaved, who might eventually be reconciled to their loss, but never again be whole or restored. The language of this definition is encumbered by difficulties such as these. We are fully cognizant of the limitations of our conventional usages, and intend no offense.

A number of modest objectives have guided this immodest product. We recognize a dizzying array of "restorative justice" applications, a range of visions and practices that, taken together, simply cannot be reconciled. The best face we might put on this trend is to compare the problem to a public health controversy in the U.S. some years ago, where former

Health, Education, and Welfare Secretary Joseph Califano characterized swine flu as a "slippery concept." The seemingly straightforward definition of its epidemiology did not stand up to the politics of immunization policy. Swine flu and restorative justice may share such a problem. At its worst, we fear retributive and punitive programs are simply being repackaged as "restorative justice" initiatives, a reflex of the growing popularity of the concept, and/or the availability of financial resources. For our part, we are proposing the contours of restorative justice practice in the hopes of ferreting through intended and unintended consequences of our work, articulating values into practice, doing what we claim, and reaching towards possibilities. We seek to be unambiguous in how we conceive of restorative justice. Having said that, however, we do not believe that any single definition will ever be likely, or even particularly useful. Again, we value its fluid nature, and above all, its responsiveness to the needs of key stakeholders in the justice equation. From among these objectives, perhaps the most ambitious task is to lay groundwork for addressing some of the sobering realities of informal, community-based, alternative justice practice in the United States.

EVALUATING JUSTICE PRACTICE

Our experience in program development and evaluation suggests some significant problems in coming to terms with the impact of restorative justice practice. Certainly, there is a heterogeneity of restorative-styled programs that makes generalizing difficult to begin with. Undeniably, there is a paucity of research and evaluation from which to draw conclusions about the impact of such programs. There are fewer efforts still to consider what standards of restorative practice are, or even the measures that are most appropriate to its value orientation. We find that restorative justice programs are resistant to evaluation to begin with, where evaluation is viewed as a threat, and/or where programs are too exhausted from the efforts to ensure day-to-day (financial) survival to bother with the more esoteric demands of assessment. Evaluations that are conducted are often done too early, before a program "hits its stride," though waiting for this moment is also a problem, as many programs do not survive for long. Often, evaluations are conducted on exemplary programs that may not be, due to high funding levels or other support, representative of most other community-based restorative justice initiatives. As the idea of responsiveness to the community is integral to our conception of restorative justice practice, incorporating the community variable into the evaluation design

50   H. ZEHR AND H. MIKA

invariably complicates the process. In the main, the most unfortunate problem is that often, conventional justice practice and outcomes are so marginal that doing anything else might be better. Such a frame of reference is a very poor incentive for programs to critically assess their works, and to improve performance.

Having said these things about the problems of assessing the impact of restorative justice programs, we would be remiss to suggest nothing is known about alternative practices of local justice that have been designed to address the shortcomings of conventional justice. We suggest the following distinct possibilities, where most alternative justice programs appear to:

- retain a conventional punishment prerogative, and an almost exclusively control mandate;
- conduct overwhelmingly offender-oriented services;
- address only less serious crimes and offenders;
- remain marginalized in the local justice continuum;
- become caught-up in the struggle to survive and are unable to effectively promote an alternative vision of justice;
- refuse to become involved in interpersonal violence (hence, do not serve the critical needs of classes of victims, such as women, minority, poor, youth);
- define impact and effectiveness very narrowly if at all, limited only to perceptions of fairness and satisfaction;
- focus on relational aspects of conflict exclusively, without regard for social and community problems that shape crime and victimization;
- fail to promote alternative criteria of effectiveness more in line with their practice of alternative values;
- seek to reduce incarceration, but seldom succeed in reducing the marginalization of offenders and victims in their own communities;
- face high organizational fatality rates, due in part to lack of community support; and
- affect too few offenders, victims, and communities.

It is against this backdrop, and with a sense of urgency, that the following definition is proposed.

A DEFINITION OF RESTORATIVE JUSTICE

The elements specified below seek to address the critical components of one vision of restorative justice practice. Organizationally, the definition is composed of three major headings that define crime, obligations and liabilities, and justice practice. Under each of the headings, a number of secondary and tertiary points specify and elaborate on the general themes.

I. CRIME IS FUNDAMENTALLY A VIOLATION OF PEOPLE AND INTERPERSONAL RELATIONSHIPS.

Victims and the community have been harmed and are in need of restoration.

1. The primary victims are those most directly affected by the offense but others, such as family members of victims and offenders, witnesses and members of the affected community, are also victims.
2. The relationships affected (and reflected) by crime must be addressed.
3. Restoration is a continuum of responses to the range of needs and harms experienced by victims, offenders, and the community.

Victims, offenders and the affected communities are the key stakeholders in justice.

1. A restorative justice process maximizes the input and participation of these parties—but especially primary victims as well as offenders—in the search for restoration, healing, responsibility and prevention.
2. The roles of these parties will vary according to the nature of the offense as well as the capacities and preferences of the parties.
3. The state has circumscribed roles, such as investigating facts, facilitating processes and ensuring safety, but the state is not a primary victim.

II. VIOLATIONS CREATE OBLIGATIONS AND LIABILITIES.

Offenders' obligations are to make things right as much as possible.

1. Since the primary obligation is to victims, a restorative justice process empowers victims to effectively participate in defining obligations.
2. Offenders are provided opportunities and encouragement to understand the harm they have caused to victims and the community and to develop plans for taking appropriate responsibility.
3. Voluntary participation by offenders is maximized; coercion and exclusion are minimized. However, offenders may be required to accept their obligations if they do not do so voluntarily.

52   H. ZEHR AND H. MIKA

4. Obligations that follow from the harm inflicted by crime should be related to making things right.
5. Obligations may be experienced as difficult, even painful, but are not intended as pain, vengeance or revenge.
6. Obligations to victims such as restitution take priority over other sanctions and obligations to the state such as fines.
7. Offenders have an obligation to be active participants in addressing their own needs.

The community's obligations are to victims and to offenders and for the general welfare of its members.

1. The community has a responsibility to support and help victims of crime to meet their needs.
2. The community bears a responsibility for the welfare of its members and the social·conditions and relationships which promote both crime and community peace.
3. The community has responsibilities to support efforts to integrate offenders into the community, to be actively involved in the definitions of offender obligations and to ensure opportunities for offenders to make amends.

III. RESTORATIVE JUSTICE SEEKS TO HEAL AND
      PUT RIGHT THE WRONGS.

The needs of victims for information, validation, vindication, restitution, testimony, safety and support are the starting points of justice.

1. The safety of victims is an immediate priority.
2. The justice process provides a framework that promotes the work of recovery and healing that is ultimately the domain of the individual victim.
3. Victims are empowered by maximizing their input and participation in determining needs and outcomes.
4. Offenders are involved in repair of the harm insofar as possible.

The process of justice maximizes opportunities for exchange of information, participation, dialogue and mutual consent between victim and offender.

1. Face-to-face encounters are appropriate in some instances while alternative forms of exchange are more appropriate in others.

FUNDAMENTALS OF RESTORATIVE JUSTICE   53

2. Victims have the principal role in defining and directing the terms and conditions of the exchange.
3. Mutual agreement takes precedence over imposed outcomes.
4. Opportunities are provided for remorse, forgiveness and reconciliation.

Offenders' needs and competencies are addressed.

1. Recognizing that offenders themselves have often been harmed, healing and integration of offenders into the community are emphasized.
2. Offenders are supported and treated respectfully in the justice process.
3. Removal from the community and severe restriction of offenders is limited to the minimum necessary.
4. Justice values personal change above compliant behavior.

The justice process belongs to the community.

1. Community members are actively involved in doing justice.
2. The justice process draws from community resources and, in turn, contributes to the building and strengthening of community.
3. The justice process attempts to promote changes in the community to both prevent similar harms from happening to others, and to foster early intervention to address the needs of victims and the accountability of offenders.

Justice is mindful of the outcomes, intended and unintended, of its responses to crime and victimization.

1. Justice monitors and encourages follow-through since healing, recovery, accountability and change are maximized when agreements are kept.
2. Fairness is assured, not by uniformity of outcomes, but through provision of necessary support and opportunities to all parties and avoidance of discrimination based on ethnicity, class and sex.
3. Outcomes which are predominantly deterrent or incapacitative should be implemented as a last resort, involving the least restrictive intervention while seeking restoration of the parties involved.
4. Unintended consequences such as the cooptation of restorative processes for coercive or punitive ends, undue offender orientation, or the expansion of social control, are resisted.

RESTORATIVE JUSTICE SIGNPOSTS

Any definition of a concept contains the seeds of the values to which it subscribes. Our proposal is no different. Hence, this is obviously a community-oriented perspective, quite different in fundamental respects from other contemporary visions of restorative justice that use as their basic framework a top-down, or state promotion and practice of justice. Equally obvious is the value of including multiple stakeholders in restorative justice processes. Their roles and levels of participation should be dramatically different than those of conventional, retributive justice practice, and their needs and accountability are redefined accordingly. Their roles may continue to change in the future as well. For example, increasingly we want to consider the role of a community of victims, made up of individuals and groups variously affected by crime, safety and victimization issues, for whom some degree of healing and restoration is requisite for an improved quality of communal life.

Where conventional justice is law and punishment oriented, we conceive of restorative justice as a harm-centered approach: the centrality of victims, the obligations of offenders (and the meaning of accountability), the role of the community, and the active engagement of all parties in the justice equation are distinctive elements, we believe, of such an approach. Tony Marshall's (1996) restorative justice definition, as "a process whereby all the parties with a stake in a particular offense come together to resolve collectively how to deal with the aftermath of the offence and its implications for the future," captures this core idea of restorative justice practice as a collaborative process to resolve harms. Despite the seductiveness of his succinct definition, however, we feel it is important to be more explicit about the elemental features of a restorative approach.

To conclude, we propose a number of simple tests or principles that flow from the definition, that may in turn guide practice. We suggest that we are working toward restorative justice when we:

- focus on the harms of wrongdoing more than the rules that have been broken;
- show equal concern and commitment to victims and offenders, involving both in the process of justice;
- work toward the restoration of victims, empowering them and responding to their needs as they see them;
- support offenders while encouraging them to understand, accept and carry out their obligations;
- recognize what while obligations may be difficult for offenders, they should not be intended as harms and they must be achievable;
- provide opportunities for dialogue, direct or indirect, between victims and offenders as appropriate;

- involve and empower the affected community through the justice process, and increase its capacity to recognize and respond to community bases of crime;
- encourage collaboration and reintegration rather than coercion and isolation;
- give attention to the unintended consequences of our actions and programs; and
- show respect to all parties, including victims, offenders and justice colleagues.

Our definition and these principles imperfectly acknowledge haunting challenges to restorative justice practice. For example, we are ever-mindful of the struggle of sustaining restorative justice ideals and values in a retributive justice context, and how in practice these translate into the serious issues of credibility, legitimacy, program viability, and financial solvency. Similarly, an expanded role for the community, as the locus of trouble and justice, will mean redefining community accountability to both victims and offenders, and a local role in preventing and intervening in those conditions that precipitate conflict and impede its productive resolution. Finally, the definition moves—step, by stagger, by lurch—towards acknowledging the central role that socially structured cleavages play in the practice and realization of justice. As Ruth Morris (1995a, b) instructs us, it is the "transformative" requisite of restorative justice that is surely its stiffest test.

References

Marshall, Tony. (1996). *The evolution of restorative justice in Britain*. Unpublished manuscript, prepared for the European Committee of Experts on Mediation in Penal Matters.
Morris, Ruth. (1995a). *Not enough! Mediation Quarterly, 12*(3), 285–291.
Morris, Ruth. (1995b). *Penal abolition: The tactical choice*. Toronto: Canadian Scholars Press.

Part II
Restorative Perspectives

[5]

Restorative justice

The real story

KATHLEEN DALY
Griffith University, Brisbane, Australia

Abstract

Advocates' claims about restorative justice contain four myths: (1) restorative justice is the opposite of retributive justice; (2) restorative justice uses indigenous justice practices and was the dominant form of pre-modern justice; (3) restorative justice is a 'care' (or feminine) response to crime in comparison to a 'justice' (or masculine) response; and (4) restorative justice can be expected to produce major changes in people. Drawing from research on conferencing in Australia and New Zealand, I show that the *real story* of restorative justice differs greatly from advocates' mythical *true story*. Despite what advocates say, there are connections between retribution and restoration (or reparation), restorative justice should *not* be considered a pre-modern and feminine justice, strong stories of repair and goodwill are uncommon, and the raw material for restorativeness between victims and offenders may be in short supply. Following Engel, myth refers to a true story; its truth deals with 'origins, with birth, with beginnings. . . with how something began to *be*' (1993: 791–2, emphasis in original). Origin stories, in turn, 'encode a set of oppositions' (1993: 822) such that when telling a true story, speakers transcend adversity. By comparing advocates' true story of restorative justice with the real story, I offer a critical and sympathetic reading of advocates' efforts to move the idea forward. I end by reflecting on whether the political future of restorative justice is better secured by telling the mythical true story or the real story.

Key Words

conferencing • myths about justice • restorative justice • retributive justice

INTRODUCTION

Much has been written in recent years that damns and sings the praises of restorative justice. In contrast to the voluminous critical and advocacy literatures, there is a thin empirical record of what is happening on the ground.[1] My aim in this article is to present the 'real story' of restorative justice, one that reflects what has been learned from research on youth justice conferencing[2] in Australia and New Zealand. I am being mostly, although not entirely, ironic in proposing to tell the real story of restorative justice. There are many stories and no real one. I shall recount what I have learned on my journey in the field, which began in the early 1990s (Braithwaite and Daly, 1994) and intensified in 1995 when I moved to Australia to work with restorative justice researchers at the Australian National University and to initiate my own program of research.

It has taken me some time to make sense of the idea of restorative justice. Initially, my questions centred on what was happening in the youth justice conference process. What were victims, offenders and their supporters saying to each other? How did they relate to one another? What did the professionals (the co-ordinators and police) think was going on? Did the critiques of conferencing, especially from feminist and indigenous perspectives, have merit? I began to observe conferences in 1995; since then, I have observed close to 60 of them; and as part of a major project on conferencing in South Australia, members of my research group and I observed 89 youth justice conferences and interviewed over 170 young people (offenders) and victims associated with them, in 1998 and again, in 1999 (Daly et al., 1998; Daly, 2001b).

The more I observed conference processes and listened to those involved in them, attended sessions on restorative justice in professional meetings and read about restorative justice, the more perplexed I became. I discovered that there was a substantial gap between what I was learning from my research in the field and what the advocates and critics were saying about restorative justice. This moves me to tell the real story, and I do so by analysing four myths that feature in advocates' stories and claims:

(1) Restorative justice is the opposite of retributive justice.
(2) Restorative justice uses indigenous justice practices and was the dominant form of pre-modern justice.
(3) Restorative justice is a 'care' (or feminine) response to crime in comparison to a 'justice' (or masculine) response.
(4) Restorative justice can be expected to produce major changes in people.

Although I focus on advocates' claims, there can be as much distortion by the critics, as well. Moreover, there are debates among the advocates on the meaning and practice of restorative justice; thus, my characterization of the advocacy position is meant to show its general emphasis, not to suggest uniformity.

I use the concept of myth in two ways. First, myth can be understood simply as a partial truth, a distorted characterization that requires correction by historical or contemporary evidence. Second, myth can be understood as a special form of narrative. Following Engel (1993: 790–2), myth 'refers not to fantasy or fiction but to a "true story". . . . which is sacred, exemplary, significant'. 'The "truth" of myth differs from the "truth" of historical or scientific accounts.' Engel suggests that myths 'differ from other forms of storytelling' in that they 'deal with origins, with birth, with beginnings . . . with how something . . . began to *be*'. He discovers in his analysis of the 'origin stories' of parents of children with disabilities that they 'perceive the world in terms of a set of oppositions that originate in the diagnosis of their child' (1993: 821). A recurring origin story is that the professional (a doctor) is wrong about the initial diagnosis, and 'the parent's insights have ultimately triumphed over those of the professional' (1993: 821). As such, when parents retell their stories, 'the triumphant ending will be achieved again'. 'The very act of retelling is a way to ensure that . . . values and outcomes in the myth will triumph over pain, opposition, and disorder.' Engel says that this sense of triumph reveals the 'affirmative, creative power of myth', where myth 'abolishes time' and 'the work of myth [transcends adversity]' (1993: 823–24).

When I began this article, I used the concept of myth as partial truth, a foil against which I could write a more authoritative story. But in analysing the myths, I began to see them in a different light, in Engel's terms, as origin stories that 'encode a set of oppositions' (1993: 822). While I shall spend more analytical time telling the real story of restorative justice, using myth as partial truth, I also offer a sympathetic reading of advocates' true story of restorative justice by viewing myth as a creative device to transcend adversity. I end by reflecting on whether the political future of restorative justice is better secured by telling the real story or the mythical true story.

THE PROBLEM OF DEFINITION

Restorative justice is not easily defined because it encompasses a variety of practices at different stages of the criminal process, including *diversion* from court prosecution, actions taken *in parallel* with court decisions and meetings between victims and offenders *at any stage* of the criminal process (for example, arrest, pre-sentencing and prison release). For virtually all legal contexts involving individual criminal matters, restorative justice processes have only been applied to those offenders who have *admitted* to an offence; as such, it deals with the penalty phase of the criminal process for admitted offenders, not the fact-finding phase. Restorative justice is used not only in adult and juvenile criminal matters, but also in a range of civil matters, including family welfare and child protection, and disputes in schools and workplace settings. Increasingly, one finds the term associated with the resolution of broader political conflicts such as the reconstruction of post-apartheid South Africa (South African Truth and Reconciliation Commission, 1998; Christodoulidis, 2000 for more critical appraisal), post-genocide Rwanda (Drumbl, 2000) and post-sectarian Northern Ireland (Dignan, 2000: 12–13).

Given the extraordinarily diverse meanings of the term and the contexts in which it has been applied, it is important for analytical purposes to bound the term to a particular context and set of practices. In this article, I discuss its use in the response to individual crime (as compared to broader political conflict); and in reviewing what is known about restorative justice practices, I focus on studies of youth justice conferencing in Australia and New Zealand, giving particular emphasis to my research in South Australia. Even with a narrowed focus on responses to individual crime, there remain problems of definition. One reason is that because *the idea* of restorative justice has proved enormously popular with governments, the term is now applied after the fact to programmes and policies that have been in place for some time, or it is used to describe reputedly new policing and correctional policies (e.g. La Prairie, 1999 for Canada; Crawford, 2001 for England and Wales). Until careful empirical work is carried out, we cannot be certain what is going on or the degree to which any of these newer or repackaged practices could be considered 'restorative'.

There is great concern among restorative justice advocates to distinguish practices that are near and far from the restorative ideal, and there is debate over how to draw the line on a continuum of practices. One definition, proposed by Marshall, is that restorative justice is 'a process whereby all the parties with a stake in a particular offence come together to resolve collectively how to deal with the aftermath of the offence and its implications for the future' (1996: 37). This definition, which McCold (2000: 358) associates with the 'Purist' model of restorative justice, has been criticized by other restorative justice advocates who say that the definition is too narrow because it includes only face-to-face meetings, it emphasizes process over the primary goal of repairing a harm and actions to repair the harm may need to include coercive responses (Walgrave, 2000: 418). These latter advocates call for a 'Maximalist' model, where restorative justice is defined as 'every action that is primarily oriented towards doing justice by repairing the harm that has been caused by crime' (Bazemore and Walgrave, 1999: 48). In this debate, advocates are considering the uses of restorative justice in youth justice cases only; and yet we continue to see debate and uncertainty over the optimal size of the restorative justice 'tent' and which practices should be included in it.

McCold (2000: 401) constructed a Venn diagram to distinguish practices that he considers to be fully, mostly or only partly restorative. He suggests that fully restorative practices occur at the intersection of the three circles of 'victim reparation', 'offender responsibility' and 'communities of care reconciliation'. At that intersection are practices such as peace circles, sentencing circles and conferences of various types. Outside the intersection are practices he defines as mostly restorative (e.g. truth and reconciliation commissions, victim–offender mediation) or only partly restorative (reparation boards, youth aid panels, victim reparation). The three circles relate to the three major 'stakeholders' in the aftermath of a crime: victims, offenders and 'communities' (which include victims' and offenders' family members and friends, affected neighbourhoods and the broader society). Using McCold's diagram, the research reviewed here are of practices associated with a 'fully restorative' model, although as McCold points out (and I concur), this is no guarantee that actual practices are 'restorative'.

A selected review of the many lists of 'core elements' of restorative justice (e.g. Zehr, 1995: 211–12; Nova Scotia Department of Justice, 1998: 1–2; Dignan, 2000: 4–7; McCold, 2000: 364–72, 399–406, to name a few) shows these common elements: an emphasis on the role and experience of victims in the criminal process; involvement of all the relevant parties (including the victim, offender and their supporters) to discuss the offence, its impact and what should be done to 'repair the harm'; and decision making carried out by both lay and legal actors. While definitions and lists of core elements of restorative justice vary, all display a remarkable uniformity in defining restorative justice by reference to what it is *not*, and this is called *retributive justice*.

MYTHS ABOUT RESTORATIVE JUSTICE
Myth 1. Restorative justice is the opposite of retributive justice
When one first dips into the restorative justice literature, the first thing one 'learns' is that restorative justice differs sharply from retributive justice. It is said that:

(1) restorative justice focuses on *repairing the harm* caused by crime, whereas retributive justice focuses on *punishing an offence*;

(2) restorative justice is characterized by *dialogue and negotiation* among the parties, whereas retributive justice is characterized by *adversarial relations* among the parties; and

(3) restorative justice assumes that community members or organizations take a more active role, whereas for retributive justice, 'the community' is represented by the state.

Most striking is that all the elements associated with restorative justice are *good*, whereas all those associated with retributive justice are *bad*. The retributive–restorative oppositional contrast is not only made by restorative justice advocates, but increasingly one finds it canonized in criminology and juvenile justice textbooks. The question arises, is it right?

On empirical and normative grounds, I suggest that in characterizing justice aims and practices, it is neither accurate nor defensible. While I am not alone in taking this position (see Barton, 2000; Miller and Blackler, 2000; Duff, 2001), it is currently held by a small number of us in the field. Despite advocates' well-meaning intentions, the contrast is a highly misleading simplification, which is used to sell the superiority of restorative justice and its set of justice products. To make the sales pitch simple, definite boundaries need to be marked between the *good* (restorative) and the *bad* (retributive) justice, to which one might add the *ugly* (rehabilitative) justice. Advocates seem to assume that an ideal justice system should be of one type only, that it should be pure and not contaminated by or mixed with others.[3] Before demonstrating the problems with this position, I give a sympathetic reading of what I think advocates are trying to say.

Mead's (1917–18) 'The psychology of punitive justice' (as reprinted in Melossi, 1998: 33–60) contrasts two methods of responding to crime. One he termed 'the attitude of hostility toward the lawbreaker' (p. 48), which 'brings with it the attitudes of retribution, repression, and exclusion' (pp. 47–28) and which sees a lawbreaker as 'enemy'. The other, exemplified in the (then) emerging juvenile court, is the 'reconstructive attitude' (p. 55), which tries to 'understand the causes of social and individual breakdown, to mend. . . the defective situation', to determine responsibility 'not to place punishment but to obtain future results' (p. 52). Most restorative justice advocates see the justice world through this Meadian lens; they reject the 'attitude of hostility toward the lawbreaker', do not wish to view him or her as 'enemy', and desire an alternative kind of justice. On that score, I concur, as no doubt many other researchers and observers of justice system practices would. However, the 'attitude of hostility' is a caricature of criminal justice, which over the last century and a half has wavered between desires to 'treat' some and 'punish' others, and which surely cannot be encapsulated in the one term, 'retributive justice'. By framing justice aims (or principles) and practices in oppositional terms, restorative justice advocates not only do a disservice to history, they also give a restricted view of the present. They assume that restorative justice *practices* should exclude elements of retribution; and in rejecting an 'attitude of hostility', they assume that retribution as a justice *principle* must also be rejected.

When observing conferences, I discovered that participants engaged in a flexible incorporation of *multiple* justice aims, which included:

(1) some elements of retributive justice (that is, censure for past offences);
(2) some elements of rehabilitative justice (for example, by asking, what shall we do to encourage future law-abiding behaviour?); and
(3) some elements of restorative justice (for example, by asking, how can the offender make up for what he or she did to the victim?).

When reporting these findings, one colleague said, 'yes, this is a problem' (Walgrave, personal communication). This speaker's concern was that as restorative justice was being incorporated into the regular justice system, it would turn out to be a set of 'simple techniques', rather than an 'ideal of justice . . . in an ideal of society' (Walgrave, 1995: 240, 245) and that its core values would be lost. Another said (paraphrasing), 'retribution may well be present now in conferences, but you wouldn't want to make the argument that it *should be* present' (Braithwaite, personal communication).

These comments provoked me to consider the relationship between restorative and retributive justice, and the role of punishment in restorative justice, in normative terms. Distilling from other articles (e.g. Daly and Immarigeon, 1998: 32–5; Daly, 2000a, 2000b) and arguments by Duff (1992, 1996, 2001), Hampton (1992, 1998), Zedner (1994) and Barton (2000), I have come to see that apparently contrary principles of retribution and reparation should be viewed as dependent on one another. Retributive censure should ideally occur before reparative gestures (or a victim's interest or movement to negotiate these) are possible in an ethical or psychological sense. Both censure and reparation may be experienced as 'punishment' by offenders (even if this is not the intent of decision-makers), and both censure and reparation need to occur before a victim or community can 'reintegrate' an offender into the community. These complex and contingent interactions are expressed in varied ways and should not be viewed as having to follow any one fixed sequence. Moreover, one cannot assume that subsequent actions, such as the victim's forgiving the offender or a reconciliation of a victim and offender (or others), should occur. This may take a long time or never occur. In the advocacy literature, however, I find that there is too quick a move to 'repair the harm', 'heal those injured by crime' or to 'reintegrate offenders', passing over a crucial phase of 'holding offenders accountable', which is the retributive part of the process.

A major block in communicating ideas about the relationship of retributive to restorative justice is that there is great variability in how people understand and use key terms such as punishment, retribution and punitiveness. Some argue that incarceration and fines are punishments because they are *intended deprivations*, whereas probation or a reparative measure such as doing work for a crime victim are not punishment because they are *intended to be constructive* (Wright, 1991). Others define punishment more broadly to include anything that is unpleasant, a burden or an imposition of some sort; the intentions of the decision-maker are less significant (Davis, 1992; Duff, 1992, 2001). Some use retribution to describe a *justification* for punishment (i.e. intended to be in proportion to the harm caused), whereas others use it to describe a *form* of punishment (i.e. intended to be of a type that is harsh or painful).[4] On proportionality, restorative justice advocates take different positions: some (e.g. Braithwaite and Pettit, 1990) eschew retributivism, favouring instead a free-ranging consequentialist justification and highly individualized responses, while others wish to limit restorative justice responses to desert-based, proportionate criteria (Van Ness, 1993; Walgrave and Aertsen, 1996). For the form of punishment, some use retribution in a neutral way to refer to a censuring of harms (e.g. Duff, 1996), whereas most use the term to connote a punitive response, which is associated with emotions of revenge or intentions to inflict pain on wrong-doers (Wright, 1991). The term *punitive* is rarely defined, no doubt because everyone seems to know what it means. Precisely because this term is used in a commonsensical way by everyone in the field (not just restorative justice scholars), there is

confusion over its meaning. Would we say, for example, that any criminal justice sanction is by definition 'punitive', but sanctions can vary across a continuum of greater to
lesser punitiveness? Or, would we say that some sanctions are non-punitive and that
restorative justice processes aim to maximize the application of non-punitive sanctions?
I will not attempt to adjudicate the many competing claims about punishment, retribution and punitiveness. The sources of antagonism lie not only in varied *definitions*,
but also the different *images* these definitions conjure in people's heads about justice
relations and practices. However, one way to gain some clarity is to conceptualize
punishment, retribution and punitive (and their 'non' counterparts) as separate dimensions, each having its own continuum of meaning, rather than to conflate them, as now
typically occurs in the literature.

Because the terms 'retributive justice' and 'restorative justice' have such strong
meanings and referents, and are used largely by advocates (and others) as metaphors
for the bad and the good justice, perhaps they should be jettisoned in analysing
current and future justice practices. Instead, we might refer to 'older' and 'newer'
modern justice forms. These terms do not provide a content to justice principles or
practices, but they do offer a way to depict developments in the justice field with an
eye to recent history and with an appreciation that any 'new' justice practices will
have many bits of the 'old' in them.[5] The terms also permit description and explanation of a larger phenomenon, that is, of a profound transformation of justice forms
and practices now occurring in most developed societies in the West, and certainly
the English-speaking ones of which I am aware. Restorative justice is only a part of
that transformation.

By the *old justice*, I refer to modern practices of courthouse justice, which permit no
interaction between victim and offender, where legal actors and other experts do the
talking and make decisions and whose (stated) aim is to punish, or at times, reform an
offender. By the *new justice*,[6] I refer to a variety of recent practices, which normally bring
victims and offenders (and others) together in a process in which both lay and legal actors
make decisions, and whose (stated) aim is to repair the harm for victims, offenders and
perhaps other members of 'the community' in ways that matter to them. (While the
stated aim of either justice form may be to 'punish the crime' or to 'repair the harm', we
should expect to see mixed justice aims in participants' justice talk and practices.[7]) New
justice practices are one of several developments in a larger justice field, which also
includes the 'new penology' (Feeley and Simon, 1992) and 'unthinkable punishment
policies' (Tonry, 1999). The field is fragmented and moving in contradictory directions
(Garland, 1996; Crawford, 1997; O'Malley, 1999; Pratt, 2000).

Myth 2. Restorative justice uses indigenous justice practices and was the dominant form of pre-modern justice

A common theme in the restorative justice literature is that this reputedly new justice
form is 'really not new' (Consedine, 1995: 12). As Consedine puts it:

> Biblical justice was restorative. So too was justice in most indigenous cultures. In pre-colonial
> New Zealand, Maori had a fully integrated system of restorative justice . . . It was the traditional
> philosophy of Pacific nations such as Tonga, Fiji and Samoa . . . In pre-Norman Ireland, restora-
> tive justice was interwoven . . . with the fabric of daily life . . . (1995: 12)

Braithwaite argues that restorative justice is 'ground[ed] in traditions of justice from the ancient Arab, Greek, and Roman civilisations that accepted a restorative approach even to homicide' (1999: 1). He continues with a large sweep of human history, citing the 'public assemblies ... of the Germanic peoples', 'Indian Hindu [traditions in] 6000–2000 B.C.' and 'ancient Buddhist, Taoist, and Confucian traditions ...'; and he concludes that '*restorative justice has been the dominant model of criminal justice throughout most of human history for all the world's peoples*' (1999: 1, my emphasis). What an extraordinary claim!

Linked with the claim that restorative justice has been the dominant form of criminal justice throughout human history is the claim that present-day indigenous justice practices fall within the restorative justice rubric. Thus, for example, Consedine says:

> A new paradigm of justice is operating [in New Zealand], which is very traditional in its philosophy, yet revolutionary in its effects. A restorative philosophy of justice has replaced a retributive one. Ironically, 150 years after the traditional Maori restorative praxis was abolished in Aotearoa, youth justice policy is once again operating from the same philosophy. (1995: 99)

Reverence for and romanticization of an indigenous past slide over practices that the modern 'civilized' western mind would object to, such as a variety of harsh physical (bodily) punishments and banishment. At the same time, the modern western mind may not be able to grasp how certain 'harsh punishments' have been sensible within the terms of a particular culture.

Weitekamp combines 'ancient forms' of justice practice (as restorative) and indigenous groups' current practices (as restorative) when he says that:

> Some of the new ... programs are in fact very old ... [A]ncient forms of restorative justice have been used in [non-state] societies and by early forms of humankind. [F]amily group conferences [and] ... circle hearings [have been used] by indigenous people such as the Aboriginals, the Inuit, and the native Indians of North and South America ... It is kind of ironic that we have at [the turn of this century] to go back to methods and forms of conflict resolution which were practiced some millennia ago by our ancestors ... (1999: 93)

I confess to a limited knowledge of justice practices and systems throughout the history of humankind. What I know is confined mainly to the past three centuries and to developments in the United States and several other countries. Thus, in addressing this myth, I do so from a position of ignorance in knowing only a small portion of history. Upon reflection, however, my lack of historical knowledge may not matter. All that is required is the realization that advocates do not intend to write *authoritative histories* of justice. Rather, they are constructing origin myths about restorative justice. If the first form of human justice was restorative justice, then advocates can claim a need to recover it from a history of 'takeover' by state-sponsored retributive justice. *And*, by identifying current indigenous practices as restorative justice, advocates can claim a need to recover these practices from a history of 'takeover' by white colonial powers that instituted retributive justice. Thus, the history of justice practices is rewritten by advocates not only to authorize restorative justice as the *first* human form of justice, but also to argue that it is congenial with modern-day indigenous and, as we shall see in Myth 3, feminist social movements for justice.

In the restorative justice field, most commentators focus specifically (and narrowly) on changes that occurred over a 400-year period (8th to 11th centuries) in England (and some European countries), where a system of largely kin-based dispute settlement gave way to a court system, in which feudal lords retained a portion of property forfeited by an offender. In England, this loose system was centralized and consolidated during the century following the Norman Invasion in 1066, as the development of state (crown) law depended on the collection of revenues collected by judges for the king. For restorative justice advocates, the transformation of disputes as offences between individuals to offences against the state is one element that marked the end of pre-modern forms of restorative justice. A second element is the decline in compensation to the victim for the losses from a crime (Weitekamp, 1999).

Advocates' constructions of the history of restorative justice, that is, the origin myth that a superior justice form prevailed before the imposition of retributive justice, is linked to their desire to maintain a strong oppositional contrast between retributive and restorative justice. That is to say, the origin myth and oppositional contrast are both required in telling the true story of restorative justice. I do not see bad faith at work here. Rather, advocates are trying to move an idea into the political and policy arena, and this may necessitate having to utilize a simple contrast of the good and the bad justice, along with an origin myth of how it all came to be.

What does concern me is that the specific histories and practices of justice in pre-modern societies are smoothed over and a lumped together as one justice form. Is it appropriate to refer to all of these justice practices as 'restorative'? No, I think not. What do these justice practices in fact have in common? What is gained, and more important-ly, what is lost by this homogenizing move? Efforts to write histories of restorative justice, where a pre-modern past is romantically (and selectively) invoked to justify a current justice practice, are not only in error, but also unwittingly reinscribe an ethno-centrism their authors wish to avoid. As Blagg (1997) and Cain (2000) point out, there has been an orientalist appropriation of indigenous justice practices, largely in the service of strengthening advocates' positions.

A common, albeit erroneous, claim is that the modern idea of conferencing 'has its direct roots in Maori culture' (Shearing, 2001: 218, note 5; see also Consedine, 1995). The real story is that conferencing emerged in the 1980s, in the context of Maori politi-cal challenges to white New Zealanders and to their welfare and criminal justice systems. Investing decision-making practices with Maori cultural values meant that family groups (whanau) should have a greater say in what happens, that venues should be culturally appropriate, and that processes should accommodate a mix of culturally appropriate practices. New Zealand's minority group population includes not only the Maori but also Pacific Island Polynesians. Therefore, with the introduction of conferencing, came awareness of the need to incorporate different elements of 'cultural appropriateness' into the conference process. But the devising of a (white, bureaucratic) justice practice that is *flexible and accommodating* towards cultural differences does not mean that confer-encing *is* an indigenous justice practice. Maxwell and Morris, who know the New Zealand situation well, are clear on this point:

> A distinction must be drawn between a system, which attempts to re-establish the indigenous model of pre-European times, and a system of justice, which is culturally appropriate. The New

PUNISHMENT AND SOCIETY 4(1)

Zealand system is an attempt to establish the latter, not to replicate the former. As such, it seeks to incorporate many of the features apparent in whanau decision-making processes and seen in meetings on marae today, but it also contains elements quite alien to indigenous models. (1993: 4)

Conferencing is better understood as a fragmented justice form: it splices white, bureaucratic forms of justice with elements of informal justice that may include non-white (or non-western) values or methods of judgement, with all the attendant dangers of such 'spliced justice' (Pavlich, 1996; Blagg, 1997, 1998; Daly, 1998; Findlay, 2000). With the flexibility of informal justice, practitioners, advocates and members of minority groups may see the potential for introducing culturally sensible and responsive forms of justice. But to say that conferencing *is* an indigenous justice practice (or 'has its roots in indigenous justice') is to re-engage a white-centred view of the world. As Blagg asks rhetorically, 'Are we once again creaming off the cultural value of people simply to suit our own nostalgia in this age of pessimism and melancholia?' (1998: 12). A good deal of the advocacy literature is of this ilk: white-centred, creaming off and homogenizing of cultural difference and specificity.

Myth 3. Restorative justice is a 'care' (or feminine) response to crime in comparison to a 'justice' (or masculine) response

Myths 2 and 3 have a similar oppositional logic, but play with different dichotomies. Figure 1 shows the terms that are often linked to restorative and retributive justice. Note the power inversion, essential to the origin myth of restorative justice, where the subordinated or marginalized groups (pre-modern, indigenous, eastern and feminine) are aligned with the more superior justice form.

Many readers will be familiar with the 'care' and 'justice' dichotomy. It was put forward by Gilligan in her popular book, *In a different voice* (1982). For about a decade, it seemed that most feminist legal theory articles were organized around the 'different voice' versus 'male dominance' perspectives of Gilligan (1987) and MacKinnon (1987), respectively. In criminology, Heidensohn (1986) and Harris (1987) attempted to apply the care/justice dichotomy to the criminal justice system. Care responses to crime are depicted as personalized and as based on a concrete and active morality, whereas justice responses are depicted as depersonalized, based on rights and rules and a universalizing

Restorative justice	*Retributive justice*
Pre-modern	Modern
Indigenous (informal)	State (formal)
Feminine (care)	Masculine (justice)
Eastern (Japan)	Western (US)
Superior justice	Inferior justice

•**Figure 1 Terms linked to restorative and retributive justice**

and abstract morality. Care responses are associated with the different (female) voice, and these are distinguished from justice responses, which are associated with the general (if male) voice. In her early work, Gilligan argued that both voices should have equal importance in moral reasoning, but women's voices were misheard or judged as morally inferior to men's. A critical literature developed rapidly, and Gilligan began to reformulate and clarify her argument. She recognized that 'care' responses in a 'justice' framework left 'the basic assumptions of a justice framework intact. . . and that as a moral perspective, care [was] less well elaborated' (Gilligan, 1987: 24). At the time, the elements that Gilligan associated with a care response to crime were contextual and relational reasoning, and individualized responses made by decision-makers who were not detached from the conflict (or crime). In 1989, I came into the debate, arguing that we should challenge the association of justice and care reasoning with male/masculine and female/feminine voices, respectively (Daly, 1989). I suggested that this gender-linked association was not accurate empirically, and I argued that it would be misleading to think that an alternative to men's forms of criminal law and justice practices could be found by adding women's voice or reconstituting the system along the lines of an ethic of care. I viewed the care/justice dichotomy as recapitulating centuries long debates in modern western criminology and legal philosophy over the aims and purposes of punishment, e.g. deterrence and retribution or rehabilitation, and uniform or individualized responses. Further, I noted that although the dichotomy depicted different ideological emphases in the response to crime since the 19th century, the relational and concrete reasoning that Gilligan associated with the female voice was how in fact the criminal law is interpreted and applied. It *is* the voice of criminal justice practices. The problem, then, was not that the female voice was absent in criminal court practices, but rather that certain relations were presupposed, maintained and reproduced. Feminist analyses of law and criminal justice centre on the androcentric (some would argue, phallocentric) character of these relations for what comes to be understood as 'crime', for the meanings of 'consent', and for punishment (for cogent reviews, see Smart, 1989, 1992; Coombs, 1995). While feminist scholars continue to emphasize the need to bring women's experiences and 'voices' into the criminological and legal frame, this is not the same thing as arguing that there is a universal 'female voice' in moral reasoning. During the late 1980s and 1990s, feminist arguments moved decisively beyond dichotomous and essentialist readings of sex/gender in analysing relations of power and 'difference' in law and justice. Gilligan's different voice construct, though novel and important at the time, has been superseded by more complex and contingent analyses of ethics and morality.

But the different voice is back, and unfortunately, the authors who are using it seem totally unaware of key shifts in feminist thinking. We see now that the 'ethic of care' (Persephone) is pitched as the alternative to retributive justice (Portia). One example is a recent article by Masters and Smith (1998), who attempt to demonstrate that Persephone, the voice of caring, is evident in a variety of restorative responses to crime. Their arguments confuse, however, because they argue that Persephone is 'informed by an ethic of care as well as an ethic of justice' (1998: 11). And towards the end of the article, they say 'we cannot do without Portia (ethic of justice), but neither can we do without Persephone' (1998: 21). Thus, it is not clear whether, within the terms of their argument, Persephone stands for the feminine or includes both the masculine and feminine, or whether we need both Portia and Persephone. They apparently agree with all three

positions. They also see little difference between a 'feminine' and a 'feminist approach',
terms that they use interchangeably. In general, they normally credit 'relational justice
as a distinctly feminine approach to crime and conflict' (1998: 13). They say that 'reintegrative shaming can be considered a feminine (or Persephone) theory' and that there
is a 'fit between reintegrative shaming practice and the *feminist* ethic of care' (1998: 13,
my italics since the authors have shifted from a feminine ethic to a feminist ethic).
Towards the end of the article, they make the astonishing claim, one that I suspect my
colleague John Braithwaite would find difficult to accept, that 'reintegrative shaming is
perhaps the first feminist criminological theory'. They argue this is so because the 'practice of reintegrative shaming can be interpreted as being grounded in a feminine, rather
than a masculine understanding of the social world' (1998: 20).

There is a lot to unpick here, and I shall not go point by point. Nor do I wish to
undermine the spirit of the article since the authors' intentions are laudable, in particular, their desire to define a more progressive way to respond to crime. My concern is that
using simple gender dichotomies, or any dichotomies for that matter, to describe principles and practices of justice will always fail us, will always lead to great disappointment.[8] Traditional courthouse justice works with the abstraction of criminal law, but
must deal with the messy world of people's lives, and hence, must deal with context and
relations. 'Care' responses to some offenders can re-victimize some victims; they may be
helpful in *some cases* or for *some offenders* or for *some victims* or they may also be oppressive and unjust for other offenders and victims. Likewise, with so-called 'justice'
responses. The set of terms lined up along the 'male/masculine' and 'female/feminine'
poles is long and varied: some terms are about process, others with modes of response
(e.g. repair the harm) and still others, with ways of thinking about culpability for the
harm.

I am struck by the frequency with which people use dichotomies such as the male
and female voice, retributive and restorative justice or West and East, to depict justice
principles and practices. Such dichotomies are also used to construct normative positions
about justice, where it is assumed (I think wrongly) that the sensibility of one side of
the dualism necessarily excludes (or is antithetical to) the sensibility of the other. Increasingly, scholars are coming to see the value of theorizing justice in hybrid terms, of seeing
connections and contingent relations between apparent oppositions (see, for example,
Zedner, 1994; Bottoms, 1998; Hudson, 1998; Daly, 2000a; Duff, 2001).

Like the advocates promoting Myth 2, those promoting Myth 3 want to emphasize
the importance of identifying a different response to crime than the one currently in use.
I am certainly on the side of that aspiration. However, I cannot agree with the terms in
which the position has been argued and sold to academic audiences and wider publics.
There is a loss of credibility when analyses do not move beyond oppositional justice
metaphors, when claims are imprecise and when extraordinary tales of repair and goodwill are assumed to be typical of the restorative justice experience.

Myth 4. Restorative justice can be expected to produce major changes in people

I have said that attention needs to be given to the reality on the ground, to what is actually happening in, and resulting from, practices that fall within the rubric of restorative
justice. There are several levels to describe and analyse what is going on: first, what occurs

in the justice practice itself; second, the relationship between this and broader system effects; and third, how restorative justice is located in the broader politics of crime control. I focus on the first level and present two forms of evidence: (1) stories of dramatic transformations or moving accounts of reconciliation; and (2) aggregated information across a larger number of cases, drawing from research on conference observations and interviews with participants.

Several reviewers of this article took issue with Myth 4, saying that 'advocates are less likely to claim changes in people' or that 'there is no real evidence that restorative justice of itself can be expected to produce major changes in people'. Although I am open to empirical inquiry, my reading of the advocacy literature from the United States, Canada, Australia and New Zealand suggests that Myth 4 is prevalent. It is exemplified by advocates' stories of how people are transformed or by their general assertions of the benefits of restorative justice. For example, McCold reports that 'facilitators of restorative processes regularly observe a personal and social transformation occur during the course of the process' (2000: 359) and 'we now have a growing body of research on programs that everyone agrees are truly restorative, clearly demonstrating their remarkable success at healing and conciliation' (2000: 363). McCold gives no citations to the research literature. While 'personal and social transformation' undoubtedly occurs some of the time, and is likely to be rare in a courtroom proceeding, advocates lead us to think that it is typical in a restorative justice process. This is accomplished by telling a moving story, which is then used to stand as a generalization.

Stories of restorative justice

Consedine opens his book by excerpting from a 1993 New Zealand news story:

> The families of two South Auckland boys killed by a car welcomed the accused driver yesterday with open arms and forgiveness. The young man, who gave himself up to the police yesterday morning, apologised to the families and was ceremonially reunited with the Tongan and Samoan communities at a special service last night.

> . . . The 20-year old Samoan visited the Tongan families after his court appearance to apologise for the deaths of the two children in Mangere. The Tongan and Samoan communities of Mangere later gathered at the Tongan Methodist Church in a service of reconciliation. The young man sat at the feast table flanked by the mothers of the dead boys. (Consedine, 1995: 9)

Consedine says that this case provides:

> ample evidence of the power that healing and forgiveness can play in our daily lives . . . The grieving Tongan and Samoan communities simply embraced the young driver . . . and forgave him. His deep shame, his fear, his sorrow, his alienation from the community was resolved. (1995: 162)

Another example comes from Umbreit (1994: 1). His book opens with the story of Linda and Bob Jackson, whose house was broken into; they subsequently met with the offender as part of the offender's sentence disposition. The offender, Allan, 'felt better after the mediation . . . he was able to make amends to the Jacksons'. Moreover, 'Linda and Bob felt less vulnerable, were able to sleep better and received payment for their losses. All parties were able to put this event behind them'. Later in the book, Umbreit (1994: 197–202) offers another case study of a second couple, Bob and Anne, after their house was burglarized a second time. He summarizes the outcome this way:

> Bob, Anne, and Jim [the offender] felt the mediation process and outcome was fair. All were very satisfied with participation in the program. Rather than playing passive roles. . . [they] actively participated in 'making things right'. During a subsequent conversation with Bob, he commented that 'this was the first time (after several victimizations) that I ever felt any sense of fairness. The courts always ignored me before. They didn't care about my concerns. And Jim isn't such a bad kid after all, was he?' Jim also indicated that he felt better after the mediation and more aware of the impact the burglary had on Bob and Anne. (Umbreit, 1994: 202)

Lastly, there is the fable of Sam, an adolescent offender who attended a diversionary conference, which was first related by Braithwaite (1996) and retold by Shearing (2001: 214–15). Braithwaite says that his story is a 'composite of several Sams I have seen' (1996: 9); thus, while he admits that it is not a real story of Sam, it is said to show the 'essential features . . . of restorative justice' (Shearing, 2001: 214). This is something like a building contractor saying to a potential home buyer, 'this is a composite of the house I can build for you; it's not the real house, but it's like many houses I have sold to happy buyers over the years'. What the composite gives and what the building contractor offers us is a *vision of the possible*, of the perfect house. Whether the house can ever be built is less important than imagining its possibility and its perfection. This is the cornerstone of the true story of restorative justice, like many proposed justice innovations of the past.

Sam's story, as told by Braithwaite, is longer than I give here, and thus, I leave out emotional details that make any story compelling. Sam, who is homeless and says his parents abused him, has no one who really cares about him except his older sister, his former hockey coach at school and his Uncle George. These people attend the conference, along with the elderly female victim and her daughter. Sam says he knocked over the victim and took her purse because he needed the money. His significant others rebuke him for doing this, but also remember that he had a good side before he started getting into trouble. The victim and daughter describe the effects of the robbery, but Sam does not seem to be affected. After his apparent callous response to the victim, Sam's sister cries, and during a break, she reveals that she too had been abused by their parents. When the conference reconvenes, Sam's sister speaks directly to Sam, and without mentioning details, says she understands what Sam went through. The victim appreciates what is being said and begins to cry. Sam's callous exterior begins to crumble. He says he wants to do something for the victim, but does not know what he can do without a home or job. His sister offers her place for him to stay, and the coach says he can offer him some work. At the end of the conference, the victim hugs Sam and tearfully says good luck, Sam apologizes again and Uncle George says he will continue to help Sam and his sister when needed.

Many questions arise in reading stories like these. *How often* do expressions of kindness and understanding, of movement towards repair and goodwill, actually occur? What are the typical 'effects' on participants? Is the perfect house of restorative justice ever built? Another kind of evidence, aggregated data across a larger number of cases, can provide some answers.

Statistical aggregates of restorative justice

Here are some highlights of what has been learned from research on youth justice conferences in Australia and New Zealand.[9] Official data show that about 85 to 90 percent of conferences resulted in agreed outcomes, and 80 percent of young people completed their agreements. From New Zealand research in the early 1990s (Maxwell and Morris, 1993), conferences appeared to be largely offender-centred events. In 51 percent of the 146 cases where a victim was identified, the victim attended the conference (1993: 118). Of all the victims interviewed who attended a conference (sometimes there were multiple victims), 25 percent said they felt worse as a result of the conference (1993: 119). Negative feelings were linked to being dissatisfied with the conference outcome, which was judged to be too lenient towards the offender. Of all those interviewed (offenders, their supporters and victims) victims were the least satisfied with the outcome of the family conference: 49 percent said they were satisfied (1993: 120) compared with 84 percent of young people and 85 percent of parents (1993: 115). Maxwell and Morris report that 'monitoring of [conference] outcomes was generally poor' (1993: 123), and while they could not give precise percentages, it appeared that 'few [victims] had been informed of the eventual success or otherwise of the outcome' and that this 'was a source of considerable anger for them' (1993: 123). Elsewhere, Maxwell and Morris report that 'the new system remains largely unresponsive to cultural differences' (1996: 95–6) in handling Maori cases, which they argue is a consequence, in part, of too few resources.

The most robust finding across all the studies in the region (see review in Daly, 2001a) is that conferences receive very high marks along dimensions of procedural justice, that is, victims and offenders view the process and the outcomes as fair. In the Re-Integrative Shaming Experiments (RISE) in Canberra, admitted offenders were randomly assigned to court and conference. Strang et al. (1999) have reported results from the RISE project on their website by showing many pages of percentages for each variable for each of the four offences in the experiment (violent, property, shoplifting and drink-driving). They have summarized this mass of numbers in a set of comparative statements without attaching their claims to percentages. Here is what they report. Compared to those offenders who went to court, those going to conferences have higher levels of procedural justice, higher levels of restorative justice and an increased respect for the police and law. Compared to victims whose cases went to court, conference victims have higher levels of recovery from the offence. Conference victims also had high levels of procedural justice, but they could not be compared to court victims, who rarely attended court proceedings. These summary statements are the tip of the RISE iceberg. In a detailed analysis of the RISE website results, Kurki (2001) finds offence-based differences in the court and conference experiences of RISE participants, and she notes that RISE researchers' reports of claimed court and conference differences are not uniform across offence types.

Like other studies, the South Australia Juvenile Justice (SAJJ) Research on Conferencing Project finds very high levels of procedural justice registered by offenders and victims at conferences. To items such as, were you treated fairly, were you treated with respect, did you have a say in the agreement, among others, 80 to 95 percent of victims and offenders said that they were treated fairly and had a say. In light of the procedural justice literature (Tyler, 1990; Tyler et al., 1997), these findings are important. Procedural justice scholars argue that when citizens perceive a legal process as fair, when

PUNISHMENT AND SOCIETY 4(1)

they are listened to and treated with respect, there is an affirmation of the legitimacy of the legal order.

Compared to the high levels of perceived procedural justice, the SAJJ project finds relatively less evidence of restorativeness. The measures of restorativeness tapped the degree to which offenders and victims recognized the other and were affected by the other; they focused on the degree to which there was positive movement between the offender and victim and their supporters during the conference (the SAJJ measures are more concrete and relational measures of restorativeness than those used in RISE). Whereas very high proportions of victims and offenders (80 to 95 percent) said that the process was fair (among other variables tapping procedural justice), 'restorativeness' was evident in 30 to 50 percent of conferences (depending on the item), and solidly in no more than about one-third. Thus, in this jurisdiction where conferences are used *routinely*,[10] fairness can more easily be achieved than restorativeness. As but one example, from the interviews we learned that from the victims' perspectives, less than 30 percent of offenders were perceived as making genuine apologies, but from the offenders' perspectives, close to 60 percent said their apology was genuine.

The SAJJ results lead me to think that young people (offenders) and victims orient themselves to a conference and what they hope to achieve in it in ways different than the advocacy literature imagines. The stance of empathy and openness to 'the other', the expectation of being able to speak and reflect on one's actions and the presence of new justice norms (or language) emphasizing repair – all of these are novel cultural elements for most participants. Young people appear to be as, if not more, interested in *repairing their own reputations* than in repairing the harm to victims. Among the most important things that the victims hoped would occur at the conference was for the offender to hear how the offence affected them, but half the offenders told us that the victim's story had no effect or only a little effect on them.

How often, then, does the exceptional or 'nirvana' story of repair and goodwill occur? I devised a measure that combined the SAJJ observer's judgement of the degree to which a conference 'ended on a high, a positive note of repair and good will' with one that rated the conference on a five-point scale from poor to exceptional. While the first tapped the degree to which there was movement between victims, offenders and their supporters towards each other, the second tapped a more general feeling about the conference dynamics and how well the conference was managed by the co-ordinator. With this combined measure, 10 percent of conferences were rated very highly, another 40 percent, good; and the rest, a mixed, fair or poor rating. If conferencing is used routinely (not just in a select set of cases), I suspect that the story of Sam and Uncle George will be infrequent; it may happen 10 percent of the time, if that.

Assessing the 'effects' of conferences on participants is complex because such effects change over time and, for victims, they are contingent on whether offenders come through on promises made, as we learned from research in New Zealand. I present findings on victims' sense of having recovered from the offence and on young people's re-offending in the post-conference period. In the Year 2 (1999) interviews with victims, over 60 percent said they had 'fully recovered' from the offence, that it was 'all behind' them. Their recovery was more likely when offenders completed the agreement than when they did not, but recovery was influenced by a mixture of elements: the conference process, support from family and friends, the passage of time and personal resources such as their own resilience. The SAJJ project finds that conferences *can* have positive effects on reducing victims' anger towards and fear of offenders. Drawing from the victim interviews in 1998 and 1999, over 75 percent of victims felt angry towards the offender before the conference, but this dropped to 44 percent after the conference and was 39 percent a year later. Close to 40 percent of victims were frightened of the offender before the conference, but this dropped to 25 percent after the conference and was 18 percent a year later. Therefore, for victims, meeting offenders in the conference setting can have beneficial results.

The conference effect everyone asks about is, does it reduce reoffending? Proof (or disproof) of reductions in reoffending from conferences (compared *not only to court*, but to other interventions such as formal caution, other diversion approaches or no legal action at all) will not be available for a long time, if ever. The honest answer to the reoffending question is 'we'll probably never know' because the amounts of money would be exorbitant and research methods using experimental designs judged too risky in an ethical and political sense.

To date, there have been three studies of conferencing and reoffending in Australia and New Zealand, one of which compares reoffending for a sample of offenders randomly assigned to conference and court and two that explore whether reoffending can be linked to things that occur in conferences.[11] The RISE project finds that for one of four major offence categories studied (violent offences compared to drink-driving, property offences, shoplifting), those offenders who were assigned to a conference had a significantly reduced rate of reoffending than those who were assigned to court (Sherman et al., 2000).

As others have said (Abel, 1982: 278; Levrant et al., 1999: 17–22), there is a great faith placed on the conference process to change young offenders, when the conditions of their day-to-day lives, which may be conducive to getting into trouble, may not change at all. The SAJJ project asked if there were things that occurred in conferences that could predict reoffending, over and above those variables known to be conducive to lawbreaking (and its detection): past offending and social marginality (Hayes and Daly, 2001). In a regression analysis with a simultaneous inclusion of variables, we found that over and above the young person's race-ethnicity (Aboriginal or non-Aboriginal), sex, whether s/he offended prior to the offence that led to the SAJJ conference and a measure of the young person's mobility and marginality, there were two conference elements associated with reoffending. When young people were observed to be mostly or fully remorseful and when outcomes were achieved by genuine consensus, they were less likely to reoffend during an 8- to 12-month period after the conference. These results are remarkably similar to those of Maxwell and Morris (2000) in their study of reoffending in New Zealand. They found that what happens in conferences (e.g. a young person's expressions of remorse and agreeing [or not] with the outcome, among other variables) could distinguish those young people who were and were not 'persistently reconvicted' during a six and a half-year follow-up period.

THE REAL OR THE TRUE STORY?

Advocates want to tell a particular kind of story, the mythical true story of restorative justice. This story asks people to develop their 'caring' sides and to 'resist tyranny with

compassion' (Braithwaite, 1999: 2). It suggests that amidst adversity, there is great potential 'for doing good' for self and others (Braithwaite, 1999: 2, paraphrasing Eckel, 1997).
It rewrites the history of justice practices by celebrating a return to pre-modern forms,
and it re-colonizes indigenous practices by identifying them as exemplars of restorative
justice. The true story offers some hope, not only for a better way to do justice, but also
for strengthening mechanisms of informal social control, and consequently, to minimize
reliance on formal social control, the machinery and institutions of criminal justice.

In order to sell the idea of restorative justice to a wide audience, advocates have
painted a dichotomous, oppositional picture of different justice forms, with restorative
justice trumping retributive justice as the superior one. There is a certain appeal to this
framing of justice: it offers two choices, and it tells us which side is right. With this
framing, who could possibly be on the side of retribution and retributive justice? Only
the bad guys, of course. When we move from the metaphors and slogans to the hard
work of establishing the philosophical, legal and organizational bases of this idea, and
of documenting what actually occurs in these practices, the true story fails us. It lets us
down because simple oppositional dualisms are inadequate in depicting criminal justice,
even an ideal justice system. With respect to youth justice conferencing, extraordinary
tales of repair and goodwill may occur, but we should not expect them to occur as frequently as the advocates would have us think.

The real story of restorative justice is a more qualified one. Empirical evidence of conferencing in Australia and New Zealand suggests that very high proportions of people
find the process fair; on many measures of procedural justice, it succeeds. However, I
am finding from the SAJJ project that it is relatively more difficult for victims and
offenders to find common ground and to hear each other's stories, or for offenders to
give sincere apologies and victims to understand that apologies are sincere. There appear
to be limits on 'repairing the harm' for offenders and victims, in part because the idea
is novel and unfamiliar for most ordinary citizens. For youthful lawbreakers, the limits
also inhere in the salience of *any* legal process or adult exhortations to 'stay out of
trouble', and the problems that adolescents may have in 'recognizing the other', an
empathetic orientation that is assumed to be central to a restorative process. For victims,
the limits reside in the capacity to be generous to lawbreakers and to see lawbreakers as
capable of change. A variety of observational and interview items from the SAJJ project
suggests that a minority of conferences have the necessary raw material for restorativeness to occur. (One needs to be careful in generalizing: the frequency of restorativeness
would depend greatly on whether a jurisdiction uses conferences selectively or routinely
and what kinds of cases are in the sample, that is, the mix of violence and property, the
degree of seriousness and victim–offender relations.) Overall, the real story of restorative justice has many positives and has much to commend, but the evidence is mixed.
Conferencing, or any new justice practice, is not nirvana and ought not to be sold in
those terms.

In the political arena, telling the mythical true story of restorative justice may be an
effective means of reforming parts of the justice system. It may inspire legislatures to
pass new laws and it may provide openings to experiment with alternative justice forms.
All of this can be a good thing. Perhaps, in fact, the politics of selling justice ideas may
require people to tell mythical true stories. The real story attends to the murk and constraints of justice organizations, of people's experiences as offenders and victims and their

capacities and desires to 'repair the harm'. It reveals a picture that is less sharp-edged and more equivocal. My reading of the evidence is that face-to-face encounters between victims and offenders and their supporters *is* a practice worth maintaining, and perhaps enlarging, although we should not expect it to deliver strong stories of repair and good-will most of the time. If we want to avoid the cycle of optimism and pessimism (Matthews, 1988) that so often attaches to any justice innovation, then we should be courageous and tell the real story of restorative justice. But, in telling the real story, there is some risk that a promising, fledgling idea will meet a premature death.

Acknowledgements

This article is revised from a plenary address given to the Scottish Criminology Conference, Edinburgh, 21–2 September 2000. My thanks to the conference organizers, Lesley McAra and David J. Smith, for the invitation; and to Emilios Christodoulidis, Neil Hutton, Ian Loader, Richard Sparks and the anonymous reviewers for their comments on earlier versions.

Notes

1 Indicative examples of advocates are Umbreit (1994), Consedine (1995), Zehr (1995), Van Ness and Strong (1997), Bazemore and Walgrave (1999) and Braithwaite (1999). Among the skeptics and critics are Ashworth (1993), Pavlich (1996), Blagg (1997), Hudson (1998), Levrant et al. (1999) and Delgado (2000). Because the modern idea of restorative justice is new, publications reporting findings from research are few. Among them are contributors in collections edited by Hudson et al. (1996), Crawford and Goodey (2000), Bazemore and Schiff (2001) and Morris and Maxwell (2001).

2 Conferences are meetings where an *admitted* offender(s), his/her supporters, a victim(s), his/her supporters and relevant other people come together to discuss the offence, its impact and what sanction (or reparation) is appropriate. The conference, which is run by a co-ordinator and attended by a police officer, is typically used as diversion from court prosecution, but it may also be used to give pre-sentencing advice to judges and magistrates. Police-run diversionary conferencing is highly atypical of Australian and New Zealand conferencing, whereas it is more typical in UK and North American practices. See Bargen (1996), Hudson et al. (1996) and Daly and Hayes (2001) for overviews of jurisdiction variation in Australia and New Zealand.

3 Even when calling for the need to 'blend restorative, reparative, and transformative justice. . . with the prosecution of paradigmatic violations of human rights', Drumbl (2000: 296) is unable to avoid using the term 'retributive' to refer to responses that should be reserved for the few.

4 Drawing from Cottingham's (1979) analysis of retribution's many meanings, restorative justice advocates tend to use retributivism to mean 'repayment' (to which they add a punitive kick) whereas desert theorists, such as von Hirsch (1993), use retributivism to mean 'deserved' and would argue for decoupling retribution from punitiveness.

5 It is important to emphasize that new justice practices have not been applied to the fact-finding stage of the criminal process; they are used almost exclusively for the penalty phase. Some comparative claims about restorative justice practices (e.g. they

PUNISHMENT AND SOCIETY 4(1)

are not adversarial when retributive justice is) are misleading in that restorative justice attends only to the penalty phase when negotiation is possible. No one has yet sketched a restorative justice process for those who do not admit to an offence.

6 I became aware of the term *new justice* from La Prairie's (1999) analysis of developments in Canada. She defines new justice initiatives as representing a 'shift away from a justice discourse of punitiveness and punishment toward one of reconciliation, healing, repair, atonement, and reintegration' (1999: 147), and she sees such developments as part of a new emphasis on 'community' and 'partnership' as analysed by Crawford (1997). There may be better terms than the 'old' and 'new justice' (e.g. Hudson, 2001, suggests 'established criminal justice' for the old justice), but my general point is that the retributive/restorative couplet has produced, and continues to produce, significant conceptual confusion in the field.

7 Restorative justice advocates speak of the *harm* not of the *crime*, and in doing so, they elide a crucial distinction between a civil and criminal harm, the latter involving both a *harm* and a *wrong* (Duff, 2001).

8 In response to this point, one reader said there had to be some way to theorize varied justice forms (both in an empirical and normative sense), and thus, the disappointment I speak of reflects a disenchantment with the theoretical enterprise adequately to reflect particularity and variation in the empirical social world. This is a longstanding problem in the sociological field. What troubles me, however, is the construction of theoretical terms in the justice field, which use dualisms in adversarial and oppositional relation to one another.

9 The major research studies in the region are Maxwell and Morris (1993) for New Zealand, Strang et al. (1999) for the ACT and the RISE project and the results reported here for the SAJJ project in South Australia. See Daly (2001a) for a review of these and other studies. Space limitations preclude a detailed review of the methods and results of each study.

10 It is important to distinguish jurisdictions like South Australia, New South Wales and New Zealand, where conferences are routinely used, from other jurisdictions (like Victoria and Queensland), where conferences are used selectively and in a relatively few number of cases (although Queensland practices are undergoing change as of April 2001). When conferences are used routinely, we should not expect to see 'restorativeness' emerging most of the time.

11 Space limitations preclude a review of the definitions and methods used in the re-offending studies; rather general findings are summarized.

References

Abel, Richard L. (1982) 'The contradictions of informal justice', in R.L. Abel (ed.) *The politics of informal justice*, vol. 1, pp. 267–320. New York: Academic Press.

Ashworth, Andrew (1993) 'Some doubts about restorative justice', *Criminal Law Forum* 4(2): 277–99.

Bargen, Jenny (1996) 'Kids, cops, courts, conferencing and children's rights: A note on perspectives', *Australian Journal of Human Rights* 2(2): 209–28.

Barton, Charles (2000) 'Empowerment and retribution in criminal justice', in H. Strang and J. Braithwaite (eds) *Restorative justice: Philosophy to practice*, pp. 55–76. Aldershot: Ashgate/Dartmouth.

Bazemore, Gordon and Mara Schiff, eds (2001) *Restorative community justice*. Cincinnati, OH: Anderson Publishing.

Bazemore, Gordon and Lode Walgrave (1999) 'Restorative juvenile justice: In search of fundamentals and an outline for systemic reform', in G. Bazemore and L. Walgrave (eds) *Restorative juvenile justice: Repairing the harm of youth crime*, pp. 45–74. Monsey, NY: Criminal Justice Press.

Blagg, Harry (1997) 'A just measure of shame? Aboriginal youth and conferencing in Australia', *British Journal of Criminology* 37(4): 481–501.

Blagg, Harry (1998) 'Restorative visions and restorative justice practices: Conferencing, ceremony and reconciliation in Australia', *Current Issues in Criminal Justice* 10(1): 5–14.

Bottoms, Anthony E. (1998) 'Five puzzles in von Hirsch's theory of punishment', in A. Ashworth and M. Wasik (eds) *Fundamentals of sentencing theory: Essays in honour of Andrew von Hirsch*, pp. 53–100. Oxford: Clarendon Press.

Braithwaite, John (1996) 'Restorative justice and a better future', Dorothy J. Killam Memorial Lecture, reprinted in *Dalhousie Review* 76(1): 9–32.

Braithwaite, John (1999) 'Restorative justice: Assessing optimistic and pessimistic accounts', in M. Tonry (ed.) *Crime and justice: A review of research* 25: 1–127. Chicago, IL: University of Chicago Press.

Braithwaite, John and Kathleen Daly (1994) 'Masculinities, violence and communitarian control', in T. Newburn and E.A. Stanko (eds) *Just boys doing business?*, pp. 189–213. New York: Routledge.

Braithwaite, John and Phillip Pettit (1990) *Not just deserts: A Republican theory of criminal justice*. New York: Oxford.

Cain, Maureen (2000) 'Orientalism, occidentalism and the sociology of crime', *British Journal of Criminology* 40(2): 239–60.

Christodoulidis, Emilios (2000) '"Truth and reconciliation" as risks', *Social & Legal Studies* 9(2): 179–204.

Consedine, Jim (1995) *Restorative justice: Healing the effects of crime*. Lyttelton, New Zealand: Ploughshares Publications.

Coombs, Mary (1995) 'Putting women first', *Michigan Law Review* 93(6): 1686–712.

Cottingham, John (1979) 'Varieties of retribution', *Philosophical Quarterly* 29: 238–46.

Crawford, Adam (1997) *The local governance of crime: Appeals to community and partnerships*. Oxford: Clarendon Press.

Crawford, Adam (2001) 'The prospects for restorative youth justice in England and Wales: A tale of two acts', in K. McEvoy and T. Newburn (eds) *Criminology and conflict resolution*. London: Macmillan.

Crawford, Adam and Jo Goodey, eds (2000) *Integrating a victim perspective within criminal justice*. Aldershot: Ashgate/Dartmouth.

Daly, Kathleen (1989) 'Criminal justice ideologies and practices in different voices: Some feminist questions about justice', *International Journal of the Sociology of Law* 17(1): 1–18.

Daly, Kathleen (1998) 'Restorative justice: Moving past the caricatures', paper presented to Seminar on Restorative Justice, Institute of Criminology, University of Sydney Law School, Sydney, April. Available at: http://www.gu.edu.au/school/ccj/kdaly.html.

Daly, Kathleen (2000a) 'Revisiting the relationship between retributive and restorative justice', in H. Strang and J. Braithwaite (eds) *Restorative justice: Philosophy to practice*, pp. 33–54. Aldershot: Ashgate/Dartmouth.

Daly, Kathleen (2000b) 'Sexual assault and restorative justice', paper presented to Restorative Justice and Family Violence Conference, Australian National University, Canberra, July. Available at: http://www.gu.edu.au/school/ccj/kdaly.html.

Daly, Kathleen (2001a) 'Conferencing in Australia and New Zealand: Variations, research findings, and prospects', in A. Morris and G. Maxwell (eds) *Restorative justice for juveniles: Conferencing, mediation and circles*, pp. 59–84. Oxford: Hart Publishing. Available at: http://www.gu.edu.au/school/ccj/kdaly.html.

Daly, Kathleen (2001b) *South Australia Juvenile Justice (SAJJ) research on conferencing, Technical Report No. 2: Research instruments in Year 2 (1999) and background notes*. Brisbane, Queensland: School of Criminology and Criminal Justice, Griffith University. Available at: http://www.aic.gov.au/rjustice/sajj/index.html.

Daly, Kathleen and Hennessey Hayes (2001) 'Restorative justice and conferencing in Australia', in *Trends & issues in crime and criminal justice No. 186*. Canberra: Australian Institute of Criminology. Available at: http://www.aic.gov.au/publications/tandi/tandi186.html.

Daly, Kathleen and Russ Immarigeon (1998) 'The past, present, and future of restorative justice: Some critical reflections', *Contemporary Justice Review* 1(1): 21–45.

Daly, Kathleen, Michele Venables, Mary McKenna, Liz Mumford and Jane Christie-Johnston (1998) *South Australia Juvenile Justice (SAJJ) research on conferencing, Technical report No. 1: Project overview and research instruments (Year 1)*. Brisbane, Queensland: School of Criminology and Criminal Justice, Griffith University. Available at: http://www.aic.gov.au/rjustice/sajj/index.html.

Davis, Gwynn (1992) *Making amends: Mediation and reparation in criminal justice*. London: Routledge.

Delgado, Richard (2000) 'Prosecuting violence: A colloquy on race, community, and justice', *Stanford Law Review* 52: 751–74.

Dignan, Jim (2000) *Restorative justice options for Northern Ireland: A comparative review*. Belfast: The Stationery Office Bookshop.

Drumbl, Mark A. (2000) 'Retributive justice and the Rwandan genocide', *Punishment & Society* 2(3): 287–308.

Duff, R. Antony (1992) 'Alternatives to punishment – or alternative punishments?', in W. Cragg (ed.) *Retributivism and its critics*, pp. 44–68. Stuttgart: Franz Steiner.

Duff, R. Antony (1996) 'Penal communications: Recent work in the philosophy of punishment', in M. Tonry (ed.) *Crime and justice: A review of research* 20: pp. 1–97. Chicago, IL: University of Chicago Press.

Duff, R. Antony (2001) 'Restoration and retribution', paper presented to Cambridge Seminar on Restorative Justice, Toronto, May.

Engel, David (1993) 'Origin myths: Narratives of authority, resistance, disability, and law', *Law & Society Review* 27(4): 785–826.

Feeley, Malcolm and Jonathan Simon (1992) 'The new penology: Notes on the emerging strategy of corrections and its implications', *Criminology* 30(4): 449–74.

Findlay, Mark (2000) 'Decolonising restoration and justice in transitional cultures', in H. Strang and J. Braithwaite (eds) *Restorative justice: Philosophy to practice*, pp. 185–201. Aldershot: Ashgate/Dartmouth.

Garland, David (1996) 'The limits of the sovereign state', *British Journal of Criminology* 36(4): 445–71.

Gilligan, Carol (1982) *In a different voice.* Cambridge, MA: Harvard University Press.

Gilligan, Carol (1987) 'Moral orientation and moral development', in E. Kittay and D. Meyers (eds) *Women and moral theory,* pp. 19–33. Totowa, NJ: Rowman & Littlefield.

Hampton, Jean (1992) 'Correcting harms versus righting wrongs: The goal of retribution', *UCLA Law Review* 39: 1659–702.

Hampton, Jean (1998) 'Punishment, feminism, and political identity: A case study in the expressive meaning of the law', *Canadian Journal of Law and Jurisprudence* 11(1): 23–45.

Harris, M. Kay (1987) 'Moving into the new millennium: Toward a feminist vision of justice', *The Prison Journal* 67(2): 27–38.

Hayes, Hennessey and Kathleen Daly (2001) 'Family conferencing in South Australia and re-offending: Preliminary results from the SAJJ project', paper presented to Australian and New Zealand Society of Criminology Conference, Melbourne, February. Available at: http://www.gu.edu.au/school/ccj/kdaly.html.

Heidensohn, Frances (1986) 'Models of justice: Portia or Persephone? Some thoughts on equality, fairness and gender in the field of criminal justice', *International Journal of the Sociology of Law* 14(3–4): 287–98.

Hudson, Barbara (1998) 'Restorative justice: The challenge of sexual and racial violence', *Journal of Law and Society* 25(2): 237–56.

Hudson, Barbara (2001) 'Victims and offenders', paper presented to Cambridge Seminar on Restorative Justice, Toronto, May.

Hudson, Joe, Allison Morris, Gabrielle Maxwell and Burt Galaway, eds (1996) *Family group conferences: Perspectives on policy and practice.* Monsey, NY: Willow Tree Press.

Kurki, Leena (2001) 'Evaluation of restorative justice practices', paper presented to Cambridge Seminar on Restorative Justice, Toronto, May.

La Prairie, Carol (1999) 'Some reflections on new criminal justice policies in Canada: Restorative justice, alternative measures and conditional sentences', *Australian and New Zealand Journal of Criminology* 32(2): 139–52.

Levrant, Sharon, Francis T. Cullen, Betsy Fulton and John F. Wozniak (1999) 'Reconsidering restorative justice: The corruption of benevolence revisited?', *Crime & Delinquency* 45(1): 3–27.

McCold, Paul (2000) 'Toward a holistic vision of restorative juvenile justice: A reply to the maximalist model', *Contemporary Justice Review* 3(4): 357–414.

MacKinnon, Catharine (1987) *Feminism unmodified.* Cambridge, MA: Harvard University Press.

Marshall, Tony (1996) 'The evolution of restorative justice in Britain', *European Journal of Criminal Policy and Research* 4(4): 21–43.

Masters, Guy and David Smith (1998) 'Portia and Persephone revisited: Thinking about feeling in criminal justice', *Theoretical Criminology* 2(1): 5–27.

Matthews, Roger (1988) 'Reassessing informal justice', in R. Matthews (ed.) *Informal justice?,* pp. 1–24. Newbury Park, CA: Sage.

Maxwell, Gabrielle and Allison Morris (1993) *Family, victims and culture: Youth justice in New Zealand.* Wellington: Social Policy Agency and the Institute of Criminology, Victoria University of Wellington.

PUNISHMENT AND SOCIETY 4(1)

Maxwell, Gabrielle and Allison Morris (1996) 'Research on family group conferences with young offenders in New Zealand', in J. Hudson, A. Morris, G. Maxwell and B. Galaway (eds) *Family group conferences: Perspectives on policy & practice*, pp. 88–110. Monsey, NY: Willow Tree Press.

Maxwell, Gabrielle and Allison Morris (2000) 'Restorative justice and reoffending', in H. Strang and J. Braithwaite (eds) *Restorative justice: Philosophy to practice*, pp. 93–103. Aldershot: Ashgate/Dartmouth.

Mead, George Herbert (1917–18) 'The psychology of punitive justice', *The American Journal of Sociology* 23: 577–602.

Melossi, Dario, ed. (1998) *The sociology of punishment: Socio-structural perspectives*. Aldershot: Ashgate/Dartmouth.

Miller, Seumas and John Blackler (2000) 'Restorative justice: Retribution, confession and shame', in H. Strang and J. Braithwaite (eds) *Restorative justice: Philosophy to practice*, pp. 77–91. Aldershot: Ashgate/Dartmouth.

Morris, Allison and Gabrielle Maxwell, eds (2001) *Restorative justice for juveniles: Conferencing, mediation and circles*. Oxford: Hart Publishing.

Nova Scotia Department of Justice (1998) *Restorative justice: A program for Nova Scotia*. Halifax: Department of Justice.

O'Malley, Pat (1999) 'Volatile and contradictory punishment', *Theoretical Criminology* 3(2): 175–96.

Pavlich, George C. (1996) *Justice fragmented: Mediating community disputes under postmodern conditions*. New York: Routledge.

Pratt, John (2000) 'The return of the wheelbarrow men; or, The arrival of postmodern penality?', *British Journal of Criminology* 40(1): 127–45.

Shearing, Clifford (2001) 'Punishment and the changing face of the governance', *Punishment & Society* 3(2): 203–20.

Sherman, Lawrence W., Heather Strang and Daniel J. Woods (2000) *Recidivism patterns in the Canberra Reintegrative Shaming Experiments (RISE)*. Canberra: Centre for Restorative Justice, Australian National University. Available at: http://www.aic.gov.au/rjustice/rise/recidivism/index.html.

Smart, Carol (1989) *Feminism and the power of law*. London: Routledge.

Smart, Carol (1992) 'The woman of legal discourse', *Social & Legal Studies* 1(1): 29–44.

South African Truth and Reconciliation Commission (1998) *The report of the Truth and Reconciliation Commission*. Available at: http://www.org.za/truth/report.

Strang, Heather, Lawrence W. Sherman, Geoffrey C. Barnes and John Braithwaite (1999) *Experiments in restorative policing: A progress report to the National Police Research Unit on the Canberra Reintegrative Shaming Experiments (RISE)*. Canberra: Centre for Restorative Justice, Australian National University. Available at: http://www.aic.gov.au/rjustice/rise/index.html.

Tonry, Michael (1999) 'Rethinking unthinkable punishment policies in America', *UCLA Law Review* 46(4): 1751–91.

Tyler, Tom R. (1990) *Why people obey the law*. New Haven, CT: Yale University Press.

Tyler, Tom R., Robert J. Boeckmann, Heather J. Smith and Yuen J. Huo (1997) *Social justice in a diverse society*. Boulder, CO: Westview Press.

Umbreit, Mark (1994) *Victim meets offender: The impact of restorative justice and mediation*. Monsey, NY: Criminal Justice Press.

Van Ness, Daniel (1993) 'New wine and old wineskins: Four challenges of restorative justice', *Criminal Law Forum* 4(2): 251–76.

Van Ness, Daniel and Karen Strong (1997) *Restoring justice*. Cincinnati, OH: Anderson Publishing.

Von Hirsch, Andrew (1993) *Censure and sanctions*. New York: Oxford University Press.

Walgrave, Lode (1995) 'Restorative justice for juveniles: Just a technique or a fully fledged alternative?', *The Howard Journal* 34(3): 228–49.

Walgrave, Lode (2000) 'How pure can a maximalist approach to restorative justice remain? Or can a purist model of restorative justice become maximalist?', *Contemporary Justice Review* 3(4): 415–32.

Walgrave, Lode and Ivo Aertsen (1996) 'Reintegrative shaming and restorative justice: Interchangeable, complementary or different?', *European Journal on Criminal Policy and Research* 4(4): 67–85.

Weitekamp, Elmar (1999) 'The history of restorative justice', in G. Bazemore and L. Walgrave (eds) *Restorative juvenile justice: Repairing the harm of youth crime*, pp. 75–102. Monsey, NY: Criminal Justice Press.

Wright, Martin (1991) *Justice for victims and offenders*. Philadelphia, PA: Open University Press.

Zedner, Lucia (1994) 'Reparation and retribution: Are they reconcilable?', *Modern Law Review* 57(March): 228–50.

Zehr, Howard (1995) 'Justice paradigm shift? Values and vision in the reform process', *Mediation Quarterly* 12(3): 207–16.

KATHLEEN DALY is Associate Professor, School of Criminology and Criminal Justice, Griffith University, Brisbane. She directed a major research project on conferencing in South Australia in 1998–9, and has begun a second major project on the feminist and indigenous/race politics of restorative justice in Australia, New Zealand, Canada and the United States. Among her publications are *Gender, crime, and punishment* (Yale University Press, 1994) and an edited collection, with Lisa Maher, *Criminology at the crossroads: Feminist readings in crime and justice* (Oxford University Press, 1998).

[6]

Reconsidering Restorative Justice:
The Corruption of Benevolence Revisited?

Sharon Levrant
Francis T. Cullen
Betsy Fulton
John F. Wozniak

Restorative justice has emerged as an increasingly popular correctional paradigm that is drawing support not only from conservatives but also from liberals. Although this approach has value, its ready embrace as a progressive reform is potentially problematic in two respects. First, the risk exists that restorative justice programs will be corrupted to serve nonprogressive goals and thus do more harm than good. Second, there is little reason to anticipate that restorative justice programs will have a meaningful effect on offender recidivism. Thus, restorative justice should be viewed and implemented with caution.

Three decades have passed since the rehabilitative agenda was pushed aside for crime control policies rooted in a "get tough" philosophy. This orientation has led to harsh forms of punishment, including a dramatic increase in incarceration, the passage of "three strikes and you're out" laws, the reinstatement of the death penalty, and a return to chain gangs. Even community-based sanctions are "unabashedly fierce," emphasizing rigorous surveillance and the enforcement of increasingly stringent conditions of supervision (Clear and Hardyman 1990, p. 46). Clear (1994, p. 3) characterizes this growth in the levels of punishment as a "penal harm" movement justified by both a retributive philosophy of inflicting deserved pain on offenders and the utilitarian arguments of deterrence and incapacitation.

It is tempting to portray the penal harm movement as having achieved complete hegemony over correctional policies. To be sure, it is a powerful way of thinking with which few policy makers publicly take issue. Still, penal harm ideology has undermined but not stamped out alternative perspectives.

SHARON LEVRANT: Ph.D. Student, University of Cincinnati. FRANCIS T. CULLEN: Distinguished Research Professor of Criminal Justice, University of Cincinnati. BETSY FULTON: Ph.D. Student, University of Cincinnati. JOHN F. WOZNIAK: Associate Professor of Sociology, Western Illinois University.

4   CRIME & DELINQUENCY / JANUARY 1999

Surveys of the public, for example, reveal that citizens favor early intervention programs over prisons as a solution to crime (Cullen, Wright, Brown, Moon, Blankenship, and Applegate 1998), are willing to use community sanctions as an option instead of incarceration (Turner, Cullen, Sundt, and Applegate 1997), and continue to support rehabilitation as an important goal of corrections (Applegate, Cullen, and Fisher 1997). In accordance, the space still exists for progressive policies to be put forth that challenge the idea that harming offenders is the only, or the best, means of controlling crime.

In this context, restorative justice is emerging as an increasingly popular alternative to penal harm or getting tough. The primary focus of restorative justice is on the ways in which crime disrupts relationships between people within a community (Center for Restorative Justice and Mediation 1996). In its purest form, it is an informal approach to the criminal law that focuses on ways to repair these social relationships (Wilmerding 1997). Thus, it attempts to hold offenders accountable through both shaming and reintegration processes (Braithwaite 1989) in hopes of strengthening community bonds and providing crime victims with an opportunity to regain their personal power (Center for Restorative Justice and Mediation 1996).

Restorative justice is often contrasted with retributive justice. Within a retributive justice framework, sanctions are imposed for the purposes of inflicting pain on the offender that is proportionate to the pain that his or her offense caused to victims and communities (Newman 1978). Within a restorative justice framework, this goal of punishment for its own sake is replaced with the goal of restoration—of repairing harm and rebuilding relationships (Center for Restorative Justice and Mediation 1996). According to restorative justice advocates, the goal of restoration can only be achieved through programs and practices that extend beyond a singular focus on the offender and that are designed to meet the needs of a variety of criminal justice system clientele, including offenders, victims, and the community (Maloney and Umbreit 1995; Van Ness 1986; Wilmerding 1997).

Notably, restorative justice is not merely a theoretical paradigm but also is now influencing criminal justice policy. A 1997 statutory change in Maryland's Juvenile Causes Act, for example, called for a balanced and restorative approach to juvenile justice (State of Maryland Department of Juvenile Justice 1997). This approach is based on the belief that, in addition to offenders, clients of the juvenile justice system include the victims and communities injured by offenders. Thus, juvenile justice reform in Maryland is aimed at building a comprehensive system that balances three important goals: (1) public safety and community protection, (2) offender accountability, and (3) offender competency and character development. Maryland's vision for the future includes enhanced prevention and early intervention opportunities for at-risk youth and families, a continuum of sanctions for delinquent youth, and an active role for victims and community members in the juvenile justice process.

Similarly, the Vermont Department of Corrections has been restructured to include two primary service tracks: The risk management service track is designed to provide intensive treatment and supervision to high-risk felony offenders and the reparative service track requires low-risk, nonviolent offenders to make reparation to the victim and the community (Dooley 1996). Reparative probation boards have been instituted in the reparative service track as a means of actively involving community members in the justice process (Dooley 1996). These boards consist of five citizen-volunteers from the offender's respective community who are responsible for meeting with the offender to develop a reparative agreement that requires the offender to (1) restore and make whole the victim(s) of his or her crime, (2) make amends to the community, (3) learn about the impact of the crime, and (4) learn ways to avoid reoffending (Walther and Perry 1997).

Maryland's balanced and restorative approach to juvenile justice and Vermont's reparative service boards are just two examples of a robust restorative justice movement. By the end of 1995, 24 states had adopted or were considering juvenile statutes and procedures that reflected the restorative justice concept (Freivalds 1996). Furthermore, there has been a proliferation of programs designed to address victims' needs, including victim notification, restitution, and victim-offender mediation (VOM) programs. VOM programs have been implemented in more than 1,000 communities in North America and Europe (Umbreit, Coates, and Roberts 1997). VOMs bring victims and offenders together in the presence of a trained mediator to negotiate an agreement for the payment of restitution or for other methods of repairing the harm caused by the crime (Umbreit 1994). Although these programs are narrow in scope, they reflect the general principles of restorative justice, which hold offenders accountable for repairing harm to victims and value victims' perspectives as to how the harm is best repaired (Center for Restorative Justice and Mediation 1996).

According to Bazemore (1994), this widespread acceptance of restorative justice can be attributed to its underlying values, which provide common ground for parties who have historically disagreed about criminal justice policy. Conservatives and liberals alike support the emphasis on addressing the needs of crime victims and holding offenders accountable for the harm they cause (Clear 1994; Zehr 1990). Liberals, however, are most attracted to restorative justice because of its potentially humanistic and balanced approach to justice. Restorative justice moves away from a state-centered definition of crime to a definition that accounts for the injuries suffered by victims and communities (Van Ness 1986). Thus, rather than blaming or punishing the offender through incarceration, it focuses on repairing the harm done to victims and communities through a process of negotiation, mediation, victim empowerment, and reparation (Bazemore and Maloney 1994). In its ideal form, restorative justice balances the need to hold offenders accountable for their wrongdoing with the need for their acceptance and reintegration into the community (Braithwaite 1989; Zehr 1990). It broadens the focus of justice from offender-oriented penal harm to community-oriented peacemaking and only considers justice to be achieved when the suffering of offenders, victims, and communities has ended and crime has been reduced (Pepinsky and Quinney 1991). For all of these reasons, progressives are casting skepticism aside and readily accepting restorative justice as a viable alternative to the get tough policies now in place.

Restorative justice appeals to conservatives for different reasons. Conservatives see restorative justice as an extension of the victims' rights movement that seeks to involve victims in the criminal justice process and to compensate victims for the losses incurred from crime (Schafer 1976; Van Ness and Strong 1997). Rather than the balanced approach to justice advocated by liberal proponents, conservatives endorse restorative justice as a means of securing more justice for victims. In so doing, they often attempt to increase the punishment of offenders at the expense of restoration.

In the middle of these conflicting perspectives, restorative justice is trying to find a place in correctional policy. The question remains whether, as liberal advocates believe, restorative justice ultimately will prove to be a truly progressive reform. This article addresses this question through a critical analysis of the restorative justice movement. Two central issues are explored. First, commentators have pointed out that correctional reforms implemented with good intentions often have been corrupted to serve less admirable goals and interests (see, e.g., Cullen and Gilbert 1982; Rothman 1980). Thus, despite its benevolent possibilities, will restorative justice programs be corrupted and have untoward, unanticipated consequences? Second, given the current knowledge about changing offender behavior, there is little reason to conclude that restorative justice can have a meaningful effect on recidivism. This latter issue is critical given that a perceived failure to reduce recidivism contributed to the decline of rehabilitation and boosted the legitimacy of punitive correctional policies in recent years (Cullen and Gilbert 1982; Hahn 1998). Although not fully dismissing the potential of restorative justice, we believe that there is danger in the impetuous adoption of this model without further examination of these issues and more rigorous research on restorative justice outcomes.

THE CORRUPTION OF BENEVOLENCE?

In the 1970s, many liberals joined with conservatives in rejecting rehabilitation and in endorsing reforms, especially determinate sentencing, that constrained the discretion exercised by criminal justice officials. Believing that these reforms would result in increased justice (e.g., equity in sentencing decisions), liberals largely overlooked the possibility that their strange bed-fellows—conservatives—would use the rejection of the rehabilitative ideal as a means to achieve their goal of getting tough on offenders. In hindsight, it now appears that the liberals' benevolent hopes of doing justice were corrupted by conservatives who succeeded in passing harsh laws that ultimately increased the punishment of and harm done to offenders (Cullen and Gilbert 1982; Griset 1991).

In endorsing restorative justice, liberals once again are embracing a reform also being trumpeted by conservatives. In doing so, it seems prudent to consider the lesson of the antirehabilitation movement: Progressive sentiments are no guarantee that reforms will not be corrupted and serve punitive ends. In this context, this section explores four potential unanticipated consequences of restorative justice: (1) it will serve as a means of getting tough on offenders; (2) it will not be restorative for victims, offenders, or communities; (3) it will be more of a symbolic than a substantive reform; and (4) it will reinforce existing race and class biases besetting the criminal justice system.

Getting Tough Through Restorative Justice

According to progressive advocates, restorative justice policies offer potential benefits to offenders, including the opportunity to reconcile with their victims, a more lenient sentence, and the chance for reintegration into society. It remains to be seen, however, whether conservatives will endorse these goals and work with liberals to create a balanced reform or whether they will use restorative justice as yet another opportunity to impose more punishment on offenders. Six considerations suggest that the restorative justice movement may not achieve its progressive goals and, in fact, may increase the extent and harshness of criminal sanctions.

First, Brown (1994) notes that restorative justice systems lack the due process protections and procedural safeguards that are awarded to offenders in the more formal adversarial system. Although programs vary, counsel are generally discouraged from attending mediation hearings because they create barriers for a smooth mediation process. Furthermore, the informality of the system contributes to more lenient rules of evidence. Information presented at conferences also can be used in a formal trial if the offender fails to reach an agreement with the victim during mediation. Restorative justice advocates believe that the cost of diminished offender rights is outweighed by the benefits of accountability (Berzins and Prashaw 1997; Van Ness 1986). Brown (1994) argues, however, that the loss of rights can result in an offender receiving more severe punishment than he or she would receive through the adversarial process.

Second, despite the progressive rhetoric of restoration, offenders may be coerced into participating in the mediation process because of perceived threats of a harsher punishment if they refuse to do so (Brown 1994; Van Ness and Strong 1997). According to Brown (1994), in certain jurisdictions, prosecutors and judges can consider offenders' refusal to participate in VOM conferences in their charging and sentencing decisions. The problem of coercion can be exacerbated if people who normally would not be subjected to state controls through the formal criminal justice process are coerced into participating in restorative justice programming.

Third and relatedly, restorative justice programs can potentially widen the net of social control (Bazemore and Umbreit 1995; Umbreit and Zehr 1996; Van Ness and Strong 1997). The increased influence that the community has in sanctioning can lead restorative justice programs to target offenders who commit minor offenses and are at a low risk of reoffending. For example, market research in Vermont revealed that citizens wanted the criminal justice system to take minor offenses more seriously (Walther and Perry 1997). Thus, instead of diverting offenders from intrusive forms of punishment (e.g., electronic monitoring, intensive supervision probation, incarceration), restorative justice may place more control over the lives of nonserious offenders who may have otherwise received no formal supervision.

Fourth, Bazemore and Umbreit (1995) contend that if broad changes do not take place to make the system restorative, then restorative justice sanctions will likely increase the supervisory requirements that offenders must satisfy. A survey of offenders participating in Vermont's Reparative Probation Program revealed that offenders perceived the program to be much more demanding than regular probation (Walther and Perry 1997). Furthermore, it was discovered that contrary to the program's design, offenders were subjected to both reparative conditions and traditional probation supervision. Until a complete paradigm shift has occurred, restorative justice policies will potentially inflict additional punishment on offenders.

Fifth, as conditions of probation expand through restorative justice programs, the potential that offenders will not meet these conditions also increases. This higher level of noncompliance, combined with heightened public scrutiny and a demand for offender accountability, will likely result in the revocation of more offenders. Other community corrections reforms have experienced a similar phenomenon. For example, the closer surveillance of offenders in intensive supervision programs has led to the increased detection of technical violations (Cullen, Wright, and Applegate 1996). Because of an emphasis on stringent responses to noncompliance, detected violations in these programs have often been followed by the revocation of probation and incarceration (Petersilia and Turner 1993). Thus, restorative justice programs may not only increase social control within the community but may also result in more offenders being sent to prison because they fail to comply with the additional sanctions imposed within the restorative justice framework.

According to Braithwaite and Mugford (1994), one strategy to circumvent this problem is to provide offenders with the opportunity to have multiple conferences when they fail to fulfill the requirements of their mediation agreements. Still, if the victim-offender agreements reached at conferences are to be meaningful, limits will have to be placed on how many repeated conferences there can be before an offender must be held accountable in criminal court and risk incarceration. Even if offenders are not incarcerated for failing to comply with the mediation agreement, they will face an escalating number of conditions. Net-widening and revocation for technical violations are the likely result.

Sixth, restorative justice may increase punishment if reforms fail to develop policies and programs that are able to reintegrate offenders into society. Karp (1998) notes, however, that shaming penalties are gaining popularity because they can fulfill the retributive aims of the public. Lawrence (1991) also sees a danger in advocating shaming activities. He suggests that they may be wrongly interpreted as a revival of support for public shaming practices, such as the ducking stool and the scarlet letter, without an emphasis on the reintegrative element of community acceptance and support.

In summary, although restorative justice policies are being advocated as a benevolent means of addressing the crime problem, they may increase the punitiveness of the social control imposed on offenders in several ways: offenders may lose certain rights and privileges that they are granted through the current adversarial process, offenders may be coerced into participating in restorative justice programs because of formal pressures from practitioners within the criminal justice system, restorative justice may widen the net of social control by targeting low risk offenders, offenders may be subjected to greater levels of supervision, offenders may have a greater likelihood of incarceration for technical violations because of the increased probation conditions and scrutiny they face, and, finally, restorative justice programs may not achieve their goal of offender reintegration and therefore fail to restore fully the harmed relationships that result from the crime. This propensity for getting tough with restorative justice creates doubt about the restorative capacities of current practices.

Restoration extends far beyond the popular conception of repaying victims for their monetary losses. It involves making victims whole again, reintegrating offenders back into the community, and strengthening community bonds (Center for Restorative Justice and Mediation 1996; Van Ness and Strong 1997; Zehr 1990). Several methods have been developed to accomplish the goal of restoration. The following sections of this article will analyze the potential of these methods for restoring victims, offenders, and communities.

Are Programs Restorative for Victims?

Making victims whole again involves redressing their monetary losses, giving them a voice in the justice process, and reducing their fears regarding future victimization (Center for Restorative Justice and Mediation 1996). Several methods have been developed to restore the victims of crime. Restitution is the oldest and most familiar method of victim restoration (American Probation and Parole Association [APPA] 1994). In addition to redressing victims' monetary losses, restitution offers a means of restoring the relationship between the victim and the offender (Galaway 1977). It provides one of the few tangible ways to compensate crime victims.

Other popular methods of victim restoration include VOM programs, family-group conferences, and various forms of community-sentencing panels—all of which bring offenders, victims, and/or communities together to resolve the conflict created by crime. Research suggests that these programs have some restorative value. Evaluations of VOMs have revealed high rates of victim and offender satisfaction with resulting reparative agreements (Marshall 1992; Niemeyer and Shichor 1996; Umbreit 1994; Umbreit et al. 1997), perceptions of fair treatment (Umbreit et al. 1997), reduced fear and anxiety among crime victims, and an increased likelihood of offenders completing the restitution agreement (Umbreit 1994). Victims participating in family-group conferences have stated that the conferences provided them with a voice in the justice process, an improved understanding as to why the crime occurred, and a chance to assess the likelihood of recidivism (Maxwell and Morris 1997). Clearly, the potential exists for achieving victim restoration. Several considerations, however, may limit the restorative capacities of current victim-oriented programs.

The limits of restitution. Although restitution provides a concrete method to compensate crime victims, there are limits on the extent to which victims are fully restored. First, according to Ferns (1994), it is the victim's perspective regarding the extent of losses that must be considered when assessing whether restitution occurs. Because the financial losses experienced by a victim may exceed those stipulated for by court orders, full monetary restoration may not be achieved (APPA 1994). Even if the victim receives financial satisfaction, if the offender remains hostile toward the victim, the latter may remain emotionally dissatisfied and not be restored (Brookes 1998). Second, although all states have made some type of provisions for victim restitution, much of the restitution ordered by the court is never collected (Seymour 1996). Third, the common practice of using an intermediary to collect restitution from offenders and disburse it to crime victims (APPA 1994) would appear to limit the degree to which a relationship between the two parties is either understood or repaired.

Limits to victim-offender conferencing. Marshall (1992) suggests that the effectiveness of mediation programs depends on the involved parties being open and active during the resolution process, using the mediation to solve problems rather than to assign blame, and ensuring that the needs of all parties are heard. This implies, first and foremost, that the parties must be present and, second, that the mediator, victim, and offender possess the competencies needed for a successful mediation.

Research indicates that the rate at which offenders and victims participate in victim-offender conferences is influenced by several factors. One factor is the type of crime involved: Studies have found that victims and offenders are most likely to appear at mediations for minor personal and property crimes and least likely to appear for serious personal crimes (Niemeyer and Shichor 1996; Umbreit 1994). Another factor is the nature of the victim-offender relationship; absent a continuing relationship with the offender, the victim may be less inclined to participate (Lindner 1996). Finally, according to Maxwell and Morris (1997), many victims do not attend family-group conferences because they are not invited or are not given adequate notice. Seymour (1996) suggests that regardless of the reason, victims too often are left out of the restorative justice equation, which limits the extent to which restoration can be achieved.

Even if victims and offenders do make it to the "restorative justice table" (Seymour 1996), what evidence would indicate that community members, offenders, and victims possess the requisite skills for an effective mediation? Often, community volunteers are responsible for facilitating mediations

(Dooley 1996; Ruddell 1996). Although careful screening and training are important safeguards, it is questionable whether citizen volunteers have the capacity to effectively mediate conflict between a potentially emotional victim and a resistant offender. Walther and Perry (1997) found that Vermont's reparative board members were reluctant to involve victims in the mediation process. They speculated that this reluctance stemmed from a lack of knowledge about how to deal with victims' emotions or from a fear that victims will view the board meetings as a forum for seeking retribution.

Victims and offenders may be equally unprepared for mediation. Lindner (1996) has suggested that a face-to-face meeting with the offender could be traumatic for the victim rather than restorative. Furthermore, Maxwell and Morris (1997) found that about 25 percent of the victims participating in family-group conferences reported feeling worse after attending a conference because of their personal inability to express themselves adequately, the offender's lack of sincerity, and the family's inability to make reparation. Given these findings, it appears that inadequate attention to the competencies required for effective mediation can potentially undermine the goal of victim restoration.

Are Programs Restorative for Offenders?

As indicated previously, restorative justice practices emphasize the importance of holding offenders responsible for restoring victims of crime. Another commonly stated objective, however, is to ensure that offenders entering the criminal justice system exit the system more capable of being responsible and productive citizens (Center for Restorative Justice and Mediation 1996; Maloney, Romig, and Armstrong 1998; Zehr 1990). This objective is achieved, it is argued, by teaching offenders right from wrong through various corrective techniques and through their reintegration into the community.

Corrective techniques. Restorative justice advocates suggest that, when rooted in a restorative justice philosophy, restitution and community service can serve corrective purposes for offenders by helping them to recognize the harm that they caused to victims (Bazemore and Maloney 1994; Galaway 1977; Lawrence 1991). Berzins and Prashaw (1997), however, question the degree to which this corrective aspect of restorative justice programs can be achieved within the existing adversarial justice system. For example, the majority of criminal cases are resolved through a guilty plea process that lessens the severity of the charge and encourages the offender to evade responsibility for the real damage done to victims and communities (Center for Restorative Justice and Mediation 1996). The goal of offender correction also may be undermined by the retributive nature of many restitution and community service programs (Shapiro 1990). Within a retributive model, the goal of offender correction is likely to be displaced by the goal of offender compliance. If so, offenders may identify themselves as "victims of the justice system" and identify the victims as "privileged avengers" (Brookes 1998).

Reintegration. Restorative justice recognizes the need to ensure that offenders are given the opportunity for forgiveness after they have been held responsible for their actions (Van Ness 1986). According to Braithwaite (1989), effective "reintegrative shaming" requires the expression of disapproval for the purpose of invoking remorse, followed by gestures of forgiveness designed to accept the offender back into the community. Absent community acceptance and opportunities for change, offenders may be stigmatized, encouraged to participate in criminal subcultures, and become reinvolved in criminal activity (Braithwaite 1989). Thus, successful reintegration requires changes in the offender and in the community. Consistent with this view, Byrne (1986) suggests that a primary role for probation and parole officers should be to work with communities in an effort to increase acceptance, support, and opportunities for offenders. Similarly, Clear (1996) argues for a movement toward a "corrections of place" that broadens the role of corrections beyond the supervision of offenders to organizing community groups and developing crime prevention strategies.

This community focus, however, is potentially problematic. Similar to attempts to implement community policing, this revised focus would alter the contemporary roles and responsibilities of corrections personnel and thus would require major changes in agency operations, including the decentralization of activities and facilities, new training, and revised schedules (Community Policing Consortium 1994). Given the resource constraints currently experienced by community corrections, these changes would be difficult to achieve. Although community corrections agencies are responsible for supervising 75 percent of the correctional population, they only receive one tenth of every dollar spent on corrections (Petersilia 1996). Officers typically are burdened with unmanageable caseloads and struggle to keep up with current supervisory responsibilities. Facing these realities, how can probation officers be expected to expand their role to include community mobilization?

Aside from various corrective techniques and reintegration, the role of rehabilitation in offender restoration is seldom discussed by restorative justice proponents. If rehabilitative programming is incorporated into reparative agreements, it is often done so as an afterthought rather than as a carefully conceived plan for addressing the factors that contribute to an offender's criminal behavior. This shortcoming will ultimately affect the degree to which communities can be restored through restorative justice practices.

Are Programs Restorative for Communities?

Community restoration involves strengthening community bonds in a way that minimizes fear of crime and fortifies informal social controls (Center for Restorative Justice and Mediation 1996; Pranis 1996). Practices designed to restore communities range from community service projects by offenders to grassroots approaches that engage citizens in collective action against crime (Pranis 1996).

Community service by offenders provides the community with the tangible benefit of work and offers much needed resources to the government and to other nonprofit service organizations (Maloney and Umbreit 1995; Van Ness 1986). Engaging offenders in community service also may improve public safety by limiting offenders' opportunities for crime (Maloney and Umbreit 1995) and by developing skills and attitudes conducive to prosocial behaviors. Although a worthy starting point, a simple program of community service cannot begin to achieve true community restoration. Putney (1997) thus argues for a broader grassroots approach to restorative justice that engages communities in owning and resolving problems that reintegrates offenders and that establishes lines of mutual accountability.

The effectiveness of both narrow and broad restorative methods is bounded, however, by two factors: the degree of community interest in participating in restorative justice initiatives and the range of opportunities available to offenders (e.g., social programs, employment, education). Organizing and maintaining community involvement has been cited as one of the most perplexing implementation problems faced by community policing programs (Grinc 1994). Studies of crime prevention programs suggest that neighborhood organizations are difficult to sustain in disadvantaged communities (Garafalo and McLeod 1986; Silloway and McPherson 1985; Skogan 1990, 1996). Skogan (1996) contends that in these communities, crime and fear stimulate withdrawal from community life and limit the ability to collectively respond to local problems. Furthermore, Currie (1985, 1998) argues that without government policies that invest in poverty-stricken communities by providing support in the form of welfare, health care, and early childhood intervention programs, piecemeal restorative justice practices are not likely to reverse the structural inequality that contributes to crime. Based on the difficulties associated with changing community characteristics, community restoration appears to be a utopian goal within the restorative justice framework.

Substantive or Symbolic Reform?

Zehr (1990) contends that a paradigm shift occurs when reformers are frustrated by an existing model's inability to solve a problem. He argues that the retributive justice system is failing to solve the crime problem and needs to be replaced by programs that are better able to address issues of crime. The question remains whether the reforms that are being put forth as restorative are part of a true paradigm shift that is redefining the crime problem and responses to it or whether they are symbolic reforms that simply rename components of the current retributive justice paradigm. Three key issues are integral to determining whether an agency will achieve substantive or symbolic reform.

First, the substance of restorative justice reforms depends on the degree of staff commitment to a new philosophy of justice. Dooley (1996) recognized that the success of Vermont's Reparative Probation Boards was hindered by staff resistance to philosophical changes and subsequent changes in operations. Second, even if the staff is committed to restorative justice goals, to move toward these goals, staff members must be willing to change their roles from that of service provider to community justice facilitator (Bazemore and Day 1996). This alteration in job orientations has been difficult to achieve (Bazemore and Day 1996). For example, most community corrections agencies have had difficulty getting staff to focus on restoring victims of crime (Bazemore 1994). Immarigeon and Daly (1997) caution "that it is naive to suppose that restorative justice processes and outcomes will entirely replace those of traditional criminal justice in the foreseeable future" (p. 16). Third, organizations must secure sufficient human and financial resources to operate quality programs that are capable of achieving restoration.

The resource and organizational obstacles faced by agencies may create incentives to abandon substantive reform and merely to label current sanctioning schemes as restorative while retaining their retributive focus. The appeal of resorting to such a euphemism may be heightened because programs with restorative aims are better able to gain public support (Colson and Van Ness 1989). In the end, symbolic reform may accrue the desired organizational benefits without having to tackle the challenges of substantive reform.

Race and Class Effects

Despite their progressive underpinnings, restorative justice programs may have unintended class and racial biases that work to the disadvantage of poor and minority offenders. First, advocates have given little thought to how the quality and harshness of restorative justice will vary by the economic status of communities. Although speculative at this point, it is likely that affluent communities will have the resources to develop programs that are more integrative because they offer a greater number of quality services to offenders.

Second, within the restorative justice process, might affluent offenders be treated more favorably? In victim-offender mediation conferences, for example, it is possible that offenders who are more educated, better dressed, and more skilled verbally will negotiate more favorable sanctions. It is instructive that mediators in VOM programs tend to be White, male, and better educated—traits that may converge with those of more affluent offenders (Walther and Perry 1997). More generally, the informal, individualized nature of restorative justice provides few guarantees that racial and class inequities will be easily detected.

Third, there may be class and thus racial differences in the ability of offenders to meet the conditions of restorative sanctions and therefore to avoid harsher penalties, including the revocation of probation. The most obvious example is the requirement of providing victims with restitution—a common feature of restorative sanctions—which may be difficult for disadvantaged offenders to fulfill (Hahn 1998). On a broader level, however, it seems likely that affluent offenders will be more able to draw on family supports (e.g., private drug treatment, parental monitoring) to meet the conditions imposed by restorative sanctions. If so, then larger inequalities in society are likely to be reproduced within the framework of restorative justice.

In summary, restorative justice remains an unproved movement that risks failure and perhaps does more harm than good. Its attractiveness lies more in its humanistic sentiments than in any empirical evidence of its effectiveness. Evaluating restorative justice becomes further complicated when the issue of recidivism is considered. Bazemore and Day (1996) argue that a true assessment of restorative justice programs must involve more than examining how well they reduce recidivism. Although this may be so, the survival of a correctional philosophy is influenced by its ostensible ability to control crime (as the popularity of the get tough movement amply shows). Thus, the next section of this article will evaluate the capacity for restorative justice policies to decrease offender recidivism based on the growing body of literature about what works to change offender behaviors.

CHANGING OFFENDER BEHAVIOR:
THE UTILITARIAN CHALLENGE

Many correctional reforms over the past 20 years have developed in response to correctional crises and political pressures rather than from a careful evaluation of policy options and empirical evidence of effectiveness (Cochran 1992). In fact, the very argument that contributed to the demise of rehabilitation—that it failed to reduce recidivism and protect public safety—has been all but ignored in recent progressive reforms. Instead, liberals have tried to promote reforms that promised to reduce the use of incarceration and to advance the legal rights granted to offenders. Whatever the value of these reforms, the result has been that correctional policy has largely been forfeited to conservatives who boldly claim that crime can be reduced by locking up more offenders (Cullen, Van Voorhis, and Sundt 1996). By failing to critically evaluate the capacity for restorative justice practices to lower crime, liberal advocates are in danger of experiencing another setback in their quest for a more progressive system of justice.

Restorative justice proponents, either explicitly or implicitly, argue that crime can be lessened through restorative practices. Pranis (1996) asserts that programs rooted in a restorative justice philosophy decrease crime by strengthening community bonds and enhancing informal mechanisms of social control. Braithwaite (1989) argues that the reintegrative aspect of restorative justice policies reduces recidivism by allowing an offender to remain a part of society and to avoid the criminal subcultures and the labeling process that perpetuate delinquency. Still others claim that specific restorative justice programs have the capacity to change offender behavior. For example, it is argued that victim-offender mediation can facilitate changes in offenders' behavior by forcing them to recognize the harm that their criminal behavior causes to victims and communities (Ruddell 1996; Umbreit 1994). Bazemore and Maloney (1994) suggest that community service would be more rehabilitative in nature if it was guided by a restorative justice philosophy.

These claims, however, seem more based on wishful thinking than on a systematic understanding of how to change the conduct of offenders. Although programs with a restorative orientation may occasionally reduce recidivism (see, e.g., Umbreit 1994), the current knowledge base on offender change would suggest that restorative interventions are likely to have effects on recidivism that are modest, if not inconsequential. In the following section, we elaborate this point by assessing the extent to which restorative programs have features that coincide with the principles of effective treatment.

Effective Correctional Interventions

Since 1975, an abundance of literature reviews and meta-analyses have examined the effectiveness of various correctional interventions (Palmer 1992). There is an increasing consensus that programs that achieve a reduction in recidivism share common features (Andrews, Zinger, Hoge, Bonta, Gendreau, and Cullen 1990; Gendreau and Andrews 1990; Izzo and Ross 1990; Lipsey and Wilson 1998). These characteristics, often referred to as "the principles of effective intervention," are summarized briefly below (Andrews, Zinger, et al. 1990; Gendreau 1996; Gendreau and Andrews 1990).

Three principles of effective intervention address the importance of matching offenders to services based on their risk, need, and personal characteristics (Andrews and Bonta 1994; Andrews, Bonta, and Hoge 1990). The risk principle suggests that levels of service should be matched to the risk level of the offender (Andrews and Bonta 1994). This principle is based on several studies that have found that intensive services are necessary to achieve a significant reduction in recidivism among high-risk offenders, but that when applied to low-risk offenders, intensive services have a minimal or positive effect on recidivism (Andrews, Bonta, et al. 1990). This latter phenomenon has been called an interaction effect in which additional efforts to intervene with low-risk offenders actually increase recidivism (Clear and Hardyman 1990; Neithercutt and Gottfredson 1974).

The need principle suggests that changes in recidivism are dependent on changes in the criminogenic needs of offenders (Andrews and Bonta 1994). Criminogenic needs are dynamic factors that are potentially changeable and that are associated with recidivism, such as antisocial attitudes, substance abuse, poor family communication, and antisocial peer associations (Andrews and Bonta 1990). Thus, when these factors are reduced, there is a decreased likelihood of recidivism. The responsivity principle suggests that in addition to matching services with an offender's risks and needs, the learning styles and personality characteristics of offenders can influence treatment effectiveness (Andrews and Bonta 1990; Van Voorhis 1997). For example, high anxiety offenders do not generally respond well to confrontation (Warren 1983), whereas offenders with below-average intellectual abilities do not respond to cognitive skills programs as well as do offenders with above-average intellectual abilities (Fabiano, Porporino, and Robinson 1991).

In addition to the above-mentioned principles relevant to offender-treatment matching, effective interventions are rooted in behavioral or cognitive-behavioral models of treatment (Clements 1988; Gendreau 1996; Izzo and Ross 1990; Palmer 1996). According to Gendreau (1996), well-designed behavioral programs combine a system of reinforcement with modeling by the treatment provider to teach and motivate offenders to perform prosocial behaviors. Cognitive-behavioral models are designed to enhance perspective taking, interpersonal problem solving, and self-control techniques so as to improve offenders' responses to their environments and stressful situations (Clements 1988).

The most effective interventions possess other similar characteristics. First, they occupy 40 percent to 70 percent of high-risk offenders' time (Gendreau 1996). Second, they last at least 23 weeks (Lipsey and Wilson 1998). Third, they employ service providers who relate to offenders in interpersonally sensitive and constructive ways and who are trained and supervised appropriately. Fourth, they use relapse prevention techniques to monitor and to anticipate problem situations and to train offenders to rehearse alternative behaviors. Last, effective interventions link offenders to other services in the community that are relevant to their needs.

Meta-analyses of correctional interventions have found that programs that meet these principles are achieving, on average, a recidivism reduction of 50 percent (Andrews, Zinger, et al. 1990). Interventions that depart from these principles have a dismal success rate. For example, a meta-analysis of studies on punishment and deterrence-based programs, such as intensive supervision, boot camp, Scared Straight programs, and electronic monitoring programs, revealed that these strategies produced slight increases in recidivism (Gendreau, Fulton, and Goggin forthcoming; Gendreau and Little 1993; see also Lipsey and Wilson 1998). Given the increasing knowledge base on what works to change offender behavior, to what extent can we expect restorative justice programs to reduce recidivism? In addressing this question, the next section will examine the degree to which restorative justice programs reflect these principles.

Assessing Restorative Justice Programs

As currently implemented, most restorative justice programs fail to incorporate the principles of effective intervention, particularly as they relate to the risk, need, and responsivity principles. In restorative justice, the primary criterion for matching sanctions to offenders is the nature and extent of the harm caused by the crime. The seriousness of the offense, however, is not consistently related to an offender's risk of recidivism (Correctional Service Canada 1989; Goldkamp and Gottfredson 1985). Thus, restorative justice programs run the dual risks of producing an interaction effect in low-risk offenders and of underservicing high-risk offenders.

Traditionally, restorative justice programs have targeted low-risk nonviolent offenders for participation (Dooley 1996; Ruddell 1996). These offenders typically are unlikely to recidivate. If subjected to unnecessary sanctions and services, however, their chances for noncompliance, and hence revocation, are increased (Clear and Hardyman 1990). The opposite problems exist for high-risk offenders who increasingly are being included in restorative justice programs. Given research findings that suggest that intensive services are required to reduce recidivism among high-risk offenders, it is unlikely that, for example, a one-hour victim-offender mediation session will lessen criminal propensities among these offenders. Thus, the restorative approach runs the risk of becoming the progressives' equivalent of conservative Scared Straight programs, which attempt to shock youth into positive behavior by subjecting them to an afternoon in prison (Finckenauer 1982).

It is also highly unlikely that restorative justice programs will, as currently implemented, produce lasting changes in an offender's criminogenic needs. As discussed previously, restorative justice programs are currently implemented in a piecemeal fashion and are focused primarily on victim restoration. The only criminogenic need that is even remotely targeted by these practices is lack of empathy or sensitivity to others—a part of many offenders' antisocial values system (Gendreau, Andrews, Goggin, and Chanteloupe 1992). Victim-offender mediation and victim-impact panels are common approaches to developing an offender's empathy toward victims of crime. However, they lack the behavioral framework and relapse-prevention component needed to reinforce improved attitudes in a manner that leads to internalization and continued improvements. Instead, they provide only short-term confrontations with victims that may result in more punishment for the offender. Furthermore, these victim-oriented programs fail to help offenders make generalizations about how their behavior influences others over the long-term or fail to teach offenders alternative ways of behaving.

Findings from a study of a restitution program demonstrate the limitations of restorative justice programs that do not abide by the responsivity principle. Van Voorhis (1985) found that low-maturity offenders, as measured by Kohlberg's stages of moral development, were more likely than high-maturity offenders to view restitution as a means of obtaining a lenient sentence and were significantly less likely to provide restitution to their victims. Thus, restitution does not appear to be a viable mechanism for changing the antisocial attitudes of low-maturity offenders and, more important, for reducing the likelihood of their future criminal behavior.

More generally, meta-analyses conclude that restitution programs have modest, if not weak, effects on recidivism. In a meta-analysis of 10 restitution interventions with serious, noninstitutionalized juvenile offenders, Lipsey and Wilson (1998) found that the mean effect of restitution on recidivism across the studies was .17. Although not inconsequential, this result is modest when compared with behaviorally oriented and individual counseling programs that had an effect size in Lipsey and Wilson's analysis of .43. Even less promising results were found in Gendreau et al.'s (forthcoming) meta-analysis of 16 studies of restitution programs. They found that the mean size of the effect of restitution on recidivism was only .04.

Community service programs also have failed to incorporate the principles of effective intervention. Bazemore and Maloney (1994) suggest that to achieve the full potential of community service, the assigned activity should "bring the offender and conventional adults together" and "provide for a sense of accomplishment, closure, and community recognition" (p. 30). Programs designed in this manner would provide offenders with the modeling and positive reinforcement that are needed to motivate prosocial behavior. However, because community service has historically been imposed as an additional punishment or condition of probation supervision, little attention has been paid to such treatment goals and related practices. In fact, the image of offenders in bright orange jumpsuits picking up trash on the side of the road suggests that some community service assignments may be stigmatizing. In these instances, the extent to which offenders learn attitudes and skills conducive to prosocial behavior is likely to be limited.

In contrast, victim-impact classes conducted by the California Youth Authority may prove more effective. The primary goal of these classes is to make offenders understand the devastating effects of crime (Seymour 1996). Youth participate in a six-week course that teaches alternative ways to resolve conflict. According to Seymour (1996), the curriculum is an educational model that is culturally sensitive and appropriate for the offenders' age and cognitive development. Although too brief in duration for high-risk offenders, this curriculum appears to include the behavioral and cognitive components required to change offender behavior.

Until more programs operating within the restorative justice framework incorporate the principles of effective intervention, the likelihood of producing reductions in recidivism is limited. This, in turn, will compromise the extent to which other restorative goals can be achieved because victims and communities will continue to suffer from the criminal behavior of these repeat offenders. A truly restorative program will be rooted in empirical evidence on what works in changing offender behavior.

CONCLUSION: RESTORATIVE JUSTICE AND REHABILITATION

Restorative justice is increasingly embraced—by criminologists and by policy makers—as an alternative correctional paradigm to the prevailing view that penal harm is the solution to crime. By offering something to everyone—victims, offenders, and the community—restorative justice is, at first glance, seemingly deserving of the excitement that it is generating. Our essay, however, is a cautionary reminder that jumping on this bandwagon may be premature, if not risky. Regardless of the benevolent rhetoric that is often used to describe the goals of restorative justice (e.g., peacemaking, communitarian), there is reason to believe that this paradigm will be corrupted and may do more harm than good.

Our goal, however, is not simply nay-saying. By illuminating potential problem areas, we hope that those implementing restorative justice programs will not oversell the intervention or be blind to its dangers. We also recognize that restorative justice potentially avoids a crucial weakness in other progressive policy agendas: the charge that the intervention is a form of entitlement to offenders. This problem is readily seen in the traditionally progressive approach of rehabilitation. Given the principle of less eligibility, any provision of treatment services to offenders is open to attack because such social welfare is undeserved. In contrast, restorative justice demands a certain level of accountability from offenders. Their reintegration depends on their willingness to make efforts to restore victims and the community. Accordingly, the paradigm moves away from entitlement to the principle of social exchange.

As noted, however, a fundamental weakness of restorative justice is its failure to provide a plausible blueprint for how to control crime. This failure is critical because the substantial hegemony of the penal harm or get tough movement has been due to the compelling promise that this strategy will protect society by locking up as many wicked people as possible. In contrast, restorative justice provides few answers for how to deal with serious and persistent offenders. It is especially disturbing that advocates of restorative justice have ignored the research on the behavioral change of offenders in favor of the hope—based on a new and unproved criminological theory—that brief interludes of public shaming will change deeply rooted criminal predispositions. No progressive policy agenda will take hold, we argue, unless citizens are convinced that it will not jeopardize their safety. The failure to control crime inevitably will lead to a new round of penal harm.

Although a marriage may prove uneasy, an alternative approach is to explore bringing together the ideals of restorative justice and rehabilitation. If rehabilitation were seen as part of a process that held offenders accountable and tried to restore victims (e.g., through public service, working to pay victim restitution), then it would be less vulnerable to the criticism that it is only concerned with the welfare of offenders. Alternatively, if restorative justice embraced the logic and knowledge of the rehabilitative ideal, it would have a scientifically informed approach of how to change offenders' behavior. In short, restorative justice transforms rehabilitation from an entitlement or welfare paradigm to an accountability paradigm, whereas rehabilitation transforms restorative justice from a paradigm that speculates in questionable ways about changing offenders to one that can be the conduit through which effective services can be transmitted.

Merging these two correctional paradigms undoubtedly would be a daunting task and would not obviate the need to address other problems relating to these two paradigms. Even so, the dual concepts of restoration and rehabilitation are powerful ideas that can challenge the view that harming offenders is the only and best solution to crime. It is instructive that the public continues to support rehabilitation as an important goal of corrections (Applegate et al. 1997), and it seems likely that this support would increase if offenders, as part of their correctional service, were working to restore victims and the community. In short, beyond pure altruism or benevolent sentiments, why should citizens want to invest in or do good for offenders? One potentially compelling and progressive answer is that doing so will allow offenders to restore those that they have harmed and will make them less likely to harm again.

REFERENCES

American Probation and Parole Association (APPA). 1994. *A Guide to Enhancing Victim Services Within Probation and Parole.* Lexington, KY: American Probation and Parole Association.
Andrews, D. A. and James Bonta. 1994. *The Psychology of Criminal Conduct.* Cincinnati, OH: Anderson.
Andrews, D. A., James Bonta, and Robert D. Hoge. 1990. "Classification for Effective Rehabilitation: Rediscovering Psychology." *Criminal Justice and Behavior* 17:19-52.
Andrews, D. A., Ivan Zinger, Robert D. Hoge, James Bonta, Paul Gendreau, and Francis T. Cullen. 1990. "Does Correctional Treatment Work? Clinically Relevant and Psychologically Informed Meta-Analysis." *Criminology* 28:369-404.

Applegate, Brandon K., Francis T. Cullen, and Bonnie S. Fisher. 1997. "Public Support for Correctional Treatment: The Continuing Appeal of the Rehabilitative Ideal." *The Prison Journal* 77:237-58.

Bazemore, Gordon. 1994. "Developing a Victim Orientation for Community Corrections: A Restorative Justice Paradigm and a Balanced Mission." *Perspectives* Special Issue:19-25.

Bazemore, Gordon and Susan E. Day. 1996. "Restoring the Balance: Juvenile and Community Justice." *Juvenile Justice* 3:3-14.

Bazemore, Gordon and Dennis Maloney. 1994. "Rehabilitating Community Service: Toward Restorative Service Sanctions in a Balanced Justice System." *Federal Probation* 58 (1):24-35.

Bazemore, Gordon and Mark Umbreit. 1995. "Rethinking the Sanctioning Function in Juvenile Court: Retributive or Restorative Responses to Youth Crime." *Crime & Delinquency* 41:296-316.

Berzins, Lorraine and Rick Prashaw. 1997. "A New Imagination for Justice and Corrections." *The ICCA Journal of Community Corrections* 8 (2):22-25.

Braithwaite, John. 1989. *Crime, Shame and Reintegration*. New York: Cambridge University Press.

Braithwaite, John and Stephen Mugford. 1994. "Conditions of Successful Reintegration Ceremonies: Dealing With Juvenile Offenders." *British Journal of Criminology* 2034:139-71.

Brookes, Derek R. 1998. "Evaluating Restorative Justice Programs." *Humanity and Society* 22:23-37.

Brown, Jennifer G. 1994. "The Use of Mediation to Resolve Criminal Cases: A Procedural Critique." *Emory Law Journal* 43:1247-1309.

Byrne, James M. 1986. "Reintegrating the Concept of Community Into Community-Based Corrections." *Crime & Delinquency* 35:471-99.

Center for Restorative Justice and Mediation. 1996. *Restorative Justice: For Victims, Communities, and Offenders*. Minneapolis: University of Minnesota, Center for Restorative Justice and Mediation.

Clear, Todd R. 1994. *Harm in American Penology: Offenders, Victims, and Their Communities*. Albany: State University of New York Press.

————. 1996. "Toward a Corrections of 'Place': The Challenge of 'Community' in Corrections." *National Institute of Justice Journal* (August):52-56.

Clear, Todd R. and Patricia Hardyman. 1990. "The New Intensive Supervision Movement." *Crime & Delinquency* 36:42-60.

Clements, Carl. 1988. "Delinquency Prevention and Treatment: A Community-Centered Perspective." *Criminal Justice and Behavior* 15:286-305.

Cochran, Donald. 1992. "The Long Road From Policy Development to Real Change in Sanctioning Practice." Pp. 307-318 in *Smart Sentencing: The Emergence of Intermediate Sanctions*, edited by J. Byrne, A. Lurigio, and J. Petersilia. Newbury Park, CA: Sage.

Colson, Charles W. and Daniel W. Van Ness. 1989. *Convicted New Hope for Ending America's Crime Crisis*. Westchester, IL: Crossway.

Community Policing Consortium. 1994. *Understanding Community Policing: A Framework for Action*. Washington, DC: U.S. Department of Justice, Bureau of Justice Assistance.

Correctional Service Canada. 1989. "What Does Type of Offense Tell Us About Recidivism?" *Forum on Corrections Research* 1 (2):3-4.

Cullen, Francis T. and Karen E. Gilbert. 1982. *Reaffirming Rehabilitation*. Cincinnati, OH: Anderson.

Cullen, Francis T., Patricia Van Voorhis, and Jodie L. Sundt. 1996. "Prisons in Crisis: The American Experience." Pp. 21-52 in *Prisons 2000: An International Perspective on the Cur-*

rent State and Future of Imprisonment, edited by R. Matthews and P. Francis. New York: St. Martin's.

Cullen, Francis T., John P. Wright, and Brandon K. Applegate. 1996. "Control in the Community: The Limits of Reform?" Pp. 69-116 in *Choosing Correctional Interventions That Work: Defining the Demand and Evaluating the Supply,* edited by A. T. Harland. Newbury Park, CA: Sage.

Cullen, Francis T., John P. Wright, Shayna Brown, Melissa Moon, Michael B. Blankenship, and Brandon K. Applegate. 1998. "Public Support for Early Intervention Programs: Implications for a Progressive Policy Agenda." *Crime & Delinquency* 44:187-204.

Currie, Elliott. 1985. *Confronting Crime: An American Challenge.* New York: Pantheon.

———. 1998. *Crime and Punishment in America.* New York: Metropolitan.

Dooley, Michael J. 1996. "Reparative Probation Boards." Pp. 185-92 in *Restoring Hope Through Community Partnerships: The Real Deal in Crime Control,* edited by B. Fulton. Lexington, KY: American Probation and Parole Association.

Fabiano, Elizabeth, Frank Porporino, and Dave Robinson. 1991. "Canada's Cognitive Skills Program Corrects Offenders' Faulty Thinking." *Corrections Today* 53 (August):102-8.

Ferns, Ray. 1994. "Restorative Case Management: The Evolution of Correctional Case Management." *Perspectives* 18 (Summer):36-41.

Finckenauer, James O. 1982. *Scared Straight! and the Panacea Phenomenon.* Englewood Cliffs, NJ: Prentice Hall.

Freivalds, Peter. 1996. "Balanced and Restorative Justice Project." Office of Juvenile Justice and Delinquency Prevention Fact Sheet (July).

Galaway, Burt. 1977. "Restitution as an Integrative Punishment." Pp. 341-47 in *Assessing the Criminal: Restitution, Retribution, and the Legal Process,* edited by R. E. Barnett and H. Hagel III. Cambridge, MA: Ballinger.

Garafalo, James and Maureen McLeod. 1986. "Improving the Effectiveness and Utilization of Neighborhood Watch Programs." Presented to the National Institute of Justice from the Hindelang Criminal Justice Research Center, State University of New York at Albany.

Gendreau, Paul. 1996. "The Principles of Effective Intervention With Offenders." Pp. 117-30 in *Choosing Correctional Options That Work,* edited by A. T. Harland. Thousand Oaks, CA: Sage.

Gendreau, Paul and D. A. Andrews. 1990. "Tertiary Prevention: What the Meta-Analyses of the Offender Treatment Literature Tell Us About What Works." *Canadian Journal of Criminology* 32:173-84.

Gendreau, Paul, D. A. Andrews, Claire Goggin, and Francoise Chanteloupe. 1992. "The Development of Clinical and Policy Guidelines for the Prediction of Criminal Behavior in Criminal Justice Settings." Department of Psychology, University of New Brunswick, St. John. Unpublished manuscript.

Gendreau, Paul, Betsy Fulton, and Claire Goggin. Forthcoming. "Intensive Supervision in Probation and Parole Settings." In *Handbook of Offender Assessment and Treatment,* edited by C. R. Hollin. Chichester, UK: Wiley.

Gendreau, Paul and Tracy Little. 1993. "A Meta-Analysis of the Effectiveness of Sanctions on Offender Recidivism." Department of Psychology, University of New Brunswick, St. John. Unpublished manuscript.

Goldkamp, John and Michael Gottfredson. 1985. *Policy Guidelines for Bail: An Experiment in Court Reform.* Philadelphia: Temple University.

Grinc, Randolph M. 1994. " 'Angels in Marble': Problems in Stimulating Community Involvement in Community Policing." *Crime & Delinquency* 40:442.

Griset, Pamala L. 1991. *Determinate Sentencing: The Promise and the Reality of Retributive Justice.* Albany: State University of New York Press.

Hahn, Paul H. 1998. *Emerging Criminal Justice: Three Pillars for a Proactive Justice System.* Thousand Oaks, CA: Sage.

Immarigeon, Russ and Kathleen Daly. 1997. "Restorative Justice: Origins, Practices, Contexts, and Challenges." *The ICCA Journal on Community Corrections* 8 (2):13-19.

Izzo, Rhena and Robert Ross. 1990. "Meta-Analysis of Rehabilitation Programs for Juvenile Delinquents: A Brief Report." *Criminal Justice and Behavior* 17:134-42.

Karp, David R. 1998. "The Judicial and Judicious Use of Shame Penalties." *Crime & Delinquency* 44:277-94.

Lawrence, Richard. 1991. "Reexamining Community Corrections Models." *Crime & Delinquency* 37:449-64.

Lindner, Charles. 1996. "VORP: An Unproven Fringe Movement." *Perspectives* 20 (Winter):15-7.

Lipsey, Mark and David Wilson. 1998. "Effective Intervention for Serious Juvenile Offenders: A Synthesis of Research." Pp. 313-45 in *Serious and Violent Juvenile Offenders: Risk Factors and Successful Interventions*, edited by R. Loeber and D. P. Farrington. Thousand Oaks, CA: Sage.

Maloney, Dennis, Dennis Romig, and Troy Armstrong. 1998. *Juvenile Probation: The Balanced Approach.* Reno, NV: National Council of Juvenile and Family Court Judges.

Maloney, Dennis and Mark Umbreit. 1995. "Managing Change: Toward a Balanced and Restorative Justice Model." *Perspectives* 19 (2):43-6.

Marshall, Tony F. 1992. "Restorative Justice on Trial in Britain." Pp. 15-28 in *Restorative Justice on Trial: Pitfalls and Potentials of Victim-Offender Mediation—International Research Perspectives*, edited by H. Messmer and H. U. Otto. Boston: Kluwer.

Maxwell, Gabrielle and Allison Morris. 1997. "Family Group Conferences and Restorative Justice." *The ICCA Journal on Community Corrections* 8 (2):37-40.

Neithercutt, Michael G. and Don M. Gottfredson. 1974. *Caseload Size Variation and Differences in Probation/Parole Performance.* Washington, DC: National Center for Juvenile Justice.

Newman, Graeme. 1978. *The Punishment Response.* Philadelphia: J. B. Lippincott.

Niemeyer, Mark and David Shichor. 1996. "A Preliminary Study of a Large Victim/Offender Reconciliation Program." *Federal Probation* 60 (3):30-4.

Palmer, Ted. 1992. *The Re-Emergence of Correctional Intervention.* Newbury Park, CA: Sage.

———. 1996. "Programmatic and Nonprogrammatic Aspects of Successful Intervention." Pp. 131-82 in *Choosing Correctional Options that Work*, edited by A. T. Harland. Thousand Oaks, CA: Sage.

Pepinsky, Harold and Richard Quinney, eds. 1991. *Criminology as Peacemaking.* Bloomington: Indiana University Press.

Petersilia, Joan. 1996. "A Crime Control Rationale for Reinvesting in Community Corrections." *Perspectives* 20 (2):21-9.

Petersilia, Joan and Susan Turner. 1993. "Evaluating Intensive Supervision Probation/Parole: Results of Nationwide Experiment." Research in Brief, National Institute of Justice, Washington, DC.

Pranis, Kay. 1996. "A Hometown Approach to Restorative Justice." *State Government News* 39 (9):14-6.

Putney, Bart. 1997. "A Grassroots Approach to Restorative Justice." *The ICCA Journal on Community Corrections* 8 (2):20-1.

Rothman, David J. 1980. *Conscience and Convenience: The Asylum and Its Alternatives in Progressive America*. Boston: Little, Brown.

Ruddell, Regina. 1996. "Victim Offender Reconciliation Program." Pp. 171-2 in *Restoring Hope Through Community Partnerships: The Real Deal in Crime Control*, edited by B. Fulton. Lexington, KY: American Probation and Parole Association.

Schafer, Stephen. 1976. "The Victim and Correctional Theory: Integrating Victim Reparation With Offender Rehabilitation." Pp. 227-36 in *Criminal Justice and the Victim*, edited by W. F. McDonald. Beverly Hills, CA: Sage.

Seymour, Anne. 1996. "Putting Victims First." *State Government News* 39 (9):24-5.

Shapiro, Carol. 1990. "Is Restitution Legislation the Chameleon of the Victims' Movement." Pp. 73-80 in *Criminal Justice, Restitution, and Reconciliation*, edited by B. Galaway and J. Hudson. Monsey, NJ: Willow Tree Press.

Silloway, Glenn and Marlys McPherson. 1985. "The Limits to Citizen Participation in a Government Sponsored Community Crime Prevention Program." Presented at the annual meeting of the American Society of Criminology, San Diego, CA.

Skogan, Wesley G. 1990. *Disorder and Decline: Crime and the Spiral of Decay in Urban Neighborhoods*. Berkeley: University of California Press.

———. 1996. "The Community's Role in Community Policing." *National Institute of Justice Journal* (August):31-4.

State of Maryland Department of Juvenile Justice. 1997. *A Comprehensive Strategy for Balanced and Restorative Justice*. Baltimore: State of Maryland Department of Juvenile Justice.

Turner, Michael G., Francis T. Cullen, Jodie L. Sundt, and Brandon K. Applegate. 1997. "Public Tolerance for Community-Based Sanctions." *The Prison Journal* 77:6-26.

Umbreit, Mark S. 1994. "Victim Empowerment Through Mediation: The Impact of Victim Offender Mediation in Four Cities." *Perspectives* Special Issue:25-30.

Umbreit, Mark S., Robert Coates, and Ann W. Roberts. 1997. "Cross-National Impact of Restorative Justice Through Mediation and Dialogue." *The ICCA Journal on Community Corrections* 8 (2):46-50.

Umbreit, Mark and Howard Zehr. 1996. "Restorative Family Group Conferences: Differing Models and Guidelines for Practice." *Federal Probation* 60 (3):24-9.

Van Ness, Daniel W. 1986. *Crime and Its Victims*. Downers Grove, IL: InterVarsity Press.

Van Ness, Daniel W. and Karen H. Strong. 1997. *Restoring Justice*. Cincinnati, OH: Anderson.

Van Voorhis, Patricia. 1985. "Restitution Outcome and Probationer's Assessments of Restitution: The Effects of Moral Development." *Criminal Justice and Behavior* 12:259-87.

———. 1997. "Correctional Classification and the 'Responsivity Principle'." *Forum on Corrections Research* 209 (1):46-50.

Walther, Lynne and John Perry. 1997. "The Vermont Reparative Probation Program." *The ICCA Journal on Community Corrections* 8 (2):26-34.

Warren, Marguerite. 1983. "Application of Interpersonal Maturity Theory to Offender Populations." Pp. 23-49 in *Personality Theory, Moral Development, and Criminal Behavior*, edited by W. Laufer and J. Day. Lexington, MA: Lexington Books.

Wilmerding, John. 1997. "Healing Lives, Mending Society." *Quaker Abolitionist* 3 (2):4-5.

Zehr, Howard. 1990. *Changing Lenses*. Scottdale, PA: Herald Press.

[7]
New Wine and Old Wineskins:
Four Challenges of Restorative Justice*

Daniel W. Van Ness**

> *And nobody puts new wine into old wineskins;*
> *if he does, the wine will burst the skins,*
> *and the wine is lost and the skins too.*
> *No! New wine, fresh skins.*
>
> *Mark 2:22*

At the 1987 London conference on criminal law reform that led to the formation of the Society for the Reform of Criminal Law, Justice John Kelly of Australia delivered a remarkable address on the purpose of law.[1] Speaking to two hundred judges, legal scholars, and law reformers from common law countries, he laid aside his prepared comments and spoke with great feeling about the need for criminal law practitioners to see themselves as healers. A purpose of criminal law, he

---

** Special Counsel on Criminal Justice, Prison Fellowship, Washington, D.C., U.S.A.; B.A., Wheaton College 1971; J.D., DePaul University 1975; LL.M., Georgetown University 1993. I gratefully acknowledge the assistance of Dr. Karen Strong, David Carlson, Thomas Crawford, and Dr. Daniel Dreisbach.

[1] For a brief account of this conference, see Conference Report, *Reform of the Criminal Law*, 1 Crim. L.F. 91 (1989).

said, should be to heal the wounds caused by crime. Since "healing" is not a word frequently heard in legal gatherings, it was helpful that he illustrated what he meant.

Justice Kelly told of a case in which he had made a special effort to ensure that a rape victim felt vindicated. He had just sentenced the defendant to prison, but before calling the next case he asked the victim to approach the bench. Justice Kelly had watched the complainant throughout the proceedings, and it was clear that she was very distraught, even after the offender's conviction and sentencing. The justice spoke with her briefly and concluded with these words: "You understand that what I have done here demonstrates conclusively *that what happened was not your fault.*" The young woman began to weep as she left the courtroom. When Justice Kelly called the family several days later, he learned that his words had marked the beginning of psychological healing for the victim. Her tears had been tears of healing.

The view that justice should bring about healing is, in fact, an ancient concept, one that a growing number of commentators are developing for contemporary application under the rubric of "restorative justice." Advocates of restorative justice face legal and jurisprudential challenges, among these the challenge to abolish criminal law, the challenge to rank multiple goals, the challenge to determine harm rationally, and the challenge to structure community–government cooperation. This article will consider these four challenges in turn and suggest ways in which they might be addressed.

ROOTS

We are used to thinking of criminal law as the means through which government prohibits criminal behavior and punishes criminals.[2] We take for granted the distinction between private and public wrongs, which separates the law of torts from criminal law, a distinction

---

[2]   *See, e.g.,* Kenneth Mann, *Punitive Civil Sanctions,* 101 Yale L.J. 1795, 1807 (1992).

ingrained in our common law tradition.[3] But there is another, older understanding of law that resists this duality, affirming that no matter how we administer the law, one of the primary goals of justice should be to restore the parties injured by crime.[4]

Early legal systems that form the foundation of Western law emphasized the need for offenders and their families to settle with victims and their families. Although crime breached the common welfare, so that the community had an interest in, and a responsibility for, addressing the wrong and punishing the offender, the offense was not considered primarily a crime against the state, as it is today. Instead, a crime was viewed principally as an offense against the victim and the victim's family.[5] This understanding was reflected in ancient legal codes from the Middle East, the Roman empire, and later European polities.[6] Each of these diverse cultures responded to what we now call

---

[3]   *See, e.g.,* Atcheson v. Everitt, 98 Eng. Rep. 1142 (K.B. 1775), in which Lord Mansfield wrote: "Now there is no distinction better known, than the distinction between civil and criminal law; or between criminal prosecutions and civil actions." *Id.* at 1147.

[4]   In his highly regarded book on what he calls "primitive law," E. Adamson Hoebel wrote:

> The job [of primitive law] is to clean the case up, to suppress or penalize the illegal behavior and to bring the relations of the disputants back into balance, so that life may resume its normal course. This type of law-work has frequently been compared to work of the medical practitioner. It is family doctor stuff, essential to keeping the social body on its feet.

E. Adamson Hoebel, *The Law of Primitive Man* 279 (1968).

[5]   *E.g.,* Marvin E. Wolfgang, *Victim Compensation in Crimes of Personal Violence,* 50 Minn. L. Rev. 223 (1965).

[6]   The Code of Hammurabi (c. 1700 B.C.) prescribed restitution for property offenses, as did the Code of Lipit-Ishtar (c. 1875 B.C.). Other Middle Eastern codes, such as the Sumerian Code of Ur-Nammu (c. 2050 B.C.) and the Code of Eshnunna (c. 1700 B.C.) required restitution even in the case of violent offenses. The Roman Law of the Twelve Tables (449 B.C.) required thieves to pay double restitution unless the property was found in their houses; in that case, treble damages were imposed; for resisting the search of their houses, they paid quadruple restitution. The Lex Salica (c. A.D. 496), the earliest existing collection of Germanic tribal laws, included restitution for

crime by requiring offenders and their families to make amends to victims and their families—not simply to insure that injured persons received restitution but also to restore community peace.[7]

This can be seen as well in the language of the Old Testament, where the word *shalom* is used to describe the ideal state in which the community should function.[8] This term signifies completeness, fulfillment, wholeness—the existence of right relationships between individuals, the community, and God.[9] Crime was understood to break *shalom*, destroying right relationships within the community and creating harmful ones. Ancient Hebrew justice, then, aimed to restore wholeness.[10] Restitution formed an essential part of this process, but restitution was not an end in itself. This is suggested by the Hebrew word for "restitution," *shillum*, which comes from the same root as *shalom* and likewise implies the reestablishment of community peace. Along with restitution came the notion of vindication of the victim and of the law itself. This concept was embodied in another word derived from the same root as both *shalom* and *shillum*—*shillem*. *Shillem* can be translated as "retribution" or "recompense," not in the sense of revenge (that word in Hebrew comes from an entirely different root) but in the sense of

---

crimes ranging from theft to homicide. The Laws of Ethelbert (c. A.D. 600), promulgated by the ruler of Kent, contain detailed restitution schedules that distinguished the values, for example, of each finger and fingernail. Daniel W. Van Ness, *Restorative Justice,* in *Criminal Justice, Restitution, and Reconciliation* 7, 7 (Burt Galaway & Joe Hudson eds., 1990).

[7]   Hoebel, *supra* note 4, at 279.

[8]   We must distinguish *shalom* from the irrational belief that the world is safe and just. Psychologist Melvin Lerner has argued that human beings need to believe that people basically get what they deserve and that the world is both safe and just, even when events suggest otherwise. This self-delusion, Lerner argues, is necessary in order for people to function in their daily lives. Melvin J. Lerner, *The Belief in a Just World* 11–15 (1980). But the Hebrew word *shalom* does not imply a delusional belief that all is well. To hold healing and *shalom* as goals for society's response to crime is to recognize that hurt and injustice do exist and that they must be healed and rectified.

[9]   G. Lloyd Carr, *Shalom,* in *Theological Wordbook of the Old Testament* 931 (R.L. Harris et al. eds., 1980).

[10]   Van Ness, *supra* note 6, at 9.

satisfaction or vindication.[11] In short, the purpose of the justice process was, through restitution and vindication, to restore a community that had been sundered by crime.

This view of justice is not confined to the far distant past. Many precolonial African societies aimed not so much at punishing criminal offenders as at resolving the consequences to their victims. Sanctions were compensatory rather than punitive, intended to restore victims to their previous position.[12] Current Japanese experience demonstrates a similar emphasis on compensation to the victim and restoration of community peace.[13] The approach (as we will see later) emphasizes a process that has been referred to as "confession, repentance and absolution."[14]

For all of its tradition, the restorative approach to criminal justice is unfamiliar to most of us today. For common law jurisdictions, the Norman invasion of Britain marked a turning point away from this understanding of crime. William the Conqueror and his successors

---

[11]   How is it that a root word meaning "wholeness and unity, a restored relationship" could produce derivatives with such varied meanings?

> The apparent diversity of meanings . . . can be accounted for in terms of the concept of *peace being restored through payment* (of tribute to a conqueror, Joshua 10:1), *restitution* (to one wronged, Exodus 21:36), *or simple payment and completion* (of a business transaction, II Kings 4:7).
>   The payment of a vow (Psalms 50:14) completes an agreement so that both parties are in a state of *shalom*. Closely linked with this concept is the eschatological motif in some uses of the term. *Recompense for sin, either national or personal, must be given. Once that obligation has been met, wholeness is restored* (Isaiah 60:20, Joel 2:25).

Carr, *supra* note 9, at 931 (emphasis added).

[12]   Daniel D.N. Nsereko, Compensating Victims of Crime in Botswana (paper presented at the Society for the Reform of Criminal Law Conference on "Reform of Sentencing, Parole, and Early Release," Ottawa, Ontario, Canada, Aug. 1–4, 1988).

[13]   *See, e.g.,* Daniel H. Foote, *The Benevolent Paternalism of Japanese Criminal Justice,* 80 Cal. L. Rev. 317 (1992).

[14]   John O. Haley, *Confession, Repentance, and Absolution,* in *Mediation and Criminal Justice* 195 (Martin Wright & Burt Galaway eds., 1989).

found the legal process an effective tool for establishing the preeminence of the king over the church in secular matters, and in replacing local systems of dispute resolution.[15] The Leges Henrici, written early in the twelfth century, asserted exclusive royal jurisdiction over offenses such as theft punishable by death, counterfeiting, arson, premeditated assault, robbery, rape, abduction, and "breach of the king's peace given by his hand or writ."[16] Breach of the king's peace gave the royal house an extensive claim to jurisdiction:

> [N]owadays we do not easily conceive how the peace which lawful men ought to keep can be any other than the queen's or the commonwealth's. But the king's justice . . . was at first not ordinary but exceptional, and his power was called to aid only when other means had failed. . . . Gradually the privileges of the king's house were extended to the precinct of his court, to the army, to the regular meetings of the shire and hundred, and to the great roads. Also the king might grant special personal protection to his officers and followers; and these two kinds of privilege spread until they coalesced and covered the whole ground.[17]

Thus, the king became the paramount victim, sustaining legally acknowledged, although symbolic, damages.

Over time, the actual victim was ousted from any meaningful place in the justice process, illustrated by the redirection of reparation from the victim to the king in the form of fines.[18] A new model of

---

15   Harold J. Berman, *Law and Revolution* 255–56 (1983).

16   *Leges Henrici Primi* 109 (L.J. Downer ed. & trans., 1972).

17   Frederick Pollock, *English Law before the Norman Conquest,* 14 Law Q. Rev. 291, 301 (1898).

18   In the hands of the royal administrators after the Conquest [the king's peace] proved a dynamic concept, and, as Maitland once expressed it, eventually the King's peace swallowed up the peace of everyone else. . . . Already by the time of Bracton, in the thirteenth century, it had become common form to charge an accused in the following terms: "Whereas the said B was in the peace of

crime was emerging, with the government and the offender as the sole parties.

RESTORATION INTO SAFE COMMUNITIES OF VICTIMS AND OFFENDERS WHO HAVE RESOLVED THEIR CONFLICTS

Criminal justice policy today is preoccupied with maintaining security—public order—while trying to balance the offender's rights and the government's power.   These are, of course, vital concerns, but a restorative perspective on justice suggests that fairness and order should be only part of society's response to crime.

And, in fact, other emphases have emerged.   These include restitution,[19] victim's rights,[20] rehabilitation,[21] victim–offender reconciliation,[22] community crime prevention,[23] and volunteer-based services for offenders and victims.[24] Some of these movements incorporate proposals

---

God and of our lord the King, there came the said N, feloniously as a felon," etc.

George W. Keeton, *The Norman Conquest and the Common Law* 175 (1966).

[19]   *See* Charles F. Abel & Frank A. Marsh, *Punishment and Restitution* (1984); *Criminal Justice, Restitution, and Reconciliation, supra* note 6; Stephen Schafer, *Compensation and Restitution to Victims of Crime* (1970).

[20]   *See From Crime Policy to Victim Policy* (Ezzat A. Fattah ed., 1983); President's Task Force on Victims of Crime, *Final Report* (1982); Steven Rathgeb Smith & Susan Freinkel, *Adjusting the Balance: Federal Policy and Victim Services* (1988).

[21]   *See* Francis T. Cullen & Karen E. Gilbert, *Reaffirming Rehabilitation* (1982).

[22]   *See Criminal Justice, Restitution, and Reconciliation, supra* note 6; *Criminology as Peacemaking* (Harold E. Pepinsky & Richard Quinney eds., 1991); *Mediation and Criminal Justice, supra* note 14.

[23]   *See* Judith Feins et al., *Partnerships for Neighborhood Crime Prevention* (1983); Richard Neely, *Take Back Your Neighborhood* (1990); Wesley G. Skogan & Michael G. Maxfield, *Coping with Crime* (1981).

[24]   *See* Marie Buckley, *Breaking into Prison: A Citizen Guide to Volunteer Action* (1974); M.L. Gill & R.I. Mawby, *Volunteers in the Criminal Justice System: A*

for systemic change, but for others the criminal justice system is basically irrelevant other than to provide a framework in which (or around which) the programs can function. In any event, the current system's limitations of vision and of participants have begun to be addressed at least in piece-meal fashion.

Some writers have suggested a more comprehensive approach that combines many of these alternatives and that not only recognizes the wisdom of the ancient model but also seeks to apply that wisdom to the present realities of criminal justice. This effort has been championed by legal scholars and criminologists,[25] victim–offender reconciliation practitioners,[26] and adherents of various philosophical, political, and religious perspectives.[27] Several have called this approach "restorative justice"[28]—the overall purpose of which is the restoration into safe communities of victims and offenders who have resolved their conflicts.[29]

Comparative Study of Probation, Police, and Victim Support (1990); R.I. Mawby & M.L. Gill, *Crime Victims* (1987).

[25]   *E.g.,* Haley, *supra* note 14, at 195; Martin Wright, *Justice for Victims and Offenders* (1991).

[26]   *E.g., Mediation and Criminal Justice, supra* note 14; Mark Umbreit, *Crime and Reconciliation* (1985); Howard Zehr, *Changing Lenses: A New Focus for Crime and Justice* (1990).

[27]   *E.g.,* Wesley Cragg, *The Practice of Punishment* (1992); Daniel W. Van Ness, *Crime and Its Victims* (1986); M. Kay Harris, *Moving into the New Millennium: Toward a Feminist Vision of Justice,* 67(2) Prison J. 27 (1987); Virginia Mackey, Restorative Justice. (discussion paper available from the Presbyterian Criminal Justice Program, Lexington, Kentucky, United States, 1990).

[28]   The term "restorative justice" was probably coined by Albert Eglash, *Beyond Restitution,* in *Restitution in Criminal Justice* 91, 92 (Joe Hudson & Burt Galaway eds., 1977), where he suggested that there are three types of criminal justice: retributive justice based on punishment, distributive justice based on therapeutic treatment of offenders, and restorative justice based on restitution. Both the punishment and the treatment model, he noted, focus on the actions of offenders, deny victim participation in the justice process, and require merely passive participation by the offender. Restorative justice focuses instead on the harmful effects of offenders' actions and actively involves victims and offenders in the process of reparation and rehabilitation.

[29]   They have expressed this in different ways. Zehr, *supra* note 26, at 178–81, analogizes to a camera lens and suggests that there are two alternative lenses: retributive

The restorative model seeks to respond to crime at both the macro and the micro level—addressing the need for building safe communities as well as the need for resolving specific crimes.

How might a system of restorative justice achieve its goals? In what ways would such a system differ from current criminal justice practice? While this article is not intended to explore these questions exhaustively, several general comments can be made. First, restorative justice advocates view crime as more than simply lawbreaking, an offense against governmental authority; crime is understood also to cause multiple injuries to victims, the community, and even the offender.[30] Second, proponents argue that the overarching purpose of the criminal justice *process* should be to repair those injuries.[31] Third, restorative justice advocates protest the civil government's apparent monopoly over society's response to crime. Victims, offenders, and their communities also must be involved at the earliest point and to the fullest extent possible. This suggests a collaborative effort, with civil government responsible for maintaining a basic framework of order, and the other parties responsible for restoring community peace and harmony. The work of civil government must be done in such a way that community

---

justice and restorative justice. With regard to restorative justice, he explains that "[c]rime is a violation of people and relationships. It creates obligations to make things right. Justice involves the victim, the offender, and the community in a search for solutions which promote repair, reconciliation, and reassurance." *Id.* at 181.

   Cragg, *supra* note 27, at 203, describes restorative justice as a process of "resolving conflicts in a manner that reduces recourse to the justified use of force."

   Wright, *supra* note 25, agrees. The new model is one

> in which the response to crime would be, not to add to the harm caused, by imposing further harm on the offender, but to do as much as possible to restore the situation. The community offers aid to the victim; the offender is held accountable and required to make reparation. Attention would be given not only to the *outcome,* but also to evolving a *process* that respected the feelings and humanity of both the victim and the offender.

Id. at 112.

[30]   *See, e.g.,* Zehr, *supra* note 26, at 181–86.

[31]   *See, e.g.,* Wright, *supra* note 25, at 114–17 (proposing a system with the primary aim of restoring—or even improving—the victim's prior condition).

building is enhanced, or at least not hampered.[32]

The focus of restorative justice, then, is intentionally holistic. In a restorative paradigm, criminal justice is not merely a contest between the defendant and the state. Criminal justice must take into account, too, the rights and responsibilities of the victim and the community, as well as the injuries sustained by victim, offender, and community.

CHALLENGES

Ultimately, whole new institutional structures are likely to emerge from the restorative approach, just as the rehabilitation model gave birth to penitentiaries, probation and parole systems, and juvenile courts,[33] and as the just deserts model of fairness in sentencing gave rise to determinate sentences and sentencing guidelines.[34] One such initiative is victim–offender reconciliation, which permits these two parties to meet with a trained mediator to discuss the crime and its aftermath and to develop a strategy to "make things right."[35]

There is great value in model programs such as victim–offender reconciliation: they explore new horizons in criminal justice theory, and they provide data with which to evaluate and modify not only the programs but the theory behind them as well.[36] But more than models is needed—there is a continuing need for analytical precision in understanding the new vision, articulating purposes and outcomes, developing

---

[32]   *See* section *infra* entitled "The Challenge to Structure Community–Government Cooperation."

[33]   *See* Edgardo Rotman, *Beyond Punishment* 21–57 (1990).

[34]   *See* Dean J. Spader, *Megatrends in Criminal Justice Theory,* 13 Am. J. Crim. L. 157, 180–95 (1986).

[35]   For an excellent description of victim–offender reconciliation programs, see Zehr, *supra* note 26, at 158–74.

[36]   This phenomenon has been aptly described as "theory overtaking practice" in Wright, *supra* note 25, at 41–45.

strategies for accomplishing those purposes, and evaluating results.[37]

Legal scholars and jurists can offer an invaluable service here, since a number of legal and jurisprudential challenges to criminal law and procedure are raised by the suggestion that a fundamental purpose of criminal justice should be to promote restoration of those touched by crime. This article examines four such challenges: (1) the challenge to abolish criminal law, (2) the challenge to rank multiple goals, (3) the challenge to determine harm rationally, and (4) the challenge to structure community–government cooperation.

The Challenge to Abolish Criminal Law

Currently, both the criminal law and the civil law of torts deal with intentional behavior by one person that violates the rights of another. In criminal cases, the offender is prosecuted by an agent of the government and punished; to convict, the prosecutor must prove the offender guilty beyond a reasonable doubt. In tort cases, the defendant–offender is sued by the plaintiff–victim and is required to pay damages or otherwise make right the harm done; the plaintiff must prove the defendant liable by a preponderance of the evidence.[38] But since the underlying harmful action is basically the same in criminal and tort cases, why are the two treated differently? The answer most often given is that while civil cases are concerned with the violation of individual rights, criminal cases are concerned with broader societal rights; criminal cases should not be initiated by victims, since vindication of public policy should not depend on an individual victim's decision to institute legal proceedings.[39]

---

[37]   It must be remembered that criminal justice history is filled with visionary people whose visions failed to be realized because they neglected to engage in the requisite analytical work. This phenomenon is neatly summarized in the title of Blake McKelvey's *American Prisons: A History of Good Intentions* (1977).

[38]   For an excellent discussion of the distinctions between what he calls the criminal justice and the civil justice "paradigm," see Mann, *supra* note 2, at 1803–13.

[39]   *But see id.* at 1812 n.61, where Mann argues that while this is the conventional argument for the paradigmatic distinction between criminal and civil justice, the practical

But as we have seen, excluding victims' interests from criminal cases is a relatively recent development. How does the emphasis in restorative justice on repairing the damage caused by crime affect our understanding of criminal law? Should a separate criminal law be maintained?

Randy Barnett and John Hagel, early proponents of restitution as a new paradigm of criminal justice, have argued for what would effectively be the end of criminal law, replacing it with the civil law of torts:

> A specific action is defined as criminal within the context of this theory only if it violates the right of one or more identifiable individuals to person and property. These individuals are the victims of the criminal act, and only the victims, by virtue of the past infringement of their rights, acquire the right to demand restitution from the criminal.
>
> This is not to deny that criminal acts frequently have harmful effects upon other individuals besides the actual victims. All that is denied is that a harmful "effect," absent a specific infringement of rights, may vest rights in a third party.[40]

Barnett and Hagel define crime by examining not the offender's behavior but the victim's rights, particularly "the fundamental right of all individuals to be free in their person and property from the initiated use of force by others."[41] They agree that there may be broader social goals but argue that settling the private dispute will "vindicate the rights of the aggrieved party and thereby vindicate the rights of all persons."[42] Barnett and Hagel conclude that, among other things, this means there can be

---

distinction is blurred by RICO statutes, which authorize private prosecution, and by SEC actions, in which the government is authorized to seek compensation for private individuals.

[40]   Randy E. Barnett & John Hagel, *Assessing the Criminal,* in *Assessing the Criminal: Restitution, Retribution, and the Legal Process* 1, 15 (Randy E. Barnett & John Hagel eds., 1977).

[41]   *Id.* at 11.

[42]   *Id.* at 25.

no "victimless crimes."

But vindicating the rights of direct victims does not vindicate the rights of all other persons. Though the injuries are not easy to quantify, *secondary victims* are also injured by crime:

> [C]rime imposes three distinct kinds of costs on its indirect victims. There are, first, the *avoidance costs* that are incurred by anyone who takes steps to minimize his chances of becoming the direct victim of crime. Installing locks and burglar alarms, avoiding unsafe areas, and paying for police protection, whether private or public, all fall into this category. Indirect victims may also have to pay *insurance costs*—costs that increase as the rate of crime in an area increases. And, finally, "as crime gives rise to fear, apprehension, insecurity, and social divisiveness," indirect victims are forced to bear the *attitudinal costs* of crime.[43]

Interestingly, these costs directly affect the right to be free in person and property that Barnett and Hagel espouse. This suggests that the first rationale for maintaining criminal law is that civil law fails adequately to vindicate the rights of secondary victims.

Second, criminal law offers more than vindication of individual rights. It also provides a controlled mechanism for dealing with those accused of crossing the boundaries of socially tolerable behavior. In a thoughtful and disturbing essay entitled "Retributive Hatred," Jeffrie Murphy notes that crime arouses "feelings of anger, resentment, and even hatred . . . toward wrongdoers."[44] He argues that criminal justice should restrain these feelings. "Rational and moral beings . . . want a world, not utterly free of retributive hatred, but one where this passion is both respected and seen as potentially dangerous, as in great need of reflective

---

[43]   Richard Dagger, *Restitution, Punishment, and Debts to Society*, in *Victims, Offenders, and Alternative Sanctions* 3, 4 (Joe Hudson & Burt Galaway eds., 1980) (citations omitted).

[44]   Jeffrie G. Murphy, Retributive Hatred: An Essay on Criminal Liability and the Emotions 2 (paper presented at a conference on "Liability in Law and Morals," Bowling Green State University, Bowling Green, Ohio, United States, Apr. 15–17, 1988).

and institutional restraint."[45] While one may argue with his description of the desires of "rational and moral beings," few would dispute that the retributive impulse must be restrained.

Third, there are procedural advantages to governmentally prosecuted criminal cases. The experience of European countries that permit varying degrees of victim participation in the prosecution of criminal cases bears this out.[46] The victim typically lacks the expertise, financial resources, and time to prosecute. Furthermore, the goals of consistency, fairness, and efficiency can best be pursued by coordinated governmental action, since public prosecutors can weigh decisions in light of stated policies and rely on the help of investigatory agencies. Moreover, prosecutors are presumably less influenced than are victims by personal motivations such as revenge.[47]

In summary, maintaining the criminal law is desirable inasmuch as it provides an effective method of vindicating the rights of secondary victims, it restrains and channels in acceptable ways retributive emotions in society, and it offers procedural efficiencies in enforcing public values.

The Challenge to Rank Multiple Goals

Given that the overall purpose of restorative justice is to resist crime by building safe and strong communities, this goal can be achieved only when multiple parties (victims, offenders, communities, and governments) pursue multiple goals (recompense, vindication, reconciliation, reintegration, atonement, and so forth). Is it possible for so many parties

---

[45]   *Id.* at 31.

[46]   *See, e.g.,* Matti Joutsen, *Listening to the Victim: The Victim's Role in European Criminal Justice Systems,* 34 Wayne L. Rev. 95 (1987).

[47]   *But see* Abraham S. Goldstein, *Defining the Role of the Victim in Criminal Prosecution,* 52 Miss. L.J. 515, 555 (1982). Governmental prosecution of offenses also has its limitations: the prosecutor administers an agency of government with its own administrative, political, investigative, and adjudicative objectives, any of which can lead prosecutors to focus less on a just resolution of the particular case and more on the effective use of limited resources. In addition, political forces may lead prosecutors to cater to, rather than restrain, retributive impulses in the community.

to pursue so many goals in such a way as to achieve restoration?

The current criminal justice system faces the challenge of balancing multiple goals,[48] usually expressed as deterrence, incapacitation, rehabilitation, and retribution (desert). The first two can be classified as utilitarian, with the focus on crime control. The third can either be similarly classified or be justified as a social value in and of itself. The last limits the nature and extent of the sentence, emphasizing proportionality. Paul Robinson has suggested that the attempt to pursue these four goals raises questions at two levels. First, does any one of them (such as crime control or proportionality) take precedence as an overarching goal of criminal justice? Second, which of the goals have priority when they cannot all be accommodated (when, for example, rehabilitation is prevented by a sentence sufficiently harsh to deter others)?[49]

At first glance, this confusion appears to grow geometrically under the restorative justice model, which adds such goals as recompense and vindication. But, in fact, the more holistic perspective of restorative justice may actually help society successfully manage multiple goals because it identifies restoration as the overarching goal of criminal justice.

How can the goals of deterrence, incapacitation, rehabilitation, and retribution be organized so that they help achieve the overarching purpose of restoration? Robinson, a former member of the U.S. Sentencing Commission, has explored approaches that permit multiple goals to interact with each other in a principled and consistent way. He proposes that a first step is to clarify which goals *determine* the sentence and which simply *limit* the nature or duration of the sentence.[50] A "determining goal" requires that certain features be included in the sentence; it recommends a sentence. A "limiting goal," in contrast, requires that certain features be excluded.[51] So, for example, rehabilitation as a determining goal might produce a recommendation of an indefinite period of treatment, whereas desert as a limiting goal would

---

[48]   Paul H. Robinson, *Hybrid Principles for the Distribution of Criminal Sanctions,* 82 Nw. U. L. Rev. 19 (1987).

[49]   *Id.* at 25–28.

[50]   *Id.* at 29–31.

[51]   *Id.*

establish maximum and minimum periods of time.

   Although this approach was designed to rank sentencing purposes under the current paradigm, it could be adapted by restorative justice advocates. For example, with regard to specific crimes, the determining goal of the criminal justice process would be resolution of the conflict; community safety would be a limiting goal only. This means that restitution would be presumed and that sentences providing for incarceration, which effectively precludes or substantially delays restitution (since most offenders are impoverished and few prison industry programs exist), should be used solely as a last resort. Any social controls imposed on the offender should not unduly obstruct the determining goal of resolution.

   Likewise, with reference to crime as a community phenomenon, the determining goal of the community and the government would be safety, with specific strategies limited by the need appropriately to resolve individual crimes when they occur. Similar analysis is needed in considering the other subsidiary goals: recompense and redress through the formal criminal justice system; rehabilitation and reconciliation through community-based programs. The challenge is to prioritize restorative outcomes over procedural goals. The test of any response to crime must be whether it is helping to restore the injured parties.

The Challenge to Determine Harm Rationally

The current paradigm of criminal justice gives scant attention to the harm resulting from the offense and focuses instead on the offender's actions and state of mind. The extent of harm to victims and their neighbors is, with some exceptions, ignored. When this form of injury is considered in offenses such as theft, it is only to establish the seriousness of the crime (misdemeanor versus felony), and the inquiry is typically limited to whether the property was worth more or less than a specific statutory amount.[52] Under recent sentencing and parole guidelines, the extent of harm also has been considered to determine the

---

[52]   *See, e.g.*, Ill. Ann. Stat. ch. 720, § 5/16-1(b) (1993) (providing that theft of property under $300 is a misdemeanor, and over that amount a felony).

length or severity of the sentence,[53] but again the categories are broad and general, and typically they are used to determine the amount of punishment as opposed to the amount of reparation.

In a restorative justice model, however, victim reparation is a determining goal. Consequently, calculating the amount of loss sustained by victims assumes great importance; to do such calculations, there must first be clarity about the kinds and extent of harms to be considered. This means that three categories of issue will need to be addressed: the kinds of victim to be reimbursed, how harms should be quantified, and how questions of disparity should be addressed.

WHAT KINDS OF VICTIMS SHOULD BE REIMBURSED?

Most people would intuitively define the victim as the person directly harmed by the offense—the person whose house was burglarized, for example. That person is certainly the primary victim. But others are also affected adversely by crime. Family members and neighbors may suffer increased fear, as well as direct and indirect financial costs. The criminal justice system (and the community as well) may be called on to expend resources. An employer may lose money because of the absence of a victim who is at court or in the hospital. And so on.

Which victims should be considered for reparation? The answer to this question may vary depending on the offense. For example, immediate family members of a homicide victim might be made eligible to recover the costs of psychiatric counseling, while members of a theft victim's family might not. But at a minimum, two groups of victims should always be eligible for restitution: the direct victim and the community, with the direct victim having priority over all secondary victims, including the community.

Alan Harland and Cathryn Rosen have made an excellent case for differentiating direct victims from their communities and, therefore, for treating restitution differently from community service:

> [U]nlike victim restitution that is based upon (and limited by) a case-by-case determination of victim injuries, the "harms" on

---

[53] *E.g.*, Albert W. Alschuler, *The Failure of Sentencing Guidelines*, 58 U. Chi. L. Rev. 901, 908–15 (1991).

which the offender's community service liability is predicated are far less specific, and the metric against which the amount of service owed is assessed tends to be no less arbitrary than the amount of a fine, probation, incarceration, or any other penal rather than compensatory sanction . . . . [I]t is perhaps not unreasonable to question whether community service has any claim at all to be part of the presumptive norm of restitution, and to ask why it is useful to continue to treat the two sanctions as merely different examples of a uniform concept.[54]

Harland and Rosen are right on all counts. But while this does not necessarily preclude the use of community service as a form of reparative sanction, it does require that we clarify the nature and extent of the harm done to the community, as well as the most appropriate means for the offender to repair that harm.

HOW DO WE QUANTIFY THE HARM THAT SHOULD BE REPAIRED?

While society incurs indirect costs as a result of crime, it is impossible to quantify with absolute accuracy the indirect costs related to a particular crime. But it is reasonable and necessary to make an effort at approximating these costs. Here the concept of "rough equivalences" developed by Norval Morris and Michael Tonry might be helpful.[55] They argue that pure equivalence between similar offenders is neither possible nor desirable. Instead, Morris and Tonry propose that the ideal should be to achieve "a rough equivalence of punishment that will allow room for the principled distribution of punishments on utilitarian grounds, unfettered by the miserable aim of making suffering equally painful."[56]

A similar approach could be taken in relating reparative sentences to levels of harm. While Harland and Rosen are right that such a system

---

[54]   Alan T. Harland & Cathryn J. Rosen, *Impediments to the Recovery of Restitution by Crime Victims,* 5(2) Violence & Victims 127, 132 (1990).

[55]   Norval Morris & Michael H. Tonry, *Between Prison and Probation: Intermediate Punishments in a Rational Sentencing System* (1990).

[56]   *Id.* at 31.

is more arbitrary than case-by-case restitution, it is certainly less arbitrary than current, entirely punitive sanctions. Criteria must be established and applied uniformly throughout the entire sentencing structure within a jurisdiction. Great Britain did this several years ago by devising guidelines for restitution. Ironically, they look a great deal like the Anglo-Saxon King Ethelbert's restitution schedules promulgated fourteen hundred years ago:

> Under guidelines sent to the country's 27,710 magistrates, attackers can be forced . . . to compensate their victims by the punch. Sample penalties: $84 for a simple graze, $168 for a black eye, $1,428 for a broken nose, $2,940 for a fractured jaw, and as much as $13,440 for a serious facial scar. Said Home Office Minister John Patten: "I am anxious that the victims get a better deal."[57]

Two things should be noted about the modern British approach: it restricts compensable harms to direct victims and it uses rough equivalences for the amount of restitution to be ordered.

   While it is neither feasible nor, perhaps, desirable to attach monetary values to every conceivable type of harm, a serious effort to grapple with the issue is necessary. Otherwise, types and amounts of reparation may be simply arbitrary and no different in nature from the abstract "fine," except for who receives the money. If victims are to be paid back, and if offenders are to see their reparation as linked to the specific harm done, then restitution, like community service, should be as closely related to the particular injury as possible.

How Do We Avoid Unwarranted Disparity?

This leads us directly into the question of disparity—whether particular offenders or victims will receive orders for restitution that are not comparable to those given to other offenders or victims. Disparity can happen in several ways.

---

[57]   *World Notes: Socking It to the Bad Guys,* Time, Oct. 3, 1988, at 43; *see* Home Office Circ. No. 85/1988; Magistrates' Ass'n of England and Wales, *Sentencing Guidelines* at iv (1992).

First, if each offender is sentenced according to the type of offense alone, the restitution order may fail to reflect the actual harm caused, because similar offenders committing similar crimes can bring about dramatically different injuries. Consider two burglaries in which a vase is stolen—if one is from a five-and-ten-cent store while the other is an authentic Ming, treating the offenders alike because their actions were similar would have a disparate effect on the two victims.

Second, if each offender is sentenced according only to the actual harm caused, then similar illegal conduct may result in dramatically different sentences. In the preceding example, the offender who stole the Ming vase could take years to repay the victim, while replacing the dime-store vase would be a matter of days or hours. Both victims and offenders would therefore receive significantly different treatment.

Finally, differing circumstances on the part of victims and offenders may lead to a disparate effect even when the offense and the financial loss are the same. Wealthy offenders may be able to complete their sentences simply by writing a check, while impoverished offenders may have to work long and hard to satisfy the judgment. Similarly, wealthy victims may have far less trouble recovering from crime than those who are without adequate financial resources.

Of course, not all disparity is wrong, nor is it possible to avoid it entirely. However, justice requires that victims and offenders be treated consistently, and that as much as possible outcomes not fall more heavily on some than on others for social, economic, or political reasons.

The earlier discussion on balancing multiple goals may offer guidance here. Should the emphasis be on *consistency* in dealing with offenders' actions or on victims' *harms?* This question calls for a prioritization of goals. Since restoration is the determining goal, the issue of fairness becomes a limiting goal.[58] Therefore, in a restorative justice system, guidelines outlining minimum and maximum amounts of restitution might be established for particular offenses. These would be related to typical losses of primary and secondary victims. If an agreement were not reached through negotiation, victims would present evidence of their actual losses to the sentencing judge, who would then

---

[58]   In the United States, it is likely that constitutional provisions requiring equal protection and prohibiting cruel and unusual punishment would yield this result.

set an amount within the pertinent range.[59] If the actual loss were less than the minimum established, the victim would receive only the actual loss, and the balance would be set aside into a victim compensation fund for those victims whose loss exceeded the range.

A similar approach might help address the issue of economic imbalance between otherwise comparable offenders. The Swedish "day fine" approach, which bases the sanction on the offender's daily wages, multiplied by a figure that represents the seriousness of the offense, could be adopted here as well.[60] Once again, the determining goal would be reparation to the victim, and fairness would be a limiting goal. Under this approach, one offender might actually be ordered to pay less than the indicated amount of restitution, with the balance made up from a compensation fund; another offender might be required to pay more, with the excess going into that fund.

The Challenge to Structure Community–Government Cooperation

Under restorative justice, it is argued, civil government and the community cooperate both in enabling the victim and the offender to resolve the crime successfully and in building safe communities. Is this kind of cooperation feasible? Two concerns have been raised in this connection.

First, can community-based programs be linked with agencies of the criminal system without losing their restorative values? This concern has been sparked by the experience of some reconciliation and mediation programs in the United States and England, which started with visionary objectives and then found those goals being redirected by a much larger criminal justice system with its own—and different—vision. For example, a reconciliation program may begin to be measured by the *number* of offenders it diverts from prison, rather than by the peacemak-

---

[59]   "[G]iving offenders opportunities to demonstrate a willingness to accept responsibility for their offences is not incompatible with treating like cases alike and assuring that sentences arrived at reflect in appropriate ways the gravity of the offences committed." Cragg, *supra* note 27, at 216.

[60]   Martin Wright, *Making Good: Prisons, Punishment, and Beyond* 87–88 (1982).

272   Criminal Law Forum   Vol. 4 No. 2

ing results of the mediation.[61]

Howard Zehr, a pioneer in reconciliation program development, has suggested three reasons that dependence on the criminal justice system can distort the vision of such programs: the criminal justice system's interests are retributive not restorative; its orientation is with the offender not the victim; and its inclination when challenged is self-preservation.[62] To these could be added the observation that the procedures of traditional criminal justice systems are coercive, which tends to mitigate against reconciliation or mediation.[63]

A second concern is that community–government collaboration will result in expanded state control. This is the well-known problem of net widening, and it happens in subtle ways.[64] Suppose, for example, that to develop credibility a community-based diversion program agrees to accept referrals of minor offenses from the local court. The court may respond by referring cases that are so minor they would have been dismissed otherwise. If offenders who fail to comply with the reconciliation agreement are then brought back before the judge and sentenced to jail or prison, the unintended effect of this arrangement, which was designed to be an *alternative* to incarceration, may actually be that more offenders are locked up.[65]

---

[61]   Zehr, *supra* note 26, at 232–36.

[62]   Dependence on the criminal justice system is one of three forces that Zehr argues can lead to distortion of vision; the other two are nongovernmental. They include the "dynamics of institutionalization" — such as the need for easily quantified and achieved administrative goals and measurements to justify the organization's existence; the tendency for programs to take on the values of their funding sources; differences between the goals of leaders and staff; and the difficulty of building "prophetic" functions into the organization's structure. The second of these is the design and operation of the program. If goal conflicts are not identified and resolved early on, they carry the potential of diverting the organization from a visionary mission. A succession of seemingly small policy decisions may change the long-range direction of the organization. *Id.* at 233–35.

[63]   Cragg, *supra* note 27, at 199.

[64]   *See, e.g.,* Thomas G. Blomberg, *Widening the Net: An Anomaly in the Evaluation of Diversion Programs,* in *Handbook of Criminal Justice Evaluation* 572 (Malcolm W. Klein & Katherine S. Teilmann eds., 1980).

[65]   *See, e.g.,* Christa Pelikan, *Conflict Resolution between Victims and Offenders in Austria and in the Federal Republic of Germany,* in *Crime in Europe* 151, 164–65 (Frances

But government does not exist apart from society; it is part of society, with specific powers and interests. This observation suggests that community–government cooperation must be fluid and dynamic in keeping with the nature of society itself. And it permits us to draw certain conclusions about what can make the cooperation effective. First, such an undertaking requires that both parties share the same overarching goal, and not just *any* goal. It is likely even now that government and community share the common goal of security. If the mutual goal is to be restoration of the victim, as well as of community safety, then a significant political and public education campaign lies ahead. This is true in the community, as well as in the governmental sphere.

Second, influence flows both ways. Thus, community programs themselves have affected the structure and the goals of the criminal justice system. Peter Kratcoski has outlined a pattern of evolving volunteer activity in criminal justice. At the outset, private groups set up new programs. These programs then have to turn to government assistance when services outstrip existing private resources. At some point, however, the government begins to underwrite the program fully, using volunteers to fill in gaps.[66] An example is the probation system, which grew out of a volunteer program initiated by John Augustus in 1842. Eventually the program was absorbed into the criminal justice system, but with a continuing mission to help offenders.[67]

Third, although government and community must seek the same overarching goal, they also play different roles not only in responding to individual offenders and victims but also in establishing community safety. Both of these objectives must be pursued with equal vigor.

Heidensohn & Martin Farrell eds., 1991). Pelikan describes a pilot program in which prosecutors were granted discretionary authority to divert juvenile offenders into a mediation program, as well as the steps taken to avoid net widening.

[66]   Peter C. Kratcoski, *Volunteers in Corrections*, 46(2) Fed. Probation 30 (1982).

[67]   A report several years ago from the Missouri Probation and Parole Department stated that it viewed its mission as helping the community determine its goals for offenders under supervision and then helping the community achieve them. On this program, see Steve German, *Knowledge Is Not Enough: Addressing Client Needs in Probation and Parole*, in *Community Corrections* 15, 17 (Amer. Correctional Ass'n 1981).

While the obstacles to accomplishing this collaboration are daunting, we can be encouraged by reports from Japan. According to John Haley, criminal justice in that nation operates on two tracks. One is similar to the formal criminal justice system found in Western nations:

> Paralleling the formal process, however, is a second track to which there is no Western analogue. A pattern of confession, repentance and absolution dominates each stage of law enforcement in Japan. The players in the process include not only the authorities in new roles but also the offender and the victim. From the initial police interrogation to the final judicial hearing on sentencing, the vast majority of those accused of criminal offenses confess, display repentance, negotiate for their victims' pardon and submit to the mercy of the authorities. In return they are treated with extraordinary leniency; they gain at least the prospect of absolution by being dropped from the formal process altogether.[68]

To illustrate this leniency, Haley notes that prosecutors proceed in only about 5 percent of all prosecutable cases. The vast majority of such cases are handled in uncontested summary proceedings in which the maximum penalty is a fine of $1,000–1,350. By the time cases have reached this point, the offender has demonstrated remorse, paid restitution, and secured the victim's pardon. Haley concludes:

> In this respect the West, not Japan, should be considered remarkable. The moral imperative of forgiveness as a response to repentance is surely as much a part of the Judeo-Christian heritage as the East Asian tradition. . . . Whatever the reason, unlike Japan Western societies failed to develop institutional props for implementing such moral commands. Instead the legal institutions and processes of Western law both reflect and reinforce societal demands for retribution and revenge.[69]

---

[68]   Haley, *supra* note 14, at 195 (citation omitted).

[69]   *Id.* at 204. Other observers have written about the distinctive role of apology and settlement in how the Japanese respond to crime. *See, e.g.,* Foote, *supra* note 13;

For a pattern like Japan's to develop in Western justice systems, victims and offenders (as well as the formal criminal justice system) will need to work together. But what if they fail to interact in the cooperative and voluntary way Haley describes? Clearly they cannot be forced to participate in community-based, informal mechanisms for repairing injuries; only the government is authorized to use this kind of force to secure participation in the criminal justice system.

Current criminal justice procedures are highly coercive for both victims and offenders. They are built on the reasonable assumption that not all defendants will willingly take part in the trial process or voluntarily complete their sentences. But they are also predicated on the assumption that not all *victims* will cooperate in the prosecution of their offenders; unwilling victims may have to be subpoenaed to testify at trial.

Restorative justice, with its emphasis on full and early participation of the parties in addressing the injuries caused by crime, places a premium on *voluntary* involvement. For offenders, this demonstrates willingness to assume responsibility for their actions. For victims, it reduces the likelihood that they will be victimized a second time by the formal or informal responses to crime. When such involvement is not forthcoming, however, what should happen? How this question is answered depends to a certain extent on whether the uncooperative party is the victim or the offender.

An uncooperative offender will need to have sufficient coercion applied to ensure participation in the criminal justice system. However, it should be the least amount of coercion necessary, and voluntary assumption of responsibility should be encouraged. Of course, there is no such thing as completely voluntary action in a coercive environment (as when an offender agrees to restitution during a victim–offender reconciliation meeting conducted before sentencing). But assumption of responsibility by the offender should be encouraged.

Victims may also choose to participate or not in the process. If they choose not to, they should be permitted to waive any rights they may have to pursue restitution as a part of the criminal case. The offender should then be required to make compensation payments to the

Hiroshi Wagatsuma & Arthur Rosett, *The Implication of Apology: Law and Culture in Japan and the United States*, 20 Law & Soc'y Rev. 461 (1986).

victim compensation fund. However, there may be situations in which
the actual and potential injuries to the community may necessitate the
victim's involvement in order to secure a conviction. Under such
circumstances, the government should have the authority (as it does
today) to subpoena the victim as a witness. Yet even this should be done
in a context that will be as protective and supportive as possible, in order
that the victim's participation, though coerced, will still contribute to a
measure of restoration.

CONCLUSION

Dissatisfaction with the current paradigm of criminal justice is leading
to new programs with different visions. Some, such as restitution, can
be incorporated into existing structures. Others, such as victim–offender
reconciliation, point to a possible new approach to criminal justice—restorative justice. In some ways, restorative justice is simply a new
application of an ancient vision. It is new wine from old vines. But
those of us who celebrate the harvest are advised to remember the
parable of new wine and old wineskins. Before we begin to pour—before
we insert restorative features into familiar responses to crime—we would
do well to reflect on what the consequences may be.
      This article has considered four likely consequences: the
challenge to abolish criminal law, the challenge to rank multiple goals,
the challenge to determine harm rationally, and the challenge to structure
community–government cooperation. Although each challenge is
significant, I have argued that all can be effectively addressed. Indeed,
they must be if criminal justice is to become—using Justice John Kelly's
image—a means of healing the wounds of crime.

[8]

Restorative Police Cautioning in Aylesbury—From Degrading to Reintegrative Shaming Ceremonies?

By Richard Young and Benjamin Goold*

Centre for Criminological Research, University of Oxford

Summary: *This article presents the findings of an exploratory study of a new form of police cautioning in which victims and others affected by an offence are invited to participate in a cautioning session. The sessions are influenced by John Braithwaite's theory of reintegrative shaming as well as by the philosophy of "restorative justice". It is argued that whilst elements of "old-style" cautioning persist in Aylesbury, the advent of restorative cautioning nonetheless represents an important and welcome shift in policing practices.*

Introduction

Virtually all cautions in the Aylesbury police area are administered by the Restorative Cautioning Unit, consisting of two Thames Valley Police constables (one of whom works part-time) and one civilian support worker.[1] The most distinctive feature of the Unit's cautioning process lies in its commitment to invite those affected by an offence, most notably the victim, to attend and take part in the cautioning session. The cautioning police officer seeks to facilitate discussion of the harm caused by the offence and of how any of the interests or relationships damaged might be restored by the offender.

The process is inspired by a cluster of ideas that have become known as "restorative justice", the central tenet of which is that crime should be conceptualised as primarily a matter concerning the individuals affected by an offence rather than as a breach of a more abstract "public interest". In cases where an offender is apprehended, the achievement of a reparative outcome is given priority over any more "objective" standard of justice.[2] The process is also based on the

---

* Thanks are due to our colleague Dr Carolyn Hoyle and to Ralph Perry, Sarah Shooter, Helen Edwards and Bob Gregory of Thames Valley Police, for their helpful comments on an earlier draft of this article.

[1] The practices analysed here are part of a broader Thames Valley Police initiative in restorative justice. From April 1998, all cautions administered by Thames Valley officers are meant to be restorative in character. Whilst the Aylesbury Unit's style of work is not necessarily representative of the Thames Valley Police's restorative cautioning programme, it may be regarded as a prototype of the significant shift in police practice intended by Thames Valley Police headquarters. In the year beginning April 1, 1996 the Unit administered 167 cautions and in the following year 435.

[2] Space constraints preclude consideration of the wide variety of theories and practical approaches associated with "restorative justice". See further, A. von Hirsch and A. Ashworth, *Principled Sentencing* (2nd ed., Oxford: Hart, 1998), Chap. 7.

criminological theory of John Braithwaite known as "reintegrative shaming".[3] This argues that crime is most effectively controlled by making offenders ashamed of their behaviour but in a way which promotes their reintegration into their community.[4] In essence, the Aylesbury cautioning process seeks to achieve restorative outcomes through a process of reintegrative shaming.

The Unit in Aylesbury has attracted much attention, including that of the Home Secretary, Jack Straw, who observed one of its cautions in September 1997. There is no doubt that the media interest has centred on the apparent impact of restorative cautioning on recidivism.[5] This article represents the first attempt, however, to subject the work of the Restorative Cautioning Unit to independent evaluation. It is not our intention here to present a critical discussion of the theories underlying restorative justice and reintegrative shaming. Rather, on the basis of a small-scale empirical study conducted in 1997, the aim is to examine the extent to which the Aylesbury cautioning process is consistent with these theories and to explore its impact on those who experience it. The research reported here helped pave the way for a three-year study of restorative cautioning as practised by Thames Valley Police,[6] and the discussion in this article is necessarily of an exploratory and preliminary nature.

Research methodology

We carried out the bulk of our study in the months of July and August 1997. The staff of the Restorative Cautioning Unit agreed to provide whatever information we required, including unfettered access to the Unit's filing system and database. We concentrated our efforts on exploring in detail a small number of cases from a variety of perspectives. We selected the cases to be studied ourselves to avoid any risk of being invited to attend only on days when the Unit expected the cautions to be successful, dramatic, difficult or otherwise "interesting". The key selection criterion was that the cautions observed should be broadly representative of the caseload of the Unit whilst allowing us to observe both police officers at work.[7]

We secured the permission of all participants to our observing and tape-recording the 15 cautioning sessions.[8] Immediately after each caution, we talked in confidence

---

[3] J. Braithwaite, *Crime, Shame and Reintegration* (Cambridge: Cambridge University Press, 1989).

[4] See *ibid*. pp.12–13: "the distinction is between shaming that leads to stigmatization—to outcasting, to confirmation of a deviant master status—versus shaming that is reintegrative, that shames whilst maintaining bonds of respect or love, that sharply terminates disapproval with forgiveness, instead of amplifying deviance by progressively casting the deviant out."

[5] For example, on October 18, 1997 it was reported in *The Guardian* that "Thames Valley police . . . yesterday claimed they had lowered the numbers of young people reoffending from 30 per cent to 4 per cent".

[6] The larger study, which began in April 1998, is directed by Carolyn Hoyle and Richard Young of the Oxford Centre for Criminological Research, and is funded by the Joseph Rowntree Foundation.

[7] Four of the cautions observed were for possessing cannabis, four for criminal damage, two for theft, two for assault, and one each for burglary, cycling on a pavement and possession of an offensive weapon. In the year to March 31, 1997, 69 of the 167 cautions administered were for theft, and nearly all of these were for shoplifting. The next largest categories of offence for which cautions were given were possession of cannabis (14 per cent of the total), and criminal damage and assault (at around 8 per cent each).

[8] One offender allowed us to observe but not tape-record his caution. He subsequently agreed to us conducting a tape-recorded interview with him.

with the key participants, interviewing 15 of the 17 offenders observed, all six victims[9] and 10 other participants (all were offenders' supporters—no victims' supporters attended the observed cautions).[10] Everyone we approached for permission to conduct a tape-recorded interview agreed to grant it. In all 15 cases we carried out a tape-recorded interview with the cautioning police officer.

After transcribing the tapes of the 44 completed interviews, data analysis was carried out by both authors independently of one another, as a way of checking whether there was agreement about the major themes and issues emerging from the data. Having satisfied ourselves that this was so, we then identified the cases which would best illustrate these major themes and issues. In the next section we examine the nature of what we shall refer to as "old-style" police cautioning, thus allowing us to highlight subsequently how "restorative cautioning" differs from previous practice.

The police caution as degradation ceremony

A caution is administered in person by a police officer, usually at a police station, and Home Office guidelines envisage it taking the form of an explanatory warning:

> "The significance of the caution must be explained: that is, that a record will be kept of the caution, that the fact of a previous caution may influence the decision whether or not to prosecute if the person should offend again, and that it may be cited if the person should subsequently be found guilty of an offence by a court."[11]

One of the theories underlying the evolution of police cautioning has been that this type of low-key response to a relatively minor offence avoids the risk of a courtroom appearance degrading offenders and ultimately confirming them in a deviant self-identity.[12] The widespread assumption that cautioning operates to protect offenders from degradation was challenged by Maggy Lee in the only extensive research on the process of cautioning as experienced by offenders.[13] She argued that a punitive ethos permeated the cautioning process, centred on a belief in individual and parental culpability for offending behaviour. Drawing on the work of Garfinkel,[14] Lee contended that cautioning sessions functioned as "degradation ceremonies",

---

[9] Victims attend less than half of all cautions administered by the Unit and a high proportion of those who attend are representing large town-centre shops.

[10] In two instances, two offenders' supporters were interviewed together, thus making a total of 29 interviews with participants rather than 31.

[11] *National Standards for Cautioning (Revised)*, Note 2D, issued as an attachment to Home Office Circular 18/1994, "The Cautioning of Offenders".

[12] For critical discussion of this "labelling" perspective, and the evidence bearing on its validity, see Braithwaite, *op. cit.*, pp.16–21, and K. Williams, *Textbook on Criminology* (3rd ed., Blackstone Press, 1997), pp.418–424.

[13] M. Lee, "Pre-Court Diversion and Youth Justice", in L. Noaks *et al.* (eds), *Contemporary Issues in Criminology* (Cardiff: University of Wales Press, 1995).

[14] H. Garfinkel, "Conditions of Successful Degradation Ceremonies" (1956) 64 *American Journal of Sociology* 420.

and that "the degrading tactics were directed towards the parents as much as the young people".[15]

She highlighted five key features of the cautioning process that contributed to this degradation. First, it was impressed upon offenders that they were being given a second chance by not being taken to court and that any subsequent offending would result in automatic prosecution. Thus, rather than the caution being presented as a proportionate, fair response to relatively trivial wrongdoing, an attempt was made to make those cautioned appreciate their good fortune in escaping "real punishment". Secondly, in asking questions about the offence and the background of the offender, the police looked for respect for private property and authority from parents and offenders alike, and made it obvious that they were dissatisfied with the level of respect displayed by those in front of them. Thirdly, the police would seek to stage the caution in such a way that would most effectively "dress-down" and maximise the discomfort of the offender, as by forcing eye-contact or by manipulating the spacing arrangements. As one officer told Lee: "If it is a first-time offender, I'll sit on a chair, make him or her stand in front of me, parents behind so the child won't be distracted."[16] Fourthly, the cautioning officer would seek a "heart-to-heart talk", focusing in particular on how a criminal record would disadvantage a young person in the employment market. Fifthly, the young person's status was condemned as criminal, as in the following example Lee quotes[17] from her research notes:

> "Inspector: So [this offence] makes you what?
> P: A thief. [Almost in tears]
> Inspector: A thief, ugh!"

To the extent that one can generalise from Lee's findings,[18] labelling theory would suggest that cautioning is an effective intervention (in the sense of minimising the risk of reoffending) *despite* the manner in which it is administered. John Braithwaite's important contribution to theoretical thinking in this area was not discussed by Lee, however.[19] Whilst accepting that stigmatising degradation ceremonies can increase the risk of reoffending, he rejects the view that moral condemnation of criminal behaviour is therefore best avoided. To ensure that such condemnation has positive consequences it is necessary that it is bounded rather than of open-ended duration and that efforts are made "to maintain bonds of love or respect throughout the finite period of suffering shame".[20]

Braithwaite's work has provided theoretical inspiration for a number of cautioning schemes seeking to promote dialogue between those affected by an offence, most notably the police-led "community conferencing" initiative in Wagga Wagga,

---

[15] Lee, *op. cit.* p.320.

[16] *ibid.* p.324.

[17] *ibid.* p.326.

[18] Lee's focus was on "delayed cautions" administered by a senior officer, usually an inspector. She does not discuss the "instant caution", typically administered quickly by custody sergeants shortly after arrest as an expedient way of disposing of minor cases: see C. Hoyle and R. Young, *A Survey of Restorative Cautioning within the Thames Valley* (Oxford: Centre for Criminological Research, 1998), p.13. Such cautions are probably more bewildering than degrading for offenders.

[19] Nor does she discuss Braithwaite's work in a fuller account of her study of cautioning: M. Lee, *Youth, Crime and Police Work* (Basingstoke: MacMillan Press, 1998).

[20] Braithwaite, *op. cit.* p.101.

Australia.[21] Based on their observation of a small number of "community confer-ences", Braithwaite and Mugford have argued that it is possible to identify a number of key conditions under which degradation ceremonies can be transformed into successful reintegrative ceremonies.[22] These conditions include ensuring that the offence, and not the offender, is made the focus of condemnation, as well as giving victims and other participants (such as the offender's supporters) control over the process of reintegration and the conduct of the ceremony. It was these insights that underpinned the Aylesbury Unit's aspiration to replace "old-style" cautioning with "restorative cautioning".

The Aylesbury cautioning process

All cases considered as suitable for a caution by the multi-agency panel in Aylesbury[23] are passed to the Restorative Cautioning Unit for it to make the arrangements for the cautioning session.[24] On arrival at the Unit's premises, participants are shown into a large room containing a circle of office chairs, and the cautioning police officer invites each party to speak in turn according to a script derived from the Wagga Wagga model.

Although the cautioning officer attempted to structure all cautions in a similar way, we noted that in practice the style of cautioning differed according to the age of the offender. Where offenders were adults, the cautioning sessions more frequently took the form of a dialogue and the cautioning officer's role was less prominent and less directive. For example, in three of the eight adult cautions (including two where victims were present) spirited discussion took place concern-ing the background to the offence and the fairness of the offender taking all the blame for what had happened. In these sessions the police officer's role drifted away from that envisaged by the standard script for facilitating a restorative caution towards that of an impartial mediator. Even where the offence was clear-cut (for example, the three adult cautions for possession of cannabis) the police officer and the offender tended to talk to one another in a conversational manner: reintegrative shaming techniques were not a prominent feature of these exchanges.

Where the cautioning sessions involved young offenders, by contrast, the role of the police officer was more dominant and the shaming of the offending behaviour more obvious, clear-cut and uncontested. Offenders said comparatively little in these sessions, and their contributions were prompted by directive questioning by the police officer. Even where victims and supporters of offenders were present, there was little in the way of dialogue not involving the police officer. The dominance of the police officer in these sessions was confirmed by a rudimentary

[21] See D. Moore with L. Forsythe, *A New Approach to Juvenile Justice: An Evaluation of Family Conferencing in Wagga Wagga, A Report to the Criminology Research Council* (Wagga Wagga: Centre for Rural Social Research, 1995).

[22] J. Braithwaite and S. Mugford, "Conditions of Successful Reintegration Ceremonies: Dealing with Juvenile Offenders" (1994) 34 *British Journal of Criminology* 139–171. See also S. Jackson, "Family Group Conferences in Youth Justice: The Issues for Implementation in England and Wales" (1998) 37 *Howard Journal* 34.

[23] Most of those referred are "first-time" offenders. The Unit's original policy of not carrying out "repeat" restorative cautions is no longer applied rigidly.

[24] At the time of the research, offenders, victims and their respective "supporters" were asked by letter to attend the session, whereas current practice is for one of the Unit's police officers to explain the cautioning process by telephone or in person.

form of content analysis in which we examined the spoken contributions of each participant. In six of the seven juvenile cautions the police officer's questioning and comments accounted for between 58 and 70 per cent of the words spoken.[25] By contrast, in six of the seven taped adult cautions the officer's contributions took up between 21 and 53 per cent of words.[26] Of course, the dominance of the police officer was affected by other factors such as the number of persons present at the cautioning session, and whether victims were present, but by far the most important factor appeared to be the age of the offender. Thus, for example, in two adult criminal damage cautioning sessions involving five and three participants, the police officer's "dominance factor" was 31 and 21 per cent respectively, compared with 58 per cent in a juvenile criminal damage case involving six participants.

In the rest of this article we focus primarily on the cautioning process as experienced by young offenders. This is for three reasons: first, the great majority of those cautioned nationally (and in Aylesbury) are juveniles; secondly, Lee's study of "old-style" cautioning was restricted to young offenders, thus providing us with a basis for comparison only in relation to those offenders; and thirdly, the core sequence observed in juvenile cautions was much more consistent than in the adult cautions, thus allowing us to describe the process in a reasonably succinct manner.

One striking difference between "old-style" cautions and restorative cautions for young offenders is the elaborate structure of the latter, usually running to 30–40 minutes in length, and sometimes much longer. Usually the officer began with some words of welcome, designed to put the offender at ease and to describe the purpose and informality of the meeting. Then the offender was asked to provide "their side of the story". In the majority of the juvenile conferences we observed, the offender readily provided this, if somewhat nervously at first. These "stories" were for the most part largely factual—none of the offenders we saw cautioned denied that they had committed the offence. The facilitators used questions to draw out the details of the story, to clarify certain points and to focus the session on the harm caused. A typical sequence of questions was as follows:

> "Facilitator: OK. So interviewed, on tape? Finger-printed, photographs, DNA test?
> Offender: Yeah.
> Facilitator: OK. What was all that like for you?
> Offender: I didn't really know what was going on, because I didn't really think I'd done that much wrong. But like I was being treated like a criminal. But, you know, it was a foolish thing to do, but I didn't feel like I was a criminal.
> Facilitator: How did the interview go?
> Offender: Well, I answered the questions and I felt sorry after, especially seeing my mum as well.
> Facilitator: Mum was upset was she?
> Offender: Mmm."

[25] In the other juvenile case the offenders had left home and were leading a near-adult lifestyle. The tone of the session was similar to that of an adult caution, thus helping to account for the officer's relatively low dominance (at 32 per cent).

[26] In the remaining taped adult case the offender appeared to be under the influence of cannabis, and the officer, unsurprisingly, did most of the talking (71 per cent).

"Facilitator: Who do you think you caused harm to, by what you did?
Offender: Um, the people who were scared by what I did.
Facilitator: Anybody else?
Offender: My friend who was there and . . . mum and dad.
Facilitator: I think there's one other person that you've left out, but I'll come
               on to that in a minute." (Case 9)

At this stage the police officer used similar questions to encourage any victims
present to explain how the offence had caused harm to them and, where
appropriate, their family or friends. On those occasions where the victim had chosen
not to attend, the officer attempted to present their point of view, often stressing the
extent of the victim's anger, dismay, and the harm caused by the offence. The
various supporters present (typically the parents of the offender) were then invited
to explain how the incident had affected them. On those occasions where they
expressed a sense of responsibility for an offender's behaviour the officer stressed
that they should not blame themselves. Where possible, the facilitator attempted to
draw out comments on the extent to which the offending behaviour had caused
them to feel hurt or disappointment. In all but one of the conferences we observed
where an offender's supporter was present, at least one of those supporters
indicated that they would find it difficult to trust the offender in the future. The
following extract from Case 13 demonstrates this point well:

"Supporter: If I thought I could do something that'd stop him, then I'd be
               happier, but I don't know that I could.
Facilitator: So how's this affected you?
Supporter: I've just been watching him all the time.
Facilitator: Why?
Supporter: Because I don't know what he's going to do. Because he's done
               one thing you worry that he's going to do something else."

Immediately after all participants had spoken in turn, the facilitator attempted to
impress upon the offender the nature and extent of the harm that he or she had
caused. If the offender had failed earlier in the conference to identify themselves as
one of those who had suffered as a consequence of their behaviour, then the
facilitator now expressed the view that the offender must have experienced stress as
a result of being caught up in the criminal process. Following on from this, the
facilitator would ask the offender whether there was anything they wanted to say to
anyone present. On those occasions where an apology or expression of regret was
not offered, no further effort was made by the facilitator to extract one from the
offender. Where the offender did apologise, however, the facilitator was quick to
acknowledge this: "I've got to say this, I've had people in here who couldn't even
apologise, who aren't as big a man as you are. And just couldn't do it. But, you
know, more power to you. Because you're able to do it." (Case 8)

In all of the cases we observed, the facilitator at this point shifted the focus of the
conference to the question of what could be done to repair the harm caused to both
the victim and the offender's relationship with their supporters. Supporters were
asked what they most wanted to get out of the session, and the usual answer was
some reassurance that no further offence would be committed. The offender was
encouraged by the police officer to identify ways of keeping out of trouble and
regaining the respect or trust of their supporters, such as more frequent attendance

at school. Where an identifiable victim was involved, an agreement to make some form of compensation or to offer a written apology was often negotiated at this stage. Finally, the facilitator addressed the offender directly for several minutes, and in the tone of a "heart-to-heart talk", developed a number of key themes, most notably:

(i) *You have begun the process of putting things right*: "Thanks, all of you. It's not been easy, but I certainly think you've gone some way to repairing the harm. I mean there's still a lot of work to do. Your mum's very upset, she said the trust has gone a bit, and she worries even more. You've got to work hard to put that right, and it won't be easy." (Case 9)

(ii) *You are in a web of caring relationships*: "You're lucky, because you've got all this help. People are desperate to help and guide you. Because they care about you. If they didn't care, they wouldn't be here. And you obviously care too because I can see that you're upset." (Case 11)

(iii) *You're not stupid, but you did something dumb*: "You can turn this around because I'm not looking at some dumb knuckle-dragging kid. I'm looking at a bright intelligent kid who's made a mistake, that's all." (Case 9)

The officer concluded the cautioning session by explaining the legal aspects of the caution, and the offender was asked to sign a form to acknowledge that this explanation had been given. It was emphasised that any further offence would result in automatic prosecution and a criminal conviction, and that this might make travelling abroad problematic and obtaining a job nigh impossible. Finally, the officer gave all the participants a short questionnaire form seeking views on the cautioning session.

Observations on the Aylesbury process

By comparison with "old-style" cautioning, typically delivered by officers using idiosyncratic and often highly questionable methods, the Aylesbury process represents a significant and welcome shift in policing practices. Consistent with the theory of reintegrative shaming, central to all of the cautions observed was a commitment on the part of the facilitator to ensure that it was the criminal behaviour which was the focus of shaming, and not the offenders themselves. Moreover, we saw no instance of a police officer seeking deference from offenders by telling them, for example, to "speak up", "sit up straight" or "look at me when you're talking". The officers appeared to us to be genuinely concerned with the future welfare of these young people and were committed and dedicated in their approach. All of those present at the cautioning session were treated with respect and invited to take part in the process.

It is also possible, however, to point to a number of similarities between the restorative approach practised in Aylesbury and the "old-style" cautions observed by Lee. Perhaps most significantly, the police officer remains the dominant figure in the process. This is despite the fact that, according to the theory of reintegrative shaming, it is essential for those with a direct stake in the resolution of the offence and its aftermath to be given "centre stage" if any meaningful or lasting impression is to be made upon the offender. On occasion, it was apparent that the facilitator was attempting to mould the comments and interactions of the participants to conform to an ideal envisaged by the "cautioning script" rather than allowing them to express themselves freely or communicate directly with one another. This sometimes provoked forms of resistance, as in the following example taken from Case 13:

> "Facilitator: So what's it been like since you knew you were going to get a caution?
> Offender: Nothing really, just acted like normal and tried to get it out of my mind.
> Facilitator: But it's always come back? [Asked rhetorically]
> Offender: Occasionally. Not much.
> Facilitator: But enough.
> Offender: Mmm. [Not really agreeing with this]
> Facilitator: Mmm, so it's been a constant worry, and stress on you and . . .
> Offender: [Interrupting] Not really stress.
> Facilitator: No?
> Offender: Not really, it didn't really bother me that much."

Another similarity with old-style cautioning was the emphasis placed on the consequences of any further offence. While the facilitator would often be at pains to distinguish between the offender and his or her behaviour, it was invariably underscored (and this was true of adult cautions too) that although on this occasion offenders had been "given a break", the next time they would be prosecuted, regardless of the seriousness of any future offence. This seemed to us to send a mixed message. Offenders were told on the one hand that they had made an out-of-character stupid mistake whilst on the other they were treated as if requiring stern individual deterrent messages. This deterrent aspect to the cautioning session could also be seen in the way in which the facilitator sought to "talk up" the harm caused by the offence, as in the exchange quoted above. Another example of such apparent exaggeration was seen in a case of criminal damage caused by two youths kicking a fence (Case 6). The police file recorded the victim's views (as expressed to the arresting officer) in the following manner: "The complainant wanted the youths in question to be spoken to and given a stern warning. He wasn't bothered about making a formal complaint re: the minor damage. (However, I'm sure he could be persuaded to . . .)". This victim chose not to attend the caution, and his views were summarised by the facilitating police officer as follows:

> "Well, he didn't want nothing to do with it, because the people who own the fence are absolutely *gutted* by your behaviour because, you know, as both your mums have pointed out, you aren't kids, you are not stupid little morons, you are young adults, who know better and shouldn't have done it and they *do not* want to see you, they are *that* angry. In fact I don't think, in all the time I've been doing this kind of work, I've come across people who are more angry. I've dealt with you know, incredible things, but they're *absolutely* livid, because it's where they live and they don't feel safe by what you've done."(original emphasis).

There was, in other words, an element of "case construction" in the practice of the Restorative Cautioning Unit. A number of studies have explored the social processes by which police and prosecutors assemble cases for or against prosecution, for example by emphasising or filtering out certain "facts".[27] What we observed in Aylesbury was the constructing of cautions with a view to making the greatest possible impression on young offenders. This strategy is, we think, ethically questionable, and, as we explore below, it may even be counter-productive in that it could undermine the legitimacy of the process in young offenders' minds.

Assessments of the cautioning process by offenders, victims and other participants

Taken as a whole, assessments of the restorative cautioning sessions as expressed to us in interview were clearly positive. For example, when participants (other than the facilitator) were asked to say which of a limited number of pre-coded answers best described their views about the caution the answers given were mainly favourable. This was true of both adult and juvenile cautions and we have accordingly aggregated the responses of all our interviewees.[28] Eighteen interviewees said they were "very positive" or "positive" in their attitude to the meeting, seven had "mixed" feelings, three were "negative" and one "very negative". Attitudes towards the police officer who handled the caution were overwhelmingly positive with 20 out of 29 interviewees declaring themselves "very satisfied" (all eight of the supporters, five of the six victims and seven of the 15 offenders), a further seven interviewees as "satisfied" (six offenders, one victim), whilst two offenders had "no attitude". It was clear from the answers to our more open-ended questions that the sources of any dissatisfaction varied from caution to caution and defied extensive generalisation. It did appear, however, that the most common source of discontent was a feeling amongst young offenders that they had not been given enough explanation about the process before coming to the caution.[29] Whereas they generally expected to be shouted at and told off, they found themselves instead being asked a long series of questions. Despite finding it difficult to formulate answers when "put on the spot" like this, they considered the process overall to be considerably less punitive than they had feared, as in the following example.

> "[Beforehand] I was scared, frightened and that . . . because I thought they would like shout and have a go at you and stuff like that. But they didn't. Then I thought, that's *amazing* isn't it?! I think to be honest that's what they normally do don't they, 'Get in there!' and all that . . . Mmm. It was a surprise, I thought, they done a good job and that, hadn't they? . . . [The officer] was very kind." (Interview 29)

The young offenders to whom we spoke typically perceived themselves as having committed relatively minor offences which had not caused much direct harm. The *overall* police response to their behaviour was therefore seen as disproportionate. The structure of the *cautioning session* itself, however, was perceived as basically fair:

[27] See, in particular, M. McConville, A. Sanders, and R. Leng, *The Case for the Prosecution* (Routledge, 1991).
[28] A rider should be added that adult offenders were more positive than were juveniles in their evaluations of restorative cautioning.
[29] Since we completed our research, the Unit has changed its practice so as to give more information to participants in advance of the cautioning session.

offenders valued the chance to put their side of the story, and were glad that their supporters were present. As one explained:

> "I don't like the way it was handled by the police. Like they were taking all these DNA tests and everything. I didn't think that was necessary. I didn't know what I was doing was illegal . . . But today it was definitely fair, yeah . . . [The police officer] was just really nice all the way through it." (Interview 12)

Offenders quite often conceded that the session had reinforced or deepened their understanding of the multiple harms caused by their behaviour. Whilst finding it difficult to articulate their feelings about whether the cautioning session would make any difference to their relationships with parents or guardians, some of their comments suggested that the process may well have had a reintegrative effect, as in this example:

> "It was good that I could find out how [my mum] was feeling, but that's what I expected her to say anyway . . . Hearing her say all that like, it was quite upsetting . . . [I see what I did as] more serious now . . . [because] I didn't know how upset she would be about it, and I didn't know about how in the future I wouldn't be able to go abroad and stuff if it was on my record." (Interview 39)

The cautions we observed may also have had some deterrent effect in that the offenders clearly understood that a record of the caution would be kept and that they now needed to keep out of trouble if they were to avoid prosecution in future. All offenders expressed relief that their contact with the criminal process was at an end, and that they had avoided a court appearance and the stigma of conviction. This was the overriding evaluation of the significance of the caution—that the courtroom had been avoided.

It was clear from our interviews with offenders' parents and guardians (and with the one victim we observed take part in a juvenile caution) that other participants are broadly sympathetic to the way in which the police are using the cautioning process to confront offenders with the harm their actions have caused. These interviewees generally wished, however, to reserve final judgment on the value of the process until enough time had elapsed for them to see whether it had made any difference to the behaviour of the offender.

Our interviews with the cautioning police officers revealed that they were confident about the value of their cautioning model, but not complacent about their use of it—indeed their evaluations of how effective and well-handled each session had been were generally less positive than those of the other participants. We deduced from these interviews, and from our perusal of 600 case files, that the cautioning officers assess whether a particular caution was successful by the extent to which the offender showed visible signs of remorse or shame. Where such signs were perceived to be lacking the notes in the files frequently expressed concern about the likelihood of reoffending. As one would expect, given the strong emphasis on the theory of reintegrative shaming in the Unit's work, the litmus test of success is regarded by the officers as being the impact of this type of caution on recidivism. Due to the exploratory nature of this study we did not attempt ourselves to measure any such impact but we did explore with the staff of the Unit the way in which it was monitoring the apparent effects of the cautioning process.

The impact of restorative cautioning on recidivism

The notion that the Restorative Cautioning Unit has "slashed"[30] reoffending by those cautioned from 30 to 4 per cent appears to have taken a hold in some influential circles. However, the press reports which quoted these figures left out many important caveats. The "baseline" 30 per cent figure was taken from a Home Office *nationwide* study of recorded reoffending within five years of a caution for a "standard list offence".[31] No accurate record exists of known reoffending following a caution (whether for a "standard list" offence or not) within the Aylesbury police area prior to the introduction of "restorative cautioning". The figures, therefore, are not based on a comparison of like with like. Moreover, the 4 per cent recidivism figure was based on the Aylesbury Unit's own monitoring of "repeat business". When its "clients" committed further offences which were dealt with outside the Aylesbury police area, or which were referred immediately for prosecution within the Aylesbury area (thus by-passing the multi-agency panel), they did not come to the attention of the Unit immediately and many may never do so. Finally, no standard follow-up period was used in calculating the "reoffending rate". Whether the caution took place a month or a year ago made no difference—if the Unit had yet to hear of a further offence committed by the individual concerned, the case counted as a "success". The upshot is that the reoffending rate as expressed in the national media is almost certain to have considerably overstated the "success' achieved through restorative cautioning. We simply do not know whether the Aylesbury Unit or any restorative or reintegrative initiative anywhere in the world is achieving any significant reduction in reoffending rates. To obtain reliable evidence on this requires a large-scale longitudinal study, preferably one in which criminal cases are randomly assigned to a "restorative" or "traditional" process and in which reoffending is rigorously monitored through a self-report study completed after a standard and sufficient follow-up period. One notable experiment along these lines is underway in Canberra, Australia, and data on reoffending will be available within the next year or so.

Conclusion

It is clear from the above analysis that the shift from degrading cautioning ceremonies to reintegrative shaming sessions is as yet incomplete. There is, however, a strong commitment within Aylesbury to refine and improve its restorative cautioning model in the light of emerging experience and data. With that in mind, we conclude with some reflections about the future development of this model.

There is no reason to think that the Aylesbury model of cautioning will not endure. Its underlying philosophy is certainly in line with that expressed by section 37 of the Crime and Disorder Act 1998 which stipulates that the principal aim of the youth justice system is to prevent offending. The planned replacement (sections 65 and 66) of cautioning with a system of reprimands and final warnings (being piloted

---

[30] *Evening Standard*, October 17, 1997.

[31] The study thus excluded those cautioned for less serious types of summary offence: D. Dulai and M. Greenhorn, "The criminal histories of those cautioned in 1985, 1988 and 1991", *Research Bulletin*, Number 37 (Home Office Research and Statistics Department, 1995), p.75.

for 18 months from September 1998) is also consistent with the deterrent and reintegrative elements of the Aylesbury process.[32]

We believe that it would be wise, however, to place less stress in future on the possible impact of restorative cautioning on reducing reoffending. In our view, the cautioning session should be regarded primarily as an opportunity to allow all those affected by an offence to express their own sense of harm and need for repair in a safe environment, and also as a more accountable, open and discursive form of criminal justice than old-style cautioning.[33] We adopt this position in part because we think that current expectations of what restorative cautioning can achieve are unrealistic and need to be moderated if a media-inspired backlash at some future date is to be avoided. There are good theoretical reasons for believing that cautioning based on the principles of reintegrative shaming will have more of an impact on recidivism than "old-style" cautioning, but equally good theoretical reasons for doubting that the impact will be spectacular. Even the best designed and implemented programmes for offenders rarely produce reductions in reoffending of more than a dozen percentage points.[34]

But we hold to this position for another reason. In our view the emphasis we saw in Aylesbury on "promoting behavioural change" was sometimes excessive. Most young offenders do not "need" the strong deterrent messages communicated in Aylesbury—most will not come to the attention of the police again whatever the content of the cautioning process. Moreover, where harm was exaggerated, or too much remorse expected, the intended additional deterrent effect may have been offset or even outweighed by the sense of unfairness this could engender in offenders.[35] There is evidence that people obey the law (and co-operate with its agents) partly because they acknowledge legal institutions such as the police to be legitimate.[36] Restorative cautioning sessions constitute important encounters between offenders, other members of the public, and the police. If they are perceived to be unfair by those taking part in them, the damage to the legitimacy of the police may be significant. It would be ironic if a cautioning process aimed at reparation resulted in such damage. With that in mind we welcome the emphasis on fair process and proportionality in Thames Valley Police's guidelines for facilitators issued in June 1998. This guidance should help to ensure that practice in Aylesbury and across Thames Valley Police is further shifted away from "old-style" cautioning.

[32] See the articles by Fionda [1999] Crim.L.R. 36 and Dignan [1999] Crim.L.R. 48.

[33] On the accountability of the cautioning process see R. Evans, "Challenging a Police Caution Using Judicial Review" [1996] Crim.L.R. 104.

[34] For a recent discussion of this complex issue see P. Goldblatt and C. Lewis (eds), *Reducing Offending*, Home Office Research Study 187 (London: Home Office, 1998).

[35] For an argument that placing strong expectations on relatively minor offenders to show high levels of remorse may lead to stigmatisation see J. Vagg, "Delinquency and Shame: Data from Hong Kong" (1998) 38 *British Journal of Criminology* 247 at 260.

[36] See the important study by T. Tyler, *Why People Obey the Law* (New Haven: Yale University Press, 1990), and the brief discussion in Goldblatt and Lewis (eds), *op. cit.* p.72.

Part III
Juridical Perspectives

[9]

RESPONSIBILITIES, RIGHTS AND RESTORATIVE JUSTICE

Andrew Ashworth*

Restorative justice is much advocated as a new and fruitful response to offending. This article argues for further debate about the proper division of functions between state, victims, offenders and 'communities', and for greater emphasis upon procedural safeguards and substantive limits in the pursuit of the apparently beneficent goals of restorative justice.

Restorative justice is practice-led in most of its manifestations (see Miers 2001). Although the writings of John Braithwaite (e.g. 1989, 1993, 1999), Howard Zehr (1990), Martin Wright (1996) and others may be a source of inspiration for some practitioners and policy makers, there is also a certain reflexivity at work. The theory of restorative justice has to a large extent developed through practice, and will probably continue to do so. One consequence of this is that there is no single notion of RJ, no single type of process, no single theory. Tony Marshall suggests that a commonly accepted definition of restorative justice would be: 'a process whereby parties with a stake in a specific offence collectively resolve how to deal with the aftermath of the offence and its implications for the future' (Marshall 1999: 5). This usefully identifies three central elements in restorative justice: the importance of process, the notion of stakeholders, and the fairly wide-ranging aspirations for outcomes.

In terms of restorative process, the keynotes are empowerment, dialogue, negotiation and agreement. Professionals should not be dominant: the voices of the stakeholders should be the loudest. The stakeholders are assumed to be the victim, the offender and the community. Turning to restorative outcomes, what is to be restored is broadly stated as 'whatever dimensions of restoration matter to the victims, offenders and communities affected by the crime' (Braithwaite 1999: 6). Restoration is often seen as a form of reintegration, of the community and of individuals. Outcomes are measured chiefly by the satisfaction of the stakeholders in each case, and not by comparison with the outcomes of like cases.

One of the aims of the restorative justice movement is to replace forms of state justice for a wide range of offences and offenders. This means changing the focus of the term 'criminal justice' itself, away from the assumption that it is a matter concerning only the state and the defendant/offender, and towards a conception that includes as stakeholders the victim and the community too. However, it will be argued here that such a process of change should not have the effect of depriving defendants/offenders of safeguards and rights that should be assured to them in any processes which impose obligations as the consequence of committing an offence. Important steps have been

* Vinerion Professor of English Law at All Souls College, University of Oxford. An earlier version of this paper was discussed at a colloquium on 'Restorative Justice in Theory and Practice' in Cambridge, October 2000. Some of the arguments were worked into a separate paper on restorative justice and the English youth justice system, published in the 2001 volume of Current Legal Problems. I am grateful to Kathleen Daly, Antony Duff, Roger Hood, Carolyn Hoyle, Paul Roberts, Prince Saprai, Andrew von Hirsch, Richard Young and Lucia Zedner for comments on earlier versions.

and are being taken to ensure that appropriate standards are respected in restorative processes and outcomes, notably in the United Nations draft 'Basic Principles on the Use of Restorative Justice Programmes in Criminal Justice Matters' (United Nations 2000; see further Braithwaite, this issue). However, there are further and deeper issues to be confronted.

The aim of this article is to generate discussion on four of those issues. First, what should be the role of the state and its organs in the administration of criminal justice and in the determination of criminal justice outcomes? Second, if it is argued that the community should have a more central role in criminal justice, what implications does this have? Third, what are the rights and responsibilities of victims in matters of criminal justice? And fourth, if it is accepted that there must be some kind of 'default system' to deal with cases that cannot be handled through restorative justice, what form should it take?

The Responsibilities of the State

It is central to the philosophy of restorative justice that the stakeholders should be able to participate in dialogue about the offence. Undoubtedly the offender is one stakeholder, but who are the others? It may be claimed that the community and the victim also have a stake in the response to the offence, but what about the state? At a time when statist assumptions are crumbling, when 'neo-liberal' and 'advanced liberal' analyses (e.g. Rose 2000; Shearing 2000) point to the changing role of the state and governmentality, what should be the role of the state in matters of criminal justice?

It is common to refer to the 'public interest' in preventing or prosecuting crime: what does this mean? What is the significance of the phrase 'a crime against society'? The idea seems to be that, when it is decided to make certain conduct a crime rather than simply a civil wrong, this implies that it should not be merely a matter for the victim whether some action is taken against the malefactor; and even that there is a public interest in ensuring that people who commit such wrongs are liable to punishment, not merely to civil suit (Cretney *et al.* 1994). Thus Antony Duff argues for a category 'of "public" wrongs that are properly condemned and dealt with as wrongs by the community as a whole' (Duff 2000: 62), and he illustrates this with crimes of 'domestic' violence:

But whatever else is unclear about the rights and wrongs of a domestic dispute . . . such violence should surely not be seen as a matter for negotiation or compromise. It should be condemned by the whole community as an unqualified wrong; and this is done by defining and prosecuting it as a crime. (Duff 2000: 62)

These are not propositions with which a restorative justice advocate would necessarily disagree. But another element of the argument is more contentious: that it is the responsibility of the state to ensure that there is order and law-abidance in society, and to establish a system for the administration of criminal justice.

In crude terms, the political theory would be that citizens agree to obey laws in return for protection of their vital interests, though keeping their right of self-defence for occasions of emergency when state protection is unavailable. As David Garland puts it, 'over time, the effective control of crime and the routine protection of citizens from criminal depredations had come to form elements of the promise that the state holds out to its citizens' (Garland 2001: 109–10). This serves as the basis of the justification for maintaining a police force, a system of public prosecutions, the courts, and other aspects of the criminal justice system. Thus Duff regards it as obvious 'that the state owes it to its citizens to protect them from crime' through the criminal law and its administration (Duff 2000: 112).

If a community is, through the legal organs of the state, to take seriously the public wrong done to a citizen, it must not only sympathize with the victim but also censure the offender. It owes it to the victim, whose wrong it shares, and to the offender as a member of the normative community, to try to get the offender to recognize the wrong and to make a suitable apology for it. (Duff 2000: 114)

These arguments in favour of the state's responsibility for criminal justice[1] are joined by other consequential justifications for the state taking over the administration of criminal justice from victims and other individuals—partly to avoid placing on victims the additional burden of having to bring offenders to justice (Reeves and Mulley 2000: 130), and partly to avoid the social instability that would result if people had to 'take the law into their own hands' in responding to offences, which might encourage vigilantism (MacCormick and Garland 1998: 22, 27).

None of this is to rule out some delegation of this function by the state (in whole or in part) to others, either by moving it down to the level of the local community (MacCormick and Garland 1998: 27) or by elements of privatization. Recent decades have seen increasing decentralization and 'responsibilization' in criminal justice (Garland 2001), for a variety of political reasons; one aspect of the restorative justice movement, too, is a relocation of authority over responses to crime (Bayley 2001: 212). It is important to question whether these changes are right in principle, but first we must acknowledge two major failures of the statist approach.

First, in many political systems the prevailing statist approach has neglected (some would say, reinforced) social inequalities. Thus Kent Roach writes of disadvantaged groups having to 'rely on the criminal sanction's false promise of security and equality' (1999: 117), and argues that the state's responsibility for protecting citizens should be viewed in the wider context of public health, and therefore tackled as one element in a social programme to improve the conditions of life of groups who are disproportionately victimized and are not in a position to buy private security or healthcare (*ibid.*: 261). This is a timely reminder of the limitations of focusing criminal policy initiatives on the criminal justice system, rather than locating them in the wider social structure.

Second, and more deeply, there are countries in which the legitimacy of the state and its apparatus, including the criminal justice system, has suffered a serious collapse-obvious examples were South Africa (van Zyl Smit 1999; Shearing 2001) and Northern Ireland (McEvoy and Mika 2001). Some of the restorative justice initiatives in the most difficult social conditions are as much about social control as about responses to crime (see McEvoy and Mika 2001 on Northern Ireland). In still other countries it is possible to say that there have been or are legitimacy deficits, particularly in respect of certain groups (Blagg 1997; Tauri 1999), which suggest that reality lies some distance from basic democratic theory. Conditions of this kind may provide fertile soil for initiatives based on restorative justice, with its emphasis on greater participation and community

---

[1] This is an inevitably crude and truncated discussion of political theory. For another approach, see e.g. Raz (1986: ch. 3).

RESPONSIBILITIES, RIGHTS AND RESTORATIVE JUSTICE

involvement, although even restorative justice initiatives intended to tap into the culture of indigenous communities court the risk of increasing the extent of official power over them (Cunneen 1997; Blagg 1997; cf. Braithwaite 1997).

These deficiencies in relation to social disadvantage and governmental legitimacy have led many restorative justice advocates to the view that the state should not have a prominent position in the administration of criminal justice, and should instead have a residual role in providing facilities and in enforcing post-offence agreements reached by conferences, etc. The facilitative state would leave restorative conferences with deliberative space in which to decide on the most appropriate response to an offender's crime, from which it seems to follow that they might select (within ill-defined outer limits) whatever approach the particular conference prefers. Would this confine the state's role too narrowly? Are there duties that the state should retain, no matter that there are elements of 'rolling back' or 'hollowing out' the state's functions which lead to a measure of privatization and responsibilization?

The focus of these questions must be on the process of responding to crime, a process that (even within restorative justice) involves a measure of public censure and the placing of obligations on offenders. Garland identifies:

an emerging distinction between the *punishment of criminals* which remains the business of the state (and becomes once again a significant symbol of state power) and the *control of crime*, which is increasingly deemed to be 'beyond the state' in significant respects. And as its control capacity comes to be viewed as limited and contingent, the state's power to punish takes on a renewed political salience and priority. (Garland 2001: 120)

What reasons can be given for state control over punishment and official responses to offences? Two arguments are that criminal justice must be administered 'in the public interest', and that it should ensure respect for human rights. Since, as argued above, a defining feature of criminal offences is that they are offences against the state or collectivity, it is right that the state should ensure that the response is based on general principles duly established and applicable throughout the jurisdiction. This connects closely with the second argument about respect for human rights. The state surely owes it to offenders to exercise its power according to settled principles that uphold citizens' rights to equal respect and equality of treatment. Decisions on sentence should be taken by independent and impartial tribunals (see below), operating on principle and transparently, within a legal framework. There is an important distinction between tribunals responding in a principled manner to relevant factual differences between cases, and responding on the basis of their own views or preferences. The latter is contrary to the rule of law, and at odds with the notion of a *Rechtsstaat*. As John Gardner has argued, one of the implications of acting according to the 'rule of law' is 'that questions of how people are to be treated relative to one another always come to the fore at the point of its application'. This is not to rule out mitigation or mercy in sentencing, but to assert that 'what falls to be mitigated is none other than the sentence which is, in the court's [judgment], required by justice' (Gardner 1998: 36–7). In other words, the power exercised by imposing obligations on offenders in response to their offending ought, in principle, to be exercised consistently as between citizens, according to settled standards.

Although the list of failures of state justice is a lengthy one, the state must, as the primary political authority, retain control over criminal justice and its administration. It must do so for pragmatic reasons concerned with security (Bayley 2001: 218), and it must do so in order to ensure respect for the rule of law and human rights standards. This is not to ignore the shortcomings of human rights declarations and their enforcement, or to overlook the malleability of the 'rule of law' principle. Rather it is to argue that these remain fundamental ideals, which should be taken more seriously rather than discarded. The state ought, out of fairness to the people in respect of whom its coercive powers are being exercised, to insist on 'rule of law' principles and so ensure consistency of response to offences. Insofar as restorative justice approaches are adopted, the state's responsibility should be to impose a framework that guarantees these safeguards to offenders—an aim no less worthy in those societies where state legitimacy is contested. The recent draft UN standards amount to a small but welcome step in this direction (United Nations 2000; Braithwaite, this issue). We should also recall that the state has responsibilities towards victims: in the context of restorative justice, this means that it is wrong in principle to place burdens on victims as part of any criminal justice initiative (Reeves and Mulley 2000).

The Empowerment of Communities

It is the hallmark of many restorative justice approaches that they draw into criminal justice both victims and the wider community (although there is no unanimity on this: some regard the involvement of community members as 'at odds with the principles underlying conferencing': Morris and Maxwell 2000: 215). Garland is among those who have argued for the delegation of sentencing powers to communities (to 'authorities intermediate between the state and the individual': MacCormick and Garland 1998: 27). He does this for reasons similar to those of many restorative justice theorists—that the closer the adjudicators and enforcers are to the offender, the more likely they are to be effective in bringing about the desired changes in behaviour (partly, perhaps, because their legitimacy is more likely to impress itself on the offender).

Much depends, of course, on the conception of community on which reliance is being placed. Every citizen may be seen as a member of several cross-cutting communities: each of us has 'a number of community attachments, articulated in terms of factors such as race, ethnicity, class, gender, age, sexuality, occupation' (Lacey 1998: 144). Some restorative justice advocates would probably claim to have an open and inclusive approach to 'community', but in practice most schemes seem to involve the families of victim and offender, and yet to regard the community (where there are 'community representatives') as a geographical entity. If this means that local communities can adopt separate standards, the result is likely to be a form of 'justice by geography' or 'postcode lottery'. Indeed, the empowerment of communities, howsoever defined, might involve a sacrifice of 'rule of law' values such as consistency, which, it was argued, ought to be standards for criminal justice. Is it right for the state, or for bodies exercising authority delegated by the state, to use its coercive powers differently against each of two people, one who commits an offence in one locality and another with exactly similar background who commits a similar offence in a different locality? Surely not; it happens in both 'conventional' and restorative justice systems, but the difference is that in the former it is regarded as a malfunction to be removed whereas in the latter it may be thought beneficial. The conflict can be represented as one between principle and pragmatism, since there are those who regard the use of local knowledge and local ordering as an

RESPONSIBILITIES, RIGHTS AND RESTORATIVE JUSTICE

essential element of successful social control in contemporary societies (e.g. Braithwaite 2000: 232, and Shearing 2001; cf. van Ness 1993). It is certainly true that policing policies are increasingly responsive to local concerns; and, as one looks across European countries or American states, there may be stark differences in criminal justice policy between neighbouring jurisdictions—federal systems differ, for example, in respect of the allocation of responsibility for the administration of criminal justice. The issue cannot be argued to a conclusion here, but the very least that is required by the principle of the consistent use of state power over offenders is that local decision making should be constrained by general standards of procedural and substantive justice.

Turning from restorative processes to restorative outcomes, what is meant by the goal of 'community restoration'? This is regarded by most advocates as one desirable outcome of restorative justice processes, but its practical meaning turns on two issues which remain unsettled. One is the conception of community that is being used. If the broad aim is to restore the 'communities affected by the crime' (Braithwaite 1999: 6), as well as the victim and victim's family, this will usually mean a geographical community; but where an offence targets a victim because of race, religion, sexual orientation etc., that will point to a different community that needs to be restored. This leads to the second issue: what exactly is community 'restoration', and on what criteria are the form and amount of community restoration to be calculated? Reintegration is a term often used in this context, but its practical implications remain unclear. Many restorative justice theorists and others (e.g. Zedner 1994; Walgrave 1995; Duff 2000: 99–106) regard as the paradigm of community restoration some form of community service (now termed 'community punishment orders' in England and Wales). This is largely a symbolic form of restoration, and therefore it must be necessary to devise a scale of 'wrongs to the community' and to match it with a register of degrees of community restoration (cf. Meier 1998). There seems to be little endeavour among restorative justice theorists to deal with this issue, and certainly nothing comparable to the efforts of desert theorists to work out parameters of proportionality (cf. van Ness 1993 with von Hirsch and Jareborg 1991, and von Hirsch 1993: chs 2 and 4).

A further issue of principle concerns impartiality. It is one thing for critics of 'conventional' criminal justice systems to argue that those systems fail to sentence 'objectively', despite their aspirations, because they fail to avoid discrimination on grounds of class, race or gender. It is quite another thing to devise a system that would avoid problems of bias, or of informal hierarchies growing up, or of local power structures tending to dominate (Lacey 1998: ch. 5). Advocates of community justice stress the importance of inclusion rather than exclusion, and the concept of community is often associated with self-regulation, consent and agreement (Pavlich 2001). There may be examples of sentencing circles and restorative justice conferences that appear to avoid these difficulties, but there is always the danger that, as Adam Crawford has warned, 'the normative appeal of community [may be] confused with empirical reality':

the ideal of community should be forced to confront the empirical reality, which reminds us that communities are often marked (and sustained) by social exclusion, forms of coercion, and the differential distribution of power relations. (Crawford 2000: 290–1; cf. McEvoy and Mika 2001)

Among the problems here might be that majorities in some communities might disagree with certain criminal laws, perhaps laws intended to protect the weak against the strong or to eradicate drunk driving (Johnstone 2001: 55–7). Allowing community-based

ASHWORTH

tribunals to determine the response to such laws is fraught with difficulty. Impartiality is a key value in justice processes, and yet in restorative justice theory it stands in tension with other values such as participation, involvement and empowerment (see Johnstone 2001: 153–8). But the tension is not insoluble, since it would be possible to concede the case for greater participation by members of affected communities while insisting that the power of decision making remains in impartial hands.

Rights and Responsibilities of the Victim

It is common for those writing on restorative justice to insist that all parties 'with a stake in the offence' ought to be able to participate in the disposition of the case, through a circle, conference, etc. (e.g. Llewellyn and Howse 1998: 19). The victim certainly has 'a stake', and Christie's (1977) assertion that the 'conflict' in some sense 'belongs' to the victim has become a modern orthodoxy among restorative justice supporters (e.g. Morris and Maxwell 2000: 207, who write of 'returning the offence to those most affected by it and encouraging them to determine appropriate responses to it'). The approach has ancient roots (Braithwaite 1999: 1–2 for a summary and references), although the growing awareness of the existence of secondary victimization (e.g. Morgan and Zedner 1992 on child victims) demonstrates the complexity of the issues arising.

The politico-historical argument is that most modern legal systems exclude the victim so as to bolster their own power. Originally the state wanted to take over criminal proceedings from victims as an assertion of power, and what now passes for 'normal' is simply a usurpation that has no claim to be the natural order. My concern is not to dispute this rather romantic interpretation of criminal justice in early history (Daly 2000 does this splendidly; also Johnstone 2001: ch. 3) but rather to raise three points of principle which have a bearing on the nature and extent of victims' rights: the principle of compensation for wrongs, the principle of proportionality, and the principle of independence and impartiality.

The first point of principle is the most direct of all in its target. What I want to argue is that the victim's legitimate interest is in compensation and/or reparation from the offender, and not in the form or quantum of the offender's punishment. The distinction between punishment and compensation is not widely appreciated: when a court fines an offender £300 for careless driving in a case where death resulted (but where there was no conviction for the more serious offence of causing death by dangerous driving), newspapers will often report comments such as 'my son's life has been valued at just £300'. However, the size of the fine will usually be related to the offender's culpability (and financial resources), and will not be a 'valuation' of the loss. Compensation for loss, from whatever source, is a separate matter. It may not require a separate civil case: English criminal courts are required to consider ordering the offender to pay compensation to the victim or victim's family, so far as the offender's means allow. However, in many cases the offender will not have the funds to pay realistic compensation. It is now recognized as part of the state's responsibility for criminal justice that it should provide a compensation fund for victims of crimes of violence, at least (see Ashworth 1986 and, on the current scheme, Miers 1997). This is not to deny that victims primarily have a right to compensation from the offender: that is clear on legal and moral grounds, if not always practical.

RESPONSIBILITIES, RIGHTS AND RESTORATIVE JUSTICE

The key question is whether the victim's legitimate interest goes beyond reparation or compensation (and the right to victim services and support, and to proper protection from further harm), and extends to the question of punishment. It would be wrong to suggest that the victim has no legitimate interest in the disposition of the offender in his or her case, but the victim's interest is surely no greater than yours or mine. The victim's interest is as a citizen, as one of many citizens who make up the community or state. In democratic theory all citizens have a right to vote at elections and sometimes on other occasions, and to petition their elected representatives about issues affecting them. If I am an ardent advocate of restorative justice or of indeterminate imprisonment for repeat offenders, I can petition my MP about it, or join a pressure group. Just because a person commits an offence against me, however, that does not privilege my voice above that of the court (acting 'in the general public interest') in the matter of the offender's punishment. A justification for this lies in social contract reasoning, along the lines that the state may be said to undertake the duty of administering justice and protecting citizens in return for citizens giving up their right to self-help (except in cases of urgency) in the cause of better social order. This returns to the earlier argument about the state's responsibility, and to the 'rule of law' values of impartiality, independence and consistency in the administration of criminal justice.

This principle is not opposed by all those who advocate a version of restorative justice. Thus Michael Cavadino and James Dignan (1997) draw a strong distinction between the victim's right to reparation and the public interest in responding to the offence. In their view it is right to empower victims to participate in the process which determines what reparation is to be made by the offender, and reparation to the victim should be the major element of the response. In serious cases some additional response (punishment) may be considered necessary, and they then insist on a form of limiting retributivism in which proportionality sets upper and lower boundaries for the burdens placed on offenders (and also serves as a default setting for cases where a conference or circle proves impossible or inappropriate). It is a matter for regret that few restorative justice theorists refer to Cavadino and Dignan's attempt to preserve as many of the values of restorative justice as possible whilst insisting upon principled limits. They rightly see the distinction between compensation and punishment as crucial, even though their proportionality constraints are looser than many desert theorists would require, and they regard victim involvement as a value to be enhanced where possible. 'Victim personal statements' must now be taken into account by English courts before sentencing: Edna Erez claims that 'providing victims with a voice has therapeutic advantages' (1999: 555; cf. Edwards 2001), but findings from the English pilot projects indicated no great psychological benefits to participant victims and some evidence of disillusionment (Sanders *et al.* 2001: 450).

The second point of principle concerns proportionality. Sentencing is *for* an offence, and respect for the offender as a citizen capable of choice suggests that the sentence should bear a relationship to the seriousness of the offence committed. To desert theorists this is axiomatic: punishment should always be proportionate to the offence, taking account of harm and culpability (von Hirsch 1993: ch. 2), unless a highly persuasive argument for creating a class of exceptional cases can be sustained. It is a strong criticism of deterrent sentencing and of risk theory that they accord priority to predictions and not to the seriousness of the offence committed: von Hirsch and Ashworth (1998: chs 2, 3). The proportionality principle is not the sole preserve of desert theorists: on the contrary, versions of it are widely accepted as limiting the quantum of

ASHWORTH

punishment that may be imposed on offenders, whether as a major tenet of the Council of Europe's recommendation on sentencing (1993: para. A4) or as an element in Nicola Lacey's communitarian approach to punishment (Lacey 1988: 194). Other important functions of the proportionality principle are that it should ensure consistency of treatment among offenders, and that it should give protection against discrimination, by attempting to rule out certain factors from sentencing calculations. It is not being suggested that existing sentencing systems always pursue these principles successfully, but it is vital that they be recognized as goals and efforts made to fulfil them.

The principle of proportionality goes against victim involvement in sentencing decisions because the views of victims may vary. Some victims will be forgiving, other will be vindictive; some will be interested in new forms of sentence, others will not; some shops will have one policy in relation to thieves, others may have a different policy. If victim satisfaction is one of the aims of circles and conferences, then proportionate sentencing cannot be assured and may be overtaken in some cases by deterrent or risk-based sentencing. Two replies may be anticipated. First, it may be argued that in fact the involvement of victims assures *greater* proportionality (Erez and Rogers 1999; Erez 1999; cf. Sanders *et al.* 2001: 451): the actual harm to the victim becomes clear, and in general victims do not desire disproportionate sentences. But these are aggregative findings, whereas the point of the principle is to ensure that in no individual case is an offender liable to a disproportionate penalty. A second reply would be to concede that victim involvement should be subject to proportionality limits, so that no agreement reached in a circle or conference should be out of proportion to the seriousness of the offence. The significance of this concession depends on the nature of the proportionality constraint. There is a range of possible proportionality theories: desert theory requires the sentence to be proportionate to the seriousness of the offence, within fairly narrow bands (von Hirsch 1993: chs 2 and 4), whereas various forms of limiting retributivism recognize looser boundaries. Michael Tonry, for example, argues against the 'strong proportion-ality' of desert theorists and in favour of 'upper limits' set in accordance with a less precise notion of proportionality (Tonry 1994). Among restorative justice theorists, Braithwaite refers to 'guaranteeing offenders against punishment beyond a maximum' (1999: 105), but it is unclear whether his 'guarantee' adopts as much of proportionality theory as Tonry seems prepared to accept, and whether it imposes similar constraints or even less demanding ones. Most restorative justice theorists would insist that one of their objectives is to reduce levels of punitiveness, not to increase them; but some questions will be raised below about the contours of the 'background' penal system which is envisaged for cases where restorative justice processes fail or are rejected.

The third point is that everyone should have the right to a fair hearing 'by an independent and impartial tribunal', as Article 6.1 of the European Convention on Human Rights declares. This right expresses a fundamental principle of justice. Under the European Convention it applies to the sentencing stage as much as to trials. Do conferences and other restorative justice processes respect the right? Insofar as a victim plays a part in determining the disposition of a criminal case, is a conference 'independent and impartial'? The victim cannot be expected to be impartial, nor can the victim be expected to know about the available range of orders and other principles for the disposition of criminal cases. All of this suggests that conferences may fail to meet the basic standards of a fair hearing, insofar as the victim or victim's family plays a part in determining the outcome.

RESPONSIBILITIES, RIGHTS AND RESTORATIVE JUSTICE

Most restorative justice supporters will be unimpressed with this, because the argument simply assumes that what has become conventional in modern criminal justice systems is absolutely right. But the issue of principle must be confronted, since it is supported by the European Convention, the International Covenant on Civil and Political Rights and many other human rights documents. One reply from restorative justice supporters might be that the required 'impartiality' and 'objectivity' produce such an impersonal and detached tribunal as to demonstrate exactly what is wrong with conventional systems, and why they fail. But that reply neglects, or certainly undervalues, the link between independence, impartiality and procedural justice. Might it be possible to sidestep the objection by characterizing conferences and other restorative justice processes as alternatives to sentencing rather than as sentencing processes, and therefore not bound by the same principles? This might be thought apposite where any agreement reached in the conference or circle has to be submitted for approval by a court, and where the offender may withdraw from the conference and go to the court at any time.

This is an appropriate point at which to question the reality of the consent that is said to underlie restorative justice processes and outcomes. The general principle is that 'restorative processes should be used only with the free and voluntary consent of the parties. The parties should be able to withdraw that consent at any time during the process' (UN 2000: para. 7). This suggests that the offender may simply walk out and take his or her chances in the 'conventional' system. However, the result of doing so would usually be to propel the case into a formal criminal justice system that is perceived to be harsher in general, or that the offender may expect to be harsher on someone who has walked away from a restorative justice process. On some occasions, then, as in plea-bargaining (Sanders and Young 2000: ch. 7; Ashworth 1998: ch. 9), the 'consent' may proceed from a small amount of free will and a large slice of (perceived) coercion. Where the 'consent' is that of young people, and it is the police who explain matters to them, the danger of perceived coercion may be acute (Daly 2001). The United Nations draft principles attempt to deal with some of these issues, by providing that failure to reach agreement or failure to implement an agreement 'may not be used as a justification for a more severe sentence in subsequent criminal justice proceedings' (UN 2000: paras. 15, 16). But it is right to remain sceptical of the reality of consent, from the offender's point of view.

Returning to the right to an independent and impartial tribunal, is it breached if the victim makes a statement about sentencing, written or oral, to the court or other body that is to take the sentencing decision? This refers to statements that go beyond a victim impact statement, and are not limited to the issue of compensation. The ruling of the European Commission on Human Rights in *McCourt* v. *United Kingdom* (1993) 15 EHRR CD110 may be taken to suggest that such a statement on sentence could prejudice the impartiality of the tribunal, but this might be thought to go too far, not least because defendants have the right to make a 'plea in mitigation', in which their lawyers usually argue against certain outcomes and (sometimes) for a certain sentence. A stronger argument here is to return to the principles of compensation and of proportionality, discussed above, and to assert that the victim's view as to sentence should not be received because it is not relevant. Consider the case of *Nunn*, where the defendant had been sentenced to four years' imprisonment for causing the death of a close friend by dangerous driving. When Nunn's appeal against the sentence came before the Court of Appeal, the court had before it some lengthy written statements by the victim's mother and sister, recognizing that some punishment had to follow such a terrible offence, but stating that their own grief was being increased by the thought of the victim's close friend being in prison for so long. They added that the victim's father and other sister took a different view. In the Court of Appeal, Lord Justice Judge said this:

We mean no disrespect to the mother and sister of the deceased, but the opinions of the victim, or the surviving members of the family, about the appropriate level of sentence do not provide any sound basis for reassessing a sentence. If the victim feels utterly merciful towards the criminal, and some do, the crime has still been committed and must be punished as it deserves. If the victim is obsessed with vengeance, which can in reality only be assuaged by a very long sentence, as also happens, the punishment cannot be made longer by the court than would otherwise be appropriate. Otherwise cases with identical features would be dealt with in widely differing ways, leading to improper and unfair disparity, and even in this particular case . . . the views of the members of the family of the deceased are not absolutely identical. (*Nunn* [1996] 2 Cr. App. R. (S) 136, at p. 140; see also *Roche* [1999] 2 Cr. App. R. (S) 105)

This statement captures the principles well.[2] Neither one victim's forgiveness of an offender, nor another's desire for vengeance against an offender, should be relevant when the community's response to an offence (as distinct from compensation) is being considered. The plea in *Nunn* was for leniency in the outcome, as also in the New Zealand case of *Clotworthy* (see Braithwaite 1999: 87–8). There are other cases where victims and their families campaign for severity, some with a very high profile (e.g. the case of Thompson and Venables, convicted at the age of 11 of the murder of James Bulger, whose family campaigned, with considerable support from the mass media, in favour of prolonging the imprisonment of the offenders). In dismissing an application by James Bulger's father for judicial review of the tariff set by the Lord Chief Justice, the Queen's Bench Divisional Court noted with approval that Lord Woolf had invited the Bulger family to make representations about the impact of their son's death on them, 'but had not invited them to give their views on what they thought was an appropriate tariff' (*R v. Secretary of State for the Home Department, ex parte Bulger, The Times*, 16 February 2001).

The above discussion of the three principles of compensation for wrongs, of independent and impartial tribunals, and of proportionality of sentence, suggests that the substantive and procedural rights of victims at the stage of disposal (sentence) ought to be limited. This should apply whether the rights of victims are being considered in the context of restorative justice or of a 'conventional' sentencing system. The rights of victims should chiefly be to receive support, proper services, and (where the offender is unable to pay) state compensation for violent crimes. There are arguments for going further, so as to achieve some measure of victim participation: this would require the provision of better and fuller information to victims, and the objective would be to enable some genuine participation in the process of disposal 'without giving [victims] the power to influence decisions that are not appropriately theirs' (Sanders *et al.* 2001: 458). This would be a fine line to tread, as the debate following the decision of the US Supreme Court to allow victim impact statements in capital cases demonstrates: *Payne v. Tennessee* (1991) 111 S Ct 2597, discussed by Sarat 1997.

[2] The *Nunn* case also points to the practical problem arising where two or more victims have different views on the proper response to the crime. A further complication would be where there is a disagreement between the victim and the community representatives over outcome (cf. Law Commission of Canada 1999: 38), although this should be resolved on the basis that the victim's interest lies in reparation and compensation whereas the state's (or community's) interest lies in measures going beyond that.

RESPONSIBILITIES, RIGHTS AND RESTORATIVE JUSTICE

Exploring the 'Default Setting': When Restorative Justice Runs Out

Although some restorative justice practitioners and writers express themselves as if there are no aspects of criminal justice with which restorative justice could not deal, most are realistic enough to recognize that provision must be made for some cases to be handled outside restorative justice processes. We have noted that Cavadino and Dignan provide for a 'default system' to deal with cases in which a circle or conference does not prove possible, perhaps because the necessary consents are not forthcoming. Certain writers make much stronger claims for the ability of restorative justice to handle a wide range of disputes in criminal justice, schools, industry, and business regulation (e.g. Wachtel and McCold 2001). But even some of those recognize that there must be some form of 'background system' in place (Braithwaite 1999). If one adds together the groups of offenders for whom such a system may be needed—those who refuse to participate in restorative justice, or whose victims refuse to participate,[3] or who have failed to comply with previous restorative justice outcomes—the numbers might be considerable. It has been argued above that some restorative justice processes themselves are incompatible with principles of justice on independence, impartiality, proportionality, and so on. How does the 'default' or 'background' system measure up to these principles?

Braithwaite explains his background system by reference to this enforcement pyramid, developed in relation to regulatory enforcement (1999: 61):

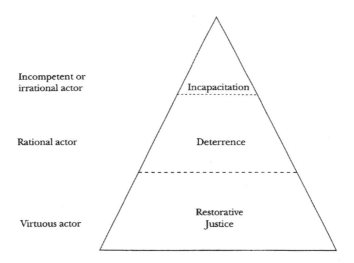

The idea is that one starts with restorative justice at the base of the pyramid. It may be tried more than once. If it clearly fails, then one would move to an 'active deterrence' strategy, which Braithwaite distinguishes carefully from the 'passive deterrence' described in most of the punishment literature (see Ayres and Braithwaite 1992: ch. 2).

---

[3] Some RJ schemes are prepared to proceed with a conference in the absence of the victim, which expands the role of the facilitator or coordinator: see, e.g. Daly (2001) on South Australia.

To have this kind of deterrence in the background helps restorative justice to work, in Braithwaite's view. Nonetheless, he warns that:

The problem is that if deterrent threats cause defiance and reactance, restorative justice may be compromised by what sits above it in a dynamic pyramidal strategy of deterrence and incapacitation . . . The challenge is to have the Sword of Damocles always threatening in the background but never threatened in the foreground. (Braithwaite 1999: 63-4)

From the point of view of principle, this approach is troubling. It seems that, once we leave the softly, softly world of restorative justice, offenders may be delivered into raging deterrent and incapacitative strategies, with rogue elements like Uncle Harry calling the shots (see the remarkable paragraphs in Braithwaite 1999: 66-7, on Uncle Harry), and with only the vaguest of gestures towards 'guaranteeing offenders against punishment beyond a maximum' (*ibid.*: 105). When Philip Pettit and John Braithwaite state that, in pursuit of the goal of 'community reassurance', sentencers should take account of 'how common that offence has become in the community' and 'how far the offender is capable of re-offending again' (1993, excerpted in von Hirsch and Ashworth 1998: 326), the glass becomes very dark, and the excesses of the 'risk society' seem to beckon.

Braithwaite and Pettit (1990: ch. 7) would answer that current maximum penalties should provide the guarantee in the first instance, and that there should then be a 'decremental strategy' of lowering those maxima progressively so as to reduce levels of punitiveness. But statutory maximum sentences are often very high, and certainly much higher than most proportionality theorists (including Tonry's looser approach to limits) would accept. It is also countered that desert-based critics are not paying attention to the difference between the usual run of consequentialist theories based on ('passive') deterrence and incapacitation, and the meaning of those strategies within a 'republican' framework which respects the dominion of each individual (Braithwaite and Pettit 1990). We should not find these aspects of Braithwaite's restorative justice theory threatening, it is contended, if we looked at the practical meaning of the pyramid of enforcement and took account of the emphasis on penal parsimony in a republican system. But it is not enough to proclaim penal parsimony and yet to give such prominence, even in a 'background system', to deterrent and incapacitative strategies. What types of deterrent strategy are permissible, within what kinds of limits? What forms of incapacitation? To what extent does the background system permit, nay encourage, sentencing on the basis of previous record rather than present offence? The answers to these questions about restorative justice and recalcitrant offenders remain unclear (see von Hirsch and Ashworth 1998: 317–35), but the need for firm safeguards against undue severity does not disappear if a system is labelled 'restorative'. Penal history yields plenty of examples of apparently benign policies resulting in repressive controls.

Conclusions

It has been argued that, despite the decline of statism and the rise of neo-liberal and 'advanced liberal' programmes for the responsibilization of other agencies of security, it should still be acknowledged to be a fundamental role of the state to maintain a system for the administration of justice and to ensure that proper standards of procedural protection are applied. It is recognized that there have been and are failures of state-led criminal justice, just as there have been and are manifest failures of states to deliver

RESPONSIBILITIES, RIGHTS AND RESTORATIVE JUSTICE

security (Garland 2001: ch. 5). The growth of restorative justice schemes is encouraged by both these phenomena. However, it should remain the responsibility of the state towards its citizens to ensure that justice is administered by independent and impartial tribunals, and that there are proportionality limits which should not only constrain the measures agreed at restorative justice conferences etc. but also ensure some similarity in the treatment of equally situated offenders. If the state does delegate certain spheres of criminal justice to some form of community-based conference, the importance of insisting on the protection of basic rights for defendants is not diminished.

Many of the innovations urged by restorative justice advocates ought to be tested and evaluated—the effect on victims and on offenders of face-to-face meetings, the value of apologies, the effect on victims and offenders of reparation agreements, the effect on victims and offenders of victim participation in conferences, and so forth. Too often, however, enthusiasm for such processes leads proponents either to overlook the need for safeguards, or to imply that they are not relevant. The steps being taken to develop standards for restorative justice processes are important in this respect (see UN 2000; Braithwaite, this issue), but they must be accompanied by a re-examination of deeper issues. In order to ensure that there is no deficit of procedural justice or human rights, it was argued above that governments must retain a primary role, that community-based processes and outcomes should be scrutinized closely, and that the proper role of the victim in criminal justice processes should be reappraised. Thus any restorative justice processes for offenders who might otherwise go to court should (a) be led by an independent and impartial person;[4] (b) be required to submit its decisions for court approval; (c) allow the participation of the victim, the offender, and their families or significant others; (d) make provision for access to legal advice before and after any restorative justice processes, at a minimum (Council of Europe 2000, para. 8; cf. UN 2000: para. 12); (e) focus on apology and on the appropriate reparation and/or compensation for the offence; and (f) be required to respect relevant principles, such as not imposing on the offender a financial burden that is not means-related. If, contrary to the argument here, a restorative justice conference is permitted to make proposals for community restoration or other responses going beyond reparation to the individual victim(s), there should be clear and circumscribed proportionality limits for those measures. However, the practical implications of 'restoration of the community' call for closer examination than they have hitherto received.

Criticisms of this kind seem to leave many restorative justice practitioners baffled, however. They may protest that restorative justice processes are not about punishment anyway; that all the safeguards are about offenders, not victims; and that in practice restorative justice encounters no problems about undue severity, etc. On the first point, Kathleen Daly (2000) rightly calls for caution among those restorative justice advocates

---

[4] This raises the question of police-led conferences, used in England in certain types of case (Young 2001). Braithwaite asks 'whether there is something wrong in principle with the police facilitating a conference. Does it make the police investigator, prosecutor, judge and jury?' (1999: 99). He never answers the question of principle, and instead points out the need to have someone assume the role of facilitator, and suggests that police involvement might have beneficial effects on police culture. But the question of principle must surely be answered by stating that this is wrong. It is not appropriate for the police to take on what is a quasi-judicial role, when they are so heavily involved in investigations. More strongly, it is inappropriate for the police to be involved in any 'shaming' of offenders (cf. Cunneen 1997 and Blagg 1997 with Braithwaite 1997). It is insufficient to reply that offenders who have misgivings can withdraw their consent: as stated above, the 'consent' in these situations may take a severely diluted form. This critique is, of course, no less applicable to the ongoing practice of police cautioning of adults.

ASHWORTH

who claim not to be in the punishment business but to be engaged in constructive and non-punitive responses to wrongdoing. Even if one were to adopt a narrow definition (that only measures intended to be punitive count as punishment), many restorative justice outcomes satisfy that definition inasmuch as they are known to impose obligations or deprivations on offenders: Johnstone 2001: 106–10; cf. Walgrave 2001. The argument that such obligations or deprivations proceed from full consent is, as we have seen, unconvincing. So far as the bias of rights towards offenders is concerned, it must be conceded that most human rights documents do not incorporate victims' rights into their framework—although there are well-known (separate) declarations of victims' rights. This imbalance ought to be rectified, but only after focusing on the arguments presented above. The third point (the absence of severity) may be generally true, since most of those interested in promoting restorative justice seem to oppose penal severity; but attention was drawn above to Braithwaite's 'background system', and even within restorative justice clear limits are important to prevent violations of rights behind a mask of benevolence. Once it is conceded that restorative justice cannot deal with absolutely all criminal cases, the relationship between the formal system and any restorative justice processes must be carefully crafted so as to avoid inequities. This third point is particularly important where enthusiasm for restorative justice leads a government to 'parachute' elements of restorative justice into a system suffused with rather different principles and practices, as has been done with youth justice in England and Wales (Morris and Gelsthorpe 2000; Ball 2000).

REFERENCES

Ashworth, A. (1986), 'Punishment and Compensation: State, Victim and Offender', *Oxford Journal of Legal Studies*, 6: 86–122.

——(1998), *The Criminal Process*, 2nd edn. Oxford: Oxford University Press.

Ayres, I. and Braithwaite, J. (1992), *Responsive Regulation: Transcending the Deregulation Debate*. New York: Oxford University Press.

Ball, C. (2000), 'The Youth Justice and Criminal Evidence Act 1999: A Significant Move towards Restorative Justice, or a Recipe for Unintended Consequences?', *Criminal Law Review*, 211–22.

Bayley, D. (2001), 'Security and Justice for All', in H. Strang and J. Braithwaite, eds., *Restorative Justice and Civil Society*, 211–21. Cambridge: Cambridge University Press.

Blagg, H. (1997), 'A Just Measure of Shame? Aboriginal Youth and Conferencing in Australia', *British Journal of Criminology*, 37/4: 481–501.

Braithwaite, J. (1989), *Crime, Shame and Reintegration*. Cambridge: Cambridge University Press.

——(1993), 'Shame and Modernity', *British Journal of Criminology*, 33/1: 1–18.

——(1997), 'Conferencing and Plurality: Reply to Blagg', *British Journal of Criminology*, 37/4: 502–6.

——(1999), 'Restorative Justice: Assessing Optimistic and Pessimistic Accounts', *Crime and Justice: A Review of Research*, 25: 1–110.

Braithwaite, J. and Pettit, P. (1990), *Not Just Deserts*. Oxford: Oxford University Press.

Cavadino, M. and Dignan, J. (1997), 'Reparation, Retribution and Rights', *International Review of Victimology*, 4: 233–71.

Christie, N. (1977), 'Conflicts as Property', *British Journal of Criminology*, 17/1: 1–15.

RESPONSIBILITIES, RIGHTS AND RESTORATIVE JUSTICE

COUNCIL OF EUROPE (1993), *Consistency in Sentencing*, Recommendation R (92) 18. Strasbourg: Council of Europe.

——(2000), *Mediation in Penal Matters*, Recommendation R (99) 19. Strasbourg: Council of Europe.

CRAWFORD, A. (2000), 'Salient Themes towards a Victim Perspective and the Limitations of Restorative Justice', in A. Crawford and J Goodey, eds., *Integrating a Victim Perspective within Criminal Justice*. Aldershot: Ashgate.

CRAWFORD, A. and GOODEY, J., eds. (2000), *Integrating a Victim Perspective within Criminal Justice*. Aldershot: Ashgate.

CRETNEY, A., DAVIS, G., CLARKSON, C. and SHEPHERD, J. (1994), 'Criminalizing Assault: The Failure of the "Offence against Society" Model', *British Journal of Criminology*, 34/1: 15–29.

CUNNEEN, C. (1997), 'Community Conferencing and the Fiction of Indigenous Control', *Australia and New Zealand Journal of Criminology*, 30: 297–320.

DALY, K. (1999), 'Does Punishment Have a Place in Restorative Justice?', unpublished paper presented to the ANZ Criminology conference; www.gu.edu.au/school/ccj/kdaly.html.

——(2000), 'Restorative Justice: The Real Story', unpublished paper presented to Scottish Criminology Conference; www.gu.edu.au/school/ccj/kdaly.html.

——(2001), 'Conferencing in Australia and New Zealand: Variations, Research Findings and Prospects', in A. Morris and G. Maxwell, eds., *Restorative Justice for Juveniles: Conferencing, Mediation and Circles*. Oxford: Hart Publishing.

DUFF, R. A. (2000), *Punishment, Communication and Community*. New York: Oxford Univesity Press.

EDWARDS, I. (2001), 'Victim Participation in Sentencing: The Problems of Incoherence', *Howard Journal of Criminal Justice*, 40: 39–54.

EREZ, E. (1999), 'Who's Afraid of the Big Bad Victim? Victim Impact Statements as Empowerment and Enhancement of Justice', *Criminal Law Review*, 545–56.

EREZ, E. and ROGERS, L. (1999), 'Victim Impact Statements and Sentencing Outcomes and Processes: The Perspectives of Legal Professionals', *British Journal of Criminology*, 39/2: 216–39.

GARDNER, J. (1998), 'Crime: In Proportion and in Perspective', in A. Ashworth and M. Wasik, eds., *Fundamentals of Sentencing Theory*. Oxford: Oxford University Press.

GARLAND, D. (2001), *The Culture of Control: Crime and Social Order in Contemporary Society*. Oxford: Oxford University Press.

JOHNSTONE, G. (2001), *Restorative Justice*. Cullompton: Willan Publishing.

LACEY, N. (1988), *State Punishment*. London: Routledge.

——(1998), *Unspeakable Subjects*. Oxford: Hart Publishing.

LAW COMMISSION OF CANADA (1999), *From Restorative Justice to Transformative Justice*, discussion paper. Ottawa: Law Commission.

LLEWELLYN, J. J. and HOWSE, R. (1998), *Restorative Justice: A Conceptual Framework*. Ottawa: Law Commission of Canada.

MACCORMICK, N. and GARLAND, D. (1998), 'Sovereign States and Vengeful Victims: The Problem of the Right to Punish', in A. Ashworth and M. Wasik, eds., *Fundamentals of Sentencing Theory*. Oxford: Oxford University Press.

McEVOY, K. and MIKA, H. (2001), 'Punishment, Policing and Praxis: Restorative Justice and Non-Violent Alternatives to Paramilitary Punishments in Northern Ireland', *Policing and Society*, 11.

MARSHALL, T. F. (1999), *Restorative Justice: An Overview*. London: Home Office Research, Development and Statistics Directorate.

MEIER, B.-D. (1998), 'Restorative Justice?A New Paradigm in Criminal Law?', *European Journal of Crime, Criminal Law and Criminal Justice*, 6: 125–36.

ASHWORTH

MIERS, D. (1997), *State Compensation for Criminal Injuries*. London: Blackstone.

——(2001), *An International Review of Restorative Justice*. London: Home Office.

MORGAN, J. and ZEDNER, L. (1992), *Child Victims*. Oxford: Oxford University Press.

MORRIS, A. and GELSTHORPE, L. (2000), 'Something Old, Something Borrowed, Something Blue, but Something New?, Comment on the Prospects for Restorative Justice under the Crime and Disorder Act', *Criminal Law Review*, 18–30.

MORRIS, A. and MAXWELL, G. (2000), 'The Practice of Family Group Conferences in New Zealand: Assessing the Place, Potential and Pitfalls of Restorative Justice', in A. Crawford and J Goodey, eds., *Integrating a Victim Perspective within Criminal Justice*. Aldershot: Ashgate.

PAVLICH, G. (2001), 'The Force of Community', in H. Strang and J. Braithwaite, eds., *Restorative Justice and Civil Society*, 56–68. Cambridge: Cambridge University Press.

PETTIT, P. with BRAITHWAITE, J. (1993), 'Not Just Deserts, Even in Sentencing', *Current Issues in Criminal Justice*, 4: 222–32.

REEVES, H. and MULLEY, K. (2000), 'The New Status of Victims in the UK: Opportunities and Threats', in A. Crawford and J Goodey, eds., *Integrating a Victim Perspective within Criminal Justice*. Aldershot: Ashgate.

ROACH, K. (1999), *Due Process and Victims' Rights: The New Law and Politics of Criminal Justice*. Toronto: University of Toronto Press

ROSE, N. (2000), 'Government and Control', *British Journal of Criminology*, 40/2: 321–39.

SANDERS, A., HOYLE, C., MORGAN, R. and CAPE, E. (2001), 'Victim Impact Statements: Can't Work, Won't Work', *Criminal Law Review*, 447–58.

SARAT, A. (1997), 'Vengeance, Victims and the Identities of Law', *Social and Legal Studies*, 6: 163–84.

SHEARING, C. (2000), 'Punishment and the Changing Face of Governance', *Punishment and Society*, 203–20.

——(2001), 'Transforming Security: A South African Experiment', in H. Strang and J. Braithwaite, eds., *Restorative Justice and Civil Society*, 14–34. Cambridge: Cambridge University Press.

TAURI, J. (1999), 'Exploring Recent Innovations in New Zealand's Criminal Justice System: Empowering Maori or Biculturising the State?', *Australia and New Zealand Journal of Criminology*, 32: 153–70.

TONRY, M. (1994), 'Proportionality, Parsimony and Interchangeability of Punishments', in A. Duff, S. Marshall, R. E. Dobash and R. P. Dobash, eds., *Penal Theory and Practice*. Manchester: Manchester University Press.

UNITED NATIONS (2000), *Basic Principles on the Use of Restorative Justice Programmes in Criminal Matters*, www.restorativejustice.org/.ents/UNDecBasicPrinciplesofRJ.htm.

VAN NESS, D. W. (1993), 'New Wine and Old Wineskins: Four Challenges of Restorative Justice', *Criminal Law Forum*, 4: 251–76.

VAN ZYL SMIT, D. (1999), 'Criminological Ideas and the South African Transition', *British Journal of Criminology*, 39/2: 198–215.

VON HIRSCH, A. (1993), *Censure and Sanctions*. Oxford: Oxford University Press.

VON HIRSCH, A. and ASHWORTH, A., eds. (1998), *Principled Sentencing: Readings on Theory and Policy*. Oxford: Hart Publishing.

WACHTEL, T. and MCCOLD, P. (2001), 'Restorative Justice in Everyday Life', in H. Strang and J. Braithwaite, eds., *Restorative Justice and Civil Society*, 114–29. Cambridge: Cambridge University Press.

WALGRAVE, L. (1995), 'Restorative Justice for Juveniles', *Howard Journal of Criminal Justice*, 34: 228–49.

RESPONSIBILITIES, RIGHTS AND RESTORATIVE JUSTICE

——(2001), 'On Restoration and Punishment', in A. Morris and G. Maxwell, eds., *Restorative Justice for Juveniles*, 17–40. Oxford: Hart.

WRIGHT, M. (1996), *Justice for Victims and Offenders*, 2nd edn. Winchester: Waterside.

YOUNG, R. (2001), 'Just Cops Doing "Shameful" Business: Police-Led Restorative Justice and the Lessons of Research', in A. Morris and G. Maxwell, eds., *Restorative Justice for Juveniles*, 195–226. Oxford: Hart.

ZEDNER, L. (1994), 'Reparation and Retribution: Are They Reconcilable?', *Modern Law Review*, 57: 228.

ZEHR, H. (1990), *Changing Lenses: A New Focus for Criminal Justice*. Scottsdale, PA: Herald Press.

[10]

THE USE OF MEDIATION TO RESOLVE CRIMINAL CASES: A PROCEDURAL CRITIQUE

*Jennifer Gerarda Brown**

TABLE OF CONTENTS

* Associate Professor, Quinnipiac College School of Law. I am grateful to Howard Anawalt, Ian Ayres, June Carbone, Morgan Cloud, Mary Coffield, Thomas Heller, Linda Meyer, Marc Miller, Robert Weisberg, and Deborah Young for helpful comments and conversations. Todd Cleary provided excellent research assistance.

1248   EMORY LAW JOURNAL   [Vol. 43

INTRODUCTION

In the ancient days of Western legal systems, criminal offenders could settle with victims and their families to avoid prosecution.[1] For some criminal offenders in the United States, privatized criminal law survives: Victim-Offender Mediation ("VOM") allows offenders to avoid public prosecution or punishment by mediating criminal cases with their victims.[2] An offender may be given the opportunity to participate in VOM at various stages in the criminal justice process.[3] VOM may even divert cases from the criminal justice system, with little or no involvement by state officials unless the mediation fails to resolve the case. Today, more than 100 VOM programs exist in the United States.[4] In 1993, U.S. programs disposed of 16,500 cases involving 12,931 victims and 14,059 offenders.[5]

Offenders participate in VOM in order to reduce their expected pun-

---

[1] *See infra* Part I.A.

[2] Victim-offender mediation programs can be defined as programs that: (1) "involve a face-to-face meeting, conducted by a trained mediator, between a person who has been victimized by a crime and the perpetrator of that crime;" (2) operate within the context of the criminal justice system rather than the civil court system; (3) not only facilitate negotiation of restitution agreements, but also strive for " 'closure' — however we operationalize the concept: reconciliation, expression of feelings, greater understanding of the event, of each other." PACT INSTITUTE OF JUSTICE, VICTIM-OFFENDER RECONCILIATION & MEDIATION PROGRAM DIRECTORY 1 (Harriet Fagan & John Gehm eds., 1993) [hereinafter DIRECTORY].

[3] The mediation could take place following arraignment but prior to any plea or adjudication of guilt; after the offender enters a guilty plea but prior to sentencing; as part of the sentence imposed on the offender; or as a condition of probation. In some programs, the mediation can take place in prison after the offender is convicted. As I will explain *infra* Part I.D, a "typical" VOM program is difficult to describe. Remarkable lack of uniformity characterizes the more than 100 VOM programs in the United States.

[4] *See* DIRECTORY, *supra* note 2, at 1 (the 1993 directory lists 123 programs in the U.S. and "an additional 63 non-U.S."). *See also* HOWARD ZEHR, CHANGING LENSES 159 (1990).

[5] DIRECTORY, *supra* note 2, at 1.

ishment.[6] An offender who participates may be rewarded by dismissal of charges or reduction of penalties. An offender who refuses to participate or fails to reach an agreement with the victim, on the other hand, returns to the criminal justice system for possible prosecution or sentencing.[7] The outcome of the mediation can influence judges, parole boards, and prosecutors as they decide how to charge or punish the offender.[8] And the outcome of the mediation turns in large part upon the victim's satisfaction.

Thus, VOM transforms the criminal justice paradigm by placing victims at the center, rather than on the periphery, of the criminal process. In effect, VOM transfers the power to resolve all or part of a criminal case from the state to a private party—the victim. As a result, VOM represents a return to an earlier model of criminal justice. In VOM, as in ancient criminal practice, the victim controls the offender's fate.

The thesis of this Article is that placing such control in the hands of the victim is inconsistent with the character and purpose of the criminal law as it has evolved since ancient times.[9] As currently structured, VOM's relationship to the criminal justice system disserves the interests of victims, offenders, and the state.

VOM disserves the interests of victims by stressing forgiveness and rec-

---

[6] ROBERT B. COATES & JOHN GEHM, VICTIM MEETS OFFENDER: AN EVALUATION OF VICTIM-OFFENDER RECONCILIATION PROGRAMS 4 (1985) (surveyed offenders said that their primary goal in participating in VOM was to "avoid harsher punishment"). Indeed, Mark Umbreit, a proponent of VOM who has written extensively on the subject, admits that offenders often feel coerced into participating: "once they're in the criminal justice arena, there's a large amount of state coercion." Wendy Benedetto, *Victims, Offenders Meet Face to Face*, USA TODAY, September 9, 1991, at 11A col. 1 (interview of Mark Umbreit) [hereinafter Interview]. *See also* Mark S. Umbreit, *Mediation of Victim Offender Conflict*, 1988 J. DISP. RESOL. 85, 89 (1988) ("The rhetoric of much of the literature in the field . . . would imply that offender participation in the mediation process is also voluntary. Actual practice in the field would suggest something quite different.").

[7] Umbreit, *supra* note 6, at 91 ("If victim and offender are unable to agree upon the amount or form of restitution, the case is referred back to the referral source (oftentimes the sentencing judge), with a good likelihood that the offender will be placed in a different program.").

[8] *See, e.g.*, Victoria E. Lawry, *Victim Offender Reconciliation Program in Polk County*, IOWA LAW ALERT, April 1992, at 1 (the defendant's participation in VOM "may result in a reduction in charge, or an agreement by the prosecutor not to resist probation in lieu of a harsher sentence"). Much of VOM is designed to displace conventional punishment, as reflected in the literature of the Elkhart, Indiana program, which states that the mediation "is not to be used as an additional penalty tacked on a standard sentence." HOWARD ZEHR ET AL., THE VORP BOOK III-20 (1983) [hereinafter THE VORP BOOK].

[9] *See infra* Part V.

onciliation before victims have the vindication of a public finding that the offender is guilty. In addition, VOM suppresses victims' outrage and loss by assuming that these negative feelings can be expressed and resolved in the course of a few hours spent meeting with the offender.

VOM disserves offenders in three ways: by using selection criteria that are not clearly related to the goals of the program; by eliminating procedural protections such as the right to counsel or rules of evidence; and by using the leverage of pending criminal process to gain advantages for the victim, a private party. If offenders believe that they will be worse off in the ordinary criminal justice system should they fail to reach a mediated agreement satisfactory to their victims, the offenders may have an unduly strong incentive to mediate and reach agreement, no matter what the psychological or monetary cost.

VOM characterizes many crimes as private disputes that fracture relationships between individuals; the state's interest in these disputes is minimal.[10] The structure of VOM often belies this assumption, however, because the mediation occurs before a backdrop of state involvement and coercion.[11] Victims of crime negotiate not only with their own individual bargaining strength, but also with the threat of enhanced state punishment should the parties fail to reach agreement.[12] The victim appropriates some of the state's leverage over the offender because both the victim and

---

[10] Dave Gustafson, *Debunking the Myths: Victim-Offender Reconciliation in Serious Crime*, 2(1) VICTIM-OFFENDER MEDIATION 8-9 (1990) (rejecting the notion that "the more serious the offense, the more essential it is to increase the role of the state in the justice process, reducing the victim's role to that of [a government] witness, and leaving the community (to which the offender must one day return) out of the equation altogether"); MARK S. UMBREIT & ROBERT COATES, VICTIM OFFENDER MEDIATION: AN ANALYSIS OF PROGRAMS IN FOUR STATES OF THE U.S. 1 (1992) ("The development of victim offender mediation in recent years has occurred within the larger context of restorative justice theory . . . 'Restorative justice' emphasizes that crime is a violation of one person by another, rather than simply against the State."); THE VORP BOOK, *supra* note 8, at II-4 (victim-offender mediation "recognizes that crime involves a conflict between people, that one person has violated another, and that ways must be found to make things right, to repair the wrong").

[11] Sally Engle Merry, *Myth and Practice in the Mediation Process*, in MEDIATION & CRIMINAL JUSTICE 239, 244 (Martin Wright & Burt Galaway eds., 1989) [hereinafter MEDIATION & CRIMINAL JUSTICE] ("Mediation risks creating a coercive process under the rhetoric of voluntariness, participation, and community involvement.").

[12] Martin Wright, *Introduction* to MEDIATION & CRIMINAL JUSTICE, *supra* note 11, at 1, 9 (stating that mediation will be "free from any coercion" only if the prosecutor decides beforehand to drop the criminal case unconditionally); FORUM FOR INITIATIVES IN REPARATION AND MEDIATION, AN INTERIM RESPONSE TO "REPARATION: A DISCUSSION DOCUMENT" (1986) (suggesting separation of mediation from the criminal justice process, because "the offender should not feel constrained

the offender know that the offender is more likely to be prosecuted or incarcerated if the victim is not satisfied with the negotiation.[13]

VOM disserves the interests of the state because it devalues the substantive and procedural norms observed in public processes. Despite proponents' claims that VOM can resolve criminal cases according to the substantive standards of the "community" in which the crime occurred, such a community rarely exists in the United States today apart from the state itself. When centralized rules of criminal law are rejected in the name of a "community" that may not even exist, any standard may fill the vacuum to resolve individual cases. Success is measured by the victim's satisfaction with the outcome rather than consistency with substantive legal rules. VOM programs ignore procedural norms because the end (the parties' ability to reach agreement) often justifies the means (lack of counsel for the offender, coercion prior to and during the mediation).[14]

This Article calls for a decoupling[15] of mediation from the criminal justice system: the success or failure of the mediation should have no impact on the offender's prosecution or punishment. The Article suggests several procedural rules to effect such a separation. A "Chinese wall" between VOM and the criminal justice system is necessary to protect the integrity of the system and the integrity of mediation as a fundamentally voluntary process.

A Chinese wall would address the dangers of VOM to victims, because

---

into admitting guilt and taking part reluctantly in mediation by the prospect of risking a custodial sentence otherwise").

[13] *See* Jennifer Gerarda Brown, *Blackmail as Private Justice*, 141 U. PA. L. REV. 1935, 1968 (1993). Some victim-offender mediation programs may unwittingly create a dynamic between victim and offender that is dangerously close to blackmail. *See also* James Lindgren, *Unraveling the Paradox of Blackmail*, 84 COLUM. L. REV. 670 (1984) (blackmail occurs when a person appropriates the leverage or bargaining power of the state for his or her own gain). Both blackmail and VOM arguably involve "private" justice. Both are decentralized. Both involve "bargaining in the shadow of the (criminal) law." *See* Robert Mnookin & Lewis Kornhauser, *Bargaining in the Shadow of the Law: The Case of Divorce*, 88 YALE L.J. 950 (1979). And both undermine or at least dilute the state's power to interpret and apply the criminal law, and thereby declare societal norms. Brown, *supra*, at 1969.

[14] This use of desirable results to justify suspect methods is ironic, since a more general utilitarian justification of the criminal law based upon theories of deterrence would meet with disapproval from most VOM proponents. *See infra* note 67.

[15] *See* JOHN HAGAN, STRUCTURAL CRIMINOLOGY 100 (1989) (observing that U.S. courts are part of a "loosely coupled" system, which "can take on new appendages . . . while at the same time ignoring the activities of those appendages").

it would preserve an independent process and the opportunity for catharsis that a public process could offer. The dangers to offenders would be decreased if a Chinese wall were in place because the separation would reduce incentives for prosecutors and program administrators to coerce offender participation. The dangers of VOM to the state would be reduced if the process were separated from the criminal justice system because the Chinese wall would preserve the public forum for public purposes.

These conclusions are subject to an important qualification: If VOM proponents and prosecutors could show that VOM does promote deterrence or rehabilitation, then it might be reintegrated into the criminal justice system.[16] This qualification is consistent with a larger theme: public coercion should only be used to vindicate public interests. To the extent that mediation is shown to further the goals of rehabilitation or specific deterrence, conditioning prosecution on mediation and its results is appropriate.

But the standard for proving that VOM promotes the traditional goals of the criminal law should be rigorous. And even if the system incorporates victim-offender mediation to resolve criminal cases, additional process is required to insure that selection criteria are fair, that the process and its outcomes are as noncoercive as possible (within an admittedly coercive system), and that the public is afforded some opportunity to monitor mediation and its results through regular judicial review. This Article suggests various procedural guidelines that might reduce the dangers, including the provision of counsel for indigent offenders who participate in

---

[16] Little empirical work has been done to determine the consequences of VOM and its effects on victim and offender. *See* UMBREIT & COATES, *supra* note 10; Stella P. Hughes & Anne L. Schneider, *Victim-Offender Mediation: A Survey of Program Characteristics and Perceptions of Effectiveness*, 35 CRIME & DELINQ. 217 (1989); Stella P. Hughes & Anne L. Schneider, *Victim Offender Mediation: A Survey of Program Characteristics and Perceptions of Effectiveness*, 2(1) VICTIM-OFFENDER MEDIATION 4 (1990); Mark S. Umbreit, *Victim/Offender Mediation: A National Survey*, L(4) FED. PROBATION 53 (1986); Mark S. Umbreit & Robert B. Coates, *The Impact of Mediating Victim Offender Conflict: An Analysis of Programs in Three States*, 3(3) VICTIM-OFFENDER MEDIATION 3 (1992). Although VOM programs may, because of their diversity and small size, be particularly difficult to study, it should be noted that some VOM advocates have drawn questionable conclusions from research projects suffering from very small samples or other methodological flaws. *See, e.g.*, Mark Stein, *A View of Two Counties: When Fully Utilized, Victim-Offender Mediation Reduces Convictions, Prison Commitments*, 3(2) VICTIM-OFFENDER MEDIATION 8 (1992) (differences in conviction rates of two "small, rural southern Indiana count[ies]" attributed to the fact that one had VOM and the other did not).

VOM, court monitoring of mediation agreements, and strict enforcement of rules that exclude from trial and sentencing any evidence of failed mediation attempts.

By proposing a separation between mediation and the criminal justice system, I intentionally seek to eliminate one of the stated goals of most VOM programs: to serve as an alternative to incarceration. Allowing offenders to buy their way out of prison with monetary and nonmonetary compensation to victims unacceptably confounds the private goals of mediation and the public goals of criminal law.[17] If a jurisdiction is serious about creating alternatives to incarceration, then the state, rather than crime victims or private administrators of VOM programs, ought to decide whether offenders are entitled to such alternatives. And the state should place these alternatives in the hands of private parties only after they have fully accounted for the "process dangers"[18] of such a change.

In Part I, the Article presents a brief history of the VOM movement, describes in greater depth the variety of VOM programs currently operating, and explains VOM's relationship to the broader "victims' rights" movement. Part II argues that the coupling of mediation with the criminal justice system creates an unacceptably coercive context for the parties' decision to take part in mediation and for the mediation itself. Parts III through V argue that as currently structured VOM disserves the interests of victims, offenders, and the state. The Article concludes by recommending a decoupling of mediation and the criminal justice system that will reduce the potential for unfair processes and results.

---

[17] Some commentators note that a complete separation of mediation from the criminal justice system, and a commitment by judges not to take mediated restitution into account when sentencing, could "make the offender feel that he has paid twice for his offence." Martin Wright, *Introduction* to MEDIATION AND CRIMINAL JUSTICE, *supra* note 11, at 11. Because a crime gives rise to both public and private harm, however, "paying twice" may be the most appropriate sanction for the offender. *See* Frieder Dünkel & Dieter Rössner, *Law and Practice of Victim/Offender Agreements*, in MEDIATION AND CRIMINAL JUSTICE, *supra* note 11, at 152; David Watson et al., *Reparation for Retributivists*, in MEDIATION AND CRIMINAL JUSTICE, *supra* note 11, at 212.

[18] The phrase is taken from the title of Trina Grillo's fine article, *The Mediation Alternative: Process Dangers for Women*, 100 YALE L.J. 1545 (1991). Her thoughtful examination of mediation's pitfalls in the context of divorce has informed much of the analysis in this Article. Professor Grillo reminds us that even as we celebrate the promise of mediation, we must guard against applications of the process that might undermine its credible use in more appropriate contexts.

I. BACKGROUND AND HISTORY

A. *Criminal Law Evolved to Reduce the Role of Victims*

Originally, criminal cases were prosecuted by private individuals, often by means of "blood feuds." Remedies focused on compensating individual victims rather than achieving public goals of deterrence, retribution, or rehabilitation. Over time, however, the law gradually changed; the criminal action became state property. This transformation occurred for a variety of economic, sociological, political, and philosophical reasons.

Although we tend now to think of the criminal law as inherently public,[19] in the early days of Western legal systems, private individuals prosecuted criminals and meted out punishment. The criminal law was primarily concerned with victims' compensation or revenge.[20] Criminal law became a matter of public interest with the close of the Anglo-Saxon period in English history and the rise of feudalism. In the Middle Ages, the system of "composition" combined public punishment with private damages so that crime victims and their families could collect satisfaction from wrongdoers.[21] Increasingly, however, intentionally harmful acts were considered offenses against the monarch's peace rather than individual victims, and a structured court system developed to redress these public wrongs.[22]

---

[19] Blackstone's Commentaries, so influential in England and the United States, are representative: "Upon the whole, we may observe that in taking cognizance of all wrongs, or unlawful acts, the law has a double view, *viz.*, not only to redress the party injured, by either restoring to him his right, if possible, or by giving him an equivalent . . . but also to secure to the public the benefit of society, by preventing or punishing every breach and violation of those laws which the sovereign power has thought proper to establish, for the government and tranquillity of the whole." J.W. EHRLICH, EHRLICH'S BLACKSTONE 731 (1959).

[20] The Torah, the Code of Hammurabi, ancient English and Germanic law, Greek law, and Roman law all provided for compensation for victims of crime. *See* STEPHEN SCHAFER, COMPENSATION AND RESTITUTION TO VICTIMS OF CRIME (2d ed. 1970); Note, *Victim Restitution in the Criminal Process: A Procedural Analysis*, 97 HARV. L. REV. 931, 933 n.18 (1984).

[21] Interestingly, even composition relied upon centralized authority sufficiently strong to "enforce the expedient of composition upon a reluctant and revengeful family." L.T. Hobhouse, *Law and Justice*, in CONSIDERING THE VICTIM: READINGS IN RESTITUTION AND VICTIM COMPENSATION 8 (Joe Hudson & Burt Galaway eds., 1975) [hereinafter READINGS].

[22] Some historians argue that crime and punishment as matters of public interest in England stemmed from the strength of the Church and the adoption of Roman law around the twelfth century. Other historians contend that criminal law grew simply to justify the king's appropriation of part of the victim's compensation. *See* SCHAFER, *supra* note 20, at 4-7 ("In Saxon England, the Wer or payment for homicide and the Bot, the betterment or compensation for injury, existed alongside the

As the state established a monopoly on punishment, the rights of crime victims were gradually severed from the criminal law.[23] The system of the "blood feud" and revenge as the principal remedy for wrongdoing became obsolete. However, as L.T. Hobhouse observes, the transformation of the criminal law from private to public enforcement was a mixed blessing for offenders: "[I]f the kindred be no longer allowed to avenge themselves, the corresponding right of the offender to make peace with the kin is also withdrawn. A crime is now a public affair."[24]

In Colonial America, crime remained a private matter, and victims were responsible for apprehending and punishing criminals. Victims could arrest offenders themselves, or pay sheriffs to make the arrests. Victims would hire private attorneys to prosecute cases, and they could collect damages from the convicted defendants, bind them to servitude, or pay for their incarceration by public authorities.[25] By the early 1800s, however, imprisonment became the most prevalent form of criminal punishment and the victim's role diminished dramatically.[26] The rise of imprisonment occurred as crime came to be considered more a breach of the general peace than a private injury to the victim. The state set out to punish and deter, shifting its focus to the offender and concentrating less on compensation to the victim.

B. VOM is a Product of the "Victims' Rights" Movement

Although the state achieved its monopoly in criminal law enforcement centuries ago, in recent years activists have worked to swing the pendulum back toward greater involvement by victims in the criminal process. As one mechanism to increase victims' roles, VOM has been lauded by some

---

Wite or fine paid to the king or overlord.") (footnotes omitted). Richard Laster argues that these various approaches are consistent because "without the rise of kingship, a structured court system, and the acceptability of punishment as an aim of the law, a system of fines payable to a centralized authority might never have been instituted." Richard E. Laster, *Criminal Restitution: A Survey of its Past History and An Analysis of its Present Usefulness,* in READINGS, *supra* note 21, at 23.

[23] *See* SCHAFER, *supra* note 20, at 7 ("[C]omposition, as the obligation to pay damages, became separated from the criminal law and became a special field in civil law.") (citations omitted).

[24] READINGS, *supra* note 21, at 18.

[25] ROBERT ELIAS, THE POLITICS OF VICTIMIZATION 11-12 (1986); Karen L. Kennard, *The Victim's Veto: A Way to Increase Victim Impact on Criminal Case Dispositions,* 77 CAL. L. REV. 417, 419-20 (1989); William F. McDonald, *Towards a Bicentennial Revolution in Criminal Justice: The Return of the Victim,* 13 AM. CRIM. L. REV. 649 (1976).

[26] Kennard, *supra* note 25, at 420.

activists as a benefit to victims.[27] Other victims' advocates have been skeptical of VOM.[28] A substantial body of literature has grown to document the existence of a rising victims' rights movement. The movement to amend state constitutions to include some provisions for victims' rights began in the early 1980s, when President Reagan's Task Force on Victims of Crime recommended that the Sixth Amendment to the U.S. Constitution be changed to guarantee that "the victim, in every criminal prosecution, shall have the right to be present and to be heard at all critical stages of judicial proceedings."[29] Soon after that, California became the first state to grant constitutional status to a Victims' Bill of Rights.[30] Rhode Island followed with a constitutional amendment granting victims the right to restitution, to submit victim impact statements at sentencing, and to be treated "with dignity and respect."[31] According to the National Victim Center, thirteen states have enacted constitutional amendments recognizing victims' rights.[32]

In addition to their work on constitutional measures, advocates have sought to make procedural rules more sensitive to the needs of victims. Though varied, these proposals often are designed to: (1) keep suspects in custody following arrest; (2) reduce delay between arrest, preliminary hearing, and trial; (3) eliminate plea bargaining or give victims greater input in that process; (4) minimize or eliminate cross-examination of victims by defense counsel; (5) discard the exclusionary rule; (6) allow vic-

---

[27] *See, e.g.*, T. CRAWFORD ET AL., RESTORATIVE JUSTICE: PRINCIPALS 6 (1990) (VOM seen as a reform that "addresses the needs of victims"); Lawry, *supra* note 8, at 1 (VOM programs are "first and foremost victim oriented").

[28] Lisa G. Lerman, *Mediation of Wife Abuse Cases: The Adverse Impact of Informal Dispute Resolution on Women*, 7 HARV. WOMEN'S L.J. 57 (1984); Kelly Rowe, Comment, *The Limits of the Neighborhood Justice Center: Why Domestic Violence Cases Should Not Be Mediated*, 34 EMORY L.J. 855 (1985).

[29] NATIONAL VICTIM CTR., A CHRONOLOGY OF THE VICTIMS' RIGHTS CONSTITUTIONAL AMENDMENT MOVEMENT (June 1991).

[30] CAL. CONST. art. I § 28.

[31] R.I. CONST. art. I § 23.

[32] These states are Arizona (ARIZ. CONST. art. II § 2.1); California (*supra* note 30); Colorado (COLO. CONST. art. II § 16A); Florida (FLA. CONST. art. I § 16); Illinois (ILL. CONST. art. I § 8.1); Kansas (KAN. CONST. art. XV § 15); Michigan (MICH. CONST. art. I § 24); Missouri (MO. CONST. art. I § 32); New Jersey (N.J. CONST. art. I ¶ 22); New Mexico (N.M. CONST. art. II § 24); Rhode Island (*supra* note 31); Texas (TEX. CONST. art. I § 30), and Washington (WASH. CONST. art. I § 35). Additional states have passed legislation authorizing a constitutional amendment that requires voter ratification or have introduced legislation dealing with victims' rights.

tims to participate in sentencing; (7) guarantee that victims receive full restitution;[33] and (8) grant victims a right to mediate with the offender.[34]

C. VOM Seeks to Include Victims When Resolving Criminal Cases

Victim-offender mediation can be viewed in some ways as an attempt to turn back the clock of legal history to a time when the criminal law retained its focus on victims and compensating their losses. In this Section, I provide some descriptive background on VOM and one influential type of victim-offender mediation called Victim-Offender Reconciliation Programs ("VORP"). VORP ideology and agendas have had tremendous influence on the development of victim-offender mediation, even in programs that do not use the VORP label.

1. A Short History of VOM

One night in 1974, two young men in Kitchener, Ontario vandalized the property of twenty-two people: They broke windows, slashed tires, and damaged churches, stores, and cars. They pled guilty to twenty-two charges. The offenders did not pay restitution to the court clerk's office, however. Instead, in an experiment jointly administered by the probation department's volunteer program and the Mennonite Central Committee, the two young offenders met with each victim.[35] It was hoped that meeting with the victims would help the offenders to see the restitution payments less as fines and more as compensation to real people for the losses they had suffered. Within six months, the young men had fulfilled their

---

[33] Lynne N. Henderson, *The Wrongs of Victim's Rights*, 37 STAN. L. REV. 937, 967-68 (1985) (footnotes omitted).

[34] An Indiana statute provides in pertinent part that "[i]n a county having a victim offender reconciliation program (VORP)," the victim shall have an opportunity, "if the accused person or the offender agrees," to:

(A) Meet with the accused person or the offender in a safe, controlled environment;

(B) Give to the accused person or the offender, either orally or in writing, a summary of the financial, emotional, and physical effects of the offense on the victim and the victim's family; and

(C) Negotiate a restitution agreement to be submitted to the sentencing court for damages incurred by the victim as a result of the offense.

IND. CODE ANN. § 33-14-10-5(a)(7) (Burns 1992).

[35] One of the probation officers involved in the case admitted that the methods used to facilitate these meetings were crude: "We were pretty brutal . . . . We walked up to the door. They [the boys] knocked. We stood back with our note pads." ZEHR, *supra* note 4, at 159.

restitution obligations in full. Many see this case as the birth of VOM, because the success of this experiment encouraged others to continue to develop the program.[36]

In the mid-1970s similar programs were developing in the United States. The Minneapolis Restitution Center, for example, offered criminal offenders the opportunity to live and work outside the prison setting in order to make restitution payments to the victims of their crimes.[37] As part of the program, offenders would meet with their victims in the presence of a program counselor to discuss the terms of restitution payment.[38] A comparable program in the state of Oklahoma began to require juvenile offenders to make contact (in person or by letter) with the victims to whom they owed restitution.[39]

VOM programs have multiplied dramatically. Today, more than 100 VOM programs exist in the United States.[40] In 1993, U.S. programs disposed of 16,500 cases, involving 12,931 victims and 14,059 offenders.[41] The growth of victim-offender mediation parallels an increased interest in restitution for victims of crime.[42] VOM is seen as a cheap, informal way

---

[36] *See* HOWARD ZEHR, MEDIATING THE VICTIM-OFFENDER CONFLICT 2 (1980).

[37] Burt Galaway & Joe Hudson, *Introduction: Towards Restorative Justice, in* CRIMINAL JUSTICE, RESTITUTION, AND RECONCILIATION 1 (Burt Galaway & Joe Hudson eds., 1990).

[38] MARK UMBREIT, VICTIM OFFENDER MEDIATION: CONFLICT RESOLUTION AND RESTITUTION 1 (1985).

[39] *Id.* It might be important to know the factors that established similarity between offenders. An alternative explanation for the higher performance rate in the mediated group is that more responsible, mature offenders were more likely to participate in mediation. It is not clear, as the study suggests, that mediation caused participants to behave more responsibly.

[40] *See* DIRECTORY, *supra* note 2, at 1 (the 1993 directory lists 123 programs in the U.S. and "an additional 63 non-U.S."). *See also* ZEHR, *supra* note 4, at 159.

[41] DIRECTORY, *supra* note 2, at 1.

[42] *See generally* BARBARA SMITH ET AL., IMPROVING ENFORCEMENT OF COURT-ORDERED RESTITUTION 1 (1989) ("Over the past several decades, restitution for crime victims has received favorable attention from judges, corrections officials, legislators, and the public as an appropriate criminal sanction for defendants."); ELMAR GEORGE & MARIA WEITEKAMP, RESTITUTION: A NEW PARADIGM OF CRIMINAL JUSTICE OR A NEW WAY TO WIDEN THE SYSTEM OF SOCIAL CONTROL 47 (1989) ("While restitution has been around in various forms for a thousand years, it became more visible in the early 1970s as a distinct and separate form of the criminal justice system."); Alan Harland, *Monetary Remedies for the Victims of Crime: Assessing the Role of the Criminal Courts*, 30 UCLA L. REV. 52, 55-56 (1982) ("Legislative and judicial interest in pursuing restitution through the criminal process has been paralleled in this decade by a rapid growth in the number of restitution programs, operated by every type of agency in the system, from police to parole authorities.") (citations omitted); Kevin McLean, *The Propriety of Imposing Joint and Several Restitutionary Liability as a Condition of a Criminal Offender's Probation*, 51 BROOK. L. REV. 809, 811 (1985) ("Victim

to determine the amount of restitution to be paid, while at the same time allowing for some interaction between victim and offender.[43] The expectations for that interaction vary highly from one program to another. Some victim-offender mediation programs strive not just to establish restitution agreements, but actually to effect some "reconciliation" between the victim and the offender, resolving conflict that the crime has created.[44] These more ambitious goals are frequently found in mediation programs that operate under the name "VORP"—Victim-Offender Reconciliation Programs.[45]

2. *Victim-Offender Reconciliation: the Christian Roots of VOM*

VORP is an important root of victim-offender mediation. Even many programs that do not publicly broadcast a VORP orientation continue internally to follow a VORP-directed agenda of "reconciliation."[46] This agenda permeates many VOM programs that are administered by state officials and community organizations, and is not limited to church-based programs.

---

restitution, as an element of the criminal justice system, is currently the focus of considerable public and legislative attention.") (citations omitted); Note, *Victim Restitution in the Criminal Process: A Procedural Analysis*, 97 HARV. L. REV. 931, 931-932 (1984) ("In their search for new sentencing options, legislatures and commissions have increasingly turned to restitution.") (citations omitted).

[43] ZEHR, *supra* note 36, at 16 (listing cost savings as one of the advantages of VOM to the criminal justice system).

[44] *See* John Gehm, *Introduction*, in THE VORP BOOK, *supra* note 8, at 2 ("VORP is not meant to be simply court-ordered restitution in which the victim and offender meet in the presence of a criminal justice official to determine how much restitution can be paid, and how soon.").

[45] A note about terminology may be appropriate at this point. Not all programs involving victim-offender mediation are VORP programs. Many programs that are called VORP have retained the spirit of the original programs without an explicit affiliation with the Mennonite church. Some programs are called VORP but stress restitution almost exclusively and do not consider reconciliation to be a goal of the program at all. As the editors of the most recent VOM program directory note:

> What's in a word? How programs self-identify within the broader fields of mediation and dispute resolution is of some interest. Fully 65 programs [out of 186], both old and new, use the word "VORP" (Victim-Offender Reconciliation Program) to describe what they do; 32 use the word "mediation" to describe their program.

DIRECTORY, *supra* note 2, at 1.

[46] *See* Tony Dittenhoffer & Richard V. Ericson, *The Victim/Offender Reconciliation Program: A Message to Correctional Reformers*, 33 U. TORONTO L.J. 315, 332 (1983) (describing a training manual for volunteer mediators which explicitly instructs that "the word 'reconciliation' is never to be used in gaining the support of the victim and that a discussion and payment of losses are given as the essential reasons for a meeting").

Initiated by Mennonite reformers in Canada and the United States—principally in the Midwest—VORP programs generally aspire to different goals than the criminal justice system. The Justice Fellowship, a research and policy institute based in Washington D.C. that promotes victim-offender mediation, has declared its aspirations for criminal justice reform:

> 1. To provide victims and offenders in every community with opportunities for reconciliation through church-based programs;
> 2. To offer victims of crime in every community crisis intervention services through local churches;
> 3. To sentence nondangerous offenders to reparative sanctions rather than to prison; and
> 4. To grant victims a formal role in the criminal justice system, including the right to participate (with legal representation) in criminal cases to pursue restitution.[47]

Although VORP proponents assert that the methodology of the process is consistent with a variety of criminal justice goals—such as rehabilitation, crime prevention, and restitution—the "primary" goal of VORP is "reconciliation."[48] The writers of one guide to VORP explain:

> We recognize that this is an unusual goal in criminal justice circles, and that [it] is a difficult goal to define and measure. However it is defined, though, we mean that our first priority is on relationships: we focus on the relational aspects of crime. Attitudes, feelings and needs of both victims and offender[s] must be taken very seriously. Healing is important.[49]

VORP programs are driven by a strong Christian theological foundation. Indeed, Howard Zehr, who has written extensively on restorative justice and VORP, says that the church should play a "critical" role in maintaining and nurturing VORP: "VORP embodies a vision of justice

---

[47] CRAWFORD ET AL., *supra* note 27, at 6. The frontispiece to this monograph includes the following note: "Justice Fellowship's mission is to promote biblical standards of justice in the American criminal system by working for reforms based on restorative justice principles. Its strategy is to restore balance by giving priority to reforms which address the needs of victims."

[48] THE VORP BOOK, *supra* note 8, at II-5. Proponents also say that VORP is consistent with encouraging accountability and creating an alternative to incarceration, though one might ask how "traditional" these goals are.

[49] *Id.*

that is inherently biblical and thus provides an arena where the church can implement its vision."[50] The VORP Book, a kind of operations manual for victim-offender mediation programs, states that "[t]he VORP concept is deeply rooted in Judeo-Christian concepts and is uniquely suited to the ministry of the church."[51]

That vision, according to Zehr, includes an understanding of justice radically different from the "retributive" perspective adopted by the existing criminal justice system.[52] Zehr contrasts "retributive" and "restorative" justice according to various factors. While retributive justice assumes that "crime violates the state and its laws," restorative justice assumes that crime violates "people" and "relationships."[53] The retributive paradigm grants a "state monopoly on response to wrongdoing," while restorative justice recognizes "victim, offender, and community roles."[54] Justice in a retributive system is "tested by intent and process," while in the restorative system, justice is "tested by its 'fruits.' "[55] The values underlying each system are also contrasted: Retributive justice promotes "competitive, individualistic values," while restorative justice encourages "mutuality and cooperation."[56] These are among more than thirty such dichotomies that Zehr uses to distinguish "restorative" justice from "retributive" justice.[57]

---

[50] ZEHR, *supra* note 4, at 173. Interestingly, many VORP programs operate in the context of state-run sentencing or probation systems. Even these state-run programs sometimes retain the "VORP" moniker. How much of the original philosophy and theology remains in the administration of the program and the training of mediators? Is it possible that such programs could give rise to problems of separation of church and state?

[51] THE VORP BOOK, *supra* note 8, at III-4.

[52] ZEHR, *supra* note 4, at 150. It is interesting that one of VOM's greatest proponents chooses retribution as the defining characteristic of our criminal justice system, despite the system's other, arguably more important, goals. *See infra* Part I.D.

[53] ZEHR, *supra* note 4, at 153.

[54] *Id.* at 212.

[55] *Id.* at 213. Indeed, the emphasis on substantive outcome rather than procedural regularity is a striking feature of much of the literature advocating VOM. This may be VOM's most radical departure from the criminal justice tradition in this country.

[56] *Id.* at 214.

[57] Zehr's distinctions between "retributive" and "restorative" perspectives quickly reveal his advocacy for one and rejection of the other. For example, in an extensive comparative chart late in the book, Zehr attributes to the "retributive" perspective the following qualities: "[o]ne social injury added to another," "[v]ictims' suffering ignored," "[p]rocess alienates," and "[i]mposition of pain considered normative." In contrast, Zehr describes the "restorative" perspective with the following language: "[p]roblem-solving central," [r]esponsible behavior encouraged," and "[m]akes possible win-win outcomes." *Id.* at 212-14.

D. *How VOM Programs Work*

Most VOM programs involve face-to-face meetings between crime victims and offenders in the presence of trained mediators.[58] Beyond this basic description, VOM programs defy generalization. The programs vary in two important ways: They aspire to different goals and they exploit different degrees of state coercion. The differences are significant because they affect the extent to which VOM serves the interests of victims, offenders, and the state.

VOM programs aspire to various ends. Sometimes their goals are not articulated explicitly, but are reflected in operational details of the programs, such as the criteria used to select cases for mediation. Some VOM programs focus on cases involving misdemeanors—mostly nonviolent property crimes.[59] Some programs limit their cases to felonies.[60] Most programs mediate some combination of misdemeanors and felonies.[61] Some proponents of VOM even encourage its use in select cases of violent felonies, including homicide, armed robbery, and rape.[62] Selection criteria reflect the different program goals. The more serious the crimes a program is willing to mediate, the more that program probably aspires to serve as an alternative to incarceration. In addition, programs that mediate more serious crimes reflect a willingness to displace some of the state's

---

[58] Some programs do not require face-to-face meetings, but allow parties to meet with the mediator by phone, or allow the mediator to act as a go-between, caucusing with each party individually to work out a restitution agreement. *See* Dittenhoffer & Ericson, *supra* note 46, at 329 ("Frequently, there was no victim/offender meeting throughout the process."). Some programs do not train their mediators at all. *See* Hughes & Snyder, *supra* note 16, at 5.

[59] Most common are cases of vandalism, burglary, or simple assault. A 1992 survey conducted by the U.S. Association for Victim Offender Mediation revealed that only 11% of the programs responding accepted exclusively misdemeanor cases. *See generally* DIRECTORY, *supra* note 2.

[60] In the 1992 survey, 10% of the responding programs accepted only felony cases. *See generally id.*

[61] For example, the Elkhart, Indiana VORP reported that 82% of the cases the program handled were felony-level cases. DIRECTORY, *supra* note 2, at 13.

[62] *See* Mark S. Umbreit, *Violent Offenders and Their Victims, in* MEDIATION AND CRIMINAL JUSTICE, *supra* note 11, at 99, 111 (though urging caution in these extended applications, Umbreit notes that "some of the most fundamental goals of the VORP model appear to be even more relevant when applied in some cases involving violent victim/offender conflict"). *See also Sonya Live* (CNN television broadcast, Jan. 28, 1993) [hereinafter, CNN Transcript] (featuring shooting victim in armed robbery who mediated case with man who shot him, and son of murdered woman who mediated case with his mother's killer); *Real Life with Jane Pauley* (NBC television broadcast, May 26, 1991) (case of rape mediated).

authority, since states presumably take a greater interest in resolving more serious cases.

The diverse goals of programs involving victim-offender mediation are also reflected in their relative entanglement in the criminal justice system. Most VOM programs are distinguishable from standard community mediation programs (even though community mediation programs may also handle cases involving technically criminal conduct) because the VOM programs mediate cases in which the participants' roles as victim and wrongdoer are more clearly determined.[63] Indeed, community mediation programs receive referrals primarily from civil, rather than criminal, courts. Community mediation programs provide an alternative to the adversary system altogether, diverting cases before they even enter the criminal justice system.[64] Referrals to VOM, in contrast, are usually made by law enforcement or criminal court personnel after an offender has entered the criminal justice system; often the adversary system takes the case to the point of conviction (following adjudication or a plea).

A final way in which the goals of VOM programs differ is the degree of importance placed on "reconciliation of the conflict (*i.e.*, the expression of feelings; greater understanding of the event and each other; closure)."[65] While many programs concern themselves primarily with hammering out restitution agreements, others also seek to address emotional issues surrounding the crime. This difference can have an especially strong effect on victims. While the potential benefits of "reconciliation" may be great, a program's strong emphasis on this goal could harm victims who are not ready or willing to forgive their offenders.[66]

In addition to different goals, VOM programs display a varying willingness to exploit state coercion. The timing of the mediation can have a tremendous effect on the level of coercion experienced by an offender.[67]

---

[63] *But see infra* Part III.C. (arguing that even in VOM, process tends to be less focused on laying blame than the adversarial system is, and this failure to condemn can harm the victim).

[64] THE VORP BOOK, *supra* note 8, at III-21.

[65] *See* Umbreit, *supra* note 16, at 54.

[66] *See infra* Part III.C.

[67] As Mark Stein made clear in his workshop on starting a VOM program, presented at the 1992 U.S.A. VOM Conference, earlier points of referral to mediation (after the offender has been charged but before the offender enters a plea) may be optimal, for several reasons:

(1) if charges are pending, offenders will recognize that they might be able to mediate and then pay restitution before their cases even come up for hearing;

VOM programs conduct mediation at various points in the criminal justice process: on the early side, some mediations occur after arrest and before any charges are filed; on the late side, some mediations follow an offender's conviction and sentencing. As an offender's case progresses through the system, the offender may gather information about the evidence, the severity of the charges, and the likelihood of conviction. The fear of state punishment may lead offenders to agree both to mediation generally and to a victim's demands specifically.

Programs that conduct mediation early in the criminal process, when the offender still lacks information about the likely outcome of the case, can more effectively exploit the offender's fear of state punishment in order to secure the offender's cooperation. A VOM program appears to lack some of the state's coercive power, because the offender can refuse to mediate. But the offender's freedom to reject mediation can be constrained if the offender fears indirect punishment for the refusal to mediate (this could occur if the offender's failure to cooperate in mediation is taken into account at the time of sentencing).[68] Even if the VOM program does not actively exercise coercive power, it can exploit the offender's fear of state coercion by scheduling mediation at a time when the offender's uncertainty is greatest.[69]

The differences among VOM programs, outlined above, make it diffi-

---

(2) earlier mediation can "take the sting out of what the prosecutor wants to do," thus potentially improving the offender's situation within the system;

(3) the earlier the referral in the process, the more a mediation program can offer to ease the burdens on the court system;

(4) finally, the earlier the referral, the more a VOM program can claim to be an alternative to the system.

Paradoxically, however, the earlier a referral, the greater an offender's uncertainty regarding the likely outcome of his case in the criminal court. Because the offender fears state process and punishment he has not yet begun to experience, the VOM program is able to exploit that potential state coercion to encourage the offender's participation. If the referral occurs later in the criminal justice process, on the other hand, the offender has already absorbed much of the state's coercive power and the VOM program is less able to exploit the offender's fear. *See supra* notes 11-13 and accompanying text.

[68] *See infra* notes 155-57 and accompanying text.

[69] Merry, *supra* note 11, at 245:

The ambiguity of the relationship of mediation to the court, particularly in the case of a court annexed and sponsored programme, fosters genuine uncertainty in the minds of disputants about its voluntary nature and may indeed tempt mediators and programme staff to enhance the authority of the mediation process itself by drawing on the legitimacy and power of the court.

cult to formulate a "typical" model for VOM. For the sake of discussion and argument in this article, let us assume a VOM program that exclusively takes adult offenders.[70] The program receives most of its case referrals from courts and probation officers before the offenders enter a formal guilty plea or receive their sentence. Once referred, each case is assigned to a mediator—in most programs, a volunteer from the community—who contacts the victim and offender individually. If the parties agree to mediate, the mediator sets a time and place for the mediation to be held and conducts the mediation. If the parties reach agreement, they enter into a written contract outlining the provisions of their agreement, both monetary and nonmonetary. The mediator returns a written report[71] of the mediation and a copy of the contract to the VOM program office, and the administrator of the program forwards the contract (often with a copy of the report as well) to the referring agency. In most programs, VOM program staff monitor performance of the contract; in some systems, the probation office will also check to insure that the restitution is paid if it is a condition of probation.[72] If, on the other hand, one of the parties refuses to mediate or the parties cannot resolve the case in mediation, the case is returned to the referring agency—the prosecutor's office, the court, or the probation office. There, the offender will be subject to state prosecution and sentencing. Sometimes the mediator will report back to the referring agency about the case. If the offender was somehow responsible for the failure to resolve the case (by refusing to mediate or agree to the victim's demands), the case will return to the system with the mediator's report and "the judge will have to decide whether to order restitution or alter the sentence in some way."[73] Similarly, if the victim's uncooperative attitude prevented the parties from mediating or reaching agreement, a judge subsequently setting a restitution amount could also be made aware of the

---

[70] Juvenile justice raises special policy issues and therefore the use of VOM for juvenile offenders may not be subject to some of the critique contained in this article. American courts have treated juvenile offenders differently from adults for the better part of the twentieth century. This difference in treatment is epitomized, of course, by the existence of separate juvenile courts. Juvenile courts have emphasized rehabilitation of offenders and restitution of victims more than adult courts. *See generally* Barry C. Feld, *The Transformation of the Juvenile Court*, 75 MINN. L. REV. 691 (1991).

[71] Generally, the report is a summary of the mediation, including preliminary contracts, the meeting between the parties, and the restitution contract. *See* THE VORP BOOK, *supra* note 8, at VI-6 (summarizing the information to be included in the volunteer's report, and suggesting that "[i]t is also helpful to include any reconciliation that may have occurred at the meeting").

[72] For an overview of the VOM process, *see* THE VORP BOOK, *supra* note 8, at II-14.

[73] *Id.* at II-8.

victim's actions.[74] When such consequences can flow from the parties' decisions, serious questions about voluntariness naturally arise. We now turn to this issue.

II. VOLUNTARINESS AND THE VICTIM-OFFENDER DILEMMA

Both the victim and the offender may agree to participate in mediation despite their preference for adjudication because the prosecutor can create a "victim-offender dilemma" and exploit the parties' lack of information about what will happen in the criminal justice system.[75] Because their fates turn in part upon the actions of the other party, with whom they cannot communicate or contract in a binding way, the parties may agree to mediation despite their mutual preference for adjudication. In addition to the coercion created by this victim-offender dilemma, prosecutors can use uncertainty and ignorance to secure participation in mediation.

Because victims do not waive or compromise any civil rights of action simply by agreeing to participate in VOM, VOM proponents may assume that the voluntariness of a victim's decision to participate is not an important issue. After all, if the mediation fails to produce an agreement, the victim may still sue the offender civilly[76] or collect restitution in the criminal court (as part of the offender's punishment).

If the victim is approached by law enforcement officials, however, the fact that the state or its surrogate initiates the discussion may create pressure to take part. Influence on the victim to participate may be especially acute when the relevant government actor has something to gain if mediation occurs in lieu of adjudication. In addition to the pressure inherent in interactions with government representatives, the victim may feel some moral or psychological pressure to participate. The very rhetorical appeal of the program may induce a sense of guilt in a reluctant victim. If the victim is asked to take part in a program that is intended to "enable the

---

[74] *Id.* at II-7 (if the court "feels the victim is too uncooperative, [it] could decide to forgo restitution"). *See also* MARTIN WRIGHT, VICTIM/OFFENDER REPARATION AGREEMENTS 10 (1983) (suggesting that courts should not be informed of the reason the parties failed to reach agreement, but should be allowed to assume that the victim refused to cooperate).

[75] Throughout much of this discussion, I will refer to the prosecutor, but the actor could be any state or private actor (such as a VOM program administrator) who is empowered to make representations to the victim and the offender about the likely result of their agreement or refusal to mediate.

[76] But the cost of private litigation may make this option illusory.

parties to communicate and reach some understanding, rather than to force an outcome,"[77] the victim may feel obstructionist, selfish, or uncooperative if she chooses not to participate. This could be traumatizing to victims who may already be experiencing a sense of vulnerability and loss of control.

Likewise, when offenders participate pursuant to court order, they are bound to feel coerced, and rightly so.[78] But even when a court order is not involved, the offender may often sense that participation is mandatory.[79] Because offenders know that the result of VOM can affect criminal proceedings pending against them, they may believe that if they refuse to participate their refusal may be held against them within the system.[80]

The pressure brought to bear on offenders is suggested by the mediator training handbook for one VOM program. Noting that parties to a case will sometimes try to back out of a mediation session on the day it is scheduled, the manual advises that "[a]s a caseworker, you may need to do some reality testing *re* the implications of rescheduling" and "[i]t is generally easier to encourage the accused to follow through on the agreed-upon

---

[77] East Bay Catholic Charities Victim Offender Reconciliation Program, What Happens When Victim & Offender Meet Face to Face (on file with the author).

[78] See Mark S. Umbreit, Victim-Offender Mediation: Conflict Resolution and Restitution 26 (U.S. Dep't of Justice Nat'l Inst. of Corrections, PACT Inst. of Justice 1985). Orders to participate in mediation as part of a sentence or as a condition of probation cannot be justified by arguing that the offender's rights following conviction are qualified and at that point standards of voluntariness can be relaxed. See Henderson, *supra* note 33, at 1015 (asserting that "once a person is convicted, his or her rights are 'merely conditional' and therefore no formal trial is necessary to determine the amount of restitution required") (citations omitted); *see also* Note, *supra* note 42, at 944. As Professor Henderson has observed, "this argument ignores the fact that if a convicted offender is sued in tort, he does not sacrifice the procedural and evidentiary benefits that other tort defendants have. To treat him differently in the criminal context undermines the purpose of the safeguards in the civil context." Henderson, *supra* note 33, at 1015 n.347.

[79] See Coates & Gehm, *supra* note 6, at 7 ("Contrary to the rhetoric of VORP staff which emphasizes the voluntary nature of participation, offenders participate because they believe they must. This view is also shared by criminal justice officials.").

[80] It is extremely difficult to find any official statement from VOM programs about the consequences of offenders' refusal to participate in VOM, but at least one VOM program administrator has admitted that when offenders refuse to participate in VOM that refusal can sometimes be considered by judges and prosecutors. Mark Stein, Setting Up a VOM Program, Presentation at U.S.A. VOM Conference (June 1992) (notes on file with the author). *See also* Interview, *supra* note 6, at 11A, col. 1 Coates & Gehm, *supra* note 6, at 7 ("[O]ffenders participate because they believe they must."); (Mark Umbreit admits that offenders' participation cannot always be characterized as purely voluntary, because "once they're in the criminal justice arena, there's a large amount of state coercion.").

date; one may need to be a bit more accommodating with the complainant."[81] Another mediation handbook implicitly recognizes the ambiguous nature of offender consent to mediation when it discusses the relative merit of programs geared to juveniles: "In some senses, juveniles are easier to work with [than adults]; there are fewer due process protections and it is easier to get them into the program."[82]

If the offender is led to believe that refusing to participate will bring negative consequences in the system, the offender's consent to VOM is achieved under circumstances that increase the coercion already existing in the system. Similarly, victim participation may be coerced if the prosecutor suggests that a lack of cooperation from the victim may lead to a less desirable outcome in the court system (such as a lower restitution award or a lighter sentence for the offender). Even if the prosecutor does not affirmatively pressure the parties to participate in VOM, the framing of their "choices" can have a tremendous impact on voluntariness. Prosecutors and VOM program administrators may secure the participation of victim and offender by creating a "victim-offender dilemma" much like the famous prisoners' dilemma, exploiting uncertainty about the likelihood and severity of punishment in the criminal court system.[83]

---

[81] YVONNE LESAGE & DOROTHY BARG NEUFELD, CASEWORK MANUAL 7 (1991) (on file with the author).

[82] THE VORP BOOK, *supra* note 8, at III-9.

[83] The "prisoner's dilemma" refers to the tension experienced by two hypothetical suspects who are taken into police custody, charged with a crime, and separated so that they cannot communicate. The prosecutor tells each of them, for example, that if neither confesses to the crime, they will both be prosecuted on a lesser charge and (if convicted) receive a one-year sentence. If they both confess, both will receive an eight year sentence. If one confesses but the other does not the confessor will receive a wrist slap (a few months in jail) and the suspect who does not confess will receive a very harsh sentence of 10 years. The dilemma for each prisoner is that although the prisoners realize that they are jointly better off if they both remain silent, each has an individual incentive to confess regardless of the other's action. *See* STEVEN GOLDBERG ET AL., DISPUTE RESOLUTION 53 (1992). *Cf.* DAVID LAX & JAMES SEBINIUS, THE MANAGER AS NEGOTIATOR: BARGAINING FOR COOPERATION AND COMPETITIVE GAIN 38-41 (1986) (describing the "negotiator's dilemma").

The dilemma assumes that the victim gets satisfaction from punishment of the offender, and feels dissatisfaction if the offender receives little jail time. Empirically, there is some evidence that many victims react this way to the treatment of the offender. *See* Irene Hanson Frieze et al., *Describing the Crime Victim: Psychological Reactions to Victimization*, 18 PROF. PSYCHOL. RES. & PRAC. 299 (1987); U.S. DEP'T OF JUSTICE, SOURCEBOOK OF CRIMINAL JUSTICE STATISTICS 203, 206 & 210 (1991) (public opinion surveys show people think courts deal "not harshly enough with criminals," and worry "criminals are being let off too easily," but they were also divided on whether "it is more important to punish [offenders] for their crimes, or more important to get them started 'on the right road';" 38% said punish and 48% said rehabilitate) [hereinafter SOURCEBOOK].

The victim-offender dilemma can affect not only the parties' decision to participate in VOM, but also their agreement to a particular outcome in mediation. Because offenders know that the outcome of VOM can affect their cases in court (satisfying the victim can help them, and failing to reach agreement can hurt them), they can feel coerced into agreeing to victims' demands. The very context of the mediation could thus create leverage that the victim might exploit against the offender. When mediation can affect a case within the criminal justice system, the assumptions about voluntariness that we would ordinarily entertain about mediation no longer apply. Too often, programs do not make clear the consequences of failing to reach agreement in VOM. The fact that a huge percentage of cases that go to mediation reach agreement could be due to the offender's willingness to meet victim demands rather than meet an uncertain fate back in the criminal court system.[84]

Uncertainty can pressure people away from their ordinary preferences. In VOM, this can undermine voluntariness both for the offender and the victim. As *The VORP Book* describes the process preceding mediation, it reveals the difficult choices participants face:

> As with most mediation programs, a number of cases are dropped because one party—most likely the victim—is unwilling or screened out for some other reason. Such cases would be returned to the court along with a report. The court decides how to proceed from there. *If the offender has been cooperative but the victim unwilling, that is included in the report. The court then may decide simply to require some restitution, but if it feels the victim is too uncooperative, could decide to forgo restitution.* At any rate, a failure to meet under such circumstances should not work to the offender's disadvantage.[85]

The writers of The VORP Book elsewhere display an almost cynical will-

---

[84] *See* Mark Umbreit & Robert Coates, *The Impact of Mediating Victim Offender Conflict: An Analysis in Three States*, 43 JUV. & FAM. CT. J. 21, 24 (1992) (of the 415 mediations studied, 403 resulted in agreements); *cf.* COATES & GEHM, *supra* note 6, at 16 (98% of the face-to-face meetings in the study led to contracts).

[85] THE VORP BOOK, *supra* note 8, at II-7 (emphasis added). Of course, if programs tell the judge when the offender is willing to mediate but the victim is not, then in all other cases where parties fail to meet, the judge can infer that the offender is unwilling. Thus, even if programs refrain from telling judges when the offender is unwilling (so as not to pressure the offender's participation), the judge will know. *See generally* WRIGHT, *supra* note 74 (courts should not be informed of the reason parties failed to reach agreement, but should be allowed to assume victim refused to cooperate).

ingness to exploit the risks for the victim and the offender in the criminal court system, as they discuss the comparative ease with which programs can obtain parties' consent relative to civil mediation programs: "Consent to cooperate by both victim and offender may be easier to obtain because of the *implied threat of the criminal justice process*."[86]

In addition to coercing the parties through the victim-offender dilemma, VOM can undermine voluntariness by giving the parties inadequate information on which to base their decisions. VOM programs vary with respect to the amount of information conveyed to the parties when attempting to gain their consent to participate in the mediation. To guard victims' privacy and security, some VOM programs might tell the victims more about the offenders than they tell offenders about the victims. It would seem important for victims to know something about the offenders that they might face in the mediation. For example, if the offender feels that he has been treated unfairly by police or other law enforcement officials, this attitude could affect the mediation in a way the victim would like to be able to predict.

It could be difficult to balance the need for such information with legitimate concerns about privacy, both for the victim and the offender. Creators of programs need to think carefully about standards of materiality and privacy. Yet it does not appear that most VOM programs have thoroughly addressed the procedures for gaining victim consent to determine what sorts of information to share with the victims.

Nor do VOM programs take steps to ensure that the offender gives informed consent to the mediation. In criminal justice, fairly well-accepted standards have emerged for measuring the voluntariness of a defendant's decisions, such as the decision to plead guilty, to waive a jury trial, or to proceed pro se.[87] The judge is specifically charged with the responsibility to establish on the record that the accused has been advised of her rights

---

[86] THE VORP BOOK, *supra* note 8, at III-21 (emphasis added).

[87] *See, e.g.*, McCarthy v. United States, 394 U.S. 459 (1969) (defendant who pleads guilty simultaneously waives right to confront accusers, but for such waiver to be valid under the Due Process Clause, it must be intentional relinquishment or abandonment of a known right or privilege); Bute v. Illinois, 333 U.S. 640 (1948) (to be valid, a waiver of the constitutional right to assistance of counsel must be given voluntarily, knowingly, and intelligently); Roseman v. United States, 364 F.2d 18 (1966), *cert. denied*, 386 U.S. 918 (1967) (waiver of right to jury trial must be freely and intelligently given, but waiver was not coerced when record showed that each defendant had separate counsel, who waived jury trial in open court after detailed interrogation by trial judge).

and that she knowingly and voluntarily waives those rights. These potentially prejudicial decisions receive far greater scrutiny than the offender's decision to participate in VOM, which may not be counseled or reviewed by a court at all. The decision to leave the justice system and enter VOM should require no less rigorous a judicial review to insure that the offender's decision is informed and voluntary.[88]

The identities of the parties could create imbalances of power and experience at the bargaining table. Offender participants are likely to be juveniles[89] and first-time offenders,[90] two groups who often lack the kind of experience and knowledge of the criminal justice system that might increase their bargaining strength. For example, an offender with greater experience in the criminal justice system might know better when the state's evidence against her is weak, or when, for various substantive and procedural reasons, the state might drop the prosecution even in the absence of an agreement emerging from the mediation. If an offender lacks experience and knowledge of the system, she could be more easily threatened and thus persuaded to participate in VOM or to agree to a victim's demands. Though inexperienced offenders are disadvantaged at almost every turn within the criminal justice system, the dangers are especially grave in VOM, which does not require or even encourage offenders to obtain a lawyer's advice or representation.[91]

---

[88] For example, to be fully informed the offender might need to hear and understand the alternatives to VOM available within the criminal justice system. This is especially important because in many VOM programs, the offender, to some extent, must admit guilt before participating. Offenders should be briefed on the potential benefits and costs of participating.

[89] COATES & GEHM, *supra* note 6, at 6 (78% of the 1983 sample of offenders referred to VORP were juveniles); Mark S. Umbreit, *Victim Offender Mediation and Judicial Leadership*, 69 JUDICATURE 202, 203 (1986) (in Valparaiso, Indiana program "nearly 80 percent of the cases (victim/offender combinations) involved juvenile offenders"); Umbreit & Coates, *supra* note 84, at 21-23 (1992) ("The majority of victim offender mediation programs . . . focus primarily upon juvenile offenders" and the average offender's age is 15). Although this Article has focused on the use of VOM for adult offenders rather than juveniles, it may be important that much of VOM occurs in cases where one party is an adult and the other is a juvenile. The VOM program in Polk County, Iowa, for example, regularly places a juvenile offender in mediation with the victim, a mediator, and an attorney from the county prosecutor's office. When asked whether a juvenile might feel intimidated by having so many adults in the room, one administrator of the program admitted that a little intimidation of the offender (to bring home to the offender the gravity of his actions) is one purpose of the program. Betty Brown, Remarks at the Polk County Attorney's Neighborhood Mediation Center, U.S.A. VOM Conference (1992).

[90] *See* COATES & GEHM, *supra* note 6, at 6 (81% of offenders sampled had no prior convictions).

[91] *See infra* notes 158-59 and accompanying text.

Victim participants may in some cases possess far greater knowledge of the system or have greater bargaining savvy. Sometimes the "victim" at the mediation is an organization, such as an insurance company that may be a "repeat player" in VOM.[92] In many cases, this asymmetry in the identity and background of the individuals who sit at the bargaining table will correlate with disparities in education and resources (for even the organizational participants must send an individual to speak for the organization).

When the mediation involves such an imbalance, the mediator's role is altered considerably. Ordinarily, for example, a mediator may function as an "agent of reality," impressing upon parties the likely consequences of a failure to reach agreement.[93] In VOM, however, the mediator will have difficulty performing this function without seeming to threaten the offender, because "reality checking" with the offender is likely to require the mediator to reiterate the threat of criminal prosecution.[94] Again, the coercive context of the mediation affects the internal dynamic of the mediation, even if representatives of the court system, such as judges or prosecutors, are absent.[95]

---

[92] Dittenhoffer & Ericson, *supra* note 46, at 328-29 (in VORP cases authors studied, two-thirds of the victims were business establishments, not individuals; one in five of the cases "required the reimbursement of insurance companies," even though "insurance companies can only be described as indirect victims"); *see also* Lorraine Stutzman Amstutz, *Mediators*, 1(4) VICTIM OFFENDER MEDIATION 8, 9 (Special Issue 1990).

[93] Mediators often provide the parties with a reality check in order to help them set realistic goals. *See* STEPHEN P. DOYLE & ROGER S. HAYDOCK, WITHOUT THE PUNCHES: RESOLVING DISPUTES WITHOUT LITIGATION 91 (1991); LINDA R. SINGER, SETTLING DISPUTES: CONFLICT RESOLUTION IN BUSINESS, FAMILIES, AND THE LEGAL SYSTEM 20 (1990); *cf.* NANCY H. ROGERS & CRAIG A. MCEWEN, MEDIATION: LAW, POLICY, PRACTICE 9 (1989).

[94] Reality checking is a function that the mediator performs when he or she converses with a party—often in private—about the likely result of a failure to reach a negotiated agreement. *See supra* note 81 and accompanying text. The mediator will often perform this function when it appears that a party has an overly optimistic view of his or her situation. *See* Jennifer Gerarda Brown & Ian Ayres, *Economic Rationales for Mediation*, 80 VA. L. REV. 323, 325 (1994). When a mediator serves as an agent of reality with the victim, the mediator might remind the victim that the offender has offered to pay as much or more than the victim is likely to collect in civil damages or court-ordered restitution. Though this might at times exert some pressure on the victim to agree to a restitution amount or payment schedule, it seems inherently less threatening than the specter of criminal prosecution and possible incarceration that the mediator discusses with the offender.

[95] Merry, *supra* note 11, at 245 ("Some of the disputants I interviewed in various mediation programmes even thought that they had been to court and seen the judge.").

III. DISSERVING THE INTERESTS OF VICTIMS

This Part argues that while VOM grows out of the victims' rights movement, it only selectively addresses victims' concerns. Given the vital emotional issues at stake for most victims, VOM may actually harm victims recovering from crime. Proponents and policy-makers should be sensitive to the risks of a process that asks victims of crime—sometimes violent crime—to face their offenders and negotiate the cases to resolution.[96] This Part analyzes the impact of VOM, emphasizing the risks of the process from a victim's perspective.

A. *Discerning Victims' Interests*

As powerful and important as the victims' rights movement has proven to be, it does not always capture or promote the interests of all victims of crime. Professor Lynne Henderson has argued forcefully that "genuine questions about victims and victimization have become increasingly co-opted by the concerns of advocates of the 'crime control' model of criminal justice."[97] The term "victims' rights", she observes, "has come to mean some undefined, yet irreducible right of crime victims that 'trumps' the rights of criminal defendants."[98] The needs of victims, she argues, are not necessarily served by such measures. Instead, she asserts, we should recognize that the encounter with crime—violent crime, particularly—causes many people to confront "the reality of the unpredictable, the threat of death, the dilemma of meaning, the responsibility for choice, and the reality of isolation" and that people concerned with the interests of victims can "only seek to avoid interfering with or denying the individual victim's efforts to resolve these questions."[99]

Henderson reminds us that a victim's recovery in the wake of crime is a delicate process, and generalizing about what is best for victims is very difficult and dangerous. When analyzing the role of the victim in VOM, then, it is important that we think carefully and inclusively about the

---

[96] VOM programs are supposed to be completely voluntary on the part of the victim, but the structure and rhetoric of some programs may bring subtle pressures to bear on victims, encouraging participation. *See supra* notes 83-85 and accompanying text.

[97] *See* Henderson, *supra* note 33, at 951.

[98] *Id.* at 952.

[99] *Id.* at 965.

preferences and expectations of crime victims. Rushing to judgment about victims and their needs could lead to poor policy choices, and "reforms" of the system that only cause victims greater potential harm. In some respects the VOM movement is consistent with various strands of the victims' rights movement. VOM offers the victim both an opportunity to confront the offender and to receive restitution for the harm done. Aside from monetary compensation, VOM promises healing and reconciliation that many victims may desire. VOM programs give victims an opportunity to see and speak to their offenders, with the hope that such contact will help victims resolve some of their fears of future victimization. This may in turn give victims a greater sense of mobility and freedom to enjoy life instead of taking excessive precautions to avoid harm. In some respects, however, VOM may betray the interests of the victims it seeks to protect. VOM's emphasis on "reconciliation" may inhibit victims' expression of anger and pressure them to forgive their offenders.

B. Deemphasizing the Past and Victims' Need to Express Anger

Some VOM sessions suppress or redirect anger in ways that may be destructive for victims. This suppression may occur if a mediator in VOM enforces the ground rules that generally apply to mediation. Ground rules that forbid blaming and extended discussion of past events facilitate a more forward-looking, problem-solving outlook. In many disputes, such ground rules are appropriate; they focus the parties' discussion on their problem and the means of solving it. In the context of a criminal case, however, these ground rules can be harmful to victims.

Professor Trina Grillo has argued that mediation has its own set of norms for the participants' behavior, and even voluntary mediation can exert subtle pressures on the parties to comply with the "rules" of the process.[100] Grillo writes about this dynamic in the context of divorce and custody mediation, but similar conditions could make people susceptible to pressure in victim-offender mediation: "[T]hey often experience what seems to them a threat to their very survival. Their self-concepts, financial well-being, moral values, confidence in their . . . abilities, and feelings of being worthy of love are all at risk."[101] As Grillo points out, if these con-

---

[100] Grillo, *supra* note 18.
[101] *Id.* at 1556.

ditions cause participants to feel insecure, responses they receive from authority figures and people associated with the justice system can exert particularly powerful influence.[102]

Like mediation generally, victim-offender mediation at some point in the process imposes a "prospectivity" rule; the parties must discuss the future rather than the past.[103] At the same time, victim-offender mediation is supposed to help the parties come to a shared understanding of what happened. A tension between past and future focus exists, then, that is not easily resolved.

If VOM focuses too much attention upon the future, it may actually inhibit discussion of the past, despite its claim to contextualize the crime in ways not possible in the criminal justice system.[104] Most victim-offender mediation sessions include a discussion of "facts and feelings." The mediator might even be trained to raise these topics explicitly.[105] In the course of a mediation, however, the mediator or the offender could decide that the parties have sufficiently established the facts relating to the crime, while the victim wants to continue to discuss the crime and the harm she has suffered in its wake. If VOM imposes the prospectivity rule on victims, it may harm them by disregarding their need to discuss and understand past events.

It has been said of VOM that "in these types of confrontations the victim often has difficulty expressing anger."[106] From a victim's perspec-

---

[102] *See id.*

[103] JAY FOLBERG & ALISON TAYLOR, MEDIATION 14 (1984) ("In mediation past history of the participants is only important in relation to the present or as a basis for predicting future needs, intentions, abilities, and reactions to decisions."); ZEHR, *supra* note 36, at 211 (while "retributive" justice keeps "focus on past," "restorative" justice puts "focus on future"); Grillo, *supra* note 18, at 1563 ("The chief means by which mediators eliminate the discussion of principles and fault is by making certain types of discussion 'off limits' in the mediation.").

[104] Grillo, *supra* note 18, at 1564.

[105] *See, e.g.,* THE VORP BOOK, *supra* note 8, at V-13 (in mediator training materials, writers recommend the discussion of "facts and feelings" before the discussion of restitution).

[106] *Attempted Murder: Confrontation* (Home Box Office, Final Script 14 1991) [hereinafter HBO Transcript]. *But see* Henderson, *supra* note 33, at 996-97. Henderson explains that retaliation may be the victim's first impulse but not the last or the definitive one. While the passage of time may not end a crime victim's anger, it may diminish the retaliatory impulse. Thus, what people choose to alleviate their feelings of anger, particularly after the initial shock of the harm has passed, can vary enormously from physical retaliation to withdrawal, to efforts to prevent future harms, to forgiveness of the offender.
(citation omitted).

tive, adjudication may allow a more satisfying expression of anger than mediation. Professor Trina Grillo has noted that "[d]espite the rational pursuit of self-interest that underlies the adversary system in theory, in practice there is much room for the expression of anger . . . in a formal constrained way through the ritualized behavior of the lawyers."[107] In VOM, on the other hand, victims must speak and act for themselves, and the directness of their contact with offenders may actually inhibit them.

VOM mediators may discourage expressions of deep or volatile anger in the mediation session. For example, Howard Zehr suggests that even after a case has been selected for VOM, if a volunteer senses a very "high level of hostility," the case may be rejected.[108] This recommendation suggests that VOM can only tolerate certain levels of hostility, and victims sensing this may try to keep the feelings they express within the acceptable range.

Some mediators instruct the mediating parties to "own their own feelings" instead of projecting them onto the other party.[109] This requires that they frame the expression of their feelings in a descriptive rather than attributive way: "When you did x, I felt y." "Owning their own feelings" prevents attribution of negative qualities to the listener, focusing instead upon the listener's behavior and its consequences for the speaker.[110] But "owning one's feelings" can also reduce the causal link between the listener's action and the speaker's feeling. When victims are encouraged to "own their own feelings," they may feel compelled to state their experiences in ways that deny the offender's responsibility for causing that emotion.

---

[107] Grillo, *supra* note 18, at 1573.

[108] ZEHR, *supra* note 36, at 11.

[109] Mark Umbreit mediated a case involving Susan Molhan, whose son had been murdered, and the man who killed her son. Discussing the mediation at the U.S.A. VOM Conference in June of 1992, Umbreit emphasized repeatedly that in "coaching" the parties prior to the mediation, he instructed the mother of the victim to "own her feelings" rather than simply accusing the offender and attributing to him an evil character.

[110] *See, e.g.*, Alan Patureau, *Hot & Bothered*, ATLANTA CONST., August 2, 1993, at B1 ("Unfortunately, the angry or uncomfortable person doesn't own his own feelings; he'll blame another person for his discomfort when he should blame the world at large.") (quoting Dr. Loring).

C. *Overemphasizing the Future and Victims' Desire to Forgive Offenders*

The role of forgiveness in VOM is complicated, and it is dangerous to assume that a victim necessarily wants to or can forgive an offender. Some victims of crime may desire a sense of "reconciliation" with offenders, a chance to come to terms with the crime and grant the offender some forgiveness.[111] Although VOM promises such victims the opportunity to meet with their offenders in an atmosphere that might lead to apology and forgiveness, a necessary precondition for forgiveness and reconciliation is an expression of accountability on the part of the offender. VOM cannot force offenders to accept the responsibility and vulnerability that make forgiveness possible. Unless the atmosphere of the mediation is sufficiently normative that some fault can be identified and allocated to the offender, the victim may never get the opportunity to forgive the offender, because their dialogue will never include a shared acknowledgement that the offender requires forgiveness.

When mediation focuses on the future relationship between the parties rather than past interactions, it may avoid allocating blame for events that took place in the past.[112] Some historical analysis is often necessary if the parties are to achieve the goals of "naming, blaming, and claiming" necessary for the recognition and resolution of injury.[113] As Professor Grillo notes, mediation can sometimes impede this process:

> "Naming" involves saying to oneself that a particular experience has been injurious . . . . "Blaming" occurs when a person attributes fault to another (rather than to an impersonal force, such as luck or

---

[111] *See* Henderson, *supra* note 33, at 998 ("Forgiveness alone retains the uncontested authorship essential to responsibility and resolution. Forgiveness, rather than vengeance may, therefore, be the act that eventually frees the victim from the event, the means by which the victim may put the experience behind her.").

[112] *See, e.g.*, Paul Rice, *Mediation and Arbitration as a Civil Alternative to the Criminal Justice System—An Overview and Legal Analysis*, 29 AM. U. L. REV. 17, 23 (1979) ("It is important to recognize that the government's goal need not always be to determine fault, to label conduct criminal, and to level blame at any single person. Mediation/arbitration programs approach antisocial behavior with this awareness. They emphasize the personal responsibility of each party rather than the narrow assessment of legal fault."); John W. Palmer, *The Night Prosecutor*, 59 JUDICATURE 22 (1975) (victim-offender mediation does not require that the parties or the mediator determine the facts precisely, and it does not require stigmatization or allocation of guilt).

[113] *See* William Felstiner et al., *The Emergence and Transformation of Disputes: Naming, Blaming, Claiming . . .* , 15 L. & SOC'Y REV. 631, 633 (1980-81).

the weather). One cannot arrive at "claiming," that is, the assertion of rights, without passing through "blaming." By making blaming off limits, the process by which a dispute is fully developed—and rights are asserted—cannot be completed.[114]

Unless the parties engage in some normative discussion, laying blame on the offender where appropriate, the victim may not be affirmed strongly enough that he or she has behaved appropriately and the offender is the "dysfunctional" party in the case.[115] In many criminal cases, only one party has behaved in a "dysfunctional" manner: the defendant. Yet the victim too often is led to search for ways in which she also shared some blame for the incident.[116]

This danger is of course mitigated by the fact that the mediation occurs in a context in which one person is labeled "offender" and the other "victim."[117] The labels themselves may be enough to vindicate the victim and provide some "blaming" of the offender. On the other hand, one of the goals of VOM is to reposition the parties and to characterize the crime as a wound suffered by both of them.[118] This reframing may reduce the "blame" placed on the offender.

For example, in 1991, HBO broadcast portions of a mediation between Tommy Brown, a man convicted of attempted murder, and Gary Smith,

---

[114] Grillo, *supra* note 18, at 1565 (citations omitted).

[115] *See id.* at 1562 n.72 (observing that, in divorce mediation, the "equal blame theory" "causes the nondysfunctional partner . . . to share the responsibility for the dysfunctional partner's behavior in a way that adversely affects the mediation outcome for the nondysfunctional partner").

[116] *See, e.g.,* William L.F. Felstiner & Lynne A. Williams, *Mediation as an Alternative to Criminal Prosecution: Ideology and Limitations,* 2 LAW & HUM. BEHAV. 223, 236 (1978) (citing illustrative case in which wife agreed not to "nag" her husband in exchange for his promise not to hit her).

[117] In contrast, parties are often sent to community mediation because judges and/or prosecutors believe that neither party is completely innocent and they must share some fault for the incident. *See generally* SALLY ENGLE MERRY, GETTING JUSTICE AND GETTING EVEN (1990) (cases in which the parties are thought to share fault are ejected from the court system, referred to as "garbage cases"). *See also* William J. Kunkle, Jr., *Punishment and the Criminal Justice System: A Prosecutor's Viewpoint,* in CRIME AND PUNISHMENT: ISSUES IN CRIMINAL JUSTICE 63 (Bauman and Jenssen eds., 1989) (contrasting "garbage cases" with "real cases"); CHARLES E. SILBERMAN, CRIMINAL VIOLENCE, CRIMINAL JUSTICE 311 (1978) (comparing "garbage" cases to "real" cases).

[118] ZEHR, *supra* note 36, at 184-85. *See also* Richard W. Evarts, *Compensation Through Mediation: A Conceptual Framework,* in CRIMINAL JUSTICE, RESTITUTION, AND RECONCILIATION 17 (Burt Galaway & Joe Hudson eds., 1990) ("[T]he victim must repair the harm within his power to address. This may take the form of . . . forgiving the perpetrator and contributing to a better social order that will not foster conditions under which crime arises.").

his victim. Brown was serving time in a New York state prison for the crime, and the mediation occurred there. Smith was still recovering from the injuries he had sustained in the attack. Two and a half years before the mediation took place, Brown—under the influence of drugs and alcohol—had interrupted a baseball game that Smith was playing with some teenagers in the physical education class he taught at a nearby high school. Brown had lost a ring on the playground and he wanted some help to search for it. When Brown could not find the ring, he became enraged, grabbed a baseball bat, and beat Smith severely.[119]

As Brown reconstructed the facts in the mediation, he stressed that he just "wasn't thinking" about his actions when he attacked Smith.[120] Brown explained that he became angry when Smith "didn't go out of [his] way to help" him look for the lost ring. In the mediation, Brown said to Smith: "The reason why it happened is because I had a lot of rage, a lot of stress. And when I came to you in that particular situation you didn't help me and at that point in time I needed help. . . . At that stage I was at a boiling point and you was the one that I took it out on."[121]

Thus a senseless crime is rationalized, but in a way that causes the offender to shift some blame for the event outside himself, even onto the victim—who is accused of not helping Brown but was really guilty only of being in the wrong place at the wrong time. When Smith reminds Brown that he traumatized additional victims—the children who witnessed the crime—Brown responds, "You see, I understand that a lot of victims were out there, mentally and physically but at that point I acted off of instinct. I didn't care. . . . See now when I look upon what I've done I can say, 'Man, I was wrong' but it was done. You understand what I'm saying?" Smith: "I understand."[122]

After explaining his actions, Brown listened to Smith explain the impact the crime has had on his life (he lost one eye and had to stop teaching completely). This leads Brown to "apologize"[123] for what happened and

---

[119] HBO Transcript, *supra* note 106, at 2-4.

[120] *Id.* at 12.

[121] *Id.* at 10.

[122] *Id.* at 12.

[123] It is interesting that Brown expresses his remorse or desire for forgiveness only in active terms—as something he does—rather than in terms of a feeling (such as feeling sorry) or in terms of a request (such as asking the victim to forgive him). *Cf.* IRVING GOFFMAN, RELATIONS IN PUBLIC 113

for what he did to the victim:

> See, the reason why I wanted to meet you is because I wanted to tell
> you it wasn't your fault. It wasn't deliberate. Like I said, it was the
> ghetto. All that stress. And I apologize for doing damage to your life
> and your family. I apologize. But see now I have to go on with
> mines. And it's hard for me too. I know what I've done. And I feel
> bad about it when I think about it because I was young and I was
> stupid. But see now I know better. In some ways I'm glad this expe-
> rience is happen to me. Because if it hadn't I wouldn't be right here
> talking to you. I think I'd be 6 feet under somewhere. But like I say
> I apologize.[124]

And where is the reconciliation for which this process is praised? It
seems significant that a major motivation for the offender's participation
in this case was his desire that the victim "understand" his position, even
if the victim couldn't forgive him:

> One thing about this meeting I was weighing out the pros and cons
> of it and I thought about it, meeting you, and I was asking myself,
> no I don't want to meet you because it will just bring back every-
> thing. That's what I thought, but see now that I'm, now that I've
> explained to you how I felt that day, and you explained to me how
> you felt, I'm alright. I can kind of put this aside. It's not going to be
> totally forgotten. It'll never be totally forgotten, but I put this aside
> and say alright, I'm not totally forgiven, but he understands where
> I'm coming from. That's all. I don't expect to be forgiven for an act
> like that. I don't expect to just as long as you understand where I'm
> coming from.[125]

Perhaps offenders can more easily ask for understanding than for forgiveness, which after all requires a confession of wrongdoing. When the offender says, "I don't expect you (i.e., I don't ask you) to forgive me—only
that you try to understand," the offender may actually retain more, rather
than less, power in the negotiation. If the victim refuses, the offender
moves forward believing he was not understood, perhaps feeling himself

---

(1971) ("An apology is a gesture through which an individual splits himself into two parts, the part
that is guilty of an offense and the part that dissociates itself from the delict and affirms a belief in the
offended rule.").

[124] HBO Transcript, *supra* note 106, at 12.
[125] *Id.* at 13.

victimized. If, on the other hand, the offender asks for forgiveness (acknowledging that he needs it) and the victim refuses, the offender moves forward tainted, unforgiven, unredeemed. But an offender may be so self-protective that he never achieves the ability to request forgiveness, and instead the victim must merely "understand."[126]

When Robert Coates and John Gehm surveyed participants in VOM, they discovered that many offenders participated because they wanted the victims to "listen" to them.[127] Victims, on the other hand, reported that "the amount of time required to participate in VORP was a point of some dissatisfaction."[128] As one victim stated: "it's like being hit by a car and having to get out and help the other driver when all you were doing was minding your own business."[129] Thus, the process may ask more of victims than it does of offenders. What many victims want most from offenders—true remorse, and an acknowledgement of responsibility for the harm they've done—may be unavailable in many cases. Instead, VOM asks victims to "listen," to "understand," and to accept the offender's explanation of the crime.[130]

IV. DISSERVING THE INTERESTS OF OFFENDERS

The preceding section sketched the ways in which VOM disserves victims of crime. The resolution of criminal cases is not a zero-sum game, however, and the disadvantages VOM poses for victims do not create corresponding advantages for offenders. VOM also disserves the interests of offenders by using biased selection criteria and by failing to provide the kinds of procedural safeguards that insure due process and equal protection within the criminal justice system.

---

[126] Toni Massaro suggests that "offenders may blush at different things than nonoffenders." Toni Massaro, *Shame, Culture, and American Criminal Law*, 89 MICH. L. REV. 1880, 1918 n.199 (1991).

[127] COATES & GEHM, *supra* note 6, at 10 (noting that offenders were most satisfied with "meeting the victim and discovering the victim was willing to listen to them") (emphasis added).

[128] *Id.* at 9.

[129] *Id.*

[130] CNN Transcript, *Sonya Live* 21 (January 28, 1993) (NEXIS) [hereinafter, "CNN Transcript"] (Stuart Kleinman, M.D., noting that offenders who "can't feel remorse or are unable to feel the pain of another person, and don't feel guilt" must be distinguished from offenders who "have the ability to feel a genuine human connection" to others). To their credit, VOM administrators may be conscious of this problem. *See infra* note 149.

A. *Biased Selection Criteria*

In this section, I review the criteria that various VOM programs use to decide whether an offender can participate in mediation with the victim. Professor Paul Rice notes, "Of those who might successfully participate in such a program, some may be more deserving than others of the opportunity to avoid the stigma of a criminal record."[131] As VOM programs seek the "more deserving," they may unfairly exclude some offenders from participation based upon factors that bear little relationship to the stated goals of VOM.[132]

It may be very difficult to formulate criteria for selection that actually correlate with successful mediation.[133] One approach is to consider the nature of the conflict that exists in the wake of the crime and determine whether negotiation is likely to resolve all or part of it. Howard Zehr writes, "For a victim-offender conflict to be a good candidate for VORP there should be something to negotiate and/or feelings that need to be dealt with."[134] This description is overinclusive, of course, since almost every crime will produce "feelings that need to be dealt with." Whether the crime also produces "something to negotiate" is perhaps a more interesting question. The parties might be able to negotiate an amount of restitution that the offender will pay to compensate the victim, or the wording and thrust of an apology that the victim hopes to receive from the offender. Viewed this way, almost every crime produces some conflict or

---

[131] Rice, *supra* note 112, at 26.

[132] The argument that offenders are unfairly excluded from VOM is in tension with my argument above that VOM pressures some offenders to mediate although they prefer to stay in the court system. *See supra* Part II. This tension recalls the joke in which two people trade contradictory complaints about a restaurant: "What terrible food!" "Yes, and such small portions!" Though the concerns expressed about selection criteria appear to clash with the argument that offenders are pressured to participate, these concerns are not really inconsistent. Offenders deemed "appropriate" by the VOM program may experience pressure to participate though they would prefer not to do so; on the other hand, mediation might be preferable to adjudication for some offenders who might be excluded on grounds unrelated to their ability to mediate with the victim.

[133] Part of the difficulty here is that the goals of the programs are not always clear. But those goals clearly determine the appropriate criteria for selection, as proponents of VOM have recognized. For example, if a VOM program is to serve as an alternative to incarceration, by necessity it will limit participation to those people involved in more serious crimes or offenders with more extensive criminal records. *See* THE VORP BOOK, *supra* note 8, at III-7 (observing that when VORPs are getting started and setting criteria for participation, they must bear in mind the goals of the program).

[134] ZEHR, *supra* note 36, at 11.

debt that could be subject to negotiation. Zehr's threshold criterion is not likely to draw very helpful distinctions between cases.

Even if a program administrator finds that a case might be appropriate for VOM based on Zehr's threshold criterion, Zehr makes clear that the screening process is ongoing: "If, after talking to victim and offender separately, the volunteer has serious questions about whether an encounter will be profitable, suspects some ulterior motive on the part of one of the parties or senses a very high level of hostility, the case may be rejected."[135] This list of excluding factors reveals how difficult it is for VOM programs to articulate the criteria that make cases appropriate for mediation.

A volunteer's "serious questions about whether an encounter will be profitable" are left unspecified, and they provide a highly subjective standard for deciding whether the victim and offender should attempt to negotiate a resolution of the case. The volunteer might have his or her own standard for determining whether "an encounter will be profitable," and that standard might not relate closely to the goals of the VOM program, much less the criminal justice system generally.

The suspicion that one of the parties might have an "ulterior motive" for participating is also a strange basis for preventing mediation. A party's reasons for mediating could be many, and participants might often wish to keep their motives a secret. Almost any offender who is offered the opportunity to avoid prosecution through mediation will probably be motivated not by an affirmative desire to mediate, but rather by a desire to avoid prosecution.[136] Likewise, victims may participate only because they hope to increase their chances of collecting restitution.[137] Requiring that participants express these motivations may be unrealistic and unfair.[138]

Finally, Zehr does not specify the point at which hostility reaches "a very high level." One would expect most victims to feel extremely hostile

---

[135] *Id.*

[136] Indeed, Coates and Gehm found that this was the primary motivation for most offenders' participation. *See* COATES & GEHM, *supra* note 6, at 4 (concluding that offenders participate in VOM in order to "[a]void harsher punishment").

[137] *See id.* at 3 (observing that victims participate in VOM in order to "[r]ecover loss").

[138] *See* Gustafson, *supra* note 10, at 9 (victims wanted to participate in VOM to recover their loss and to help the offender); Washington Crime News Service, *Victim-Offender Reconciliation Programs May be an Effective Alternative to Incarceration*, 5(1) CRIM. JUST. DIG. 1, 7 (1986) (victims wanted to "receive restitution and hear remorse on the part of the offender").

toward their offenders; if high levels of hostility are enough to keep a case out of VOM, then VOM may cause victims to suppress their anger in order to have the opportunity to participate. This can be destructive for victims, as explained above.[139] Thus, programs that screen potential participants by relying upon volunteers' subjective assessments of hostility and motivation may create structural opportunities for bias to enter the selection process.[140]

Many programs screen potential participants by using criteria intended to be more objective; thus these programs consider the offenders' criminal records and allow them to participate only if they have committed no prior offenses. In a 1983 study of VORP participants, eighty-one percent had no prior conviction, and ninety-three percent had no prior incarceration, even if some had prior convictions.[141] Prior convictions presumably signal a pattern of wrongdoing and a suggestion that the offender may be "hardened," less amenable to negotiation with the victim. But since absence of convictions is no guarantee that the offender has been crime-free prior to the incident in question, it may send more noise than signal.[142] Moreover, even if it were certain that the offender had a prior criminal record, such past experiences would not necessarily disable the offender from mediating; some VOM programs concentrate efforts on cases that would ordinarily send offenders to prison, and thus practically require that the offender have a prior criminal record.

Some evidence suggests that selection criteria create or enhance a racial disparity in participant populations. In a 1983 sample, ninety-two percent of the offender participants in VOM were caucasian.[143] Some of this might be explained by the fact that many victim-offender mediation projects are run in rural areas or urban centers—such as Minneapolis/St. Paul—where the black and Latino populations are very small. Additional

---

[139] *See supra* Part III.B.

[140] *See* Hughes & Schneider, *supra* note 16, at 5 (stating that some VOM programs excluded cases with "overly angry victims").

[141] COATES & GEHM, *supra* note 6, at 6. *See also* UMBREIT, *supra* note 78, at 25-26.

[142] Howard Zehr has also raised the problem that VORP was initially conceived as an alternative to incarceration, and to fulfill that purpose, it must be capable of serving the more "serious," or repeat, offender who is most likely to be incarcerated. THE VORP BOOK, *supra* note 8, at III-7 ("Ideally, 'alternative programs' would be structured in such a way that they would be real alternatives. It is possible, for example, to accept only certain kinds of cases which would have gone to jail otherwise.").

[143] COATES & GEHM, *supra* note 6, at 6.

study is necessary, however, to determine why such a disproportionally large number of offender participants are white.[144] Administrators of VOM programs have also reported that they have experienced difficulty recruiting and retaining blacks, Latinos, and Asians to serve as mediators and members of advisory boards for VOM programs.[145]

In addition to race, wealth—or lack of it—may inappropriately exclude some offenders from participating in VOM. Although it would strike many as repugnant to punish criminal offenders according to their wealth, many VOM programs may facilitate just such a system.[146] Some VOM programs allow offenders to participate only if they are likely to be able to make restitution payments to the victim. Although this is a legitimate criterion if the sole purpose of the mediation is to gain restitution for the victim, most VOM programs claim broader goals. Even indigent offenders might be able to mediate with their victims to achieve alternative goals of the programs (e.g., the victims' expression of anger, the offenders' expression of remorse).

But when programs use the offenders' ability to express remorse as a criterion for participation, they also run into difficulty. Administrators of VOM programs sometimes say that offenders are permitted to participate in mediation only if they will admit guilt.[147] Victim offender mediation is no place, they say, for offenders who want to contest liability or shift some of the blame onto victims. This, they recognize, could be worse for the victim than no mediation at all. But if only offenders who can effectively express remorse and accountability are chosen for VOM, the programs could disadvantage offenders who are poor communicators or who are reluctant to confess their guilt, lest they waive procedural and substantive rights.[148] The "smooth talkers" may get more favorable treatment while

---

[144] The more subjective the criteria used to determine offender participation, the more likely that subtle and perhaps unconscious racial bias could become a part of the selection process. The amount of remorse that offenders show when they talk to program administrators is one subjective criterion that could serve as an outlet for racial bias.

[145] Proceedings of 1993 U.S.A. VOM Conference, Chicago, Illinois (June 1993) (forthcoming in VICTIM OFFENDER MEDIATION (Winter 1994)).

[146] Indeed, in Tate v. Short, 401 U.S. 395 (1971), the Court struck down a sentencing scheme that required convicted criminals who were unable to pay a fine immediately to spend time in prison, while those who could pay immediately were released.

[147] See Hughes & Schneider, supra note 16, at 4-5 (stating that in 80% of the VOM programs surveyed, some kinds of offenders were excluded, including "offenders showing no remorse").

[148] In Brady v. United States, 397 U.S. 742, 748-49 (1970), Justice White wrote for the Court

the tongue-tied languish in the system.[149]

Psychologists, sociologists, and scholars of communication theory have long understood that people of different backgrounds and cultures often communicate with different styles and emphases.[150] Differences in communication style could cause some administrators to exclude offenders who are different from them, particularly if the administrators are looking for an expression of remorse or guilt. Offenders who have committed similar crimes but communicate in ways more comfortable to program administrators could be allowed to participate, even though their mediations with victims are no more likely to succeed than those offenders who were excluded.

In sum, VOM is offered as a diversion from or alternative to the criminal justice system, but the criteria used to screen offenders often degenerate to mere subjective assessments on the part of program administrators and volunteer mediators. This is particularly dangerous if an administrator's or volunteer's judgment that an offender is not suitable for VOM is taken into consideration in the prosecution or punishment of the offender within the system.

---

and reiterated "[t]he importance of assuring that the defendant does not plead guilty except with a full understanding of the charges against him and the possible consequences of his plea." Of course, the offender's admission of guilt sufficient to qualify for participation in VOM may fall far short of a guilty plea. The broader principle of *Brady*, however, is that confessions of guilt by a criminal defendant must be accompanied by sufficient process to assure that they are voluntary and well-informed; this is a proposition of fundamental fairness that should adhere when offenders decide whether to participate in VOM. *See supra* notes 78-83 and accompanying text.

[149] *See* Dittenhoffer & Ericson, *supra* note 46, at 326 (observing that VORP workers "requested that only offenders who have 'some limited verbal skills' be referred" to mediation). Stuart Kleinman observes, however, that verbal ability does not always correlate with sincerity:

> But there is a whole other group of people, and these people can't feel remorse or are unable to feel the pain of another person, and don't feel guilt. Now, what's to stop those types of people from doing it again? Those types of people are the dangerous ones, because they can learn the right words, learn the right ways of behaving, and then, possibly fool someone.

CNN Transcript, *supra* note 130, at 13. As experience has shown, an offender will not necessarily make good on commitments and fulfill the obligations of a restitution agreement simply because the offender has expressed remorse effectively. The empty promises of offenders can lead to disappointment on the part of victims, as the research of Robert Coates and John Gehm has revealed. They found that the element of VOM least satisfying to victims was a "lack of adequate follow-up and leverage on the offender to fulfill the agreed upon contract." COATES & GEHM, *supra* note 6, at 9.

[150] *See, e.g.*, CAROL GILLIGAN, IN A DIFFERENT VOICE: A THEORY OF WOMEN'S PSYCHOLOGICAL DEVELOPMENT (1984); THOMAS KOCHMAN, BLACK AND WHITE STYLES IN CONFLICT (1966); DEBORAH TANNEN, THAT'S NOT WHAT I MEANT (1986).

B. *Offenders Often Need the Protection of Public Processes*

Though Jeremy Bentham strongly urged that compensation of victims be an important goal of the criminal law,[151] he also recognized the importance of public processes to determine guilt and compensation:

> Without publicity, all other checks are insufficient: in comparison of publicity, all other checks are of small account. Recordation, appeal, whatever other institution might present themselves in the character of checks, would be found to operate rather as cloaks than checks; as cloaks in reality, as checks only in appearance.[152]

Public determination of restitution could more effectively reassure people that harms would not go unaddressed; the people's fear of victimization would be better calmed if they could observe the procedure. Bentham also appeared to distrust private processes for setting restitution because he did not believe that the parties to the case could be objective as they negotiated the amount to be repaid. He preferred instead a neutral party to set the amount in a manner that appeared fair to the public.[153] Fairness in the eyes of the public is not just a function of the substantive outcome of a case; it also has to do with the procedures that are followed to reach that outcome.[154]

---

[151] Bentham believed that forcing offenders to pay restitution to victims could have a deterrent effect: "Satisfaction is necessary in order to cause the evil . . . to cease, and reestablish everything in the condition it was before the offense; to replace the individual who has suffered in the lawful condition in which he would have been if the law had not been violated." Jeremy Bentham, *Political Remedies for the Evil of Offenses, in* WORKS OF JEREMY BENTHAM 371 (J. Brow ed., 1970).

[152] 1 JEREMY BENTHAM, RATIONALE OF JUDICIAL EVIDENCE 524 (1827).

[153] But we must make one essential observation here. In order to take away the alarm, it is sufficient that the satisfaction should appear complete to the eyes of the observers, which it may not be so to the eyes of the persons interested. How shall we judge if the satisfaction be perfect, with respect to him who receives it? The balance in the hands of passion will always incline to the side of interest. To the miser you can never give enough: to the revengeful, the humiliation of his adversary never appears sufficiently great. It is necessary, then, to imagine an impartial observer, and to regard as sufficient the satisfaction which would make him think that, for such a price, he would hardly regret to receive such an injury."
Jeremy Bentham, *Political Remedies, in* READINGS, *supra* note 21, at 30.

[154] Although a public trial "hedged with procedural protections and conducted with conspicuous respect for the rule of law" is perhaps the most important way to demonstrate the "fairness of the law" to the public, a court's open review on the record of a plea bargain or restitution award, complete with findings regarding voluntariness and the basis for the plea or award, can serve a similar function. Richmond Newspapers v. Virginia, 448 U.S. 555, 595 (1980).

1288   EMORY LAW JOURNAL   [Vol. 43

Just as victims often need vindication and "catharsis" through public process, offenders may often need the protection of public process to insure that their rights are not unfairly compromised. Public processes can protect offenders through various safeguards: the right to counsel, judicial review to ensure offenders are informed and act voluntarily, rules of evidence that exclude irrelevant information from proceedings to determine guilt and punishment, and uniform sentencing schemes to make sure that punishment is reasonably related to the crime committed rather than being based upon the individual who committed it. Because victim-offender mediation stresses substantive outcomes rather than procedural regularity, it cannot protect offenders from unfairly subjective assessments of their culpability or from well-intentioned but unrestrained exercise of discretion by program administrators.

Rules of evidence promote fairness in public proceedings. Under the Federal Rules of Evidence, for example, civil courts may not admit offers of compromise into evidence to show fault.[155] Similar protections may be lacking, however, when offenders offer to "compromise" in VOM but later return to the criminal justice system for trial or sentencing. At the U.S. Association for Victim Offender Mediation Conference in 1991, Mark Stein conducted a workshop that allowed participants to view a mock mediation and interrupt each time the model departed from the procedures followed in their own programs. One matter that "differed greatly between programs" was whether "information obtained in mediation" could be used by prosecutors if a mediated case later went to the court for trial or sentencing.[156] Not only is such lack of uniformity a potential cause for concern, but it is not even clear that parties to VOM are thoroughly briefed on the policy their program follows; thus they can be unaware of the extent to which their statements in mediation will be held confidential. The confidentiality of mediation generally is a controversial issue, and absent a clear statutory privilege protecting the mediation, considerable information about it may become available to people and institutions outside the mediation.[157] VOM programs may try to reassure participants that

---

[155] FED. R. EVID. 407 ("When, after an event, measures are taken, which, if taken previously, would have made the event less likely to occur, evidence of the subsequent measures is not admissible to prove negligence or culpable conduct in connection with the event.").

[156] *But We Do It This Way*, Summary of Presentation by Mark Stein at 1991 USAVOM Conference, 3(1) VICTIM-OFFENDER MEDIATION 9 (Fall 1991).

[157] GOLDBERG ET AL., *supra* note 83, at 112; Jonathan M. Hyman, *The Model Mediator Confi-*

everything they say will be kept confidential, but the truth is that often they cannot make such guarantees. When so much is at stake for an offender, such misrepresentations can be especially costly.

Another important procedural right in criminal cases is the right to be represented by competent counsel. VOM programs have no consistent rules about requiring or encouraging counsel to be present at the mediation. If the offender attends the mediation alone, there seems to be no consistent encouragement to get the advice of counsel prior to signing the mediation agreement. VOM lacks uniform rules to clarify the lawyers' roles even when lawyers do attend. Indeed, some programs actively discourage counsel from attending because their focus on "rights" is thought to obstruct the mediation process. Paul Rice asserts that in victim-offender mediation programs, "the presence of counsel at the dispute resolution stage of the mediation/arbitration program would detract from the atmosphere the program is trying to create."[158] If a program could show that counsel's presence "would be so detrimental that it would jeopardize the ultimate success of the program," he argues, then mediation programs might be "justified" in forbidding counsel to attend the mediation.[159]

But the offender's right to counsel can be important even in mediation. If the victim has retained counsel to assist in the negotiations, the offender's lack of counsel will only aggravate the offender's inherent vulnerability. Of course the mediator is always expected to watch for and seek to balance such inequality, but the mediator cannot serve the function of counsel to the offender.[160]

In addition to its impact on the balance of power in negotiations, the offender's lack of counsel can have constitutional ramifications. Defendants have a constitutional right to the advice of counsel when they reach a "critical stage" of the criminal process. Mediation in VOM programs is such a "critical stage" because the events at the mediation can "substan-

---

dentiality Rule: A Commentary, 12 SETON HALL LEG. J. 17 (1988); Note, *The Sultans of Swap: Defining the Duties and Liabilities of American Mediators,* 99 HARV. L. REV. 1876 (1986); *Confidentiality in Mediation: An Annotated Bibliography,* 12 SETON HALL LEG. J. 57 (1988).

[158] Rice, *supra* note 112, at 65.

[159] *Id.* at 66.

[160] *See* Victim Offender Reconciliation Program of Seattle/King County, Neutrality: Is it Passive or Power, VORP REP.?, Spring 1992, at 1, ("The mediator must . . . guard against imposing her own judgements and values.").

tially prejudice the offender's full defense at trial."[161] Paul Rice has argued that VOM does not represent such a "critical stage" because it "requires no admission of guilt," and "no rights are waived by participating." Moreover, he argues, "[a]ssuming all communications are privileged, the offender cannot be harmed by anything be says in mediation if criminal charges are later pursued."[162]

Contrary to Rice's conclusions, however, VOM can require admission of guilt.[163] Moreover, as discussed above, not all communication in VOM is necessarily protected from discovery or use in the criminal justice system, because no clear "mediation privilege" exists.[164] Both the fact that mediation occurred and its results (the agreement or failure to reach one) can be considered by judges and prosecutors.[165] Even if a "mediation privilege" could shield the mediator from testifying, the victim might pass on to prosecutors the confessions of guilt made by the offender in the course of the mediation. Once damaging information has been revealed by the offender, the victim's memory cannot be erased and the prosecutor might be able to find an independent source for the information.

Finally, Rice may be correct about lawyers' insistence on procedural regularity undermining the "atmosphere" of a VOM program, but this should lead to closer scrutiny of VOM, not an exclusion of lawyers from the process. The notion that VOM programs must conflict with the system in order to be effective seems quixotic.[166] To assume, as Rice does,

---

[161] A "critical stage" is a point in a criminal proceeding, before or during trial, at which the Sixth Amendment requires assistance of counsel for the accused. United States v. Wade, 388 U.S. 218, 228 (1967). The Supreme Court has defined critical stages as times when "counsel's absence . . . might derogate from [the] right to a fair trial." *Id.* at 228. If the participation in mediation itself is a critical stage, then the decision whether to participate would also appear to be a critical stage at which offenders should have advice of counsel.

[162] Rice, *supra* note 112, at 64.

[163] THE VORP BOOK, *supra* note 8, at III-9 ("Obviously, there must be some admission of guilt for VORP to work; that is one basic case criteria [sic]"); Hughes & Schneider, *supra* note 16, at 4-5 (offenders excluded if they show no remorse or deny involvement).

[164] *See supra* notes 156-57 and accompanying text.

[165] *See* THE VORP Book, *supra* note 8, at II-7.

[166] Russ Immarigeon, a VOM advocate who typifies a profound distrust for "criminal justice practitioners" and their concern for "official, professional control over case process and case outcome," writes:

  VORP challenges at least two central premises of current criminal justice practice: By (a) empowering victims and offenders to have some significant say in the outcome of their cases, VORP in effect tries to reduce official, professional control over case process and case

that for VOM to succeed it must deemphasize rights of the accused seems dangerous as well.[167]

V. DISSERVING THE INTERESTS OF THE STATE

Professor Barbara Babcock has recognized that public, adversarial processes help to strike a balance between an individual's interest in procedural rights and the society's interest in collective, substantive norms. She observes that

> the trial is an important occasion for dramatic enactment, the symbolic representation of the community's most deeply held values. On the one hand, we desire the reassurance of safety and the satisfaction of revenge; this is the catharsis of which the Supreme Court spoke . . . . On the other hand, we require the reaffirmation of our individualist values, of the separateness and sanctity of every individual; these are the values expressed in the rights and restrictions, even the "technicalities," embedded in our criminal procedure. The criminal trial, as the most vivid and visible intersection of state and individual, simultaneously affirms the needs of both our collective and separate selves.[168]

Because VOM deemphasizes both the procedural rules that protect individuals and the substantive laws that represent society's collective interest in behavioral norms, it cannot promote the state's interests.

---

outcome. Failure to understand the reasons for official resistance can lead to changes in program operation which do not address the true cause of the difficulties a program may be experiencing. By (b) stressing reconciliation instead of punishment, incapacitation or deterrence, VORP is advocating an approach to criminal justice processing which is categorically different than the approach taken presently by the criminal justice system. This difference in approach is fundamental. Initial conflicts between VORP practitioners and criminal justice practitioners should be seen as a natural part of VORP's implementation process. In the absence of such conflict, a VORP practitioner might ask what is going wrong? Does a lack of conflict mean that criminal justice practitioners have accurately integrated VORP into their operations, without diluting VORP's goals: Or, does it mean that VORP is being used by criminal justice practitioners for other purposes?"
Russ Immarigeon, *VORP and the Criminal Justice System: Conflict & Challenge*, 1(4) VICTIM-OFFENDER MEDIATION 14, 15 (1990).

[167] *See* Grillo, *supra* note 18, at 1597-99 (noting that lawyers can serve a useful function in mediation as protectors of rights and as "insulation").

[168] Barbara A. Babcock, *Fair Play: Evidence Favorable to an Accused and Effective Assistance of Counsel*, 34 STAN. L. REV. 1133, 1140 (1982) (referring to argument by Thurman Arnold).

A.   VOM Invokes the Interest of an Undefined or Nonexistent "Community"

Often proponents argue that VOM rests upon an alternative paradigm of criminal justice; VOM assumes that the conflict not only involves the offender and the state, but also affects the victim and "the community."[169] Thus, proponents say, one of the strengths of VOM is that it allows disputes to be resolved with "community" involvement or with some sensitivity to "community norms."[170] But when pressed to identify the community they have in mind, proponents are not forthcoming.[171] In the United States today, few "communities" can be identified that would yield meaningful standards to be used in VOM.[172] Even if such community standards existed, nothing about the VOM process ensures that community standards will be integrated into the mediation or used to resolve the case.

There is some question about whether the "community" so celebrated by VOM proponents even exists.[173] Too often, "community" is discussed in contrast to "some aspect of modern life that is found to be lacking."[174]

---

[169] *See, e.g.,* ZEHR, *supra* note 36, at 184 (observing that crime injures the victim, "interpersonal relationships," the offender, and the community).

[170] THE VORP BOOK, *supra* note 8, at II-4 (arguing that VORP "recognizes the community's responsibility in the conflict"); ZEHR, *supra* note 36, at 15 ("A community-controlled program empowers a community to solve its own problems, helping to reverse the tendency among Americans to look to the state for solutions."). Lynne Henderson writes about victim participation at sentencing as having a potentially "democratizing function." *See* Henderson, *supra* note 33, at 1003. It is possible that VOM could serve a similar purpose.

[171] "The ongoing community-based reform movement has faltered in part because the existing community conditions do not match the reformers' assumptions about the community's structure, behavior, values, and beliefs." Massaro, *supra* note 126, at 1928.

[172] I am arguing that community standards separate from law are not useful in VOM or in criminal contexts generally. I do not deny, as some do, that communities exist that bind together large groups of people apart from the community of citizens who adhere to a body of law. *See* Timothy P. Terrell & James H. Wildman, *Rethinking "Professionalism,"* 41 EMORY L.J. 403-22 (1992). I have elsewhere argued that communities do exist with which people can identify and in which they can claim membership. *See* Jennifer Gerarda Brown, *Rethinking "The Practice of Law,"* 41 EMORY L.J. 451, 451 n.3 (1992).

[173] The modern cry in Western countries for community alternatives to the established systems of crime control is a belated realization of the need for social simpler solutions to crime than repression by helicopters, electronics, computerization of records, and armed policemen. Unfortunately, the "communities" referred to are often not in existence so that despite the awareness, such lessons are difficult to learn from the advanced urban complexes.

WILLIAM CLIFFORD, CRIME CONTROL IN JAPAN 175 (1976).

[174] Dan A. Lewis & Cheryl Darling, *The Idea of Community in Correctional Reform: How*

Because the concept lacks substance, it fails to drive VOM in a meaningful way. As Dan Lewis and Cheryl Darling have observed:

> The justification of community alternatives, for the most part, lacked conceptual clarity, and this shortcoming was reflected in the way these ideas were operationalized. Therefore, what the phrase community corrections means is unclear. . . . Community alternatives have represented a critique, rather than a clearly conceived call for action.[175]

Professor Sally Merry has analyzed the challenges facing "community mediation programs" and has concluded that "the social features of American neighborhoods differ from the characteristics of situations in which mediation emerges naturally."[176] According to Merry, "The ease of avoiding disputes by exiting from a local social system, the interconnectedness and durability of social networks, the degree of consensus on moral norms, and cultural values about disputing all influence whether mediation is appropriate in a particular social context."[177] These factors, she says, have "important implications for the ability of [community mediation] centers to function as they were intended."[178]

Village and pastoral societies, where mediation is common, are generally "stable, closed and bounded social systems" where "individuals cannot escape from their local communities without sacrificing much of their social lives and often their economic livelihood."[179] American cities, in contrast, contain more mobile populations for whom the community is not so well defined. Even if a community could be identified, escape from it would have much less serious consequences.[180] As a result, the commu-

---

Rhetoric and Reality Join, in ARE PRISONS ANY BETTER? 95, 96-97 (John W. Murphy & Jack G. Dison eds., 1990) ("In the world of corrections, community is contrasted with institutions. If institutions are bad, then that which is not an institution, in this case the community, is good.").

[175] *Id.* at 98-99.

[176] Sally Engle Merry, *Defining "Success" in the Neighborhood Justice Movement* 175, *in* NEIGHBORHOOD JUSTICE: ASSESSMENT OF AN EMERGING IDEA (R. Tomasic & M. Feeley eds., 1987).

[177] *Id.* at 177.

[178] *Id.* at 175.

[179] *Id.*

[180] This mobility undermines the development of mores sufficiently uniform that a VOM program can be expected to detect and apply them. Without a uniform social code arising from the "community," VOM cannot elicit remorse from the offender based upon his or her betrayal of those community values. *See* Massaro, *supra* note 126, at 1935 ("Residential and occupational mobility,

nity, to the extent it exists, cannot easily enforce its norms upon individuals.

Professor Merry also notes, "Societies that commonly rely on mediation are often more homogeneous in norms and values than American neighborhoods." American neighborhoods, in contrast, rarely claim the sorts of "shared expectations and customs to resolve agreements" that make mediation work so well elsewhere.[181] Without this set of "shared expectations," VOM cannot impress upon an offender the disapproval of a community apart from the state whose values the offender has breached.[182] As Toni Massaro notes, "American subculturalism, or cultural pluralism, is pronounced enough to make broad conclusions about our moral coherence suspect."[183] VOM aims to generate shame and remorse in an offender, and "reconciliation" absolves the offender of the guilt she has experienced and expressed. But without a cohesive community, it is not always clear that the offender will feel the requisite shame or that the VOM process will be able to elicit such feelings from the offender. When VOM occurs between people who lack consensus about right and wrong, the process loses much of its authority.[184]

Howard Zehr, perhaps the most visionary of VOM's proponents, does not recognize the difficulty of "*re*conciling" people who were never connected. He calls for a paradigm of criminal justice that emphasizes "rituals of lament and reordering" and the "offender's integration in to community."[185] But Zehr does not explain how to create a cultural context in which such rituals and reintegration make sense. In this respect, VOM is subject to the same criticism that Robert Weisberg has leveled against John Braithwaite's theory of crime and reintegration:

> [He] locates the key to crime prevention and cure in social ceremonies of reintegrative shaming that induce moral behavior through

---

coupled with a generally eroded sense of community, can undermine the effectiveness of stigma punishments, even for the social groups traditionally most sensitive to stigma.").

[181] Merry, *supra* note 176, at 175.

[182] *See* Massaro, *supra* note 126, at 1922 (observing that the "cultural complexity" of the United States "can give rise to different definitions of shame, which may confound official efforts to deter crime through shaming").

[183] *Id.* at 1923.

[184] *Id.* at 1906 n.120 ("If consensus about good and evil erodes, then authority that is based on the 'guilt' concepts of 'sin,' 'transgression,' or 'forgiveness' loses its force.")

[185] ZEHR, *supra* note 36, at 213.

loving guilt . . . . [He] is circular in that he leaves us working backward to imagine transforming American culture into something that can fulfill this daunting task.[186]

VOM seems to long for a simpler, more homogeneous time when individuals could readily identify with and implement the norms of their "community." The more culturally complex this country becomes, however, the less likely it is that such norms can be identified or imposed upon offenders through mediation. Community standards are relevant to the resolution of criminal cases, but the law as enacted by the legislature may most accurately reflect those norms. VOM claims to rely instead upon "community values" as intuited by the victim, the offender, and a volunteer mediator—"a self-selected group of individuals who do not necessarily represent the norms of the community."[187]

Finally, the prevailing American legal culture, based on a "belief in individual rights," is different from cultural values about disputes and disputing found in societies in which mediation is common. In such societies, the success of the disputant "depends much less upon a claim of right and more upon the individual's ability to marshall allies and present her needs as consonant with the needs of the family, group, class, or state."[188] In the United States, both victims and offenders can be expected to care about their individual rights and desires;[189] they are less concerned with the desires of a "community" which they might not even share. In such a setting, it is no surprise that the promise of restitution, rather than a desire to reconcile with the offender, is the primary motivation for most victim participants in VOM.[190]

---

[186] Robert Weisberg, *Criminal Law, Criminology, and the Small World of Legal Scholarship*, 63 U. COLO. L. REV. 521, 556 (1992).

[187] *See* Henderson, *supra* note 33, at 1003 ("In fact, if ensuring that community norms prevail is the goal, jury sentencing would be more representative than victim participation.").

[188] Merry, *supra* note 176, at 176.

[189] *See* Sally Engle Merry, *Concepts of Law and Justice Among Working Class Americans: Ideology as Culture*, 9 LEGAL STUD. F. 59, 67 (1985) (noting that working class Americans see themselves as possessors of legal rights).

[190] *See* COATES & GEHM, *supra* note 6, at 7 (stating that recovering loss was ranked first as motivation for participating in VOM).

B. VOM's Puzzling Relationship to the Traditional Purposes of Criminal Law

At times cooperative, at other times openly hostile,[191] the rhetoric of VOM proponents lacks a clear theory of how VOM relates to the traditional goals of criminal justice—retribution, deterrence, rehabilitation, and incapacitation.[192] Instead, proponents trumpet the process as "inherently right,"[193] as if further justification were unnecessary. But such declarations do not adequately explain VOM's relation to the criminal justice system. D.F. Greenberg has criticized proponents of community corrections for their failure to "relate their advocacy of sanctions imposed in the community to a defensible philosophy of the justifications of punishment and the constraints to which it should be required to conform."[194] VOM is subject to the same criticism, for in the name of "reconciliation," VOM proponents too readily dismiss the traditional goals of the criminal law and fail to reconcile their programs' procedures and results with those of the larger criminal justice system.[195]

---

[191] *See* Immarigeon, *supra* note 166.

[192] The United States Federal Sentencing Guidelines, for example, require sentencing judges to consider

> the need for the sentence imposed . . . to reflect the seriousness of the offense, to promote respect for the law, and to provide just punishment for the offense; . . . to afford adequate deterrence to criminal conduct; . . . to protect the public from further crimes of the defendant; and . . . to provide the defendant with needed educational or vocational training, medical care, or other correctional treatment in the most effective manner.

18 U.S.C. § 3553(a) (1988). *See also* Marc Miller, *Purposes at Sentencing*, 66 S. CAL. L. REV. 413, 414 (1992) (observing that actual sentencing in most systems seems "unconnected" to the traditional purposes of sentencing: "retribution, deterrence, incapacitation, and rehabilitation").

[193] THE VORP BOOK, *supra* note 8, at III-7 (asserting that "unlike most sanctions or programs, VORP can be viewed as being inherently right" and thus applicable to cases of varying gravity); John Gehm, *Introduction*, *in* THE VORP BOOK, *supra* note 8, at 4 (stating that "there is something intrinsically right about the VORP process").

[194] David F. Greenberg, *Problems in Community Corrections*, 10 ISSUES IN CRIMINOLOGY 1 (1975).

[195] This does not mean, however, that VOM proponents fail to recognize the potential inconsistency. *See, e.g.*, THE VORP BOOK, *supra* note 8, at III-8 ("Is it possible, for example, to operate a program whose aim is reconciliation in conjunction with a system whose aims are somewhat different? Clearly there will be tensions.").

1. VOM Rejects Retribution and Incapacitation

When the U.S. Supreme Court ruled in *Richmond Newspapers v. Virginia*[196] that court proceedings in criminal cases could not be closed to the public, the Court acknowledged the importance of retribution in the scheme of the criminal law. Although "societies withdraw both from the victim and the vigilante the enforcement of criminal laws," the Court said, "they cannot erase from people's consciousness the fundamental, natural yearning to see justice done—or even the urge for retribution."[197] While the retributive goal has been criticized by some scholars,[198] it gains greater appeal when recast as an effort to "reflect the seriousness of the offense, to promote respect for the law, and to provide just punishment for the offense."[199] When proponents of VOM repeatedly state that mediation is an alternative to punishment, and not designed to be in any way punitive,[200] they seek to "erase from people's consciousness" the "urge for retribution."

Despite the designs of its administrators, VOM is often perceived as punishment by victims and offenders.[201] But the perceptions of victim and offender are not sufficient to transform VOM—a private process—into the sort of punishment that allows people to "see justice done." VOM offers no guarantee that the victim's or the offender's view of "justice" or "just deserts" will comport with the views of their fellow citizens.

Perhaps VOM's most dramatic departure from the traditional goals of the criminal justice system is its wholesale rejection of incapacitation. VOM was originally intended to be an alternative to incarceration, and several of its adherents continually call for application of VOM to very serious offenses, even violent crimes, for which incarceration would be the

---

[196] 448 U.S. 555 (1980).

[197] *Id.* at 571.

[198] *See generally* Markus D. Dubber, Note, *The Unprincipled Punishment of Repeat Offenders: A Critique of California's Habitual Criminal Statute*, 43 STAN. L. REV. 193, 203 n.66 (1990); Christopher A. Thorn, Note, *Retribution Exclusive of Deterrence: An Insufficient Justification for Capital Punishment*, 57 S. CAL. L. REV. 199 (1983).

[199] 18 U.S.C. § 3553(a)(2)(A).

[200] *See* UMBREIT, *supra* note 141, at 29.

[201] Seventy percent of the victims surveyed thought that the offender was adequately "punished" through VOM; 24% thought that VOM alone would be too little punishment. As for the offenders, 65% considered themselves adequately punished, but 35% thought they received too much punishment. COATES & GEHM, *supra* note 6, at 12-13.

expected sanction.[202] Although VOM proponents acknowledge the need to incapacitate dangerous offenders, they reject incarceration as a value for most offenders.[203]

2. VOM Does Not Promote General Deterrence

Although it has been argued that a certain obligation to pay restitution would discourage people from crime,[204] VOM proponents do not attempt to justify VOM on a general deterrence basis. The reasons for rejecting deterrence as a rationale for VOM seem to be twofold. First, proponents cannot show that the potential obligation to participate in VOM does in fact deter people from committing crimes.[205] Second, general deterrence rests in large part upon a utilitarian notion—that one person should be punished in order to have a beneficial effect on others, or one person suffers for the greater good—and utilitarian philosophies are judged morally bankrupt by many advocates of VOM.[206]

VOM might be reconciled with deterrence goals by arguing that the

---

[202] *See, e.g.*, THE VORP BOOK, *supra* note 8, at III-7 (asserting that "[i]deally, 'alternative programs' would be structured . . . to accept only certain kinds of cases which would have gone to jail otherwise" and thus serve as a "real alternative"); GEHM, *Introduction, in* THE VORP BOOK, *supra* note 8, at 4 ("Is it responsible, given prison overcrowding and prison conditions, to offer any sentencing options—even VORP—unless it is a genuine alternative to incarceration?"); Immarigeon, *supra* note 166, at 14 ("Sadly, VORP is apparently rarely used as an alternative to imprisonment.").

[203] *See* Henderson, *supra* note 33, at 1012 (arguing that restitution's ability to force "an acknowledgement of moral responsibility" seems "ideally suited to moral retributionist goals," but is "unworkable" in cases of serious crime and that "[a]s a society, we want the rapist, mugger, or robber imprisoned on proportionality and incapacitation grounds; in many instances, the victim does also")

[204] "If offenders were persuaded that . . . they could in no wise evade the obligation to repair the damage of which they have been the cause, the ensuing discouragement to the criminal world . . . would be far greater than that produced by temporary curtailment of their liberty." BARON RAFFAELE GAROFALO, CRIMINOLOGY 419 (1914).

[205] In fairness, deterrent effects of conventional punishment are controversial as well, and difficult to prove. *See* ROBERT COOTER AND TOM ULEN, LAW AND ECONOMICS 524-28 (1988) (concluding that increasing the probability or severity of penalty will reduce crime); DETERRENCE AND INCAPACITATION: ESTIMATING THE EFFECTS OF CRIMINAL SANCTIONS ON CRIME RATES (Alred Blumstein et al. eds., 1978); RICHARD A. POSNER, ECONOMIC ANALYSIS OF LAW 224 n.1 (4th ed. 1992); Alred Blumstein & Daniel Nagin, *The Deterrent Effect of Legal Sanctions on Draft Evasion*, 29 STAN. L. REV. 241 (1977); Isaac Ehrlich, *Participation in Illegitimate Activities: A Theoretical and Empirical Investigation*, 81 J. POL. ECON. 559, 561 (1973). Certainly, the proposition that crime can be optimally deterred through heavy penalties is not uncontroversial. The causes of crime are many, and increasing penalties will probably not deter crimes that stem from some of these causes.

[206] *See* ZEHR, *supra* note 36, at 54.

cost of the crime to the offender is increased when he or she must face the victim and hear about the consequences of the crime. This might cause the offender to internalize some of those consequences.[207] Though VOM proponents do not claim to care about deterrence, they might begin to emphasize this aspect more to "sell" VOM to skeptical prosecutors and judges. VOM proponents might argue that even if deterrence is a valid goal in the abstract, VOM's competition (the status quo criminal justice system) fails utterly to deter, and thus VOM can be judged no worse than the status quo with respect to this element. To have general deterrent effect, however, the costs associated with facing the victim would have to be publicized more, so that potential criminals would know the fate that might await them if their contemplated crime is detected. In addition, participation would have to be mandatory because, as long as VOM remains voluntary, offenders who will experience pain when they face their victim might simply refuse to mediate. Thus they could avoid internalizing the costs now borne by the victim. In sum, because VOM is voluntary and private, it does not generally deter crime.

3. VOM Might Promote Specific Deterrence and Rehabilitation

Even if VOM fails to deliver general deterrence of potential criminals, it still might offer specific deterrence among the offenders who participate. One 1979 study found that offenders who made contact with their victims had significantly lower recidivism rates than those who did not.[208] Other more recent studies have been inconclusive, and have found little if any

---

[207] Henderson argues that because "[t]he focus of general deterrence is public and nonindividualized [a]chieving specific deterrence does not require victim participation at sentencing, rather it requires a calculation of the appropriate level of punishment to teach the offender to abstain from wrongdoing in the future." Henderson, *supra* note 33, at 988-89. One might argue, however, that severity of punishment is not just a matter of how many months the defendant spends in prison, but also a qualitative question—what kind of pain/costs are imposed on the defendant. If the victim's participation somehow makes the sentence more painful for the defendant—and not just because the victim's testimony is likely to lead the judge to impose a longer sentence—it could theoretically have a deterrent effect.

[208] UMBREIT, *supra* note 141, at 33-34 (summarizing Leonard J. Guedalia, "Predicting Recidivism of Juvenile Delinquents on Restitutionary Probations from Selected Background, Subject, and Program Variables" (1979) (unpublished doctoral dissertation, American University, Washington, D.C.)).

evidence that participation in VOM discourages future crime by the offenders.[209]

One of VOM's strongest claims to consistency with traditional criminal justice goals is that VOM helps to rehabilitate the offender. VOM is designed to help victim and offender see each other less as stereotypes and more as real people. Coates and Gehm found such an attitude change in one-third of the cases they studied, but did not indicate whether one or both of the participants reported this change, and if only one, whether it was the offender.[210] Disturbingly, Coates and Gehm's data suggests that in at least two-thirds of the cases that go through VOM, offenders perceive no change in their attitudes toward potential victims. This might not be surprising in light of the compulsion to participate reported by many offenders in the same study.[211] If VOM could lead offenders to recognize the costs of their behavior to other people and to see those effects as important, then it could achieve some rehabilitation.

One difficulty with the rehabilitative justification for VOM is that it assumes some kind of shame or remorse on the part of the offender. The hope is that dialogue with the victim will lead the offender to feel remorse he or she would not experience in the criminal justice system. For many offenders, VOM may indeed have this effect. But for some offenders remorse does not come easily, and victims may not be the best equipped or most appropriate people to determine whether offenders feel genuine remorse.[212] To the extent VOM claims a rehabilitative function, it places

[209] Laurie Ervin & Anne Schneider, *Explaining the Effects of Restitution on Offenders: Results from a National Experiment in Juvenile Courts*, in Galaway & Hudson, *supra* note 37, at 183, 191 (although restitution programs appear to suppress subsequent offending to a greater degree than traditional court programs, the effect could not be explained by a deterrence model). *See also* Mark Umbreit, *Cross-Site Analysis of Victim Offender Mediation*, 4(1) VICTIM-OFFENDER MEDIATION 4, 5 (1992) (study showing that within a one-year period following mediation, juvenile offenders who participated in VOM committed "considerably fewer and less serious additional crimes" than similar offenders who did not participate in VOM, though conceding that this finding was "not statistically significant").

[210] COATES & GEHM, *supra* note 6, at 10-11. *See also* UMBREIT, *supra* note 141, at 29.

[211] COATES & GEHM, *supra* note 6, at 7 ("offenders participate because they believe they must"). *See* UMBREIT, *supra* note 141, at 25; Henderson, *supra* note 33, at 1011 ("Whether restitution orders under the threat of imprisonment do serve a rehabilitative function is an open question.").

[212] Massaro, *supra* note 126, at 1907 n.120 ("Of course, an offender who feels guilt or remorse may not need public 'spanking' to feel punished, whereas a remorseless offender might."). *See also supra* note 149 (some offenders will manipulate the process by feigning remorse).

too much responsibility on victims to make these decisions.[213]

VOM proponents also argue that VOM has rehabilitative effects because an offender's ability to complete a restitution contract and fulfill a promise to the victim reinforces desirable behavior and gives the offender a sense of gratification. But making and meeting a commitment is only gratifying to an offender if the offender has already learned to value commitments and the fulfillment of promises. VOM lacks sufficient contact with the offender to have substantial behavior-modifying effects.[214]

Martin Wright states: "It appears that the most consistent case for mediation and reparation is based on regarding them as ends in themselves. The traditional ends of criminal justice might occur as desirable side-effects, but in the main would be treated separately." But the traditional goals of the criminal law represent the state's rationale for exercising coercive power to punish its citizens. VOM's inability to reconcile its effects with these traditional goals causes VOM to expand the reach of state coercion to achieve goals the public may not value. Meanwhile, VOM compromises the state's ability to use its coercive power to achieve retribution, incapacitation, and general deterrence.[215]

VI. RECOMMENDATIONS FOR PROCESS DESIGN AND REGULATION

Because of the multiple dangers outlined in this Article, mediation should presumptively have no impact on criminal cases. A "Chinese wall" should separate VOM and public proceedings to determine guilt and punishment. Participation in VOM should neither help nor hurt a defendant

---

[213] "In a few instances, rehabilitation-oriented sentences may seem to depend upon, or benefit from, victim cooperation. . . . This is quite different, however, from giving the victim a role in determining what sentence to impose. Instead, it gives the victim a role in implementing the sentence." Henderson, *supra* note 33, at 990 (emphasis in original).

[214] *See* Umbreit, *supra* note 62, at 110 (victims and offenders in violent crimes may need "more extended counselling and support services than the more typical VORP case," and "[t]he average time per case is probably going to be closer to 15-20 hours, rather than the 4-6 hours per case" most VOM programs spend).

[215] *See* SOURCEBOOK, *supra* note 83, at 203-210. Public opinion polls revealed that: large majority of respondents believe courts in their area are "not harsh enough" with criminals (Table 2.35); large majority believe criminals are "let off too easily" (Table 2.36), and; large majority believe victims should have a right "to be paid for stolen or damaged property or injuries received in crime" (Table 2.38). When asked about the relative importance of punishment and rehabilitation in prisons, 38% believed it more important to "punish [offenders] for their crimes," and 48% believed it more important to "get them started 'on the right road' " (Table 2.43).

in the system. In this Part, I explain how this separation might be accomplished. I also explain the limited conditions under which VOM might be integrated into the criminal justice system.

One option for separating mediation from the criminal system is to allow mediation to occur only after the offender's guilt has been determined and a sentence is set. If the mediation takes place only after adjudication and sentencing, the offender would be subject to far less pressure to capitulate to victim demands.[216] This later timing, with its corresponding reduction in pressure on the offender, would still yield some of the theoretical advantages of VOM for the victim. The victim could still negotiate for payment of restitution and experience some healing from confronting the offender.[217] The victim might benefit from talking with the offender, learning that he is not so monstrous, and consequently reducing her fear in the future.[218] And because the offender's case would be resolved publicly one way or another—by trial or by a plea—the victim would have had the satisfaction of seeing society condemn the offender's act.

Timing the mediation after the offender has been found guilty and punished would also yield benefits for the offender. If the mediation were to occur at this later point, the offender would still have the opportunity to apologize to the victim and thus receive some of the rehabilitative advantages of mediation. Because the offender would have already been convicted and punished, however, the threat of public proceedings (including parole hearings for the incarcerated offender)[219] could no longer serve as

---

[216] Even after sentencing, however, the victim may have additional leverage if the sentence is subject to revision depending upon the outcome of the mediation. The victim might also be able to exploit some leverage if the offender is incarcerated at the time of the mediation, because the offender might be thinking ahead to parole proceedings, hoping that his willingness to participate in VOM would reflect positively on his application.

[217] *See* Carleton Bryant, *Report Suggests Alternatives to Jail Terms*, WASH. TIMES, January 11, 1991, A3 (quoting Ann Seymour, public affairs director for the National Victim Center, advocating the use of "victim impact panels" because "[a] face-to-face encounter like that helps the offender understand the impact of his crime on the victim . . . and is rehabilitative for the victim").

[218] Lawry, *supra* note 8, at 2 (following an "extremely emotional" mediation, a burglary victim said that he could go home to his wife and tell her that the "defendant was not an ogre").

[219] *See* Richard Belsha, *Caring and Concern Evolve from Victim Offender Meeting*, 4(1) VICTIM-OFFENDER MEDIATION 9 (1992) (victim relates his suspicion of the offender during the mediation: "I actually started liking and admiring him for the smooth way in which he conducted himself. But I managed to keep things in perspective by remembering that he was trying to get paroled and could be trying to portray himself in a better light.").

leverage to pressure the offender's participation in VOM. There would likewise be less leverage in the negotiation itself.

Finally, mediation following conviction and punishment could also better serve state interests. When mediation can affect pending or potential criminal proceedings, the victim can appropriate public leverage in what is essentially a private negotiation.[220] If the victim thus achieves a private goal but not the public purpose to which the state directs its power to punish (such as deterrence or retribution), then the state is harmed. Delaying the mediation would prevent such appropriation by the victim and preserve the state's interest.

Postponing the mediation until conviction and punishment are complete might impose heavy burdens on some victims because such a rule could cause a delay of years in many cases. Victims might need some control over timing if mediation is to facilitate their healing after a crime has occurred. Therefore, lawmakers could decide that mediation should be allowed to occur before conviction and punishment are complete. Indeed, if the victim has a private right of action arising from the criminal event, he is free to sue the offender and settle the suit, perhaps through mediation. Therefore, the victim should have the right to mediate with the offender even before the criminal case is resolved.

To retain the advantages of postponed mediation, however, certain procedural rules should be followed to ensure that the mediation and its results would not affect the criminal case. A "Chinese wall" of confidentiality and evidentiary exclusion could help to achieve such separation. Judges and juries in criminal cases would remain ignorant of the mediation and its results, so that the mediation would not distract them from the merits of the criminal case. In most jurisdictions, however, very few criminal cases are actually tried, so hiding the mediation from judges and juries would not be sufficient to erect a barrier. Ideally, the separation would be so complete that government attorneys would disregard the mediation

---

[220] Ordinarily, criminal and contract law will invalidate contracts made under threat of criminal charges because such contracts violate "a more general principle, to wit, that legal processes should not be used outside their proper sphere or to secure an unrelated or improper benefit." ALAN WERTHEIMER, COERCION 43 (1987). Although Wertheimer does not explain how one determines the "proper sphere" of legal processes, or how to determine whether a benefit is "unrelated" or "improper," one might rely upon the traditional goals of the criminal law to assess its proper sphere and then determine whether the victim's benefit falls within the ambit of those goals.

when deciding prosecution, plea bargaining, and sentencing strategy.[221] In practice, however, this goal would be hard to achieve. Prosecutors would usually know about the mediation and its results because they often work closely with victims, who might be important witnesses. If the victim mediates a satisfactory resolution of the case, the prosecutor can easily exercise discretion and drop the case. Thus, it is probably impossible to insulate the system from the mediation and its effects.

If the prosecutor determines that the criminal case should proceed despite the mediation some procedural changes could help to preserve the government's case in the wake of mediation. For example, victims could be deposed prior to the mediation to ensure that their testimony does not change—to favor or disfavor the offender—in the wake of the mediation.[222] If the victim were deposed prior to the mediation, she would have to commit to a version of the events without knowing how cooperative or remorseful the offender might be. If the victim successfully mediated a satisfying agreement with the offender and then sought to make her testi-

---

[221] Prosecutors have tremendous power and discretion in the criminal system. Prosecutorial power and discretion is reflected, perhaps most dramatically, by the prevalence of plea bargaining in most jurisdictions. Although statistics on plea bargaining fluctuate widely depending upon the jurisdiction, estimates range from 60% to 90%, and the majority fall within 5 points of 90%. If the mediation is to remain separate from that system, prosecutors must remain ignorant of mediation results when they decide whether and how to charge or prosecute the offender, and what sentence to recommend. *See, e.g.*, Reynolds Holding, *Black Defendants, White Victims*, SAN FRANCISCO CHRON., April 7, 1993, at A1, A8 (90% of all criminal cases end in plea bargains); Katherine Bishop, *Mandatory Sentences in Drug Cases: Is the Law Defeating Its Purpose?*, N.Y. TIMES, June 8, 1990, at B16, (95% of federal criminal cases involve plea bargains); Chris Spolar & Angela Walker, *Date Rape*, WASH. POST, Sept 4, 1990, at Z12, Z16 (in D.C. Superior Court, 90% of cases were resolved by plea bargain).

[222] In jurisdictions that distinguish between evidentiary and discovery depositions, the deposition of the victim should be treated as an evidentiary deposition. In this way, any risk of altered testimony by the victim in the wake of mediation could be eliminated; the victim's deposition, rather than live testimony, would be offered into evidence. The Confrontation Clause ordinarily requires, however, that testimony against a criminal defendant be presented live, in open court, and subject to cross examination; the prosecution's ability to introduce an out-of-court statement into evidence is conditioned upon a showing that the declarant is "unavailable" and that the prosecution made a "good faith effort" to produce the witness in court. *See* Ohio v. Roberts, 448 U.S. 56, 74 (1980); Barber v. Page, 390 U.S. 719 (1968). If mediation becomes a fixture in the criminal process, some statutory revision may be necessary to ensure that the victim is deposed prior to the mediation and the offender has a meaningful opportunity to confront and cross-examine the victim (with a concomitant right to counsel) during the deposition. *See* JOHN STRONG ET. AL., MCCORMICK ON EVIDENCE § 253 at 129-38 (1992).

mony more favorable to the offender, prosecutors could use the premediation deposition to impeach this altered testimony.[223]

Similarly, if the mediation were to take place while the offender served a prison sentence following conviction, the victim might execute a statement supporting or resisting the offender's parole before the mediation occurred. If, for example, a victim who had opposed the offender's parole reconsidered following the mediation and offered to testify at a parole hearing in the offender's favor, the state could bring to the parole board's attention the victim's change of heart. This might not lead members of the parole board to disregard or exclude the victim's testimony, but it would give them valuable information about the victim's newly found forgiveness. Offenders would lose a potential advantage ex post, but gain some protection from coercion ex ante.

In order to keep mediation separate from the criminal justice system, courts could enforce rules that would exclude from evidence any statements about the mediation or its results. Ordinarily, the offender's participation in the mediation might be noted as a mitigating or aggravating circumstance at sentencing. A Chinese wall approach would prevent such use, effectively declaring the mediation irrelevant to prosecution and punishment. Thus, any attempt to introduce evidence about the mediation, by the government or the defense, would be rejected.[224] Although this deprives the offender of a possible advantage in the criminal court, it also protects the offender from harsher treatment by the prosecutor or judge if the mediation fails.

My recommendation that VOM should not affect the offender's case is subject to an important qualification: If VOM could be shown to promote deterrence or rehabilitation, then the state might appropriately condition prosecution on mediation and its results. Currently, evidence that VOM promotes the traditional goals of the criminal law is scarce. While many

---

[223] Indeed, the state might even prosecute for perjury.

[224] In capital cases, the defendant has a right to introduce any evidence in mitigation. Because the defense determines for itself what evidence qualifies as mitigation, an offender might want to introduce evidence that she participated in mediation with the family of her victim. The offender's right to do so would have to be preserved despite the "Chinese wall" that would exclude such evidence in other non-capital cases. See Lockett v. Ohio, 438 U.S. 586, 604 (1978) (sentencer should "not be precluded from considering, as a mitigating factor, any aspect of a defendant's . . . record . . . that the defendant proffers as a basis for a sentence less than death").

VOM proponents deny the importance of mediation's consequences (stressing instead the inherent value of the process), others have attempted to show that VOM has a deterrent effect. Their efforts, however, have been somewhat half-hearted: The studies either produce ambiguous results or suffer from such small sample size that their statistical significance is undermined.[225] Before policy-makers allow mediation to influence the outcome of criminal cases, they should demand more compelling evidence that mediation furthers the traditional goals of the criminal law.[226] This qualification is consistent with a more general theme of this Article: Public coercion should be used only to vindicate public interests.

If VOM is allowed to influence proceedings in the criminal justice system, it should be accompanied by greater formality and uniformity than it currently possesses. Rules for integrating mediation into criminal justice might be modeled upon "compromise" statutes, which already exist in several jurisdictions. Compromise statutes typically provide that when criminal conduct gives rise to a civil cause of action on the part of the victim, if the offender can negotiate a resolution of the case that meets with the victim's satisfaction, the criminal case may be discharged.[227]

To achieve such compromise, the victim must appear before the court in which the criminal case is pending and acknowledge that he has received satisfaction for his injury. At that point the court can exercise its discretion and discharge the criminal case, entering into the record "the reasons for the order." A California court has listed three issues a court ought to consider when exercising discretion under the compromise statutes: (1)

---

[225] *See supra* notes 16 and 209 and sources cited therein.

[226] Lawmakers might also want to integrate VOM into the criminal justice system because they would like to save the expense of determining guilt and punishment in a public forum. Thus, VOM might be seen to promote the public interest in part by saving resources. Despite its potential cost savings, however, VOM should not be considered consistent with the public interest without strong evidence that VOM deters crime and rehabilitates offenders.

[227] *See, e.g.,* ALASKA STAT. §§ 12.45.120-.140 (1993); ARIZ. REV. STAT. ANN. § 13-3981 (1993); CAL. PENAL CODE §§ 1377-79 (West 1994); IDAHO CODE §§ 19-3401 to -3403 (1992); MASS. ANN. LAWS ch. 276, § 55 (Law. Co-op. 1994); MISS. CODE ANN. §§ 99-15-51 to -53 (1994); NEV. REV. STAT. ANN. §§ 178.564-.568 (Michie 1992); N.Y. CODE CRIM. PROC. § 170.40 (Consol. 1993); N.D. CENT. CODE §§ 29-01-16 to -19 (1991); OKLA. STAT. tit. 22, §§ 1291-94 (1994); OR. REV. STAT. §§ 135.703-.705 (1994); PA. STAT. ANN. tit. 42, § 314 (1993); WASH. REV. CODE §§ 10.22.010-.020 (1991). The original New York statute was 1 N.Y.R.L (1813) p.499 §9 and many modern statutes are based upon it. *See, e.g.,* State v. Nelles, 713 P.2d. 806, 807-808 (Alaska Ct. App. 1986) ("It appears that Alaska's civil compromise statutes derived from the same source as most other similar statutes, a 1813 New York statute.").

whether the civil injury is "coextensive with the criminal violation;" (2) whether "the injury to the public" will be "fully vindicated" through private settlement; and (3) whether the victim's agreement to settle is "completely voluntary."[228] If mediation were integrated into the criminal justice system, courts could similarly review mediation agreements and enter findings on the record regarding the nature of the criminal violation, the mediation's impact on the public interest, and the voluntariness of the parties' agreement.[229]

In order to insure that the parties voluntarily entered the agreement, the judge would have to examine the parties to make sure that they were told and understood their options before agreeing to mediate. If the program is to be voluntary, then the parties must be assured that refusal to mediate will not bring reprisals in the court system. Instead, the parties need a candid, accurate prediction of the likely adjudicative outcome. If the evidence against the offender is weak and would be unlikely to support a finding of guilt, the offender needs to know that remaining in the court system might be an attractive option. Gaining the offender's consent to mediation by exploiting fear and uncertainty is inconsistent with voluntariness. If the parties receive full and accurate information prior to consenting to mediate, voluntariness can be enhanced.

If offenders are to be fully informed they will at times require the advice of counsel. Because both the agreement to mediate and a mediated restitution contract will affect the offender's criminal case, the offender may need the advice of counsel to determine the legal and financial risks of any agreement. If an offender has counsel, she will be less vulnerable to unfair leverage in the negotiations, because counsel may give her a realistic assessment of the likely adjudicative outcome should the mediation fail.

Under these circumstances and with additional procedural protections

---

[228] People v. Moulton, 182 Cal. Rptr. 761, 767-68 (Cal. Ct. App. 1982).

[229] The first factor—whether the civil injury is "coextensive with the criminal violation"—forces courts to consider carefully the nature of the injury caused by a criminal violation. The compromise statutes and the courts applying them seem to assume, as VOM does, that some criminal acts are more important as private wrongs than as public ones. Some criminal acts produce an identifiable victim; others more generally harm the public. Both VOM and the compromise statutes require the existence of an identifiable victim. Both seem to assume that once such a victim has been identified, that individual can represent the public and measure "satisfaction" following a settlement. Unlike VOM, however, the compromise statutes require some judicial review to insure that the participants and the public are protected.

in place, the state might appropriately condition prosecution on VOM and its results. Unless such safeguards can be implemented, however, a decoupling of mediation from the criminal justice system is necessary to preserve the integrity of each.

CONCLUSION

In June of 1992, I attended a conference about victim-offender mediation held in Berkeley, California. Administrators and mediators involved in VOM from around the country—indeed, from around the world—attended. Reflecting on the conference, I had conflicting reactions to VOM. I hoped that the programs might facilitate compensation for victims and rehabilitation for offenders, but feared that VOM might involve dangerous levels of coercion. Hope and fear may be reasonable reactions to VOM's maddeningly middle ground. VOM advances neither of the parties' positions as fully as the adversarial system. Instead, it establishes its own normative scheme for the parties at the outset, based more upon an agenda of "reconciliation" than on the real interests of the victim, offender, or community. VOM assumes a compromise of all parties' needs before their interactions have even begun.

This Article has demonstrated that, as currently structured and administered, victim-offender mediation disserves the interests of victims, offenders, and the state. VOM straddles the private and public spheres: It characterizes cases as private disputes affecting individuals rather than the state, and it rejects the state's substantive legal rules for resolution of criminal cases. At the same time, however, VOM uses the state's coercive power to distort parties' choices about participation, agreement, and performance. This Article seeks to shift VOM firmly into the private sphere, and calls for a decoupling of mediation from the criminal justice system. The mediation should not affect public proceedings against the offender. A Chinese wall is necessary to protect the integrity of the criminal justice system and the integrity of mediation as a fundamentally voluntary process.

To achieve this decoupling, I have suggested several procedural reforms. Ideally, the occurrence and result of mediation should be hidden from the prosecutor, the judge, and the jury in the criminal proceedings. Inevitably, however, the prosecutor is likely to know that mediation has occurred. Any evidence regarding the mediation or matters discussed in it should be deemed irrelevant at trial and sentencing. To insulate the criminal justice system further, any victims who wish to participate in VOM could be deposed prior to the mediation to insure that their testimony does not change in the wake of the mediation.

These recommendations are premised on VOM's failure to promote the traditional goals of criminal law. If additional study demonstrates to the satisfaction of policy makers that VOM does promote deterrence or rehabilitation, then mediation might be more formally integrated into the criminal justice system. Should that occur, however, additional formality would facilitate several goals: Selection criteria would be more objective and more clearly tailored to the goals of the mediation programs; the parties would receive complete information—including legal advice—about likely adjudicative outcomes and the various alternatives to any agreement they might negotiate; and the public would be afforded some opportunity to monitor mediation results through regular judicial review. With such safeguards in place, the integration of mediation into the criminal justice system could be achieved in a manner consistent with my general thesis—public power should be used only to vindicate public interests.

[11]

PROSECUTING VIOLENCE: A COLLOQUY ON RACE, COMMUNITY, AND JUSTICE

Goodbye to Hammurabi: Analyzing the Atavistic Appeal of Restorative Justice

Richard Delgado*

A recent innovation in criminal justice, the restorative justice movement has serious implications for the relationship among crime, race, and communities. Restorative justice, which sprang up in the mid-1970s as a reaction to the perceived excesses of harsh retribution, features an active role for the victims of crime, required community service or some other form of restitution for offenders, and face-to-face mediation in which victims and offenders confront each other in an effort to understand each other's common humanity.

This article questions whether restorative justice can deliver on its promises. Drawing on social science evidence, the author shows that the informal setting in which victim-offender mediation takes place is apt to compound existing relations of inequality. It also forfeits procedural rights and shrinks the public dimension of disputing. The article compares restorative justice to the traditional criminal justice system, finding that they both suffer grave deficiencies in their ability to dispense fair, humane treatment. Accordingly, it urges that defense attorneys and policymakers enter into a dialectic process that pits the two systems of justice, formal and informal, against each other in competition for clients and community support. In the meantime, defense attorneys should help defendants find and exploit opportunities for fair, individualized treatment that may be found in each system.

* Jean Lindsley Professor of Law, University of Colorado-Boulder. J.D., 1974, U.C. Berkeley. I gratefully acknowledge the assistance of Andrea Wang in the preparation of this essay.

Apr. 2000]   *RESTORATIVE JUSTICE*   753

INTRODUCTION

The relationship among race, crime, and community is complex and multiform. Although every crime is a violation of community,[1] community concerns acquire special significance with interracial and interclass crimes where offenses can easily be seen as injuries one of *you* inflicted against one of *us*.[2]   Enforcement of crime may also take on an interclass or intergenerational dimension, such as when police enforce anticruising ordinances against teenage drivers or antigraffiti laws against inner-city youth.[3] *Non*enforcement can also raise class and community concerns as well, such as when the black community charges the police with lax enforcement of street crime because of subconscious racism and devaluation of black life.[4]

The prosecution and defense of crime may take on an implicit or explicit community dimension as well. Consider, for example, a defense attorney who advances a cultural defense that, if successful, will mitigate his or her client's punishment but only at the cost of stigmatizing the defendant's group as subcultural, violent, or bizarre.[5] In these cases, the community issue is what one of us (the defendant) is doing to the rest of us (the community).[6] Finally, sexual violence cases demonstrate how the manner of prosecuting a case may affect the community. When a victim of sexual assault is forced to recount her sexual history on the stand, all women receive a warning not to complain of mistreatment at the hands of men.[7]

This essay addresses a recent dynamic movement that seeks to address the effects of crime on community. Restorative justice, which began in the mid-1970s as a reaction to perceived excesses of incarceration, as well as

---

1. This is so because the community defines crime and punishes those whose actions violate these standards. On the role community condemnation plays in the criminal law, see Henry M. Hart, Jr., *The Aims of the Criminal Law*, 23 LAW & CONTEMP. PROBS. 401, 402-06 (1958).

2. *See, e.g.*, JODY DAVID ARMOUR, NEGROPHOBIA AND REASONABLE RACISM: THE HIDDEN COSTS OF BEING BLACK IN AMERICA 81-101 (1997); KATHERYN K. RUSSELL, THE COLOR OF CRIME: RACIAL HOAXES, WHITE FEAR, BLACK PROTECTIONISM, POLICE HARASSMENT, AND OTHER MACROAGGRESSIONS 1-13 (1998).

3. *See* John Larrabee, *Cities Wish Artists Would Find Another Canvas*, USA TODAY, June 29, 1999, at 4A; Roesslein, *These Motorists Are Cruising for Trouble*, MILWAUKEE J. SENTINEL, Sept. 8, 1998, at 14.

4. *See* RANDALL KENNEDY, RACE, CRIME, AND THE LAW 76-135 (1997) (arguing that nonenforcement of crime in black neighborhoods erodes quality of life). *But see* Regina Austin, *"The Black Community," Its Lawbreakers, and a Politics of Identification*, 65 S. CAL. L. REV. 1769, 1771-72 (1992) (noting that some black communities rally behind certain offenders).

5. *See, e.g.*, Peter Margulies, *Identity on Trial: Subordination, Social Science Evidence, and Criminal Defense*, 51 RUTGERS L. REV. 45, 53-54 (1998) (pointing out that cultural defenses can stigmatize the defendant's community). *See generally* Leti Volpp, *(Mis)Identifying Culture: Asian Women and the "Cultural Defense,"* 17 HARV. WOMEN'S L.J. 57 (1994).

6. *See* Margulies, *supra* note 5, at 46-47, 53-57.

7. *See, e.g.*, SUSAN ESTRICH, REAL RAPE 51-53 (1987) (giving examples of victim humiliation at trial).

inattention to the concerns of victims, offers a new paradigm for structuring the relationship among crime, offenders, and communities.[8] Featuring new ways of conceptualizing crime, along with innovative mechanisms for dealing with it, restorative justice constitutes a radically new approach to criminal justice.

Part I reviews the origins and ideology of restorative justice, including what it hopes to accomplish and its purported advantages over the current system. Parts II and III then critique the movement, first offering an internal assessment that evaluates the new approach on its own terms, followed by an external critique that examines it in light of broader values. Part IV reviews some of the deficiencies in our current system, particularly for disadvantaged, minority, and young offenders. Part V offers suggestions for strengthening community bonds while dealing fairly and consistently with those who have breached them.

I. THE RESTORATIVE JUSTICE MOVEMENT AND VICTIM-OFFENDER MEDIATION

In ancient times, crime was dealt with on an interpersonal level, with restitution or even private resources, rather than official punishment, the main remedy.[9] The state played little part. For example, the Code of Hammurabi provided that individuals who had injured or taken from others must make amends, in service or in kind.[10] Other early systems, such as the Torah and Sumerian Code,[11] required that offenders make their victims whole, as

---

8. For excellent overviews of the new movement, see generally PACT INST. OF JUSTICE & MCC OFFICE OF CRIMINAL JUSTICE, THE VORP BOOK (Howard Zehr ed., 1983); DANIEL VAN NESS & KAREN H. STRONG, RESTORING JUSTICE (1997); MARTIN WRIGHT, JUSTICE FOR VICTIMS AND OFFENDERS: A RESTORATIVE RESPONSE TO CRIME (2d ed. 1996); Mark S. Umbreit, *The Development and Impact of Victim-Offender Mediation in the United States*, 12 MEDIATION Q. 263 (1995); Daniel W. Van Ness, *New Wine and Old Wineskins: Four Challenges of Restorative Justice*, 4 CRIM. L.F. 251 (1993); Henry J. Reske, *Victim-Offender Mediation Catching On*, A.B.A. J., Feb. 1995, at 14, 14; David Van Biema, *Should All Be Forgiven?*, TIME, Apr. 5, 1999, at 55, 55; Howard Zehr, *Restorative Justice: The Concept*, CORRECTIONS TODAY, Dec. 1997, at 68.

For critiques and evaluations of the restorative justice movement or victim-offender mediation, see generally RESTORATIVE JUSTICE ON TRIAL (Heinz Messmer & Mans-Uwe Otto eds., 1992); Andrew Ashworth, *Some Doubts About Restorative Justice*, 4 CRIM. L.F. 277 (1993); Jennifer Gerarda Brown, *The Use of Mediation to Resolve Criminal Cases: A Procedural Critique*, 43 EMORY L.J. 1247 (1994); Terenia Urban Guill, *A Framework for Understanding and Using ADR*, 71 TUL. L. REV. 1313 (1997); Sheila D. Porter & David B. Ells, *Mediation Meets the Criminal Justice System*, 23 COLO. LAW. 2521 (1994).

9. *See, e.g.*, VAN NESS & STRONG, *supra* note 8, at 8; Van Ness, *supra* note 8, at 253-56; Brown, *supra* note 8, at 1254 (discussing blood feuds and private vengeance).

10. *See, e.g.*, VAN NESS & STRONG, *supra* note 8, at 8-9.

11. *See id.; see also* Fred Gay & Thomas J. Quinn, *Restorative Justice and Prosecution in the Twenty-First Century*, THE PROSECUTOR, Sept./Oct. 1996, at 16 (noting that the Sumerian method has roots in the 600 A.D. Laws of Ethelbert). On the Torah's preference for compensation of vic-

did Roman law.[12] Then, in the eleventh century, William the Conqueror expanded the king's authority by declaring certain offenses crimes or "breaches of the king's peace," redressed only by action of the king's courts.[13] Accordingly, private vengeance was forbidden, fines were paid directly to the state, rather than to the victim, and punishment, rather than restitution or making amends, became the main sanction for antisocial behavior.[14] This approach, with the state wielding monopoly power over the prosecution and punishment of crime, has reigned unchallenged until recently.

A. *Restorative Justice*

Many proponents of restorative justice believe that our current approach to criminal justice should be reexamined and that we should try to recapture many of the values of the earlier, pre-Norman approach. Specifically, restorative justice advocates argue that incarceration offers little in the way of rehabilitative opportunities for offenders. Many emerge from prison more hardened and angry than when they entered, setting up a cycle of recidivism that serves neither them nor society.[15] Moreover, although the victims' rights movement has begun to clamor for restitution as a part of court-ordered sentencing,[16] relatively few victims receive compensation for their injuries, and fewer still receive anything resembling an apology from the perpetrator.[17]

The movement's proponents argue that the traditional criminal justice system does a second disservice to victims, by forcing them to relive their ordeal at trial.[18] Because the American criminal justice system conceptualizes crime as a wrong against the state, it uses the victim for her testimony, while offering little, if anything, in the way of counseling services or sup-

---

tims, see STEVEN SCHAFER, COMPENSATION AND RESTITUTION TO VICTIMS OF CRIME (2d ed. 1970); Brown, *supra* note 8, at 1254 n.20; *Victim Restitution in the Criminal Process: A Procedural Analysis*, 97 HARV. L. REV. 931, 933 n.18 (1984).

12. *See* VAN NESS & STRONG, *supra* note 8, at 8-9. Early Saxon justice had similar provisions. *See* SCHAFER, *supra* note 11, at 3-7; Brown, *supra* note 8, at 1254-55 n.22.

13. *See, e.g.,* VAN NESS & STRONG, *supra* note 8, at 9-11; Van Ness, *supra* note 8, at 255-56.

14. *See* VAN NESS & STRONG, *supra* note 8, at 9-11; WRIGHT, *supra* note 8, at 14 (noting that collecting fines and forfeits proved to be profitable); Van Ness, *supra* note 8, at 256.

15. *See, e.g.,* VAN NESS & STRONG, *supra* note 8, at 43; WRIGHT, *supra* note 8, at 11, 40; Van Ness, *supra* note 8 at 257-60.

16. On the victims' rights movement, which advocates restitution and a more participatory role at trial for victims of crime, see, e.g., NATIONAL VICTIM CTR., CHRONOLOGY OF THE VICTIMS' RIGHTS CONSTITUTIONAL AMENDMENT MOVEMENT (1991). For a critique of this movement, see Lynne N. Henderson, *The Wrongs of Victim's Rights*, 37 STAN. L. REV. 937 (1985).

17. *See* Brown, *supra* note 8, at 1255-57 (describing the nascent victims' rights movement, which is attempting to address these perceived differences).

18. *See* NATIONAL INST. OF CORRECTIONS, DEP'T OF JUSTICE, RESTORATIVE JUSTICE: WHAT WORKS 3 (1996); Umbreit, *supra* note 8, at 263.

756   *STANFORD LAW REVIEW*   [Vol. 52:751

port.[19] For the same reason, district attorneys rarely consult with the victim at key times during the course of the trial, so that he experiences a lack of control as key events take place without his input.[20]

In response to these perceived shortcomings, proponents of the Restorative Justice Movement believe that those affected most by crime should play an active role in its resolution. The movement intends to redefine crime as an offense against an individual, providing a forum for the victim to participate in the resolution and restitution of that crime.[21] This is achieved through programs in which the victim, offender, and community play an active role.

B. *Victim-Offender Mediation: Restorative Justice in Action*

Of the numerous programs bearing restorative justice roots, Victim-Offender Mediation (VOM) is the most well established.[22] Although VOM takes slightly varying forms,[23] all share the same basic structure. Most receive referrals from the traditional justice system, are predicated on an admission of guilt, and, if successful, are conducted in lieu of a conventional trial.[24] The VOM process generally consists of four phases: Intake, Preparation for Mediation, Mediation, and Follow-up.[25] During intake, a pre-

---

19. This limitation is inherent in the prosecutor's role—she prosecutes in the name of the state. Unlike a tort lawyer who sues on behalf of an assigned client and, of course, is under a professional obligation to consult with that client at critical stages, the victim of a crime is not the client of either the prosecutor or defense counsel and has no right, under conventional law or professional codes, to be consulted as to his wishes at critical stages. *See* Henderson, *supra* note 16, at 942-53 (describing recent changes affording victims a measure of participation rights).

20. *See* Brown, *supra* note 8, at 1256-57 (describing the beginnings of a movement to provide victims such input).

21. *See* VAN NESS & STRONG, *supra* note 8, at 43; Mark S. Umbreit & William Bradshaw, *Victim Experience of Meeting Adult vs. Juvenile Offenders: A Cross-National Comparison*, 61 FED. PROBATION, Dec. 1997, at 33, 33. On the general movement to reincorporate the victim in our treatment of crime, see generally DAVID W. VAN NESS, CRIME AND ITS VICTIMS (1986).

22. *See* Gordon Bazemore & Curt Taylor Griffiths, *Conference, Circles, Boards, and Mediations: The "New Wave" of Community Justice Decisionmaking*, FED. PROBATION, June 1997, at 25, 27; Zehr, *supra* note 8, at 268-70.

Other restorative justice programs include community policing, community corrections, and family conferencing circles. *See* Bazemore & Griffiths, *supra*; Russ Immarigeon & Kathleen Daly, *Restorative Justice: Origins, Practices, Contexts, and Challenges*; 8 ICCA J. ON COMMUNITY CORRECTIONS 13, 13-16, 26, 28-30, 35, 37-39 (1997). On various aspects of community corrections, see ROBERTA C. CRONIN, NATIONAL INST. OF JUSTICE, BOOT CAMP FOR ADULT AND JUVENILE OFFENDERS, OVERVIEW AND UPDATE (1994) (describing boot camp punishment, youth leadership camps, and similar programs for offenders); NATIONAL INST. OF CORRECTIONS, STRIVING FOR SAFE, SECURE AND JUST COMMUNITIES (1996) (essays on approaches to community corrections that emphasize community and neighborhood participation and control).

23. *See* Brown, *supra* note 8, at 1264 (describing the different implementations of VOM).

24. *See* Mark S. Umbreit, *Mediation of Victim Offender Conflict*, 1988 J. DISP. RESOL. 85, 88 (1988).

25. *See id.* at 87.

screening occurs. Here, the mediator, who is either a trained community volunteer or a staff person,[26] accepts the victim and offender into the VOM process if both parties express a readiness to negotiate and show no overt hostility toward each other.[27] In the Preparation for Mediation stage, the mediator talks with the victim and the offender individually and schedules the first meeting. If the mediator does not feel she has effectively established trust and rapport with each of the parties, the case is remanded to court.[28] In the Mediation stage itself, the parties are expected to tell their versions of the story, talk things over, come to understand each other's position, and agree upon an appropriate solution, usually a restitution agreement or work order.[29] If they cannot do so, the case is remanded to court. A final Follow-up stage monitors the offender's performance and cooperation with the work or restitution agreement, with the goal of assuring compliance.[30]

1. *VOM success: far-reaching and still growing.*

While the majority of VOM programs concentrate on first- and second-time juvenile offenders,[31] some include adult felons, including alleged killers, armed robbers, and rapists.[32] In a recent year, VOM dealt with 16,500 cases in the United States alone, while the number of programs in the United States and Canada approached 125.[33] Endorsed by the ABA,[34] the movement shows no sign of slowing.[35]

2. *VOM's departure from today's criminal justice system.*

Like other programs born of the Restorative Justice Movement, VOM seeks to cure perceived problems with the traditional criminal justice process. While an adversarial dynamic may create the appearance of greater justice, it also provides minimal emotional closure for the victim and little direct

---

26. *See* MARK S. UMBREIT & NATIONAL INST. OF CORRECTIONS, DEP'T OF JUSTICE, VICTIM OFFENDER MEDIATION: CONFLICT RESOLUTION AND RESTITUTION 9 (1985).

27. *See id.*

28. *See* Umbreit, *supra* note 24, at 88.

29. *See id.* at 90-91.

30. *See id.* at 92; Brown, *supra* note 8, at 1265-67.

31. *See* Umbreit, *supra* note 8, at 270; Mark S. Umbreit & Jean Greenwood, *National Survey of Victim-Offender Mediation Programs in the United States*, 16 MEDIATION Q. 235, 239 (1999).

32. *See* MARK S. UMBREIT, PACT INST. OF JUSTICE, VICTIM OFFENDER MEDIATION WITH VIOLENT OFFENSES 11-18 (1986); WRIGHT, *supra* note 8, at 90, 159 (noting that VOM is beginning to be considered for cases of domestic violence and sexual assault); Brown, *supra* note 8, at 1262; Barbara Hudson, *Restorative Justice: The Challenge of Sexual and Racial Violence*, 25 J.L. & SOC'Y 237, 245-53 (1998); Umbreit & Greenwood, *supra* note 31.

33. *See* Guill, *supra* note 8, at 1327.

34. *See* Reske, *supra* note 8.

35. *See* Mike Dooley, *The NIC on Restorative Justice*, CORRECTIONS TODAY, Dec. 1997, at 110.

accountability by the offender to the victim.[36] On the other hand, VOM deals more openly with the direct human consequences of crime. Through a face-to-face meeting and discussion, the victim is able to receive information about the crime, express to the offender the impact his actions have had on her, and, it is hoped, gain a sense of material and emotional restoration.[37] Similarly, the offender is forced to face the consequences of his actions and accept responsibility for them, while also playing a role in fashioning the remedies.[38] The offender's restitution should also lead to increased public confidence in the fairness of the system.[39] A further advantage for the offender is that VOM offers an alternative to the ravages of incarceration: Because successful mediation serves in lieu of a trial, a defendant who cooperates and performs the agreed service will escape confinement entirely.

In summary, proponents of VOM maintain that the program will empower the victim while reducing recidivism among offenders.[40] It offers the hope that victims and offenders may come to recognize each other's common humanity and that offenders will be able to take their place in the wider community as valued citizens. Through restitution, the victim will gain back what was lost. Accordingly, VOM proponents advocate the program as "a challenging new vision of how communities can respond to crime and victimization. . . . deeply rooted in . . . the collective western heritage . . . of remorse, forgiveness, and reconciliation."[41]

II. CAN RESTORATIVE JUSTICE DELIVER ON ITS PROMISES? AN INTERNAL CRITIQUE

Critics of the Restorative Justice Movement and VOM voice two concerns: (1) they charge that restorative justice does not deliver what we expect from a system of criminal justice, and (2) they contend that the movement

---

36. *See* Umbreit, *supra* note 8, at 266.

37. *See* Van Biema, *supra* note 8, at 55-56; *see also* Hon. Robert Yazzie, *"Hozho Nahasdlii"—We Are Now in Good Relations: Navajo Restorative Justice,* 9 ST. THOMAS L. REV. 117, 123-24 (1996) (discussing a traditional parallel system of restorative justice among the Navajo).

38. *See* UMBREIT & NATIONAL INST. OF CORRECTIONS, *supra* note 26, at 3; Guill, *supra* note 8, at 1327-28; Yazzie, *supra* note 37, at 123.

39. *See* Gordon Bazemore & Mark Umbreit, *Rethinking the Sanctioning Function in Juvenile Court: Retributive or Restorative Responses to Youth Crime,* 41 CRIME & DELINQ. 296, 297-98, 302-03 (1995).

40. *See* William R. Nugent & Jeffrey B. Paddock, *The Effect of Victim-Offender Mediation on Severity of Reoffense,* 12 MEDIATION Q. 353, 363, 365 (1995).

41. Umbreit, *supra* note 8, at 275. *But see* Brown, *supra* note 8, at 1295 (arguing that this goal is unrealistic in a culturally diverse society and that VOM advocates hunger for a "simpler, more homogeneous time").

may render a disservice to victims, offenders, or society at large. The following two sections discuss these two sets of criticisms in turn.[42]

A. *Can Restorative Justice Deliver What We Expect from a System of Criminal Justice?*

Among the elements that society may reasonably expect from a criminal justice system are consistency, equality of bargaining power, due process, punishment, state control, and widespread applicability.

1. *Consistency.*

Consider first the problem of inconsistent results. The traditional criminal justice system aims at uniformity, employing a system of graded offenses and sentencing guidelines designed to assure that like cases are treated alike.[43] Although far from perfect in realizing this goal, the system at least holds consistency up as an ideal and includes measures designed to bring it about.[44] Moreover, judges, prosecutors, and defense attorneys are repeat players who tend to see cases in categorical terms (e.g., a car accident: pedestrian versus driver) rather than in terms of ascribed qualities of the participants (e.g., black driver, white pedestrian).[45] However, VOM lacks both an obvious "metric" (e.g., what is the appropriate number of hours of community service for a shoplifting offense?[46]) and the repeat-player quality of formal adjudication.[47] The mediator may have seen many cases similar to the one at hand, but the victim and the offender will most likely be in their

---

42. The term "internal critique" describes a critique or assessment that takes as its point of departure goals and values that its new movement professes, or that reasonably may be attributed to it.

43. *See, e.g., A Symposium on Sentencing Reform in the States,* 64 U. COLO. L. REV. 645 (1993).

44. *See, e.g.,* Leonard Orland & Kevin R. Reitz, *Epilogue: A Gathering of State Sentencing Commissions,* 64 U. COLO. L. REV. 837, 844 (1993).

45. The "social contact hypothesis," a leading school of social science thought, holds that interacting with large numbers of people of different races diminishes prejudice, because the individual learns, through experience, that people of different races and ethnicities are similar to those of her own group—some good, some bad. For a summary of this theory and its leading contender, the "confrontation theory," see Richard Delgado, Chris Dunn, Pamela Brown, Helena Lee & David Hubbert, *Fairness and Formality: Minimizing the Risk of Prejudice in Alternative Dispute Resolution,* 1985 WIS. L. REV. 1359, 1385-87 (summarizing social science studies suggesting that a regime of firm rules and sanctions is best calculated to suppress racist impulses, even the unconscious kind).

46. On this lack of a readily available metric for compensatory justice, see Ashworth, *supra* note 8, at 280-85, 290-94 (noting that harms to "the community" are especially hard to quantify).

47. In mediation, the mediator may be somewhat of a repeat player (although not so much as a judge), but the victim and offender are likely to be first-time (or at least infrequent) participants. *See* Delgado et al., *supra* note 45, at 1365.

situation for the first time.[48] Without any prior experience, different victims and offenders may decide similar cases differently, leading to inconsistency in punishment.

2. *Inequality of bargaining power.*

VOM gives great power to the victim, and mediators and judges reinforce that power, placing defendants in an almost powerless position. For example, the mediator frequently advises the offender that he will be referred back to the court system for trial if he and the victim cannot reach a restitution agreement.[49] The mediator may also tell the offender that the judge will take his lack of cooperation into account at the time of sentencing. This leaves the victim with the power to price the crime based on her subjective reaction, while at the same time confronting the offender with a harsh choice: cooperate or go to jail.[50]

3. *Waiver of constitutional rights.*

Related to the above-mentioned coercive quality of mediation is the issue of waiver of constitutional rights.[51] Enacted during a period when the "king's peace" view of crime and criminal justice prevailed, rather than during the earlier period when private restitution served as chief remedy,[52] our Constitution and Bill of Rights guarantee the criminally accused certain rights, including the right to confront witnesses, to be represented by counsel, and to avoid self-incrimination.[53] Fearing abuse by the powerful state, the Framers incorporated these protections against overzealous prosecution and police practices.[54] However, because VOM pressures offenders to accept informal resolution of the charges against them and to waive representation by a lawyer, trial by jury, and the right to appeal, it would seem to stand on constitutionally questionable ground.[55] Moreover, mediation takes place early in the criminal process, at a time when the offender may be un-

---

48. *See* note 45 *supra* and accompanying text.

49. *See* Brown, *supra* note 8, at 1267, 1269-70.

50. *See* note 46 *supra* and accompanying text; *see also* Brown, *supra* note 8, at 1249.

51. *See* notes 28-31, 48-50 *supra* and accompanying text.

52. *See* notes 9-14 *supra* and accompanying text.

53. *See* U.S. CONST. amend. V, VI; *see also* JEROLD H. ISRAEL, YALE KAMISAR & WAYNE R. LAFAVE, CRIMINAL PROCEDURE AND THE CONSTITUTION 33-54 (1999) (discussing the way in which these rights were extended to all criminal defendants).

54. *See* WAYNE R. LAFAVE & JEROLD H. ISRAEL, CRIMINAL PROCEDURE § 2.1 (2d ed. 1992).

55. *See* notes 28-31, 48-50 *supra* and accompanying text.

aware of the evidence against him, or the range of defenses available.[56] Furthermore, social science evidence compiled by VOM's defenders is one-sided, adulatory, and lacking basic elements of scholarly rigor—such as blind studies, controls for variables, and randomization—that one would wish in connection with a widespread social experiment.[57] In the current state of research, neither offenders nor their advisors can predict what mediation will really be like.[58] Thus, a defendant may be unable to waive his rights "knowingly and intelligently" as required by the Constitution.[59]

4. *Punishment.*

Our society has further expectations of any system of criminal adjudication. These include the traditional goals of criminal punishment—deterrence, rehabilitation, increased societal safety, and retribution.[60] Mediation may accomplish some of these objectives in individual cases, but only incidentally and as a byproduct of its principal objectives of compensating the victim and avoiding incarceration for the offender.[61] During mediation, if an offender is willing to apologize and make restitution, he is released immediately into society with little check on whether he is fully rehabilitated.[62] Accordingly, society's need for retribution or vengeance remains unsatisfied. This is not surprising: Most restorative justice theorists consider retribution an illegitimate relic of a more barbaric age.[63]

5. *State control.*

Another troubling aspect of VOM is that it may upset social expectations by casting a wider net of state control than we expect. One way this may happen is that minor cases that ordinarily would have been dismissed or treated summarily in the traditional system receive full-blown treatment under VOM.[64] Indeed, one study showed that VOM *increased* incarceration

---

56. *See* Brown, *supra* note 8, at 1263-64.

57. *See, e.g.,* Elmar Weitenkamp, *Can Restitution Serve as a Reasonable Alternative to Imprisonment?*, in RESTORATIVE JUSTICE ON TRIAL, *supra* note 8, at 84, 94.

58. *See id.; see also* Guill, *supra* note 8, at 1327-28 (arguing that the literature is dismissive of problems and objections).

59. *See* Johnson v. Zerbst, 304 U.S. 458, 465 (1938) (holding that waiver of constitutional rights must be knowing and voluntary).

60. On these four classic goals of criminal punishment, see JOSHUA DRESSLER, CASES AND MATERIALS ON CRIMINAL LAW 21-35 (1994).

61. *See* text accompanying notes 9-41 *supra* (discussing the objectives and ambitions of restorative justice).

62. *See* Robert Carl Schehr, From Restoration to Transformation: Victim Offender Mediation as Transformative Justice 19-21 (1999) (unpublished manuscript, on file with author).

63. *See, e.g.,* WRIGHT, *supra* note 8, at 133, 135; Van Ness, *supra* note 8, at 251-52, 258-59, 266.

64. *See* Weitenkamp, *supra* note 57, at 81-84.

because many offenders who would not have received jail time entered into a restitution agreement, but then failed to carry it out. These offenders were then referred back to court, where they were sentenced for failure to complete their restitution bargain.[65]

6. *VOM's limited applicability.*

Finally, mediation cannot be applied, without radical modification, to victimless crimes, such as drug offenses or crimes of attempt, or to offenses against the state or a corporation.[66] In these cases, no ordinary victim is available to meet with the perpetrator and discuss restitution, nor has the perpetrator victimized a specific individual or community who could be made whole.

B. *Disservice Toward Particular Groups*

Defenders of restorative justice and VOM frequently assert that this type of informal justice is beneficial to society, offenders, and victims. What they neglect to mention, however, is that informal justice may also have a number of downsides for both victims and offenders.

1. *Victims.*

Mediation may disserve victims by pressuring them to forgive offenders before they are psychologically ready to do so.[67] Mediators, who typically want both parties to put aside their anger and distrust, may intimate that victims are being obstructionist or emotionally immature if they refuse to do so. Such victims may in fact harbor perfectly understandable anger and resentment over the crime.[68] A victim who already blames herself may magnify that self-blame; this risk is most severe if the offender is an acquaintance or intimate partner of the victim.[69] Furthermore, VOM casts the victim in the role of sentencer, holding the power of judgment over the offender. Not only does this lead to a lack of proportionality and consistency,[70] but it may also place an unwelcome burden on the victim who will end up determining the

---

65. *See, e.g., id.*

66. In these cases, either no victim exists, or the harm is so diffuse as to make restitution and compensatory justice impracticable. *See* WRIGHT, *supra* note 8, at 147-48 (noting that where no individual victim exists, restitution might go to the community as a whole, or it may not be required if the victim does not want it); Ashworth, *supra* note 8, at 284.

67. *See,* Brown, *supra* note 8, at 1273-76.

68. *See id.* at 1266, 1273.

69. *See id.* at 1278-81.

70. *See* text accompanying notes 43-48 *supra.*

fate of an often young and malleable offender. Not every victim will welcome this responsibility.[71] In pressuring the victim to "forgive and move on" and handing him the power of sentencer, VOM may end up compounding the injury received from the crime itself.

2. *Offenders.*

At the same time, VOM may disserve offenders, who lose procedural guarantees of regularity and fair treatment.[72] Offenders are urged to be forthcoming and admit what they did, yet often what they say is admissible against them in court if the case is returned.[73] Finally, as mentioned earlier, mediation may not meet social expectations for a system of criminal justice: It dismisses retribution, a valid social impulse; abjures incapacitation, even for serious offenses; offers little in the way of deterrence (a forty-five minute session is not unpleasant enough); and reduces recidivism little, if at all, perhaps because offenders' basic attitudes are unchanged, and the compulsory nature of the mediation induces only superficial expressions of shame and regret.[74]

III. EXTERNAL CRITIQUE: LARGER, SYSTEMIC PROBLEMS WITH RESTORATIVE JUSTICE AND VICTIM-OFFENDER MEDIATION

As we have seen, restorative justice, in some respects, falls short of achieving its professed goals, or, indeed, those that any system of criminal justice, even narrowly understood, should be expected to accomplish. This section examines restorative justice in light of broader political and social values, such as its ability to spark needed social change, moral reflection, or altered relationships between offender and victim communities. As will be seen, restorative justice raises troubling issues when viewed through this lens as well.

A. *Restoration of the Status Quo Ante*

One difficulty with restorative justice inheres in the concept itself. Restorative justice, like tort law, attempts to restore the parties to the status quo ante—the position they would have been in had the crime not occurred—through restitution and payment.[75] But if that status quo is marked by radical

71. *See* Brown, *supra* note 8, at 1266-67.

72. *See* notes 54-55 *supra* and accompanying text; Brown, *supra* note 8, at 1284-86 (noting that VOM may be especially hard on minorities and the tongue-tied).

73. *See* Brown, *supra* note 8, at 1288-90 (noting the risk of self-incrimination).

74. *See* note 85 *infra* and accompanying text; *see also* WRIGHT, *supra* note 8, at 27 (describing punishment as the "deliberate infliction of pain" and rehabilitative sanctions as constructive measures); Ashworth, *supra* note 8, at 283-86 (doubting whether society is prepared to forfeit retributive punishment in favor of a restorative justice approach).

ugh restitution and payment.[75] But if that status quo is marked by radical inequality and abysmal living conditions for the offender, returning the parties to their original positions will do little to spark social change. The mediation agreement ordinarily requires payment from the offender to the victim, when in many cases it will be the offender who needs a better education, increased job training, and an improved living environment. Offenders rarely are assigned work that will benefit them or lead to new job opportunities; rather, they end up performing menial services for the victim, such as cutting his grass, painting his porch, or making simple repairs.[76] When the offender performs services for the community, they typically take the form of unskilled labor, such as clearing brush, picking up trash in city parks, or painting over graffiti.[77]

A key component of VOM consists of shaming the offender—making him feel the full force of the wrongfulness of his action, thus causing him to experience remorse.[78] Yet, this adjustment is all one-way: No advocate of VOM, to my knowledge, suggests that the middle-class mediator, the victim, or society at large should feel shame or remorse over the conditions that led to the offender's predicament. Of course, many offenders will be antisocial individuals who deserve little solicitude, while many victims will have well-developed social consciences and empathize with the plight of the urban poor. But nothing in restorative justice or VOM encourages this kind of analysis or understanding.[79] In most cases, a vengeful victim and a middle-class mediator will gang up on a young, minority offender, exact the expected apology, and negotiate an agreement to pay back what she has taken from the victim by deducting portions of her earnings from her minimum-wage job. Little social transformation is likely to arise from transactions of this sort.

---

75. *Cf.* WRIGHT, *supra* note 8, at 124, 129 (acknowledging that restitution can be regressive, but noting that this is not a frequent concern); Schehr, *supra* note 62 (noting that restitution is arguably inherently conservative, since its goal is to restore parties to the situation that prevailed before their interaction took place).

76. On the range of work assignments, see Bazemore & Griffiths, *supra* note 22, at 28; Schehr, *supra* note 62, at 3-5, 21-22 (on menial work assignments, in general); Reginald A. Wilkinson, *Community Justice in Ohio*, CORRECTIONS TODAY, Dec. 1997, at 100-01.

77. *See* note 76 *supra*.

78. On shame as an ingredient in VOM and restorative justice, see generally VAN NESS & STRONG, *supra* note 8; Brown, *supra* note 8. On shame as a crime control strategy, see generally JOHN BRAITHWAITE, CRIME, SHAME, AND REINTEGRATION (1989). For critiques of the shaming approach, see generally Toni M. Massaro, *Shame, Culture, and American Criminal Law*, 89 MICH. L. REV. 1880 (1991); Robert Weisberg, *Criminal Law, Criminology, and the Small World of Legal Scholarship*, 63 U. COLO. L. REV. 521 (1992).

79. *See generally* Schehr, *supra* note 62.

B. *Unlikelihood of Sparking Moral Reflection and Development*

By the same token, it seems unlikely that VOM will produce the desired internal, moral changes in the offender.[80] In theory, bringing the offender to the table to confront the victim face-to-face will enable him to realize the cost of his actions in human terms and to resolve to lead a better life.[81] Some offenders may, indeed, have a crisis of conscience upon meeting the person she has victimized. But a forty-five minute meeting is unlikely to have a lasting effect if the offender is released to her neighborhood and teenage peer group immediately afterwards.[82] If the offender-victim encounter is brief and perfunctory, and the ensuing punishment demeaning or menial, young offenders will learn to factor the cost of restitution into their practical calculus the next time they are tempted to commit a crime and to parrot what is expected of them when caught. Most offenders are at an early stage of Kohlberg's moral development, seeing right and wrong in pragmatic terms— the action is right if you can get away with it, wrong if you are caught and punished.[83] A short encounter with a victim is unlikely to advance them to a higher stage. Reports of young offenders show that most have little self-esteem,[84] yet both the mediation and the ensuing work an offender performs for the victim or his community come perilously close to degradation rituals. Rarely, if ever, is the offender ordered to do something that will benefit him. For all these reasons, VOM is apt to do little to make an offender a better person; indeed, in a few studies, recidivism increased, compared to a similar group subject to the ordinary criminal justice system.[85]

C. *Inequality of Treatment of Offenders and Victims*

Mediation treats the *victim* respectfully, according him the status of an end-in-himself, while the offender is treated as a thing to be managed, shamed, and conditioned.[86] Most surveys of VOM programs ask the victim if he felt better afterwards. By contrast, offenders are merely asked whether

---

80. On the hope that VOM will transform hardened criminals into thoughtful, law-abiding citizens, see Brown, *supra* note 8, at 1259-61.

81. *See id.* at 1259-60.

82. In other words, the reinforcing effect of the neighborhood and peer group is likely to be much more enduring and influential than that of mediation.

83. *See* JAMES Q. WILSON & RICHARD J. HERRNSTEIN, CRIME AND HUMAN NATURE 392-93 (1985); Bruce A. Arrigo & Robert C. Schehr, *Restoring Justice for Juveniles: A Critical Analysis of Victim-Offender Mediation*, 15 JUSTICE Q. 629, 653 (1998).

84. *See, e.g., Turning Society's Losers into Winners, an Interview with Dennis A. Challeen*, 19 JUDGES J. 4, 5 (1980).

85. *See* P. R. SCHNEIDER, RESTITUTION AS AN ALTERNATIVE DISPOSITION FOR SERIOUS JUVENILE OFFENDERS (1982); Weitenkamp, *supra* note 57, at 84. *But see* VAN NESS & STRONG, *supra* note 8, at 10 (finding small, insignificant reductions in recidivism).

86. *See* notes 12-18, 36-40 *supra* and accompanying text.

they completed their work order and whether they recidivated.[87] Offenders sense this and play along with what is desired, while the victim and middle-class mediator participate in a paroxysm of righteousness. In such a setting, the offender is apt to grow even more cynical than before and learn what to say the next time to please the mediator, pacify the victim, and receive the lightest restitution agreement possible.

The offender's cynicism may not just be an intuition; it may be grounded in reality: Informal dispute resolution is even more likely to place him at a disadvantage than formal adjudication. In court, a panoply of procedural devices serve as a brake against state power and overzealous prosecution.[88] Each defendant is assigned a lawyer, who has a prescribed time and place for speaking.[89] The state bears a heavy burden of proof.[90] Moreover, visible features of the American Creed, such as the flag, the robes, and the judge sitting on high, remind all present that principles, such as fairness, equal treatment, and every person receiving his day in court, are to govern, rather than the much less noble values we often act upon during moments of informality.[91] In less formal settings, the same individuals who will behave with fairness during occasions of state will feel much freer to tell an ethnic joke or deny a person of color or a woman a job opportunity.[92] This "fairness and formality" thesis, solidly grounded in social science understandings of the dynamics of prejudice,[93] counsels against using VOM for offenders who are

87. *See, e.g.,* MARK S. UMBREIT, VICTIM MEETS OFFENDER: THE IMPACT OF RESTORATIVE JUSTICE AND MEDIATION (1994) (reporting studies of satisfaction in four juvenile courts that employed victim-offender mediation); WRIGHT, *supra* note 8, at 129; William Bradshaw & Mark S. Umbreit, *Crime Victims Meet Juvenile Offenders: Contributing Factors to Victim Satisfaction with Mediated Dialog*, JUV. & FAM. CT. J., Summer 1998, at 17, 19, 21-24; Stella P. Hughes & Anne L. Schneider, *Victim-Offender Mediation: Characteristics and Perceptions of Effectiveness*, 35 CRIME & DELINQ. 217, 229 (1989) (finding victims satisfied and offenders unlikely to recidivate); Schehr, *supra* note 62; Mark S. Umbreit & Jean Greenwood, *National Survey of Victim-Offender Mediation Programs in the United States*, 16 MEDIATION Q. 235, 244-45 (1999) (asking survey victims about their feelings and degree of satisfaction and focusing on whether offenders completed the restitution agreement).

88. *See* notes 54-55 *supra* and accompanying text; Delgado et al., *supra* note 45, at 1367-75, 1402.

89. *See* Delgado et al., *supra* note 45, at 1402.

90. *See e.g.,* DRESSLER, *supra* note 60, at 8-9 (discussing the burden of proof in criminal cases).

91. *See* Delgado et al., *supra* note 45, at 1383-84 (pointing out that at moments of intimacy and informality, individuals are more likely to tell a racist joke, favor friends in job searches, or disparage minorities or women).

92. *See id.* at 1383-85, 1388.

93. *See id.* at 1375-83, 1402-04 (discussing the social science foundation of the fairness-and-formality hypothesis).

young, black, Latino, or otherwise different from the white, middle-class norm many Americans implicitly embrace.[94]

D. *Racial and Social Inequality*

The prime architects of the VOM movement seem to believe that mediators can balance, or counter, inequalities among the parties.[95] However, their own writing about race is replete with stereotypes.[96] Rather than

---

94. *See id.* at 1387-89, 1402-04 (noting that deformalized adjudication exacerbates preexisting power differentials among the participants and increases the likelihood of a biased outcome).

95. *See* Umbreit, *supra* note 8, at 270 (expressing this faith).

96. For example, a leading proponent of VOM, addressing the problem of mediation when one of the parties is a minority group member, writes of African Americans that "understanding the cultural base from which the client is operating" is key. MARK S. UMBREIT, NATIONAL INST. OF CORRECTIONS INFO. CTR., VICTIM OFFENDER MEDIATION IN URBAN/MULTI-CULTURAL SETTINGS 12 (1986). Citing other authorities, seemingly with approval, this author goes on to assert that this understanding includes that blacks are church-oriented, share "child care, food, money, and emotional support," and affirm "a value system which embraces a sense of 'we-ness.'" *Id.* at 13. Moreover, blacks supposedly exhibit an interpersonal style that is "'animated, interpersonal and confrontational,'" while whites are cool and impersonal. *Id.* Black talk is said to be "'heated, loud, and generates affect.'" *Id.* Whites use argument to express anger; blacks, routinely, use argument when trying to persuade. *See id.* at 13-14. Blacks have no respect for authority—merely because something is published "or in some other way certified by experts in the field is not sufficient for many blacks to establish its authority." *Id.* at 14 (citing authorities). Blacks are said to follow a value system in which it is permissible to interrupt, "rather than waiting for their turn," and in which spontaneity of expression is routine. *Id.* They do not understand rules regarding generalization, so that statements like "'white people are racists'" are "not intended to be all inclusive." *Id.* at 15. "Within black culture, the applicable rule is 'If the shoe fits, wear it.'" *Id.*

Further generalizations about blacks related by the same author deal with eye contact, "hot" versus "cool" interactive style, use of titles and surnames, and boastfulness (tolerated and approved of in the black community). *See id.* at 16-17.

Latinos ("Hispanic people") do not come off much better. Latinos are supposedly deeply respectful of authority. "Whether the locus is nature, fate, age, God, or authority, it tends to be more external than internal," in contrast to Anglos who see themselves in charge of their fates. *Id.* at 6-7. Challenging a person's opinion is evidence of "disrespect," a major sin. *Id.* at 7. Hispanic people live in a "hierarcial [sic] world," in which respect and calling people by their last names are of utmost importance. *Id.* at 7-8. The culture is said to encourage dependency, so that the mediator or social worker must "be sure the individual understands you through use of language that is clear, concise, and simple. Second, be warm and personal . . . (yet not) overly friendly, effusive. . . ." *Id.* at 8.

For further stereotypes about minority communities, see Howard H. Irving, Michael Benjamin & Jose San-Pedro, *Family Mediation and Cultural Diversity: Mediating with Latino Families*, 16 MEDIATION Q. 325, 327-30 (1999), which includes the following wisdom about Latinos for fellow mediators:

- Group-oriented (family over all);
- Obsessed with machismo and honor;
- "Sensitive to insult or criticism;"
- Devoid of any sense of time urgency (time is flexible);
- "Emotions are close to the surface;"
- Prone to escalating conflict rapidly, and unable to let it go; and
- Susceptible, in the case of men, to "shame, which in turn promotes marital . . . desertion . . . and divorce."

breaking down the barriers and preconceptions that parties bring to the table, mediation is apt to compound preexisting power and status differentials even more systematically and seriously than formal, in-court resolution.[97] VOM sets up a relatively coercive encounter in many cases between an inarticulate, uneducated, socially alienated youth with few social skills and a hurt, vengeful victim. This encounter is mediated by a middle-class, moralistic mediator who shares little background or sympathy with the offender, but has everything in common with the victim. To label this encounter a negotiation seems a misnomer, for it is replete with overt social coercion.

E. *Prompting Recognition of Common Humanity*

Nothing is wrong with requiring persons who have harmed others without justification to make restitution. But forcing a needy person who has stolen a loaf of bread to do so is regressive, unless accompanied by measures aimed at easing his poverty.[98] In VOM, all the onus is placed on the offender to change; the victim is required only to come to the bargaining table, discuss how the crime has affected him, negotiate a restitution agreement, and accept an apology. Why not require victims to take a bus tour of the offender's neighborhood and learn something about the circumstances in which he lives? In traditional adjudication, judges, prosecutors, defense attorneys, and jurors will all be privy to this information and be able to consider it when charging and sentencing, but with mediation, the mediator and the victim often will not. Mediation aims at emotional closure,[99] but without a reciprocal exchange of information, any closure is apt to occur only on the most superficial level. If the objective of VOM is to have both sides recognize their common humanity, measures of this sort ought to be considered. Why not even encourage the *victim*, in appropriate cases, to perform service to the offender or his or her community as a condition of receiving restitution (for example, by serving as a mentor or big brother/sister to a youth like the of-

---

Mediators are urged to cultivate patience, respect the existing hierarchy and macho practices, and be ready for a parade of "allusions, proverbs, folk tales, storytelling, humor, metaphor, and reframing." *Id.* at 332-33. Because of Latinos' concept of extended time, mediators also need to be ready for clients who miss appointments or show up late. *See id.* at 334; *see also* Cherise D. Hairston, *African Americans in Mediation Literature: A Neglected Population*, 16 MEDIATION Q. 357, 360-61 (1999) ("A review of mediation literature indicates minimal awareness of and sensitivity to historical, political, societal, and cultural influences.").

    97. *See* Delgado et al., *supra* note 45, at 1388-89, 1402-03; text accompanying notes 116-123 *infra*.

    98. Recall the famous line from Anatole France about how the law, in its majesty, forbids rich and poor alike from sleeping under bridges or stealing bread. *See* DICTIONARY OF QUOTATIONS 363 (Bergen Evans ed., 1968).

    99. *See* Brown, *supra* note 8, at 1263; Reske, *supra* note 8, at 14-15; Mark S. Umbreit, *Restorative Justice through Mediation*, J.L. & SOC. WORK, Spring 1995, at 1, 2.

fender)? Countless studies of mediated crime adopt the feelings of the victim as the principal measure of success or failure—the better the victim feels afterwards, the more successful the mediation.[100] Yet, sometimes in a successful mediation, the victim should feel *worse*, or at least realize that matters are not as simple as she might have thought.

F. *Which Community is to be Restored?*

In a similar vein, VOM will frequently lead to a restitution agreement that includes service to "the community."[101] Indeed, one of the principal advantages of VOM is said to be its ability to repair the breach that the offender's crime has opened between himself and that same community.[102] Yet proponents of restorative justice rarely focus on the precise nature of that community. In a diverse, multicultural society, many collectivities may vie for that status. To which does the offender owe restitution? If, for example, the offender is to rake leaves, should he be required to do it in a park near where the victim lives? In a large municipal park serving the entire city? In one in his own neighborhood? Descriptions of successful mediation abound with stories of offenders made to perform services to victims' churches, for example.[103] Apart from obvious issues of separation of church and state, such privatized, particularized service is troublingly reminiscent of peonage and prison labor gangs.

G. *Erasing the Public Dimension of Criminal Prosecution*

Moreover, such particularized mediation atomizes disputes, so that patterns, such as police abuse or the overcharging of black men, do not stand out readily. It forfeits what Owen Fiss and others call the public dimension of adjudication.[104] Mediation pays scant attention to the public interests in

---

100. *See* Reske, *supra* note 8; Van Biema, *supra* note 8 (using feelings as a measure of success).

101. *See, e.g.*, text accompanying note 77 *supra*; Bazemore & Griffiths, *supra* note 22, at 28. For critiques of the notion that, in a diverse society like ours, anything like a unitary community exists, see Massaro, *supra* note 78, at 1922-23; Sally Engle Merry, *Defining "Success" in the Neighborhood Justice Movement*, *in* NEIGHBORHOOD JUSTICE 172, 175-77 (Roman Iomasic & Malcolm M. Feeley eds., 1987); Daniel R. Ortiz, *Categorical Community*, 51 STAN. L. REV. 769 (1999).

102. *See* note 77 *supra* and accompanying text; Bazemore & Griffiths, *supra* note 22, at 28.

103. *See* Bazemore & Griffiths, *supra* note 22, at 25 (describing a work assignment under which the offender was sent to work in a food bank sponsored by victim's church); *see also* WRIGHT, *supra* note 8, at 151 (warning that restitution can be corrupted to serve private gain); Burt Galaway, *Victim Participation in the Penal-Corrective Process*, 10 VICTIMOLOGY: AN INT'L J. 617, 624-25 (1985) (addressing the concern that restitution can be corrupted to serve private gain).

104. *See* Owen Fiss, *Against Settlement*, 93 YALE L.J. 1073, 1085 (1984). Mediation, as observed earlier, takes place in private settings, and the results are rarely recorded or reported in a newspaper or anywhere else.

criminal punishment, particularly retribution.[105] It also lacks the symbolic element of a public trial, trying instead to compensate by formalized talking among private participants. The criminal justice system, of course, is a principal means by which society reiterates its deepest values; loss of that opportunity is cause for concern.

The timing of VOM's advent is also curious: It first appeared when the United States' demographic composition was beginning to shift rapidly in the direction of a majority nonwhite population.[106] Juries were beginning to contain, for the first time, substantial numbers of nonwhite members, and at least one scholar of color would soon encourage black jurors to acquit young black men, who are, in their view more useful to the community free than behind bars.[107] Could it be that VOM arose, consciously or not, in response to the threat of jury nullification?

H. *Treating Conflict as Pathology*

Perhaps the above concerns can be captured in the notion of conflict as pathology.[108] Like many forms of mediation, VOM treats conflict as aberrational, and the absence of it as the desired state.[109] Yet, in a society like ours, tension among groups may be normal, and not a sign of social pathology.[110] With a history of slavery, conquest, and racist immigration laws, the United States today exhibits the largest gap between the wealthy and the poor of any Western industrialized society.[111] Until recently, Southern states segregated school children by race[112] and criminalized marriage between whites and blacks.[113] Surely, in such a society, one would expect the have-nots to attempt to change their social position (by legal or illegal means), and the

---

105. *See* notes 60-63 *supra* and accompanying text; Albert W. Alschuler, *Mediation with a Mugger: The Shortage of Adjudicative Services and the Need for a Two-Tier Trial System in Civil Cases*, 99 HARV. L. REV. 1808, 1809-10 (1986) (questioning whether mediation satisfies the public's demand for accountability); Ashworth, *supra* note 8, at 284 (also questioning whether mediation satisfies the public's demand for accountability).

106. In the late 1970s and early 1980s, when society was first becoming aware of the growth in minority populations.

107. *See generally* Paul Butler, *Racially Based Jury Nullification: Black Power in the Criminal Justice System*, 105 YALE L.J. 677 (1995). For a forerunner of the Butler thesis, see Austin, *supra* note 4, at 1771-72.

108. *See* Richard Delgado, *Conflict as Pathology: An Essay for Trina Grillo*, 81 MINN. L. REV. 1391 (1997) (first coining the term).

109. *See id.* at 1397.

110. *See id.* at 1397, 1400-02.

111. *See* Tom Teepen, *It's True: Rich Just Get Richer; Poor, Poorer*, MILWAUKEE J. SENTINEL, Sept. 7, 1999, at 10.

112. *See* Brown v. Board of Education, 347 U.S. 483 (1954).

113. *See* Loving v. Virginia, 388 U.S. 1 (1967).

haves to resist these attempts. Conflict is a logical and expected result.[114] One also would expect the majority group to use the criminal law, at least in part, as a control device—a means of keeping tabs on any behavior of subordinate groups that threatens or irritates, such as loud music, congregating on sidewalks, writing graffiti on freeway overpasses, and shoplifting.[115] Insofar as restorative justice aims at smoothing over the rough edges of social competition and adjusting subaltern people to their roles, it is profoundly conservative. While restoration and healing are emotionally powerful objectives, it is hard to deny that they can have a repressive dimension as well.

IV. "BUT CONSIDER THE ALTERNATIVE": THE CRIMINAL JUSTICE SYSTEM

Before rejecting restorative justice and VOM for the reasons mentioned in Parts II and III of this essay, it behooves us, as its advocates urge, to consider the alternative—the conventional criminal justice system. For if informal adjudication of offenders is imperfect, the traditional system may be even worse. And when one does examine the traditional system, one discovers that it is far from the safe haven that formal settings generally provide for the disempowered. Instead, as a result of a slow evolution, our criminal justice system has emerged as perhaps the most inegalitarian and racist structure in society. Our prisons are largely black and brown.[116] Indigent defendants are assigned a lawyer from the underfinanced public defender's office and encouraged to plead guilty to a lesser offense in return for a shorter sentence, even if they are innocent or have valid defenses to the charges against them.[117] Minority defendants receive harsher sentences than middle-class whites charged with the same offense, while black men convicted of murdering whites receive the death penalty ten times more often than do whites who kill blacks.[118] Police focus on minority youth congregating on street corners; they stop black motorists and Latino-looking men at airports so regularly that the black community refers to the traffic stops as "DWBs"

---

114. *See* Delgado, *supra* note 108, at 1397-1402.

115. On the use of the criminal law to demonize and control minority groups of color, see Richard Delgado, *Rodrigo's Eighth Chronicle: Black Crime, White Fears: On the Social Construction of Threat*, 80 VA. L. REV. 503 (1994).

116. *See generally* MARC MAUER, THE SENTENCING PROJECT: YOUNG BLACK MEN AND THE CRIMINAL JUSTICE SYSTEM: A GROWING NATIONAL PROBLEM (1990) (discussing disproportionate number of black men in penal institutions).

117. On the difficult conditions under which most public defenders work, see James M. Doyle, *"It's the Third World Down There!": The Colonialist Vocation and American Criminal Justice*, 27 HARV. C.R.-C.L. L. REV. 71 (1992).

118. On the racial gap in sentencing, see MAUER, *supra* note 116; Andrea Blum, *Jail Time by the Book: Black Youths More Likely to Get Tough Sentences Than Whites, Study Shows*, A.B.A. J., May 1999, at 18. On the death penalty, see DAVID C. BALDUS, GEORGE WOODWORTH & CHARLES A. PULASKI, JR., EQUAL JUSTICE AND THE DEATH PENALTY (1990) (examining the role of racial bias in the application of the death penalty).

("Driving While Black").[119] Meanwhile, the war on drugs causes police to target minority communities, where drug transactions tend to be conspicuous, rather than in middle-class areas where use is more covert.[120] Black judges face recusal motions more often than their white counterparts often from white litigants concerned that the judge may rule against them because of their race.[121] Studies of the behavior of mock jurors show that baby-faced defendants are acquitted more often than less attractive ones against whom the evidence is exactly the same.[122]

The criminal justice system, then, may be the lone institution in American society where formal values and practices are worse—more racist, more inegalitarian—than the informal ones that most citizens share. As previously mentioned, the situation in this society is generally the opposite: Our formal values, the ones that constitute the American Creed, are exemplary—every person is equal, everyone deserves full respect as a moral agent, one person one vote—while informality harbors risks for women, blacks, and members of other outgroups.[123] In our criminal justice system, however, the opposite situation prevails. There alone, as in South Africa under the old regime, the formal values are implicitly or explicitly racist. Just as in South Africa, in former times, a black, such as a stranded motorist, might receive kind treatment from the occasional white traveler while the official police would pass him by, members of stigmatized groups today are apt to receive harsher treatment from U.S. police, judges, and juries than they might get, with luck, at a mediation table. As with Jews in Holland during the Third Reich, private kindness is at least possible; the official kind, unlikely. Despite the main drawbacks of privatized, decentralized, informal mediation, offenders will often be better off taking their chances within VOM than within the formal system.

---

119. *See generally* City of Chicago v. Morales, 527 U.S. 41 (1999) (striking down anti-gang ordinance that prohibited congregating on the streets as impermissibly vague). On "driving while black," see AMERICAN CIVIL LIBERTIES UNION, DRIVING WHILE BLACK: RACIAL PROFILING ON OUR NATION'S HIGHWAYS (1999); Michael A. Fletcher, *Driven to Extremes: Black Men Take Steps to Avoid Police Stops*, WASH. POST, Mar. 29, 1996, at A1; Kevin Johnson, *ACLU Campaign Yields Race Bias Suit*, USA TODAY, May 19, 1999, at 4A. On profiling of Latinos, see Julie Amparano, *Waiting to Celebrate*, A.B.A. J., July 1999, at 68, 69.

120. On the racial impact of the war on drugs, see Andrew N. Sacher, *Inequities of the Drug War: Legislative Discrimination on the Cocaine Battlefield*, 19 CARDOZO L. REV. 1149 (1997).

121. *See* Sherril A. Ifill, *Judging the Judges: Racial Diversity, Impartiality and Representation on State Trial Courts*, 39 B.C. L. REV. 95, 114 (1997) (describing case in which defendants insisted that Judge Leon Higginbotham disqualify himself for this reason).

122. For a study of the role that baby-faced features and physical attractiveness play in determining length of sentence, see Michael G. Efran, *The Effect of Physical Appearance on the Judgment of Guilt, Interpersonal Attraction, and Severity of Recommended Punishment in a Simulated Jury Task*, 8 J. RES. PERSONALITY 45 (1979).

123. *See* Delgado et al., *supra* note 45, at 1367-75, 1383-85, 1402-03.

V. WHAT, THEN, TO DO? A DIALOGIC APPROACH BASED ON COMPETITION BETWEEN THE TWO SYSTEMS

Assuming they have a choice, blacks, Latinos, and others subject to prejudice should examine both systems carefully before opting for one or the other. In white-dominated regions, as Rodney Hero has recently pointed out, blacks are apt to receive poor formal treatment;[124] they may be better off taking their chances with VOM. Where, by contrast, the jury pool is racially mixed and the judge sympathetic, formal adjudication may be the better choice. While these pragmatic calculations are taking place, conscientious legislators and reform-minded lawyers should work to improve both systems.

A. *Within the Formal Criminal Justice System*

Within the formal system of courtroom justice, defense lawyers should serve as guides and native informants, helping defendants find and exploit any known niches of sympathy and fair treatment. Examples include regions where the jury pool is racially and economically mixed, where judges are trained to look behind police testimony and a record of prior convictions for possible bias and overcharging.[125] Because the formal values have become corrupted by an overlay of discriminatory practices, participants must constantly remind everyone to follow the American Creed. Legislators and community groups should urge "superformality"—new layers of formality aimed at keeping the police, prosecutors, and other agents of official power honest. Examples include police and prosecutor review boards, laws requiring the police to keep statistics on traffic stops, and instructions aimed at encouraging members of the jury to consider whether race is affecting their judgment.[126] In short, progressive lawyers and community activists should bolster the in-court version of criminal justice by expanding any informal

---

124. *See* RODNEY HERO, FACES OF INEQUALITY: SOCIAL DIVERSITY IN AMERICAN POLITICS 74-79 (1998) (examining the racial makeup of judges and juries in state courts).

125. *See generally* Doris Marie Provine, *Too Many Black Men: The Sentencing Judge's Dilemma*, 23 L. & SOC. INQUIRY 823 (1998) (discussing the problems of avoiding disproportionate conviction and sentencing of African American males); Katheryn K. Russell, *"Driving While Black": Corollary Phenomena and Collateral Consequences*, 80 B.C. L. REV. 717, 728 (1999) (describing Judge Nancy Gerstner's refusal to sentence a black motorist to a long term under a "three-strikes" type statute, because of the way police target black motorists for zealous enforcement). On the need for skepticism over eyewitness identification in cross-racial settings, see John Gibeaut, *"Yes, I'm Sure That's Him,"* A.B.A. J., Oct. 1999, at 26.

126. *See* Matt Ackerman, *Special Jury Instructions Needed if Cross Racial ID Uncorroborated*, N.J. L.J., Apr. 19, 1999, at 1, 1; Gibeaut, *supra* note 125 (noting that social scientists support the need for caution in cross-race situations); Cynthia Lee, *Race and Self-Defense: Toward a Normative Conception of Reasonableness*, 81 MINN. L. REV. 367, 482 (1996) (urging a "race switching" jury instruction aimed at requiring jurors to consider whether their verdict would be the same if the defendant and the victim were of different races).

links to justice, while seeking to impose new levels of formal oversight on the rest of the system.

B. *Within Alternative, Informal Justice*

Reformers and critics need to call attention to the way mediation's informality can easily conceal race and class bias underneath an overlay of humanitarian concern.[127] Minority communities need to understand how this happens, so they can avoid its seductive appeal. Minorities should also lobby for structural improvements to VOM, such as more mediators of color, participation by defense attorneys, and studies that test some of VOM's overenthusiastic claims. Where VOM seems fairer than the formal justice system, defendants should "take the bait" and opt for it, while keeping alert for possible abuse and unfairness. The defense bar should attempt to counteract the powerfully conservative, status-quo-enforcing thrust of restorative justice by insisting that community and religious groups (its main sponsors) reform it. For example, minority groups could demand that work assignments benefit the offender and her community, rather than merely enhancing the middle-class or suburban communities where most victims live. Just as mediation now provides for a full airing of the victim's story, mediation should allow the offender's history be heard as well. If the offender is inarticulate, someone should be appointed to speak for him, so that those present become better informed of the social conditions that give rise to crime in a substantial sector of the population. Optimistically, this knowledge will inspire further social reform.

C. *Short and Long-Term Strategies*

In short, persons dissatisfied with both approaches to criminal justice should adopt a short-term and a long-term strategy. The short-term would consist of steering defendants to the system where they are likely to experience the fairest treatment. The long-term strategy would focus on forcing dialog and competition between the two systems, drawing comparisons between them, making criticism overt, and attempting to engraft the best features of each onto the other. This frank merging and borrowing should promote dialog between practitioners of conventional, courtroom justice and informal mediation—something that, except in a few locations, is not taking place now. Both systems should be made to compete with each other for resources, participants, and approval in the eyes of the various constituencies that make up the criminal law's public.

---

127. *See* notes 88-95 *supra* and accompanying text.

This process, if carried out persistently and intelligently, can harness two principal theories for controlling prejudice—confrontation and social contact[128]—by challenging the conventional system and the emerging one, reminding each of its myths and values, and demanding that each equal or exceed the other in pursuit of the common goal of racial and social justice. Ultimately, no form of criminal justice, either of the traditional or the restorative variety, will work if the target community lacks a hand in designing and operating it. Blacks, Latinos, whites, middle-class, and blue-collar people must be permitted, indeed encouraged, to work together to counter exploitative arrangements that oppress them and render our society one of the most fearful and crime-ridden in the Western developed world.

---

128. *See* note 45 *supra* (explaining these two approaches).

[12]

Reparation and Retribution: Are They Reconcilable?

Lucia Zedner*

Introduction

The recent history of criminal justice contains an apparent anomaly: the simultaneous renaissance of retributive and reparative models of justice. This article will explore the genesis and competing claims of these two models, how it is that their fortunes have coincided, and with what consequences. Many writing in this field have felt driven to champion the claims of one or the other.[1] Some of these writings read like missionary tracts whose proselytising purposes tend to obstruct measured analysis. Yet the greatest possibilities for illuminative debate have arisen where rival champions have entered into battle with one another to expose the inadequacies or undesirability of the other's model.[2] The consequence, however, is that positions have become polarised. Retributive and reparative justice are posed as antinomies whose claims rival one another and whose goals must be in conflict. The most radical writers propose a major paradigm shift in which reparation would take priority over punishment as the goal of the criminal justice system.[3] From the opposing camp, adherents of retributivism generally argue that reparation is merely incidental to the main purpose of punishment. According to this latter view, the place of reparation within the criminal justice system serves pragmatic purposes but is conceptually anomalous. More recently, welcome attempts to bridge the gap traditionally posed between reparation and retributivism have been mooted by those who question the usefulness of this dichotomised approach to penal theory.[4]

---

*Law Department, London School of Economics.

This article draws upon my contribution to a comparative project 'Wiedergutmachung im Strafrecht/ Reparation in Criminal Law' at the Max Planck Institute for Foreign and International Criminal Law, Freiburg. The project looks at the relationship between punishment and reparation at the level of both theory and practice in sixteen countries. I am grateful to Andrew Ashworth, Michael Cavadino, James Dignan, Nicola Lacey, Andrew von Hirsch and Susanne Walther for their comments and suggestions.

1 The best of such writings include: on reparative justice, Barnett, 'Restitution: A New Paradigm for Criminal Justice' (1977) 87 *Ethics* 279; Wright, *Justice for Victims and Offenders* (London: Sage, 1991); and on retributivism, von Hirsch, *Doing Justice* (Boston: Northeastern University Press, reprint 1986); Ashworth, 'Criminal Justice and Deserved Sentences' (1989) CLR 340.

2 For example, see the debate between Braithwaite and Pettit, and von Hirsch and Ashworth: Braithwaite and Pettit, *Not Just Deserts: A Republican Theory of Criminal Justice* (Oxford: Oxford University Press, 1990); von Hirsch and Ashworth, 'Not Not Just Deserts: A Response to Braithwaite and Pettit' (1992) 12 OJLS 83 and reply by Braithwaite and Pettit, 'Not Just Deserts, Even in Sentencing: A Reply to von Hirsch and Ashworth' (1992) 4(3) *Current Issues in Criminal Justice* 225—239; Ashworth and von Hirsch, 'Desert and the Three Rs' (1993) 5(1) *Current Issues in Criminal Justice* 9. Another such debate is Van Ness, 'New Wine and Old Wineskins: Four Challenges of Restorative Justice' (1993) 4(1) *Criminal Law Forum*, and Ashworth, 'Some Doubts about Restorative Justice' (1993) 4(2) *Criminal Law Forum* 1.

3 See, for example, Barnett, *op cit* n 1; Abel and Marsh, *Punishment and Restitution: A Restitutionary Approach to Crime and the Criminal* (Westport, Connecticut: Greenwood Press, 1984); Fattah, 'From a Guilt Orientation to a Consequence Orientation' in Kueper and Welp (eds), *Beitraege zur Rechtswissenschaft* (Heidelberg: C.F. Mueller Juristischer Verlag, 1993) 771—792.

4 See Watson, Boucherat and Davis, 'Reparation for Retributivists' in Wright and Galaway (eds), *Mediation and Criminal Justice: Victims, Offenders and Community* (London: Sage, 1989); Cavadino and Dignan, 'Reparation, Retribution and Rights,' unpublished paper delivered at the British Criminology Conference, Cardiff, 1993.

This article asks whether the penal system can or should embrace both punitive and reparative goals simultaneously. It does so by analysing the genesis and the claims of retributive and reparative justice; by examining the central criticism of reparation — that it fails as punishment; and, finally, by asking whether and in what respects reparation and retribution can be reconciled. If reparation does have a place within the penal system, then what is, or ought to be, that place? This is neither a missionary 'tract nor a determined attempt at reconciliation. Rather, it seeks to subject both retributive and reparative justice to critical examination in order to tease out strands of congruity and accord as well as those of difference and incompatibility. In a criminal justice system which is characterised above all by diversity and tension, it would be curious for sentencing to enjoy unity or even coherence of aim. Sentencing embraces an array of diverse functions and rightly so. Pluralism is a necessary feature of our penal system and we should resist the temptation to seek intellectual elegance or unanimity at all costs.

A Punishment as Retribution

Before examining the genesis and claims of reparative justice, let us briefly recapitulate the present state of discussion regarding the purposes of our penal system. This history is familiar and it serves little purpose to rehearse it at length here. This said, if the import of the potential paradigm shift proposed by reparative justice is to be fully appreciated, then an overview of the prevailing paradigm is essential.

Since the heyday of welfarism in the 1960s, the political agenda in sentencing has changed markedly: disillusionment with the welfare model of justice prompted growing calls for a 'return to justice', a movement which signifies both renewed regard for due process and the renaissance of retributivism in sentencing.[5] Propounded first and most vigorously in the United States by Andrew von Hirsch,[6] desert theories have more recently become highly influential in Britain. Using classical notions of free will, moral responsibility and culpability, desert theory reifies corresponding notions of censure and sanction as the 'just' response to offending behaviour. Within this framework, it claims to grade the gravity of crimes in order that sanctions of comparable severity may be applied. In Britain many academics, most notably Andrew Ashworth, have welcomed the attempt made by desert theory to develop a coherent, structured approach to sentencing and have applauded the move toward certainty and consistency in the imposition of penalties which it is said to promote.[7] Early proponents of desert theory envisaged that it would serve to delimit levels of punishment, or even bring about a general lowering of the tariff. Instead, since the political swing towards conservatism in Britain in the 1980s, the retributivism of desert theory has been appropriated to serve demands for tougher penalties for serious crime.[8]

---

5 See Ashworth, *Sentencing and Criminal Justice* (London: Weidenfeld and Nicolson, 1992) 66–68, for a discussion of the return to retributivism.

6 von Hirsch, *Past or Future Crimes* (Manchester: Manchester University Press, 1986); von Hirsch and Ashworth (eds), *Principled Sentencing* (Edinburgh: Edinburgh University Press, 1992); von Hirsch, *Censure and Sanctions* (Oxford: Oxford University Press, 1993).

7 Ashworth, *op cit* n 1, 350.

8 Hudson, *Justice through Punishment: A Critique of the 'Justice' Model of Corrections* (Basingstoke: Macmillan, 1987) 22.

Replacing the prevailing 'cafeteria system' of choices with a clear commitment to proportionality, the Criminal Justice Act 1991 was hailed as the most important sentencing legislation in 40 years.[9] The preceding White Paper furnished perhaps the most useful statement of the Government's objective of achieving 'better justice through a more consistent approach to sentencing, so that convicted criminals get their "just desserts"' (*sic*).[10] In outlining the aims of this new sentencing system, the Government declared that 'the first objective for all sentencies is denunciation of and retribution for the crime.' In so doing, it sought to relegate other purposes of 'public protection, reparation and reform of the offender' secondary to this main aim.[11] Scarcely had the Act come into force,[12] however, than it was subject to intense criticism from sentencers who resented the 'straight-jacket' imposed upon their exercise of discretion. Most controversial was the requirement that proportional sentences be handed down without reference to the offender's past record. Under attack from magistrates, judges and, most fiercely, from Lord Chief Justice Taylor, the Government rapidly abandoned its adherence to desert theory.[13] Just nine months after the 1991 legislation had come into force, the Criminal Justice Act 1993 once more gave sentencers the discretion to consider previous convictions.[14]

The current abandonment of desert theory in Britain probably owes more to certain political shibboliths concerning the independence of the judiciary than to doubts about its internal coherence or ability to deliver justice. However, retributivism is not free from criticism on philosophical, moral and, indeed, social grounds. Desert theory is predicated on assumptions of free moral choice and ignores the social context of structural disadvantage in which many offenders act.[15] Emphasis on proportionality thus seeks to detach justification for punishment from wider theories of social justice. Moreover, despite the importance it ascribes proportionality, it gives little concrete guidance as to the appropriate level of penalty. To say that a penalty should be proportional is immediately appealing. It appears instinctively 'right' that a penalty should be no more or less than that merited by the offence. But closer reflection raises difficult questions about whether one can so readily match the gravity of an offence with a number of years of imprisonment, still less with the myriad forms and conditions of probation. The problem becomes particularly acute in respect of more complex or diffuse crimes such as fraud, blackmail or perjury where it is far from obvious what the 'proportionate' punishment might look like.[16] Moreover, the quantum of punishment is always liable to shift according to extraneous criteria such as policy

---

9 Ashworth, *op cit* n 5, p 308. The Criminal Justice Act 1991, s 2(1)(a) and s 6(2)(b) both state that the sentence should be 'commensurate with the seriousness of the offence.'
10 Home Office, *Crime, Justice and Protecting the Public* (London: HMSO, 1990) 2.
11 *op cit* n 10, p 6.
12 In October 1992.
13 Some flavour of these criticisms can be gleaned from the following quotation from a contemporary editorial in *The Times*: 'the Criminal Justice Act should not become an instrument for the statutory suppression of common sense . . . The problems which afflicted the Criminal Justice Act in its first six months illustrate the difference between sensible guidelines and rigid prescription . . . the scales of justice cannot be reduced to an algorithm,' *The Times*, 23 March 1993.
14 It has been argued that the provisions of the 1993 Act provide sentencers with even greater discretion than they enjoyed prior to the 1991 Act: see Thomas, 'Custodial Sentences: The Criterion of Seriousness,' *Archbold News* (London: Sweet & Maxwell, 1993) 14.
15 Hudson, *op cit* n 8.
16 Lacey, *State Punishment* (London: Routledge, 1988) 17. The difficulties entailed in arriving at a proportional punishment for these 'more complex' crimes are recognised even by desert theorists; see von Hirsch and Jareborg, 'Gauging Criminal Harm: A Living-Standard Analysis' (1991) 11 OJLS 34.

considerations, availability of resources and priority given to criminal justice expenditure. Thus, although just deserts may provide a framework for internal order and consistency, the scale itself is susceptible to external political, moral and economic pressures. The danger is that just deserts, far from introducing objectivity and fairness into punishment, will create a sentencing framework very much at the mercy of the prevailing political climate.[17] Finally, and perhaps most fundamentally, desert theory derives from eighteenth-century notions of divine justice which inevitably fail to address many of the problems of social order which late twentieth-century criminal justice is called upon to regulate.[18]

B The Renaissance of Reparative Justice

The renaissance of reparative justice derives its impetus from an even earlier historical tradition, for it harks back to the origins of Anglo-Saxon law when little distinction was made between public and private wrongs. Both were dealt with by a system for gaining compensatory redress via monetary payments known as the 'bot' whose sum was fixed according to the nature and extent of the harm done.[19] Only with the growth of royal jurisdiction in the twelfth century was direct restoration to the victim sacrificed to the wider purposes of securing the 'King's Peace.'[20] Crimes were differentiated from other social wrongs on the grounds that they were so serious as to offend not only against the interests of the victim but against King and community as well. Accordingly, the rights of the victim to compensation were usurped by fines payable to the Crown and personal apologies were supplanted by demands for atonement to God. Over time, the original restorative purpose of the 'bot,' the claim of the victim to redress and, indeed, the interest of the offender in making good have been effectively submerged beneath the wider social purposes of maintaining order.

Only in the late twentieth century have proponents of reparative justice revived the argument that crime should be seen not only as a wrong against society but also as a dispute between offender and victim requiring resolution.[21] Particularly influential were the demands of Nils Christie that the criminal justice system recognise and restore the property rights of participants to 'their' conflict.[22] But one might go further and argue that not only has the State 'stolen' the conflict, by the artifice of legal language it has transformed the drama and emotion of social interaction and strife into technical categories which can be subjected to the ordering practices of the criminal process. That small proportion of conflicts which enter the criminal justice system undergo an elaborate process of inquiry, classification and judgment by police, lawyers and judges by means of which they are translated to fit the legal categories of crime. The criminal justice process may thus be seen as a means of repackaging conflicts in order to render them amenable

---

17 von Hirsch has argued that 'a sentencing theory cannot, Canute-like, stop the waters from rising: where the law-and-order pressures in a particular jurisdiction are sufficiently strong, punishments will rise, and no penal theory can stop that'; von Hirsch, 'The Politics of "Just Deserts"' (1990) *Canadian Journal of Criminology* 402. The possibility remains, however, that desert theory is particularly susceptible to such pressures.

18 As Fattah argues, belief in an avenging God who is satisfied only when wrongdoing is met with the infliction of equivalent pain has little resonance in our increasingly secular society; Fattah, *op cit* n 3:

19 Roebuck, *The Background of the Common Law* (Oxford: Oxford University Press, 1988) 29.

20 Greenberg, 'The Victim in Historical Perspective' (1984) 40 *Journal of Social Issues* 79.

21 Wright, *Justice for Victims and Offenders* (London: Sage, 1991).

22 Christie, 'Conflicts as Property' (1977) 17 *Brit J Criminology* 1.

to legal regulation. The adversarial system further distances and embattles the two parties, whilst high standards of proof demand absolute attribution of culpability. The intimate relations between many victims and offenders involved in crimes against the person,[23] the blurred distribution of victim and offender status and of causal responsibility which are inimical to securing a conviction are diminished and denied.[24]

The renaissance of reparative justice may be seen in part, therefore, as a rebellion against law's dominion and the reassertion of populist rights of participation. The proliferation of academic research about victims has contributed to this debate.[25] And public attitude surveys have been particularly influential in revealing that many victims would welcome the opportunity to seek some reparation from, or even reconciliation with, 'their' offender in place of traditional punishment.[26] These findings come at a time when confidence in the criminal justice system to 'do anything' about crime is low. Disillusionment among many academics, policy makers and criminal justice professionals with the existing paradigm of punishment fuelled hopes that some limited good might be achieved by compensating victims for the wrongs they had suffered.[27] Politically also, reparative justice has attracted widespread support across the spectrum. Those on the Left see compensation to victims as a natural extension to national insurance and as an important corollary to welfarism. Conservative interest has been characterised as representing the softer face of the 'Law and Order lobby,' though one should note that the image of the deserving victim has also been used effectively as grounds for demanding tougher punishments. More generally, the financial backing given to Victim Support, to compensation, mediation and reparation schemes by the Conservative government during the 1980s has been seen as entirely consistent with its wider search for lost 'community.'[28]

The arguments advanced for incorporating reparative elements into the criminal justice system are for the most part pragmatic and economic ones. At the most basic level, reparative justice is supported on the grounds that it is functional for the state to secure the payment of compensation or to support other ventures which seek to repair the damage done by crime. To the extent that reparative ventures are actually perceived by victims as having desirable effects, they reduce the possibility of a disgruntled victim taking the law into his or her own hands to seek redress. In the same vein, they lessen the likelihood that the victim will become so disaffected that they themselves turn to crime. Moreover, the prospect of

23 Fattah, *Understanding Criminal Victimisation: An Introduction to Theoretical Victimology* (Canada: Prentice-Hall, 1991) ch 7.
24 McBarnett, *Conviction: Law, the State and the Construction of Justice* (London: Macmillan, 1981).
25 For example, Shapland *et al*, *Victims and the Criminal Justice System* (Aldershot: Gower, 1985); Maguire and Pointing (eds), *Victims of Crime: A New Deal?* (Milton Keynes: Open University Press, 1988); Morgan and Zedner, *Child Victims: Crime, Impact and Criminal Justice* (Oxford: Oxford University Press, 1992). For an overview, see Zedner, 'Victims', in Maguire, Morgan and Reiner (eds), *The Oxford Handbook of Criminology* (Oxford: Oxford University Press, 1994).
26 Hough and Moxon, 'Dealing with Offenders: Popular Opinion and the View of Victims' (1985) 24 *The Howard Journal* 160.
27 This approach also raised questions about the responsibility of the state to compensate victims and was instrumental in the establishment of the Criminal Injuries Compensation Board in 1964. The provision of state-funded compensation has little bearing, however, on the questions concerning the purposes of punishment discussed here.
28 In 1990, the British Government announced the 'Victim's Charter' which reaffirmed the rights of victims, amongst other things, to compensation from the offender and the state. Though it should be noted that with these rights come also new responsibilities, see Miers, 'The Responsibilities and Rights of Victims' (1992) MLR 482.

reparation may encourage victims to report crimes, to cooperate with the police and to appear at trial, hence increasing the efficacy of the criminal justice process.[29] Given that the vast majority of crimes are detected only with the aid of the general public, it must be desirable for these forms of cooperation to be encouraged.

A consequentionalist variant on this view is the recognition that to the social costs of crime are added the further costs of punishment. The financial costs of traditional punishments (above all imprisonment) to the taxpayer or to society generally are a heavy burden. To the extent that these penalties are seen to fail, their costs become unjustifiable. Reparative sentences, by contrast, lessen the financial burden on the taxpayer and further shift the burden onto the offender (via the payments of fines, compensation orders and through community service). The cost of the criminal justice process to victims is also recognised: victims are required to give considerable time and energy to reporting crimes and assisting police investigations. For a few, there is the additional trauma of being required to give evidence as a witness in court. Reparation, it is argued, recognises the reliance of the criminal justice system on victims, either by ensuring that they receive financial compensation from the offender, 'paying' for their cooperation or compensating them for the further 'secondary victimisation' suffered at the hands of the criminal justice system. Finally, proponents of reparation suggest that the costs suffered by the offender (the stigma of conviction, the pains of imprisonment, the disadvantages faced on release from custody) are so burdensome as to be counterproductive. Reparative sentences would, it is argued, not only lessen the burden of punishment on the offender but offer the possibility for constructive, forward-looking sentencing. Making good, whether via monetary compensation or other reparative endeavour, is also applauded as having psychological advantages over traditional retributive penalties. Reparation, it is argued, relieves the offender's feelings of guilt and alienation which may precipitate further crimes. The effect is said to be restorative not only to the victim but also to the offender, increasing their sense of self-esteem and aiding reintegration.[30]

These pragmatic purposes are largely uncontroversial, such controversy as exists arising mainly from doubts about the ability of reparation to achieve them. The theoretical reorientation posed by a fully developed reparative schema is more challenging. Such a schema would demand the abandonment of culpability of the offender as the central focus of sentencing and, in its place, pay much closer attention to the issue of harm. It would reconceive crimes less as the willed contraventions of an abstract moral code enshrined in law but, more importantly, as signals of social disfunction inflicting harm on victims (and perhaps also offenders) as well as society. According to this view, criminal justice should be less preoccupied with censuring the code-breakers and focus instead on the process of restoring individual damage and repairing ruptured social bonds.[31] In place of meeting pain with the infliction of further pain, a truly reparative system would seek the holistic restoration of the community. It would necessarily also challenge the sole claim of the state to respond to crime and would instead invite (or perhaps demand) the involvement of the community in the process of restoration.

---

29 Though the ultimate consequence of full victim cooperation might be that the criminal justice system becomes impossibly overloaded with cases.
30 Braithwaite, *Crime, Shame and Reintegration* (Cambridge: Cambridge University Press, 1989).
31 Van Ness, *op cit* n 2.

Whilst early proponents of reparative justice hailed it as a new paradigm which should replace the existing model of punishment, such claims ring rather hollow now. Increasingly, demands for an entirely new paradigm have been abandoned in favour of more muted discussion about the possibilities of integrating reparative into prevailing retributive schema. At the level of practice, the criminal justice system has always embraced an eclectic array of aims and initiatives, but at a theoretical level this bid for reconciliation has met with resistance. Is reparative justice no more than a conceptual cuckoo in the criminal law nest?[32]

C What is Reparative Justice?

Before going on to consider the relationship between reparation and retribution in detail, it is worthwhile pausing to reflect upon what exactly is meant by reparative justice. For although it has attracted many proponents, it is far from clear that they share a common vision as to its shape and purpose.[33] The tendency of the 'movement' toward reparative justice (if one can call it that) to embrace an array of possibilities is reflected in the slippery quality of the language used to convey its key concepts. 'Making good' is suggestive only of restoration to the victim and conveys little of what involvement in reparative schemes may mean for the offender. 'Compensation' suggests a civil purpose analogous to damages and misses the penal character inherent in such disposals. 'Mediation' purports to be orientated toward dispute resolution, but commonly refers to projects which are often more concerned to divert offenders from prosecution or mitigate their sentence than to take account of the interests of the victim.[34] 'Restitution' seems to be too narrow a term, suggesting little more than the returning of property or its financial equivalent to the person from whom it was unlawfully taken.[35] As such it tends to conflate the functions of civil and criminal law.

'Reparation' is not synonymous with restitution, still less does it suggest a straightforward importation of civil into criminal law. Reparation should properly connote a wider set of aims. It involves more than 'making good' the damage done to property, body or psyche. It must also entail recognition of the harm done to the social relationship between offender and victim, and the damage done to the victim's social rights in his or her property or person. According to Davis, reparation 'should not be seen as residing solely in the offer of restitution; adequate reparation must also include some attempt to make amends for the victim's loss of the presumption of security in his or her rights.'[36] This way of thinking echoes, consciously or not, the concept of 'dominion' developed by Braithwaite and Pettit.[37] For dominion to be restored, what is sought is some

---

32 A question posed by Campbell, 'Compensation as Punishment' (1984) 7 Univ New South Wales LJ 338.

33 Cavadino and Dignan have developed a typology which embraces six possible models of reparative justice (Conventional model with limited elements of reparation; 'Victim allocution model'; Diversion model; Separatist model; Court-led hybrid model; and Integrated 'restorative justice' model), *op cit* n 4, p 4.

34 Davis, *Making Amends: Mediation and Reparation in Criminal Justice* (London: Routledge, 1992).

35 Hodgson Committee, *Profits of Crime and their Recovery* (London: Heinemann, 1984) 5.

36 Davis *et al*, *Preliminary Study of Victim-Offender Mediation and Reparation Schemes in England and Wales* (London: Home Office RPU, 1987) 7.

37 'An agent enjoys negative liberty . . . if and only if he is exempt from the constraints imposed by the intentional or at least the blameworthy actions of others in choosing certain options'; Braithwaite and Pettit, *op cit* n 2, p 61.

evidence of a change in attitude, some expression of remorse that indicates that the victim's rights will be respected in the future. Achieving such a change in attitude may entail the offender agreeing to undergo training, counselling or therapy and, as such, these may all be seen as part of reparative justice. A forced apology or obligatory payment of compensation will not suffice; indeed, it may even be counterproductive in eliciting a genuine change of attitude in the offender. But is 'symbolic reparation' alone sufficient? According to Braithwaite, if reparation is not to come too cheap it must be backed up by material compensation.[38] Accepting Braithwaite's view, the distinctions made between material and non-material or symbolic reparation tend to lose significance. It would seem that in most cases for full reparation to be achieved some mixture of the two will be required. Let us examine each in turn.

The most obvious and concrete form of reparative justice is compensation.[39] Monetary compensation recognises the fact that crime deprives its victim of the means to pursue life choices: it seeks to recognise that deprivation and to restore access either to those means which have been denied or to comparable alternative means. Compensation orders payable by the offender were introduced by the Criminal Justice Act 1972, which gave the courts the power to make an ancillary order for compensation in addition to the main penalty in cases where 'injury, loss or damage' had resulted. Ten years later, under the Criminal Justice Act 1982, it became possible to make compensation orders as the sole penalty against an offender. Where fines and compensation orders were given together, the 1982 Act required that payment of compensation should take priority over the fine. The importance given to compensation was enhanced further under the Criminal Justice Act 1988, which required the courts to consider making a compensation order in every case of death, injury, loss or damage and, where the court failed to give such an order, to furnish reasons for not doing so.[40] Difficulties remain in determining what constitute reasonable grounds for failing to make such an order or, where such an order is made, in determining the degree of harm caused and hence the level of compensation payable. In practice, compensation orders are set with reference to the ability of the offender to pay and, given that the majority of offenders are of limited means, they rarely result in complete restoration. In so far as reparation also seeks to promote the reintegration of the offender, it would surely be counterproductive to heap intolerable burdens on him. Although in seeking to embrace both reintegration and restoration simultaneously, reparative justice is necessarily riven by tensions, we should not see these aims as competing or necessarily in conflict: they are rather two sides of the same coin.

Less tangible but nonetheless important is what we might call 'symbolic reparation.' This might be an apology made by the offender to the victim or other attempts at reconciliation. The reparation here is 'symbolic' in that it does not

---

38 Braithwaite, *Crime, Shame and Reintegration* (Cambridge: Cambridge University Press, 1989).

39 For extensive discussion of the role and form of compensation, see Miers, *Compensation for Criminal Injuries* (London: Butterworths, 1990).

40 In 1991, 58 per cent of offenders sentenced in magistrates' courts for offences of violence, 37 per cent for burglary, 40 per cent for robbery, 51 per cent for fraud and forgery, and 58 per cent for criminal damage were ordered to pay compensation. Overall, 26 per cent of offenders sentenced for indictable offences in magistrates' courts were ordered to pay compensation. In Crown Courts, the figures were lower — only 12 per cent of those sentenced (partly because compensation orders are not normally combined with custodial penalties). The comparable figures of those ordered to pay compensation are proportionately lower: 25 per cent for violence, 8 per cent for burglary, 18 per cent for fraud and forgery, and 19 per cent for criminal damage. Barclay, *Digest 2: Information on the Criminal Justice System in England and Wales* (London: HMSO, 1993) 20.

entail the return of money or material goods. Proponents of reparative justice argue that if the apology is not merely an empty gesture but one which conveys remorse and a genuine change of attitude, then such symbolic reparation is quite as important as more tangible returns.[41] Mediation seeks to provide a way for parties to resolve disputes without recourse to the vagaries of the courts. It aims to allow both parties to retain control over the dispute and to voice their grievances under the supervision of a mediator, whether a trained professional or lay volunteer.[42] In theory, the mediator acts only as a conduit and ideally any resolution is reached by the mutual agreement of the two parties. In practice, the form and organisation of mediation schemes vary considerably and it is worth examining a little more closely their development and form.

One of the first mediation schemes in Britain arose out of a discussion group set up by Philip Priestley in 1969 on behalf of NACRO.[43] This initiative sought to provide a forum in which both victims and offenders could express their views and feelings. Many early mediation and reparation schemes, however, were as much concerned with diverting the offender from punishment as with the interests of the victim.[44] Reparation 'in the service of diversion' both saved the offender from the pains of punishment and reduced the ever growing burden on the courts.[45] Early initiatives begun by Juvenile Liaison Bureaux (for example, in Devon and Northamptonshire) focused mainly on young offenders. Used in conjunction with police cautions, these schemes aimed to promote diversion of young offenders out of the criminal justice system. It was less clear what benefits they provided to victims. The National Association of Victim Support Schemes,[46] as the voice of the victims' lobby, was notably circumspect about the benefits of mediation for victims and remained reluctant to give wholehearted support.

The early 1980s saw several important developments in the promotion of reparative programmes. Probation services were instrumental in establishing local mediation schemes, the first being in South Yorkshire and the West Midlands in 1983.[47] Those seeking to promote mediation and reparation schemes joined together in 1984 to found a central organising body — FIRM (Forum for Initiatives in Reparation and Mediation).[48] In 1984, the then Home Secretary Leon Brittan agreed to fund a number of reparation projects in Cumbria, Leeds, Wolverhampton and Coventry on an experimental basis. These and other voluntary schemes take a variety of forms. Most seek to bring about some communication between victim and offender (though not necessarily face-to-face) using a mediator (often a probation officer). Their aims also vary from simply providing a conduit for communication enabling the parties better to understand one another, to eliciting an apology or some tangible form of restitution from the

---

41 Indeed, Launay claims that 'British victims are reluctant to accept material reparation from their offenders and are usually content with their explanations and apologies': Launay, 'Victim-Offender Conciliation' and McGurk *et al* (eds), *Applying Psychology to Imprisonment: Theory and Practice* (London: HMSO, 1987) 12.
42 Davis, *op cit* n 34; Davis *et al*, *op cit* n 36.
43 The National Association for the Resettlement and Care of Offenders.
44 Davis, *op cit* n 34, p 23.
45 Davis *et al*, 'Reparation in the Service of Diversion: The Subordination of a Good Idea' (1988) 27 *The Howard Journal* 129.
46 NAVSS has since been relaunched as Victim Support.
47 Though given the role of the probation service, it is hardly surprising that these early schemes focused primarily on the offender.
48 Later relaunched as Mediation UK.

offender (often with the hope of a reduced sentence in return), to attaining resolution of the conflict or even reconciliation.[49]

Mediation may be introduced into the criminal justice process at various points. Some schemes operate primarily as agents of diversion at the pre-prosecution stage, for example the police may issue a formal caution but recommend mediation.[50] Most pre-prosecution schemes are organised by Juvenile Liaison Bureaux as a means of diverting young offenders from court.[51] Others may be court-based providing for mediation before court proceedings or on adjournment before sentence. In England and Wales it is possible for the prosecutor or the court to discontinue, but not defer, a case in its preliminary stages and recommend mediation.[52] In Scotland the Procurator Fiscal may defer cases for mediation provided that they are deemed to be of sufficient seriousness to merit prosecution. Yet another type of mediation is introduced after conviction but before sentence.[53] Finally, mediation may take place post-sentence, for example in relation to Intermediate Treatment, as a condition of probation or community service, or (more rarely) during a prison sentence. The latter type of mediation scheme was developed at the youth custody centre in Rochester, Kent.[54] Under the so-called Victims and Offenders In Conciliation (VOIC) programme, young offenders serving sentences for burglary meet with victims of burglary in groups for one and half hour sessions over three weeks to discuss the impact of the crime.

Sceptics continue to question whether mediation schemes can ever really operate properly 'in the shadow of the court.' Victim Support has warned of the additional burdens — in terms of time, energy and goodwill — which mediation may place on victims.[55] As a consequence, its development has been slow. By 1990 there were just fourteen mediation schemes in operation. In the consultation period preceding the 1991 Act, the Government was anxious to glean attitudes towards schemes which elicited direct reparation, whether by some personal service or an apology to the victim. They found that court-based reparation schemes, in particular, enjoyed 'little support . . . there was often confusion whether reparation was for the benefit of the victim or a means of rehabilitating the offender.'[56] Moreover, it was found that victims felt under pressure to cooperate, a consequence which the Government considered wholly undesirable. As a result, 'the Government has concluded that reparation to victims should not be a requirement of orders made by the courts.'[57] This waning of support at the level of central government has dulled, but certainly not eradicated, enthusiasm for mediation at the local level.

---

49 Davis *et al*, *op cit* n 36. A study by the Home Office over two years (1985—87) found that in six schemes dealing with juveniles cautioned by the police, 57 per cent of all agreements involved an explanation and apology with just over 25 per cent involving material reparation. Marshall, 'Victim-Offender Mediation,' *30 HORS Research Bulletin* (London: HMSO, 1991) 9.
50 As in Exeter, London, Corby and Northamptonshire.
51 Davis *et al*, *op cit* n 36, p 3.
52 Though under s 23 of the Prosecution of Offences Act 1985, the accused can demand that the prosecution be continued: Wright, *op cit* n 21, p 86.
53 As in Home Office funded schemes set up in Leeds, Coventry and Wolverhampton or locally funded schemes in Rochdale, South Glamorgan, South Yorkshire and Southampton. Most court-based schemes deal with less serious adult offenders appearing in magistrates' court; an exception is the Leeds scheme, set up explicitly to deal with high-tariff offenders.
54 Launay, 'Bringing Victims and Offenders Together: A Comparison of Two Models' (1985) 24 *The Howard Journal* 200.
55 Reeves, 'The Victim and Reparation' (1984) 31 *Probation Journal* 136.
56 Home Office, *op cit* n 10, p 24.
57 *ibid*.

Mediation is, as we have seen, modelled (even predicated) upon the bringing together of two individuals to express their views and seek resolution. But what should happen, for example, where the offender is a large corporation and the victim is the community? Who then should speak on their respective behalves? The problem of the absence of 'authoritative consent' to speak on behalf of a group has been recognised by Fiss in respect of civil dispute resolution: it is no less pressing in criminal cases.[58] The problem is particularly acute where the victim is a 'nebulous social entity,'[59] such as an ethnic or racial minority group subject perhaps to persistent criminal damage, abuse and assaults but who have no formal organisational structure and lack procedures for generating authoritative consent. Is it possible to envisage a model of reparative justice which might deal adequately with such a problem? Proponents of reparative justice might respond in two ways. First, it is not difficult to think of ways by which a representative might be elected to speak on behalf of the victim group. Nor must mediation necessarily take the form of bilateral negotiation; rather, it might well bring together the various parties in group discussion.[60] Second, even if there are problems of who should speak, at the very least the reparative model acknowledges the right of the parties to retain some say over resolution. In court neither party is allowed a voice other than in so far as their knowledge is deemed legally relevant to establishing the facts of the case. Any voice, it might be argued, is better than none.

It was argued above that it is theoretically desirable that reparation entail both material and symbolic elements. Happily, it would appear that in practice the dichotomy between material and non-material reparation is rarely so complete as it may first appear. Sums paid in compensation seldom approach the actual value of the loss suffered and the significance of the payment may often be largely symbolic. In turn, mediation may lead to practical actions making good damage done, and thus its impact is also material.[61] So far so good, but the question remains in what proportions respectively should the material and the symbolic (or perhaps better, the psychological) elements of reparation apply and who should determine the nature and weight of these ingredients.[62] The danger remains that, without careful consideration of questions such as these, the 'recipe' for reparation remains elusive.

D   Is Reparation Compatible with Punishment?

So far we have explored the case for reparative justice and how it might best be realised. But if its aims are to be pursued within the terrain of the criminal process, the question arises whether, or to what extent, reparation can plausibly fulfil the purposes of punishment.[63] To answer this we need to ask rather basic questions about the nature of punishment and the principles upon which it should be applied.

---

58 Fiss, 'Against Settlement' (1984) 93 Yale L Rev 1078.
59 *ibid* 1079.
60 As in the VOIC programme discussed above.
61 For example, young offenders who commit acts of vandalism may be called upon to make good the damage done or to do other practical work for the victim.
62 An analogous point is made by Ashworth and von Hirsch respecting the problematic relationship between 'recognition and recompense' in Braithwaite's promotion of restorative justice, 'Desert and the Three Rs,' 5(1) *Current Issues in Criminal Justice* 10.
63 Though this begs the question whether a just response to crime must necessarily be punitive. A more radical critique of the prevailing paradigm might well challenge the assumption that offending behaviour must always be met by the infliction of further pain in order for justice to be done.

This is not the place to enquire into the philosophical foundations of the criminal law nor to explore at length theories of punishment. It is enough to recognise that certain basic elements of the prevailing paradigm must be fulfilled if reparation is to claim a place within it. These include: first, the imposition of 'pain';[64] second, that the sanction is invoked in response to social wrongs (crimes); and, third, that it is applied against culpable offenders. Reparative justice must satisfy each of these elements if it is to escape the tag of 'conceptual cuckoo'. Let us examine them in turn.

(a) Punitive Quality

Perhaps the most telling objection to reparative justice is that it has no intrinsic penal character and that to enforce civil liabilities through the criminal courts is not, of itself, to punish. Lacey argues that 'there must be some idea of additional loss, inconvenience or stigma in order to preserve ... a genuine distinction between punishment and compensation.'[65] To the extent that a disposal is solely concerned with securing compensation, its punitive quality seems to be in doubt. In 1970, the Advisory Council on the Penal System supported compensation orders solely on the grounds that it was unreasonable to expect most crime victims to pursue claims for damages through the civil courts.[66] The Dunpark Committee (1977), which examined the role of compensation within the Scottish system, likewise concluded that restitution could only be justified on the grounds of 'doing something for victims.'[67] In the view of the Committee; compensation orders had no penal function, providing no more than a convenient means of settling civil suits within the criminal process. In 1974 the Court of Appeal described them as 'a convenient and rapid means of avoiding the expense of resort to civil litigation.'[68] Certainly, the argument for pragmatism has some merits. It is unnecessarily burdensome on victims' time and resources to expect them to pursue a separate claim via the civil courts. Neither does it make good administrative or economic sense to require a separate court to consider the case all over again. On grounds of efficiency, therefore, the victim is spared the effort of a civil action to obtain redress. To accept this view would be to conclude that although the pursuit of reparation may be pragmatic, it is conceptually incoherent.

It is questionable, however, whether a compensation order can properly be seen as no more than a civil instrument riding on the back of a criminal trial. Unlike the French device of the *partie civile*,[69] compensation in English law is fully integrated into the criminal process and has the formal status of a penalty. Moreover, a shift in the attitude of the courts is discernible. A decision of the Court of Appeal in 1984 established that a criminal court may make a compensation order against an offender even where there was no right to sue in the civil courts.[70] The Lord Chief Justice stressed that although compensation orders

---

64 Or what Lacey terms 'unpleasant consequences,' *op cit* n 16, p 7.
65 *ibid* 35.
66 Advisory Council on the Penal System, *Reparation by the Offender* (Widgery Report, 1970) para 50.
67 Lord Dunpark, *Reparation by the Offender to the Victim in Scotland* (Edinburgh: HMSO, 1977) Cmnd 6802.
68 Scarman J in *Inwood* (1974) 60 Cr App R 70, 73.
69 Or the German *Adhaesionsverfahren*, though interestingly this device for attaching civil proceedings to the criminal process is rarely used; see Mueller-Dietz, 'Compensation as a Criminal Penalty?' in Kaiser, Kury and Albrecht (eds), *Victims and Criminal Justice* (Freiburg: Eigenverlag Max-Planck-Institut, 1991) 202.
70 Chappell (1984) Cr App R 31.

were commonly used as an easy means of ensuring that a victim received compensation without the expense of resort to civil proceedings, it was not the case that 'the criminal remedy is the mirror of an underlying civil remedy.' The implication here was that compensation orders were an integral part of the criminal process, justifiable even where no civil liability existed.[71] One might conclude that compensation orders do not have a 'given' meaning but can become more or less punitive according to the manner in which they are imposed.

It is significant also that compensation orders extort money which, in the vast majority of cases, offenders would not otherwise have been required to pay. First, the action for recovery is brought about without financial cost to the victim. And, secondly, the state has the coercive mechanisms to ensure that repayment is actually made. In this sense, it may be said that the compensation order inflicts 'pain' which is 'additional' to that which civil law would otherwise exact. These factors also help to ensure that compensation orders are perceived both by offenders and society as 'real' punishment. But the danger here is that to claim compensation orders operate as a punishment may lead us to the unhappy conclusion that for the offender the compensation order is undifferentiated from the fine and has little or no reparative quality. If the goal of restoring the recipient to a position akin to that which existed prior to the offence is obscured in the offender's mind by the punitive bite of the penalty, then it is unlikely that its avowed reintegrative aspects will be effective.

The objection that compensation lacks 'penal value' becomes even more difficult to maintain in light of the fact that, since 1973, it has been possible to impose compensation as the sole penalty.[72] Stigma attaches to conviction whatever the subsequent penalty and, where compensation is ordered alone, it too is accompanied by the shaming mechanism of the guilty verdict. We might do well to separate out notions of censure and sanction. It is possible to argue that the public drama of the trial, the naming of the defendant and, in particular, the formal attribution of guilt goes a long way toward fulfilling the requirements of censure. Once the demands of reproof have thus been met, is it not excessive to demand that penal sanctions also be endowed with censuring qualities?[73]

In respect of mediation and reparation, the issue of punitive quality becomes more complex still. Purists might argue that the offender must enter into the process voluntarily and participate willingly in seeking an outcome. To the extent that participation is coerced, the reintegrative impact of mediation may be lost. But such a view is predicated upon reaching a resolution which is fully agreed upon by both parties. If the offender is a less than willing participant who agrees only reluctantly and under pressure, then it is more likely that he or she will fail to abide by the resolution reached. How, then, should enforcement be assured? Should mediation agencies have access to the full coercive powers of the court and, if they were to do so, would there not be a danger that the reparative potential would be undermined? Proponents of reparative justice might argue that discussion about enforcement is to miss the very point of mediation — that the outcome should be freely agreed and its terms willingly met. The experience of mediation in other

---

71 See also Campbell, *op cit* n 32, for the development of this view. Cf. *Att Gen's Ref No. 10 of 1992 (R v Cooper)* [1993] Crim. L.R. 631.

72 Powers of the Criminal Courts Act 1973, s 35(1).

73 The answer may vary according to the broader social context in which the criminal justice process operates. On the relationship between censure and sanction, and the counterarguments for adding sanctions or 'hard treatment' to censure, see Narayan, 'Appropriate Responses and Preventive Benefits: Justifying Censure and Hard Treatment in Legal Punishment' (1993) 13 OJLS 166. See also von Hirsch, *op cit* n 6, ch 2.

areas (for example, the settlement of family disputes)[74] suggests that we would do well, however, to reflect further on what should happen if offenders fail to fulfil their part of the bargain. Should offenders be brought back to court, as would happen on breach of any other community disposal, and, if so, by whom and with what consequences?

(b) Recognition of Social Wrong

As we have seen, the original appeal to reparative justice was made through an evocation of a nostalgic vision of a bygone community in which disputes were settled by the parties to them.[75] Present mediation practice reflects this view and tends to treat crime as a personal issue between offender and victim. Not only does mediation take the private conflict as its sole object, but its organisational context sets it apart from the public symbolic processes of criminal justice. Most schemes promote mediation as an alternative to formal procedures, as a way of diverting the offender away from public prosecution. They host discussions between the immediate parties alone with only the mediator in attendance and shield their participants from media exposure. Whilst proponents might argue that all these measures are purposively designed to ensure that the parties retain a sense of ownership over 'their' dispute, such tactics tend also to overlook the wider interests at stake. They tend also to strip the process of its power to signify public disapprobation and to inflict shame upon the offender. To this extent, it is arguable that reparation, narrowly conceived, fails to recognise that it is not only the victim but also society that has been wronged by the disregard shown for its norms and the general threat posed to public dominion. Another objection is that to make reparation to identifiable victims the primary aim of criminal justice would be effectively to decriminalise the mass of 'victimless' offences. The model of mediating a dispute between two parties may operate with some plausibility in respect of interpersonal crimes of violence or theft, but offers little by way of resolution to crimes such as motoring violations, vandalism or public order offences.

It is surely possible, however, to put forward a broader conception of reparative justice which recognises that the rights infringed by crime are not those of the victim alone but are held in common socially.[76] It is this social aspect which distinguishes crime from the private harms inflicted by torts. Thus, even where there is no identifiable victim, reparation to the wider community for actual harms or public 'endangerment' is owed. Is it possible also for reparative forms of justice to fulfil the public functions (both recognition of the social wrong and public shaming) demanded by infringement of the criminal law? Proponents might legitimately argue that it is misplaced to look upon compensation and mediation as the only means to reparation and that penalties such as community service orders are better placed to make reparation to the wider community. One might then ask how far, or indeed whether, the community feels itself to be 'repaired' by such activities. Until there is empirical research which offers evidence as to the psychological impact of 'community service' on the community it purports to serve, it is probably unwise to make assertions about its wider reparative quality.

---

74 Roberts, 'Mediation in Family Disputes,' 46 MLR 537.
75 Christie, *op cit* n 22.
76 See Watson, Boucherat and Davis, 'Reparation for Retributivists' in Wright and Galaway (eds), *Mediation and Criminal Justice* (London: Sage, 1989) 19. See also Braithwaite and Pettit, *op cit* n 2.

Even to propose such research raises questions about the very entity of 'community' and whether it actually refers to more than the geographical location in which mediation, reparation or community service orders take place.

If reparative justice, as currently conceived, fails to respond adequately to the social wrong which has been perpetrated, is it possible to envisage modifications which would allow it better to fulfil the public purposes of punishment? One would be to open up the mediation process, either by allowing the public to observe the proceedings or by permitting the media to report on both process and outcome. This would meet the requirement that the offender's offence be publicly known and censured. The danger in using the media as instruments of censure in this way is, however, that, as Dignan has pointed out, 'the kind of shaming indulged in by much of the media is highly stigmatising and might well make the process of reintegration all the more difficult.'[77] A stronger and perhaps more controllable version of public participation would be to elevate the mediator from the position of go-between in an essentially bilateral negotiation to that of a third party representing the public interest. If mediation is to respond adequately to the social wrong which has been done, then it must take due heed of the wider social purposes of the criminal trial. These include the reassertion of normative order, the reestablishment of the rights and obligations of citizens, the interpretation and development of doctrinal law and of policy, and even the elaboration and maintenance of legal ideology.[78] One may debate how and to what ends these goals should be pursued, but a system which wholly failed to acknowledge their place would scarcely merit the label of criminal justice.

(c) Response to Culpability

A third charge laid against reparative justice is that it shifts the focus on to harm and, in so doing, risks ignoring the fundamental basis of criminal liability for serious offences — the offender's *mens rea*. Ashworth has argued that a reparative approach:

> ignores one cardinal element in serious crimes — the offender's mental attitude . . . Criminal liability and punishment should be determined primarily according to the wickedness or danger of the defendant's conduct: that should depend on what he was trying to do or thought he was doing, not upon what actually happened in the particular case.[79]

To make harm the focus of the debate thus ignores the current centrality of intent as the determinant of moral wrong. Attempts, conspiracy, conduct crimes (such as careless driving), precursor offences (such as possessing firearms or explosives), fraud and theft (which requires no more than the intention permanently to deprive) are all deemed to be criminal irrespective of any harm done. Some attempts, most notably attempted murder, are serious crimes involving high levels of culpability, though the physical harm caused may be negligible. Is there not a danger that a penal system predicated upon response to harm would miss much that we currently conceive of as crime?

---

77 Dignan, 'Reintegration through Reparation: A Way Forward for Restorative Justice?' (unpublished paper delivered at the Fulbright Colloquium: *Penal Theory and Penal Practice*, University of Stirling, September 1992) 7.
78 See the analogous arguments made in respect of settlement and the civil process in Fiss, *op cit* n 58, p 1085.
79 Ashworth, 'Punishment and Compensation: Victims, Offenders and the State' (1985) 6 OJLS 97.

In answering this question, we should recall that the vast majority of petty (and not so petty) offences are crimes of strict liability. Here the requirement of moral responsibility has long been abandoned in recognition of the need to regulate and sanction a wide variety of socially harmful actions.[80] An appraisal of the Canadian criminal statistics leads Fattah to the dramatic conclusion that 'while the abstract concept of moral guilt does still have some proponents in the legal community, it has lost any practical significance and could easily be abandoned without dire consequences.'[81] A less radical response may be to argue that to pose culpability and harm as antinomies fails to recognise the intimate relationship which generally exists between them. Responding to harm necessarily entails close attention to its origins, although under a reparative schema the emphasis may shift away from attributing moral guilt to ascertaining causal responsibility.[82] Moreover, if reparation is to respond appropriately and in a symbolically apt way, then it will need to differentiate between more or less responsible offenders. According to this view, whilst culpability would no longer be the primary determinant of punishment, the offender's state of mind would nonetheless remain integral to the choice of disposal.

It is also worth questioning whether a harm-orientated system would necessarily draw a penal map so very different from that which we currently employ. The answer depends rather on the scope of our notion of harm. It may be possible to fashion a broader understanding of harm based on the presumption that we have the right as citizens to go about our lives without fear of others intentionally or recklessly injuring us in any way. According to this view, to the extent that an offender threatens our presumption of security, he or she inflicts harm upon us and should be held liable for so doing. Thus attempts, conspiracies and even recklessness which threaten the social and legal order, and our place within it, can all be seen as potential harms. Critics might object that this is to stretch the notion of harm too far, but the evidence of criminological research clearly indicates that the impact of crime extends far beyond the person formally noted in police records as the victim.[83] A generalised sense of insecurity is a major social cost of crime which constrains life choices and diminishes quality of life.[84] To recognise these costs as harms would allow us to bring within the reparative model offences which are normally considered to be 'victimless'. For example, the Second Islington Crime Survey revealed that fear of crime in the city arises largely in reaction to 'local incivilities' such as graffiti, vandalised street lighting, boarded-up shop fronts, youths or drunks loitering on street corners and other signals of a hostile environment.[85] The sense of insecurity thus engendered may lead those vulnerable to remain at home at night, to limit their movements outside the home to 'safe' areas and even to move to another 'safer' neighbourhood. Whilst we might readily concur that these are real and tangible harms, correlating the relationship between them and actual crimes is highly problematic. To relate diffuse harms such as these with the culpability of individual offenders is probably impossible and it is

---

80 It has been estimated that over half the 7,000 offences in English criminal law require no proof of fault; see Ashworth, *Principles of Criminal Law* (Oxford: Oxford University Press, 1991) 142.
81 Fattah, *op cit* n 3, p 774.
82 A complicating factor is that the causal responsibility of the victim may also acquire a new importance: see Fattah, *op cit* n 23.
83 See, for example, Morgan and Zedner, *Child Victims: Crime, Impact and Criminal Justice* (Oxford: Oxford University Press, 1992) 27ff.
84 Maxfield, *Fear of Crime in England and Wales* (London: Home Office Research Study 78, 1984).
85 Crawford *et al, The Second Islington Crime Survey* (Middlesex, 1990) 82.

questionable upon what grounds liability might then be imposed. The danger here is that, in responding to the cumulative impact of such 'incivilities', we overstate our collective claim to protection and condone intrusion into the lives of vandals, drunks and young delinquents out of all proportion to their, individually petty, offences.

Finally, whilst culpability is the central component of criminality, we should not overlook the place of harm in determining the gravity of the offence. In many areas of crime, harm already determines which offence will be charged and what sentence will follow. An obvious example arises in the case of interpersonal violence. Without any change in the offender's *mens rea*, the crime charged may vary between simple assault and manslaughter, depending on the degree of harm caused.[86] Harm here (and in many other areas of crime) is a determinant both of liability and of the seriousness of the crime. But as von Hirsch and Jareborg have pointed out: 'virtually no legal doctrines have been developed on how the gravity of harms can be compared.'[87] By explicitly recognising that harm has a place alongside culpability in determining both liability and offence seriousness, something already tacitly recognised by criminal law and penal practice, a reparative approach might offer the possibility of developing a more coherent basis for our penal system.

The case for full and proper recognition of harm as a basis for liability can be made most strongly in respect of modern environmental and corporate crimes which have the potential to cause very grave and widespread harms.[88] Under the present system, as Fattah has argued:

> grave negligence causing a serious nuclear disaster and claiming hundreds of thousand lives or irreparable harm to the environment leads to much more lenient response than the wilful killing of a single individual because in the first instance there was no deliberate intent to cause harm.[89]

The orientation toward culpability limits both the scope of the criminal law and its ability to respond adequately to the proliferating array of crimes in which culpability is often low but where the consequences for the community are liable to be very high.

E   Can Reparation Comply with the Principles of Punishment?

So far we have examined the capacity of reparative justice to mirror or incorporate the chief elements of punishment. If reparative justice is to claim a full place within the penal system, then it must also accord with the principles which delimit the intrusive powers of the state. Can reparation satisfy the requirements for fairness, consistency and proportionality which currently underpin and frame our penal system? Once again, let us look at each element in turn.

---

86 If no harm ensues the crime would be simple assault attracting a maximum of six months imprisonment (Criminal Justice Act 1988, s 39); if injury follows then the maximum rises to five years imprisonment for assault occasioning actual bodily harm (Offences Against the Person Act 1861, s 47); and finally, if the victim dies, then the offender might be guilty of constructive manslaughter and liable to a maximum of life imprisonment.

87 von Hirsch and Jareborg, *op cit* n 16. See also Feinberg, *Harm to Others* (Oxford: Oxford University Press, 1984).

88 The examples of Bhopal, Chernobyl, Exxon Valdez, Piper Alpha and Zeebrugge immediately spring to mind.

89 Fattah, *op cit* n 3, p 782.

(a) Fairness

A primary criticism faced by the reparative approach is that it would create a system of penalties which would have little regard to the means of the offender and so impinge differently on rich and poor. At worst it might allow the very rich to 'buy' their way out of punishment by paying off their victim for harms suffered. Such payments might even become part of the calculus carried out by the rational offender as an 'acceptable cost' readily offset by the benefits of the crime. Particular problems arise in respect of reparative conduct by the offender put forward in mitigation at trial, the difficulty being that an offender with the means to make good may receive a more lenient sentence than an impoverished one. In the case of *Crosby and Hayes* (1974)[90] the two offenders sought to make amends, one had the means to pay compensation and the other had not. On appeal, it was held that it was wrong in principle to give differential sentences on grounds of financial means. As Ashworth has argued, to allow mitigation in such cases could become a source of discrimination contravening the principle of equality before the law and allowing rich offenders to be treated more leniently than poor ones.[91] The point was reiterated in *Copley* (1979) in which Lord Lane insisted that it should not be open to offenders to buy their way out of prison or to secure shorter sentences by offering money in the way of compensation.[92] On the same logic, neither should impoverished offenders suffer longer sentences because of their inability to compensate.

In practice, in the interests of fairness to the offender, the amount payable in compensation is often scaled down below that which is proportional to the harm done. Critics of reparation would argue that it is right that fairness to the offender should take priority over that to the victim. But a pure restitutionist approach might insist that the harm be 'made good' at whatever cost is necessary. Can it be right that an offender with meagre resources suffers, in real terms, a greater punishment than the wealthy offender for whom the payment is no burden at all? Is it desirable that an impoverished offender might work for years to pay off a compensation order (perhaps to a victim whose own wealth makes the sum received negligible)? All these factors clearly do considerable damage to the idea of fairness in criminal law. Yet one might argue that this conception of justice is predicated on being fair to the offender and that an alternative version might equally well be predicated on the rights or interests of the victim and be prepared to sacrifice fairness to the offender to this end.

(b) Consistency

The attempt made by desert theory to develop a coherent, structured approach to sentencing has been applauded as a move toward certainty and consistency.[93] For the same reason Ashworth has objected to reparative justice on the grounds that it would allow the victim to influence sentencing, as happens in the United States through the use of victim-impact and victim-opinion statements. In so doing, it would be damaging to the pursuit of consistency.[94] If victims are given the

90 *Crosby and Hayes* (1974) 60 Cr App R 234.
91 Ashworth, *op cit* n 5, pp 179–180.
92 *Copley* (1979) 1 Cr App R (S) 55. This point has been reaffirmed in *Att Gen's Ref No. 10 of 1992 (R v Cooper)* [1993] Crim. L.R. 631 and *Att Gen's Ref No. 5 of 1993 (R v Hartland)* [1993] Crim. L.R. 794.
93 Asworth, *op cit* n 1, p 350.
94 Ashworth, 'Victim Impact Statements and Sentencing' (1993) CLR 498–509.

right to influence the penalty, a twofold danger arises. Both the form of the penalty (be it reparative or retributive) and its size (be it monetary value or duration) may vary according to the temperament of the victim. But are such criticisms well-grounded?

First, there is a danger of presuming that the objective calculus posited by desert theory is in practice feasible or realistic. Individual sentences will always depend in part on subjective assessments regarding the gravity of the offence made by the sentencer. Thus, while just deserts may promise consistency, it cannot guarantee it.[95] Second, Ashworth's objection makes certain assumptions about the reparative justice model which are questionable. It is not necessarily the case that reorientating the system around 'making good' must inevitably entail allowing the victim to usurp the role of the state in determining the appropriate sentence. Reparation is owed not just to the victim but to all those whose interests are threatened, and the author would agree that it is not appropriate for the victim to determine the nature or extent of reparation.[96] The harm suffered is a social one and it is for society to determine what is necessary to effect reparation. Just as the state now makes judgments about the seriousness of the offence and the severity of punishment deserved or, indeed, about the harm done and the quantum of compensation owed, so within a reparative model the state could retain the right to determine the penalty. One might even envisage a system which imports a standardised scale for determining the seriousness of harm analogous to that suggested by von Hirsch and Jareborg in their development of a 'living standard analysis' for gauging criminal harm.[97] Whereas their model is backward-looking and concerned solely with 'how much harm a standard act of burglary did,'[98] a reparative schema would need to furnish criteria for assessing what would be necessary to 'make good' the harms done. Within this schema, victim-impact statements might furnish necessary information about the harm inflicted and the consequent needs of the victim upon which impartial judgments might be made about the reparation required. By developing a framework for making such judgments systematically, the risk that offenders would find themselves at the whim of vindictive or overly forgiving victims is surely overcome.

(c) Proportionality

The final and most important claim of desert theory is that it secures proportionality between offence and punishment.[99] If reparative penalties are to be made proportional to the harm done, by what standard is compensation to be made? Should the car thief who has stolen a Mercedes pay ten times that demanded of the thief who has taken only a Mini though the intention in each case is to steal? Or should one base the calculation on the basis of the harm actually suffered by the victim? Or, as has been suggested above, should it reflect what is necessary to 'make good'? It may be that the owner of the Mercedes is a wealthy woman who

---

95 Above all in a criminal justice system which places such a high value on the independence and the exercise of discretion by sentencers. The mechanistic formulae of the Minnesota Guidelines would simply not be acceptable in England, as the judicial response to the attempts to impose proportionality under the Criminal Justice Act 1991 bears witness.
96 Ashworth, *op cit* n 2.
97 von Hirsch and Jareborg, *op cit* n 16.
98 *op cit* n 16, p 16.
99 Though see criticisms of this claim above.

has a fleet of cars and the loss of one is immaterial, whereas the owner of the Mini relies on her car as the sole means of mobility. Desert theory requires that the car thief should bear responsibility only for his own conduct, but reparative justice would insist that responsibility extends to the harm caused by his conduct. In deciding to 'throw the dice,' the offender must bear responsibility for the way it falls.[100] A particular difficulty arises in respect of mitigation or incapacity. The offender who is drunk, drugged or insane may bear less culpability but his victim suffers no less harm as a consequence of his actions. Why should the victim of an intoxicated offender receive less compensation than the victim of a fully competent offender inflicting the same level of harm?

The difficulties which arise in relating monetary payments to loss or damage to property become infinitely greater in respect of loss of life or limb, or psychological harm. Critics question the feasibility of assessing harm done without recourse to extensive medical and/or psychiatric evidence, victim impact statements and the like. More tellingly still, they argue that there can be no rational relationship between monetary payments and these forms of loss. Yet tort law relies every day on making just such calculations. Similarly, desert theory relies on making tenuous estimations of proportionality between offence and sentence length. Deciding how many years imprisonment are merited by a rape or a robbery is no more or less contrived than fixing on some value (monetary or other) in relation to harm. And even if the calculation is based on a series of inadequate equivalences, at the very least reparation provides for some tangible or symbolic compensation to the victim, whereas punishment alone provides none at all.

Conclusion: Can Reparation and Punishment be Reconciled?

In reality, reparation in its pure form has nowhere replaced the paradigm of punishment. In Britain, demands for the replacement of punishment by reparative justice have been muted. Instead, provision for compensation only to identifiable victims is incorporated into the existing stigmatising and retributive array of penalties. Incapacitation, for example, is generally regarded as appropriate for the most serious of crimes such as murder, rape and assault. Yet an offender imprisoned is effectively deprived of their ability to repay in the very cases where the harm caused (and therefore the claim to compensation) is greatest. Whilst it is often possible for compensation to run in tandem with other penalties, problems arise where the two are in conflict: custody may be inimical to compensation. For example, in *Huish*, Croom-Johnson LJ stated that 'very often a compensation order is made and a very light sentence of imprisonment is imposed, because the court recognises that if the defendant is to have an opportunity of paying the compensation he must be enabled to earn the money with which to do so.'[101] In general, however, unless an offender clearly has the means to pay[102] or has good prospects of employment on release from prison, it would be inappropriate to impose a compensation order alongside custody. The concern is that the burden of

---

100 Honoré, 'Responsibility and Luck' (1988) 104 LQR 530; O'Malley, 'Punishment and Moral Luck' (1993) Irish CLR 40.
101 *Huish* (1985) 7 Cr App R (S) 272.
102 See *Dorton* (1987) 9 Cr App R (S) 514, in which the Court of Appeal commented that where a court is satisfied that the offender has, or will have, funds available then a compensation order in addition to a custodial sentence was appropriate.

paying compensation on release from a custodial sentence is liable to be 'counterproductive and force him back into crime to find the money.'[103]

Difficulties also ensue where retributive and reparative sentences are in competition with one another. For example, fines and compensation orders both make financial demands on the offender's, often limited, resources: which, then, should take priority? Since 1982, English law has given priority to the imposition of a compensation order over a fine.[104] The effect is for courts to reduce the sum payable as a fine or to refrain from fining altogether in order to allow the compensation order to be paid. In this respect, it might be said that the compensation order does indeed allow the offender to 'buy his way out of the penalties for crime.'[105] More recently, the Court of Appeal has conceded that other penalties may be reduced to enable a compensation order to be paid. Most acute of all are the problems faced when different rationales point to differential levels of punishment: the harm caused in the instant case may be slight but the malice of the offender great. Which penalty should then prevail?

So far attention has been focused on areas of conflict and difficulty. Let us close by considering some points at which reparation and retributive punishment coincide. First, both retribution and reparation are predicated upon notions of individual autonomy. Unlike rehabilitative or 'treatment' orientated models of justice, both reparation and retribution presume that offenders are rational individuals able to make free moral choices for which they may be held liable. The offender may thus be legitimately called to account, whether by making good or suffering a proportionate punishment. However, both approaches are open to the objection that they ignore the structural imperatives of deprivation and disadvantage under which many offenders act. Both assume that all offenders are rational, free-willed individuals despite the disproportionate incidence of mental illness and disorder, social inadequacy and poor education among our offending population.

Secondly, it might be argued that both reparation and retribution derive their 'authority' from the offence itself and impose penalties according to the seriousness of the particular crime. Unlike the utilitarian aims of general deterrence or rehabilitation which import wider notions of societal good, both retribution and reparation exclude (or nearly exclude) consideration of factors beyond the particular offence. The offender's personal history, the social or economic causes of crime or the need to prevent future offending (all of which extend the limits of intrusion by the state under deterrent or rehabilitative theories) are here deemed irrelevant. As such, both retributive and reparative justice, it is said, impose strict constraints on the intrusion of the state into the lives of offenders. This apparent congruity is not, however, as close as it first seems. The seriousness of the offence is set according to two different sets of criteria. Retribution demands punishment proportional primarily to the intent of the offender, whereas reparative justice derives its 'proportionality' from the harm inflicted on the victim. Whilst intent is generally focused on outcomes, and intent and harm may thus coincide, the two may point to very different levels of gravity. If reparation and retribution were to be wholly reconciled, then it would be necessary to devise a measure which integrated intent and harm in setting offence

---

103 *Inwood* (1974) 60 Cr App R 70.
104 Criminal Justice Act 1982.
105 Wasik, 'Sentencing' in Murphy (ed), *Blackstone's Criminal Practice* (London: Blackstone, 1992) 1714. Though this view assumes that compensation has no penal value.

seriousness. A greater difficulty still is that, if reparative justice is to be more than a criminal analogue to civil damages, then it should go beyond the offence itself to enquire about its wider social costs and the means to making them good.[106]

Finally, reparation and retribution have been described by Davis as each a 'species of distributive justice, the root metaphor in each case is that of justice as balance, the object being to restore the distribution of rights which existed prior to the offence.'[107] Whilst one seeks to restore equilibrium by depriving the offender of his rights, the other pursues the same goal by recompensing those whose rights were injured by the crime. This redistribution of rights is analogous to Ashworth's notion of criminal justice as a 'form of social accounting.'[108] In respect of mitigation, for example, laudable social acts by the offender are balanced against crimes to arrive at the appropriate penalty. Ashworth suggests that this calculus is based upon rehabilitative reasoning which sees the offender's subsequent conduct as evidence of his reform. Another possible view is that mitigation is justified here on the grounds that some restoration of the legal order has been made.

These 'distributive' or 'accounting' metaphors go some way to describing the common ethos of retributive and reparative justice. But they rely on a very narrow conception of reparative justice as solely restitutive in intent, seeking only to return to the preceding legal order.[109] Moreover, the legitimacy of a justification based on 'restoring the balance of rights' is open to question on a number of counts. First, to use the criminal justice system solely as a means of restoring the balance of rights which existed prior to the offence is to condone the reinforcement of pre-existing social inequality. Secondly, many of those activities defined as criminal and those groups identified as offenders reflect the interests and values of a socially dominant group. If reparation, with retribution, seeks to restore the values which criminalisation underpins, it is likely not merely to recreate but to accentuate social inequality.[110] Thirdly, as Davis has also argued, to demand that offenders bear the full burden of restoring the distribution of rights is to expect too much from that 'unrepresentative and generally impecunious group of citizens who come to the attention of the criminal courts,' both practically and as a matter of principle.[111] A powerful objection to the increased use of compensation orders, for example, is that they ignore the fact that very many offenders are in straitened financial circumstances. To impose further financial burdens upon impoverished offenders may simply be counterproductive.

In the light of these conceptual links, the concurrent re-emergence of retributive and reparative thinking is perhaps less surprising than it first appears. Ironically, however, the very points at which reparative and retributive justice coincide appear on closer inspection to be the points of greatest weakness within the

---

106 The danger here is that this process of making good will necessarily entail wider social intervention of the sort that was so troublesome in respect of traditional crime prevention. Though we should remember that it is also arguable that retribution should properly take into account structural factors which limit the free will or culpability of the offender.

107 Davis, *op cit* n 34, p 11.

108 Ashworth, *op cit* n 5, p 133.

109 They may also be inadequate as the foundation for desert theory. Significantly, von Hirsch has also now disavowed his earlier subscription to the idea that sanctions can be justified on the basis of restoring a balance, on the grounds that this does not provide a sufficient reason to invoke the coercive powers of the state, nor does it provide an adequate basis for determining 'how much' punishment is owing under a retributivist schema: von Hirsch, 'Proportionality in the Philosophy of Punishment' (1990) 1 *Criminal Law Forum* 265.

110 Hudson, *op cit* n 8. Though victim surveys have gone a long way toward illustrating that the least powerful in society are most likely to suffer as victims of crime.

111 Davis, *op cit* n 34, p 12.

reparative justice model. Its frailty is greatest in respect of its 'redistributive' purposes which, while theoretically attractive, are predicated on a fictitious just society in which the only imbalance of rights is caused by crimes themselves. A truly reparative model might better recognise that much crime is not simply a cause but also the consequence of social injustice and that the victim, the community *and* the offender are probably in need of repair if criminal justice is to contribute toward a more reintegrated society.

We began with the questions 'can and should' the penal system embrace both punitive and reparative goals: let us return to them by way of conclusion. From our discussion it would seem that whilst 'making good' entails certain difficulties within a criminal justice system, reparation is quite capable of fulfilling the basic demands of punishment and, thus far, is reconcilable with retribution.[112] The danger, however, is that the attempt to accommodate reparative justice to the rationale of punishment so perverts its underlying rationale as to strip it of much of its original appeal, not least its commitment to repairing ruptured social bonds. We are accustomed to seeing criminal justice as the repressive arm of the state, but might it not better be conceived as one end of a continuum of practices by which social order is maintained? Punishment has a very limited ability to control crime and, to the extent that it is disintegrative, it inflicts further damage on society. Given that the high profile 'law and order policies' of the past decade have done little to stem spiralling crime figures, perhaps it is time to explore the integrative potential of reparative justice on its own terms.

---

112 A conclusion also reached by differing routes by Campbell, *op cit* n 32, and Watson *et al, op cit* n 4.

Part IV
Race and Gender Perspectives

[13]

A JUST MEASURE OF SHAME?

Aboriginal Youth and Conferencing in Australia

Harry Blagg*

This article explores the limits of 'reintegrative shaming' and family conferencing as encapsulated in the 'Wagga Model' currently popular in Australia. I question the relevance of the model to the task of reducing the over-representation of Aboriginal people in custody. I argue that the model represents an 'Orientalist' appropriation of a Maori decolonizing process and is based on a one-dimensional reading of the New Zealand experience which involved a significant reduction in police powers. The product being franchised in Australia (and marketed internationally) promises to intensify rather than reduce police controls over Aboriginal people. There is also danger in assuming that all indigenous peoples are amenable to conference-style resolutions and that all operate within shaming structures of social control.

Australian states have tended to lag behind overseas countries with similar policing and judicial structures, such as Britain and New Zealand, in the introduction of diversionary options for juvenile offenders.[1] Since the early 1990s, however, considerable interest has focused on the potential for increased diversion from the formal system offered by police cautioning and Family Group Conferences (FGC). The Family Group

* Crime Research Centre, University of Western Australia. This paper draws on a number of research projects including: a research visit to New Zealand hosted by the Department of Social Welfare, Wellington, 1991; research and consultations with Aboriginal people in Western Australia on the introduction of culturally relevant justice systems, 1991–92; national research on young people and police powers in Australia (see Blagg and Wilkie 1995); research on Aboriginal youth and the juvenile justice system in Western Australia (see Crime Research Centre 1996). I am grateful to Linda Kazazi for her assistance and encouragement: thanks also to Anna Farrante, Frank Morgan, David Indermaur, Meredith Wilkie, Rod Broadhurst, Mat Hakiaha and Basil Sansom.

[1] South Australia has been one of the few states to adopt a diversionary approach (Seymour 1983). The state developed a system of screening panels, with social work and police involvement, which were successful in achieving high rates of diversion from court (Naffine *et al.* 1990). There are concerns that the introduction of police led conferencing as an alternative has reduced rates of diversion (Blagg and Wilkie 1995).

HARRY BLAGG

Conferencing system, adopted from the schemes in operation in New Zealand, has become firmly associated with the practice of 'shaming' as set out by Braithwaite and his associates. The combination of the two has aroused considerable interest and sparked controversy in Australia (Alder and Wundersitz 1994). In Australia some of the interest in Maori-style Family Group Conferences was generated by the 1989 Royal Commission into Aboriginal Deaths in Custody which called on Australia's states to implement strategies to reduce the over-representation of Aboriginal youth in the criminal justice system and increase the involvement of Aboriginal people themselves in the justice process.

The purpose of this paper is to explore the limits of one particular interpretation of the Family Group Conference system as elaborated in a number of texts (Braithwaite 1989, 1993, 1994; Braithwaite and Mugford 1994; O'Connell 1992) and operationalized in a number of Australian initiatives led by the police. Particular attention is paid to the situation in Western Australia, which traditionally has had one of the highest rates of over-representation of Aboriginal youth in the criminal justice system. This is, therefore, not intended as a totalizing critique of Braithwaite's thesis on shaming: rather it is intended to identify its limitations in relation to one specific region of criminal justice practice. I am less concerned, here, with the issue of shaming as a solution to the problem of delinquency *per se*, or of its place within criminological theory. My intervention has relevance to situations where the apparatuses of the criminal justice system confront people from other cultures and ethnic backgrounds. I argue that the lessons of the Maori experience as it relates to youth from indigenous backgrounds and criminal justice systems, are currently obscured by an Orientalist representation of a Maori process. This process is currently being represented as a kind of shaming ceremony: a representation which disregards its function as a strategy of empowerment. Most of all, this appropriation of the conferencing system neglects the radical reforms which took place in New Zealand to reduce the over-policing of Maori youth. Justice systems have a tendency to generate and reflect mono-culturalist narratives and values: indeed, they play a role in constructing 'the other' (Nelken 1994: 5). Many encounters in the criminal justice system take place *across*, rather than *within*, cultural divisions—encounters between non-Aboriginal police and courts and Aboriginal people representing one of the most common such encounters in some parts of Australia. The meaning attached to involvement in the criminal justice system (i.e. whether it is a source of shame) may not be simply reflecting universal cultural processes but may also be shaped by historically specific relationships between dominant and subordinate cultures (Zhang 1995).

A number of voices in Australia have accepted the Wagga model as relevant to the Aboriginal justice issues (Lincoln and Wilson 1995: Hazlehurst 1995) and there are signs that it is being franchised for consumption in the United States.[2] In practice the model in Australia has led to the supplementation and extension of already significant police powers over young people (Blagg and Wilkie 1995; Sandor 1994). What has been called the 'Wagga Model' has become the master pattern for schemes in Australia which

[2] A number of people, known now as the 'original innovators of Family Group Conferences' (Real Justice Forum 1995) such as Moore, McDonald and O'Connell are introducing the product to the USA.

have explicitly set out to increase the police role.[3] The South Australian scheme was devised to 'increase the involvement of the police in the juvenile justice system' and reduce the role of welfare agencies (Alder and Wundersitz 1994: 84; South Australia Parliament 1992). Variants of this arrangement are currently in operation in most Australian states. Reservations have been expressed by Maori observers of the Australian schemes that they have 'substituted the police for the people' (Brown 1994). What is taking place currently in Australia is not a reform but a *reconfiguration* of the juvenile justice system; increasing the scope of police powers in those areas once considered to be the domain of welfare and giving the police a very direct and overt (as opposed to simply indirect and covert) role in the deployment of punishments (Blagg and Wilkie 1995; Bargen 1995; National Children's and Youth Law Centre 1995; see also various contributions by White, Polk and Sandor in Alder and Wundersitz 1994). There are also significant doubts as to whether the system can reduce rates of recidivism (Coumarelos and Weatherburn 1995). The introduction of conferencing, I will suggest, reflects the dominant preoccupation with resolving Australia's version of the 'crisis of penological modernism' (Garland 1991: 72) as it relates to the juvenile crime problem, rather than empowering indigenous people.

Orientalism and Cultural Appropriation

Contemporary quests for an alternative to the dominant mode of criminal justice have led to the rediscovery of pre-modern mechanisms of resolving conflict (Marshall 1995; Christie 1977) and new discourses of 'relational' and 'restorative' justice, involving face to face, victim/offender mediation, rely heavily on non-judicial metaphors of social cohesion for legitimacy. The so-called New Zealand model of Family Group Conferences,[4] presents as one source of ceremonial reintegration of offenders which avoids the problems inherent in the bureaucratized realms of the court. I want to suggest that a number of fashionable readings of the Maori experience in this area fall into the category of what Edward Said calls *Orientalism*. Orientalist discourses are, primarily, powerful acts of representation that permit Western/European cultures to contain, homogenize and consume 'other' cultures. It is through such techniques of representation that we identify what is essentially 'knowable' about them: and our knowledge of them then becomes a kind of cultural capital, the accumulation of which serves to reinforce our nascent cultural superiority. Our knowledge of the cultural 'other' has been achieved though, among other things, 'a distribution of geopolitical awareness into aesthetic, scholarly, economic, sociological, historical and philological texts' (Said 1995: 11) (one might add criminological to the list). Orientalist discourses have the capacity to 'essentialize' other cultures and denude them of their indigenous histories. The discourse established by the Wagga model's appropriation of the Maori conference is Orientalist in a number of senses.

---

[3] I will use the term the 'Wagga Model' here to describe the forms of 'conferencing' or 'Family Group Conferencing' currently in operation in Australia even though the terminologies employed by schemes themselves is evolving; for example the Wagga Wagga scheme was originally called an 'Effective Police Cautioning Scheme'; this was changed to 'Community Accountability Conference'. Other terms used to describe the process are communitarian justice and 'republican' justice.

[4] For reasons which will become clear I will use the term Maori to identify its origins as a popular process rather than as a New Zealand 'model', 'programme' or other 'technique'.

HARRY BLAGG

First, it imposes a westernized interpretation of Maori justice reform, denuding the process of its history, context and internal structures of meaning and 'representing' it as simply a regional, albeit exotic, variation on a universal theme (i.e. one model of a shaming ceremony).[5] In this respect Braithwaite's attempt to give shaming a universal currency places it in the discourse of 'anthropological meta-projects', as described by Cohen (1994), which have likewise attempted to identify globally applicable values, structures and norms. While gesturing in the direction of a specifically Maori 'tradition' in relation to the ceremony (Braithwaite and Mugford 1994) and acknowledging that Maori people have had a raw deal from the system; their reading, and also, to a lesser extent, that of Maxwell and Morris (1993), attaches little significance to what is historically conjunctural and political about this intervention as part of a broader power struggle between *Pakeha* and Maori cultures. The creation of the Family Group Conference system, in this political sense, represented a *counter-hegemonic* reform on a truly Gramscian scale: in that it has both created new structures and has shifted the balance of forces in a crucial region of Maori concern. This, of course, is not the only reading of the situation; it can be read as a reform of the juvenile justice system through reintegration conferences, a system of 'restorative justice',[6] a means of involving victims and making offenders accountable, but—if we are to capture what is, in relation to Aboriginal peoples, its most innovative characteristic—it must also be read as an empowering and *de-colonizing* process which has led to the recovery of lost authorities, social relationships and ceremonies: while reducing the extent of welfare and penological colonialism. In this sense it constitutes a *reclamation* of the child from non-Maori institutions, rather than a *reintegration* ceremony.[7]

Secondly, and relatedly, because Braithwaite *et al.*'s intervention in the Maori domain is *over-determined* by their own 'awareness' and 'scholarly texts' (e.g. it provides an example of a specific intervention in delinquency theory; it demonstrates the universality of 'reintegrative shaming'), this ultimately colours their approach which takes on a positivist and utilitarian cast: i.e. what can we learn from this specific programme? So, while it is acknowledged that western (*Pakeha*) cultures, institutions and penologies have 'failed' and are 'culturally inappropriate', the failure is presented as essentially a correctional failure, a failure to prevent Maori juvenile crime with all its consequences for society and victims. The issues are reduced, therefore, to a positivistic

---

[5] The Maori system is, at least in Australia, being *read through* the works of Braithwaite and his colleagues in much the same way that the Orient was 'read through the complex rewritings' of Orientalists from which 'the actualities of the modern Orient were systematically excluded' and its 'actual identity is withered away into a set of consecutive fragments' (Said 1978:177, 179). Hence the *Maori* system is being represented as simply another 'programme', or 'model of restorative justice' (La Prairie 1995: Lincoln and Wilson 1995) and, as we shall see, thus measured, it can be found wanting when compared with other 'programmes' and 'models' of conferencing (such as Wagga Wagga in Australia) in relation to such criteria as 'success' with victims (we are informed it is a 'failure' in this regard) (Braithwaite and Mugford 1994: 49). Braithwaite and Mugford go on to express concern about the New Zealand schemes 'half hearted commitment to victims' (155n). In other work Braithwaite claims it for 'republican' justice (Braithwaite 1994: 5), a stunning act of 'systematic exclusion' given the profoundly monarchist history of Maori society.

[6] The term 'restorative' can be read in different ways: the dominant reading is one of *restoring* relations between victims and offenders, while the contrapuntal reading is one of *restoring* Maori systems of social control and restoring the child to its *whanau*. The 1989 legislation reflected Maori beliefs that a child could not be treated as an individual outside this context, see the influential report by the Ministerial Advisory Committee on a Maori Perspective (1986).

[7] A dimension of the process which is undervalued in Braithwaite and Mugford's emphasis on the ceremony is the range of activities conducted with *whanau* outside of the ceremony. While not minimizing the FGCs's significance Maori youth justice co-ordinators referred to it as the 'tip of the iceberg' (Hakiaha, personal communication).

and behavioural level; a something works/nothing works equation of programmatic solutions, in keeping with 'the instrumental means to an end conception of punishment' (Garland 1990:7) characterizing our penological era: as opposed to a moral issue of resistance to injustice, cultural genocide, oppression, alien laws and an historical denial of human rights.[8]

In opposition to this symptomatic and utilitarian representation of the Maori experience, therefore, I want to establish what might be called, following Said, a 'contrapuntal' reading (Said 1994), one which situates justice for indigenous peoples within a shared problematic of decolonization. The system established in New Zealand, following ground-breaking legislation, was part of a process of *re*-establishing Maori dominion and the mapping out of a distinctly Maori jurisdiction. The theme has resonance in Australia in relation to the 'de-colonization of the Aboriginal domain' (Rowse 1992: 100; see also Rowse 1993). I can only sketch out briefly here some of the salient features of this quest for jurisdictional sovereignty (for a full review see Maxwell and Morris 1993).

The 1989 legislation[9] placed family decision making at the centre of both youth justice and children's protection processes. The youth justice section of the Act did not just restrict the power of welfare professionals, however. Strict controls were also placed upon police powers to arbitrarily stop, question, search and detain young people. The Act set down strict procedures for the police to follow when approaching and arresting young people (ss. 214–32) and when conducting interrogations, similar to those set out in the codes of practice under the Police and Criminal Evidence Act 1984 in England. The over-representation of Maori children and young people in custody and entrenched hostility between Maori youth and the police was a central concern. Previously existing screening panels and diversionary mechanisms had been by-passed by the police where Maori youth were concerned (Morris and Young 1987). The legislation created new mechanisms, the family group conference, and new gatekeepers, the youth justice co-ordinators. All youth justice matters had, by law, to be referred to the youth justice co-ordinator, with the police being unable to by-pass the processes in the old way. Supporters of the Wagga model maintain that the process in New Zealand expanded police 'options for dealing with young offenders' (Moore and McDonald 1995). The significant dimension of the process from a Maori perspective was the degree to which it did precisely the opposite and *restricted* police discretion—a critical polarity in interpretation that defines the dominant ideology of conferencing in Australia.[10]

This emphasis on family in this manner transformed a process targeted towards reproducing the UK model of victim/offender mediation and diversionary systems management, to one premised upon family decision making as the defining moment in the process (Doolan 1991). In this crucial respect many Australian observers have missed the point about the novelty of the scheme. In one commentary Braithwaite refers

[8] Thus, also, reinforcing the view that Maori over-representation in the justice system is purely a consequence of high Maori crime rates, with over-policing playing no part.

[9] The 1989 Children, Young Persons and their Families Act (CYPFA).

[10] It is open to doubt whether the New Zealand police feel that their options have increased considering their fierce denunciation of the restrictions placed on their powers to stop, search, question and arbitrarily detain youths under s.125 of the 1989 CYPFA (see their submissions to the Ministerial Review Committee 1991).

to the moment in the family group conference where all the professionals leave the room and the family works on a plan (in the Maori sense takes back responsibility) is literally relegated to the status of 'break in proceedings':[11] while Maori youth justice co-ordinators, a prominent Maori judge and other justice professionals in New Zealand, considered this to be a major breakthrough in the empowerment of Maori people and an aspect of the scheme of which sets it apart from others.[12] Within the Wagga reading of the conferencing system nothing of any significance takes place when it is not under the gaze of the police.

The system has been exhaustively reviewed by Maxwell and Morris (1993). While they acknowledged that victim satisfaction was low (although they also suggest that this may have partly been due to the lack of experience with victims and the fact that the processes were not established with victims in mind, rather than anything inherently wrong with the system itself) and that Maori people saw many aspects of the system as reflecting *pakehia* (European) values, they, nevertheless suggest that families have been more involved in the process and have felt empowered by it. The prominence given to Maori forms of conflict resolution is reflected in the use of the *marae*, the community meeting place, as the site for many conferences (Consedine 1993). Clearly, no matter how tentatively, a specifically Maori jurisdiction is being mapped out here: one that may act as the basis for the regeneration of indigenous narratives.[13] The point I wish to make before moving on to look at the situation in Australia is this: *the processes of cultural regeneration in New Zealand, as exemplified by the conferencing system, are engaged not simply with the retrieval of lost practices but the removal of alien ones.* If we allow this distinction to inform the current discourse around shaming and reintegration in relation to Australia's indigenous peoples we may see more clearly the limitations of the Wagga model.

From its inception the model attracted pilgrims from Australia; including academics, government, the judiciary and the police.[14] The Wagga model was the outcome of one pilgrimage by a police sergeant from Wagga Wagga in New South Wales who borrowed the conferencing element of the process to supplement police cautioning. In this interpretation of the system, police officers, rather than youth justice workers, run conferences. The model has become firmly yoked to the practice of 'reintegrative shaming'.

'Shaming' may very well be reintegrative when the ceremonies reflect and harmonize with the embedded values of a particular community. The structures of feeling which underpin interpretative and speech communities act to reconcile conflicts and provide

---

[11] 'In New Zealand, it is usual to have a break in the proceedings during which the offender's family meets on its own to prepare a plan of action' (Braithwaite 1994: 154n).

[12] From interviews conducted in 1991, observations at five conferences in Auckland and personal correspondence.

[13] I am not suggesting here a return to some idealized Maori world. Aspects of traditional justice would be unacceptable to most Aboriginal and Maori people. Cultures and traditions change and adapt through narrative and other processes; current debates in New Zealand and Australia suggest that even ideas about 'parallel' systems are underpinned by reference to human rights treaties, patriarchal structures, due process, etc.; see Tauri and Morris (1995), Hazlehurst (1996), Law Reform Commission (1986).

[14] A number of Australian States sent delegations and a variety of models were constructed on the strength of these visits. South Australia's system, on paper, resembles most the New Zealand format, although the police have more influence than in New Zealand. The 'Wagga model' no longer exists in its previous form in Wagga Wagga now that New South Wales has created its own state-wide conferencing system run by the Ministry of Justice, however it has found a new home in Canberra ACT. In all the schemes the police are very prominent in terms of participation in conferences and their monopoly of the referral process, even in those such as NSW where there has been a nominal transfer of powers (Blagg and Wilkie 1995; Bargen 1995).

a framework within which normal relationships can be reconstructed. This is acknowledged within Braithwaite's re-working of Garfinkel's notion of the degradation ceremony. Garfinkel (1956) indicates that the successful ceremony hinges upon mutual acceptance of a cluster of shared cultural values: 'the supra-personal values of the tribe' (Garfinkel 1956: 423). Like so many seemingly spontaneous and situationally constructed encounters in the ethnomethodological universe they are, in fact, predicated upon a highly structured underlying system of social reality: in Braithwaite's terminology 'communitarian' values. This bed-rock of consensus acts as a fulcrum upon which the world of the offender can be realigned and brought into harmony with the constellation of significant others around him/her. This particular thesis, for reasons I will demonstrate shortly, may not have the universality claimed by its proponents. In reality we are being invited to accept not one but two contentious propositions, the first involving a theory of reintegrative shaming and the second one of agency—that is the processes through which reintegrative shaming is realized. In relation to contemporary Australia both propositions are suspect.

Beyond the shaming community

There are at least two principal objections to this shaming model as it relates to Aboriginal people. First, it is doubtful that Australia's indigenous peoples live within the boundaries of the particular imagined community and its modes of comprehension, speech and interpretation: how can they, therefore, be participants in police-led *re*-integration ceremonies? Secondly, Australian Aboriginal cultures may not operate within a shaming paradigm of social controls, as we would understand the terms. It is in keeping with an Orientalist appropriation to assume that because the conferencing format, or 'sentencing circle' (LaPrairie 1995*b*), reflects aspects of 'indigenous culture' then it is somehow readily transportable to other indigenous cultures (Maxwell 1995).[15] There is a tendency to assume that all of these cultures manifest similar mechanisms for ensuring adherence to accepted standards of behaviour and that all societies maintain a similar balance between social structures and emotions such as shame. We are informed that the 'communitarian approach which underpins family group conferencing, has been used by Aboriginal people *all over the world for ages*' (Real Justice Forum 1995: 2, emphasis added).[16] The current interest in shaming conferencing as a solution to Aboriginal juvenile crime, for example, assumes that Aboriginal culture traditionally operates on the lines of 'shaming' as we would understand it. While not wishing to present an essentialist view of 'traditional' Aboriginal culture myself, I would like to establish another contrapuntal theme and suggest that perhaps it may not.

---

[15] This is in keeping with post-modern modes of 'Food Hall multi-culturalism', as revealed in contemporary appropriations of 'indigenous' cultures through, 'new-age', 'world music' mixes (e.g. a bit of pigmy rain-forest singing, mixed with didjiridu and some Peruvian Indian pipe music). This is having serious implications for Australia's indigenous people who are struggling against a new and virulent form of cultural neo-colonialism where their artefacts are being stolen and their culture desecrated.

[16] The problems created by this melding of 'indigenous' tradition with shaming and conferences and this ensemble then being 'read through' the Wagga model is present in LaPrairie's statement that 'The concept of shame is central to many new justice activities including the community consultation strategies in Australia and New Zealand, the diversion project at Indian Brook and the sentencing circles at Yukon' (1995*a*: 534).

HARRY BLAGG

Anthropological theories link shaming to 'social honour' and to the emergence of 'corporate' and hierarchical civil societies (Peristiany 1965). In this sense Maori society, with its highly organized hierarchies of family and tribal association and its elaborately structured warrior system, may, in some respects, have more in common with western society than with Australia's Aboriginal peoples. Shaming as a social practice is intricately bound up with public presentations of self within a tightly bound polity. Shame is linked to personal honour and is based upon shared, collective views of the world (Pitt-Rivers 1965). It is at its most developed and elaborate within highly 'corporate' societies where social relations are displaced and refracted through an intricate spectrum of homologous and mimetic relationships (Baroja 1965). Symbols of authority, in such cultures, tend to be highly abstracted and people come to associate themselves with a multiplicity of others through *intermediary symbols* (such as badges, emblems, flags, etc.) which then lock them into large scale, imagined collectivities. In corporate societies ones 'reputation' has a certain autonomous life which leads to 'a concern for repute, both as a sentiment but also as the public recognition of that sentiment. It is what makes a person sensitive to the pressure exerted by public opinion' (Pitt-Rivers 1965: 42).

Some readings of Australian Aboriginal society would lead us to question the extent that they operate on such corporate principles or publicly displaced forms of association. The term 'mob' (Sansom 1980) as a description of Aboriginal collectivity: suggesting only loose affiliation, beyond labile groupings of 'clan', 'family group', or 'countrymen', would suggest that notions of collective shame are of limited relevance. There is no fixed, hierarchically structured tribalism as there is, for example, in New Zealand, tying *whanau, iwi* and *hapu* together, but a 'fluid, negotiable and transitory quality of corporate life' as well as a strong emphasis on 'autonomous individual action' (Rowse 1993: 57), which tends towards 'disaggregation' and 'sits awkwardly with administrative notions and technologies which are inclined towards aggregation, the unification of sovereignties across space and the persistence of corporate forms through time' (p. 99).[17] This produces highly localized constituencies of people 'working against hierarchy and authoritarianism' (Langton 1981: 74). 'Public opinion' and 'reputation' may only have a limited impact on, and meaning for, behaviour. In Aboriginal cultures the whole idea of 'representation' is highly contentious, particularly that contained within wholly exterior, adjudicatory structures such as the courts, and there is only limited scope for individuals to 'speak for' others.[18] Another

[17] Braithwaite and Mugford (1994) criticize Ericson's statement that many degredation ceremonies are irreversible as 'overly deterministic' (1994: 141) and postulate that '. . . most kids labelled as delinquents never go to jail as adults' (p. 141). In relation to Aboriginal youths, however, Ericson's statement has some validity.

[18] Finding the appropriate person 'invested with the right in the name of ultimate values' (Garfinkel 1956: 423) to 'represent' Aboriginal people is a hard task. Speaking to others can also present points of difference within indigenous cultures. One Aboriginal elder I discussed the question of conferencing with, suggested that his own people would tend not to confront one another so directly in a 'one-off' or 'face-to-face' conference, much Aboriginal etiquette is designed to avoid and deflect conflict. Discussion, he said, would take place 'over a campfire' (the fire itself absorbs some of the potential conflict, and allows people to avoid direct eye contact). There are inherent features of Australian Aboriginal culture which would raise problems in conferences e.g. Aboriginal culture operates through avoidance mechanisms and language turns which deflect rather than bring on confrontation, showing respect for others (particularly adults) entails not looking in their eyes, speaking in a very low voice etc., which, within the gaze of the criminal justice system, may be interpreted as sullen, remote, not showing remorse, not bothered, shifty, and so on. The mis-reading of Aboriginal language and culture is a constant problem in the criminal justice system (Eades 1988).

A JUST MEASURE OF SHAME?

problematic feature (problematic, that is, for non-Aboriginal processes) in relation to the issue of involving family, lies in the unique patterns of authority and socialization within Aboriginal society which separates out biological parenthood from child socialization, discipline and, particularly, the processes of indoctrination into customary law. The child's biological parent may have little authority in relation to issues of law infraction (either customary and introduced) and may feel not the slightest sense of shame when their biological child commits breaches of either law[19]: while those charged with responsibility for the child's behaviour under Aboriginal law, such as an 'uncle', may still have no responsibility where infractions of non-Aboriginal law are concerned. This should make us hesitant about the efficacy of intervention by 'authority figures' and parsimonious when defining any networks of significant others whose own 'shame' in the face of public disapproval would then impact on the child.

The savagery of white colonization has left a situation where, as one anthropologist expressed it, 'Aboriginal people are not shamed by having white values shouted at them' (Basil Sansom, personal communication): recalling Frantz Fanon's caustic comment that the violence with which 'universal human values' of Europeans were imposed on the colonized meant that, 'in revenge the native laughs in mockery when Western values are mentioned in front of him' (Fanon 1991: 43).[20]

It is naive to imagine that the invitation to participate in a 'shaming' ceremony will not be decoded by Aboriginal people as a further imposition on them: or what may seem to Braithwaite *et al.* as simply a vehicle for the reinforcement of *universal* cultural values will not be received as yet another regime intended to impose some *specific*, non-indigenous practices on them. Moreover, levels of contact with the most degrading elements of the system are such that to have had dealings with the police, lock-ups, courts and prisons is hardly a source of shame or stigma within Aboriginal collectivities (Crime Research Centre 1996).[21]

For the ceremony (be it intended to degrade or integrate) to be meaningful for the actors involved, relationships within the ceremony must be analogous, or in some way compatible, to those existing between people in the everyday world. We must have an image of us all 'getting along' and having a place in some civil realm of everyday life beyond the ceremony—we must have something to lose or to gain. However, as Rowse (1993: 32) demonstrates, such images of 'civil equality' remain at variance with the reality of 'ruthless dispossession and accompanying racist contempt' that have characterized the history of relationships between Aboriginal and non-Aboriginal

---

[19] When Aboriginal people use the term 'shame' they tend to mean something rather different from established usage; Eades suggests that it '. . . refers to the mixture of embarrassment and shyness which come from a variety of situations, particularly being singled out from a group either for rebuke or praise' (Eades 1991).

[20] Fanon goes on, 'when the native hears a speech about Western culture he pulls out his knife—or at least he makes sure it is within reach' and 'when Western values are mentioned they produce in the native a sort of stiffening or muscular lockjaw' (p. 43).

[21] I am not suggesting that Aboriginal people have remained immune to the real degradation, upheavals, institutionalizations, forced assimilations and other strategies designed to eliminate them as a race; because they are not shamed does not mean that they are not damaged in other ways. Only recently has the full story and its appalling legacy in terms of broken lives begun to be told (see, for example, Royal Commission into Aboriginal Deaths in Custody 1991 (RCIADC)). In 1995 the Federal Government commissioned the Human Rights Commission to begin a study into the impact of policies (in place until the late 1960s) which allowed the police and Native Welfare departments to remove Aboriginal children from their families and raise them in institutions and missions and allow them to be adopted into white families; many were told they were orphans, many Aboriginal adults still do not know their real families; half of the Aboriginal people who died in custody were of this 'stolen

HARRY BLAGG

Australia:[22] a reality that the police themselves have done much to cement and perpetuate and in many ways represent for Aboriginal people. How can they be accorded a 'lower social status' (Garfinkel 1956) from a ceremony than they already have? Shame is bound up with anxieties about a loss of social status—a feared mortification of a public self. A reintgrative shaming ceremony exploits this fear of loss, not just for the child but for others, such as parents, whose own social status is, by homology, also under threat. How can this hope to be meaningful for those who have no public status to lose? In this sense any intervention with Aboriginal youth and their families designed to use shaming strategies as a means of reintegration back into the community must struggle first with the continuing reality that Aboriginal people were never living within the community in the first place.[23]

   Justice for indigenous peoples has involved not simply an act of recovery but has also taken them into the international arena where a discourse of human rights holds sway, as a means of protecting them from their own governments which historically have been the greatest threat to their survival. Hence, Aboriginal groups are increasingly turning to international instruments and protocols (Council for Aboriginal Reconciliation 1993; Blagg and Wilkie 1995) for protection; there has been considerable interest by international human rights organizations such as Amnesty International on the Australian scene (Amnesty International 1993, 1996). Indeed, we are confronted with a number of the 'dense, complex and contradictory' (Cohen 1994: 99) aspects of the human rights discourse. We have 'conservative' forces advocating historical amnesia, collective denial and reconciliation where past injustices to Aboriginal people are concerned; and we have the counter discourse of rights for indigenous peoples. We also have the discourse constructed by 'victimology' and, in relation to this, we find those same conservative forces concerns are with 'street crime, making offenders accountable, encouraging self reliance and advocating retributive justice' (Cohen 1994: 100). The crux of it is this: while indigenous peoples may wish to develop alternative justice structures as a means of retrieving lost cultures and as an alternative to the dominant system's colonizing tendencies, these conservative groupings are only concerned with such alternatives in so far as they provide a better mechanism for ensuring outcomes for victims (who are most often non-Aboriginal) and more effective punishment for the offenders (who are most often Aboriginal). This remains the dominant mode of appropriation of the Maori system in Australian justice discourses and reflects the mainstream preoccupation with white victims of Aboriginal offenders: it is leading to what, in the Canadian context, has been called the 'indigenization of social controls' (Harding 1991; Haverman 1988) a process whereby elements of indigenous tradition are reconstructed to increase neo-colonial forms of control. Statements by Moore *et al.*,

---

[22] Rowse also demonstrates the limitations of Goffman-style methodologies derived from symbolic interactionism that presuppose some kind of shared social realm.
   [23] Western history reveals instances where the most elaborately defiling aspects of the apparatuses of shame, proved to be impotent in the face of another cultures rejection of the rules of the game. The British Poor Laws, for example, established the 'outsider' status of the pauper as the most stigmatizing and feared social position in society. The Irish, however, refused to be shamed in this way. The Work House (that 'New Bastille') and the Courts were treated with 'good humored contempt' by indigent Irish folk who found the 'rulers' laws and religion alien' and 'there was no community sanction which found prosecution in the English courts *a cause of shame*' (Thompson 1971: 476, emphasis added). Because the Irish 'adhered to a different value system to that of the English', they were able to adopt a 'cheerfully predatory attitude' to English social rules. One contemporary source bemoaned the fact that the Irish took, 'parochial relief without the *least sense of shame*' (Thompson 1971: 477, emphasis added).

that the Wagga scheme has a better record with victims, need to be read in terms of this dominating Orientalist narrative which has structured the way Australian officials, academics and others have appropriated the Maori system.

Even within these terms of reference there are no guarantees that 'police-led' schemes necessarily produce more victim satisfaction. Some research evidence suggests that they can, in some circumstances leave victims very dissatisfied indeed: Blagg and Smith (1989) found that many victims were unhappy with police-led reparation initiatives in the UK. The police are as capable of manipulating, 'recruiting' victims for their own ends (to punish offenders) as social workers are for their ends (treatment via a 'learning experience').

Having dealt with the issue of the shaming ceremony in relation to neo-colonialistic, essentialistic and Orientalist appropriations of the Maori system, I will now turn to the second dimension or dynamic of the process as set out in the communitarian justice approach, the question of the police as 'agency'. Supporters of the Wagga model make the claim that it has surpassed the 'New Zealand model' because it is more 'communitarian' and, because of the police role, is less dependent on 'state officials' (what are the police?) than New Zealand (Moore 1993: 19).[24] This is a remarkably tendentious claim when read within the context of the construction of Australian society. The police were the states' sharp instrument of conquest.

Policing terra nullius

Australia's indigenous people have yet to be accorded a place in the community. There is a history of genocide, dispossession and exclusion. Aboriginal people were cleared from the country along with the native bush as a *prerequisite* for the introduction of 'community' (Reynolds 1989). Australia's indigenous peoples were not invited to participate in the process of 'state-building' (Deas 1993), neither was any 'social contract' (Dodson 1991) agreed between them and white settlers which would cement a place for them in the new society.

There are clear parallels with the experience of Maori people and the Canadian Indians here. Furthermore the criminal justice system in these societies has been identified as having perpetuated their marginalization and destroyed indigenous social structures, patterns of authority and customary laws (see Royal Commission into Aboriginal Deaths in Custody 1991; Canadian Law Reform Commission 1991; Alberta Task Force on Criminal Justice 1991). The position of Australia's indigenous peoples is worse in some respect: the doctrine of *terra nullius* (that the continent was 'no man's land' before invasion) and the absence of treaties such as *Waitangi* in New Zealand, has meant that they have been among the most dispossessed of dispossessed peoples. The enforced separation of Aboriginal people from mainstream society and their still

---

[24] Leaving aside for the moment this somewhat fanciful notion that the police are not state functionaries, the ethnocentrism inherent in the Wagga reading of the New Zealand situation is reflected in their tendency to reduce the issues to a populist anti-statism; e.g. the 'state' versus the 'community'. The particular functionaries criticized by Moore, youth justice co-ordinators, have a high complement of Maori (some 40 per cent) . Indigenous people involved in reclaiming their collective destiny may not be able to afford this rather precious disdain for working from within state agencies; they often need the protection of the state, particularly the law and human rights instrumentalities, to protect them from some sections of the 'community'—and, of course, sections of the police.

unresolved status as the 'other', immediately problematizes any appeals to shared 'communitarian' traditions.[25]

The police were the principal instrument of dispossession in some regions of Australia where policing was shaped by 'frontier conditions' (Connell and Irving 1989: 32): the protection of settlers from hostile natives being its primary purpose. This was a role carried out in other frontier societies, such as the USA and Canada, by the army; inevitably they became implicit in acts of genocide (Green 1995). From its outset the policing of Aboriginal people had an 'exceptional' character and operated outside the normal forms of 'accountable' policing which were developing in urban areas. There was nothing remotely *neutral* about their role. The police fulfilled a broad range of functions in relation to the 'relocation and maintenance of controls over Aboriginal people' (Cunneen 1991: 5). This was to include the removal of children from their families under legislation designed to 'assimilate' them by placing them in missions and welfare institutions—a practice which, some maintain, lives on in the present through the massive over-representation of Aboriginal youth in custody (Cunneen 1995). Some criminologists maintain that high rates of Aboriginal offending and the reactions of the system to those problems suggest that a 'frontier' style struggle is still active (Broadhurst 1996; Harding *et al* 1995).[26] In Western Australia the police have historically had enormous powers over Aboriginal people which they have supplemented by a grip on the judicial and penological systems in regional areas.[27]

The 'Wagga' model, therefore, raises a number of concerns as it relates to Aboriginal people. It places a question mark against the extent to which the police and the police station can really be neutral territory that 'favours neither victim nor offender' (Moore 1992: 205). The use of the police station for holding victim/offender meetings may, indeed, 'lend a certain gravity to the proceedings' but the formal symbolism here may have resonance diametrically opposite to Moore's meaning: signifying 'white-fella law' rather than neutrality. The idea of police stations being neutral territory flies in the face of the historical and contemporary reality of police/Aboriginal relations as described above and the role played by police cells and lock-ups in the capture enclosure and genocide of Aboriginal people (Royal Commission into Aboriginal Deaths in Custody 1991). Criminal justice professionals and representatives of Aboriginal organizations interviewed for a study of youth/police relations (Blagg and Wilkie 1995) were sceptical that the police could be viewed as 'facilitators and mediators' or 'umpires' (O'Connell 1992: 224; Moore 1992: 271) by Aboriginal people. The same consultations found widespread concern among these groups about the increase of police powers accorded by their control over diversionary schemes. There were calls

---

[25] The groundwork for an Australian 'moral community' which includes Aboriginal people is only now being mapped out after the 'Mabo' High Court Ruling which accepted that 'Native Title' existed prior to invasion, hence finally acknowledging Aboriginal forms of land ownership and officially ending the legal fiction of *terra nullius* (see Rowse 1993).

[26] The notion of the 'frontier' here is strongly linked to the idea of the 'outback' which is less a place than a 'metaphorical side of a mythical partitioning of nationhood into primeval and civilised aspects' (Rowse 1988: 67).

[27] It is also lucrative. The practice of paying meal allowances to police officers to cover the cost of meals for detainees in rural areas, has been held responsible for high levels of incarceration. The practice was condemned by the 1905 Roth Royal Commission (Royal Commission on the Condition of Natives 1905) and recently by the Aboriginal Justice Advisory Council (1995) and the Aboriginal Social Justice Task Force (1995). The practice is being phased out. Anecdotal evidence from police suggests a dramatic reduction in incarceration levels for those towns which now receive frozen meals from local prisons.

for suitably trained and accredited bodies to run conferences (along the lines of youth justice co-ordinators in New Zealand) in some quarters, as an alternative to the police (Blagg and Wilkie 1995).

How successful then are the processes of police cautioning and conferencing at providing communitarian justice in relation to Aboriginal people? I will now turn to the situation in one Australian State where both have been recently introduced.

Aboriginal youth and justice in Western Australia

Police cautioning was only instituted formally in Western Australia in 1991 and has led to a reduction in the number of arrests and charges. The rate of decrease for Aboriginal children and young people, however, is significantly lower than for non-Aboriginal children and young people. Aboriginal juveniles are arrested by police more often than non-Aboriginal juveniles (Crime Research Centre 1996).

In one country region of the state (the South Eastern region) more than 28 out of every 100 young Aborigines were arrested *at least once* in 1994 and faced an average of more than five charges each.[28] Aboriginal youth are less likely to be cautioned by the police than non-Aboriginal youth. Of the 12,887 juveniles cautioned by police between August 1991 and December 1994, only 12.3 per cent were Aboriginal. When set against their levels within the age population (they are roughly 4 per cent of the youth/child population in Western Australia) this may appear unproblematic, even progressive. Placed against their over-representation in the criminal justice system it begins to look sinister. Aboriginal youth represent just under half of all juvenile admissions to police lock-ups, the over-representation rate being particularly high for Aboriginal girls, with twice as many being detained as non-Aboriginal girls. Aboriginal children and young people between the ages of 10 and 14 years of age were 32 times more likely to be charged by the police than non-Aboriginal children and young people. Of particular concern is the young age at which these young people have contact with the police. One in five Aborigines detained in 1994 was 14 years or under. Of these, 91.6 per cent already had an arrest history (Crime Research Centre 1996). This picture is no aberration but the continuation of business as usual (Harding *et al.* 1995). Once they are in the system, furthermore, they easily become enmeshed. Aboriginal youths in Australia are 18.6 times more likely to be imprisoned than non-Aboriginal youths. In Western Australia this difference is even greater and Aboriginal youth are 32.4 times more likely to be imprisoned (the over-representation at the custody level neatly matching their over-representation at the arrest stage).

Criminologists are becoming increasingly aware of the crucial role police decisions play in the development of Aboriginal criminal careers. Research in New South Wales on Aboriginal youth and police discretion found that a 'small but compounding bias' against Aboriginal youth in police decisions, such as not to caution, contributed to high levels of custody (1995: 7). The high arrest and prosecution rates of Aboriginal youths

[28] Such levels of incarceration are not unusual for adults either. It was calculated that in one Western Australian country town in 1994 the number of separate individuals detained exceeded 'any estimate of the towns population itself' (Aboriginal Legal Service 1995: 5).

HARRY BLAGG

in Australia are seen as a consequence of 'over-policing' and a tendency to 'initiate confrontation' with Aboriginal people (Findlay *et al.* 1994: 272).

Police discretion in Western Australia remains virtually unchecked by any secondary screening processes aimed at minimizing the impact of over-policing, such as those provided by mandatory inter-agency discussion and the Crown Prosecution Service in Britain or youth justice co-ordinators in New Zealand.[29] The rules governing encounters between the police and youth, including regulations on stop and search, name checking and interrogations, are weak and are contained within non-binding Police Routine Orders (Blagg and Wilkie 1995).

While the police in Western Australia have resisted reforms to their systems of policing they have not been slow in latching on to the idea of shaming. Braithwaite confesses to being 'regularly surprised' by the 'imaginative' ways the police are using the idea of 'reintegrative shaming' (Braithwaite, 1993: 387). In April 1994 the Western Australian Government introduced amendments to the Police Act to tackle the graffiti problem. A headline in the Western Australian *Sunday Times* (1993) quoted a police spokesperson saying that 'graffiti artists' were 'marked for shame' and 'the ultimate humiliation' described the scheme, which would see children and parents clean graffiti, as 'designed to shame offenders':

> The approach we're taking is the shaming effect—not only for kids but for their families . . . Vandals would be humiliated during clean ups.

Imaginative indeed.

This approach has become an exemplar for other police forces. In Queensland the police are about to target four areas as sites for Diversionary Conferences for minor offenders, or 'villains' (*Courier Mail* 1995), at which victims would confront offenders to 'bring home the shame' according to police sources. The report maintains that these would-be young 'villains' who would otherwise just be cautioned.

Western Australia's Juvenile Justice Teams

In 1991, the same year as the introduction of cautioning, two pilot Juvenile Justice Teams were established in Perth, Western Australia. These have since been expanded to four with others in the planning stage: a variant of the scheme has also been established in country areas.[30] The model operating in Western Australia has features in common with the Wagga and South Australian models in that it leaves significant discretion with the police (Hakiaha 1994). It differs from these others in that the conferencing system itself is managed by a multi-agency team comprising a police officer, youth justice worker, education officer and an Aboriginal community worker in appropriate areas. Although the teams are co-ordinated by juvenile justice personnel from the Ministry of Justice the police ultimately control access to teams. In Western

---

[29] Police control goes deep into the system in most parts of Australia. Not only do they make the key gatekeeping decisions they also prosecute the overwhelming majority of cases in court. In country regions, in particular, where the police presence is particularly marked, this prosecutor role fuels Aboriginal perceptions that the police are 'boss of the courts' and 'despair of justice being done . . . the police have more power than the courts' (Dodson 1991: 160).

[30] For administrative purposes the state is separated into the Perth metropolitan and county areas.

A JUST MEASURE OF SHAME?

Australia, as in the majority of Australian States, the 'gatekeeper' is the arresting officer and there are few controls by senior personnel, other agencies only being brought into play once the significant decisions have been made by the police. This factor, along with rigid schedules in the 1994 Young Offenders Act , which prevent diversion for a wide range of offences, greatly restrict the scope for diversion.

The initial model of the inter-agency teams was intended to be a part of a much broader strategy aimed at involving Aboriginal people in the justice system and the teams themselves were envisaged as building blocks in an ongoing process of reconfiguring the justice system and building in the direction of a New Zealand-type scheme (State Government Advisory Committee on Young Offenders 1991). Raising the cautioning rate was seen as a 'structural prerequisite', along with the introduction of a specialist Youth Aid section in the police, a recommendation also of other high level committees in Western Australia (Police/Youth Task Force 1993; Select Committee on Youth Affairs 1992; State Government Advisory Committee on Young Offenders 1991). The Aboriginal worker would link in with family and community groups and ensure that there were networks into which to direct the child (State Government Advisory Committee on Young Offenders 1991). Unfortunately this has become an optional extra rather than an imperative under the 1994 Young Offenders Act. The ideas for the project had been strongly endorsed by Aboriginal people in the Perth area at a number of consultative meetings (State Government Advisory Committee on Young Offenders 1990). The conferencing scheme as it was actually instituted, however, rested on an unreconstructed police prosecutory system.[31] The underpinning reforms that modified police actions in New Zealand (similar to those under the Police and Criminal Evidence Act 1984 in England and Wales) were entirely absent—instead the police have been largely allowed to determine referrals to the projects. The political climate at the time of the project's introduction was largely responsible for the emasculation of the reform process.[32] Police in other Australian States, with the exception of South Australia, came in for criticism from human rights watchdogs, lawyers, Aboriginal organizations, academics and others involved in the youth and children's rights area for their failure to adhere to due process regulations and laws (Blagg and Wilkie 1995; Alder *et al.* 1992).

The Western Australian scheme was evaluated 'in house' by the Justice Ministry in 1994 (Ministry of Justice 1994). Police referrals tended to be of a less serious nature than those from the courts (the scheme allows for both police and court referrals)— 47 per cent of court referrals having had previous court appearances as opposed to 10 per cent of police referrals. Referral rates for Aboriginal youth were low. At 16 per cent the referral rate for Aboriginal youth was consistent with their rates of cautioning. The picture in 1994/5 shows little improvement. Rates of Aboriginal referral to conferences by the police show no sign of increasing and are set at around 16 per cent of all referrals in the Perth region. Western Australia is in a position roughly comparable

---

[31] Aboriginal support for the diversionary schemes was based on their desire to be involved with their young people and conditional on having Aboriginal workers employed on diversionary teams as per the recommendations of the Royal Commission into Aboriginal Deaths in Custody (State Government Advisory Committee on Young Offenders 1991).

[32] In the same year the Crime, Serious and Repeat Offenders Act was passed following a massive moral panic about Aboriginal juvenile crime, particularly car theft. The Act introduced mandatory terms in custody for certain categories of 'repeat offender' (see Harding 1993).

to New Zealand in the mid-1980s, prior to the introduction of the 1989 legislation, when the police cautioning scheme was diverting around 50 per cent of cases (roughly equivalent to the present rate of diversion in Western Australia) but failing to make inroads into the high rate of arrests and court appearances of Maori children and young people. The lack of adequate gatekeeping of the conferencing referral process has seen the Juvenile Justice Teams deluged with trivial cases of a kind that would be cautioned, or even dealt with by an informal warning, in New Zealand or the UK (Crime Research Centre 1996).

Aboriginal people and conferencing

The low rates of referrals for Aboriginal youth to the teams in the Perth metropolitan area represented just one of a number of problems for an initiative designed as a strategy of involving Aboriginal people in the justice system. Even where Aboriginal youths are referred for conferences in Western Australia there has been considerable difficulties in involving them and their families in the process. Aboriginal workers in the Juvenile Justice Teams, who conduct the family visits and encourage Aboriginal involvement in the process, identified a diversity of reasons why this was the case. An Aboriginal person working in the Wangara team (in the northern suburbs of Perth), for example suggested that Aboriginal people have been conditioned to expect non-Aboriginal authorities to provide controls over their young people since they took over responsibility following settlement. Other Aboriginal workers suggested that families feared involvement in the process because the police play too prominent a role. Mistrust of the police was a factor in the reluctance of young Aboriginal people, in particular, to attend a family meeting; workers frequently found that a youth had moved to live with another member of his family group when the day of the conference arrived. It was also said that Aboriginal youth who attended conferences would simply 'clam up' when police were present. A number of Aboriginal workers reported that they had sometimes asked the police officer to leave meetings for a time, finding that children were more communicative when this occurred. Aboriginal people also suggested that Aboriginal police aides[33] should be more involved in the process, as an alternative to non-Aboriginal police. Others (and a number of non-Aboriginal professionals) suggested that the police should be required to wear civilian clothes when attending conferences.

Juvenile Justice Teams established in country areas of Western Australia found it hard to engage with Aboriginal people, who, one worker in a justice team said, had a 'profound fear and loathing of the police and welfare' authorities. Only in those parts of the country region where the police were playing a less active role in the process (due to a number of reasons; unwillingness in some cases but also lack of management direction and training) and Aboriginal workers from the Ministry of Justice were dealing with the youth and his/her community, were there clear reports of Aboriginal willingness to be involved.

---

[33] Police aides are Aboriginal auxiliaries. In theory they liaise with Aboriginal communities and are not involved in mainstream social order policing or crime investigation.

A JUST MEASURE OF SHAME?

Conclusion

Returning to a point I made in my introduction, I have deep misgivings that Aboriginal people will 'fail' at conferencing. This will be a double failure because it is, after all, an indigenous people's system. Rural Aboriginal people are highly mobile (as are, to a lesser extent, urban Aborigines) and difficult to pin down for meetings. One worker said that 'they are in South Australia before we can organize a meeting'. They are not in the *marae* or long houses or *wigwams* waiting to have meetings. Aboriginal ceremony involves an emphasis not on place as much as on *movement*, the ritual passages along the 'song lines' and dreaming tracks, replenishing their links with kin groups, sacred sites and 'country', settling for a time on traditional campsites and camp fires. Processes intended to involve Australia's Aboriginal people in the criminal justice system must go in train with processes designed to free them from its destructive devices: in Cohen's terms, the victimology must be balanced with an acknowledgement of genocidal crimes and steps must be taken to reform the structure and culture of the police.

In this paper I have raised some questions about the relevance of shaming to Aboriginal people in Australia. I have questioned the extent to which these shaming ceremonies, as currently constructed, can have relevance to the needs of Aboriginal Australians. In relation to the relevance of the Maori system I suggest that attention needs to be paid to the totality of the Maori experience, rather than simply extracting the conferencing element, if we are to increase levels of Aboriginal involvement in the criminal justice process in Australia. The representations of the Maori system, found in the works of proponents of Wagga-style conferencing, rest upon Orientalist appropriations of a Maori process intended to reclaim their children from justice and welfare colonialisms, repackaged as a model of communitarian justice. Ironically, but wholly consistent with Orientalist appropriations, the indigenous process is then designated as inferior to the brand 'franchised' by the Orientalists as the 'real thing'. I have also raised questions about the viability of the 'shaming' solution to the problem of Aboriginal over-representation and stress instead, as a prerequisite for any meaningful reform process, the need thoroughly to transform the systems of policing as they impact on the lives of Aboriginal people. It is noteworthy in this regard that many Aboriginal people in Western Australia are focusing their energies on developing their own forms of policing through Aboriginal Patrols (Crime Research Centre 1996; Blagg forthcoming), continuing the work of defining their own 'domain'. The Patrol system may provide the basis for some indigenous methods of conflict resolution to emerge at a local level. Low levels of Aboriginal participation in conferencing may be the result of a combination of factors not all related to their 'occidentalist' structure: lack of investment in Aboriginal support services to the teams remains an ongoing problem, there is a lack of co-ordination with Aboriginal organizations and scant thought has been given to developing culturally appropriate options for conferences to refer young people on to. However, Aboriginal workers on the teams and personnel from Aboriginal organizations remained optimistic that the conferencing system could be made to operate in a way that would fulfil a key recommendation of the Royal Commission into Aboriginal Deaths in Custody in relation to juvenile justice:

. . . the primary sources of advice about the interests and welfare of Aboriginal juveniles should be the families and community groups of the juveniles and specialist Aboriginal organizations, including Aboriginal Child Care Agencies. (RCIADC 1991: Recommendation 235)

REFERENCES

ABORIGINAL JUSTICE ADVISORY COUNCIL (1994), *Getting Strong on Justice: 1994 Report of the AJAC.* Department of Aboriginal Affairs, Perth, WA.

ABORIGINAL LEGAL SERVICE (1995), *Counting the Cost: Policing in Wiluna 1994.* Perth: Aboriginal Legal Service.

ALBERTA GOVERNMENT (1991), *Justice on Trial, Report of the Task Force on the Criminal Justice System and its Impact on Indian and Metis People.* Attorney General of Alberta, Edmonton.

ALDER, C., O'CONNER, I., WARNER, K. and WHITE, R. (1992), *Perceptions of the Treatment of Juveniles in the Legal System.* Canberra: National Youth Affairs Research Scheme.

ALDER, C. and WUNDERSITZ, J.,eds. (1994), *Family Group Conferencing and Juvenile Justice: the Way Forward or Misplaced Optimism?* Canberra: Australian Institute of Criminology.

AMNESTY INTERNATIONAL (1993), *Australia: A Criminal Justice System Weighted Against Aboriginal People.* Sydney: Amnesty International.

——(1996), 'Aboriginal Deaths in Prison Reach Record High', *Amnesty International News*, 26: 1.

BARGEN, J. (1995), 'A Critical View of Conferencing', *Australian and New Zealand Journal of Criminology*, Special Supplementary Issue: 100–4.

BAROJA, J. C. (1965), 'Honour and Shame', in J. G. Peristiany, ed., *Honour and Shame: the Values of Mediterranean Society.* New York: Weidenfeld and Nicolson.

BLAGG, H. and SMITH, D. (1989), *Crime, Penal Policy and Social Work.* Essex: Longmans.

BLAGG, H. and WILKIE, M. (1995), *Young People and Police Powers in Australia.* Sydney: Australian Youth Foundation.

BRAITHWAITE, J. (1989), *Crime, Shame and Reintegration.* Melbourne: Cambridge University Press.

——(1993), 'Beyond Positivism: Learning from Contextual Integrated Strategies', *Journal of Research in Crime and Delinquency*, 50: 383–400.

——(1994), 'Resolving Crimes in the Community: Restorative Justice Reforms in New Zealand and Australia,' in C. Martin, ed., *Resolving Crime in the Community: Mediation in Criminal Justice.* London: ISTD.

BRAITHWAITE, J. and MUGFORD, S. (1994). 'Conditions for Successful Reintegration Ceremonies', *British Journal of Criminology*, 32: 139–72.

BROADHURST, R. (1994), 'Aborigines, Cowboys, "Firewater" and Jail: the view from the frontier', *Australian and New Zealand Journal of Criminology*, 27: 50–7.

——(1996), 'Aborigines and Crime in Australia', *Crime and Justice: A Review of Research*, 21: 408–68.

BROWN, M. (1994), '*New Zealand and Youth Justice*'. Paper delivered to the Australian Labour Lawyers Conference, Fremantle.

CANADIAN LAW REFORM COMMISSION (1991), *Aboriginal People and Criminal Justice: Equality, Respect and the Search for Justice*, LRCC No. 34.

CHRISTIE, N. (1977), 'Conflicts as Property', *British Journal of Criminology*, 17: 1–15.

COHEN, S. (1993), 'Human Rights and Crimes of the State: The Culture of Denial', *The Australian and New Zealand Journal of Criminology*, 26: 97–116.

498

A JUST MEASURE OF SHAME?

CONNELL, R. T. and IRVING, T. H. (1980), *Class Structure in Australian History Documents: Narrative and Argument.* Melbourne: Longman.

CONSEDINE, J. (1993), *Restorative Justice: Healing the Effects of Crime.* Lyttleton: Ploughshare.

COUMARELOS, C. and WEATHERBURN, D. (1995), 'Targetting Intervention Strategies to Reduce Juvenile Recidivism', *Australian and New Zealand Journal of Criminology,* 28: 54–72.

COUNCIL FOR ABORIGINAL RECONCILIATION (1993), *The Position of Indigenous People in National Constitutions.* Canberra: Council For Aboriginal Reconciliation.

Courier Mail, Brisbane, 9 May 1995.

CRIME RESEARCH CENTRE (1996), *Aboriginal Youth and the Juvenile Justice System in Western Australia.* Perth: University of Western Australia.

CUNNEEN, C. (1994), 'Enforcing Genocide? Aboriginal Young People and the Police,' in R. White and C. Alder, eds., *The Police and Young People in Australia.* Melbourne: Cambridge University Press.

DEAS, E. I. (1993), 'Address to the Conference', *The Position of Indigenous People in National Constitutions.* Canberra: Council for Aboriginal Reconciliation.

DODSON, P. (1991), 'Underlying Issues in Western Australia', *Royal Commission into Aboriginal Deaths in Custody.* Canberra: AGPS.

DOOLAN, M. (1991), Youth Justice: Legislation and Practice, unpublished paper. Wellington: Department of Social Welfare.

EADES, D. (1988), 'They Speak An Aboriginal Language, Or Do They', in I. Keene, ed., *Being Black: Aboriginal Cultures in Settled Australia.* Canberra: Aboriginal Studies Press.

——(1991), *Aboriginal English and the Law.* Brisbane: Continuing Legal Education Department, Queensland Law Society.

FANON, F. (1991), *The Wretched of the Earth.* New York: Grove Weidenfeld.

FINDLAY, M., ODGERS, S. and YEO, S. (1994), *Australian Criminal Justice.* Melbourne: Oxford University Press.

GARFINKEL, A. (1956), 'Conditions for Successful Degradation Ceremonies', *American Journal of Sociology* 61: 420–44.

GREEN, N. (1995), *The Forest River Massacres.* Fremantle: Fremantle Arts Press.

HAKIAHA, M. (1994), 'Youth Justice Teams and the Family Meeting in Western Australia', in C. Alder, and J. Wundersitz, eds., *Family Group Conferencing and Juvenile Justice: the Way Forward or Misplaced Optimism?* Canberra: Australian Institute of Criminology.

HARDING, J. (1991), 'Policing and Aboriginal Justice', *Canadian Journal of Criminology,* 33: 363–85.

HARDING, R., ed. (1993), Repeat Juvenile Offenders: The Failure of Selective Incapacitation in Western Australia, Research Report No. 10.

HARDING, R., BROADHURST, R., FERRANTE, A. and LOH, N. (1995), *Aboriginal Contact with the Criminal Justice System and the Impact of the Royal Commission into Aboriginal Deaths in Custody.* Sydney: Hawkins Press.

HAVERMAN, P. L. (1988), 'The Indigenization of Social Control in Canada' in B. Morse and G. R. Woodman, eds., *Indigenous Law and the State.* Dordrecht, Holland: Forrsest.

HAZELHURST, K. M. ed (1995) *Legal Pluralism and the Colonial Legacy.* Aldershot: Avebury.

LANDAU, S. F. and NATHAN, G. (1983), 'Selecting Delinquents for Cautioning in the London Metropolitan Area', *British Journal of Criminology* 23: 128–49.

LANGTON, M. (1981), 'Urbanising Aborigines—the Social Scientists' Grand Deception', *Social Alternatives,* 2: 73–9.

LAPRAIRIE, C. (1995a), 'Community Justice or Just Communities?', *Canadian Journal of Criminology,* 37: 521–47.

——(1995*b*), 'Altering Course: New Directions in Criminal Justice, Sentencing Circles and Family Group Conferences', *Australian and New Zealand Journal of Criminology*, Special Supplementary Issue: 78–100.

LAW REFORM COMMISSION, AUSTRALIA (1986), *Recognition of Aboriginal Customary Laws*, 2 vols, Report No. 31. Canberra: AGPS.

LAW REFORM COMMISSION OF CANADA (1991), *Aboriginal People and Criminal Justice: Equality, Respect and the Search for Justice*, LRCC: 34.

LINCOLN, R. and WILSON, P. (1995), 'Aboriginal Offending: Patterns and Causes', in D. Chappell and P. Wilson, eds., *The Australian Criminal Justice System: the Mid 1990s*. Sydney: Butterworth.

LUKE, G. and CUNNEEN, C. (1995), Aboriginal Over-representation and Discretionary Decisions in the NSW Juvenile Justice System. Sydney: Juvenile Justice Advisory Council of NSW.

MARSHALL, T. F. (1995), *Alternatives to Criminal Courts*. Aldershot: Gower.

MAXWELL, G. M. (1995), 'Some Traditional Models of Restorative Justice from Canada, South Africa and Gazza', *Criminology: Aotearoa/New Zealand*, Victoria: University of Wellington, New Zealand.

MAXWELL, G. M. and MORRIS, A. (1993), *Family, Victims and Culture: Youth Justice in New Zealand*, 4: 6–7. Victoria: University of Wellington, Social Policy Agency, Institute of Criminology.

MINISTERIAL ADVISORY COMMITTEE ON A MAORI PERSPECTIVE FOR THE DEPARTMENT OF SOCIAL WELFARE (1986), *Puao-te-ata-tu (Daybreak)*. Wellington: Department for Social Welfare.

MINISTERIAL REVIEW TEAM (1992), *Ministerial Review of the 1989 Children, Young Persons and their Families Act*. Wellington: Department of Social Welfare.

MINISTRY OF JUSTICE (1994), *Juvenile Justice Teams: A Six Month Evaluation*. Perth: Ministry of Justice.

——(1992), 'Facing the Consequences', *National Conference on Juvenile Justice*. Canberra: Australian Institute of Criminology.

MOORE, D. (1993), 'Shame, Forgiveness and Juvenile Justice', *Criminal Justice Ethics*, Winter/ Spring: 3–24.

MOORE, D. B. and McDONALD, J. M. (1995), 'Achieving the "Good Community": A Local Police Initiative and its Wider Ramifications', in K. M. Hazlehurst, ed., *Perceptions of Justice*. Aldershot: Avebury.

MORRIS, A. and YOUNG, W. (1987), *Juvenile Justice in New Zealand: Policy and Practice*, Study Series 1. Wellington: Institute of Criminology.

NAFFINE, N., WUNDERSITZ, J. and GALE, F. (1990), 'Back to Justice for Juveniles: the Rhetoric and Reality of Law Reform', *Australian and New Zealand Journal of Criminology*, 23: 4.

NELKEN, D., ed. (1994), *The Futures of Criminology*, London: Sage.

O'CONNELL, T. (1992), 'Wagga Wagga Juvenile Justice Cautioning Program: It May Be The Way To Go', *National Conference on Juvenile Justice*. Canberra: Australian Institute of Criminology.

PARLIAMENTARY SELECT COMMITTEE ON YOUTH AFFAIRS (WA) (1992), *Youth and the Law*. Government of Western Australia.

PERISTIANY, J. G., ed. (1965), *Honour and Shame: the Values of Mediterranean Society*, New York: Weidenfeld and Nicolson.

PITT-RIVERS, T. (1965), 'Honour and Social Status', in J. G. Peristiany, ed., *Honour and Shame: the Values of Mediterranean Society*. New York: Weidenfeld and Nicolson.

POLICE /YOUTH TASK FORCE (1991). Report. Perth: The Minister for Police.

Real Justice Forum (1995), Family group conferencing newsletter.

REYNOLDS, H. (1989), *Dispossession: Black Australia and White Invaders*. Sydney: Allen and Unwin.

A JUST MEASURE OF SHAME?

ROWSE, T. (1988), 'Middle Australia and the Noble Savage: a Political Romance', in Beckett T. ed., *Past and Present—the Construction of Aboriginality*. Canberra: Aboriginal Studies Press.

——(1992), *Remote Possibilities: The Aboriginal Domain and the Administrative Imagination*. Darwin: North Australian Research Unit, Australian National University.

——(1993), *After Mabo: Interpreting Indigenous Traditions*. Carlton, Victoria: Melbourne University Press.

ROYAL COMMISSION ON THE CONDITION OF NATIVES (1905), Report. Perth: Government of Western Australia.

ROYAL COMMISSION INTO ABORIGINAL DEATHS IN CUSTODY (1991), Reports 1–5. Canberra: AGPS.

SAID, E. W. (1995), *Orientalism: Western Conceptions of the Orient*. Harmondsworth: Penguin.

——(1993), *Culture and Imperialism*. London: Vintage.

SANDOR, D. (1994), 'The Thickening Blue Wedge in Juvenile Justice', in C. Alder and J. Wundersitz, eds., *Family Group Conferencing and Juvenile Justice: the Way Forward or Misplaced Optimism?* Canberra: Australian Institute of Criminology.

SANSOM, B. (1980), *The Camp at Wallaby Cross: Aboriginal Fringe Dwellers in Darwin*. Canberra: Australian Institute of Aboriginal Studies.

SELECT COMMITTEE ON YOUTH AFFAIRS (1991), *Youth and the Law*, Discussion Paper 3. Legislative Assembly, Western Australia.

SEYMOUR, J. (1983), *Juvenile Justice in South Australia*. Melbourne: Law Book Company.

SOUTH AUSTRALIAN PARLIAMENT: SELECT COMMITTEE ON THE JUVENILE JUSTICE SYSTEM (1992), *Interim Report*. South Australia: Government Printer.

STATE GOVERNMENT ADVISORY COMMITTEE ON YOUNG OFFENDERS (1992), *Police Questioning of Juveniles*. Perth: Government of Western Australia.

——(1991), *Pilot Priority Projects for Local Involvement in Juvenile Justice*. Perth: Government of Western Australia.

Sunday Times, Perth, 19 December1993.

TAURI, J. and MORRIS, A. (1995), 'Maori Justice Practices', *Criminology: Aotearoa/New Zealand*. Victoria, New Zealand: University of Wellington.

TASK FORCE ON THE CRIMINAL JUSTICE SYSTEM AND THE IMPACT ON THE INDIAN AND METIS PEOPLE OF ALBERTA (1991), *Justice on Trial*. Alberta Taskforce Report.

TASK FORCE ON ABORIGINAL SOCIAL JUSTICE (1994), *Report of the Task Force*, vol. 1. Perth: Government of Western Australia.

THOMPSON, E. P. (1971). *The Making of the English Working Class*. Penguin, Harmondsworth.

ZHANG, S. X. (1995), 'Measuring Shame in an Ethnic Context', *British Journal of Criminology*, 35/2: 248–62.

[14]

Community Conferencing and the Fiction of Indigenous Control*

Chris Cunneen†

The paper analyses the use of community conferencing for young people in various jurisdictions in Australia in the light of its impact in Indigenous communities. It argues that the manner in which these programs have been introduced has ignored Aboriginal rights to self-determination and has grossly simplified Indigenous mechanisms for resolving conflicts. In most jurisdictions, community conferencing has reinforced the role of state police and done little to ensure greater control over police discretionary decision-making. The changes have also been introduced in the context of more punitive law and order policies, including mandatory minimum imprisonment terms and repeat offender legislation for juveniles. The end result is likely to be greater bifurcation of the juvenile justice system along racialised boundaries, with Indigenous youth receiving more punitive outcomes.

Introduction

There is now widespread and systematic empirical research carried out throughout Australia which clearly indicates a number of central features in the relationship between Indigenous young people and juvenile justice systems. For the purposes of this article they can be summarised as follows. First, there is long-standing and extreme over-representation of Indigenous young people throughout State and Territory juvenile justice systems (Cunneen & McDonald 1997). Second, Indigenous young people are most over-represented at the most punitive end of the system, in detention centres (Gale et al 1990; Wilkie 1991; Crime Research Centre 1995; Luke & Cunneen 1995; Criminal Justice Commission 1995). Third, Indigenous young people are less likely to receive the benefit of diversionary options and are more likely to receive adverse decisions when police utilise discretionary powers (Gale et al 1990; Wilkie 1991; Crime Research Centre 1995; Luke & Cunneen 1995; Criminal Justice Commission 1995; Wundersitz 1996; Dodson 1996).

The purpose of this article is to explore the impact of family group conferencing within the context established above. Can we expect the process of conferencing to positively impact on the situation by facilitating the move of more Aboriginal and Torres Strait Islander young people into diversionary processes and out of Children's Court and detention centres? A related and equally important question is: what relationship does family group conferencing have to the principle of Indigenous self-determination and the commitment that governments have to working within this framework of negotiation? All State and Territory Governments have committed themselves

* Received: 6 May 1997; accepted in revised form: 27 August 1997.
† Senior Lecturer, Institute of Criminology, Sydney University Law School, 173–5 Phillip St, Sydney 2000, email: chriscu@law.usyd.edu.au

to implementing recommendation 62 of the Royal Commission into Aboriginal Deaths in Custody which requires negotiated solutions for dealing with Indigenous youth (Cunneen & McDonald 1997:170).

In general terms, 'diversionary schemes' refer to the mechanisms and programs available which *divert* young people away from the formal processes of the Children's Court. Diversionary schemes *may* involve some type of community input into the design and administration of the scheme, although this is by no means a necessary feature. From an Indigenous perspective, one of the most critical issues in relation to the development of diversionary schemes has been the lack of Indigenous consultation, negotiation and control. The schemes are seen as frequently rigid in their structure and not designed in close consultation with Indigenous communities or adapted to local circumstances (Dodson 1996). According to Dodson, diversionary schemes are:

> packaged in remote 'policy' units and driven or posted into communities. We see diversion delivered to us in a package because 'they' know what is best for 'us'. The paternalism of such diversion reflects the earlier policies of 'care and protection' and 'assimilation' that permitted the removal of Indigenous children from their families up until the 1970s (1996:31).

The development of simple models of diversion and dispute resolution often fails to understand the complex reality of Indigenous communities, including the history of those communities and their relationship with colonial states. They also ignore fundamentally the principle of self-determination. They promote what has been referred to as a 'one size fits all' approach to Indigenous criminal justice and juvenile justice matters (Dodson 1996:61; Canadian Royal Commission on Aboriginal Peoples 1996:219).

In recent years, 'family group conferencing' has become a favoured option for diversion and for ensuring individual accountability and responsibility. Conferences are intended to bring together young offenders and their support persons with the victim and their supporters to develop a sense of responsibility on the part of the offender for the offence. They are also intended to reach a mutually agreeable resolution for the harm that has been caused by the offence and to reintegrate the offender back into the community. Various forms of 'conferencing' have been established in most areas of Australia. By and large, they adapt and modify parts of the New Zealand system of family group conferences. The New Zealand system derives from extensive consultation with Maori communities and is reflective of Maori traditions.[1]

At a theoretical level, the use of conferences has been closely associated with Braithwaite's (1989) theory of reintegrative shaming. Reintegrative shaming is said to demonstrate disapproval for the offending behaviour while maintaining a level of respect for the offender. The person is not labelled as deviant and there is a process by which the individual is decertified as deviant. Reintegrative shaming is the opposite of stigmatisation which is disrespectful and humiliating of the offender. With reintegrative shaming the offender is given the opportunity to re-enter society through recognition of their wrongdoing, through recompense to the victim and by reassurance to the community that the offending behaviour will not be repeated. Family group conferences or community conferences are seen as a process through which

294   (1997) 30 The Australian and New Zealand Journal of Criminology

reintegrative shaming can and does occur (Braithwaite 1989; Braithwaite 1992; Braithwaite & Mugford 1994).

It should also be noted that the introduction of family group conferencing has occurred within a particular political climate. In South Australia, the Young Offenders Act 1993 abolished screening panels and Children's Aid Panels and replaced them with a system of diversionary options including police cautioning and family group conferencing. When introducing the new bill into Parliament, the relevant Minister claimed that the new legislation was needed because, 'the penalties handed down by the Children's Court are considered to be too lenient in many cases, with young offenders not being held accountable for, nor made to confront, the consequences of their actions' (quoted in Roach Anleu 1995:37). It has been argued that the new legislation, of which family group conferencing is a key part, represents a shift from giving primary emphasis to rehabilitation and welfare to a concentration on community protection, victim participation and juvenile accountability (Roach Anleu 1995:37). Section 3(2) of the legislation states that statutory policies of juvenile justice must include 'sufficiently severe' sanctions against illegal acts to provide for an appropriate level of deterrence and for adequate community protection. The discourse speaks of individual responsibility and deterrence (Cunneen & White 1995:192).

The South Australian legislation reflects a key paradox surrounding the introduction of family group conferences in Australia. The legislation rests on a 'just deserts' model of criminal justice with its emphasis on children and young people as individuals who make rational choices and who are responsible for their actions (Sarre 1994). Punishment for wrongdoing should be proportional to the seriousness of the offence, to protect the community and to ensure specific and general deterrence. The irony is that, although family group conferencing has been introduced within this 'just deserts' framework, the underlying theoretical approach relies more on restorative justice principles. Indeed restorative justice and reintegrative shaming have been developed in part as a critique of, and alternative to, the 'just deserts' model (Braithwaite & Pettit 1990). As noted previously, the use of family group conferencing is considered a part of the restorative justice framework.

This apparent contradiction in the philosophical and political underpinning of recent juvenile justice legislation should alert us to the possibility that conferencing is merely one strategy within a complex of approaches designed to gain compliance and ensure the regulation of young people. Conferencing sits within the context of greater bifurcation in treatment between those defined as minor and serious offenders. Conferencing has been established for minor offenders. Penalties have been increased for more serious offenders, and there has been a move to shift a greater number of offences out of the jurisdiction of the Children's Court and into the higher courts in jurisdictions such as South Australia (Roach Anleu 1995:44) and Queensland (Cunneen & McDonald 1997:173). In addition there have been significant changes in dealing with repeat offenders through the use of indeterminate sentences and mandatory terms of imprisonment in Western Australia and Northern Territory (Cunneen & McDonald 1997:129).

Australian adaptations of conferencing have been the subject of criticism by many commentators. Stubbs (forthcoming) provides a useful summary of the wide range of concerns which have developed around conferencing with juvenile offenders in Australia. These include: absence of due process safeguards and inconsistent outcomes; the centrality and/or dominance of the police role in conferencing and lack of police accountability; imbalances of power between conference participants; problems with victim attendance and victim satisfaction; inequities based on gender; lack of cultural sensitivity/suitability; and problems associated with resource requirements for efficient conferences. The Australian Law Reform Commission reference on children and the law is also considering the development of conferencing. The reference commissioner, Kathryn Cronin, has noted that children and young people in the juvenile justice system represent 'some of the most disadvantaged, damaged and least articulate young people in the community', yet are expected to benefit from being shamed while confronting angry and emotional victims, acknowledging their wrongdoing and making appropriate reparation (Cronin 1997:2).

There is also a developing literature which looks specifically at the impact of family group conferencing on Indigenous people in Australia (Blagg, forthcoming; Dodson 1996; Bargen 1995), as well as numerous reports which provide evaluative and empirical data (Aboriginal Legal Rights Movement and the Aboriginal Justice Advisory Committee 1994; Wundersitz 1996; Cunneen & McDonald 1997). Much of this literature has been implicitly or explicitly critical of the impact of the new processes on Indigenous youth. The Australian adaptations of the New Zealand model have been referred to as 'hybrids' with 'the real spirit of the diversionary process completely lost in all but a few cases' (Dodson 1996:42). These criticisms can be summarised as follows.

- There has been a failure to negotiate and consult with Aboriginal communities and organisations.
- The police exercise significant discretionary powers over access to conferencing, the operation of the process and the agreement which is reached.
- Cultural differences are inadequately dealt with.
- Bifurcation is occurring with more punitive processing of Indigenous offenders.
- Conferencing undermines self-determination through its tokenistic recognition of Indigenous rights.

The failure to consult and negotiate

Some recent research suggests that there has been inadequate consultation with Aboriginal communities during development of new models of conferencing. In addition, where consultation has occurred there has been insufficient regard paid to Indigenous views (Dodson 1996:33). The absence of consultation and negotiation can fundamentally compromise the development of family group conferencing in Indigenous communities. For example, the trial conferencing project in Alice Springs occurred without Aboriginal community consultation and Aboriginal organisations were of the view that Aboriginal young people were unlikely to receive benefits from the program. Repeat offenders were not being considered for conferencing, which effectively excluded the bulk of Aboriginal young people (Cunneen &

McDonald 1997:171). In South Australia, the Pitjantjatjara Council noted that they had barely seen any impact of change as a result of the new juvenile justice legislation which introduced conferencing. There was no knowledge of any conferencing panels in the Pitjantjatjara lands (Cunneen & McDonald 1997:171). Indeed it appears that the part-time conference co-ordinator's position which was to service the Pitjantjatjara lands has been abolished (Wundersitz 1996:119).

Part of the failure to consult and negotiate is reflected in inadequate resourcing for conferencing in Indigenous communities. Independent evaluation of barriers to the use of alternatives in South Australia, noted in relation to the Anangu Pitjantjatjara Lands that:

> The local Youth Justice Co-ordinator has insufficient resources to organise Family Conferences. The most time consuming and culturally difficult task involves the identification of family members who are appropriate to participate in the conference and then subsequently arranging for them to come together for a Conference. Very few victims of offences are involved in family conferences resulting in a central feature of the scheme being omitted from the process (Planning Advisory Services 1995:27).

In Western Australia, Aboriginal organisations have argued that there is a lack of empowerment for Aboriginal families or communities which would assist in utilising the diversionary options which are offered. The 'current systemic discrimination against Aboriginal youth in the operation of the diversionary processes will be perpetuated by the new legislation' (Ayres 1994:20).

The lack of commitment to Indigenous involvement and to fundamentally shifting the balance of power in decision-making marks an enormous divergence between the New Zealand model of conferencing and what has occurred in Australia. In New Zealand the change,

> . . .has both created new structures and has shifted the balance of forces . . . if we are to capture what is, in relation to Aboriginal peoples, its most innovative characteristic, it must be read as an empowering and de-colonising process which has lead to the recovery of lost authorities, social relationships and ceremonies; while reducing the extent of welfare and penological colonialism (Blagg, forthcoming).

By and large, conferencing in Australia has been an add-on feature to more punitive changes in juvenile justice legislation. It is couched in 'Indigenous friendly' terms because it is argued that it enables greater Indigenous input into the process of juvenile justice decision-making. Yet the available evidence suggests that negotiation with Aboriginal communities has been poor. In addition, Indigenous juvenile incarceration rates have been rising rapidly (NISATSIC 1997:498).

In general, Aboriginal organisations have not been completely condemning of the conferencing process and instead have tended to adopt a critical attitude of watching how the system operates in the longer term (see, for instance, Aboriginal Legal Rights Movement and Aboriginal Justice Advisory Council 1994:25). The Aboriginal and Torres Strait Islander Social Justice Commissioner has argued that panels and family conferencing can be successful with adequate cultural sensitivity and Aboriginal community involvement 'but schemes which increase alienation and which are imposed by police on families of the offender and the victim will not succeed' (Dodson 1996:199). ATSIC has supported greater evaluation of the potential benefits of the scheme to Indigenous young people (ATSIC 1996:42).

The role of police in the process

Police control over the conferencing process is a significant problem. The major procedural concerns relate to the power police wield at various stages of the decision-making process. Aboriginal organisations are sceptical that police can be viewed as independent arbiters in the process (Blagg & Wilkie 1995). Power and control over diversionary options are being extended to police without screening or regulatory processes over decision-making (Dodson 1996:33; Blagg, forthcoming). In South Australia, Western Australia and the pilot conferencing programs in Northern Territory, ACT, Tasmania and New South Wales the police control some or all of the following points of decision-making: access to conferencing, the operation of the process, and a veto over the final agreement which is reached.

In Western Australia, the Juvenile Justice Teams were supposed to model the New Zealand family group conferencing process. However, the composition of the team may include only a representative from the police, the Ministry of Justice, a responsible adult and the young person. Referral to the team can be made by the police or the Children's Court. The Aboriginal Legal Service Western Australia suggests that the 'Juvenile Justice Team model is a half-baked and inadequate version of the New Zealand model that will not live up to its potential' (Aboriginal Legal Service Western Australia 1996:348). The teams are inadequate because: they have restricted membership; the conferences lack specific time frames; they are restricted to dealing with minor non-scheduled offences, and are only available to first offenders; there are no legal safeguards for the young person; and the police have control over who is referred to the teams (Aboriginal Legal Service Western Australia 1996:348; Beresford & Omaji 1996:103–5).

In Western Australia, the available evidence shows that Indigenous young people are not being referred as frequently to Juvenile Justice Teams (to hold conferences) as non-Indigenous youth. A survey in metropolitan Perth of the first 39 weeks of the operation of the Teams concluded that 'only a small percentage of Aboriginal young people are being referred to the Teams and ... this percentage is gradually decreasing' (Western Australian Government 1996: Exhibit Number 19 Appendix 4). Other research has confirmed that rates of referral of Aboriginal youth to the conferences in Western Australia are low (Crime Research Centre 1995:6).

Similarly, in South Australia, Indigenous young people are less likely to be referred by police to the conferences and more likely to be referred to court. Indigenous young people comprise 12% of referrals to conferences, but 19% of referrals to court. In addition Indigenous young people (36%) are almost twice as likely as non-Indigenous youth (19%) to be referred straight to court without the benefit of either a conference or a police caution (Dodson 1996:33; Wundersitz 1996:204). In Queensland the Juvenile Justice Legislation Amendment Act 1996 establishes 'community conferences' as an available diversionary option. Only police officers are authorised to make

298   (1997) 30 The Australian and New Zealand Journal of Criminology

referrals to a community conference as an alternative to court, although the court can refer a matter to a conference *after* a hearing and guilt has been determined (s 18). Given that Aboriginal and Torres Strait Islander young people in Queensland are already disadvantaged by police discretionary decisions to utilise existing diversionary alternatives such as cautioning (Criminal Justice Commission 1995), there is nothing in the new legislation which will shift the way police already decide who will receive the opportunity of a diversionary option. In other words, there is no reason to believe that conferencing will in any way alter the existing progression of Indigenous youth through to the most punitive end of the system.

In NSW, it has been recommended that the pilot Community Youth Conferencing scheme be abandoned partly because of attitudinal problems on the part of police (Bargen 1995) and lack of referrals of Indigenous youth to the conferences (Dodson 1996). A new system is being introduced called 'accountability conferences' which limits more directly the power of police in relation to referral by proposing that referrals also be made by the court and the Director of Public Prosecutions. The new legislation places a presumption in favour of conferencing for a greater number of offences. However, the number of prior police cautions or conferences must be considered by police when deciding the eligibility of the young person for a diversionary option (NSW Young Offenders Act 1997, s 37). In Tasmania the draft Youth Justice Bill proposes that referrals be made by way of the court.

The problems associated with the police role in the conferencing process show how different the systems developed in Australia are to the original New Zealand model. There were significant reforms to policing practices in New Zealand at the same time as the introduction of family group conferences. These reforms included stricter controls on police powers in relation to young people. The Australian variations have simply seen conferencing as expanding the options available to police. Blagg argues that 'the significant dimension of the process from a Maori perspective was the degree to which it did precisely the opposite and restricted police discretion' (forthcoming). The South Australian Young Offenders Act 1993 is an example where the legislation has formally expanded the police role over young people who admit offences through the use of conferencing and cautioning (Roach Anleu 1995:39). This is precisely the issue which is of major concern to Indigenous organisations. The new South Australian legislation has given police 'enormous discretionary powers without, it appears, any form of control or vigilance over their discretion' (Aboriginal Legal Rights Movement and the Aboriginal Justice Advisory Committee 1994:23). Given the widespread research which already exists concerning the problematic way in which police discretion is exercised in relation to Indigenous youth, it is not surprising that the extension of police powers into new areas of diversion is cause for concern.

The role of police in the conferencing process also raises a number of theoretical issues concerning the function that police might play within the shaming process. It has been argued that one factor which will determine the nature and effectiveness of a police role in reintegrative shaming is the climate of respect for police (Findlay 1993:29). Whether police authority is seen as legitimate or not will have direct consequences for actions which require respect such as reintegrative shaming. Police respect and authority will also be affected by the use of discretion. Findlay has noted that, 'If police discretion becomes consistently perceived by the public as unworthy of respect rather than as ensuring it, then . . . the legitimacy of police authority for the exercise of discretion will be undermined' (1993:32). This relationship between respect, authority and the use of shaming mechanisms such as conferencing has particular importance in understanding how police are likely to be perceived by Aboriginal communities. Lack of respect for police authority and lack of acceptance of the legitimacy of police actions already significantly undermine Aboriginal/police relations.

The introduction of conferencing in Australia has increased police powers in a formal sense as 'gate keepers' to the various levels of the juvenile justice system. However, it has also increased police power in a symbolic sense through the conferencing process itself.

> It would seem that the police maintain a powerful stance throughout the entire process from when the young person is initially apprehended until the outcome of the Family Group Conference . . . The impact of racism and harassment experienced by many young Aboriginal people is no doubt intensified when the police wield an amount of power in a situation where the young person has very little. This can be compounded by an historical sense of 'them and us' that has existed between most Aboriginal people and the police over generations (Aboriginal Legal Rights Movement and the Aboriginal Justice Advisory Committee 1994:24–5).

It has been noted that where police authority relies on community endorsement and where there is a framework of 'community conscience' which regulates police practice, then the potential for reintegrative shaming will be greater (Findlay 1993:36). This is precisely what is missing in the relationship between Aboriginal communities and state police. The police function has a particular resonance for Indigenous communities given the history of child removal, forced relocations and heavy police intervention in day-to-day life. The use of police, combined with cultural differences and language difficulties, may well cause Indigenous young people and their families to appear 'un-cooperative' within a conferencing framework (Dodson 1996:46–7). Indeed, research in Western Australia has indicated that the police presence increases the reluctance of Aboriginal people to attend meetings and contributes to a non-communicative atmosphere for those Aboriginal youth that do attend (Aboriginal Justice Council 1995:44; Crime Research Centre 1995:28).

Shaming and community conferencing rest on idealised notions of community consensus around the role of policing. Police are thought of as drawing their legitimacy from this consensus built on the images of community policing and a homogenous community. Yet we know that police roles are highly differentiated and that organisational and legal structures orient policing towards different social groups in different ways (Findlay 1993). In relation to Indigenous young people, conflict in public places, unequal treatment in the use of discretion and ongoing complaints about the use of excessive force are key issues which structure the relationship between the two groups (Cunneen & White 1995; Cunneen & McDonald 1997). In this context the police role in the conferencing process may do little more than create the symbolic appearance of 'community policing' while at the same time reinforce the separation and removal of

300   (1997) 30 The Australian and New Zealand Journal of Criminology

Indigenous young people from the imagined consensual 'society'. In practical terms, Aboriginal and Torres Strait Islander youth will find themselves still at the hard edge of the juvenile justice system: more likely to be brought before the courts and more likely to be incarcerated. The available empirical data already suggest that conferencing has not altered this feature of Aboriginal involvement in the juvenile justice system.

The role of police in conferencing undermines Braithwaite's own preference for not placing too much emphasis on state policies for dealing with offenders after they have been identified (Braithwaite 1992:16). A significant part of the problem in relation to Indigenous communities is the failure to recognise the centrality of the principle of self-determination.[2] The recognition of the principle of self-determination is not inconsistent with the republican view of 'dominion'. Furthermore, dominion is seen as the measuring point for whether criminal justice intervention is justified. Rather than support further penetration of non-Indigenous state bureaucracies into the fabric of Aboriginal communities through police-run conferences or half-hearted attempts at reform where some magistrates 'allow' Indigenous young offenders to be dealt with by their communities, a thorough-going commitment to Indigenous self-determination (dominion) would support the development of a separate Indigenous jurisdiction or forms of shared jurisdiction where this is the wish of the community.[3] Such a position would also be consistent with Braithwaite's preference for support of social movements which seek to extend dominion (Braithwaite 1991; Braithwaite & Pettit 1994).

Cultural differences and colonial discourses

The 'one size fits all' approach to Indigenous communities has been noted above. As Dodson (1996) indicates, Indigenous people are themselves keenly aware of this failing in government policy towards Indigenous communities. In practical terms, the application of the model from New Zealand has rested on the spurious assumption that there are homologous social structures among Indigenous cultures (Blagg, forthcoming). In other words, Indigenous people all over the world are seen as the same. Family group conferencing grew out of Maori traditions; Maori people are Indigenous; therefore all Indigenous people will benefit from family group conferencing.[4] Ultimately such a view is racist, ascribing as it does some essentialist core to what it is to be authentically 'Indigenous' without cultural, spatial or temporal difference.

The presumed applicability of reintegrative shaming and its expression in a conferencing model grossly simplify Indigenous cultures in a number of ways. First, it assumes that Indigenous cultures in Australia operate on a model that prioritises a simple confrontational shaming process in resolving disputes and conflict. Second, it assumes that Indigenous young people can operate effectively within an imposed model without suffering significant disadvantage because of cultural difference. Third, it fails to adequately grasp the relationship between Indigenous communities and non-Indigenous colonial state formations.

In relation to the first point, an example of cultural difference centres on the need for the victim to face the offender. Such a meeting is held to be central to a successful reintegration ceremony (Braithwaite & Mugford 1994). Yet this is a simplistic view of how disputes are worked out in Indigenous societies. For example, Blagg (forthcoming) has noted the extent to which Indigenous societies in Australia seek to avoid the open conflict between victim and offender which is at the heart of the conferencing process. Support for this view can be found in careful and extensive analysis of dispute management in Aboriginal communities such as that undertaken by Williams (1987). Rather than some simplistic process of shaming, she discusses a variety of sanctions used by Yolgnu people in Arnhemland including temporary exile, temporary internal exile, withdrawal and restitution (Williams 1987:96–106). Many of these sanctions are clearly based on avoidance rather than confrontation. Similarly, elders groups dealing with Indigenous young people in northern Queensland still rely on various forms of exile through the use of outstations. In central Australia managing disputes and preparing for the intervention of the non-Indigenous criminal justice system may involve complex arrangements between various clan groups in the absence of the offender or the victim (Intjartnama 1994).

In relation to the second point above, observations of conferencing in South Australia have suggested that 'the most striking aspect of the model developed *for* Indigenous people are the problems encountered with cultural difference' (Dodson 1996:46). These differences include inadequate understanding of Indigenous social structure, language barriers, different communication patterns and different spatial and temporal patterns which derive from cultural obligations. Indigenous observers of conferencing in South Australia have noted that questions may be directed to the wrong person in the family group, causing some people to feel disgruntled because of the failure to show proper respect and others to become silent because of embarrassment (Collings 1996). Problems communicating in standard English can also cause silence. The end result can be that the silence is interpreted as 'sullenness', the victim feels more anger and the young offender feels alienated (Dodson 1996:46–7). Not only do the desired outcomes of the process fail to materialise, but the young person is likely to be pushed into the potentially more punitive reaches of the juvenile justice system.

There is now a significant body of literature which outlines the difficulties which face Indigenous people in the formal legal process (Eades 1995; Criminal Justice Commission 1996; Mildren 1997). These difficulties primarily derive from cultural and communicative (verbal and non-verbal) differences but also may include medical conditions (such as middle ear infection leading to hearing loss). They are part of the structural parameters which prevent Indigenous people receiving fair treatment in the non-Indigenous legal process. In addition, leaving aside the layers of rhetoric which construct family group conferencing as an 'alternative', the process is still firmly a part of the formal juvenile justice system in terms of referral, determinations and sanctions for non-compliance.

The third point relates more directly to the *relationship* between Indigenous communities and the non-Indigenous state. 'Reintegrative shaming' is a practice which is based in communicative processes (Braithwaite 1989). The communicative process through which shaming rather than stigmatisation occurs presupposes respect for the offender and some equality of power. In conferencing however, the non-Indigenous procedure and the 'law' from which it gains legitimacy may be fundamentally oppressive. In this instance, the process of 'communication' may reflect an ethic of silencing and denial, where inequality and domination structure the communicative process to the extent that the experience of the oppressed cannot be communicated, and indeed the practices of exclusion and silence are perpetuated (Fraser 1992).

The silencing can operate in a number of ways. At the practical level this occurs in such examples referred to earlier in this article where the police presence 'silences' Indigenous young people and their families, or where individual participants feel alienated from the process because of the failure to understand and respect Indigenous structures and processes for inter-personal communication. There is also the more general effect of silencing and delegitimising existing forms of Indigenous social control where these exist. It has become increasingly commonplace to describe Indigenous communities in terms of social disorganisation and lack of interdependencies (Broadhurst 1996; La Prairie 1997). Yet as Braithwaite acknowledged two decades ago, apparent social disorganisation may conceal informal social control mechanisms within a particular community. The application of formal intervention mechanisms may disrupt these existing forms, particularly where official involvement is likely to be clumsy and bureaucratically controlled (Hogg 1988:43–4; Braithwaite 1979:96–7). In the context of Australian Indigenous communities, government intervention may also be unsympathetic to or unaware of localised and culturally distinct solutions.

A further dimension to the 'silencing' aspect of non-Indigenous law is the resistance shown by Indigenous adults and youth who refuse to speak. There is no doubt that an important political tactic for some Indigenous people has been the *refusal* to accept the legitimacy of a non-Indigenous criminal justice jurisdiction. Part of this refusal is held in the view that Indigenous people have been refused citizenship rights, subjected to genocide and terror, and are now essentially political prisoners within a colonialist and neo-colonialist legal structure (de Graff 1993; Cunneen 1996). Reintegrative shaming rests on a process of recognition, recompense and reassurance by the offender towards the victim, which will result in reconciliation. It may well be that in particular circumstances reconciliation by Indigenous offenders is seen as unacceptable. Unable and/or unwilling to comply with the demands of a conferencing process, the offenders are then seen as suitable for more punitive forms of intervention, including incarceration (de Graff 1993:17).

It is perhaps not surprising that the empirical evidence suggests that Indigenous young people are less likely to experience a 'successful' conference than non-Indigenous youth (Wundersitz 1996:204). The process may well degenerate into further stigmatising of Indigenous young people as 'incorrigible' and their families as 'uncaring' or 'incompetent'. The effects of seeing Indigenous youth as 'incorrigible' will be discussed below. For the moment it is important to consider the outcome of seeing Indigenous families as 'failures'. White (1991) has noted that the blaming of parents for juvenile offending has developed a particular currency which serves to displace other structural explanations of juvenile crime such as poverty, unemployment and racism. What has been referred to as the 'criminalisation of inadequate parenting' has particular ramifications for Indigenous families given that welfare intervention during the assimilationist period was partially justified by pathologising Indigenous family structures and parenting styles. Indigenous children were removed on welfare grounds because Indigenous families could not provide a 'proper' home environment. There are still widespread complaints among Indigenous people that welfare authorities assume that Indigenous people are 'bad' parents (NISATSIC 1997). Conferencing as it is currently being introduced may see the same type of 'blaming' of Indigenous families and reinforce the perceived need for greater forms of bureaucratic surveillance and intervention.

Bifurcation along racialised boundaries

At the beginning of this article it was noted that conferencing models have been introduced in the context of a greater *bifurcation* in juvenile justice system within Australia. In other words, juvenile justice systems are responding to two categories of offenders: those who are minor offenders and those who are serious and/or repeat offenders. Minor offenders are channelled into the various diversionary programs such as police cautioning and conferencing schemes. Serious and repeat offenders, on the other hand, become ineligible for diversionary programs and are dealt with more punitively through sentencing regimes that are more akin to adult models. Amendments to the Northern Territory Juvenile Justice Act provide for mandatory minimum terms for some categories of offences and in Western Australia the Young Offenders Act has provisions for indeterminate sentences for some categories of offenders.

The bifurcation of juvenile justice systems has been discussed in the literature for a decade (Pratt 1989). What is significant in the Australian context is the extent to which bifurcation between 'minor' and 'serious' juvenile offenders is occurring along *racial* boundaries. O'Connor (1994) noted that greater bifurcation was arising partly as a result of a greater reliance on 'justice' models of juvenile justice. 'The bifurcatory processes embedded in justice model practice inevitably result in the problematization and incarceration of "serious offenders" ie Aboriginal offenders' (O'Connor 1994:210). Recent juvenile justice legislative changes in South Australia, Western Australia, Queensland and the Northern Territory have refocussed attention on treating 'serious' offenders more seriously. At the same time, the incarceration rate per 100,000 for Indigenous youth have risen by 24% between 1993 and 1996. The non-Indigenous juvenile rate rose by less than 5% for the same period (NISATSIC 1997:498). In other words, not only are more Indigenous young people being locked up but the rate of over-representation is actually increasing as well.[5]

In Western Australia both the Crime Research Centre (1995) and the Aboriginal Legal Service Western Australia (1996) have noted that Aboriginal young people are not receiving diversionary outcomes or are seen as 'failing' the alternatives. The results are then compounded. 'The courts may perceive Aboriginal youth to have "failed to respond" to diversionary options such as cautioning and family group conferences and consequently "up-tariff" them, that is, give them a more severe disposition than justified by the current offence alone' (Crime Research Centre 1995:13).

Similarly, in South Australia the Aboriginal Legal Rights Movement (1994:24) noted that where Aboriginal young people either refuse to attend a

304   (1997) 30 The Australian and New Zealand Journal of Criminology

conference or fail to comply with the agreed upon sanction then the matter is referred directly to the Youth Court. The judge or magistrate may well see the apparent non-compliance as contemptible and, as a result, impose an unwarranted penalty.

The restrictions that have been placed on the use of conferences also directly limit their potential application for Indigenous young people. In Western Australia and the Northern Territory conferencing is only available to first offenders. However, the empirical evidence has consistently shown that Indigenous young people come into the system at an earlier age and at any one time those being formally dealt with by the system are far more likely to have a record of previous convictions (Gale et al 1990; Luke & Cunneen 1995; Crime Research Centre 1995). These restrictions, coupled with restrictions on the type of matters which can be dealt by conferences (Crime Research Centre 1995; Dodson 1996), will structurally exclude many Indigenous youth from the process. Similarly in New South Wales, although the new Juvenile Justice Act 1997 has a presumption in favour of the use of the least restrictive form of sanction (s 7), police are also required to consider prior cautions, conferences or convictions when determining how to proceed with a young person.

When the these structural limitations are then coupled with the likely adverse use of police discretion, potential cultural inappropriateness of conferencing, and array of tougher sentencing options at the court end, it is perhaps not surprising that Australia is witnessing a further increase in the number of Indigenous youth behind bars.

Tokenism or self-determination?

There is nothing in the current or proposed Australian conferencing schemes which allow for conferencing models to be significantly developed by Indigenous communities. Provisions in existing or proposed legislation which stipulate that conferencing should be 'culturally appropriate' are nothing more than tokenism if there is no framework provided for significant Indigenous input or control over the form and substance of conferences. The eleventh (and last) 'guiding principle' of the New South Wales Accountability Conferences is that 'it should be culturally appropriate' (NSW Attorney-General's Department 1996:38). The legislation which was introduced stipulates that measures for dealing with children 'are to be designed so as to be culturally appropriate, wherever possible' and that the sanctions imposed 'take into account the gender, race and sexuality' of the child (New South Wales Juvenile Justice Act 1997, s 34(1)(a)(v) and s 34(1)(c)(iv)). What does 'culturally appropriate' mean? Who will decide what it is, when it is possible, and what processes will guarantee its implementation? The South Australian Government has noted that the Department of Family and Community Services 'is committed to a model of conferencing with Aboriginal people that will facilitate the sharing of responsibility for planning, decision making, care and action' (South Australian Government 1996:44). However, there is no statutory obligation to consider cultural issues, the model itself is assumed to be appropriate, and the problem to be resolved is essentially one of overcoming 'logistic' problems such as distance and developing the 'processes' which will ensure Aboriginal family inclusion. The South

Australian Young Offenders Act 1993 lists in s 3(2) a number of statutory policies. Subsection (e) provides for the proper regard of a youth's sense of racial, ethnic or cultural identity. However, there are no specific requirements in relation to either police cautions or family conferencing for culturally appropriate Indigenous participation — let alone decision-making.

The Western Australian Young Offenders Act 1994 requires that, when the person being dealt with is a 'member of an ethnic or other minority group', the team should include a person nominated by members of an ethnic or minority group, *where practicable*. In New South Wales the only recognition of cultural difference is that the administrator of conferences, when choosing a Convenor to run the conference, 'would need to consider among other things, whether it is possible to match the young person with a Convenor from the same cultural background, distance considerations, and so on' (NSW Attorney-General's Department 1996:xv). Again, Indigenous involvement is seen as essentially an administrative issue to be dealt with, rather than a right based on the principle of self-determination.

The model of conferencing has been imposed on Indigenous communities without consideration of Indigenous cultural values, and without consideration of how communities might wish to develop their own Indigenous approaches to the issue. It should be noted that even in new proposals for conferencing such as those in NSW and Tasmania where the police role in referral is somewhat circumscribed, there is no provision for Indigenous organisations and communities to make decisions about whether their children would be best served by attending a conference. The best that is included in new proposals is that when conferences are held which involve Indigenous youth, then an elder or other representative of the young person's community must be invited (s 30(2)(c)(v) of the Tasmanian Youth Justice Bill).

Some governments have identified the problem associated with conferencing in Indigenous communities. 'The organisation, systems and delivery of service have evolved from non-Aboriginal frameworks, and are based on a Western system of thought, culture and values that is very different to Aboriginal traditions and culture. Aboriginal people are, therefore, inevitably alienated to some degree from the systems and structures that exist to provide them with services' (South Australian Government 1996:42). Similarly, the Western Australian Government, in response to the lack of Indigenous involvement in family group conferencing, identified factors such as remoteness, the difficulty of locating the whereabouts of families because of mobility, failure or refusal to attend and 'a wary attitude towards a justice system that is alien to most traditional values and has never really worked for them' (quoted in NISATSIC 1997:526).

However, governments appear unable to identify any solution based on a respect for Indigenous rights which would allow Aboriginal and Torres Strait Islander people to develop their own solutions. Ironically, governments commit themselves on paper to recognising the right to self-determination but consistently fail in practice (Dodson 1996; Cunneen & McDonald 1997). The solution proposed by the South Australian Government is essentially one of greater Aboriginal involvement in service delivery — in making the existing framework of non-Indigenous laws and policies culturally appropriate. 'The development of culturally appropriate models of service delivery, and fostering the self-determination of Aboriginal people, is an ongoing challenge' (South Australian Government 1996:42). Yet the solutions which are proposed are, in essence, about making the existing non-Indigenous system 'work' for Aboriginal people. Thus the recent review of the South Australian juvenile justice system recommends in relation to conferencing that a separate Aboriginal conferencing team be established to increase Aboriginal attendance, provide information, determine appropriate support people, act as co-ordinators, and seek feedback from the community 'regarding the development of more culturally appropriate conferencing processes' (Wundersitz 1996:125). Nowhere in the general recommendations relating to Aboriginal youth is there recognition of a decision-making role for Aboriginal communities or their organisations as a right of self-determination (Wundersitz 1996:208).

A corollary to the issue of incorporating Indigenous people within diversionary processes such as conferencing is the way in which Indigenous social processes may be compromised and changed in the process of adaptation and rationalisation by state agencies. As Matthews (1988:9) has noted, informal social processes are unlikely to re-emerge in their original form once they have been absorbed into state processes. The apparent informalism exhibited in processes like family group conferencing may represent a move towards 'a more normative, inclusive and decentralised mode of regulation . . . a form of governmentality involving a change in the distribution and organisation of power' (Matthews 1988:19). For Indigenous peoples in Australia, the new forms of regulation may represent an apparent incorporation of Indigenous modes of dispute resolution ('all Indigenous people use shaming, therefore conferencing must be better suited to *them*') at the same time as extending further regulation into the community particularly where conferencing is used for trivial matters, while simultaneously incarcerating more Indigenous youth as serious/repeat offenders. Indigenous communities may end up getting the hard end and the soft end of the stick at the same time.

There *are* successful examples of Indigenous diversionary schemes, such as the Koori Justice Workers in Victoria and the community justice groups in a number of Queensland communities (Cunneen & McDonald 1997). The essential feature of these schemes is that they have developed from community involvement in finding solutions to specific problems. The communities have received funding from State departments but the control, content and form of intervention is determined by the community. The schemes which are successful have an inherent respect for developing solutions founded on the principle of self-determination. From an Indigenous perspective, 'the success of these programs . . . require a collaborative, intelligent, co-ordinated approach which honours the principle of self-determination . . . Empowering our old people and revitalising dispute resolution through community programmes have the potential to restore a greater degree of social control and divert our kids from custody' (Dodson 1996:59).

Developing community justice solutions within a context of self-determination is essentially a practical task. Governments are not required to relinquish their responsibilities, but they are required to relinquish control over decision-making for Indigenous communities. The lesson of successful Indigenous community justice responses is efficient, practical and ongoing support from governments to facilitate communities in the difficult process of finding acceptable solutions (Cunneen & McDonald 1997).

The available theoretical, observational and empirical evidence strongly suggests that family group conferencing, far from being a panacea for offending by Indigenous young people, is likely to lead to harsher outcomes for these young people. Indigenous youth do not receive the same benefits of diversionary options as non-Indigenous young people. Of fundamental importance is that the diversionary options are not of Indigenous making. In other words, the diversionary options in most instances are 'alternatives' created by the non-Indigenous juvenile justice system and imposed on Indigenous young people and their communities. Indigenous communities and families have been punished by Anglo-Australian law for more than two centuries, and with what result? The policies of government towards Indigenous children and young people during the first seven decades of this century have been found to constitute genocide, and the contemporary level of removals through juvenile justice systems at least parallels those earlier policies (NISATSIC 1997). Perhaps if there is any shaming to be done it should be directed at those 'whitefellas' who, in the face of this history, continue to remain presumptuous enough to claim that they have all the right answers. There are solutions to be found, but they will not be located in any simple or singular panacea. They require respect for the political rights of Aboriginal peoples and practical support to communities.

Acknowledgements

Some short sections of this paper have been published in the report of the National Inquiry into Separation of Aboriginal and Torres Strait Islander Children from their Families (1997). The author was a consultant to the Inquiry. The views expressed in this article do not necessarily reflect the views of the Inquiry. This article has also benefited from earlier discussions with Neva Collings and Barbara Salgado at the Aboriginal and Torres Strait Islander Social Justice Commission, HREOC, and comments from Jenny Bargen and David Dixon.

Notes

1. The NZ Children, Young Persons and Their Families Act 1989 provides for family group conferences (FGCs). There is extensive literature discussing both the NZ model and Australian adaptations (for example, see Alder & Wundersitz 1994; Hudson et al 1996). For an Australian Indigenous perspective on NZ FGCs see Dodson (1996:42–5).
2. See NISATSIC (1997:562–80) for a discussion of the right of Indigenous peoples to self-determination.
3. Space precludes a discussion of the relationship between the right of Indigenous peoples to self-determination and the potential development of Indigenous criminal justice jurisdictions. See NISATSIC (1997:562–80) for further discussion of the issue.

308   (1997) 30 The Australian and New Zealand Journal of Criminology

4. Blagg cites a reference from the US newsletter *Real Justice* which states that 'the communitarian approach which underpins family group conferencing has been used by Aboriginal people all over the world for ages' (Blagg, forthcoming).
5. The rate ratio of over-representation is derived by comparing the relevant rate per 100,000 of Indigenous and non-Indigenous young people incarcerated.

References

Aboriginal Justice Council (1995) *Getting Stronger on Justice*, Aboriginal Affairs Department, Perth.

Aboriginal Legal Rights Movement and the Aboriginal Justice Advisory Committee (1994) *107 Recommendations — Have They Been Implemented?, A Joint Response to the South Australian Government's 1993 Implementation Report*, ALRM/AJAC, Adelaide.

Aboriginal Legal Service Western Australia (1996) *After the Removal, A Submission to the National Inquiry into Separation of Aboriginal and Torres Strait Islander Children from Their Families*, ALSWA, Perth.

Alder, C & Wundersitz, J (eds) (1994) *Family Conferencing and Juvenile Justice*, Australian Institute of Criminology, Canberra.

ATSIC (1996) *Submission to the National Inquiry into Separation of Aboriginal and Torres Strait Islander Children from Their Parents*, ATSIC, Canberra.

Ayres, R (1994) 'Way out west: implementation of the Royal Commission into Aboriginal deaths in custody recommendations in Western Australia', *Aboriginal Law Bulletin*, vol 3, June 1994, pp 18–20.

Bargen, J (1995) 'A critical view of conferencing', *Crime, Criminology and Public Policy, The Australian and New Zealand Journal of Criminology, Special Supplementary Issue*, pp 100–103.

Beresford, Q & Omaji, P (1996) *Rites of Passage. Aboriginal Youth, Crime and Justice*, Fremantle Art Centre Press, South Fremantle.

Blagg, H (forthcoming) 'A just measure of shame?: Aboriginal youth and conferencing in Australia', *British Journal Of Criminology*.

Blagg, H & Wilkie, M (1995) *Young People and Police Powers*, Australian Youth Foundation, Sydney.

Braithwaite, J (1979) *Inequality, Crime and Public Policy*, Routledge and Kegan Paul, London.

Braithwaite, J (1989) *Crime, Shame and Reintegration*, Cambridge University Press, Melbourne.

Braithwaite, J (1991) 'The political agenda of republican criminology', Paper presented to the British Criminology Conference, York, 27 July 1991.

Braithwaite, J (1992) 'Diversion, reintegrative shaming and republican criminology', Paper given at an International Symposium entitled 'Diversion and Social Control: Impacts on Justice, Delinquents Victims and the Public', Bielfeld, Germany, 27–29 May 1991.

Braithwaite, J & Mugford, S (1994) 'Conditions of successful reintegration ceremonies', *British Journal of Criminology*, vol 34, pp 139–71.

Braithwaite, J & Pettit, P (1990) *Not Just Deserts*, Oxford University Press, Melbourne.

Braithwaite, J & Pettit, P (1994) 'Republican criminology and victim advocacy', *Law and Society Review*, vol 28, pp 764–76.

Canadian Royal Commission on Aboriginal Peoples (1996) *Bridging the Cultural Divide, A Report on Aboriginal People and Criminal Justice in Canada*, Canada Communication Group, Ottawa.

Collings, N (1996) 'Travelling through family conferencing', *Aboriginal and Torres Strait Islander Social Justice Commissioner News*, June 1996.

Crime Research Centre (1995) *Aboriginal Youth and the Juvenile Justice System of Western Australia*, University of Western Australia, Nedlands.

Criminal Justice Commission (1995) *Children, Crime and Justice in Queensland*, Research Paper Series, vol 2, September 1995.

Criminal Justice Commission (1996) *Aboriginal Witnesses in Queensland Criminal Courts*, Goprint, Brisbane.

Cronin, K (1997) 'The failings of federalism: juvenile justice issues in Australia', Paper presented to the Institute of Criminology Seminar, Children and the Law: What About Justice?, New South Wales Parliament House, 28 April 1997.

Cunneen, C (1996) 'Detention, torture, terror and the Australian State: Aboriginal people, criminal justice and neocolonialism' in Bird, G, Martin, G & Nielsen, J (eds), *Majah. Indigenous Peoples and the Law*, Federation Press, Annandale, pp 13–37.

Cunneen, C & McDonald, D (1997) *Keeping Aboriginal and Torres Strait Islander People Out of Custody, A Evaluation of the Implementation of the Recommendations of the Royal Commission into Aboriginal Deaths in Custody*, ATSIC, Canberra.

Cunneen, C & White, R (1995) *Juvenile Justice. An Australian Perspective*, Oxford University Press, Melbourne.

Dodson, M (1996) *Aboriginal and Torres Strait Islander Social Justice Commissioner Fourth Report*, AGPS, Canberra.

Eades, D (ed) (1995) *Language in Evidence*, UNSW Press, Kensington.

Findlay, M (1993) 'Police, authority, respect and shaming', *Current Issues in Criminal Justice*, vol 5, pp 29–41.

Fraser, D (1992) 'The shame file', *Australian Journal of Law and Society*, vol 8, pp 106–8.

Gale, F, Bailey-Harris, R & Wundersitz, J (1990) *Aboriginal Youth and the Criminal Justice System*, Cambridge University Press, Cambridge.

de Graff, P (1993) 'The poverty of punishment', *Current Issues in Criminal Justice*, vol 5, pp 13–28.

Hogg, R (1988) 'Taking crime seriously: Left realism and Australian criminology' in Findlay, M & Hogg, R (eds), *Understanding Crime and Criminal Justice*, Law Book company, North Ryde, pp 24–51.

310 (1997) 30 The Australian and New Zealand Journal of Criminology

Hudson, J, Morris, A, Maxwell, G & Galaway, B (1996) *Family Group Conferences. Perspectives on Policy and Practice*, Federation Press, Annandale.

Intjartnama Consultants (1994) *A Plan to Increase the Involvement and Employment of Aborigines in the Justice Process and the Delivery of Non-Custodial Sentencing Where They Live [Intjartnama Report]*, Northern Territory Department of Correctional Services, Darwin.

Luke, G & Cunneen, C (1995) *Aboriginal Over-Representation and Discretionary Decisions in the NSW Juvenile Justice System*, Juvenile Justice Advisory Council of NSW, Sydney.

Matthews, R (ed) (1988) *Informal Justice?*, Sage, London.

Mildren, D (1997) 'Redressing the imbalance against Aboriginal in the criminal justice system', *Criminal Law Journal*, vol 21, pp 7–22.

NISATSIC [National Inquiry into Separation of Aboriginal and Torres Strait Islander Children from Their Families] (1997) *Bringing Them Home*, Report of the National Inquiry into Separation of Aboriginal and Torres Strait Islander Children from Their Families, HREOC, Sydney.

New South Wales Attorney-General's Department (1996) *Report of the New South Wales Working Party on Family Group Conferencing and the Juvenile Justice System, Discussion Paper*, New South Wales Attorney-General's Department, Sydney.

Planning Advisory Services & Larkin, C (1995) *Barriers to Alternatives to Custody*, Report to the South Australian Department of State Aboriginal Affairs, Adelaide.

Pratt, J (1989) 'Corporatism: the third model of juvenile justice', *British Journal of Criminology*, vol 29, pp 235–54.

Roach Anleu, S (1995) 'Lifting the lid: perspectives on social Control' in Simpson, C & Hil, R (eds), *Ways of Resistance. Social Control and Young People in Australia*, Hale and Iremonger, Sydney, pp 22–50.

Sarre, R (1994) 'The role of the 1994 Youth Court Act and Young Offenders Act in the pursuit of better Police/Aboriginal relations', *Aboriginal Justice Issues Conference II*, Australian Institute of Criminology, Townsville, 14–17 June 1994.

South Australian Government (1996) *Interim Submission to the National Inquiry into Separation of Aboriginal and Torres Strait Islander Children from Their Families*, Adelaide.

Stubbs, J (forthcoming) 'Shame, defiance and violence against women: a critical analysis of "communitarian" conferencing' in Bessant, J & Cook, S (eds), *Violence Against Women: An Australian Perspective*, Sage, Thousand Oaks, California.

Western Australian Government (1996) *Submission to the National Inquiry into Separation of Aboriginal and Torres Strait Islander Children from Their Parents*, WA Government, Perth.

Wilkie, M (1991) *Aboriginal Justice Programs in Western Australia*, Research Report No 5, Crime Research Centre, Nedlands.

Community Conferencing and the Fiction of Indigenous Control   311

White, R (1991) 'Taking custody to the community', *Current Issues in Criminal Justice*, vol 3, pp 171–84.

Williams, N (1987) *Two Laws, Managing Disputes in a Contemporary Aboriginal Community*, Australian Institute of Aboriginal Studies, Canberra.

Wundersitz, J (1996) *The South Australian Juvenile Justice System. A Review of Its Operation*, Office of Crime Statistics, Adelaide.

[15]

DOMESTIC VIOLENCE AND THE RESTORATIVE JUSTICE INITIATIVES: THE RISKS OF A NEW PANACEA

By Stephen Hooper* and Ruth Busch**

I. Introduction

In the middle of 1995 Waikato Mediation Services began the process of drafting protocols for a restorative justice programme to be piloted in Hamilton, New Zealand. One of the first issues that needed to be addressed was what categories of offences should be included (and/or excluded) from the ambit of the project. A complex debate immediately ensued about whether the programme should deal with cases involving domestic violence.

Because of the similarities in philosophical perspectives and process techniques between mediation and the processes used to implement restorative justice, the controversy about the appropriateness of adopting a restorative justice approach for domestic violence cases is embedded in the more general debate about utilising mediation processes to deal with domestic violence situations.[1] Battered women's advocates have long argued that mediation is inherently unfair and potentially unsafe for their clients. They suggest that women are better served by the traditional adversarial process.[2] Mediation proponents, on the other hand, contend that in all but the most serious cases, the mediation process is more empowering and more effective for victims than engaging in court proceedings.[3] A third view posits that the mediation process may be

---

* LLB (Hons) (Canterbury), Lecturer in Law, University of Waikato, Co-ordinator of, and mediator in, the Hamilton Restorative Justice Programme.

** BA (University of Wisconsin), JD (Hons) (University of Connecticut), Advanced Senior Lecturer in Law, University of Waikato, Member of the Pilot Review Panel of the Hamilton Restorative Justice Programme.

[1] Boshier, J, Beatson, L, Clark, K, Henshall, M, Priestley, J, and Seymour, F, *A Review of the Family Court: Report for the Principal Family Court Judge* (1993) 119. The 1993 Review of the Family Court recognised domestic violence as "a reflection of power" and recommended that wherever it exists, "mediation should be avoided by the judicial process as a legitimate means of dispute resolution."

[2] Hart, "Gentle Jeopardy: The Further Endangerment of Battered Women and Children in Custody Mediation" (1990) 7 Mediation Quarterly 317, 325.

[3] Corcoran and Melamed, "From Coercion to Empowerment: Spousal Abuse and Mediation" (1990) 7 Mediation Quarterly 303, 314.

helpful but that a case-by-case determination of appropriateness must be made.[4]

Recent restorative justice initiatives in New Zealand and Australia have extended the parameters of this debate from family mediation to the criminal justice arena. It has been suggested that a restorative justice model offers opportunities for victims[5] and offenders[6] to effectively address domestic violence situations that have come to the notice of police, community groups and/or the criminal courts.[7] We suggest, however, that this conclusion should not be reached lightly. The purpose of this paper is to critically evaluate arguments about the use of a restorative justice model for domestic violence cases and to propose specific protocols which we believe should be implemented in the very limited number of domestic violence situations for which restorative justice may be applicable. Our analysis presumes that the primary goals of any intervention in domestic violence situations -including restorative justice programmes - must entail the prioritisation of the safety and autonomy of victims over any other

---

[4]   Erickson and McKnight, "Mediating Spousal Abuse Divorces" (1990) 7 Mediation Quarterly 377, 378 and Girdner, "Mediation Triage: Screening for Spouse Abuse in Divorce Mediation" (1990) 7 Mediation Quarterly 365, 375-6.

[5]   In this article, we will refer to the abused spouse as a "victim". We are aware that the term "victim" does not encapsulate the entirety of this person's identity; s/he is clearly more than just a victim. Within the criminal justice context, however, we seek to differentiate between the violent offender and the target of his abuse. "Target of abuse" seems inappropriate because it may mask the fact that *a person* has been the recipient of abuse. The use of the word "complainant" is not always an accurate description as police often lay charges in domestic violence-related offences. So, reluctantly and with full awareness of the debates about this issue, we retain the concept of "victim".

[6]   We use the words "offender," "abuser", and "perpetrator" interchangeably in this article. As well, we adopt the convention of referring to offenders as male and to adult victims as female. We recognise that there are male victims of intimate violence but as Gelles has stated:
"It is categorically false to imply that there are the same number of battered men as there are battered women. Although men and women may hit one another with about the same frequency, women inevitably suffer the greatest physical consequences of such violence. Women victims of intimate violence also suffer more emotional and psychological consequences than do men."
Gelles, RJ, *Violence Toward Men: Fact or Fiction?* (Unpublished Paper presented at the American Mediacal Association Council on Scientific Affairs, September 28, 1994).

[7]   Carbonatto, "Expanding Intervention Options for Spousal Abuse: The use of Restorative Justice" Occasional Paper in Criminology New Series: No. 4, Newsletter of the Institute of Criminology (March 1995) 2, 5.

outcomes, including the reconciliation or conciliation of the parties. Our definition of "safety", moreover, includes freedom from the risk of exposure to further physical and psychological abuse as a result of the utilisation of specific processes.

II. THE MODELS OF RESTORATIVE JUSTICE

In devising the Hamilton restorative justice programme, two existing models were considered, namely victim-offender mediation[8] and the Family Group Conference model (renamed by the programme "the Community Group Conference")[9]. While a hybrid process was ultimately developed by Waikato Mediation Services, the attempt to decide which aspects of the two approaches would be utilised in the programme involved examining the perceived advantages and drawbacks of these existing models, especially their implications for cases involving domestic violence.

1. Victim-offender Mediation

The victim-offender mediation process involves the victim and the offender taking part in a face-to-face meeting. The aim of the process is to enable victims to recover from the effects of crime and to obtain an element of emotional closure. The model endeavours to allow victims to fully articulate the consequences of the offending for them and to have a voice in structuring the response to the offending, which typically takes the form of a restitution agreement.

To date, the victim-offender mediation process has mainly been used for property offences such as burglary[10] and then generally only after the offender has pleaded and been found guilty. While the process has typically been utilised for what may be categorised as minor or non-violent cases, it has at times been used to address the effects of more serious offences,

---

[8]   This is based both on the VORP (Victim Offender Reconciliation Program) model used in the United States and Canada or the VOM (Victim-Offender Mediation) model used in the United Kingdom and Australia.

[9]   The name comes from the paper by McElrea, F W N, *Restorative Justice in The New Zealand Youth Court: A Model for Development in Other Courts?* (Unpublished Paper prepared for the National Conference of District Court Judges, Rotorua, 6-9 April 1994), 12. Hereafter, Family Group Conferences will be referred to as "FGCs" and Community Group Conferences will be referred to as "CGCs".

[10] The Hamilton programme by contrast has mainly dealt with driving offences (such as careless driving causing death or injury) and cases of stranger assault.

including aggravated assault and murder. The mediation of these more serious crimes has occurred only after extensive case preparation and after a sentence has been imposed.[11]

In victim-offender mediation, the parties are each encouraged to tell their sides of the story. Both parties get the opportunity to ask questions and discover each other's perspectives about the factors which contributed to the incident and its on-going consequences. Parties are then given the opportunity to negotiate an agreement which provides for restitution by the offender, where appropriate. These agreements may take the form of the payment of money, the completion of work, or a commitment to undergo rehabilitative assistance or counselling. Mediators in the traditional mediation process act as neutral facilitators.

Research findings on existing victim-offender mediation projects have shown that they can deliver high levels of victim and offender satisfaction. Evaluations of these programmes have demonstrated excellent results in terms of both victims' and offenders' perceptions of the fairness of the mediation process relative to the Court process[12] and in relation to the successful performance of restitution agreements by offenders.[13] The model, moreover, appears to be able to generate satisfactory outcomes for the parties. The Umbreit study, for instance, indicated that those who chose to participate in victim-offender mediation programmes in four different American cities were able to negotiate restitution agreements in 95% of the mediations.[14] Eighty-six percent of the victims found it helpful to talk with the offender. In addition, they reported being significantly less upset

---

[11] The Hamilton Programme deals with offences in the period between conviction and sentencing. The authors believe that mediation might be appropriate in certain cases of domestic violence *after* the victim has had counselling and had an opportunity to deal with the major effects of the violence. Given that this would rarely occur prior to sentencing, this issue is not explored in this paper. For a discussion about the use of mediation for serious offences, see Umbreit, M, *Mediating Homicide Cases: A Journey of the Heart Through Dialogue and Mutual Aid* (Unpublished Paper, March 1994) and Umbreit, "The Development and Impact of Victim-Offender Mediation in the United States" in Galaway, B and Hudson, J (eds), *Criminal Justice, Restitution and Reconciliation* (1990) 263, 273.

[12] Participants in mediation overwhelmingly felt that the restitution agreements were fair to the victim. Nine out of ten victims and 95% of offenders believed that the agreement was fair to the victim. Nine out of ten victims and 88% of offenders felt that the agreement was fair to the offender. Umbreit, M S, *Victim Meets Offender: The Impact of Restorative Justice and Mediation* (1994) 19-21.

[13] Ibid., 18-19.

[14] Ibid., 8.

about the crime and less fearful of being re-victimised by the same offender after having met with him in mediation.[15] The model requires the voluntary participation of both victims and offenders in the process, clearly a crucial factor in maintaining the integrity of the mediation. In a study by Umbreit, a high proportion of victims (91%) and offenders (81%) felt that their participation had indeed been voluntary.[16]

2. *The Assumptions and Limitations of the Victim-Offender Mediation Process in Relation to Domestic Violence Offences*

The most commonly used victim-offender mediation process shares a number of basic assumptions with the traditional mediation process.[17] These assumptions include a consensus approach to justice and an emphasis on concepts of neutrality and power balancing. These premises are of major significance to, and limit the impact of, victim-offender mediation in the domestic violence area.

There are, obviously, significant differences in the types and degree of violence used in domestic violence cases. As well, there are important differences in the forms and quality of resources available to victims of such violence. However, the power imbalances and dynamics of control which characterise many domestic violence relationships suggest that, in most instances, the victims of violence do not have the capacity to negotiate freely and fairly with their abusers.[18] To reach a consensus, the parties must have the capacity to negotiate with each other. There must be at least some capacity for accord, a willingness to be honest, a desire to settle the dispute and some capacity for compromise.[19] The relationships between perpetrators and victims in domestic violence situations, moreover, are

---

[15] Umbreit and Coates, "The Impact of Mediating Victim Offender Conflict: An Analysis of Programs in Three States" [1992] Juvenile & Family Court Journal 4.

[16] Umbreit, supra n. 12, at 63.

[17] By the term "traditional mediation process" we are referring to problem-solving mediation. The restorative justice models used in other parts of the world, such as the VORP model, have relied heavily on traditional problem-solving approaches. These approaches have been developed from the work of the Harvard Negotiation Project and are reflected in the landmark work of Fisher, R, Ury, W and Patton, B *Getting To Yes* (2nd ed 1991). The narrative mediation model used by Waikato Mediation Services focuses less strongly on the generation of an agreement and attempts to leave behind the problems of neutrality in favour of transparency and client accountability.

[18] Astor, "Swimming Against the Tide: Keeping Violent Men Out of Mediation" in Stubbs J (ed), *Women, Male Violence and the Law* (1994) 147, 151.

[19] Idem.

not typically characterised by consensuality, honesty, mutuality and compromise.[20]

In many cases, the perpetrator's pattern of dispute resolution is characterised by coercion and intimidation. In an attempt to avoid further violence, the victim's responses often involve compliance and placation of his wishes. Mediation in the traditional sense requires victims to assert and negotiate for their own needs and interests.[21] Mediation carried out against the backdrop of domestic violence, however, requires the victim to negotiate effectively on her own behalf although her experiences have in all likelihood led her to renounce or adapt her needs in an attempt to avoid repetitions of past violence. There is a strong likelihood, therefore, that a battered woman will negotiate for what she thinks she can get, rather than press for more major changes on the part of the offender.[22]

In 1994, Newmark, Harrell and Salem carried out a research study in the Family Courts of two centres in the United States, Portland, Oregon and Minneapolis, Minnesota.[23] The purpose of the study was to assess the perceptions of men and women involved in custody and access cases where there had been a history of domestic violence.[24] The study found that there were significant differences in the perceptions of women who had been the victims of violence as opposed to those who had not been abused during their relationships.[25] Women who had been abused were more likely than women who had not to feel that they could be "out-talked" by their partners.[26] They also felt that their partners were more likely to retaliate against them if they held out for what they wanted. Newmark et al reported that abused women were "afraid of openly disagreeing with [their partner] because he might hurt [her] or the children if [she did]".[27] This accords with comments made by some New Zealand women interviewed following their involvement in Family Court mediation and counselling.[28]

---

[20] Idem.

[21] Ibid., 152.

[22] Idem.

[23] Newmark, L. , Harrell, A. and Salem, P, *Domestic Violence and Empowerment in Custody and Visitation Cases An empirical Study on the impact of Domestic Abuse* (Paper published by the Association of Family and Conciliation Courts, 1994), 6.

[24] Ibid., 1.

[25] Ibid., 15.

[26] Ibid., 35-6.

[27] Ibid., 14-15.

[28] See case study interviews with New Zealand women concerning their experiences in Family Court mediation and counselling in Busch, R, Robertson, N, and Lapsley, H, *Protection From Family Violence* (1992).

In addition, the Newmark study indicated that there were significant differences between the women who had been abused and those who had not in terms of their assessments of their partners' power to control decisions about finances, social and sexual relationships and child rearing. The abused women perceived that their partners had much more decision-making power than did the non-abused women.

Perceived risks of harm and decreased involvement in decision-making indicate a diminished ability on the part of battered women to participate assertively and effectively in the mediation process.[29] Fears of future violence clearly exert an intimidating and coercive effect on the willingness of a victim to state her wishes and expectations during the mediation process.[30]

Two further factors combine to make it unlikely that mediation will be able to provide the answer to the problem of spouse abuse. The first is the apparent passivity and learned helplessness of the battered woman. While acknowledging the inherent limitations of the theory of learned helplessness,[31] researchers have found that it is often difficult for battered women to believe that they can stop the violence through their own assertive actions.[32] They are apt to be more worn down, more suggestible and less able to confront their partners than other disputants in a mediation.[33] Second, negotiation is more difficult for the victim because of her fear of the batterer. Threats of retaliation, whether direct or indirect, may give the batterer an additional advantage in a mediation session. Even in the absence of overt threats, the fact that she may leave the session and go home with her batterer may make a battered woman unwilling to assert her own needs for fear of antagonising her partner.[34] The early referrals to

---

[29]   Newmark et al, supra n. 23, at 22.

[30]   Ibid., 22.

[31]   Walker, "Post-Traumatic Stress Disorder in Women: Diagnosis and Treatment of Battered Women's Syndrome" (1991) 28 Psychotherapy 21, 24. Lenore Walker has stated that "learned helplessness" should not be taken as meaning that women respond to battering with total helplessness or passivity. Rather, she comments that the history of abuse "narrows battered women's choices...(as they opt)...for those that have the highest predictability of creating successful outcomes." Walker concludes that, for battered women, getting the violence to stop constitutes the most desired 'successful outcome'.

[32]   Rowe, "Comment: The Limits of the Neighbourhood Justice Center: Why Domestic Violence Cases Should Not be Mediated" (1985) 34 Emory Law Journal 855, 863.

[33]   Ibid., 864.

[34]   Ibid., 865.

Waikato Mediation Services highlighted these safety concerns. The mediators met victims briefly and then left the parties to address the issues raised in the mediation.[35] The mediators were unable to deal with on-going issues, such as the distress arising from "reliving" the experience of victimisation. As well, the mediators were unable to guarantee the on-going protection of the victims in cases of domestic violence. There was no process, for instance, for dealing with the risk of retaliation against the victim for statements made by her during the mediation itself.

The traditional mediation process relies heavily on the judicial model of neutrality and impartiality. Like judges, however, mediators are not exempt from the politics of gender, class, race and culture. Moreover, it is naive to suggest that mediators, even with appropriate training, are immune from the minimising, trivialising and victim-blaming attitudes towards battered women which are so commonly found in judicial and psychological discourses about domestic violence.[36] In addition, because mediation techniques are unfamiliar to most parties, there is the danger that a mediator's own goals will predominate during a mediation session. The parties may tend to rely on the claimed expertise of the mediator and the latter may be tempted to steer the meeting in his or her own direction rather than in that of the parties.[37]

Another fundamental problem is that violence creates power imbalances between the parties. Violence against women is characterised by intentional measures by the offender to control the actions of the victim. Such control, which may be exerted in a myriad of ways,[38] has been described as having the purpose of getting a victim to do what the offender wants her to do, or punishing her for doing what the offender has told her she may not do.[39]

---

[35] This has been addressed in the Hamilton programme by acquainting victims with the process and the difficulties that may arise. They are urged to have a support person present before, during and after each session to assist them in dealing with the issues raised.

[36] See, for example discussions of judicial and psychological discourses in Robertson and Busch, The Dynamics of Spousal Violence: Paradigms and Priorities" in Seymour, F and Pipe, M (eds), *Psychological perspectives on Family Law in New Zealand* (1996) and in Busch, "Don't Throw Bouquets at Me: Judges Will Say We're in Love" in Stubbs, J (ed), supra n. 18, at 104.

[37] Marshall, T F and Merry, S, *Crime and Accountability : Victim/Offender Mediation in Practice* (1990) 205.

[38] See discussion of the range of power and control tactics in Pence, E. and Paymar, M., *Power and Control: Tactics of Men who Batter* (1990).

[39] Robertson and Busch, supra n. 36, at 84.

A risk entailed in giving the process over to the parties (even if overseen by an impartial third party) is that any decisions will simply reflect the power differences which exist between the parties.[40] This problem is magnified in the area of domestic violence where power imbalances may be extreme.[41] Unless the process of mediation can compensate for these power imbalances, there is a major risk that the agreements reached will reflect the views of and outcomes desired by the dominant party.

It is claimed that the issue of power balancing can be addressed by process changes, such as dictating who goes first or ensuring that the less dominant party has access to adequate legal advice.[42] Extensive experience as a mediator has shown one of the authors that while these interventions can compensate for minor differences in power, they are not capable of re-establishing equality where violence has occurred.

Some argue that power imbalances can be addressed through the use of "shuttle" diplomacy or indirect mediation.[43] It is suggested that this will contribute to the protection of the victim by ensuring that the parties do not meet. Although the use of shuttle diplomacy is not uncommon in victim-offender mediation, research has shown that such indirect mediation is time consuming and, ultimately, less effective than a face-to-face victim-offender meeting.[44] This is because a key purpose of the process is to enable the victim and the offender to become directly involved with one another in discussing what response is necessary to "put things right". This is less likely where the parties do not meet. As well, the use of shuttle diplomacy fails to address a very real question. If the parties are unable to negotiate face-to-face because one party fears confronting the other, does the use of shuttle diplomacy merely provide an illusion of safety? For instance, if the perpetrator makes it clear that he desires a specific form of restitution agreement, how can a mediator ensure that a victim's fear of post-mediation retaliation will not affect the outcome of the shuttle mediation?

Shuttle diplomacy can place the mediator in the invidious position of having to make a decision about whether to pass on a threat by one person

---

[40]   National Committee on Violence Against Women, *Position Paper on Mediation* (December 1991) 10.

[41]   Idem.

[42]   Moore, C W, *The Mediation Process Practical Strategies for Resolving Conflict* (1991) 271-282.

[43]   Carbonatto, supra n. 7, at 4.

[44]   Marshall and Merry, supra n. 37, at 243.

to another. If the mediator passes the threat on "word for word", he or she
colludes in the re-victimisation of the victim. Moreover, what can one
think of a restitution agreement reached as a result of the mediator repeating
the perpetrator's threats verbatim to the victim? If the mediator refuses to
pass on the threats, however, the mediator imposes his or her version of
the events on the parties. Indeed, in that situation the real danger that the
victim may be in (should she refuse to reach an agreement with the
offender) may be masked. Finally, the mediator's influence on the content
of the mediation is at its highest during shuttle mediation. This heightens
the risk that biases and preferences of the mediators will predominate.

In the area of domestic violence, it is claimed[45] that mediation enables the
parties to focus on relationship issues in a way which is not possible during
Court proceedings. Because many women do reconcile with their abusers
or, even if not, the relationship between the parties may continue long
after the court case has finished, it is said that mediation can help both
parties to develop ways of achieving a relationship based on trust and
non-violence.[46] This claim ignores an important fact about domestic
violence. It is one of the characteristics of men who are violent towards
their partners that their violence often escalates at the time of separation.
Indeed, domestic homicides are most likely to occur when the woman
first attempts to separate or during the first year after separation.[47]
Mediations occurring during this period, including restorative justice
mediations, take place when the perpetrator is often using particularly
aggressive efforts to control the target of his violence.[48] These mediations
also have the consequence of suggesting that domestic violence is
inherently a "couple problem" which can be addressed by offering
conciliation to the parties. The use of violence reflects a serious social
problem on the part of the batterer rather than a defect in the relationship.

When establishing the Waikato Mediation Services project, one of the
primary goals was the protection and prevention of further harm to both
the victim and the offender during -and after- the mediation process. From
the past experience of one of the authors, it is clear that some perpetrators

---

45   Carbonatto, supra n. 7, at 4.

46   Ibid., 8.

47   Hart, "The Legal Road to Freedom" in Hansen, M and Harway, M (eds), *Battering and
      Family Therapy* (1993).

48   Astor, supra n. 18, at 151, and Liss and Stahly, "Domestic Violence and Child Custody" in
      Hansen and Harway (eds), ibid.

use mediation as an opportunity for further contact with the victim.[49] Of particular concern in relation to cases of domestic violence was the reality that there were often insufficient resources to guarantee the protection of the victim during the mediation itself, let alone after the session is completed or after she has returned home.[50]

Several final issues about victim-offender mediation need to be mentioned. First, the labelling of crime as "conflict" is an integral part of the restorative justice process. In situations of domestic violence, it can be misleading to define violent acts as simply an escalation in the conflict level. This labelling tends to have the effect of muting the perpetrator's responsibility for the behaviour. Violence is not an escalation in conflict. It is one thing to have a difference of opinion. It is quite another to attack someone physically.[51] Second, in the past, there had been social acceptance of spousal violence. Such violence has only recently come to be understood or treated as a criminal offence. In the past, there had been a general refusal on the part of the criminal courts to interfere in family matters. The focus had instead been on individual and marital privacy and the desire to preserve the family as an intact unit.[52] All of these factors have in the past contributed to the trivialisation of domestic violence and the creation of a veil of secrecy which is only now being lifted. There is a danger that these outdated paradigms of secrecy and marital privacy may be legitimised by the confidentiality of the mediation process at a time when they seem to be losing their hold.

3. Family Group Conferences

The Family Group Conference (FGC) model was the second approach considered by Waikato Mediation Services in the formulation of its restorative justice protocols. The FGC approach was adopted in New

---

49   This is referred to as "negative intimacy" and is clearly a factor influencing the appropriateness of mediation. See discussion in National Working Party on Mediation, *Guidelines for Family Mediation: Developing Services in Aotearoa-New Zealand* (1996). In one instance, a party who requested mediation as part of the community mediation project had non-violence, non molestation orders and trespass orders against him. The trespass notice was in respect of his partner's solicitor's offices. The mediation did not proceed.

50   National Committee on Violence Against Women, supra n. 40, at 24.

51   Zehr, H, *Changing Lenses* (1990) 183.

52   Rowe, supra n. 32, at 875. For an analysis of domestic-violence related cases in the New Zealand criminal courts, see chapter 13 in Busch et. al., supra n. 28.

Zealand in 1989 as the centrepiece of youth justice initiatives codified in the Children, Young Persons and Their Families Act (CYP&F Act). Under that Act, the conferencing process applies to children and young offenders under 17 years of age.

In considering whether to adopt the FGC model, Waikato Mediation Services began by analysing the assumptions underpinning the FGC approach and evaluating whether similar assumptions would be relevant to offences committed by adults. In making this assessment, it needed to consider the implications of the process for the range of possible offences to be dealt with within the programme. Given the number of "male assaults female" prosecutions presently being heard in the Hamilton District Court,[53] it was quickly realised that a major issue involved the appropriateness of the conferencing approach for domestic violence offences.

Within the CYP&F Act, there is both a formal and an informal system, with Family Group Conferences having a central role in each process.[54] In the informal process, once the police have established an intention to charge, they are able to direct a youth justice co-ordinator to convene a Family Group Conference without reference to the Youth Court.[55] If the family is able to achieve an agreement and the offender completes the plan, the matter may not be referred to court. If agreement is not reached, the matter may be referred back to the court. On the other hand, if a young offender is arrested the formal youth justice process operates. The young offender will appear in court without entering a plea and, if the charge is not denied, the judge will direct the youth justice co-ordinator to convene a Family Group Conference.

Although there is no prescribed conference format, the co-ordinators have developed routine procedures for conducting FGCs.[56] Once a case has been referred to the conference, the co-ordinator sets up an appointment

---

[53] Accused are charged under section 194 of the Crimes Act. For a discussion of the reasons for the increase in prosecutions under section 194, see Dominick, C, *Overview of the Hamilton Abuse Intervention Pilot Project (HAIPP) Evaluation* (April 1995) 42.

[54] New Zealand Ministry of Justice, *Restorative Justice: A Discussion Paper* (October 1995) 26.

[55] Maxwell, G and Morris, A, *Family, Victims and Culture: Youth Justice in New Zealand* (1993) 69.

[56] Ibid., 87.

to meet with the young person and his or her family.[57] At this visit the process is explained to the family and to the young person and a determination is made about whether the young person will admit or deny the charges.[58] The young person's attitude to the offence is assessed and he or she is briefed about the meeting processes, including the issues around meeting with the victim.[59] On some occasions the co-ordinator will outline the possible outcome results available to the family including the resources, programmes and facilities available.[60]

At the conference itself the co-ordinator welcomes the participants as they arrive and attempts to put them at ease.[61] The co-ordinator will normally check with the family about whether they wish to open with a prayer, blessing or other introductory statement.[62] When all parties are present, the conference begins with introductions. In some areas this is preceded by a prayer or karakia and a welcome in Maori.[63]

The co-ordinator then explains the procedure to be followed. It is important that all of the participants have a clear understanding of what will happen during the conference.[64] In addition to providing a necessary opportunity for the parties to ask questions and settle in, this step allows the co-ordinator to assess the "mood" or atmosphere of the conference.[65]

The Youth Aid Officer then reads a summary of the facts and asks the young offender whether the facts are accurate.[66] It is rare for him or her to deny the accuracy of the fact summary.[67] The young person is then asked to state clearly whether he or she accepts responsibility for the offence. This is often the first opportunity for the young offender to assume

---

[57]   Stewart, T, "Family Group Conferences With Young Offenders in New Zealand" in Hudson, J, Morris, A, Maxwell, G, and Galaway, B (eds), *Family Group Conferences: Perspectives on Policy and Practice* (1996) 75.

[58]   Idem.

[59]   Idem.

[60]   Maxwell, G and Morris, A, "The New Zealand Models of Family Group Conferences" in Alder, C and Wunderersitz, J (eds), *Family Conferencing and Juvenile Justice The way Forward or Misplaced Optimism* (1994) 15, 23.

[61]   Stewart, supra n. 57, at 76.

[62]   Ibid., 75.

[63]   Maxwell and Morris, supra n. 55, at 87.

[64]   Stewart, supra n. 57, at 77.

[65]   Ibid., 75.

[66]   Maxwell and Morris, supra n. 55, at 87.

[67]   Ibid., 87.

responsibility for his or her actions.[68] If the information in the summary of facts is disputed, it is possible to correct an error at this time.[69] If, however, the young person denies responsibility for the offence, the FGC is terminated and the matter is referred back to the police.[70]

Once an admission is made, the co-ordinator asks the victim to speak.[71] Alternatively, if the victim is not present, the reported views of the victim are read to the conference.[72] The purpose of this step is to allow the victim to detail the effects of the offending on her and to raise questions about what happened and why. The young offender is asked to listen to the victim's statement without interruption. The young person's family may, however, ask questions. At the conclusion of the victim's presentation, there is often an emotionally charged silence while conference participants await the response of the young offender[73] who is then asked to explain how he or she felt upon hearing the victim's side of the story.[74]

The co-ordinator will then ask whether other members of the family would like to speak. All participants in the process are asked to provide information which may be relevant to the formulation of a decision of the issues. Family members and counsellors may speak about the offender's life in order to paint a total picture of the young person's situation.[75]

Once all of the information has been presented and after a general discussion of possible conference outcomes, the family is left in private to consider and resolve the issues raised in its own unique way.[76] A plan, in theory generated by the family, is then formulated.[77] The plan commonly covers three main elements. First, "putting things right" in the form of an

---

[68]   Stewart, supra n. 57, at 75.

[69]   Maxwell and Morris, supra n. 60, at 21.

[70]   Idem.

[71]   Ibid., 27.

[72]   Maxwell and Morris, supra n. 55, at 88.

[73]   Stewart, supra n. 57, at 78.

[74]   Idem.

[75]   Fraser, S and Norton, J, "Family Group Conferencing in New Zealand Child Protection Work" in Hudson et. al.(eds), supra at n. 57, 39.

[76]   Idem.

[77]   In some regions, social workers, police and facilitators have not withdrawn from the FGCs. This raises the concern that these professionals may have "construct[ed] the family's decisions" by selecting the issues to be addressed and influencing the outcomes. Maxwell and Morris, supra n. 55, at 113-15.

apology.[78] Second, addressing the issue of reparation.[79] For example, the family may suggest that there be regular payments to the victim from part-time earnings or the sale of an asset.[80] The third element of the plan involves a penalty.[81] This may entail the young person engaging in unpaid work either for the benefit of the victim or for an organisation suggested by the victim.

Once the plan is formulated by the family, there may be some negotiation between all the conference participants about the content of the plan. The victim and the police may veto the terms of the proposed plan. In that event, the matter is referred back to the court for resolution. If the plan is accepted by the victim and the police, its exact details are finalised and then recorded by the co-ordinator and a review date is set for one week prior to the young person's fulfilling the plan's requirements.[82] The participants are asked to make any final comments[83] and the meeting is closed with a final statement thanking the parties for participating in the process.[84]

4. Strengths of the conferencing approach over the victim-offender mediation process

One of the advantages of the Family Group Conferencing process is the sharing of information with the extended family. This removes some of the secrecy that can surround offending and enables the family to support the parties in dealing with the effects of the offending. This is a particular problem with the traditional two party victim-offender mediation process with its strong emphasis on confidentiality. Things which have in the past only been "whispered behind closed doors" can now be brought into the open.[85] A number of families involved in Waikato Mediation Services' programmes who have begun to openly discuss their problems have found that their family and friends have willingly supported and affirmed them.

It is fundamental to the family group conferencing process that the parties

---

[78]   Stewart, supra n. 57, at 79.

[79]   Idem.

[80]   Idem.

[81]   Idem.

[82]   Stewart, supra n. 57, at 80.

[83]   Idem.

[84]   Maxwell and Morris supra n. 55, at 88.

[85]   Barbour "Family Group Conferences: Context and Consequences" (1993) 5 Social Work Review 16, 18.

should be able to participate in decisions which affect them.[86] Since the basis for the FGC is non-adversarial, it encourages the family to find the resources from within rather than to rely on a solution imposed by "experts". In one of the first of the court referrals to Waikato Mediation Services, the family involved resolved independently to discuss the relevant issues among themselves without the need for mediators to convene a conference. Holding a conference despite the family's opposition would have said to the family: "Yes, we (the experts) know that you think you are coping fine but we know better". This respect for the family decision-making remains an important ingredient in the conferencing process used by Waikato Mediation Services.

It has been suggested that the family decision-making process can change the way in which families think and function.[87] The very fact that participants are able to meet and discuss issues openly can begin the healing of family relationships. In one of the first referrals to the Hamilton restorative justice programme, for instance, a son had repeatedly denied that he had any involvement with alcohol or drugs. This lie was uncovered when his family found a "bong" in his room which he admitted that he had used to smoke marijuana. During the conference, the mediators explored with him what actions he believed were necessary to win back his parents' trust. By the end of the conference, certain steps were agreed to in order to start him "on the road to self responsibility". When three weeks later, he was accused of taking things from his father's garage, he "owned up" to his actions rather than denying them as he had done on numerous previous occasions. He openly discussed with his parents what further steps he could take to remedy this very recent breach of trust. In the context of this young man's previous behaviour, this acknowledgment represented a positive change. By looking at the agreement he had made during the conference, he re-committed himself to taking responsibility for his actions.

Waikato Mediation Services has adopted a conferencing model which includes not only families as participants but also people drawn from the victim's and offender's communities. This community conference approach draws on the wide range of knowledge within the parties' social networks to support change.[88] It enables the parties to realise the array of

---

[86] "Introduction" in Hudson et. al. (eds), supra at note 56, at 2.

[87] Barbour supra n. 85, at 19.

[88] Idem.

resources available to them within their families and communities. Since, in most cases, funding for conferencing allows the offender and victim access to mediators for only a few hours, it is essential that parties utilise the strengths of their on-going family and community networks to complete their rehabilitation work.

The conferencing process enables participants to find wide-ranging options to address the causes of the offending and its effects.[89] These can include options which were not readily apparent at the time the conference was called. For instance, in the Canadian provinces of Newfoundland and Labrador, the outcomes of community conferences have included dealing with a party's or family's needs for fire wood or a refrigerator as well as more obvious solutions of counselling for substance abuse or sex abuse.[90]

In assessing the appropriateness of the conferencing approach for adult offenders, Waikato Mediation Services has been particularly attracted to its family empowerment and community re-integration aspects. In addition, the conferencing process seems capable of meeting the needs of specific cultural groups because of its commitment to the involvement of extended family groups.[91] These benefits are less evident in the previously discussed two party victim-offender mediation model. The conferencing process that Waikato Mediation Services has recently implemented has, as a key element, a commitment to separate conferences for offenders' and victims' families and communities. This enables victims' support networks to explore the effect of the offending on the victim and on his or her family and friends without the negative dynamics that may arise because of the presence of the offender.

5. Limitations of the Conferencing Approach in relation to domestic violence offences

There are several aspects of the Family Group Conference model which make its use problematic for domestic violence offences. Some issues, like the importance accorded to mediation techniques and consensus

---

[89]   Ibid., 18.

[90]   Burford, G. and Pennell, J. *Family Group Decision Making Project Implementation Report Summary* (1995) 33.

[91]   We are conscious that the conferencing process has at times been accused of being tokenistic, pakeha dominated, and unresponsive to cultural difference. While the use of Maori mediators can ameliorate certain problems inherent in the FGC approach, WMS understood that nothing short of a parallel legal system could address the issues of pakeha gatekeeping and control of the process.

decision-making, are concerns that have already been discussed in terms of the victim-offender mediation model. As in the latter model, the emphasis of the FGC is on consensus decision-making arrived at through mediation between the parties. The conference facilitator fulfils the role of the mediator who negotiates between parties who may have widely differing perspectives on the offending.[92] A number of the problems already discussed in terms of traditional mediation and its application to domestic violence are, therefore, inherent in the conferencing process. Other problems are specific to the conferencing model itself and involve concerns about community support for victims in domestic violence situations, safety of participants at conferences, and negative research findings that have emerged from recent evaluations of FGCs.

As discussed, the family group conference posits a communitarian approach to offender accountability. It relies on the notion of a family, or community of people, with shared values who are capable of exercising surveillance and control over the offender's future behaviour.[93] The conferencing process is a reflection of re-integrative shaming proposed by Braithwaite.[94]

One concern about the conferencing process is the assumption that the offender in a domestic violence situation will be shamed into changing his behaviour. In domestic violence cases, the concept of re-integrative shaming posits the view that each member of the offender's community will accept that domestic violence is unacceptable.[95] It needs to be acknowledged, however, that in New Zealand at present there is no such societal consensus about domestic violence.[96] Instead, researchers have found that an offender's abusive behaviour takes place within a social context which often legitimises, condones and even supports his use of violence.[97] There is no reason to believe that violent men will readily be shamed into accepting that their violent acts are wrong.[98] As well, the

---

92 Maxwell and Morris supra n. 55, at 87.

93 Stubbs, J, "'Communitarian' Conferencing and Violence Against Women: A Cautionary Note" (Unpublished Paper, 1996) 17.

94 Braithwaite, J, *"Crime, Shame and Reintegration"* (1989). It is noted that the work of Braithwaite has had a greater influence on the Australian Family Group Conferences than the New Zealand FGC process.

95 Stubbs, supra n.93, at 17.

96 Idem.

97 Supra n. 38.

98 Stubbs, supra n. 93, at 17.

parties' families or communities may not be supportive of a victim's attempts to hold the perpetrator accountable for his actions.

In order to see the use of the conferencing model as appropriate in domestic violence cases, it is necessary to understand how a family or community seeks to "explain" the occurrence or causes of abuse.[99] Some of these explanations attribute the responsibility for violence wholly, or in part, to the victim. Others assume that the use of violence may, in certain circumstances, be an acceptable response to a conflict situation. Given that the conferencing model relies heavily on the participation of the victim's and offender's community for the generation of "solutions" or responses to the offending, the discourses of the community will influence the discussion of the causes of and proposals to resolve the abuse.

It is our belief, however, that from the conferencing perspective, the most dangerous explanations are those which site the cause of abuse in the relationship between the partners. If violence is defined as a "symptom of a problem in the relationship"[100] rather than a *real* problem of itself, the conference outcomes will, in all likelihood, reflect commonly held justifications and excuses for violence (eg "she provoked him", "it takes two to tango", "they're a dysfunctional family"). A focus on the relationship as the cause of violence may mask the impact of the violence on the victim and her on-going need for protection. The ways in which social attitudes legitimise the use of power and control tactics ("he's the head of the family"), and the issue of who benefits and loses from the perpetrator's use of violence may also be hidden. Most importantly, a relationship focus often may fail to hold the perpetrator accountable for his violence, and indeed, reconciliation or conciliation may be prioritised over the victim's need (and legal right) to safety.

Another major concern about adopting the conferencing model for adult offenders arises from research which has found that victims or their representatives have attended only 46% of conferences.[101] For those victims who have been present, statistics indicate that 38% felt worse after attending the conference.[102] Although there have been attempts to explain these disappointing statistics in terms of inadequate preparation

---

[99] Jenkins, A, *Invitations to Responsibility - The therapeutic engagement of men who are violent and abusive* (1990) 25-28.

[100] See discussion of "interactional" theories of domestic violence in Robertson and Busch, supra at n. 36.

[101] Maxwell and Morris, supra n. 55, at 75.

[102] Ibid., 119.

of victims and unrealistic expectations of conference outcomes, victim dissatisfaction may in fact reflect the underlying objects of the FGC which focus primarily on the offender and his family. One can only query whether a victim would be more likely to participate if the offender were an intimate who had a (lengthy and on-going) history of violent behaviour toward her rather than a stranger who had committed a non-violent property offence.

There is also concern about the low levels of actual participation in the FGC process by offenders. Research indicates that 34% of offenders believed that they had been actively involved in the decision-making process while another 11% believed that they had only been partly involved. Forty-five percent of offenders believed that they were not involved in the process at all.[103] Although these figures may be related to the ages of the offenders involved in FGCs, they suggest an important concern for using this approach with adults. In the area of domestic violence, it is especially important that the real participation of offenders is high in order to ensure their acceptance of responsibility for their violence and of conference outcomes.

A further concern is that two-thirds of FGC facilitators describe hostility being directed either at family members or at Department of Social Welfare staff during the conferences.[104] This hostility has included shouting, verbal abuse, threats and even physical violence.[105] Over half of the facilitators reported that the safety of at least one party had been threatened during Family Group Conferences.[106] Anecdotal evidence also exists to support these views. One facilitator reported to one of the authors that she had had to hurriedly abort a care and protection conference when a husband told his battered wife: "One more f...... word from you and I'll throw you out this bloody window."[107] Another facilitator described how at a FGC held to deal with the effects on the children of witnessing their mother's repeated beatings, the perpetrator was able to force his partner to forego the support of her family by simply snapping his fingers and pointing to the empty chair next to him. The wife had initially sat down with her family but moved "automaton-like to his side" immediately after his

---

103   Ibid., 109-110. Ten percent expressed no opinion about whether or not they had participated.

104   Robertson, J. "Research on Family Group Conferences in Child Welfare in New Zealand" in Hudson et al (eds), supra at n. 57, 54.

105   Idem.

106   Idem.

107   Personal interview between Ruth Busch and care and protection panel facilitator, February 1996.

gesture. A year later, the woman was killed and her partner has now been found guilty of her murder.

Clearly there is a risk that the safety of participants may be compromised during FGCs. This is of particular concern in cases of domestic violence where there has been a previous history of threats and intimidation and where the perpetrator has used physical violence as a means of getting his own way. This risk may extend beyond the perpetrator's typical targets of violence (eg, his spouse and/or his children) and influence the participation of all family and community members at the conference.

Facilitators themselves may be fearful of challenging abusers' behaviours and belief systems because of worries about their own safety. As an example, one of the authors recently facilitated a mediation involving an assault. When he openly confronted the offender about his use of violence, the mediator immediately began to feel nervous about pressing on with that line of questioning. The offender had a history of explosive episodes of violence and the mediator was concerned about putting himself at risk by continuing to confront him.

What is the message to a perpetrator and his victim if the conference facilitator and participating family members refuse to challenge his use of power and control tactics? Alternatively, if threats are made or violence is used, what should the facilitator do to ensure the safety of the victim and other conference participants? The present approach seems to be for the facilitator to abort the conference, but how does this help to ensure the safety of an abused spouse? Another approach is to omit known batterers from the conference but this calls into question the utility of holding a conference in such circumstances. In informal meetings with CYPS supervisors and co-ordinators, a repeated observation has been that all too often the perpetrator's violence is neither confronted nor dealt with at FGCs, precisely because of this fear factor.[108]

6. The Burford and Pennell Conferencing Model

Gale Burford and Joan Pennell are currently trialing the use of the conferencing model for child abuse and family violence cases in Newfoundland and Labrador. Their initial report details some of their findings and outlines in detail the process used by them.[109] Two central

---

[108] Personal interview between Ruth Busch and social worker, June 1996.

[109] Burford and Pennell, supra n. 90.

principles are used to guide the project.[110] The first is that family violence does not stop by itself; there must be mandatory intervention by government authorities such as probation or child welfare workers.[111] Second, the best long range solutions are those which give the affected parties the opportunity to come up with solutions that are appropriate for their families, their communities and their culture.[112]

Cases are referred to the project by child welfare workers where abuse against the child is confirmed through investigation.[113] The project appears, therefore, to be initiated by reference to the safety needs of children. Approximately three to four weeks of preparation occurs before the conference takes place. During this period the facilitators contact the parties and discuss steps to protect the safety of participants during the process.[114] The conference participants include family members (defined to include extended families), friends, support people or guardians, and other significant social supporters including statutory agency representatives. The process relies heavily on the work of Braithwaite and the use of re-integrative shaming as a method to change the offender's actions.[115] Where the conference co-ordinators believe that the victim's (or victims') safety may be at risk, abusers are excluded from the conference.[116] Where abusers are excluded, their views are expressed either by letter or through a representative. Cases involving the most serious criminal offences are excluded from the process.[117]

These conferences follow a similar process to that used in New Zealand FGCs. As with FGCs, the actual decision is made by the family group participants. The co-ordinator emphasises that the conference belongs to the family (rather than to the statutory agencies involved) and this is reinforced by the use of community facilities for the conference venue, circular seating and voluntary participation.[118] After advising the family

---

[110] Burford, G. and Pennell, J. " Attending to Context: Family Group Decision Making in Canada" in Hudson et. al. (eds), supra at n. 57, 207.

[111] Idem.

[112] Idem.

[113] Ibid., 206.

[114] Burford and Pennell, supra n. 90, at 14.

[115] Burford and Pennell in Hudson et. al. (eds), supra n. 57, at 209.

[116] Burford and Pennell, supra n. 90, at 13. It was not specified in the interim report, how many times this occurred.

[117] Ibid., 14.

[118] Burford and Pennell, in Hudson et. al. (eds), supra n. 57, at 210.

about the possible plan outcomes, the conference co-ordinators and other professionals withdraw from the room and leave the family to arrive at its decision.[119]

The initial results of the project show that the majority of family members who were invited came to the conference and participated "responsibly" in the decision-making process.[120] Based on the results of thirty-seven conferences, the findings indicate that family groups had a commitment to working together to prevent further violence.[121] Family members reported that they were satisfied with the conference process and outcomes.[122] The project, however, is in its early phases and further evaluations of additional conferences need to be performed.

The Burford and Pennell report does record one instance which causes some concern. The family involved in that conference ended up denying that any violence had occurred. In this case, it appears that the views of the mother and the children were not adequately represented[123] and the husband/father was able to intimidate the family into refusing to acknowledge the abuse. In commenting on this case, Burford and Pennell noted: "That experience confirmed a potential worst fear about how families might subordinate the abuse to other concerns".[124] They also commented that this was not the only conference where this dynamic surfaced. In other conferences, however, the family and the professionals were able to ensure that things did not get "turned around".[125]

7. The conferencing process suggested by Carbonatto

In her article outlining the appropriateness of a restorative justice approach for domestic violence, Helene Carbonatto develops a conferencing process to be used in New Zealand.[126] The conference would involve a trained facilitator, who would be responsible for bringing the parties and their "key network members" together. Participants in the meeting would include family, friends and others whom the spouses respect and who are

---

[119] Burford and Pennell, supra n. 90, at 27.

[120] Ibid., 9. What the term "responsibly" meant was not explained.

[121] Ibid., 24.

[122] Ibid., 25

[123] Ibid., 28.

[124] Idem.

[125] Idem.

[126] Carbonatto, supra n. 7, at 4.

prepared to assume responsibility for them.[127] If the situation was potentially explosive the mediations could be conducted on a "shuttle approach". Referrals would come from statutory and community agencies such as the police, women's refuge and men's groups.

The object of the conference is to end domestic violence by addressing the causes of the offending, providing support for the victim, and imposing a sanction on the offender which is decided upon "by a 'community' of people who have an interest in the lives of both the offender and the victim".[128] The role of the conference participants is to propose sanctions which will "adequately resolve family abuse".[129] Plans would be arrived at through consensus decision-making with no express provision for the victim to veto proposed sanctions. If the group's sanctions did not prevent further violence, police could become involved.

Carbonatto provides examples of the types of sanctions which might be imposed. For instance, the conference group might implement a plan for checking on the victim at "risk times", such as Friday and Saturday nights "when many incidents occur".[130] Alternatively, the plan might require members to provide the perpetrator with a bed to ensure that he stays away from home if he goes out drinking. Where perpetrators are financially secure, the plan could entail putting the family's bank accounts into the victim's name to allow her to walk out of the relationship and be financially independent if more violence occurs.

8. Problems with the Carbonatto Approach

This model is clearly only in a developmental phase, however it does cause a great deal of concern. It is a process which can be initiated without referral to the police or the judiciary. It operates under a mantle of confidentiality and there is virtually no external accountability unless further violence occurs. The process creates a situation where the sanction becomes something to be established by the conference participants alone, without reference to the wider community's interest in addressing the consequences of offending. Conferencing under this model may fail to confront the problems inherent in consensus decision-making within a family or community context.

---

[127] Idem.

[128] Ibid., 3.

[129] Idem.

[130] Ibid., 4.

In the Carbonatto model, the suggested sanctions fail to address the underlying causes of domestic violence and provide superficial responses to issues of victim safety and autonomy. Carbonatto's proposed sanctions perpetuate many of the now discredited myths of domestic violence and do not acknowledge the variety of tactics used by perpetrators to maintain power and control over their partners and children. For instance, few researchers now believe that domestic violence is caused by alcohol consumption or that it occurs only on weekends. As well, while the Carbonatto model recognises that "[the victim] may not even have a meaningful community in [her] geographical area,"[131] the common use of isolation as a tactic of power and control is not discussed. Instead, Carbonatto places the onus on the conference facilitators to manufacture a "community" for one or both of the parties so that a conference can be convened. As Carbonatto states:

The onus is on the facilitators to find such a community. Thus the need for facilitators to be inventive in mobilising key network members. This may, for example, take the form of approaching a neighbour whom the victim has only casually met (obviously with her consent).[132]

The most significant drawback in the Carbonatto model is that it does not require the perpetrator to take responsibility for his violent behaviour. By asking family and friends to supervise his actions to prevent further violent incidents during "risk periods", the focus shifts from the abuser's accountability for his violence to the adequacy of the restraints put in place by the community. In the face of future violence, the issue may well revolve around whether or not a certain support person failed to carry out the terms of the sanction rather than focus on the abuser's violence and its consequences for the victim. The agreed plan itself may provide the abuser with an excuse or justification for his violence ("If only you had checked up on things on Saturday night like you were supposed to, this would never have happened.")

As opposed to criminal justice interventions which prioritise victim's safety over reconciliation and/or conciliation concerns, the assumptions underlying the Carbonatto model tend to characterise domestic violence as a relationship issue. The sanctions suggested reflect Carbonatto's view that: "The reality is that many women return to their abusive partners and, therefore, it is necessary to develop ways to help both partners achieve

---

[131] Ibid., 3.

[132] Ibid., 3- 4.

relationships based on trust and non-violence".[133] In fact, it is often the victim's very inability to obtain adequate legal protection or financial autonomy for herself and her children which leads her to reluctantly reconcile with her abuser. This is especially true in cases of recent separation, when statistics in New Zealand[134] and overseas[135] indicate that the risks of serious injury and homicide are heightened.

There is no provision in the Carbonatto model for monitoring the perpetrator's compliance with the terms and conditions of the agreed plan. Neither is there any follow-up process outlined by which the victim's concerns and experiences can be compiled and used to further refine or amend the sanctions already in place. In addition, the Carbonatto model relies on the use of "shuttle" mediation for what she characterises as "potentially explosive situations".[136] Her definition of this phrase highlights many of the problematic aspects of her model. In an implicitly victim-blaming statement she comments: "[A potentially explosive situation is] one in which the victim does not want reconciliation with the offender but is more intent on securing her protection". Surely the object of all interventions in the domestic violence area - including mediations and other restorative justice initiatives - must prioritise the safety of the victim.[137] Moreover, as already discussed, shuttle mediation is the least effective of the mediation processes in terms of its vulnerability to abuse and influence.

9. The Community Group Conference

The process being trialed in Hamilton is a hybrid one based primarily on the victim-offender mediation approach but incorporating elements of the Family Group Conference model. In the Hamilton scheme, the District Court refers offenders to the project during the period between conviction and sentencing. Before individual meetings with any of the parties, referrals are reviewed by a Pilot Review Committee comprising representatives from community and statutory agencies and the legal profession. Presently, the Committee includes appointees from the police, community corrections, victim's support, the Hamilton Abuse Intervention Pilot

---

[133] Ibid., 4.

[134] Busch, "Safeguarding the Welfare of Children" (1995) 4 Butterworths Mental Health & the Law Bulletin 46, 48.

[135] Idem.

[136] Carbonatto, supra n. 7, at 4.

[137] Guidelines for Family Mediation, supra n. 50, at 55.

Programme, Matua Whangai, the Hamilton District Court, church groups, legal academics and criminal barristers. There is special consideration given to the gender balance of this group. The Review Panel may either reject the referral or impose conditions on its acceptance, such as the offender's and/or victim's participation in prior counselling or educational programmes.

After an intake procedure, the parties each meet separately with the mediators and then separate Community Group Conferences are held. The purpose of each separate conference is to address the effects of the offending on the parties and their respective family and friends, and to enlist future support to stop the offending. For the victim, the separate conference allows an exploration of the ways in which her reaction to the offender and the offending have strained her relationships with family and friends. For the offender, it allows conference facilitators to address his specific rehabilitation needs without the victim feeling that her issues are being ignored. One risk of dealing with rehabilitation in the joint session is that the victim will interpret this as indicating that the "real victim" is the offender.

Mutual issues are addressed in a joint session after the separate community group conferences are held. The joint session may involve family and other support people, if requested by the parties. In the Hamilton process, the victim and offender structure the restoration plan; however, they are strongly encouraged to have support people present before, during, and after the joint session. The role of these support people is usually to assist and encourage the parties to generate suitable responses to the offending and to provide an additional level of protection for the victim. In addition, follow-up sessions are built into all restoration plans in order to monitor compliance with the terms of any agreements. Plans are amended where proposals have proven to be unsatisfactory.

10. The process used by the Hamilton project in circumstances involving domestic violence

In the protocols adopted by the Hamilton scheme, mediation is generally deemed to be unsuitable for cases of domestic violence.[138] Referrals are excluded where there is evidence of domestic violence in all but the most exceptional of circumstances. Such exceptions might include instances where the violence involved an isolated incident, occurred within the

---

[138] National Committee on Violence Against Women, supra n. 40, at 35.

context of family trauma or highly unusual circumstances, and the risk of further violence was remote. The mediators would have to satisfy themselves that there has been no previous history of physical, sexual, or psychological violence against an offender's (ex) spouse, children, or others with whom either party has a domestic relationship.[139] Threatening or intimidatory behaviour as well as destruction of property and harassment each constitute "psychological violence" and it is highly unlikely that cases involving such facts would be deemed suitable for the programme. Referrals are also rejected where the offender has made suicide threats, has a psychiatric or substance abuse history, or has abducted or threatened to abduct children.[140]

In those rare instances where such referrals are accepted, they are subject to specific process protocols which have been adopted to deal with the power and control dynamics inherent in most battering relationships. The protocols are designed to ensure that the victim is fully informed of her legal rights and the other options available to her before making a decision about whether to proceed with mediation. At our first meeting, the victim is encouraged to formulate a safety plan, is briefed about her legal remedies and advised to get independent legal advice about protection orders. Finally, she is informed about the array of community and government agencies which she might need to contact for further protection (eg the Hamilton Abuse Intervention Project, the local women's refuges).

Identification of domestic violence factors is of utmost concern. Where violence forms the basis for a charge against the offender, there is less opportunity for domestic violence issues to be hidden. Charges involving breaches of protection orders and assault are, therefore, readily identifiable. In some cases, however, it is possible that the type of charge may mask the existence of such violence. For instance, if the offender has been charged with theft or damage to the property of a former partner or assault against her present spouse, it may not be apparent that domestic violence issues are involved. In order to deal with this contingency, parties are always asked whether they know the offender. Where it is revealed that the victim and the offender do know each other, the victim is asked to detail the nature of their relationship and specific questions are asked to ascertain whether there have been any previous violent incidents.

---

[139] See definition of "domestic violence" in section 3 of the Domestic Violence Act 1995.

[140] This approach coincides with the definition of "serious violence" found in Magana, and Taylor, "Child Custody Mediation and Spouse Abuse: A Descriptive Study of a Protocol (1993) 31 Family and Conciliation Courts Review 50, at 55.

In those few domestic violence situations where mediation is considered appropriate, a "narrative mediation" process is adopted as opposed to the strictly problem solving approach used in the traditional victim-offender mediation model. One of the advantages of this technique over other forms of mediation and conferencing is that it examines the social discourses which have allowed the offender to avoid responsibility for his violence. Narrative mediation facilitates a deconstruction of the perpetrator's belief system about gender roles and violence, and allows him to explore the ways that these beliefs are socially constructed and legitimised. For example, the offender in his initial separate session is asked such questions as:[141]

•   If a man wanted to control and dominate another person, what sort of strategies and techniques would he put into place to make this possible?
•   If a man desired to dominate another person what sort of attitudes would be necessary to justify this?

These questions allow the offender to consider the implications of violence generally, before examining whether, and how, he has engaged in the use of power and control tactics in his domestic relationships.

A decision to proceed further with the mediation process is conditional on the offender understanding the impact of his actions on the victim and her children and family. He also needs to accept responsibility for his actions, not blame his victim for his use of violence, and agree that it is her decision solely to determine her future involvement (if any) in their relationship. For example, the offender needs to agree to cease all unwanted contact with the victim by not telephoning or writing to her or coming to her home or workplace. In general, the offender needs to stop all behaviours which the victim might consider coercive, controlling or dominating in order to empower her to make her own decisions about her future.

Issues arising during the victim's separate session mirror the ones addressed with the offender. She is encouraged to discuss the ways in which she has accepted responsibility for his violence and how such acceptance reflects prevailing societal assumptions about gender relations and domestic violence. The session also focuses on issues of self blame, her feelings of despair and worthlessness in being unable to stop the violence, and in general women's role vis-a-vis their male partners. A primary aim of this separate session is to encourage the victim to place responsibility for the violence squarely on the offender.

---

[141] White M. "Deconstruction and Therapy" in Gilligan, S and Price, R (eds), _Therapeutic Conversations_ (1993) 22, 30.

Through the use of community group conferences, the communities of victims and offenders can be mobilised to provide support for dealing with the consequences of violence. The conference also allows participants to more openly address the issue of secrecy which can surround violence in families. Only when mediators and conference participants are satisfied that it is safe and appropriate to meet will the parties meet in a joint session. This protocol has the advantage of prioritising victim safety and offender accountability over all other issues in the mediation process.

III. Conclusion

The restorative justice process opens up new opportunities for victims and offenders to actively participate in the criminal justice system. However, the desire for change should not be allowed to blind us to the limitations of the process. These limitations arise from the dynamics of mediation and conferencing and are clearly exemplified in cases of domestic violence. In this early trial period of restorative justice initiatives in New Zealand, great care and thought should be given to whether domestic violence cases should be referred to these programmes. In our view this decision should not be taken lightly. The process should only be attempted in rare cases and then only after special protocols are followed to ensure a victim's free and informed consent and safety. It must be remembered that in most cases, an abuse victim turns to the criminal justice system for protection from on-going violence. She should not be asked to participate in any process which may compromise her safety and risk exposing her to further violence. At the very least, the system which a victim turns to for protection should not be complicit in her further victimisation.

[16]

Restorative Justice: The Challenge of Sexual and Racial Violence

BARBARA HUDSON*

The paper reviews the theory and policy proposals of recent formulations of abolitionism and restorative justice. Challenges are posed to some of the assumptions of abolitionism by considering its applicability to acts of violence against women, children, and minority ethnic citizens. In particular, the assumptions that dangerous offenders are few, and that the 'meaning' of a harmful act is negotiable between perpetrators and victims, are called into question. The symbolic function of criminalization and penalization is discussed. The paper considers whether the strategies suggested by recent proponents of forms of abolitionism and restorative justice can satisfy doubts about the adequacy of earlier abolitionist formulations in relation to both the symbolic and instrumental functions presently served by criminal law.

Whilst calls for further criminalization and penalization of racial, sexual, and domestic violence are understandable, the abolitionist case that retributive justice is more likely to increase rather than reduce such violence, and to leave victims unsatisfied, is defended.

INTRODUCTION

This paper focuses on one major theory, and reflects on one important controversy about its application, which has appeared in the writings of critical/abolitionist criminologists during the last few years. A significant development during the late 1980s and the 1990s has been the elaboration of the idea of *restorative justice*, as an alternative to retributive justice; an urgent, and as yet unresolved, controversy has been whether an abolitionist/ restorative perspective is appropriate with regard to crimes against women,

* *Professor of Criminology and Penology, Division of Sociology, University of Northumbria at Newcastle, Newcastle upon Tyne NE1 8ST, England*

An earlier version of this paper was presented at the Law and Society Association annual meeting, St. Louis, Missouri, May 1997.

children, and minority ethnic citizens. These debates reflect the significance for abolitionists and other penal reformers of the 'get tough' penal climate, and also the rise in influence of victims' movements and the successes of feminists and others in urging that sexualized and racialized violence needed to be taken more seriously by 'progressive' criminologists as well as by legislators and policy-makers.

Two publications which appeared in 1986 summarized the main currents of European abolitionist thought at that time, and gave hints of what was to be elaborated during the next ten years. Herman Bianchi and Rene Van Swaaningen's edited volume contained twenty papers which were presented at the Second International Conference on Prison Abolition in Amsterdam in 1985.[1] As the conference title implies, it was focused mainly on the abolition of imprisonment, although some papers did look towards the replacement of the whole criminal justice system with something along the lines of the 'alternative dispute settlement' procedures which existed in some places in North America. The ideas put forward in the volume were the well-known abolitionist proposals for a moratorium on prison building, decriminalization of some offences, and moving from criminal law towards civil law/community court procedures. In the main, abolitionism and the informal justice movement were separate, even if their practical proposals sometimes appeared very similar. Abolitionism was a vision without a strategy; informal justice was a practice without a theory.

In the same year, a special issue of the journal *Contemporary Crises* contained papers which tried to give abolitionism a stronger theoretical base than previously. A paper by Heinz Steinhert, for example, showed that with a different (more realistic, he claims) set of assumptions than those on which crime policy is usually based – more realistic especially than the assumption that punishment is an appropriate and effective means of reducing crime – an alternative strategy for reducing the influence of harmful behaviour could rationally be derived.[2]

In the 1990s, writers sharing or sympathetic to abolitionism or at least drastic reduction of the penal sphere have further developed ideas about procedures which could replace those of present criminal law and about changing the normative orientation of law from retribution to restoration.[3] As well as European abolitionist theory, these contemporary reformers have found theoretical grounding for their proposals in the work of Habermas and in feminist and postmodernist jurisprudence.

---

1 H. Bianchi and R. Van Swaaningen (eds.), *Abolitionism: Towards a Non-Repressive Approach to Crime* (1986).
2 H. Steinhert, 'Beyond Crime and Punishment' (1986) 10 *Contemporary Crises* 21.
3 J. Braithwaite, 'Inequality and Republican Criminology' in *Crime and Inequality*, eds. J. Hagan and R.D. Peterson (1995); R. Van Swaaningen, *Critical Criminology: Visions from Europe* (1997).

FROM ABOLITIONISM TO RESTORATIVE JUSTICE

European abolitionism is a movement as well as a theory, as Sim demonstrates with reference to England and Wales, which has campaigned for the rights of prisoners and for improvements in prison conditions, as well as for reductions in the use of imprisonment.[4] In the 1970s and 1980s, European abolitionists were much influenced by Thomas Mathiesen's succinct posing of the reform/revolution dilemma: if abolitionists propose reforms, implementation of these may strengthen the institution which they so dislike, by making it seem less oppressive or arbitrary; if they publish more radical suggestions for change or abolition, they are likely to be marginalized and have no influence on actual prisons and punishments.[5] Mathiesen therefore suggested that abolitionists should not disclose their final objectives, but should campaign against the worst aspects of imprisonment, such as punishment blocks, the use of drugs in prisons, lack of legal representation in disciplinary hearings. The result of this campaigning to rid the prisons of their worst evils rather than theorizing to formulate an alternative to a punishment system produced some important local improvements in prison conditions,[6] but left in place a repressive, punitive criminal justice system, with prison at its centre.

In the 1980s, prison numbers grew, prison conditions became harsher, and so-called alternatives to custody came to incorporate more and more of the pains of imprisonment. The work of Michel Foucault and Stanley Cohen drew attention to the 'dispersal' of the disciplinary mode of punishment that is most fully realized by the modern prison, throughout society.[7] If 'prison' was not merely a building, but a principle – the coercion of time and space[8] – then not only was abolishing some of the worst features of prisons insufficient to make the response to crime more humane and constructive, but abolition of prisons themselves was also insufficient. The target for abolition had to become punishment itself.

If prisons were to be abolished but not punishment, then there would be no check on the intrusiveness or unpleasantness of community punishments: what is the point of abolishing prisons, if electronically monitored curfews and house arrest turn homes into prisons, or if community service orders impose hard and degrading labour combined with the intrusiveness of body searches and urine testing? Only if punishment itself is called into question

---

4 J. Sim, 'The abolitionist approach: a British perspective' in *Penal theory and practice: tradition and innovation in criminal justice*, eds. A. Duff et al. (1994).

5 T. Mathiesen, *The Politics of Abolition* (1974).

6 Sim, op. cit., n. 4.

7 M. Foucault, *Discipline and Punish: the Birth of the Prison* (1977); S. Cohen, 'The Punitive City: Notes on the Dispersal of Social Control' (1979) 3 *Contemporary Crises* 339; S. Cohen, *Visions of Social Control* (1985).

8 B. Hudson, 'The rising use of imprisonment: the impact of decarceration policies' (1984) 11 *Critical Social Policy* 46.

is it clear that criticisms of prison conditions, lack of rehabilitative facilities, and so on cannot be remedied by more and better prisons, or by reproducing the prison in the 'community facility' or the 'day centre'.[9]

At the same time that the intrusiveness and pain of the punitive network was being acknowledged,[10] increasing attention was being paid to the differential impact of state punishment on the unemployed, on minority ethnic groups, on the mentally disordered: punishment was recognized as the 'penalizing circuit' of the poor.[11] It was held to be inimical to social justice and doing nothing to reduce levels of crime.

Beyond the world of academic criminological debate, the growing influence of the idea of the offender as a member of an 'underclass', committed to a criminal value-system and therefore unamenable to reform and rehabilitation was underpinning the toughening of community punishments as well as the harshening of prison regimes, whilst criminological and political recognition of the victim was adding another ingredient to the ideology of law and order. In Europe as in the United States of America, the political manipulation of the suffering of actual victims and of the fears of potential victims has provided further impetus for the move towards harsh, incapacitative penal policies. One of the ironies of recent penal developments is that a long-standing abolitionist argument against present penal systems is that all the resources of criminal justice have been used for punishment of offenders, with almost nothing being done by way of crime prevention or support or recompense to the victim – we have, as is often said, a punishment system not a justice system. Thus Nils Christie in a celebrated paper argued that the criminal law appropriates the experiences of victims, substituting the state for the individual as victim and leaving no place in the criminal justice process for victims to tell their stories.[12] Abolitionists have also argued that punishment does nothing to prevent crime – that social policy rather than penal policy is needed to reduce the pressures on people to turn to illegal means to secure their wants and necessities.[13] And yet, it is in the name of community safety and acknowledging victims' demands for both retaliation and protection that policies such as three strikes, mandatory minimums, and their English and European equivalents have developed.[14]

By the end of the 1980s, the 'negative reform' strategy advocated by Mathiesen seemed inadequate to meet the challenge of the new law-and-order climate; new theories and strategies have accordingly been developed by penal abolitionists and penal reductionists which try to address the claims of actual victims and communities of potential victims on criminal justice

9 B. Hudson, *Penal Policy and Social Justice* (1993).
10 N. Christie, *Limits to Pain* (1982).
11 B. Laffargue and T. Godefroy, 'Economic Cycles and Punishment: Unemployment and Imprisonment' (1979) 13 *Contemporary Crises* 371
12 N. Christie, 'Conflicts as Property' (1977) 17 *Brit. J. of Criminology* 1.
13 Hudson, op. cit., n. 9.
14 A. Sarat, 'Vengeance, Victims and the Identities of Law' (1997) 6 *Social and Legal Studies* 163.

systems. What has emerged as a positive alternative to retributive criminal justice, is *restorative justice*. The overall purpose of restorative justice is not to inflict punishment in proportion to the seriousness of the offence, or to incapacitate offenders so that they pose no further risk to the public, but 'the restoration into safe communities of victims and offenders who have resolved their conflicts'.[15]

The main principle of this approach is that the task of criminal justice should be the restoration of relationships, and balances of advantages and disadvantages, that have been fractured by the harmful action (the 'crime', in the present vocabulary of criminal justice). This basic principle is common to many formulations, but a particularly well-reasoned and thorough exposition is given by de Haan. He uses the term *redress*, arguing that the restorative process is started by a 'victim' claiming redress: 'To claim redress is merely to assert that an undesirable event has taken place and that something needs to be done about it.'[16]

Claiming redress would initiate a dialogue about the nature of the event that has taken place, and about what needs to be done to put matters right. The idea of redress rests on the assumptions that:

(i) what we presently call crime is a complex event, which will have a different meaning according to the circumstances of the offender, the victim, and the community, and the relationship between them;

(ii) all parties to the event deserve a hearing, and that they have claims on the justice process.[17]

The strengths of restorative justice, its proponents claim, are that it makes the perpetrator face the fact that real harm has been done to an actual victim by his or her action; that if the perpetrator is a party to the outcome, he or she is less likely than with a punitive system to displace remorse for the action into resentment of the punishment; above all, it is much more likely than the present system to provide for a balance between the needs and rights of both offenders and victims. With a punitive system, there is always a tension between recognizing the harm to the victim and protecting the rights of the offender. In terms of the critique of law posed by Derrida and other deconstructionists, 'justice' would be more closely approached than with a punitive system because the process would recognize the perpetrator and victim in their individuality, rather than approximating the crime to a general legal category and the harm to that which would be felt by a standard, average, victim.[18]

---

15 D.W. Van Ness, 'New Wine and Old Wineskins: Four Challenges of Restorative Justice' (1993) 4 *Crim. Law Forum* 251, at 258.

16 W. de Haan, *The Politics of Redress: Crime, Punishment and Penal Abolition* (1990) at 158.

17 B. Hudson, 'Restoration, reintegration and human rights: punishment in a socially just justice system' (1995) 9 (Howard League for Penal Reform seminar, 'Punishment in the year 2000', Edinburgh).

18 J. Derrida, 'The Force of Law: the Mystical Foundations of Authority' (1990) 11 *Cardozo Law Rev.* 5–6, 960; D. Cornell, *The Philosophy of the Limit* (1992) ch. 6; C. Douzinas and R. Warrington, 'The Face of Justice: A Jurisprudence of Alterity' (1994) 3 *Social and Legal Studies* 405.

The emphasis of restorative justice is on 'right relationships' rather than 'right rules'; restorative justice thus has much in common with Pepinsky and Quinney's 'peacemaking', and it also has much in common with the 'ethic of care' of feminist jurisprudence.[19]

It is, say its proponents, more likely than retributive justice to reduce the incidence of crime because of its concern for the safety of victims: as Van Ness explains, restorative justice addresses crime at the macro level as well as the micro level – addressing the need for building safe communities as well as the need for resolving specific crimes.[20]

Abolitionists have long recognized some possible problems both with the abolition of imprisonment, and with the abolition of punitive justice and its replacement by a more restorative-oriented justice. Difficulties arise with regard to reactions to persons who pose clear danger to others; to persons who will not agree to offer redress or to refrain from similar behaviour in future; to behaviour where the perspectives of perpetrator and victim are so opposed as to be non-negotiable, and to the impact of restorative procedures on the acceptability of behaviour in the community.[21] These problems are posed most acutely if one imagines replacing punitive justice by restorative justice when the behaviour concerned is violence against women, children, or minority ethnic citizens. My purpose is to consider these dilemmas, and to ask whether the most recent formulations of the restorative paradigm propose viable and appropriate remedies for these most serious kinds of harms.

THE FAILURE OF CRIMINAL JUSTICE

It is common cause among those advocating women's rights, child protection, and the protection of minority communities that traditional criminal justice has failed to provide remedies for violence against women, children, and minority ethnic victims. The failings of criminal justice are well documented, especially in the case of violence against women.[22] They include social and judicial attitudes which have regarded matters that happen in the private domain as no concern of criminal law; attitudes among police and prosecutors that victims are unlikely to sustain complaints and that therefore action is generally wasteful of time and effort; humiliating and intrusive interrogation of victims to determine issues of consent or provocation; victims' unwillingness to press charges because of fears of retaliation;

---

19 H. Zehr, *Changing Lenses: A New Focus for Crime and Justice* (1990); H. Pepinsky and R. Quinney (eds.), *Criminology as Peacemaking* (1991); Hudson, op. cit., n. 9, ch. 6; C. Smart, 'Feminist Jurisprudence' in *Law, Crime and Sexuality*, ed. C. Smart (1995).
20 Van Ness, op. cit., n. 15.
21 H. Bianchi, 'Abolition, assensus and sanctuary' in *A Reader on Punishment*, eds. A. Duff and D. Garland (1994).
22 R.E. Dobash and R.P. Dobash, *Women, Violence and Social Change* (1992).

difficulties of obtaining corroborating evidence when abuse takes place in private, and so on. These obstacles to obtaining remedy (and getting the behaviour stopped!) are especially formidable in the case of ethnic groups such as Britain's Asians, who risk rejection and hostility by their relatives and neighbours if they turn to the police and the courts.[23]

Racial violence has been difficult to measure.[24] Even when policy suggests that racist elements should be considered as aggravating circumstances leading to enhanced penalties, and when police forces take an inclusive approach to recording cases as racially-linked (including offences on the basis of victim characteristics and/or victim reporting of the offence as racially motivated, rather than excluding cases unless the arresting officer or other official assesses the case as racially motivated), the racial aspect tends to be lost as the case progresses through the various criminal justice processes. In a survey of cases recorded by Northumbria Police as racially linked, my co-researchers and I found that cases of abuse and harassment or other public order offences tended not to be prosecuted, usually for lack of evidence; in cases such as theft and robbery from Asian or other minority shops and homes, the racial link 'disappeared' from agency information systems and the cases were prosecuted and sentenced like those with white victims. Again, the usual reason given was lack of evidence for the racial motivation. A recent report by the group Human Rights Watch documents alarming levels of racial violence in England and Wales, and deplores the failure of criminal justice to prosecute and penalize the perpetrators.[25]

The most notorious case recently in Britain has been the murder of Stephen Lawrence, a black youth who was killed by a group of white youths, whilst he was waiting for a bus. Although a number of white young men have been identified as responsible for the killing, they have not been convicted because of lack of evidence. The Lawrence family and their supporters say that evidence was not obtained primarily because police approached their investigations with the view that Stephen Lawrence and his companion must have been engaged in some sort of unlawful activity, and that the death must have been the result of some sort of spontaneous fracas amongst lawless youth, rather than a law-abiding, hard-working student engaged on peaceful, proper activities being attacked by racist thugs. This case demonstrates a further difficulty which black victims have in obtaining remedy through criminal justice: they are more readily seen as 'suitable enemies' than as 'ideal victims'.[26] (This same problem, of having to fit the constructions of 'ideal victim' in order to obtain conviction of one's

23 id.
24 B. Bowling, 'Racial Harassment and the Process of Victimization: Conceptual and Methodological Implications for the Local Crime Survey' (1993) 33 *Brit. J. of Criminology* 231.
25 *Observer*, 11 May 1997.
26 N. Christie, 'The Ideal Victim' in *From Crime Policy to Victim Policy: Reorienting the Justice System*, ed. E.A. Fattah (1986).

aggressor, has affected women, for example prostitute women or other independent, sexually-active women, attempting to bring rape charges.)

Criminal justice has failed to deliver on the first demand made by feminist and anti-racist activists calling for increased criminalization or for alternative forms of justice – to make evident the extent of racialized and sexualized violence – because of the obstacles to reporting, prosecution, and conviction that it poses. Criminalization means that most offenders are left free to continue their activities, and most victims are left unprotected.

Those urging that racial and sexual violence should be taken more seriously, including groups such as the Commission for Racial Equality, have complained that even where prosecutions are successful, penalties are insufficient.[27] Fines and community penalties too often induce resentment and the desire for revenge, rather then repentance, in the perpetrator, and provide no protection for the victim or other potential victims. If criminalization and penalization are the ways of demonstrating that society is opposed to certain behaviours and takes them seriously, then the message given by the composition of prison populations in Britain, the United States of America, and similar countries is that racial and sexual violence are less serious wrongs than burglary, theft, and many other property offences. Women's groups, and anti-racist campaigners, therefore, have been demanding not only higher rates of arrest and prosecution, but also tougher penalties for those committing offences of racial and sexual violence.

Acknowledging that in Scandinavia, as elsewhere in Europe, women who would support reduced imprisonment for the property crimes of the poor, demand more and longer prison sentences for sexual and domestic violence, Liv Finstad urges abolitionists to take up the challenge of devising more constructive ways of responding to sexualized violence precisely because of its damaging, domineering, harmful nature: if these most serious of crimes could be dealt with without imprisonment, the case for abolition of imprisonment for other, less serious, crimes would be established.[28] Finstad insists that any non-imprisoning response to sexual violence must satisfy certain demands:

> Guilt and responsibility must be firmly and unequivocally attached to the perpetrator;
> protection and compensation must be effected for the victim;
> the extent and seriousness of sexualized violence must not be made invisible.

These are the demands made of justice processes by other writers who either advocate or are sympathetic to restorative justice, for example, Braithwaite and Daly.[29] I would endorse them, and again, I would insist on parallel demands for any response to racial violence.

27 Dobash and Dobash, op. cit., n. 22; M.D. Fields, 'Criminal justice responses to violence against women' in *Penal theory and practice: tradition and innovation in criminal justice*, eds. A. Duff et al. (1994).
28 L. Finstad, 'Sexual Offenders Out of Prison: Principles for a Realistic Utopia' (1990) 18 *International J. of the Sociology of Law* 157.
29 J. Braithwaite and K. Daly, 'Masculinities and communitarian control' in *Just Boys Doing Business? Men, Masculinities and Crime*, eds. T. Newburn and E.A. Stanko (1994).

RACIALIZED, SEXUALIZED, AND DOMESTIC VIOLENCE: THE POTENTIAL OF RESTORATIVE JUSTICE

Even if more cases could be prosecuted successfully, the dilemma highlighted by Finstad, Meima, Braithwaite and Daly, and others who take up the challenge of abolitionism's response to sexualized and racialized violence, is that of moving away from punitive reactions which – even when enforced – further brutalize perpetrators, without, by leniency of reaction, giving the impression that sexualized or racialized violence is acceptable behaviour.[30] As Sim summarizes the dilemma in relation to rape:

> The lenient sentences for such crimes and the symbolic messages which men take from leniency can be contrasted with the fact that longer prison sentences offer no solution to the problem of rape and indeed may simply exacerbate the problem at an individual level by placing the rapist in a masculine culture which reinforces the misogynist fantasies that were part of his behaviour patterns outside the walls.[31]

This statement points to the fact that there is an important difference between racial and sexual crimes, and the street crimes of the powerless which seem to be the behaviours which most abolitionists have most clearly in view. This difference is that, as shown above, sexual, domestic, and racial violence has not, until very recently, been taken seriously. These crimes have been over-tolerated, whereas burglary, car theft, street robbery, and the like have been over-penalized. In other words, the censuring, moral-boundary-declaring, symbolic purposes of criminal law have already been served in relation to these latter types of offences, whereas with racialized and sexualized violence, the symbolic force of criminal law has only recently, and only partially (especially in the case of racial violence) been deployed to demonstrate that society, at least in its official organization, disapproves of these forms of behaviour.

Sim's words echo Garland's description of the 'tragic quality' of punishment: that it is simultaneously necessary to symbolize the state's authoritative disapproval of certain forms of behaviour and futile in its effects at controlling that behaviour.[32] Certainly, it is desirable for society to demonstrate that it is opposed to racial and sexual violence. On the other hand, could not the response to such behaviour be organized according to a logic that makes for more effective remedies than either doing nothing (or, at most, very little), or punishing offenders by confining them in settings where their racist and sexist attitudes, and their fantasies of violence and sexuality, will be further fuelled? Garland's depiction of the tragic duality of punishment refers to its expressive and instrumental functions, which may often

---

30 Finstad, op. cit., n. 28; M. Meima, 'Sexual Violence, Criminal Law and Abolitionism' in *Gender, Sexuality and Social Control*, eds. B. Rolston and M. Tomlinson (1990); Braithwaite and Daly, id.

31 J. Sim, review of Bianchi and Van Swaaningen, op. cit., n. 1 (1990) 18 *International J. of the Sociology of Law* 97.

32 D. Garland, *Punishment and Modern Society* (1990) at 80.

be in conflict. Abolitionism and other critiques have usually concentrated on the instrumental aspects of punishments, and left its expressive tasks unaddressed. If restorative justice is to provide an adequate response to racial and sexual violence, its processes and remedies will have to address both the expressive and instrumental functions of traditional retributive criminal justice.

The argument of abolitionists such as Bianchi and Mathiesen with regard to people who pose a clear danger to the physical safety of others is generally that there are few such offenders; incapacitative institutions where they can be restrained and kept away from potential victims therefore are needed, but there is need for only a small number of such facilities, and imprisonment as the response to crime can become the exceptional rather than the normal practice. Violence against women, children, and minority ethnic citizens is, however, widespread and frequent. Chesney-Lind and Bloom report that an estimated three to four million women are battered in the United States of America every year according to a former Surgeon General; that population surveys estimate that 21 to 30 per cent of United States women will be beaten by a partner at least once in their lifetimes; that almost half of all batterers beat their partners at least three times a year.[33] The 1996 British Crime Survey reports 1 million incidents of domestic violence, with the caveat that this is likely to be an undercount.[34] As revealed by the survey, domestic violence accounted for more incidents than stranger violence of all kinds. From the figures given in the survey, domestic violence certainly appears to be a more serious problem than mugging (street robbery): 990,000 reported incidents of domestic violence compared with 390,000 reported incidents of mugging; victims were also more likely to sustain injury in domestic violence, with only 31 per cent of reported domestic violence incidents resulting in no injury compared to 67 per cent of muggings.[35]

Not only is domestic violence widespread, it is increasing, and whilst some of the apparent increase can perhaps be attributed to increased reporting, there is no doubt that the behaviour is widespread, and that it continues to be under-reported. The same sort of detailed figures are not available for racial violence, but police forces throughout England and Wales have recorded rising levels of racial attacks and harassment throughout the 1990s. Home Office figures show that police recorded 12,222 racial incidents in 1995/96, 3 per cent more than in 1994/95.[36] It is widely accepted that racial violence is significantly under-recorded, partly because of the difficulties of ascertaining racial motivation, and partly because of under-reporting by victims and their communities who lack confidence that the police and other enforcement agencies will

33 M. Chesney-Lind and B. Bloom, 'Feminist Criminology: Thinking About Women and Crime' in *Thinking Critically About Crime*, eds. B.D. MacLean and D. Milanovic (1997).
34 Home Office, *The 1996 British Crime Survey, England and Wales* (1996) at 28.
35 id, at p. 65.
36 National Association for the Care and Resettlement of Offenders (NACRO), *Criminal Justice Digest*, no. 91 (1997) at 17.

take the problem seriously. Sexual offences, including offences against children, though now revealed as more frequent than had long been assumed, remain relatively rare. 30,0436 sexual offences were recorded in England and Wales in 1995/6, in a total of more than 5 million offences overall, but of course each and every one needs to be taken seriously.

Violence against women, children and minority ethnic citizens is deplorable, but its incidence is hardly surprising in the light of current criminological theories. New understandings of the components of 'masculinities', and especially the pressures to accomplish an identity which approximates to 'hegemonic' masculinity help explain why, in a socially unequal society which pushes so many young men into economic marginality, those who cannot demonstrate the affluence of successful masculinity will be likely to exaggerate – through violence – their claims that they are racially superior, heterosexual, and 'macho'.[37]

As well as challenging the abolitionist assumption that the number of dangerous offenders is small, these offences challenge the argument that criminal justice is targeted against the powerless, on behalf of the powerful. Feminists who advocate imprisonment and 'zero tolerance' for domestic violence, as well as those who urge longer sentences for offences against children, and for racial violence, point out that the crimes are acted out on victims who within the crime relationship, lack power: the point of such offences is to dominate, for the offender to exercise power over the victim. Whilst it may be true that it is among the poor and the marginalized that such aggression is likely to lead to punishment rather than counselling, it must be acknowledged that the power relationships in domestic, sexual, and racial crime are different from those in property offences and other kinds of 'economic survival' crimes. The logic of restorative justice makes the relationship between victim and offender central, displacing that between offender and state, and it could therefore be argued that restorative processes would reproduce and reinforce the imbalance of power of the crime relationship, rather than confronting the offender with the power of the state acting on behalf of (in the place of) the victim.

Racial and sexual violence thus pose some difficulties for the domain assumptions of abolitionist theories. These behaviours challenge restorative justice to formulate strategies that can deal with large numbers of victims and offenders; that can provide protection and redress for victims; that can change social attitudes from tolerance to disapproval; that can inculcate remorse and a desire for change in perpetrators, and that can bring about a rebalancing of power within the crime relationship.

---

37 Newburn and Stanko, op. cit., n. 29; R.W. Connell, *Gender, Power and Society: the Person and Sexual Politics* (1987); J. Messerschmidt, *Masculinities and Crime: Critique and reconceptualization of theory* (1993) and *Crime as Structured Action: Gender, Race, Class and Crime in the Making* (1997).

The process model advocated by most formulations of restorative justice is that of the community forum, or, especially in the writings of John Braithwaite, the community or family conference.[38] This is a rather broader concept than 'mediation' or 'reparation' – sometimes advocated as an addition to present criminal justice processes, either as an alternative to prosecution (caution plus), or as an alternative to fines or communities penalties (or to damages and compensation payments in civil cases) – which signifies a remedy of conciliation and compensation worked out between victim and offender. Practices being termed 'restorative justice' by some police forces in England at the present time fit the 'caution plus' model rather than the conception of restorative justice under discussion here. The conference model of Braithwaite and other theorists assumes the involvement of other parties, and would address the 'safe community' objective as well as the relationships between victim and offender.

An implicit assumption in the ideas of meetings and forums put forward by the 1970s and 1980s abolitionists and proponents of various other forms of 'alternative dispute settlement' that is problematic in the case of these types of offences, is that there is some common understanding, some agreed perspective, which can be arrived at between victim and offender. As Finstad argues, the earlier model of informal or civil justice appears to presume that an account of 'what happened' can be negotiated which will be somewhere between the victim's and offender's perspectives, whereas, with sexualized violence, there are two separate, non-negotiable perspectives – his and hers.[39] This is the case, she says, wherever the offence involves huge imbalances of power between victim and perpetrator. It is also, obviously, the case where the offence involves majority and minority race or ethnicity, and even more so, when the case involves child victim and adult perpetrator.

The conference model allows for the victim to have representatives to urge her view of the events, and Braithwaite and Daly argue that one of the benefits of the model as compared with existing criminal justice processes is that a feminist – or racial/ethnic/religious – standpoint can be accommodated. Instead of having a lawyer attuned to legal criteria and world views, women's groups, community leaders, victim support movements, and the like can all be heard. The victim's perspective is made central to proceedings, whereas it is only a source of evidence (as far as rules of admissibility allow) in criminal cases. Hulsman makes a similar claim in relation to the use of civil rather than criminal procedures in cases of rape and sexual assault: the victim's definition of harm and threat is at the centre of proceedings; she is transformed from the humiliated victim of criminal proceedings to an active claimant, identifying her own requirements and drawing her own lines in future contacts with the perpetrator.[40]

38 Braithwaite, op. cit., n. 3; Braithwaite and Daly, op. cit., n. 29.
39 Finstad, op. cit., n. 28.
40 L. Hulsman, 'The Abolitionist Case: Alternative Crime Policies' (1991) 25 *Israeli Law Rev.*
    681.

The point being made by these writers is that in fact it is the conventions of present criminal law which reproduce the power relations that produce racial and sexual crime: the victim is one person, on the down-side of power, confronting, and having to conform to, the gender and racial ordering of law, which is itself reflective of the society in which that law is embedded.[41] Restorative justice, on the other hand, enables the parties to be equally represented; it enables other narratives to be heard; it empowers standpoints which are otherwise powerless and excluded, or at least circumscribed.

For the proponents of restorative justice, the desired outcome of these conferences would be that the offender acknowledges not just his own responsibility for the act, but also that he appreciates the victim's perspective: he should acknowledge that he performed the act; that it was wrong; and that it was harmful. He should be ashamed, and determined to avoid repetition of the behaviour. The contemporary restorative justice paradigm owes much to Braithwaite's idea of *reintegrative shaming*.[42] He contrasts the reintegrative shaming of the good parent – who makes clear her disapproval of bad behaviour without rejecting the child – with the stigmatizing shame of modern criminal justice. Stigmatizing shame labels the person rather than the act, and imposes a status change which has generalized, deleterious, and often irreversible consequences.[43] In the stigmatizing processes of retributive justice, the offender is given more incentives to contest the label than to repent the behaviour; the 'sin' which people try to avoid is as likely to be that of being found out as that of behaving badly. With restorative justice, the community is involved in expressing disapproval, and in providing and guaranteeing protection and redress for victims, but it is also involved in supporting the perpetrator in his efforts to change, and in maintaining him as a member of the community.

It has sometimes been asked whether 'the community' is likely to express strong enough disapproval to induce shame; that the pomp and ceremony of the court is necessary for the shaming ritual. Current experience of responses to sexual offending show that the community is somewhat in advance of judicial attitudes: lenient sentencing for rape cases; failure to imprison wife batterers and sexual attackers have been widely criticized by publics throughout Europe, north America, and Australia. Indeed, developments such as Megan's Law in the United States of America, and similar community notification schemes in the United Kingdom and elsewhere show that the community is, if anything, too strong in its disapproval and is certainly willing to provide guarantees of enforcement of remedies.

41 R. Van Swaaningen, 'Feminism, Criminology and Criminal Law' in *Gender, Sexuality and Social Control*, eds. B. Rolston and M. Tomlinson (1990).
42 J. Braithwaite, *Crime, Shame and Reintegration* (1989).
43 H. Becker, *Outsiders: Studies in the Sociology of Deviance* (1963); A. Cicourel, *The Social Organisation of Juvenile Justice* (1956).

249

Racial violence provokes less strong reaction, but few would express dissent from disapproval in a public forum. Another claim made by the restorative justice movement is that progressive views about matters such as the need to express disapproval of racial harassment and abuse, and to protect minority citizens, tend to be strengthened during discussion: dissenters feel discouraged from expressing racist views, and an emergent consensus of attitude can be firmed into a resolve to act. A narrative style of proceedings can therefore not only perform the norm-affirming expressive role of adversarial criminal justice; it can also perform an additional, norm-creating role.

Abolitionists and other advocates of restorative justice here echo or draw upon Habermas's model of 'communicative morality' or 'discourse ethics': that it is in the exposition of views, the listening to accounts of harm, the attempting to justify prejudice, that more progressive moral consensus can be reached. Habermas in his two-volume *Theory of Communicative Action* develops a dialogic view of morality, in which a plurivocal evolved consensus replaces the monologic voice of law.[44] In the dialogic process of defining and legitimating norms, moral judgments are reached not by consideration of the impartial voice of – male – judicial reason, but by the communication between 'concrete others'; between participants expressing their viewpoints and needs. The condition for such debates to generate normative categories and binding decisions is the 'ideal speech situation', the creation of a situation in which all participants can take part without constraint or oppression. Descriptions of conferences and other procedures given by Braithwaite and Daly, and by Hulsman seem very much like strategies to approximate this ideal speech situation, in which women, children, and members of minority ethnic groups will be empowered and protected to an extent that is not approached by present criminal justice processes.

Habermas's theory has been criticized by writers affirming a politics of difference on the grounds that it still presupposes a negotiated outcome (*a rational consensus*); that at times it appears to submerge the 'concrete others' into a transcendental 'universal other'; and that the situation of the ideal speech situation is as abstract and unrealizable as Rawls's 'veil of ignorance'.[45] Nonetheless, the idea of a communicative or discursive ethics, together with Braithwaite's concept of reintegrative shaming, advance both the theory and strategy of restorative justice a great deal.

To make its disapproval effective, and to deliver adequate protection, a community forum would have to have resources at its disposal: anger-management or anti-prejudice courses to which offenders could be referred; alcohol projects and other programmes and facilities to help offenders deal

44 J. Habermas, *The Theory of Communicative Action*, vols. 1 and 2 (1984 and 1987); P. Pettit, 'Habermas on Truth and Justice' (1982) *Royal Institution of Philosophy Lecture Series* 207; I.M. Young, *Justice and the Politics of Difference* (1990).
45 S. Benhabib, *Critique, Norm and Utopia* (1986); Young, id.

with personal and social conditions which had been part of the reasons for the behaviour. There would also have to be a network of holding facilities and recourse to injunctions, curfews and the like to deter further offending and protect the victim and potential victims before the conference or forum could take place. These resources would also be brought to bear on offenders who did not exhibit the necessary shame and resolve, or whose own efforts to change their behaviour needed buttressing by some stronger sanctions, both positive and negative. And of course, these resources would have to be extensive, given the amount of racialized and sexualized violence.

The facilities needed for giving effect to decisions made by community or other forums are very similar to the proposals of state-obligated rehabilitation: society should acknowledge its part in the causation of crime by providing rehabilitative facilities which the offender can have recourse to as of right; society as victim has the right to demand that the offender acknowledges his or her own willed role in the offence by agreeing to participate in whatever rehabilitative programme is recommended.[46] The difference between state-obligated rehabilitation and restorative justice is not so much in the remedies proposed, but in the processes of decision-making. Restorative justice goes further than state-obligated rehabilitation in including determination of 'what happened' in its processes of deliberation, as well as deciding the appropriate remedy. It also goes further in calling for the replacement of the adversarial, formal court of law by a form of negotiation between parties empowered as far as possible as equals.

It is, perhaps, less the 'disapproval' element of the term 'community disapproval', that is problematic, than that of 'community'. The 'death of the social' having been proclaimed, most of us now inhabit not 'communities', but shifting, temporary alliances which come together on the basis of private prudentialism.[47] Residents' associations; parents' associations; city-centre rate-payers; shopping-mall retailers; share-holders' meetings; women's groups: these are the kinds of collectivities which claim people's allegiances now, rather than communities. The weakest point of many of the restorative justice formulations, is thus not the question of how can the power between victim and offender be balanced, but what is the community; what is the community interest, and how can it be represented? Without the concern to make safer communities, restorative justice is in danger of merely substituting civil justice for criminal justice. Without the community, restorative justice is reduced to the competing perspectives of the victim and the perpetrator, and there is no social group with reference to whom the

46 P. Carlen, 'Crime, inequality and sentencing' in *Paying for Crime*, eds. P. Carlen and D. Cook (1989); Hudson, op. cit., n. 9, ch. 5.
47 P. O'Malley, 'Risk, Power and Crime Prevention' (1992) 21 *Economy and Society* 252; and P. O'Malley, 'Post-Social Criminologies: Some Implications of Current Political Trends for Criminological Theory and Practice' (1996) 8 *Current Issues in Criminal Justice* 26; N. Rose, 'The Death of the Social? Refiguring the Territory of Government' (1996) 25 *Economy and Society* 327.

offender can experience either shame or reintegration. Different versions of restorative justice or related paradigms propose different memberships of their tribunals, forums or conferences. Sometimes, 'community' appears to mean victims, offenders, those close to them, and selected 'expert' groups (for example representatives of the battered women's movement), but more often there is some fairly vague reference to wider community. All envisage some sort of 'community' representation – to arbitrate, to mobilize resources, to express disapproval, to readmit.

The problem of the offender who continues to pose danger, or who refuses to accept the account, wishes, and proposals of the victim is addressed by the various formulations, and this is an issue about which differences arise. Bianchi and some other European abolitionists propose revival of the institution of 'sanctuary', as somewhere where a person who poses danger to others can be, safe from vengeance from victims and communities, whilst awaiting processes and remedies.[48] Bianchi's description of sanctuary, however, presupposes some sort of negotiation, and upholds the right of a victim to demand a trial if the perpetrator continually refuses to negotiate. What the last resort of failed negotiations should be is unclear.

For Finstad, the last resort provision is coerced deprivation of liberty, but she invokes a medical model of hospitalization rather than a criminal model of imprisonment.[49] The danger here is that the individual becomes pathologized rather than the behaviour being condemned. Braithwaite and Daly apply the idea of an *enforcement pyramid*, with prison at its apex.[50] Depending on the willingness or otherwise of the perpetrator to accept responsibility, admit the wrongness of the behaviour, and take steps to ensure that it does not recur, an escalating repertoire of responses is provided, ranging from informal disapproval by family and friends, through reparative measures decided upon by neighbourhood conferences, through to penal sanctions and finally, for the most recalcitrant, imprisonment. Like Bianchi and other abolitionists and proponents of restorative justice, Braithwaite and Daly foresee that most offenders will come to accept their behaviour as wrong; that most victims will be content with acknowledgement of guilt, compensation/reparation, and some firm assurance (such as the undertaking of educative or therapeutic measures) that the behaviour is unlikely to recur. Unlike thoroughgoing abolitionists, however, they see that the 'big stick' of penal sanctions – including imprisonment – is necessary to reinforce the authority of restorative remedies. The big stick of imprisonment, they say, allows justice to 'speak more softly' in most cases.

The difficulty with their position is that the existence of the custodial possibility could perpetuate the present situation, which is that unless (long) prison sentences are imposed, the message of a case is that the behaviour is

48 Bianchi, op. cit., n. 21.
49 Finstad, op. cit., n. 28.
50 Braithwaite and Daly, op. cit., n. 29.

not really serious. Community disapproval, redress and attempts to change could be seen as 'getting away with it', just as the proponents of get tough sentencing designate non-custodial penalties for a range of offences now. This points to the importance of restorative responses to domestic, sexual, and racial violence being introduced in a general framework of restorative justice. They should not be used – as was the complaint against some earlier initiatives in informal justice – as second-rate justice for offences that don't really matter.[51] Braithwaite has consistently argued for across-the-board reductions in the resort to punitive sanctions and the introduction of conference procedures and restorative measures for most offence types. In such circumstances of general penal deflation, introduction of the enforcement pyramid should not mean that sexual or racial violence was taken less seriously than other offence types, but it could perpetuate one of the elements of current criminal procedures that are objected to by many advocates of tougher responses to domestic violence, which is that violence appears only to be seen as serious if it is repeated.

Existence of the 'big stick' of imprisonment might well mean, in other words, that the pronouncement of a prison sentence is still the expressive yardstick for the condemnation of behaviour. Victims and their relatives might feel that their injury was being taken less seriously than an incident which did result in imprisonment: the lynch mob, after all, exists in relation to awareness of the possibility of execution and perception that this is the mark of stern disapproval. To serve the expressive functions of punishment, restorative processes will have to devise ways of clearly separating condemnation of the act from the negotiation of measures appropriate to the relationships between the particular victim, the offender, and the community.

RESTORATIVE JUSTICE OR ENHANCED PENALTIES?

Tolerance and/or denial of the extent and seriousness of crimes against women, children, and minority ethnic citizens make the demand for increased penalization understandable, but as well as believing that the infliction of suffering generally makes people worse rather than better, my own abolitionist instincts are strengthened by fear of the punitive inflation that occurs if, whenever a group gains recognition for its harms, such recognition is expressed through increased penalization. Penal measures, as van Swaaningen argues, do not have a simple *ad hoc* validity, but always have a *general* impact.[52] Feminists may successfully persuade legislators and judges of the serious harms of domestic and sexual violence; environmentalists successfully urge the seriousness of pollution; politicians pontificate

---

51 M. Cain, 'Beyond Informal Justice' (1985) 9 *Contemporary Crises* 335; C. Harrington, *Shadow Justice? The Ideology and Institutionalization of Alternatives to Court* (1985).

52 Van Swaaningen, op. cit., n. 41, p. 218.

about the evils of car crime and drug-taking: if all these claims lead to increased punishment of offenders, the carceral society envisioned by Foucault and Cohen would indeed be a reality! As Chesney-Lind and Bloom put it in relation to domestic violence, zero tolerance activism has supplied the system with 'new men to jail, particularly men of color'.[53]

On the other hand, to forego penalization in a punitive society would look like tolerance of intolerable behaviour. Whilst it is correct to argue that racial and sexual violence will only be diminished by reducing the economic, racial, and sexual inequalities in power that exist in present societies, we cannot ask women, children, and victims of racial violence and abuse to wait for protection and compensation until the achievement of wholesale social transformation. We cannot, furthermore, reasonably expect them to give up such protection, remedy, and condemnation of violence as is afforded by criminal law, in present society with its systems of criminal rather than restorative justice.

What should be taken from feminist, anti-racist, and other 'zero tolerance' campaigners is that racial, sexual, and domestic violence should always be taken seriously. Spousal violence should not be dismissed as 'a domestic', of concern to no one outside the household; a victim's claim of racial motivation should be taken seriously; children should be listened to and any violence (sexual or non-sexual) against them should be regarded as reprehensible. From the abolitionists, however, we should learn that punishment is morally problematic in that it involves the state inflicting pain or deprivation on an individual; that it adds the suffering of the offender to the suffering already endured by the victim; that it deflects attention from the victim; that it generally offers little by way of protection and usually makes people worse rather than better. Punishment therefore needs justification, not just in general but in every particular case, and more constructive, less violent responses to the most serious forms of anti-social behaviour need to be developed with some alacrity.

The positives of restorative justice – compensation as of right; hearing the harms endured by the victim as well as weighing the evidence against the offender; considering how best to ensure the restoration of relationships between victims, offenders, and relevant communities – should be pursued as priorities. The negative reforms – abolishing imprisonment as a normal response to injury; finding restorative, rehabilitative alternatives to punishment in most cases – should be part of an overall move to a less retributive, more restorative justice. These reforms will need to be accompanied by vigorous 'policy preparation' along the lines suggested by Braithwaite and Mathiesen: that is, vigorous social education to make sure that domestic, sexual, and racial violence is behaviour which is strongly and generally disapproved, and about which perpetrators feel a strong sense of shame.[54]

53 Chesney-Lind and Bloom, op. cit., n. 33, p. 46.
54 Braithwaite, op. cit., n. 42; T. Mathiesen, *Prison on Trial: A Critical Assessment* (1990).

On the other hand, shaming should be of Braithwaite's reintegrative variety, rather than the rampaging vengeance that is being seen in some 'community' naming-and-shaming responses to sexual offending.

What abolitionists and other penal reductionists fear is that responsiveness to the legitimate claims for attention by victims, and acknowledgement of the seriousness of racial, sexual, and domestic violence will further fuel the harsh penal politics of these law-and-order times; it is also likely that unchecked punitiveness in relation to offences where corroborative evidence is difficult to obtain will lead to the adoption of civil law standards of proof, but with such cases resulting in criminal law punishments. What we also strongly suspect is that penal toughness towards racial, sexual, and domestic violence would only be inflicted on the poor and marginalized, with the powerful continuing to perpetrate their racist and misogynist behaviour behind closed doors: penal toughness will lead, to paraphrase Reiman, to the rich getting counselling and the poor getting prison.[55]

I am aware that I, like others who have addressed these difficult issues, am not coming to any firm or innovative conclusions. I can merely urge more abolitionist thinking about the problems posed by behaviour that is seriously harmful and widespread; that has not been subject to vigorous condemnation and penalization by the state, and which involves the exercise of power by offenders over victims. In particular, the problems of identifying the relevant 'community' and securing its participation, representation, and co-operation, and the problem of the last-resort sanction for recalcitrant offenders, need to be addressed.

Whatever the difficulties, however, the core principles of abolitionism hold true: the punitive power of the state needs to be curbed not expanded; penal strategies will be directed predominantly at those who are powerless and marginalized in the wider society, even if they are more powerful than their victims in the individual crime relationship; and punishment is more likely to reinforce racism, sexism, and other anti-social attitudes than to produce the chastened anti-racist and anti-sexist good citizen. The work of Braithwaite and Habermas provides a considerable advance in the theoretical resources available to restorative justice, whilst experiments with family conferences, community forums, and other processes being carried out in Australia, New Zealand, the Netherlands and elsewhere provide valuable experience in the viability of extending restorative justice processes to more serious forms of crime.

The key to reconciling the problems and possibilities of restorative justice lies in creative consideration of its relationship to formal criminal law. Problems of how to deal with recalcitrant offenders; how to ensure that restorative procedures are not seen as second-class justice; how to balance expressive and instrumental functions of justice; and above all, how to ensure that the voice of any party does not become submerged in an emergent

55 J.H. Reiman, *The Rich Get Richer and the Poor Get Prison* (1979).

unitary consensus all turn on the relationship between the discursive processes of restorative approaches and the role of formal law in modern societies in relation to defining relationships and allocating rights.

The developing perspective of 'guaranteeism' proposes a role for law as guarantor of rights, both general, in the sense of protecting human rights for all, and specific, for example, women's rights.[56] Formal law could stand behind restorative justice procedures as a guarantor of rights: that each party has certain rights which cannot be overridden by any decisions arrived at by consensus or majority. It could mean, for example, that an offender's rights would be protected against a vengeful community; that a victim's rights would be protected against a community view which did not take the harm seriously; that either party would have rights guaranteed against persuasion of the group by a stronger advocate. Guaranteeism would protect rights enjoyed in a generality of situations and contexts against the outcome of negotiations in a particular situation and context. This is quite different from the role of law in the present criminal justice system, which can adjudicate between competing rights, and which can order the suspension of certain rights (including, in the United States of America, for example, the right to life). If penality in modern societies is, as Foucault has described, a political economy of rights, then a role for law as guarantor of rights would be a progressive and appropriate development.

Further elaboration of Habermas's discursive ethics, especially as informed by feminists and those more generally engaged in developing philosophies of difference, and of perspectives such as legal guaranteeism, may solve many of the dilemmas of restorative justice. In particular, such work could enable restorative justice to maintain an orientation towards the 'others' involved in conflictual situations which is the essence of the problem-solving restorative approach in contrast to the rule-following retributive approach. Less easy to envisage, at least in present-day Britain and the United States of America, is recovery of a culture of social inclusion which would underpin and support the development of processes whose outcome is shaming that was reintegrative rather than eliminative, and where the ultimate goal is the enhancement of social justice. This is the most intractable problem in the path of restorative justice, and it is one that is beyond the ability of proponents of any theory of penal reform to solve.

---

56 T. Pitch, *Limited Responsibilities: Social Movements and Criminal Justice* (1990, English ed. 1995); Van Swaaningen, op. cit., n. 3.

Part V
Social Justice Perspectives

[17]

Conservative Conflict and the Reproduction of Capitalism: The Role of Informal Justice*

RICHARD L. ABEL

UCLA Law School, Los Angeles, U.S.A.

Informal alternatives to courts are a major preoccupation of legal reformers and scholars, not just in the United States and Europe but also in the third world, in socialist as well as capitalist nations (see generally Abel, 1982a,b). Informal legal institutions have been the subject of numerous conferences (see, for example, *70 Federal Rules Decisions*, p. 79; *76 Federal Rules Decisions*, p. 277; Fetter, 1978; Sander, 1978) and considerable scholarly research (Blankenberg, Klausa·and Rottleuthner, 1979; Cappelletti, 1978 to 1981; Felstiner and Drew, 1976; Nader, 1980) and have generated a literature large enough to inspire several lengthy bibliographies (Sander and Snyder, 1979; Wilkinson, 1980). The National Institute of Justice of the U.S. Department of Justice recently established three Neighborhood Justice Centers (Cook, Roehl and Sheppard, 1980) and these, together with alternative dispute institutions created in more than 110 cities throughout the country (McGillis, 1980), have been the subject of extensive evaluation (see, for example, Felstiner and Williams, 1980; Davis, Tichane and Grayson, 1980). The Royal Commission on Legal Services (1979, chapter 43), the Royal Commission on Legal Services in Scotland (1980, chapters 11, 14), and the Royal Commission on Criminal Procedure (1981) have all expressed interest in simplifying procedure, increasing access, and reducing delay, either by reforming the courts or by creating alternative institutions (see also Economides, 1980).

Notwithstanding all this activity, there is some danger that scholars may create (or at least exaggerate) the importance of the phenomenon of "informalism" by dwelling on it, in much the same way that the media create news. The Dispute Resolution Act of 1980 (P. L. 96–190) was enacted by

---

*An earlier version of this paper was presented at the Scandinavian–American Exchange on Conflict Management, Stavern, Norway, 31 May to 4 June 1980.

246 *R. L. Abel*

Congress but has not been funded, and is not likely to be in the present political climate. The Neighborhood Justice Centers have encountered difficulty in obtaining local support after the termination of their federal grants. Scholarly interest in disputing may say more about the poverty of theory in social studies of law than about the significance of the subject outside academia (Abel, 1980). Yet fads in scholarship and social reform merit analysis, if only to show that they are epiphenomenal. This paper explores the professed reasons for interest in informal alternatives to courts, develops a model of disputing in society that seeks to show the similarities between formal and informal legal institutions as modes of neutralizing conflict, and uses that model to assess the political significance of contemporary concern with informalism.

Informalism as Ideology

The concept of informal justice consists of two, possibly contradictory, ingredients. It clearly refers to alternatives to *courts*, i.e., these are *judicial* institutions, which they declare, modify and apply norms in the process of controlling behavior and handling conflict. What is much less clear is the sense in which these are *alternatives*. This section will therefore examine the claims that advocates of informal justice make for its differences from, and advantages over, formal legal institutions. My purpose is to demystify the ideology of informalism and show its inadequacy as a framework for analysis.

Cost

Informal alternatives are said to be less expensive than courts. But to whom do the savings accrue? To those who use informal alternatives? Would they ever have used the more expensive courts? If not, are they enjoying any savings by being diverted from other responses: two-party negotiation, endurance, or exit? Or are the proponents of informalism more interested in the benefit to those who already use the formal courts regularly and will experience shorter delays as caseload is shifted to informal institutions? And if informal institutions are less expensive perhaps this is because they are *worth* less to their users. Not only are they less well endowed with both coercive power and due process guarantees than formal courts, but participants may also invest less of themselves in the process, so little, in fact, that they get nothing significant in return (*cf.* Christie, 1977). Indeed, this seems a plausible interpretation of the fact that disputants must be compelled to use informal institutions: those alternatives that eschew compulsion tend to have much smaller clienteles (see Cook *et al.,* 1980, p. 106). Contrary to the economistic assumptions of many reformers, disputants may not be bargain hunters.

A completely different measure of expense is cost to the state (or to any other entity, such as a charitable organization) that supports the informal institution. Is the purpose of the institution to reduce the cost to those who use it by shifting some of their expense to the state? If so, we should certainly be concerned to know who is being subsidized to use the institution and who is paying that subsidy (*cf.* Landes and Posner, 1979). Or is the purpose to reduce the cost to the state by transferring litigants to less expensive informal processes? A significant consequence of the diversion of felonies to mediation in New York City, for instance, was the savings in police resources, since officers were not required to testify at arraignment or trial (Davis *et al.*, 1980, p. 67). Yet that is a highly problematic strategy, since reducing court caseloads by creating alternative institutions tends to render courts more attractive to potential litigants, thereby restoring caseloads to their former levels, with the result that the total cost to the state of subsidizing litigation *and* informal alternatives increases significantly (see Haley, 1982). An unacknowledged consequence of the creation of informal alternatives may be to redistribute dispute-settling resources, if those who use courts and those who use informal institutions constitute distinct categories, for instance, business enterprises and individuals. [This is not to deny that business enterprises frequently choose informal alternatives on the their own initiative (see Abel-Smith and Stevens, 1967, pp. 261–262; Macaulay, 1963; Mentschikoff, 1952).]

Access

Informal institutions are said to be more accessible than courts. Cost is obviously an important ingredient in access, but there are others; geography, knowledge, social distance, prior use (see Galanter, 1974; Merry, 1979). Access, like cost can have a number of different, and potentially inconsistent, meanings. It can signify availability. In this sense it is not clear whether we want informal institutions to be highly accessible and to encourage disputing, or highly inaccessible and to discourage it (*cf.* van der Sprenkel, 1962), or to appear accessible while actually being inaccessible. Do we wish to alter patterns of use because we think disputing is intrinsically good or bad or because we have a theory that relates kinds and amounts of disputing to some other social desideratum? Or are we interested in formal access regardless of actual use, in much the same way that most law reform is concerned to change the law on the books without troubling to inquire about consequent changes in the law in action? Proponents certainly want legal institutions to be *equally* available to the entire population, for this is an axiom of liberalism, but they tend to be vague about what such equality means and how it is to be attained within an unequal society. Would equality be satisfied if some disputants had access to courts but others only to informal alternatives?

Process variables and the ideal of formal justice

Informal institutions are said to offer a process that is more desirable for the particular disputes and disputants they handle, or even for all kinds of conflict.

248   *R. L. Abel*

Informal dispute processes are characterized as more humane and caring, speedier, concerned with a broader range of issues and evidence, more comprehensible (because less differentiated linguistically), and open to participation by a wider category of parties (and even non-parties). Yet again these claims are ambiguous. Is the standard of comparison a formal trial, a mediated settlement, or face-to-face negotiations (*cf.* van Velsen, 1969)? Is this the judgment of plaintiffs, defendants, or third parties? Informal processes also co-exist uneasily with the ideology of liberal legalism. In formal courts justice requires conformity with procedural and substantive laws. Why discard these criteria in informal institutions? Are we saying that legal procedures never produce formal justice? Or that they fail to do so only in certain cases? But then how do we recognize such instances? And why do we think that informal institutions can achieve formal justice in an unjust society when formal institutions cannot? Should informal institutions apply official substantive law? Are they better able to do so than formal institutions? If not, what substantive principles should the third party apply: the party's own values? In what cases is it appropriate to abandon substantive law for other normative guidelines? Are the latter preferable because they are imbued with common sense, or are more popular, or less technical? Are informal institutions more democratic in the sense that they are more permeable to diverse normative orders? Or are they better capable of reaching consensus among conflicting norms?

Lay participation

Informal institutions may be valued because they encourage greater lay participation in the process of resolving disputes. But why is it appropriate for the public to be involved in resolving some disputes and not others? And, indeed, why is public participation ever desirable: because it enhances the process, produces outcomes that are more just, or expresses democratic values? Does the public want to participate? The extreme reluctance of Americans to serve on juries (see Alker, Hosticka, and Mitchell, 1976) and the political apathy that leads half the American electorate to abstain from voting even in Presidential races, strongly suggest that most citizens feel neither political interest nor civic obligation. Finally, there is a disconcerting inconsistency between the declining role of the jury in civil cases, where the lay public really do determine outcomes (California voters recently approved overwhelmingly an initiative to halve the number of jurors in civil cases) and advocacy of an informalism in which a new breed of *professionals* (facilitators, mediators, or conciliators) actually exercise control; it is worth noting that arbitration has historically been used to *reduce* the influence of lay juries (Auerbach, 1979).

The value of conflict and litigation

The interest in informalism rests upon attitudes toward conflict and litigation that are ambivalent, perhaps even hypocritical. Advocates of informalism portray all conflict as evil (*cf.* Bohannan, 1969; Haley, 1982; Reifner, 1982) by lumping together forms of illegitimate violence and oppression, street crime, international aggression, and totalitarianism, with *resistance* to political repression, colonialism, racism, sexism, and economic exploitation. They thus identify conflict exclusively with threats to stability, obscuring the fact that many people experience the status quo as oppressive and see themselves as the victims of constant conflict. Yet because conflict is recognized as threatening it must be granted some limited expression, and informal processes are valued as ways of channeling conflict into forms that appear less violent, more just, or simply less revolutionary (Meador, 1978).

The attitude of reformers toward litigation is equally contradictory. Numerous commentators deplore what they describe as the excessive litigiousness of American society (for example, Barton, 1975; Burger, 1977; Ehrlich, 1976; Jones, 1965; Kline, 1978a,b; Manning, 1976; Rosenberg, 1971). They respond with strategies desgned to reduce litigation both by establishing alternatives to draw cases away from the courts and by intimidating potential litigants, compelling indigents to reimburse the state for their legal fees (*Los Angeles Times*, 14 December 1979, Part I, p. 7) or punishing those who litigate and lose (for instance, by imposing liability for costs, or heavier criminal sentences on those who refuse to engage in plea bargaining) (*Law & Society Review*, 1979). Yet the object is not to reduce litigation in general but to rid the courts of *certain kinds* of cases so that judges can handle more cases of other kinds, or handle them better. The attitude toward litigation is somewhat like the invective directed by business against government, except that lawyers (and to a lesser degree litigants) replace bureaucrats as the targets of abuse. The universal experience of the dilatoriness of government, the discourtesy of front-line officials (see Katz *et al.*, 1976; Katz and Danet, 1973), and the inefficiency of large public organizations (see Morris, 1980) can be mobilized, not to reduce government responsibilities but to expand them by creating new procedures and institutions in addition to those that already exist, and to reallocate them selectively.

The concept of informalism as an *alternative* to formal courts is inadequate as either description or prescription. The advantages claimed for informal institutions are vague and often inconsistent. Furthermore, they emphasize qualities internal to those institutions, especially their processual features, a myopic view that is reinforced when informal institutions are evaluated primarily in terms of the satisfaction of individual disputants (for example, Cook *et al.*, 1980, pp. 45–83). But those institutions must have *some* impact on the larger society: even in informal processes disputants win or lose, grievances are expressed or repressed, conflict is transformed, substantive rights are implemented or frustrated. An understanding of informalism must therefore set aside the programmatic assertions of its proponents and instead construct a model of conflict that seeks to identify the social consequences of different forms of legal institutionalization.

Conservative and Liberating Conflict

That the ideology of informalism exaggerates the differences between formal courts and informal alternatives is not surprising: every reform proclaims its novelty. But such distortion hides what seem to me to be far more important similarities between the formal and informal legal institutions of the capitalist state, between adjudication, arbitration, mediation, and conciliation. In order to reveal these common features I will construct two contrasting ideal-typical models of conflict. The first, which I will call conservative conflict, encompasses the processes that typify both formal courts and informal alternatives. It is repetitive, homeostatic, and it preserves the structures of domination that characterize capitalist society. The alternative I will call liberating conflict because it is transformational, disequilibrating, and it challenges those structures of domination (*cf.* Gluckman, 1965, pp. 163–66). Liberating conflict *can* occur within both formal and informal legal institutions, but I will argue below that those institutional structures *tend* to render conflict conservative. And of course conflict that occurs outside legal institutions is not necessarily liberating, the political process can be just as conservative. I want to draw attention to two features of this framework. It is explicitly normative: I am interested in the ways in which institutions shape conflict so as to preserve or challenge structures of domination and exploitation. And it is historically specific: these institutions are part of the state apparatus of advanced capitalism.

Disputant characteristics

People enter into conservative conflict imbued with the attributes that characterize them in the larger society. Among these the most important are that capital and state are organized, whereas workers, citizens, and consumers are disorganized. An extreme instance of this direct translation is the refusal of formal legal institutions to allow new forms of social organization to engage in litigation: constraints on labor unions in the nineteenth century and contemporary restrictions on class actions, intervention, and standing are examples. Individual advantages and disadvantages associated with class, socio-economic status, education, gender, age, and ethnicity retain their significance in conservative conflict. This occurs not through third-party bias, for legal decision makers claim impartiality, thereby mystifying the influence of social inequality, but through differences in the resources each adversary commands. Furthermore, these differences tend to be cumulative and irreversible. Those who are advantaged by their social standing tend to be more successful in their initial encounters and thereby are encouraged to engage in further conservative conflict, and vice versa; this positive or negative reinforcement helps to differentiate what Marc Galanter calls one-shot and repeat-player litigants (1974). Advantage can be displayed visibly (even boastfully) in the conspicuous consumption of extensive and expensive legal services, "papering the opposition to death"; but it can also enter invisibly into the preparations for conflict, including the structure of antecedent transactions, perceptions, the sense of entitlement, and expectations about success (*cf*. Abel, 1979a).

In liberating conflict, existing social structures are transformed, existing patterns of advantage inverted. Organization, for instance, can turn from a source of strength into an Achilles heel: the complex integration of the corporation or state may render it unusually susceptible to pressure on a vital part (e.g., strikes in police or fire departments, or the current political transformation in Poland). Liberating conflict organizes the disorganized, allowing them to see the commonality in their individual grievances and the power that can be gained by aggregating weakness; perceptions are changed, expectations upset. Trades unionism, civil rights, feminism, environmentalism, and consumerism, are obvious examples. But even legal institutions can sometimes be the arena for liberating conflict: revolutionary courts that consciously seek to compensate for prior class advantage illustrate this; so too (if to a far lesser degree) do small claims courts in the United States that forbid legal representation, or doctrines that require judges to disregard unconscionable agreements.

Equality of adversaries

A second, related distinction is that adversaries in conservative conflict can be unequal, even extremely unequal, and usually are, whereas opponents in liberating conflict are roughly equal. In the former the individual confronts some organized entity, either a private corporation or the state (see Galanter, 1975; Wanner, 1974, 1975). This is true whether the individual is making a claim (a dissatisfied consumer seeking a refund or a citizen requesting a welfare benefit) or resisting one (opposing collection of an alleged debt or defending a criminal prosecution). Significant inequalities may also characterize legal conflict between individuals, disputes between estranged spouses being the most frequent example. The reason that conflict between unequals is channeled into legal forms is that the ideology of liberal legalism promises equal justice for all, encouraging relatively weak supplicants to assert their legal rights and simultaneously legitimating the legal victories of corporations and the state as expressions of impersonal law rather than extralegal power. In formal processes, the appearance of equality between patently unequal opponents is enhanced by numerous devices: adversaries are represented by formally equal lawyers; the corporation or state may be replaced by an individual (an official, the prosecutor) who seems more like an equivalent of the individual party; both sides have formally identical opportunities to present evidence and arguments, etc. Prosecutions of particularly heinous crimes or of political dissidents, staged with the full panoply of procedural safeguards and impressive displays of virtuoso rhetoric by lawyers on both sides, are an important means of reaffirming the myth embodied in the iconography of blind justice.

252   *R. L. Abel*

Informal processes use other mechanisms to convey an image of equality: reducing the differentiation of third parties so that they appear equally approachable (rather than equally *un*approachable) by both sides; replacing the awesome state by the individual complainant, who seems a fairer match for the accused; seeking common ground between the two sides by de-emphasizing irreconcilable differences; characterizing proposed outcomes as "compromises", even if only one side is actually giving up anything of significance; excluding some of the more egregious instances of conflict between unequals (preferring, for instance, to handle disputes between individuals); and adopting a therapeutic posture that purports to transcend inequalities. Informalism thus reproduces within intraclass conflict the same structure that formal institutions impose on interclass conflict.

Liberating conflict, by contrast, occurs only between adversaries who are approximately equal (*cf.* Bailey, 1971, p. 19 and n. 17). This statement is certainly counter-intuitive and may even appear absurd. What I mean by it is that, despite the promise of equal treatment held out by legal institutions, (formal or informal) it only makes sense to confront an adversary of roughly equal strength. In situations of patent inequality the weaker party will refrain from asserting a claim and retreat or otherwise avoid battle if made the object of the claim. Even the stronger party may avoid conflict that occurs outside a legal institution capable of mystifying inequalities of power; weakness may thus become a hidden source of strength. International relations, labor relations, and guerilla warfare all illustrate these principles, as do struggles over racism and sexism. A party opposed by a more powerful adversary will seek to enhance its position before openly asserting or resisting a claim; deliberately provoking legal conflict may be one way of doing so. Thus either a symbolic victory (as in many famous constitutional cases) or a symbolic act of oppression (as in political prosecutions) may be a tactic for mobilizing before engaging in liberating conflict.

Normative order

In conservative conflict, the normative order is fully shared by both parties, exhaustive, and internally coherent. In formal legal institutions the judge explicitly imposes this body of norms on the disputants, attributing it to some external authority, a legislature, the constitution, or natural law. Informal institutions disguise authoritative imposition; the third party (mediator, go-between) may suggest that the norms are shared by both parties (emphasizing agreement and downplaying differences); imposition may be relatively invisible because the external authority is diffuse and inchoate (public opinion) or hidden (the threat of resort to formal institutions); or the third party may pretend that the norms are irrelevant, even obstructive. Both formal and informal legal institutions present the normative foundation of the outcome as something that antedates the conflict.

In liberating conflict there is normative dissensus. This does not mean that norms are absent or disregarded; although it is theoretically possible for inconsistent demands to be asserted without any normative justification, this rarely happens (*cf.* Eisenberg, 1976). But it is both conceivable and commonplace for claims to rest on normative bases that are wholly incompatible: an employer's offer of higher wages confronting the demand by employees for greater control over working conditions; a university's insistence upon meritocratic criteria for appointment opposing the demands of women or minorities for some specified level of representation. It is equally distinctive of liberating conflict that the parties themselves create the normative basis that permits a resolution (even if only temporary): create it because normative dissensus implies that no common norms antedated the conflict; and do so themselves because there is no third party on whom to rely.

Role differentiation

Legal conflict is characterized by a very high degree of role differentiation (*cf.* Abel, 1973). In formal institutions the most important role is clearly that of the third party who possesses the power to decide and therefore must take a vow of impartiality and ignorance with respect to both dispute and disputants. But even in informal institutions third parties are expected to be less partisan than the disputants, and this relative impartiality endows them with at least some moral suasion. Third parties are typically assisted by a host of subordinates who occupy their own distinct roles and serve to differentiate the third party still further from the disputants: clerks, bailiffs, and sheriffs in formal institutions, secretaries, intake officers, social workers, and therapists in informal institutions. Even the parties are differentiated: internally structured (corporations, unions, even voluntary associations are bureaucracies since this is the way in which individuals are organized under capitalism) and represented to the outside world by lawyers. Liberating conflict, as an ideal type, displays no role differentiation: there are no intermediaries; parties are unrepresented, internally homogeneous, and non-hierarchical. A group of urban squatters who move into vacant land or buildings might be an example. But since liberating conflict under capitalism pits undifferentiated subordinated groups against differentiated dominant entities (corporate, governmental), the former may tend to adopt a bureaucratic structure, even though this may mean winning a better outcome at the cost of coming to resemble the adversary; union-management conflict may be an example.

Conflict boundaries

Conservative conflict is confined by clearly demarcated, relatively rigid boundaries. These are temporal (conflict has a definite beginning and end), spatial (conflict may only be waged within certain arenas, e.g., the widespread

254 *R. L. Abel*

prohibition on discussing a case that is *sub judice*), institutional (jurisdictional rules ensure that only one institution will have competence), strategic (violence is prohibited, rhetoric may be restricted), even linguistic (certain forms must be used, others cannot be). Rules define the issues that may be raised and the evidence that may be introduced. Informal legal institutions also bound conflict, although the novelty or subtlety of the constraints may render them more difficult to perceive: for instance, parties may be required to abstain from controversial conduct while the dispute is proceeding (drinking, associating with friends or lovers), and the restrictions upon language may be even narrower (accusations may not be tolerated). Because informal legal institutions rely on formal ones for referrals, and frequently must report the outcome, they transpose many of the boundaries characteristic of formal institutions. Procedural rules, like the universe of substantive norms, are imposed from outside, antedate the encounter, and are agreed, exhaustive, and internally consistent. Liberating conflict begins untrammeled by procedural norms; it has no beginning or end and is waged in all arenas, even in several simultaneously. "All is permitted in love and war". Only the parties themselves can limit it; but they tend to subordinate process to outcome. Conservative conflict may be encapsulated as an incident in ongoing liberating conflict; the reverse cannot occur.

Chronological focus

The distinction just made suggests a reinterpretation of another opposition frequently encountered in the dispute settlement literature (e.g., Aubert, 1963; Nader, 1969). Conflict in formal legal institutions is said to be retrospective, concerned to evaluate past events, interested in causation and in ascertaining responsibility; informal, therapeutic institutions are prospective, preoccupied with devising a solution for the future. Though this opposition is reasonably accurate and useful I suggest that formal and informal legal institutions are similar in that they bound conflict by focusing on *either* the past *or* the future whereas liberating conflict is concerned with *both*. Regardless of what they may profess, formal legal institutions are fundamentally uninterested in the future (but *cf.* Eisenberg and Yeazell, 1980): they have a limited number of remedies to choose from and care little what happens to the parties after these remedies have been formally granted or denied (doctrines of *res judicata* and collateral estoppel preclude reconsideration). A recurrent justification for legal relief is to restore the *status quo ante*. Informal legal institutions curtail examination of the past; they prohibit the attribution of blame or praise because it may prejudice future relationships, and they tend to view people as lacking free will and urge accommodation to the inevitable. There are no final judgments for therapy never ends. Both kinds of legal institution thus render conflict conservative by ignoring either the past or the future. Liberating conflict, by contrast, engages in a normative evaluation of the past in order to influence the future (e.g., the

Nuremberg trials, the inquiry demanded by Iran into American complicity with the Shah, or Solzhenitsyn's call for an inquest into the Gulags). Thus scrutiny of the past is shaped by an interest in the future, and an acceptable future is deemed to rest on thorough historical analysis and moral assessment of the past.

Outcome

In conservative conflict the outcome, like the norms that guide and justify it, is externally imposed. The source of authority may be a judge (in formal institutions) or the diffuse sanction of public opinion (in informal institutions). In this sense both popular courts in revolutionary regimes and tribal moots in pre-industrial societies may exhibit conservative conflict. They share with formal courts the paternalistic assumption that someone other than the disputants (the judge, the state, the Party, the community) knows what is best. In liberating conflict the outcome is produced by the parties alone, though these will often be groups rather than individuals. This distinction has an ironic corollary. Conservative conflict is terminated decisively by a final judgment; yet because the parties do not construct this outcome but rather submit to it, a judicial decree is often followed by liberating conflict over whether it will be implemented. Problems of enforcement are endemic in formal legal institutions. Although we know less about conflict within informal institutions, there is every reason to expect similar problems to recur, if the aftermath of divorce (Chambers, 1979; Goode, 1956), the unenforceability of small claims judgments (Yngvesson and Hennessey, 1975, pp. 254–55), and the lack of finality in tribal dispute processing (Abel, 1973, pp. 231–32) are any guide. If and when the parties in liberating conflict finally agree upon an outcome, it will be relatively stable, unless they change their minds or are feigning agreement for tactical purposes.

The outcome of conservative conflict, like the process itself, perpetuates the status quo. By this I mean not only that distributions of wealth and power are preserved (e.g., tort and contract law both protect the income stream of tort victims and contractual parties) but even more that fundamental party characteristics are reproduced. Corporate entities, public and private, have their corporate identity strengthened. Individuals obtain remedies, pre-eminently money damages, that accentuate their individuality, distinguishing them from others by what they do and do not receive and intensifying differences of class and stratum. Liberating conflict transforms parties, disaggregating those that were corporate (for instance, by dividing public policymakers from bureaucratic staff, or capitalists from employees) and organizing previously atomistic individuals (for instance, by producing an outcome that treats them equally and corporately, involving them in new behaviours and conferring joint responsibility rather than making them the passive recipients of an award of money).

256   *R. L. Abel*

Informal Justice as Conservative Conflict

Although I argued in the previous section that both formal and informal legal institutions under capitalism tend to render conflict conservative they are not, for that reason, identical. The questions thus remain: why do we find an emphasis on informal legal institutions today, and what are their social significance?

I have suggested elsewhere (1979b), as have others (e.g., Pound, 1922, p. 54; *cf.* Galanter, 1979a), that formalism and informalism are alternatives in an endless cycle. Some have criticized this view: it is unduly idealist; the end-state of any completed cycle is always different from the beginning; this is at most a description, not an explanation, since the dynamic of the alteration is not stated. I accept these criticisms but still think there is a core of truth in the notion of cycles within capitalism. Those who manage legal institutions (judges, legislators, high executive officials, élite lawyers, legal scholars) are engaged in a continuous effort to legitimate the legal system, at least to themselves, whether or not anyone else is listening or being persuaded; they are constantly building twentieth century Potemkin villages. But the contradictions inherent in the dominant ideology of liberal legalism, between form and substance, the promise of equality and the fact of inequality, constantly erode legitimacy. Yet capitalism cannot escape from this ideology, which justifies both the exercise of state power and its limits. In the endless projects of legitimation within the legalist paradigm, informalism has the attraction of the relatively new, an untested solution whose flaws are not yet apparent. Furthermore, by focusing attention upon experimental peripheral institutions, the program of informalism deflects criticism from those older formal institutions that lie at the core of the legal system.

But this is still a very partial account; it suggests why reformers have turned away from the courts but not why they have turned toward informal institutions (to supplement courts, not to replace them). I think such an explanation must begin with the contemporary backlash to the "rights explosion" of the last few decades. The enemies of the welfare state contend that it has created too many substantive rights, placed too many restrictions upon capital, and constrained both state and capital within too many formal procedures. These forces have recently made substantial political gains, a fact that itself requires explanation, though it is beyond the scope of this paper. Formal legal rights (both substantive and procedural) express classical liberal theory, which consistently has been an important weapon of the oppressed in resisting domination and exploitation. If these rights were invented by the bourgeoisie in the course of overthrowing feudalism, the proletariat and other oppressed groups have also been able to use them in struggling against capitalism (*cf.* Marx, 1963). Informalism, by contrast, expresses positivist theories, developed in the last century and a half, which justify domination, authority, the exercise of control from above, whether in the substantive criminal law, criminal procedure, penology, mental institutions, education, or the workplace (*cf.* Christie, n.d.). Classic liberalism is the ideology of the revolutionary phase of capitalism, whereas positivism is the ideology of capitalism triumphant. The movement from formalism to informalism thus reflects and carries forward a shift in power from the less privileged to the more.

Sometimes the dominant class openly declares this to be its goal: substantive welfare rights, the minimum wage, restraints on commercial fraud and overreaching, the regulation of occupational health and safety, environmental protection, are said to be too "expensive", to reduce "efficiency" or "productivity", to render a country less competitive in the international economy. But because such explicit attacks draw attention to the opposed interests of privileged and oppressed and thus intensify political and economic conflict, the backlash to the rights explosion has generally been couched in the language of process. Process values appear neutral: informalism does not *obviously* favor any group or category. Like proposals to reorganize government or reduce bureaucracy, informalism thus promises reform without conflict, relief from expensive and pointless procedural intricacies without sacrifice by anyone.

Yet if the advocates of informalism seek to portray it as neutral, this mystifies its true significance. Informal processes commonly characterize their outcomes as compromise solutions in which nobody wins or loses. But compromise produces unbiased results only when opponents are equal; compromise between unequals inevitably reproduces inequality. Informal institutions claim to be cheaper and thus more accessible than formal, thereby appealing to the value of equality of opportunity so fundamental to liberalism. Yet enhanced opportunity leads to equal opportunity and equal use only when the potential users are themselves equal. In a class society, a slight reduction of the barriers to access will marginally enlarge the category of privileged users without altering the distinction between use and non-use or the consequences of differential use. Disputants themselves are able to see through the pretensions of informalism: although they may be willing to submit a controversy with an equal to an informal process, they strongly prefer formal institutions when confronting a clearly superior adversary (for example, Buckle and Buckle, 1980; Merry, 1982).

These preliminary examples suggest that the social significance of informalism often may best be revealed by treating its public pronouncements as Orwellian newspeak and inverting them. Let me begin with what is perhaps the central claim: that informalism represents a relaxation of authority, a reduction in domination, an amelioration of coercion. I would argue, on the contrary, that informalism has the potential to subject additional forms of behavior to legal authority, thereby expanding the scope of state control and transforming liberating conflict into conservative (*cf.* Cohen, 1979; Foucault, 1977). First, to the extent that informal institutions handle cases that would otherwise go to court (though the numbers are probably fairly small), they

258   *R. L. Abel*

reduce court caseload and thus delay, rendering courts more attractive to disputants, who may choose to litigate conflicts that previously would have been resolved outside of court. Second, to the extent that informal institutions deal with disputes that would not have been litigated they subject those conflicts, too, to the conservative influence of legal forms. This latter influence is not randomly distributed across the population: by their location, staffing, subject matter, jurisdiction, and processual characteristics, informal institutions are targeted at workers, the poor, inner-city residents, women, and ethnic minorities. They handle problems that those who are relatively privileged (in terms of wealth, income, education, ethnicity) solve without state intervention, either by dealing directly with their adversaries (for example, addressing consumer complaints to sellers) (Best and Andreasen, 1977; Hannigan, 1977) or by taking them to private therapists (for example, family conflict) (*cf.* Hollingshead and Redlich, 1958). In other words, if informal institutions render law more accessible to the disadvantaged, they also render the disadvantaged more accessible to the state, and the latter consequence may be the more significant. In assessing the validity of this hypothesis it is essential to bear in mind two contradictory pressures. On the one hand, informal institutions, like so many conspicuous reforms, are of symbolic importance; because they will be systematically underfunded, only a few exemplary institutions will probably be created. The elimination of all appropriations for the Dispute Resolution Act is symptomatic. On the other hand, those relatively few institutions that seek permanent funding will need to develop large caseloads in order to justify their existence according to the prevailing standards of bureaucratic efficiency (Cook *et al.*, 1980).

One reason why informal institutions have the potential to legalize more behavior and new kinds of behavior is that they appear non-coercive. Although there is a continuum of coerciveness, with arbitration at one end and conciliation or facilitated negotiation at the other, all informal processes present themselves as less coercive than courts or administrative agencies. Informal institutions generate this image out of a composite of elements: they blur the distinction between public and private (using private forms to implement state programs); appear to respond passively to the desires of disputants to resolve their conflicts rather than exercising state control affirmatively; involve the parties more actively in the settlement process (without actually surrendering control); frame the outcome as a compromise. But despite appearances, coercion continues to play a significant role. Non-coercive procedures are often backed by implicit coercion: the threat of initiating or reviving a criminal prosecution frequently underlies an "agreed" solution; reluctance to "agree" may be overcome, or nullified, by the residual alternative of compulsory arbitration (Davis *et al.*, 1980; Harrington, 1980). The process may itself be the punishment, judging, stigmatizing, and thereby controlling the participants in the dispute (*cf.* Feeley, 1979). All of this exemplifies a very fundamental tendency in the mode of social control under advanced capitalism: as the state perfects its monopoly of force it no longer needs to exercise power as openly or brutally and can rely, instead, on less coercive forms of control (Poulantzas, 1978, chapter 3). But as coercion becomes less visible and more subtle it is more readily extended to new areas of behavior: persuasion is appropriate in many realms of social interaction where compulsion would be obviously excessive. Furthermore, it evokes less resistance: citizens have greater difficulty in recognizing it and less justification for insisting on formal procedures as a means of protection.

The significance of informal institutions is further mystified by analogizing the state to the family. Half a century ago Jerome Frank (1931) advanced a crude Freudian interpretation of popular faith in law as expressing the need for an omnipotent, omniscient father. Harold Berman (1963) has described the conscious paternalism of Soviet criminal courts. John Griffiths (1970) has argued for a family model of the criminal law, as an alternative to both due process and law and order models. And western scholars often speak admiringly of the identification between ruler and father in eastern societies, which endows the former with the latter's authority. Once this parallel between state and family is accepted, conflict is no longer conflict; there are no truly irreconcilable interests, only misunderstandings. *All* behavior is of interest to the informal institution *qua* family. Informalism explicitly rejects the basic liberal tenet "everything that is not forbidden is allowed" substituting, instead, the principle that everything is either forbidden, or discouraged, or encouraged, or mandated, but never irrelevant or neutral. Because this model denies the possibility of structural opposition between the parental third party and the disputants, because the former is seen as motivated only by solicitude and concern, the latter possess no rights. Where the juvenile court was justified by the failure of parents to control or nurture their children, and the domestic relations court by the dissolution of the family, informal institutions have generalized the role of state as surrogate family. If disputants are children and the third party is a parent it is proper, indeed inevitable, that the former should be totally dependent on the latter. There is no punishment, only tutelage; indeed, rewards are the preferred response.

This formulation, like the characterization of informal institutions as non-coercive, is both false and dangerous. Once again we get closer to the truth if we invert the claim: the state has not come to resemble the family; rather, the family has become ever more transparent to the state (*cf.* Donzelot, 1979; Lasch, 1977). The image of the family that inspires informalism is naive, if not hypocritical. Families are not islands of calm in a sea of dissension; they are driven by sexual, generational, and sibling conflict. It is ironic that the family should be invoked as a model of harmonious interaction at a time when its principal bonds (parent–child and spousal) are both disintegrating under social and economic pressures and the object of ideological attack. But this is hardly surprising: social formations often seek legitimation by identifying with what they are displacing – capitalism with the feudal order (Polanyi, 1957), bourgeois professionalism with aristocratic patron/client relationships (Larson, 1977), the contemporary welfare state with *laissez-faire* capitalism.

State institutions, no matter how informal, cannot replicate behavior within the family and certainly not the idealization of that behavior. A third party does not really care about the disputants, at least not the way one member of a family cares about the others; the intermediary did not live with the parties before the controversy, will not be stuck with them after it is concluded, and has no strong feelings about them. The third party is parental in much the way that airlines, banks, or oil companies are "friendly" (*cf.* Simon, 1978, p. 109). The interests of the third party diverge significantly from those of the disputants: the former takes pride in possessing and exhibiting technical skills in managing people, needs (and wants) to enhance the authority of the dispute institution, and must satisfy bureaucratic pressures to move cases. And because the third party does not control significant rewards (the disputants are not really concerned what the third party thinks about them) negative sanctions must be the primary response.

Just as ostensibly non-coercive institutions insinuate coercion, so institutions that appear to proffer solicitude foster dependence, on the state if they are public bodies, on capitalist enterprises (large manufacturers and retailers, the media) if they are creatures of the latter (Palen, 1979; Ross and Littlefield, 1978). They do this by reproducing and extending the relationship between the helping professional and the needy consumer of services, a paradigmatic form of domination in advanced capitalism (Illich, 1977; Larson, 1977, pp. 241–44). The fact that these institutions are informal extends dependence by creating new categories of professionals (arbitrators, mediators, conciliators) who are less expensive to produce than legally-trained professionals (Marquart and Wheat, 1980, p. 473). The state or corporation can therefore hire more of them and use them to handle conflicts that have less monetary significance than the disputes presently taken to courts or other formal institutions. The fact that these institutions are informal also lulls the client's sense of dependence (and that of us, the observers), just as it masked coercion. But informal institutions do truly foster dependence: there is neither mutuality nor equality between professional and client; the former is competent, knowledgeable, uninvolved (even if these qualities may be less accentuated than they are in lawyers); the latter, incompetent, ignorant, and in the midst of a crisis (psychological, social, economic), is reduced to a passive consumer of the helping service. Informal conflict management is simply the latest service provided by constantly expanding welfare state bureaucracies and capitalist enterprises (the two increasingly indistinguishable) in the movement toward social democracy and corporate paternalism.

Informal institutions not only channel conflict into conservative forms, they also distract attention from conflict that is potentially liberating. Just as nineteenth century French penal institutions diverted attention from illegality by focusing on delinquency (Foucault, 1979, Part 4, Chapter 2) and contemporary American courts ignore political questions in obedience to the "passive virtues" (Bickel, 1962) or in pursuit of an illusory neutrality (Wechsler, 1961), so informal legal institutions, by circumscribing their jurisdiction, help to assign to oblivion whatever conflict is excluded.

First, they define who can claim and what they can claim. Only individuals can be grievants before most informal institutions; hence they discourage organizing (thereby reproducing existing social imbalances, since many respondents are already organized). They also rule out many possible solutions: a tenant may ask a landlord to make repairs but cannot insist on restructuring the landlord-tenant relationship; the purchaser of a defective product may request a replacement but cannot require the manufacturer to redesign the product. Control over property, the capitalist enterprise, and the state apparatus cannot be challenged.

Second, informal institutions define the locus of significant conflict – typically the neighborhood (Beresford and Cooper, 1977; Cratsley, 1978; Danzig, 1973; Fisher, 1975). Here again, as in the self-conscious identification of informalism with family, a symbol that evokes strong nostalgic yearnings (the community) is held out as a model at a time when it has almost totally atrophied as an actual pattern of behavior (in this it recalls conservative appeals to states' rights). Co-residence simply is not the primary locus for social interaction in urban America (*cf.* Sennett, 1977). Hence disputes within the neighborhood tend to be trivial, quarrels over noise, or pets, or fences (Baumgartner, 1980). The neighborhood usually does not witness conflict between worker and capitalist, subordinate and superordinate, citizen and state, human being and polluter. Even racial conflict is largely excluded by residential segregation.

Third, informal institutions define the adversaries against whom claims can be made. Often this limitation is extremely narrow: only individuals can be respondents. This may restrict the institution to managing intra-class conflict between spouses, parents and children, and neighbors. Such a limitation implicitly denies the existence or denigrates the importance of inter-class conflict, it fosters the privatization of life, the cult of the personal. But even a broader definition of respondent tends to include only the petty bourgeoisie (the local landlord or small grocery store) (Cook *et al.*, 1980) and low-level public employees (the garbageman or cop on the beat) not monopoly capitalists or those state officials who set policy. It is because such adversaries are relatively powerless, and thus roughly comparable to the grievants, that informal institutions can relax rules of procedure and present the result as fair compromise. Informal institutions thus not only define legitimate conflict as the dissatisfaction of the consumer, the disharmony between equal individuals (thereby denying the existence of irreconcilable, structural conflicts between classes or between citizen and state), they simultaneously pursue the classic strategy of domination, *divide et imperium,* in much the same way that colonial regimes tolerated or established dispute mechanisms, subjugating indigenous peoples in the name of indirect rule (*cf.* Abel, 1979c; Galanter, 1979b; Santos, 1977).

262   *R. L. Abel*

Conclusions

In this paper I have sought to understand the significance of the growth of
informal justice within the state apparatus of advanced capitalism. I began by
noting that its proponents stress the divergence from formal legal institutions in
order both to promote informalism and to present it as a major reform of the
capitalist legal system. Yet analysis of their claims reveals them to be vague,
contradictory,   and   empirically   dubious.   Furthermore,   advocates   of
informalism largely confine their vision to what happens within the legal system
and emphasize institutional style. I argued that we must, instead, examine the
impact of legal institutions on society. In particular, I urged that we ask
whether each institution renders conflict conservative or liberating. The
answer, I believe, is that the legal institutions of the capitalist, whether formal
or informal, usually render conflict conservative.

   We are familiar with the ways in which formal legal institutions have guided
many categories of potentially liberating conflict into conservative channels:
the arbitration of labor struggles; school desegregation lawsuits in response to
racial conflict; administrative hearings for complaints of sex discrimination in
employment; individualized grievance mechanisms for prisoners, consumers,
tenants, and welfare recipients; state regulatory agencies as a result of
environmental activism. Informal institutions perform a similar function but in
their own distinctive fashion. By disguising coercion, centralization, and
dominance, they extend state control to new behavior. By offering a hearing to
certain grievances (thereby cooling out the grievants) they convey the powerful
(if implicit) message that other grievances are illegitimate or insignificant. Also
unlike civil (though like criminal) courts, they direct their attention largely at
the dominated classes.

   There is some evidence that informal justice is coming to play a greater role
in controlling conflict, although the magnitude of this trend, and its
explanation, are unclear. We appear to be reaching the end of a long period,
dating back to the end of the nineteenth century, during which formal legal
institutions have been the dominant mode of managing conflict: substantive
rights   have   expanded,   administrative   agencies   have   proliferated,   the
compulsory arbitration of labor disputes has become widespread, the criminal
justice system has grown enormously, and we have seen the rise of state-funded
legal services and foundation-supported public interest law. These formal
rights, institutions, and procedures are not about to disappear, but their further
growth may be checked and they may experience significant retrenchment.
The reasons for this remain obscure. The fiscal crisis of the state may require a
reduction of services, but economic forces do not specify that these must be
mechanisms of social control. The political weakness of the dominated classes
may permit the state to withdraw welfare rights granted earlier, but the source
of this weakness is itself uncertain, though it is clearly related to the capitalist
economic crisis. Finally, though ideas alone are never a sufficient explanation

for institutional change, the dominant ideology of capitalism, liberal legalism, does appear to induce perpetual oscillation between formalism and informalism as modes of legitimation.

How successful are informal legal institutions likely to be in rendering conflict conservative? Here again the answer seems clear, they can only fail. No legal institution, formal or informal, can resolve the contradictions of capitalism or eliminate the exploitation and domination that generate conflict. Formal legal institutions repeatedly engender the liberating conflict they try to contain. Workers threatened with unsafe conditions reject the protection of regulatory agencies and the promise of compensation after they are injured and simply stop production or walk off the job (*Whirlpool Corp.* v. *Marshall*, 100 S.Ct. 883, 1980). Ethnic minorities subjected to constant police violence cannot be pacified with internal review procedures and lawsuits and will finally respond violently, as they recently did in Miami. A community faced with toxic wastes that are producing miscarriages, birth defects, and sick children, like those in the Love Canal, may shortcircuit governmental bureaucracy by taking officials hostage until residents are provided with alternative accommodation (Brown, 1980; *Los Angeles Times*, 20 May 1980, Part I, p. 20).

Informal legal institutions have their own limitations. From the viewpoint of the capitalist state, their drawback is that they cannot effectively manage conflict and remain informal. If they take the latter course they will atrophy, like the conciliation services attached to family courts. If they choose the former they will have to become more openly coercive; but this will generate opposition and compel the liberal state to respond by adopting formal procedures, witness the history of the juvenile court. Members of oppressed groups are likely to find informal procedures uncongenial for other reasons, because they want to resist exploitation and domination, not reach an accommodation with it. They want a public hearing and moral vindication; if informal institutions do not provide this, grievants will find other arenas. Finally, informal (like formal) institutions retain the potential to advance liberation. Indeed, they must express some of the aspirations of the disputants or the latter would shun them altogether. And these institutions sometimes do offer a more humane process, a mechanism for extending welfare rights, greater participation by the parties, exploration of a wider range of issues, and less dependence upon professionals.

Yet both formal and informal legal institutions under capitalism ultimately present the project of liberation with the same dilemma. Most of the time those institutions successfully contain conflict and render it conservative. But even when conflict remains liberating, those who struggle will seek to embody their success in a legal institution, formal or informal: a substantive rule, a new process, an administrative agency. They will do so for several reasons: the hegemony of liberal legalism, the high cost to the participants of continuing the struggle, and the fact that legal institutions do represent important ideals of substantive and procedural justice (if only imperfectly). But the result is the

264   *R. L. Abel*

creation of yet another legal institution that ultimately serves to render further conflict conservative and to strengthen capitalism. For the reasons sketched above, no institution can fully succeed in this task and each will engender resistance. The dialectic of liberation is unending.

Acknowledgements

I am grateful to Nils Christie for inviting me to the Scandinavian–American Exchange on Conflict Management, the German Marshall Fund for supporting the conference, and all the participants for their instruction, stimulation and comments. I have also received valuable criticism from Robert Kidder, Carrie Menkel-Meadow, Udo Reifner, my colleagues in our critical legal studies group in Los Angeles, and Boaventura de Sousa Santos, whose article in this journal (1980, **8,** 379–397) has strongly influenced me.

References

Abel, R. L. (1973) A comparative theory of dispute institutions in society. *Law & Society Review* **8,** 217–347.
Abel, R. L. (1979a) Socializing the legal profession: can redistributing lawyers' services achieve social justice? *Law & Policy Quarterly* **1,** 5–51.
Abel, R. L. (1979b) Delegalization: a critical review of its ideology, manifestations and social consequences. In *Alternative Rechtsformen und Alternativen zum Recht.* (Blankenburg, E., Klausa, E. & Rottleuthner, H., Eds). Westdeutscher Verlag: Opladen, pp. 27–47 (*Jahrbuch für Rechtssoziologie und Rechtstheorie,* band 6).
Abel, R. L. (1979c) Theories of litigation in society: "modern" dispute institutions in "tribal" society and "tribal" dispute institutions in "modern" society as alternative legal forms. In *Alternative Rechtsformen und Alternativen zum Recht.* (Blankenburg, E., Klausa, E. & Rottleuthner, H., Eds). Westdeutscher Verlag: Opladen, pp. 165–91 (*Jahrbuch für Rechtssoziologie und Rechtstheorie,* band 6).
Abel, R. L. (1980) Redirecting social studies of law. *Law & Society Review* **14,** 805–29.
Abel, R. L. (Ed.) (1982a) *The Politics of Informal Justice: The American Experience.* Academic Press: New York (forthcoming).
Abel, R. L. (Ed.) (1982b) *The Politics of Informal Justice: Comparative Studies.* New York: Academic Press (forthcoming).
Abel-Smith, B. & Stevens, R. (1967) *Lawyers and the Courts: A Sociological Study of the English Legal System, 1750–1965.* Heinemann: London.
Alker, Jr. H. R., Hosticka, C. & Mitchell, M. (1976) Jury selection as a biased social process. *Law & Society Review* **11,** 9–42.
Aubert, V. (1963) Competition and dissensus: two types of conflict and of conflict resolution. *Journal of Conflict Resolution* **7,** 26.
Auerbach, J. S. (1979) Informal (in)Justice? The Legalization of Informal Dispute Settlement in Modern America. Part I: Conciliation and Arbitration (unpublished).
Bailey, F. G. (1971) Gifts and poison. In *Gifts and Poison*(Bailey, F. G., Ed.). Blackwell: Oxford, pp. 1–25.
Barton, J. H. (1975) Behind the legal explosion. *Stanford Law Review* **27,** 567–84.
Baumgartner, M. P. (1980) Social Control in a Suburban Town: An Ethnographic Study. PhD. dissertation, Sociology, Yale University.

Beresford, R. & Cooper, J. (1977) A neighborhood court for neighborhood suits. *Judicature* **61,** 185–90.

Berman, H. J. (1963) *Justice in the U.S.S.R: An Interpretation of Soviet Law* (Rev. Ed.). Vintage Books: New York.

Best, A. & Andreasen, A. R. (1977) Consumer response to unsatisfactory purchases: a survey of perceiving defects, voicing complaints, and obtaining redress. *Law & Society Review* **11,** 701–42.

Bickel, A. (1962) *The Least Dangerous Branch: The Supreme Court at the Bar of Politics.* Yale University Press: New Haven.

Blankenburg, E., Klausa, E. & Rottleuthner, H. (Eds) (1979) *Alternative Rechtsformen und Alternativen zum Recht.* Westdeutscher Verlag: Opladen (*Jahrbuch für Rechtssoziologie und Rechtstheorie,* band 6).

Bohannan, P. (1967) Introduction. In *Law and Warfare* (Bohannan, P., Ed.). Natural History Press: Garden City, N.Y.

Brown, M. (1980) *Laying Waste: The Poisoning of America by Toxic Chemicals.* Pantheon: New York.

Buckle, L. G. & Thomas-Buckle, S. R. (1980) Bringing Justice Home: Some Thoughts about the Neighborhood Justice Center Policy. Presented at the joint meeting of the Law and Society Association and the ISA Research Committee on Sociology of Law, Madison, 5 June.

Burger, W. E. (1977) Our vicious legal spiral. *Judges' Journal* **16,** 23–24, 48–49.

Cappelletti, M. (Gen. Ed.) (1978–1981) *Access to Justice,* 5 volumes. Giuffre: Milan and Sijthoff and Noordhoff: Alphen aan de Rijn.

Chambers, D. L. (1979) *Making Fathers Pay: The Enforcement of Child Support.* University of Chicago Press: Chicago.

Christie, N. (1977) Conflicts as property. *British Journal of Criminology* **17,** 1–15.

Christie, N. (n.d.) Limits to Pain (unpublished).

Cohen, S. (1979) The punitive city: notes on the dispersal of social control. *Contemporary Crises* **3,** 339–63.

Cook, R. F., Roehl, J. A. & Sheppard, D. I. (1980) *Neighborhood Justice Centers Field Test: Final Evaluation Report.* U.S. Department of Justice, National Institute of Justice, Office of Program Evaluation: Washington, D.C.

Cratsley, J. C. (1978) Community courts: offering alternative resolution within the judicial system. *Vermont Law Review* **3,** 1–69.

Danzig, R. (1973) Toward the creation of a complementary decentralized system of justice. *Stanford Law Review* **26,** 1.

Davis, R. C., Tichane, M. & Grayson, D. (1980) *Mediation and Arbitration as Alternatives to Prosecution in Felony Arrest Cases: An Evaluation of the Brooklyn Dispute Resolution Center (First Year).* Vera Institute of Justice: New York.

Donzelot, J. (1979) *The Policing of Families.* Pantheon: New York.

Economides, K. (1980) Small claims and procedural justice. *British Journal of Law and Society* **7,** 111–21.

Ehrlich, T. (1976) Legal pollution. *New York Times Magazine* 17, (8 February).

Eisenberg, M. A. (1976) Private ordering through negotiation: dispute settlement and rule making. *Havard Law Review* **89,** 376.

Eisenberg, T. & Yeazell, S. C. (1980) The ordinary and extraordinary in institutional litigation. *Harvard Law Review* **93,** 465.

Feeley, M. (1979) The *Process Is the Punishment.* Russell Sage: New York.

Felstiner, W. L. F. & Drew, A. B. (1976) *European Alternatives to Criminal Trials and Their Applicability in the United States.* University of Southern California: Los Angeles, CA.

Felstiner, W. L. F. & Williams, L. A. (1980) *Community Mediation in Dorchester, Massachusetts.* U.S. Department of Justice, National Institute of Justice: Washington, D.C.

Fetter, T. J. (Ed.) (1978) *State Courts: A Blueprint for the Future.* National Center for State Courts: Williamsburg, VA.

Fisher, E. A. (1975) Community courts: an alternative to conventional criminal adjudication. *American University Law Review* **24,** 1253–91.

Foucault, M. (1977) *Discipline and Punish: The Birth of the Prison.* Pantheon: New York.

Frank, J. (1931) *Law and the Modern Mind.* Brentanos: New York.

266   *R. L. Abel*

Fried, C. (1976) The lawyer as friend: the moral foundations of the lawyer client relation. *Yale Law Journal* **85**, 1060.

Galanter, M. (1974) Why the "haves" come out ahead: speculations on the limits of legal change. *Law & Society Review* **9**, 95–160.

Galanter, M. (1979a) Legality and its discontents: a preliminary assessment of current theories of legalization and delegalization. In *Alternative Rechtsformen und Alternativen zum Recht.* (Blankenburg, E., Klausa, E. & Rottleuthner, H., Eds). Westdeutscher Verlag: Opladen, pp. 11–26 (*Jahrbuch für Rechtssoziologie und Rechtstheorie*, band 6).

Galanter, M. (1979b) *Justice in Many Rooms.* University of Wisconsin Law School, Disputes Processing Research Program: Madison (Working Paper 1979–4).

Gluckman, M. (1965) *Politics, Law and Ritual in Tribal Society.* Basil Blackwell: Oxford.

Goode, W. J. (1956) *Women in Divorce.* Free Press: Glencoe, IL.

Griffiths, J. (1970) Ideology in criminal procedure or a third "model" of the criminal process. *Yale Law Journal* **79**, 359.

Haley, J. O. (1981) The politics of informal justice: the Japanese experience 1922–1942. In Abel, 1982b.

Hannigan, J. A. (1977) The newspaper ombudsman and consumer complaints: an empirical assessment. *Law & Society Review* **11**, 679–700.

Harrington, C. (1980) Voluntariness, consent and coercion in adjudicating minor disputes. In *Policy Implementation: Choosing Between Penalties and Incentives.* (Brigham, J. & Brown, D., Eds). Sage Publications: Beverly Hills, CA.

Hollingshead, A. B. & Redlich, F. (1958) *Social Class and Mental Illness.* Wiley: New York.

Illich, I. *et al.* (1977) *Disabling Professions.* Marion Boyers: London.

Jones, H. W. (Ed.) (1965) *The Courts, the Public, and the Law Explosion.* Prentice-Hall: Englewood Cliffs, N.J.

Katz, D., Gutek, B. A., Kahn, R. L. & Barton, E. (1975) *Bureaucratic Encounters: A Pilot Study in the Evaluation of Government Services.* Survey Research Center: Ann Arbor, MI.

Katz, E. & Danet, B. (Eds) (1973) *Bureaucracy and the Public: a reader in official-client relations.* Basic Books: New York.

Kline, J. A. (1978a) Curbing California's colossal legal appetite. *Los Angeles Times,* Part IV, p. 1 (12 February).

Kline, J. A. (1978b) Law reform and the courts: more power to the people or the profession? *California State Bar Journal* **53**, 14.

Landes, W. M. & Posner, R. A. (1979) Adjudication as a private good. *Journal of Legal Studies* **8**, 235–284.

Larson, M. S. (1977) *The Rise of Professionalism; A Sociological Analysis.* University of California Press: Berkeley.

Lasch, C. (1977) *Haven in a Heartless World: The Family Besieged.* Basic Books: New York.

Law & Society Review (1979) Plea bargaining. *Law & Society Review* **13**, (Special Issue, Winter).

Macaulay, S. (1963) Non-contractual relations in business: a preliminary study. *American Sociological Review* **28**, 55.

McGillis, D. (1980) *Dispute Processing Projects: A Preliminary Directory.* Harvard Law School, Center for Criminal Justice: Cambridge.

Manning, B. (1976) Hyperlexis: our national disease. *Northwestern University Law Review* **71**, 767.

Marquardt, R. G. & Wheat, E. M. (1980) Hidden allocators: administrative law judges and regulatory reform. *Law & Policy Quarterly* **2**, 472–94.

Marx, K. (1963) *The Eighteenth Brumaire of Louis Bonaparte.* International Publishers: New York.

Meador, D. J. (1978) Statement. In *Hearings before the Subcommittee on Courts, Civil Liberties, and the Administration of Justice of the Committee on the Judiciary, House of Representatives, 95th Congress, 2nd Session, on S. 957: Dispute Resolution Act.* U.S.G.P.O.: Washington, DC. pp. 60–2.

Mentschikoff, S. (1952) The significance of arbitration – a preliminary inquiry. *Law and Contemporary Problems* **17**, 699.

Merry, S. E. (1979) Going to court: strategies of dispute management in an American urban neighborhood. *Law & Society Review* **13**, 871–925.

Merry, S. E. (1981) The social organization of mediation in non-industrial societies: implications for informal community justice in America. In Abel, 1982b.

Morris, C. R. (1980) *The Cost of Good Intentions: New York City and the Liberal Experiment, 1960–1975.* Norton: New York.

Nader, L. (1969) Introduction. In *Law in Culture and Society* (Nader, L., Ed.). Aldine: Chicago.

Nader, L. (Ed.) (1980) *No Access to Law: Alternatives to the American Judicial System.* Academic Press: New York.

Palen, F. S. (1979) Media ombudsmen: a critical review. *Law & Society Review* **13,** 799–850.

Polanyi, K. (1957) *The Great Transformation: the Political and Economic Origins of our Time.* Beacon Press: Boston (first published 1944).

Poulantzas, N. (1978) *State, Power Socialism.* New Left Books: London.

Pound, R. (1922) *An Introduction to the Philosophy of Law.* Yale University Press: New Haven.

Rosenberg, M. (1971) Let's everybody litigate? *Texas Law Review* **50,** 1349–68.

Ross, H. L. & Littlefield, N. O. (1978) Complaint as a problem-solving mechanism. *Law & Society Review* **12,** 199–216.

Royal Commission on Criminal Procedure (1981). *Report* H.M.S.O.: London (Cmnd 8092).

Royal Commission on Legal Services (1979) *Final Report,* vol. I. H.M.S.O.: London (Cmnd 7648).

Royal Commission on Legal Services in Scotland (1980) *Report,* vol. I. H.M.S.O.: Edinburgh (Cmnd 7846).

Sander, F. E. A. (1978) *Report on the National Conference on Minor Disputes Resolution.* American Bar Association: Chicago.

Sander, F. E. A. & Snyder, F. E. (1979) *Alternative Methods of Dispute Settlement – A Selected Bibliography.* American Bar Association, Division of Public Service Activities: Washington, D.C.

Santos, B. de S. (1977) The law of the oppressed: the construction and reproduction of legality in Pasargada. *Law & Society Review* **12,** 5–126.

Santos, B. de S. (1980) Law and community: the changing nature of state power in late capitalism. *International Journal of the Sociology of Law* **8,** 379–397.

Sennett, R. (1977) *The Fall of Public Man.* Knopf: New York.

Simon, W. H. (1978) The ideology of advocacy: procedural justice and professional ethics. *Wisconsin Law Review* **1978,** 29–144.

van der Sprenkel, S. (1962) *The Legal Institutions of Manchu China: a sociological analysis.* Athlone Press: London.

van Velsen, J. (1969) Procedural informality, reconciliation and false comparisons. In *Ideas and Procedures in African Customary Law* (Gluckman, M., Ed.). Oxford University Press: New York.

Wechsler, H. (1961) Toward neutral principles of constitutional law. In *Principles, Politics and Fundamental Law.* Harvard University Press: Cambridge.

Wilkinson, P. J. (1980) *The Social Organization of Disputes and Dispute Processing and Methods for the Investigation of Their Social, Legal and Interactive Properties: A Bibliography in Three Parts.* Centre for Socio-Legal Studies: Oxford.

Yngvesson, B. & Hennessey, P. (1975) Small claims, complex disputes: a review of the small claims literature. *Law & Society Review* **9,** 219–74.

Date received: January 1981

[18]

Truth, Reconciliation and Justice: The South African Experience in Perspective

*Kader Asmal**

The lecture examines the role and objectives of truth and reconciliation commissions in societies undergoing major political transitions, with particular reference to the model of South Africa, and compares this method to others suggested by international criminal law for accommodating both retributive and restorative responses to past conflicts and crimes against humanity.

My subject tonight is 'Truth, Reconciliation and Justice: The South African Experience in Perspective'. This plainly raises preliminary questions as to the nature of the South African experience, and what exactly the appropriate perspective might be.

In brief, the South African democracy born in 1994 succeeded nearly half a century of racial discrimination raised to a constitutional principle. It was a period of brutal oppression, hit squads, violent attacks on neighbouring states, and even research into chemical warfare and eugenics. The new Parliament chose to confront this terrible past through the establishment of a truth and reconciliation commission, a body established by an Act passed in mid-1995.[1] The objective of this Act was to deepen our country's factual and interpretative grasp of its terrible past, going back to 1960.[2] The Commission was mandated to pronounce on what had been done by whom to whom, why, and what was to be done about these past abuses in our calmer present times.

Unlike many truth commissions that preceded it,[3] our own was not solely concerned with granting amnesty to perpetrators of human rights abuses. It in addition gave a voice to the victims[4] and provided for reparation to and rehabilitation of victims.[5] Furthermore, while it indeed conferred amnesty in respect of criminal and civil liability for human rights abuses, this was subject to

---

* Minister of Education, South Africa.
This is the text of the twenty-seventh Chorley Lecture, delivered at the London School of Economics and Political Science on Thursday 4 November 1999. The author gratefully acknowledges the contribution to this lecture of Louise Asmal, Ronald Suresh Roberts, Estelle Dehon, and Charles Villa-Vicencio, while acknowledging that the responsibility for the comment and conclusions is his own.

1 Promotion of National Unity and Reconciliation Act 34 of 1995 (henceforth, 'Act').
2 Act, s 3.
3 P.B. Hayner, 'International Guidelines for the Creation and Operation of Truth Commissions: A Preliminary Proposal' (1996) 59 *Law and Contemporary Problems* 173.
4 Act, s 11.
5 Act, ch 5.

various important criteria, notably requirements that there be full disclosure of the facts surrounding the abuse;[6] that the abuse be associated with a political objective (as opposed for instance to motivation for personal gain); and that the abuse was proportionate to the political goal that it sought to advance.[7]

Much can and has been said and written about the proper interpretation of the Act and my remaining time could easily be spent addressing such questions as the proper scope of assorted statutory phrases. But here we encounter the other key theme of my address: the perspective. I doubt that, in turning our attention to truth commissions, we should allow ourselves to get lost in the details of statutory handiwork. Indeed the entire quest to establish a truth commission is best seen, in my view, as an attempt to avoid the intrusion of narrow legalism[8] into the rightly fluid context of political transitions. This is the proper context, as I see it. We are concerned not with the limited preoccupations of scriveners, like Herman Melville's Bartleby, but rather with the broad brush strokes needed to establish democracy on a firm footing and to ensure a durable climate for the pursuit of human welfare. The proper perspective from which to view the South African truth commission is the age-old quest for a better life for all.

It is, then, in the true spirit of Lord Chorley that I approach my lecture tonight. He was a renaissance lawyer: passionate about penal and prison reform yet internationally renowned as a maritime and banking lawyer. His mind was sharp as well as committed. He was a person who, as the Modern Law Review wrote on his death in 1978, spent a lifetime 'building a bridge between academic legal pursuits and the day-to-day needs of the community ... For him law was too serious a human and social concern to be used as an intellectual plaything'.[9] It was a privilege to have heard him lecture. As I look tonight at the role of law in the aftermath of political violence and repression, I could ask for no more exacting standard than Lord Chorley's: stern taskmaster; man of compassion.

The quest in our century

From the Hague Conventions at the beginning of the century to ongoing discussions as it closes about the establishment of an International Criminal Court, our era has been one wherein people have dared to hope for peace and have found their hopes dashed, and dashed again. World War I was to be the 'war to end all wars'. Then more war came. From national rivalries early in the century to internal and civil conflicts at its end, violent conflict has become bloodier and more frequent: the nineties has been our century's bloodiest decade.[10] Much of this violence has been

---

6 Act, s 20(1)(c).
7 Act, s 20.
8 For an example of the genre of narrow legalism, see A. Jeffrey, *The Truth About the Truth Commission* (Johannesburg: Institute of Race Relations, 1999) 8. The book enlists a whole raft of legalistic criteria in order to judge the transitional justice process in South Africa, but never argues why these narrowly legalistic criteria are or ought to be applicable to the kinds of dilemmas that truth commissions set out to resolve.
9 (1978) 41 MLR 121–22.
10 P. Armstrong, P. Fortier, R. St John, B. Hamilton, A. Lapointe and Mi. Zigayer, *Security Implications of Low-Probability, High-Impact Events – Assessing the Changing Traditional National Security Environment in the Context of Low-Probability, High-Impact Events* (Canadian Government, 1998) <http://policy research.Schoolnet.ca/keydocs/globalz/vol2 rap5-e.htm>. (While in the 1950s, 50 percent of the victims of armed conflicts were civilians, that figure has risen to 90 pecent today. 'In the period 1989–95, there were 87 intrastate (internal) armed conficts ... The peak was reached in 1992 when there were 53 active armed conflicts of this type. Through this period, Asia and Africa accounted for at least 65 percent of all conflicts').

imposed by governments on their own peoples, or has derived from ethnic groups tearing up the national fabric (in for example Yugoslavia and Rwanda) or autocrats pursuing narrow and corrupt self-interest (in countries such as Chile under Pinochet, or the Argentina of the Generals). Prominent among the lessons that international lawyers have taken from this century's ongoing violence is the truth that it is in fact impossible to separate large international questions of war and peace from seemingly local matters of civil disorder.[11]

What then is to be done? People have certainly not suffered in silence. This century's blood and gore have caused louder and more effective protest than ever before, through the United Nations and its organs, and international human rights non-governmental organisations. The internationalisation of human rights norms, laws and institutions, beginning in the late nineteenth century and taking a quantum leap in the late 1940s, could be described as the first wave of what today we faddishly call 'globalisation'. Like the economic and cultural globalisation of this century, the globalisation of human rights during the last century was a mixed blessing, often captive to selfish agendas. Cecil Rhodes and his Afrikaner rivals alike described themselves (however cynically) as bringers of civilised values to benighted colonial places. After World War II, the Nuremberg trials, which raised international human rights enforcement to an entirely new plane, were nevertheless an exercise in victor's justice.[12] Afterwards, the United Nations was for decades immobilised by Cold War gridlock and, in the post Cold War era, there are fears that the United States has become overly influential in determining the human rights consensus.[13]

The attempt to achieve a genuinely multicultural and global perspective is, however, complex. Professor Onuma Yasuaki of the University of Tokyo sets out in quest of 'intercivilisational' human rights, aiming to view human rights from 'an Asian perspective'. Yet he has to begin by acknowledging that 'the very notion of Asia is not Asian, but of European origin'.[14] Much the same has been said of the idea of Africa.[15] Colonialism's last laugh is the way in which it often shaped the form, if not the content, of anti-colonial mobilisation.[16]

Like postcolonial identity itself, the international human rights context has not been static. The idea of human rights is always shifting and contested, and is as complex as are our seemingly interminable moral and philosophical debates themselves.[17] These

---

11 R. Falk, *On Humane Governance: Toward a New Global Politics: The World Order Models Project Report of the Global Civilization Initiative* (Cambridge: Polity Press, 1995).

12 Y. Beigbeder, *Judging War Criminals: The Politics of International Justice*, (London: Macmillan Press, 1999) 48–49.

13 'The discourse of human rights exists, as does any other intellectual discourse, within [a] Westcentric universe of information and culture, and therefore tends to be premised on this intellectual, informational, and cultural hegemony'. Onuma Yasuaki, 'In Quest of Intercivilisational Human Rights: Universal versus 'Relative Human Rights Viewed from an Asian Perspective', Occasional Paper Number 2 of the Asia Foundation's Centre for Asian Pacific Affairs (California, March 1996) 10.

14 Onuma Yasuaki, *ibid* p 1.

15 See A. Appiah, *In My Father's House* (Oxford: Oxford University Press, 1992).

16 Though as Edward Said points out in *Culture and Imperialism* (New York: Viking, 1993), the stubborn reality of authentic resistance to colonialism, in all times and places, has, if anything, been underplayed in most received histories. See ch 3, 'Resistance and Opposition'.

17 See eg A. McIntyre, *Whose Justice? Which Rationality* (Notre Dame: University of Notre Dame Press, 1989) for a neo-Aristotelian perspective on values; S. Cavell, *The Claim of Reason: Wittgenstein, Skepticism, Morality and Tragedy* (Oxford: Oxford University Press, 1982) 247–313 for a Wittgensteinian perspective; T. Baldwin (ed), *G.E. Moore's Principia Ethica* (Cambridge: Cambridge University Press, 1992) 37–58, 142–180 for an intuitionist perspective; A.J. Ayer, *Language, Truth and Logic* (London: Dover Publications, 1949) 15–40, 66–89 for a positivist approach. Side debates over questions of definition *within* these supposed 'schools' of meta-ethics (who really *is* intuitionist, positivist, Wittgensteinian et cetera) are often as vibrant as the ostensibly main contest *between* these schools.

3

moral or meta-ethical debates feed directly into jurisprudential questions about whether and to what extent law – even in domestic systems – provides meaningful guidance for the judges who implement it: are they unconstrained moral actors, or bureaucratic functionaries effectively bereft of discretion, because the law tells them what to do and leaves them no choice to do otherwise.[18] Moreover, whatever the status and binding nature of law in domestic legal systems, whole schools of thought would deny international law the status of law at all, because (these critics suggest) international law lacks John Austin's[19] virtue of rules backed by effective and enforced sanctions.[20]

In countries which suffered the rape and pillage of colonial powers, one sees in some instances extraordinary moves being undertaken to make reparation to those who were forcibly deprived of their land and livelihoods. New Zealand and Australia have recognised that their indigenous populations have a special place in the country and have made concrete moves towards restoring some at least of the traditional land which colonisers had occupied. Past colonialism may still have its defenders, but there is no doubt that international law today would condemn the forcible acquisition of countries or territory. Internationally, both on the African continent and within America, voices are today being raised to demand compensation from the former colonial powers, or at the very least apologies, for the appalling ravages of the slave trade, which not only claimed millions of lives but in the process caused untold damage to the development of the continent from which so many were culled.

The new deadlock

Despite the contested nature of human rights consensus and even of international law itself, it is a truism now to say that with the end of the Cold War there is an opening for more genuine international human rights collaboration. The old imperial assumption that human rights belonged only to self-styled racial and class elites has fallen away. Few today would defend the imperialist triumphalism of the last century.[21] That deadlock has been undone. But now there is the risk of a second deadlock: not between the ideologies of right and left but rather between

---

18 This debate pits positivists (such as H.L.A. Hart, 'Positivism and the Separation of Law and Morals', (1958) 71 *Harvard Law Review* 593, 593–629 against adherents of legal realism (K. Llewellyn, 'A Realistic Jurisprudence – the Next Step' (1930) 30 *Columbia Law Review* 431 in George C. Christie, (ed) *Jurisprudence* (West, 1973) 720–47, of critical legal studies (as summarised by, R. Unger, *The Critical Legal Studies Movement* (Cambridge: Harvard University Press, 1983), and critical race theory (as excerpted in K. Crenshaw, N. Gotanda, G. Peller, K. Thomas (eds), *Critical Race Theory: the Key Writings that Formed the Movement* (New York: New Press, 1996)) and natural lawyers (L.L. Fuller, 'Human Purpose and Natural Law' (1958) 3 *Natural Law Forum* 68. Again, it is not always easy to describe which theorist fits where. For instance, R. Dworkin's *Law's Empire* (Cambridge: Harvard University Press, 1986) in which a fictional judge, Hercules, is able to find the 'best fit' in hard cases, can be described as positivist with residual natural law tendencies.
19 J. Austin, *Lectures on Jurisprudence* Vol 1 (London: John Murray, 1885) 33–43.
20 This is the so-called Newhaven School: see, R.J. Beck, *International Rules: Approaches from International Law and International Relations* (Oxford: Oxford University Press, 1996). For a recent popularisation of such views, see J.R. Bolton, 'The Global Prosecutors: Hunting War Criminals in the Name of Utopia' 78 no.1, *Foreign Affairs* 157 (review essay criticising A. Neier, *War Crimes: Brutality, Genocide, Terror and the Struggle for Justice* (New York: Times Books, 1998) and (less trenchantly) M. Minow, *Between Vengeance and Forgiveness: Facing History After Genocide and Mass Violence* (Boston: Beacon Press, 1998).
21 Again, see E. Said, *Orientalism* (New York: Pantheon, 1978) 31–49, showing that imperialist knowledge production claimed to advance the welfare of colonies while actually bolstering exploitation.

what might be called human rights fundamentalism, on the one hand, and cynical realpolitik on the other.

The battle of democracy against oppression, truth against power, memory against forgetting; the bleak past vanquished in favour of a beckoning brighter future – this is the sort of Manichean vocabulary that populates the field of human rights law. And this is of course rightly so: as long as the world remains a place where bad things happen, there will also be an important place for morally charged vocabulary and for the genuine and justified moral passions that underlie it.[22]

I myself speak as an international lawyer from a position well within the human rights discourse of the last five decades. And I am proud of the role that the anti-apartheid struggle has had in the evolution of international law itself.[23] Human rights campaigners have rightly resisted assorted revisionisms, for just as today there are still those who continue to deny the facts of the German Holocaust,[24] now we find latter-day apologists for apartheid in my own country at the century's end, who argue that apartheid was not a crime against humanity.[25] In these and other cases, we find time and time again that we cannot relax our judgmental guard, for the very good reason that apologists stand ready to exploit the murk and shadow of 'historical complexity'.[26]

And yet our Manichean hymn book, the one that we on the side of the angels so often employ, invites a cynical counter-vocabulary. We come up against the techno-crats of the social sciences and of international relations. These are the hard men of *realpolitik*, the mandarins of statecraft who view moralists as naïve children, lacking knowledge of the real world's harsh realities. To borrow a mildly inelegant American colloquialism, these mandarins behave as though we human rights activists 'ain't never run nothing but our mouths' – they imply that we are all talk and no organisation.

If we wish to sum up these contending attitudes, the human rights mindset as contrasted with the mandarin one, we could do worse than compare Mahatma Gandhi and Henry Kissinger. Gandhi's successful passive resistance campaign made uncompromising idealism seem like sound statesmanship, not naïveté; Kissinger on the other hand continues to influence generations of mandarins across the globe who fervently believe that morality is a luxury in statecraft.

What I would like to construct tonight is a 'third way', with apologies to Professor Giddens.[27] By this, I hasten to add, I do not mean compromise and the abandonment of principle. Alongside the polar opposites of Gandhi and Henry Kissinger, I would propose that we focus on Nelson Mandela. As the *New York Times Magazine* correctly discerned some time ago, our former South African President is not the simple saint of caricature, but also and fundamentally a shrewd politician.[28]

---

22 R. Unger, *Passion* (New York: Free Press, 1986).
23 K. Asmal, 'The Legal Status of National Liberation Movements (with particular reference to South Africa' (1983–84) *Zambia Law Journal* 37; K. Asmal, 'The Illegitimacy of the South African Regime: International Law Perspectives' (1990) 8 *International Review of Contemporary Law* 21.
24 See generally, A. Rosenbaum (ed), *Is the Holocaust Unique?* (Colorado: Westview Press, 1996).
25 H. Giliomee, 'Asmal offers 'no fresh view, no ground-breaking synthesis' of the truth', *Cape Times*, 23 October, 1996, 2.
26 T. Eagleton, *The Illusions of Postmodernism* (Oxford: Blackwell, 1996).
27 A. Giddens, *The Third Way: The Renewal of Social Democracy* (Cambridge: Polity Press, 1999). I also noticed, in the course of finalising this lecture, that Archbishop Desmond Tutu, Chairperson of the South African Commission, has employed this very phrase in characterising the South African approach. The second chapter of his *No Future Without Forgiveness* (London: Rider Books, 1999) is entitled 'Nuremberg or National Amnesia? A Third Way?' Archbishop Tutu and Professor Giddens of course employ the phrase with very different meanings.
28 'The Mandela Behind the Saint' *New York Times Magazine*, 23 March, 1997 cover story.

He has offered more than moral platitudes, he has run a country smoothly, and even held it together before the 1994 elections while it teetered constantly on the brink of flames. In short he has seen us through the worst. Many women and men in governments all over the world have faced challenges of ensuring justice during transitional eras, as countries turned away from repression.[29] But nobody has managed a political transition as successfully as has Mandela, while also emerging with his halo, as it were, intact. To preside over justice in a transitional era is almost always a moral and political poisoned chalice.[30] The compromises can be enervating, morality can indeed seem a luxury, the mandarins so easily make all the running.

It is Mandela, more than any other figure of our century, who exemplifies Max Weber's much-cited distinction between the ethics of responsibility and the ethics of conviction.[31] Thus the fact of Mandela's success his moral and political success deserves closer attention. We need to understand how it came about.

The facts of transition

The difference between *realpolitik* and naïveté can be presented as a conceptual matter, a matter of principle, as though some people are committed to *realpolitik*, while others are deliberately naïve. Yet Gandhi had his stratagems and Kissinger his misty-eyed moments. Inconvenient as it may be, the difference between *realpolitik* and naïveté often hinges on how we, the onlooking third parties, perceive the relevant facts at issue. Conceptual or supposedly principled arguments become unprincipled indulgences if inserted into a factual vacuum.

Take for instance the spirited exchange between Professor Diane Orentlicher, an academic with an interest in transitional justice, and Carlos Nino, who was a key official in Raul Alfonsin's Argentine Government when it was wrestling with the legacy of the military regime that preceded it. In an influential article published in 1991, Orentlicher argued in favour of the prosecution of offenders, suggesting that such prosecutions were required by international law and also that 'because trials secure pre-eminent rights and values, governments should be expected to assume reasonable risks associated with prosecutions, including a risk of military discontent'.[32] She adds: 'While many have asserted that prosecutions were impossible, the claim has typically been overstated'.[33] In support of these assertions, Orentlicher attaches two examples in a footnote. First, she criticizes the Government of the Philippines for its rejection of prosecutions as 'political

---

29 See eg J. Zalaquett, 'Balancing Ethical Imperatives and Political Constraints: The Dilemma of New Democracies Confronting Past Human Rights Violations' (1992) 43 *Hastings Law Journal* 1428. Zalaquett was a member of the Chilean truth commission.
30 Interestingly, A. Neier suggests that truth and justice are actually two separate phases in transitional democracies: 'What Should be Done about the Guilty?' *The New York Review of Books* (New York: NY Review Inc, 1990) 43.
31 M. Weber, *Politics as a Vocation* (Munich: Duncker and Humblodt, 1919).
32 D.F. Orentlicher, 'Settling Accounts: The Duty to Prosecute Human Rights Violations of a Prior Regime' (1991) 100 *Yale Law Journal* 2537, 2548–2549. This position is also advocated by M. Cherif Bassiouni, who scathingly criticises any process which would allow political considerations to prevent full-scale prosecutions: 'Introduction' (1996) 59 *Law and Contemporary Problems* 5. (The practice of impunity has all too frequently been the result of *realpolitik*. At times it is rationalised as a necessary evil, which is indispensable to achieving peace. While this is true in some cases, in most cases it is a cynical manipulation by governments of people's expectations that both peace and justice can be attained).
33 Orentlicher, *ibid* 2548.

suicide'. In fact, Orentlicher asserts, the government 'enjoyed considerable power relative to the armed forces in its early months in office, and was at that time in a position to press bold action without provoking a viable threat of military rebellion'.[34] Turning to the example of Uruguay, Orentlicher asserts that 'experts on Uruguay similarly believe that President Julio Maria Sanguinetti could have insisted upon some prosecutions of the military for past violations without derailing his country's transition to democracy'.[35]

Orentlicher's argument is uncomfortably caught between such factual reckonings, matters really of political judgment, on the one hand, and arguments, on the other hand, that there is a legal duty to prosecute certain offenders in times of political transition: that governments are 'not excused from their duty to prosecute human rights violations merely to placate restive military forces; the excuses are available only to avert a threat to the life of a nation'.[36] But the line between unnecessarily placating the military and prudently averting a threat to the life of the nation is fundamentally a matter of fact and of political judgment; it does not help to invoke a legal injunction. Attempting to blend these two arguments (the practical and the legalistic), Orentlicher ends up suggesting that the existence of the international law obligation can strengthen the hand of pro-democracy forces, so that legal command and practical politics might work hand in hand.

But this last claim is no less a matter of conjecture than Orentlicher's opinions on the ready scope for action in the Philippines and Uruguay. And the correct answer will necessarily differ from context to context. As Nino points out in his response, Orentlicher's criticisms ultimately resort not 'to moral or legal normative premises, but to factual ones'.[37] And the deliberate care of the study has no automatic advantages for fact-finding, especially when those facts must be assessed and responded to in the heated context of actual politics and life-or-death political contestation.

Underlying the academic literature of 'transitional justice' – underlying the debate that I have summarised between Orentlicher and Nino – is that by now familiar issue of naïveté versus *realpolitik*. Beyond the particular debating points that separate them, this is the underlying importance of their debate. Orentlicher believes that 'with every recital' of international law obligations by dissidents, the legitimacy of repressive regimes crumbles a little more – which comes across as a little wishful and naïve. Meanwhile, Nino seeks to mount the high horse of the practical man of affairs. 'A legal duty selectively to prosecute human rights violations committed under a previous regime is too blunt an instrument to help successor governments who must struggle with the subtle complexities of re-establishing democracy'.[38] In these mandarin tones, Nino comes uncomfortably close to disparaging the perspective of the victims in whose name he undertakes his subtle labours: in rebuffing 'maximalist' demands for prosecution, Nino notes the courage of the victims' groups that were pressing these demands, but, he adds 'the emotional strains various groups suffered impaired their ability to be objective'.[39] This sounds somewhat callous in view of the appalling suffering which many

---

34 *ibid.*
35 *ibid.*
36 *ibid* 2609–2610.
37 C.S. Nino, 'Response: The Duty to Prosecute Past Abuses of Human Rights Put in Context: The Case of Argentina' in N.J. Kritz (ed), *Transitional Justice* (United States Institute of Peace Research, 1995).
38 *ibid* 435.
39 *ibid* 432.

victims endured. However, in South Africa, victims did not band together to seek prosecutions; in fact the voices of the victims of the struggle were taken as central[40] rather than dismissed as lacking in objectivity. Some individuals or families have indeed opposed the granting of amnesty to the perpetrators of the crimes against them, but many have shown themselves anxious only to establish the truth about what happened.

When Nino talks of international law at all, it is through the lens of game theory:[41] he never assumes that international law is binding just because, or precisely because, it is international law.[42] He is more interested in analysing whether, and how aggressively, the alleged international obligation will in fact be converted into a demand by an international community assumed to be motivated by strategic, diplomatic and other considerations.[43] Thus, for instance, Nino doubts that there can be an obligation on the new regime to prosecute the crimes of the old because, if the new government fails in this duty, the prospect of any intense international punitive response is 'complete fantasy'.[44]

Orentlicher argues that the international law obligation to prosecute the wrongdoers of the former regime must be followed as an end in itself and also because, in practice, it strengthens the hand of the angels. Nino doubts that international law strengthens the hand of the angels, argues that it weakens their hand by de-legitimising the new regime, and suggests that only international power politics really matter at the end of the day.

One may debate whether there is room for a third way between Orentlicher's well-meaning but uncertain hybrid of international legal idealism and speculative *realpolitik*, on the one hand, and Nino's equally well-meaning but ultimately *ad hoc* pragmatism on the other. I believe that there is and I would direct our attention, once more, to South Africa. First, in deference to Nino's emphasis on facts and local complexities, I will supply a narrative of the relevant South African transitional background. This remains very much an unwritten history, for now, so I have erred on the side of the uncontroversial. Few would, I think, disagree with this basic account. After this, I will move on to describe the approach taken by our Parliament and the Truth Commission that we established, highlighting the ways in which I believe we have moved beyond the twin traps of naïveté and *realpolitik*. Finally, I turn once again to the international perspective with which we began, to link developments there with developments in South Africa.

---

40 See, L.S. Graybill, 'Pursuit of Truth and Reconciliation in South Africa' (1998) 45 *Africa Today* 103, 120.
41 'Would the structure of collective action have been different if Orentlicher's proposal [selective compulsory prosecutions] had materialised? The bargaining power of the government to carry out the trials would not have been strengthened by the prospect of international condemnation of the country for failing selectively to prosecute past human rights abuses. This international pressure would not have been seen by resilient sectors of the military as a threat to them'. Nino, n 37 above 429.
42 'I doubt the beneficial effects of a general duty which does not take into account [the] complexities' [of particular countries] Nino, n 37 above, 417.
43 'Ultimately, a necessary criterion for the validity of any norm of positive law, including positive international law, is the willingness of the governing institutions, in this case states and international bodies, to enforce it'. Nino, n 37 above, 419. This begs the question of what constitutes 'enforcement'. Customary international law develops, for instance, through repeated declarations even if the state parties issuing the declarations are impotent to alter the facts to which they object, so that the declaration itself constitutes sufficient 'enforcement'. See H. Lauterpacht (ed), *L. Oppenheim, International Law: A Treatise* (London: Longman, 1955) 5–6.
44 Nino, n 37 above, 430.

Complexities of the South African transition

The history of apartheid has several familiar phases, which comprise a necessary background to any discussion of transitional justice in South Africa. First, the narrow 1948 election victory of the National Party inaugurated a period of consolidation and caution as apartheid's whites-only electoral majority was stabilised (through a combination of constitutional shenanigans and a deepening of the National Party's all-white electoral appeal). Next, the relatively open civic agitation against apartheid in the fifties was shut down by the banning of the liberation movements, including the African National Congress (ANC), in 1960. Here began a period of underground activity and seeming quiet. Apartheid's security apparatus had gained the upper hand. By the early seventies, an increasingly confident apartheid regime had embarked on a strategic offensive within Africa as well as beyond the continent.

This apparently stable period was interrupted by the 1976 student uprising in Soweto, an event which shook South Africa more than Paris '68 ever shook France. Out of this, despite the repressive force meted out by the apartheid police, grew the agitation of the 1980s and the United Democratic Movement, which set out, in the words of the slogan of the times, 'to make South Africa ungovernable'. This strategy of ungovernability had succeeded dramatically by the late eighties, and had overwhelmed successive states of emergency imposed by an increasingly frantic P.W. Botha.

Meanwhile the anti-apartheid sanctions campaign had rocked the economy, convincing the country's business elite that it had an interest in rendering South Africa globally respectable. But this realisation was grudgingly arrived at; it was at best a surly conversion to the abolition of apartheid; there was certainly no deep well of good feeling among businesspersons towards the ANC.

By 1989, when F.W. de Klerk took office, the inability of the apartheid state to control the country made urgent the installation of a legitimate government that might have a fighting chance. De Klerk had little choice in this matter as he had sat in Cabinet and seen P.W. Botha's heavy-handed military strategies fail. The apartheid government under De Klerk calculated that it might be able to install a nominally black government, thus terminating the campaign for ungovernability, while retaining de facto control of the country through 'power sharing,' by which De Klerk intended that whites would exercise a veto power of some sort, both in Cabinet and in the legislature. This was quite explicitly De Klerk's agenda well into the transition period. The compulsory coalition, the Government of National Unity, which was installed after the 1994 election, may have owed something to this desire, but more to the fact that the balance of forces had changed in South Africa.

From the side of the African National Congress, the Government of National Unity was a form of insurance policy. The National Party had stacked the military, the civil service and the judiciary with loyalists and the ANC needed time to win these constituencies over, keenly aware of the risk of an 'ungovernability' strategy in reverse: one in which the ANC, now in government, faced a recalcitrant civil service able to sow disruption, a surly or perhaps even rebellious military, and naturally conservative financial markets that identified the National Party with the holy grail of continuity.

Between the release of Nelson Mandela in 1990 and the first democratic election in 1994, the National Party used its command of the state machinery in a merciless

9

The Modern Law Review   [Vol. 63

fashion. Hit squad activities intensified, attacks on innocent commuters were carried out by the Civil Cooperation Bureau (an Orwellian name for the state security body) and, in the killing fields of Natal, the regime funded and fuelled a civil war which it presented to the world as 'black-on-black' violence. As many people were lost to political violence between 1990 and 1994 as were killed during the entire previous history of apartheid, dating back to 1948.

Such were the realities that the incoming ANC-led government faced on its 1994 election victory. The people gave the ANC a solid 63% majority, but one coupled with high expectations for the delivery of housing, health care, water, electricity and the other elements of the 'better life for all' that had been promised by the ANC election slogan. Meanwhile the financial markets, military, civil service and the high value end of economic activity generally were all in hostile, suspicious or ambivalent hands, more or less loyal to the old order.

The South African Truth and Reconciliation Commission: morality and political transition

The South African Commission set up by Nobel laureate Nelson Mandela's Government and headed by Nobel laureate Desmond Tutu could not be mistaken for a foray into the cynical arts of 'transition management', the amoral abandonment of ethics in pursuit of the compromises that would cement social stability.[45] Our Commission was intended to have powerful moral resonances and its proceedings have even been criticised, by some, for having too many religious overtones.

These facts alone are hardly conclusive evidence of high moral intent: nor can the moral strength of the two laureates, however widely acknowledged, be sufficient in itself to persuade the cold legal mind of the value of the Commission. Indeed, there are some who have questioned the whole exercise on the grounds of the strong political views of the same two people.[46]

So let us look further. In a context where the apartheid government had tried to grant unilateral and blanket amnesties,[47] the drafters of our legislation insisted that there would be no automatic amnesty,[48] no blanket amnesty[49] and that certain

---

45 For a contrary view, see M. Cherif Bassiouni, who speaks disparagingly of truth commissions as essentially serving the end of peace and reconciliation, but not of justice. He also rules out any possibility of truth commissions addressing crimes against humanity or gross violations of human rights: 'Searching for Peace and Achieving Justice: The Need for Accountability' (1996) 59 *Law and Contemporary Problems* 9, 20.

46 L. Abrahams, 'Vision, Truth and Rationality' (1995) 23 *New Contrast* 64, 68 protests at what he sees as the global favouring of politics over truth in the form of amnesty being conferred 'on the politically motivated by the politically motivated'. This is a concern that an effective transitional justice process must address: that truth commissions are not set up in collusion with former enemies to provide a mutual blanket amnesty. See also R.A. Wilson, 'The Sizwe Will Not Go Away: The Truth and Reconciliation Commission, Human Rights and Nation-Building in South Africa' (1996) 55 *African Studies* 1, 18 (suggesting tendentiously that the South African truth commission and other human rights institutions are a mere distraction, concealing an actual disinclination to uphold human rights).

47 Further Indemnity Act of 1992, which allowed amnesty to be granted to those who had committed serious crimes, without the details of their crimes being made known.

48 Act, s 20(1).

49 s 4(a)(iv) clearly includes members of the liberation movement within the terms of reference of the TRC. See further, 'T.R.C. Moves to Quash its Own 37 Pardons' *Pretoria News*, 14 March 1998 (TRC asked the Cape High Court to overturn the amnesty committee's controversial decision to grant a blanket amnesty to 37 leading African National Congress members). Available at <www.ics-online.co.za/machx/preview/pta/index/html>.

10

offences, which were disproportionate to the alleged political objective, would receive no amnesty at all.[50] This means that criminal and/or civil liability would remain intact in respect of these offences. While the Commission itself was not a prosecutorial body, the door was left open for prosecutions to be brought in respect of all acts for which no amnesty had been sought or where, having been sought, it had been denied.[51]

The ANC is the only liberation movement that, before entering government, had already appointed commissions to investigate its own conduct. In fact, the one was conducted in 1992, when Nelson Mandela set up the 'Commission of Inquiry into Complaints by Former African National Congress Prisoners and Detainees', which focused on events at ANC detention camps located in various countries in Southern Africa. Although the ANC questioned some findings of the report, it was nevertheless released by the ANC to the public.[52]

Before the 1994 elections, there was a very real fear that the military and or upholders of the old order would refuse to accept a settlement, or would refuse to operate it. Although the ANC rejected all ideas of a blanket amnesty, part of the rationale for setting up the Truth and Reconciliation Commission (TRC) was the need to prevent further alienation of right-wing elements. This was understandable in the light of the shocking assassination of one of the principal leaders of the ANC, Chris Hani, and of the bombs and killings in the period leading up to the election.

Today however the threat of a right-wing uprising has receded. The military is in the process of reconstruction, the old generals are no longer in charge, and the situation cannot be compared to that in parts of Latin America, where the military was and often still is the prime threat.[53] Thus criminal trials, which were the central ingredient of justice in Latin America, become less central in my country.[54]

The crucial requirement of the South African transition is the need to reconstruct society and to abolish the horrendous inequalities which were produced by the apartheid system. The liberation movement has always been very clear that its major aim was not to replace a white government by a predominantly black one, but to transform the whole society. South Africa, as the ANC's Freedom Charter states, 'belongs to all who live in it' and the talents of all its citizens must be enlisted in the fight to eliminate poverty. In the longer term, if the inequalities are not reduced, the threat to South Africa could come not from right-wing violence but from a restless and alienated populace whose dream of a better future has receded. What would be the point of the struggle against injustice 'if in the end we remain subjected to a state which, even if ruled by Africans, only serves the rich and powerful'?[55] Our President, Thabo Mbeki, is fond of quoting Langston

---

50 Act, s 20(3)(f). The drafters of the Act followed international precedent set down in the Norgaard principles as to the criteria by which to grant or refuse amnesty. G.N. Barrie, 'The Norgaard Principles and the Truth Commission' (1996) 1 *SA Now: A View on Our Country* 8, 9–10.

51 In 1994, Justice Minister Dullah Omar made it clear that the aim of the TRC was not just to let bygones be bygones. L. McBlain, 'Justice For All: Interview with Dullah Omar' (1994) 7 *RSA Review* 1, 2.

52 P.B. Hayner, 'Fifteen Truth Commissions – 1974 to 1994: A Comparative Study' (1994) 16 *Human Rights Quarterly* 200, 239–240.

53 See regarding the negative effect of trials on transformation of the military, A.H. Henkin, 'Conference Report', in *State Crimes: Punishment or Pardon* (Queenstown, Maryland: The Aspen Institute, 1989) 7.

54 In different circumstances, even general political amnesty may work well, such as that granted in Spain after the end of Franco's rule. M. Albon, 'Report of the Project's Inaugural Meeting', in *Project of Justice in Times of Transition* (New York: The Charter Seventy-Seven Foundation, 1992) 9.

55 A question asked by the Angolan journal, *Poder Popular*, Casa de Angola No 6, 18 March 1975, just prior to independence in that country.

11

Hughes, the African American poet, who reminds us what happens to a dream deferred: it explodes. So South Africa must deal with the inequities it inherited and cannot finesse this challenge away[56] in a warm fog of rapprochement.[57]

But this fundamental challenge immediately places the idea of criminal trials in a new light. Criminal trials will not restore rights to those who were deprived in the past. Even though they may deter would-be criminals in the armed forces who might want to declare themselves ruling juntas, they cannot defuse a situation in which the dream has been deferred, in which an explosion may take place. This is why, from the very outset of the truth commission debate, in the midst of the transition, I personally linked the idea of a truth commission with the notion of reparations and social justice,[58] a theme which my co-authors and I carried through to our book on transitional justice in South Africa itself.[59]

We argued that transitional justice was not a mere matter of criminal trials;[60] that it had to be part of a systematic process of: acknowledging the illegitimacy of apartheid; acknowledging the need for corrective action to undo apartheid's racially skewed socio-economic legacy; establishing equality before the law, which meant reforming the criminal and other justice systems, far from placing them in the driver's seat of transition;[61] placing property rights on a legitimate footing, which means redistribution; facing up to the collective responsibility of the apartheid privileged, the majority of whom put their whites-only ballots behind the system for four decades; and acknowledging the claims of the regional and international communities, including the prevailing norms of international law.

The forms of transitional justice are diverse; it is unimaginative to think that criminal trial processes exhaust the means of achieving justice. Professor Charles Villa-Vicencio, a professor of religious studies who served as the South African Truth Commission's Director of Research, identifies at least five divergent forms that justice can take, including 'justice as the affirmation of human dignity'. These are: deterrent justice, which seeks to dissuade future perpetrators by making an example of past ones; compensatory justice, which requires beneficiaries of the old order to share in present-day restitution measures; rehabilitative justice, which attempts to remedy the maimed temperaments and or personalities of victims as well as perpetrators; justice as an affirmation of human dignity, which recognises the equal dignity of all, particularly where the prior atrocities were dealt out against categories of persons; and justice as exoneration, which rectifies the record as to those who were falsely accused, for example of being terrorists or spies.[62] If we take a sufficiently critical view of the diverse forms of justice, we begin to see

56 As Nelson Mandela noted in his Foreword to N.J. Kritz's *Transitional Justice* (United States Institute of Peace Research, 1995), xi: 'transition is accompanied by enormous challenges ... it signifies new hopes, but also difficult choices that countries must make on their road to democracy and economic progress'.
57 A compelling account of the relationship between socio-economic development and political regimes in emergent democracies is given by J.H. Herz, *From Dictatorship to Democracy: Coping With the Legacies of Authoritarianism and Totalitarianism* (Westport, CN: Greenwood Press, 1982) 287–288.
58 K. Asmal, 'Victims, Survivors and Citizens Human Rights, Reparations and Reconciliation' (1992) 8 *South African Journal on Human Rights* 490.
59 K. Asmal, L. Asmal and R.S. Roberts, *Reconciliation Through Truth: A Reckoning of Apartheid's Criminal Governance* 2nd edn (Oxford: James Currey, 1997).
60 *ibid,* 18–22.
61 For a jurisprudentially subtle account of the role of apartheid's judiciary, see David Dyzenhaus, *Truth, Reconciliation and the Apartheid Legal Order* (Johannesburg: Juta & Co, 1998), to which the author of this lecture contributed a Foreword, vii–x.
62 C. Villa-Vicencio, 'Why Perpetrators Should Not Always Be Prosecuted' (manuscript on file with the author) 12.

that truth commissions, if properly implemented, are a form of the pursuit of justice, rather than its sacrifice, as University of Cape Town Professor André du Toit has argued.[63] Certain human rights organisations have, moreover, accepted that the nature of accountability (a concept aligned with but distinct from justice) is also flexible. For example, impunity can be avoided and accountability achieved, by public disclosure of wrongdoing.[64]

Given the complexity of justice in transitional situations, the simplifications insisted upon by penal law fundamentalists are helpful neither to the South African transition, nor to transitions elsewhere. Those in the international human rights community who have a fundamentalist attachment to criminal trials have even insisted that all relevant Rwandans should be tried: yet this could reach a total of up to 100,000 people. Such a volume of trials would immobilise the judicial system of the United States, let alone that of Rwanda or of South Africa.[65]

Moreover, such trials as happened in South Africa during the transition to date did not go well: Magnus Malan, P.W. Botha's savage Minister of Defence, was put on trial for murder along with twenty-one others and was acquitted amidst recriminations within the prosecutorial team, including allegations and counter-allegations about the loyalties of the prosecutor, who previously had served the apartheid government.[66]

The central moral fact of political transitions, the circumstance that makes them morally distinctive, is that they involve a powerful desire to end the illegitimate and violent governance of the old regime, while also ensuring that the nature of governance changes forever under the new one. This means that the new government must consolidate its hold on the levers of power by coaxing the old bureaucratic functionaries away from their former loyalties, while at the same time ensuring that the new government does not forsake the cause for which it previously struggled, by inadvertently legitimising its illegitimate inheritance. As Juan Linz notes in his landmark study, 'the systematic exclusion or discrimination against the partisans of the [old regime] in many realms of public life, such as the

---

63 A. du Toit, 'The Moral Foundations of Truth Commissions: Truth as Acknowledgement and Justice as Recognition as Principles of Transitional Justice in the Practice of the South African TRC' ('the TRC's approach to transitional justice need not be construed as a moral compromise, sacrificing justice for the sake of truth and reconciliation') (manuscript on file with the author) 3, 5. See also, Graybill, n 40 above (argues persuasively at 119 that Nuremberg-type legal prosecutions would not have ensured more justice for victims than the TRC. 'It would be misleading to equate justice with the Nuremberg route and something less than justice with the TRC route'). Yet it is not impossible to find the old Manichean concepts at work in the thinking even of those who were very involved in the South African process. The Vice-Chairperson of the South African Commission, Alex Boraine, has said misleadingly that 'the central tension [in transitional justice] is between the politics of compromise and the radical notion of justice': quoted in Y. Beigbeder, *Judging War Criminals: The Politics of International Justice* (London: Macmillan Press Ltd, 1999) 122.

64 Human Rights Watch, 'Policy Statement on Accountability for Past Abuses' *Special Issue: Accountability for Past Human Rights Abuses*, (New York: Human Rights Watch, 1989) 1.

65 R. Goldstone, 'Failure to Deal with the Dark Past Spells Disaster' *South African Associated Press* 14 August 1997, quoted in Graybill, n 40 above 119. ('If one had to bring to court all the perpetrators of human rights abuses during the last 40 years, there just would not be enough courts to deal with it'). See also Neil J. Kritz, 'The Dilemmas of Transitional Justice', in N.J. Kritz (ed), *Transitional Justice* (United States Institute of Peace Research, 1995), xxiii. ('In Rwanda, after ousting a regime that organized genocidal killings of at least half a million people, if the new government were to undertake prosecution of every person who participated in this heinous butchery, some 30,000–100,000 Rwandan citizens could be placed in the dock – a situation that would be wholly unmanageable and extremely destabilizing to the transition. Moving the nation forward toward both justice and reconciliation plainly precludes an absolutist approach to the chain of responsibility'.)

66 See, 'Why McNally Lost the Malan Trial' *Weekly Mail and Guardian* (October 18, 1996). Available at <http://www.sas.upenn.edu/African_Studies/Listserv/Weekly_Mail_17980.html>.

13

bureaucracy, the armed forces, or the administration of interventionist economic policies, might push those ready to become a loyal opposition into semi- and disloyal positions'.[67] This is an extremely delicate balancing act. Criminal trials answer to the first need – a vivid line between the old illegitimacy and the new democracy – while not necessarily addressing the need to rehabilitate a bureaucracy which is needed to serve the new ideals, and so cannot be dismissed or imprisoned.[68]

This is not simply a matter of pragmatism, and of making the best in a difficult set of circumstances. It also involves a profoundly different view of what in fact constitutes justice, and whether justice is best served by taking retribution against those who have offended our view of justice, or by inducing the offender to see the error of his or her ways. The very first clause of Chapter 1, the founding provisions, of the Constitution of South Africa, states that the Republic is founded on the values of 'human dignity, the achievement of equality and advancement of human rights and freedoms'. Human dignity, equality and human rights are thus placed on an equal footing. Dignity is given pride of place, which has a strong echo of the values of traditional African society and culture in this country, where justice is not seen as a matter of adjudicating on competing rights between individuals, but on promoting cooperation between people and harmony within the community.

As Judge J.Y. Mokgoro, Judge of the Constitutional Court of South Africa, has said, 'the original conception of law [was] not as a tool for personal defence, but as an opportunity given to all to survive under the protection of the order of the communal entity'.[69]

Such insights are increasingly coming to the forefront of debates over how countries might best deal with oppressive pasts. It is a pity that, in general, the academic literature in this area has lacked the conceptual subtlety of longer running jurisprudential debates. But there are hopeful signs. Professor Ruti Teitel's book *Transitional Justice*, to be published by Oxford University Press next year, is the first attempt of which I am aware to relate the factual and conceptual challenges of transitional situations to the longer running debates. Professor Teitel faces up to the fact that law has a distinctive nature and function in situations of radical political change; that the rule of law itself must have a distinctive meaning in such circumstances. She correctly argues that we cannot simply take the notion of the rule of law that prevails in settled societies and transplant it uncritically into the different and fraught context of transitional justice. She instead identifies what she terms 'transitional jurisprudence', based on the observation that 'the transitional rule of law comprises distinctive values particular to [transitional] periods'.[70] She notes that in this sense, the Nuremberg legacy, the spectacle of perpetrators in the dock, is 'an anomalous precedent',[71] more honoured in the breach than the observance in subsequent human rights enforcement. Nuremberg encourages us to conflate justice with criminal trials, but the actual state practice of transitional justice has been more diverse.

---

67 See, J.J. Linz, *The Breakdown of Democratic Regimes: Crisis, Breakdown, and Requilibration'*, (Baltimore: Johns Hopkins University Press, 1978) 34.
68 For a persuasive argument that transitional administrations do not breach their moral duties by refraining from punishing all violators of human rights, see J. Malamud-Goti, 'Transitional Governments in the Breach: Why Punish State Criminals?' (1990) 12 *Human Rights Quarterly* 1, 5–6.
69 Judge J.Y. Mokgoro, 'Ubuntu and the Law in South Africa', paper delivered at the Colloquium, *Constitution and Law*, Potchefstroom 31 October 1997, and published by the Konrad Adenauer Stiftung, *Seminar Report of the Colloquium*, (Johannesburg: 1998).
70 R. Teitel, *Transitional Justice*, (forthcoming, Oxford: Oxford University Press, 2000) 7.
71 *ibid* 31.

14

Whatever the ultimate merits of Professor Teitel's particular jurisprudential approach,[72] her book is a hopeful sign that the conceptual depth of the study of transitional justice is at last increasing. I think that, finally, we are moving beyond Manichean platitudes.

Justice and reparations

If we move beyond the reflex assumption that justice in a political transition is measured by the number and success of criminal prosecutions, we quickly arrive again at the concept of reparations, and of restorative rather than punitive justice, a concept that in itself includes a number of important sub-debates.[73]

Within the United Nations, the debate about reparations centres on the following options:

- Restitution, requiring, *inter alia*, restoration of liberty, family life, citizenship, return to one's place of residence, and restoration of employment or property
- Compensation for physical or mental harm, lost opportunities, material damages and loss of earnings, harm to reputation or dignity, legal or expert costs
- Rehabilitation
- Satisfaction and guarantees of non-repetition.[74]

This list is not claimed to be exhaustive, but even confining ourselves to it, there are evident tensions, trade-offs, and potential incompatibilities. The restoration of citizenship or of family life suggests complex country-wide policy processes, with connotations of legislation and social reform – the issue seems to be undoing societal scars and broad injustices, averting a scenario of dreams deferred, that might explode. On the other hand, the provision of legal and expert costs suggests a

---

72 Professor Teitel's most original argument is that transitional jurisprudence has an autonomous impact on political transitions, so that law should not be seen as merely the outcome of broader political power balances. She argues passionately that 'transitional law transcends the "merely" symbolic to be the leading rite of modern political passage' (p 221). But her own arguments throughout imply that this assertion will be true in some contexts and less so in others. That law can itself make a distinct impact on the mix of factors influencing political transitions is a useful point; that it is always the leading influence is less compelling. Additionally, I believe that in some respects Teitel does not accurately characterise the arguments of the critical legal studies advocates, and therefore paints too static a picture of the rule of law in 'normal' or non-transitional settings. For instance, she argues at 25 that the fluidity of transitional justice presents an appropriate venue for the sort of 'hyperpoliticised adjudication' that critical theorists advocate. She suggests that in non-transitional situations, critical legal theorists' arguments about the highly politicised nature of law are less well placed. I myself view law as a form of congealed politics, so that I would personally be more fair to the critical theorists in the context of non-transitional justice, in normal times. This distance from the useful insights of critical legal studies becomes a significant problem when, towards the end of her book, Professor Teitel argues that 'transitional law's distinctive contribution to [political transition] is that it is both constrained by and transcendent of politics'. The idea that law – whether in normal or in transitional settings – participates at all in political 'transcendence' must give us pause after a century of legal realism.

73 See C. Villa-Vicencio. 'The Reek of Cruelty and the Quest for Healing: Where Retributive and Restorative Justice Meet' (manuscript on file with the author) 19. ('Deep healing involves more than a judicial ruling and more than monetary compensation, recognising that both are often immanently helpful. It involves the quest for a new quality of life and the creation of a milieu within which the atrocities of the past are less likely to recur in the future'.)

74 United Nations Commission on Human Rights, Note on the 'Basic Principles and Guidelines on the Right to Reparation for Victims of [Gross] Violations of Human Rights and International Humanitarian Law', submitted by the Special Rapporteur of the Sub-Commission on Prevention of Discrimination and Protection of Minorities, quoted by Beigbeder, n 63 above 105.

The Modern Law Review   [Vol. 63

narrower forum, akin to a courtroom – the issue seems to be the undoing of individual or personal injustice.

It would be convenient to skate over such issues and to say that the pursuit of individual and societal remedies are complementary rather than conflicting, or some such form of words. But in the real world of scarce resources and hard choices, this is simply not the case. If black South Africans are to be compensated in cash and individually for lost employment opportunities or forced removals alone, to take just two examples, the annual budget of our country would be wholly tied up for the foreseeable future, indeed, well into the unforeseeable future. Meanwhile, the dream of collective recovery would be deferred, and might explode. Social unrest would bring the curtain down on the well-meant programme of compensation for lost employment and forced relocations, along with much else.

Such perceptions underlay the position adopted in South Africa that reparations are to take the form not only of mandatory monetary compensation (although section 42 of the Act creates a President's fund from which payments may be made), but also of symbolic or other redress. The Commission itself recommended that a structure be developed in the President's Office to oversee the implementation of reparation and rehabilitation programmes, which would entail, among other things, financial reparation, the issuing of death certificates, the expedition of exhumations and burials and the facilitation of the resolution of outstanding legal matters relating to reported violations.[75] The Government is reviewing these proposals within the broader context of its plans for orderly societal change.

If we look again at the forms of reparation that feature in UN debates – measures to restore liberty, residence, employment and property; compensation for mental and physical deprivation and for lost dignity; rehabilitation of those who have suffered and guarantees that human rights abuses will not recur – these could easily be read as the stuff of modern governance in its entirety, rather than as a special case of the requirements of governance in transitional societies. What is unusual is that transitional societies, because we agree that they have had excessively unjust recent pasts, have an opportunity, through truth commissions and the like, to pause for introspection and to gather themselves into a new collective direction.[76]

For countries like South Africa, where the legacy is a particularly appalling institutionalised and society-wide one, the real value of truth commissions lies in their impact on the social consensus. It seems less important to me, personally and as a Minister of State, to see P.W. Botha behind bars than to see his ideological followers stalled in their quest to perpetuate his socio-economic legacies. In a system that killed far more infants through malnutrition and the unavailability of water than it killed adults with bullets and bombs, the drama to be had from placing militarists on trial might easily overshadow the equally real atrocity of the system itself. In the driest areas of South Africa, infant mortality rose to above 400 per thousand under apartheid.

---

75 *Truth and Reconciliation Commission of South Africa Report* (Cape Town: Juta, 1999) vol 5, ch 8, paras 22–23, 321.
76 M.H. Morris, 'International Guidelines Against Impunity: Facilitating Accountability' (1996) 59 *Law and Contemporary Problems* 29, 33 (truth commissions often have the credibility and authority that a private historian's account would lack). Additionally, John Hertz argues at 288 that the one factor required to constitute a minimally stable democracy is the creation of a democratic counter-image, and this in turn relies on exposing the truth about the previous regime. Therefore, there is an imperative to accomplish what the Germans call *Vergangenheitsbewaeltigung*, a coming to terms with one's past.

There is an analogy here between the longstanding debate in the international human rights community between civil and political rights on the one hand, and socio-economic rights on the other. The so-called first generation civil and political rights were for some time treated as the only real rights, but in recent times socio-economic rights have been acknowledged as equally important, not least in our own constitution, which includes rights of access to housing,[77] water, nutrition, and health.[78] Just as good governments will assure the fulfillment of first and second generation rights alike, bad governments will often flout both generations of rights (along with 'third generation' environmental rights).[79]

Our truth commission had ample legislative scope to investigate 'the entire edifice of apartheid'.[80] The Act deliberately left scope for the investigation of offences against both first and second generation rights. So it is wrong to say that the Act or the policy underlying it focused only on civil and political offences as a deliberate legislative choice.[81] In fact the Commission could and did address broad and systemic injustices. It for instance held hearings into various culpable sections of civil society, such as the medical profession, the legal profession, the business community and the judiciary.[82] But the Commission occasionally seemed hesitant to venture beyond traditional civil and political offences (particularly in relation to investigating the business community) and the media coverage of the Commission clearly focused disproportionately on the dramatic evil deeds done by those who sought amnesty from criminal prosecution. This is a failing more of the Commissioners and of their public relations machine than of the Act as passed by Parliament.

---

77 Constitution of the Republic of South Africa Act 108 of 1996, section 26. (1) Everyone has the right to have access to adequate housing. (2) The state must take reasonable legislative and other measures, within its available resources, to achieve the progressive realisation of this right. (3) No one may be evicted from their home, or have their home demolished, without an order of court made after considering all the relevant circumstances. No legislation may permit arbitrary evictions.

78 *ibid* s 27 (1) Everyone has the right to have access to: a. health care services, including reproductive health care; b. sufficient food and water; and c. social security, including, if they are unable to support themselves and their dependants, appropriate social assistance. (2) The state must take reasonable legislative and other measures, within its available resources, to achieve the progressive realisation of each of these rights. (3) No one may be refused emergency medical treatment.

79 This is not always the case. Supporters of the Pinochet regime like to trumpet its economic successes, just as the Nazis flaunted the Volkswagen and the fall in joblessness under their rule.

80 Asmal, Asmal and Roberts, n 59 above 25.

81 M. Mamdani, 'Reconciliation Without Justice' (1996) 46 *Southern African Review of Books*, available at <http://www.uni-ulmde/~rturrell/antho3html/Mamdani.html> (critiques what he takes to be the terms of reference of the Truth and Reconciliation Commission, 'whereby injustice is no longer the injustice of apartheid: forced removals, pass laws, broken families. Instead, the definition of injustice has come to be limited to abuses within the legal framework of apartheid: detention, torture, murder. Victims of apartheid are now narrowly defined as those militants victimised as they struggled against apartheid, not those whose lives were mutilated in the day-to-day web of regulations that was apartheid. We arrive at a world in which reparations are for militants, those who suffered jail or exile, but not for those who suffered only forced labour and broken homes'.) See also J. Dugard, 'Is the Truth and Reconciliation Process Compatible with International Law? An Unanswered Question' (1997) 13 *South African Journal of Human Rights* 258, 260. (The phrase 'severe ill treatment of any person' in s19(3)(b)(iii) of the Promotion of National Unity and Reconciliation Act will 'clearly be narrowly interpreted to mean physical ill treatment, as this accords with the categories of crime that precede it' in the statutory clause in question). Both these views adopt a view of the statutory scope of the Act which is not laid down in the plain language of the Act. They misread the terms of reference established by the Act. The commission was free, as my co-authors and I argued, to have interpreted the Act more broadly, so as to examine the entire socio-economic edifice of apartheid. (Asmal, Asmal and Roberts, n 59 above, 25–26.) The proper scope and interpretation of the phrase 'severe ill treatment' was in fact much more intensely debated (within the commission itself as well as in public discussion) than Dugard's rather conclusory plain language argument might suggest.

82 For a useful discussion of this aspect of the truth commission's work, see Graybill, n 40 above.

17

This is not to suggest, however, that the Act was flawless. Since only those who feared criminal prosecution under the old apartheid laws needed to apply for amnesty, the ordinary daily consequences of apartheid, which were not criminal under the old laws, did not fall within the drama of the amnesty hearings, even if they did fall within the proper scope of the legislation. It may well be that the first step in the transitional justice process ought to have been the ratification of the 1973 Convention on the Suppression of the Crime of Apartheid, which called on subscribing states to punish acts of apartheid in their local criminal justice systems.[83] This would have meant that the 'desk murderers', those who had implemented the mundane and everyday policies of apartheid, would have had to seek amnesty from criminal prosecution. The problem with this suggestion is that it would have exacerbated the risks of subversion and made more complex, perhaps impossible, the task of winning over the loyalty of the bureaucracy from their erstwhile apartheid masters. Those who insist that new governments are uniformly under an absolute obligation to prosecute human rights abusers are well intentioned, but what they advocate may turn out to be destructive rather than beneficial.[84] Even respected groups like Amnesty International can fall into this trap on occasion.[85]

One of the most poignant contributions to the discussion about truth commissions is that made by Ignacio Martin-Baro, one of six Jesuit priests murdered in El Salvador in 1989. Just before his death, he wrote in favour of truth commissions, and brought to light a point that many human rights fundamentalists miss – that the justness of amnesty depends on the process by which it has been granted: 'the problem turns on whether that pardon and renunciation are going to be established on the foundation of truth and justice, or on lies and continued injustices'.[86] This links the justice of amnesty to the justness (or otherwise) of the

---

83 N. Fritz, a researcher at the South African Constitutional Court, made this observation. See also, N. Fritz *Sighs of the Bridge: The South African Truth and Reconciliation Process and International Law Obligations*, (unpublished manuscript on file with the author), 28 (noting that in the absence of legislation criminalising socio-economic aspects of apartheid, socio-economic crimes against humanity remain outside the incentives set up by the South African commission, since socio-economic perpetrators face no liability, hence need no amnesty). Additionally, John Dugard notes that while South Africa's interim constitution (under which the founding election in 1994 was held) took no account of international crimes, the final constitution, passed by the democratic legislature in 1996, provides that everyone has the right not to be convicted for an act or omission that was not an offence 'under either national *or international law* at the time it was committed or omitted' (Constitution of the Republic of South Africa, s 35(3)(1)). J. Dugard, 'Retrospective Justice: International Law and the South African Model', in J. McAdams (ed), *Transitional Justice and the Rule of Law in New Democracies* (Notre Dame: Notre Dame University Press, 1997) 269–270. This acknowledges international law as a legitimate basis for subsequent criminal prosecution, even in the absence of a relevant criminal inhibition under the criminal law of the prior regime. Thus the question is not a lack of legal basis for prosecution, but whether prosecution would, at this juncture, advance conceptions of justice in South Africa.
84 The best recent article on the absoluteness or otherwise of the duty to prosecute is S. Michael, 'The Letter of the Law: The Scope of the International Legal Obligation to Prosecute Human Rights Crimes' (1996) 59 *Law and Contemporary Problems* 41. See generally, Orentlicher, n 32 above; and Z. Motala, 'The Promotion of National Unity and Reconciliation Act, the Constitution and International Law' (1995) 28 CILSA 338, 353–357.
85 In a policy statement in 1991, Amnesty International insisted that alleged perpetrators should be brought to trial and that their trials should include a clear verdict of guilt or innocence. Amnesty International did, however, doff its hat to restorative measures, saying that it 'took no position on post-conviction pardons': 'Policy Statement on Impunity', *Oral Statement by Amnesty International Before the United Nations Commission on Human Rights, Sub-Committee on Prevention of Discrimination and Protection of Minorities,* (Amnesty International, International Secretariat, 1991) 3–4.
86 Ignacio Martin-Baro, 'Reparations: Attention Must be Paid' (1990) *Commonwealth* 185.

society which grants it. It is noteworthy that the UN-sponsored El Salvador truth commission had called, upon the publication of its report, for uncompromising prosecution of forty named offenders – and the Government five days later passed a general amnesty, to avert the threat of military upheaval.[87] The call for aggressive prosecutions thus boomeranged and led to an end result of outright impunity. A less seemingly radical approach at the outset might have been more practically effective in saving Mr Baro's life.

International justice: beyond retribution?

Stepping back from the uncertainties of transitional justice within national political systems, from the relatively subtle and refined notions of justice that prevail there, it is striking to note that punishment-driven notions of justice, as opposed to restorative or other forms, have been prevalent in the international sphere.[88] In the 1990s, two international criminal tribunals, the International Criminal Court, and, most recently, the Independent International Commission for Kosovo have been established: the international sphere has a seemingly pro-punishment ethos. Indeed, arguably the most innovative and adventurous action taken by the Security Council since the end of the Cold War was the imaginative way it interpreted its Chapter VII powers to allow it to set up the International Criminal Tribunal for the Former Yugoslavia[89] – a step taken in the name of prosecution and punishment.

Yet, at the very heart of both International Criminal Tribunals, ostensibly pro-punishment entities, one actually finds truth commissions and a more discriminating and practical form of justice. In 1994, the UN established truth commissions in Yugoslavia[90] and Rwanda,[91] and their authoritative reports boosted the political momentum for bringing perpetrators to justice.[92] The work of the truth commissions also provided the basis for early indictments once the criminal tribunals had been set up.[93]

Given that the prosecutor-driven International Criminal Tribunal for the former Yugoslavia (ICTY) gained momentum from the prior work of a non-retributive truth commission, it is appropriate that the ICTY prosecutions themselves have shown up the inherent limitations of a purely retributive response to human rights

---

87 Hayner, n 52 above, 242.
88 For a useful account of retributive justice, including a discussion of 'positive' and 'negative' retributivism, see J. Malamud-Goti, 'Transitional Governments in the Breach: Why Punish State Criminals?' (1990) 12 *Human Rights Quarterly* 1.
89 Instead of initiating the traditional process of an international treaty, the Security Council used its powers under Article 39 of Chapter VII to 'determine the existence of any threat to the peace, breach of the peace, or act of aggression and ... make recommendations, or decide what measures shall be taken ... to maintain or restore international peace and security'. This is the first time the Security Council has created a judicial body as a means to 'restore international peace and security'.
90 See generally Final Report of the Commission of Experts Established Pursuant to Security Council Resolution 780 (1992), UN SCOR, 49th Sess, UN Doc. S/1994/674 (1994) available at <http://www.un.org/Docs/>. The ICTY has been hailed as a tremendous advance of international law, and, alongside the Rwanda Tribunal, it certainly provided an effective spur for the adoption of the International Criminal Court statute. See, for example, P. Akhavan, 'The Yugoslav Tribunal at a Crossroads: The Dayton Peace Agreement and Beyond' (1996) 18 *Human Rights Quarterly*, and Beigbeder n 63 above, 166–167.
91 See generally Final Report of the Commission of Experts Established Pursuant to Security Council Resolution 935 (1994), U.N. SCOR, 49th Sess., UN Doc. S/1994/1405 (1994), available at <http://www.un.org/Docs/>.
92 M.P. Scharf, 'The Case for a Permanent International Truth Commission' (1997) 7 *Duke Journal of Comparative & International Law* 380.
93 *ibid.*

19

abuse. Judge Richard Goldstone, a member of the South African Constitutional Court and previous chief prosecutor of the ICTY, has now increasingly spoken in favour of doing justice through truth commissions rather than through prosecutions.[94]

Ironically, the ICTY itself is beginning to come full circle, moving away from a prosecutorial style towards a process more in the style of a truth commission[95] that would be less formal and alienating than a court. In complete contrast, the Rwandans have moved consistently away from the truth commission roots of their process of facing the past. This well illustrates the fluidity that attaches to attempts to define justice during political transitions. In thus moving from punishment-based models to approaches that are more compatible with transitional fluidity, international law itself may well outlast the obituaries currently being written in its name.[96]

The violence that erupted in Rwanda in 1994 interrupted the country's slow and difficult political transition. In late 1992, the Government and the armed opposition negotiated the Arusha Accords, which contained an agreement to establish a commission of inquiry into past atrocities.[97] The Rwandan Government went so far as to petition a French organisation to set up a truth commission, but the request was declined. When the UN truth commission was established, it was given a formal welcome by the Rwandan President.[98]

The horror of the 1994 genocide changed forever the Rwandan political landscape. The truth commission approach was abandoned. As early as September 1994, the new Government itself actually proposed the establishment of an international prosecutorial tribunal, long before any serious consideration was given to the matter by other states.[99] A letter from the Permanent Representative of Rwanda to the President of the Security Council stated that the Government did not believe it possible to 'arrive at true national reconciliation' without eradicating the 'culture of impunity' which characterised Rwandan society. Essential to the construction of 'a new society based on social justice',[100] the Government now asserted, was an international criminal tribunal: retributive justice. Swift and harsh retribution alone, the Government now felt, would end the cycle of violence begun in the 1950s, and only once the rule of law was re-established could socio-

---

94 Quoted by D. Arnold. 'Speaker Goldstone Calls for Justice in War Crimes – South African Judge Praises Truth Commissions' *Stanford Daily* January 14, 1998. The article can be found at <http:// daily.stanford.org/daily97%2D98/1%2D14%2D98/news/newjustice14.html>. Indeed, Goldstone has asserted that public acknowledgement of the suffering of victims, and the giving of a voice to the voiceless – both classic functions of truth commissions – are in themselves forms of justice.

95 Three separate national war crimes commissions were established in the former Yugoslavia, and each has served some of the functions of a truth commission in that they have provided an opportunity for victims to come forward and tell their stories. In 1997, however, the leaders of the commissions acknowledged they were creating three separate and conflicting versions of history. There have increasingly been calls for the creation of one joint Bosnia-wide commission, an idea which has actively been supported by the ICTY. See N.J. Kritz, 'Coming to Terms With Atrocities: A Review of Accountability Mechanisms for Mass Violations of Human Rights' (1996) 59 *Law and Contemporary Problems* 127, 143–4.

96 Teitel, n 70 above, argues that, notwithstanding signs of life such as moves towards an International Criminal Court, 'the historical justification for framing the successor justice question in international terms has largely dissipated. Postwar hopes for developing an international criminal law today remain largely unfulfilled. The early enthusiasm for international law's advances is now tempered by sober reflection on the relative inefficiency of international mechanisms for responding to atrocity'.

97 Hayner, n 52 above 242.

98 *ibid.*

99 P. Akhavan, 'The International Criminal Tribunal for Rwanda: The Politics and Pragmatics of Punishment' (1996) 90 *The American Journal of International Law* 504.

100 *ibid* 505.

economic rebuilding be contemplated. This view is diametrically opposed to that of the South African Government on its own, different, situation.

Although the international community heeded the Rwandan Government's call for a criminal tribunal, it viewed the factual situation in Rwanda differently, and did not fully endorse the harsh, unforgiving notions of justice seen by Rwanda as imperative.[101] This divergence led Rwanda, which was a member of the Security Council, to vote against Resolution 955 establishing the Criminal Tribunal under Chapter VII. The Rwandan Government fired a barrage of criticisms at the Statute of the Tribunal, all of which stemmed from the Government's heavily retributive focus. It strongly objected that the death penalty, which was provided for in the Rwandan penal code, would not be imposed by the tribunal, and it disparaged the concurrent jurisdiction of other nations to prosecute Rwandan war criminals who were within their borders, asserting that some countries might 'be inclined to let the perpetrators of genocide go free'.[102] The Government also argued that the temporal restriction of the jurisdiction of the Tribunal to 1994 cut out the long period of planning that preceded the genocide, and was thus unacceptable; and that the seat of the Tribunal should be in Rwanda in order to 'teach the Rwandan people a lesson, to fight against the impunity to which it had been accustomed . . . and to promote national reconciliation'.[103]

Yet, hidden within this retributive focus, one can discern a more constructive aim, looking to rebuild the shattered country. As a result of the widespread carnage caused by the 1994 genocide, most of Rwanda's infrastructure was destroyed, leaving a state without a police force or a judiciary.[104] The ICTY was seen by the Rwandan Government as a vital component in the whole reconstruction project necessary to fill this void, and indeed the Tribunal did send people to Rwanda to train new judges and police. Even within a heavily retributive environment, therefore, room was still made for measures designed to reconstruct society.

The recent establishment of the Independent International Commission for Kosovo (IICK) reflects a growing uncertainty as to whether criminal trials are adequate to manage the aftermath of civil conflicts in the last decade. While the Yugoslav Tribunal's prosecutors may be able to answer the immediate calls of both the international community and ethnic Albanian refugees for high level indictments,[105] a different forum is necessary to explore how such tragedies might in future be avoided. It is instructive that the international community, appalled by witnessing, in CNN technicolour, the destructive bombardment of a country and its attendant horrors, should fall back on a political rather than a legal mechanism. Given that the IICK is free to determine its own frame of reference, it can include within its investigations a consideration of the interplay between *realpolitik* and action taken in the name of human rights. Indeed, the necessity of engaging in such an analysis has already been identified by the commission.

---

101 International opinion actually swung in the other direction and it was felt that there was a need for 'pragmatism to temper an absolutist approach to prosecution'. This resulted in the formulation of an expedited 'confession and guilty plea' procedure, which ran along the same lines as a truth commission, requiring perpetrators fully to confess their crimes and formally to apologise to their victims in order to qualify for 'a significantly reduced schedule of penalties', Kritz, n 95 above, 135–136.
102 UN Doc S/PV.3453 (1995). Available at <http://www.un.org/Docs/>.
103 *ibid.*
104 Ninety-five per cent of Rwanda's judges were killed or sent into exile. See Akhavan, n 99 above 510.
105 See M.S. Ellis 'Non-Negotiable: War Criminals Being in the Dock, Not at the Table' *Washington Post* 9 May 1999, B1. Ellis recounts his experiences in the Stenkovec refugee camp, and describes the refugees' common 'yearning for justice' through high level political leaders being held criminally accountable for orchestrating what is still euphemistically called ethnic cleansing.

The appointment of a truth commission in Nigeria in September 1999 acknowledges the usefulness of this manner of justice. The Nigerian Commission will investigate 8,000 cases submitted by the Ogoni people (whose leader, Ken Saro-Wiwa, was hanged), as well as 2,000 other cases, many of which relate to the events surrounding the cancellation of the 1993 election results by the then military government.[106]

The international community has, however, recognised in an even more fundamental way the need to accommodate both retributive and restorative responses to conflicts involving genocide, crimes against humanity and war crimes. The 1998 Rome Statute establishing a permanent International Criminal Court (ICC) acknowledges as one of its fundamental principles that national criminal systems retain jurisdiction over international crimes, and that States can validly put themselves beyond the jurisdiction of the ICC either through *bona fide* prosecution at national level, or through *bona fide* truth commission processes. The United Nations Secretary General Kofi Annan said as much in Johannesburg recently.[107] This is not by any means to say that an easy solution (or any solution at all) to the debate has as yet been found. The Court will in fact be faced with the complex and politically uncertain task of adjudicating whether decisions not to prosecute are valid, or whether they result from 'the unwillingness or inability of the State genuinely to prosecute'.[108]

The relationship between domestic forums and the ICC is also ambiguous, and the notion of complementary national and international jurisdiction is unclear. Commentators seem to agree that 'complementarity', as it has been termed,[109] is a crucial issue, which determines the role that the Court will play.[110] However, the precise meaning of this soothing term remains elusive.[111]

Closely allied to the issue of complementarity are questions about the very way in which international crimes have come to be understood. The prevailing assumption has been that the ICC would address those crimes imprinted on the collective conscience[112] by the increasing brutality of successive conflicts. Only these customary law crimes – genocide, crimes against humanity (including apartheid), war crimes and aggression – were included in the Rome Statute. A conscious decision was taken early on in the process of codifying post-Nuremberg international crimes[113] to exclude crimes without a 'political element', such as piracy, drug trafficking and counterfeiting.[114] The ensuing disputes over, for

---

106 Johannesburg *Business Day*, 20 September 1999. Available at <http://www.bday.co.za/cgi-bin/post-queryfm.cgi>.

107 Speaking after receiving an honorary doctorate of law at the University of the Witwatersrand on Tuesday, 1 September, 1998.

108 Art 17(1)(b).

109 M.C. Bassiouni, 'Introduction' in M. Cherif Bassiouni (ed*)*, *The International Criminal Court: Observations and Issues Before the 1997–97 Preparatory Committee; and Administrative and Financial Implications.* (Toulouse: Ères, 1996) 21–22.

110 See, J.L. Bleich, 'Complementarity', in M. Cherif Bassiouni (ed) n. 109 above 231–233; and Christopher Blakesley, 'Jurisdiction, Definition of Crimes and Triggering Mechanisms', in M. Cherif Bassiouni (ed) n 109 above 201–203.

111 See, generally, C. Blakesley, n 110 above. Moreover, if the experience of the ICTR is anything to go by, complementary jurisdiction is rather a hindrance to the proper function of justice. For more on this see Frederik Harhoff, 'Consonance or Rivalry? Calibrating the Efforts to Prosecute War Crimes in National and International Tribunals' (1997) 7 *Duke Journal of Comparative and International Law* 571, 583.

112 Termed *jus cogens* crimes, or norms recognised at international level as fundamental.

113 This process culminated in the production of several successive versions of the Draft Code on Crimes Against the Peace and Security of Mankind, the latest one being released in 1996.

114 L.S. Sunga, *The Emerging System of International Criminal Law: Developments in Codification and Implementation* (The Hague: Kluwer Law International, 1997) 4.

example, whether or not international drug trafficking should be included, need not concern us here, since there is no question of setting up truth commissions to deal with such crimes.

Nevertheless these competing visions of an international criminal court, and of the work that such a court might do, are a useful way to highlight, in closing, what it is that we mean when we talk about transitional justice, international law and ultimately about international justice. First, we are – or ought to be – in the realm of debate and not of arbitrary fiat. Global institutions must mature to the point where they are forums for real debate, not the forced consensus of veto powers and such exercises in vote-rigging, the sorts of mechanisms that the De Klerk government tried and failed to introduce into the national politics of South Africa.

If we lose sight of such issues – of the way in which global institutions impact on the way the world decides which injustices shall be censored or punished, and which not – then we will find our national processes of transition held hostage to global norms not of our own making.[115] This point can be illustrated even with reference to our own, ostensibly domestic, truth commission process. As I have already suggested, the global discourse of transitional justice has been conceptually simplistic to date. The tendency has been (particularly in South Africa) to extrapolate from conflicts elsewhere – notably the 'dirty wars' of Latin America – and to assume that, since there were abuses on all sides in those conflicts, there must be a similar equivalence also in South Africa.[116] Globalisation itself, including the globalisation of human rights, remains contested territory. This is a contest from which we dare not shrink.

It is up to all of us to ensure that when we talk about various national transitional experiences 'in perspective', which I have taken to mean 'in international perspective', we have exerted ourselves in advance to ensure that that perspective is as equitable as it can be.

Conclusion

Tonight I have tried to develop a third way through times of political transition, a way between the stark extremes of naivete and realpolitik. Through this perspective, I have presented the South African experience as something of a model. This is not merely my own jingoistic chest-thumping. In international debates over transitional justice, the South African experiment is increasingly seen as a rich and complex model from which much can be learned, whatever its inevitable flaws.

In South Africa, we had prosecutions of some offenders and will have prosecutions of some more. Some of those prosecutions have failed (for instance that of murderous 1980s general Magnus Malan and 21 of his colleagues), while others have succeeded (for instance that of apartheid hit-man Eugene De Kock). But we also realised that over-reliance on trials would be a wasteful diversion of administrative and political resources; that trials would traumatise the country and

---

115 O. Yasuaki, 'The Tokyo Trial: Between Law and Politics', in *The Tokyo War Crimes Trial: An International Symposium* (New York: Harper and Row, 1986), where for instance he comments on the 'contradictions between the emergence of non-Western powers in Asia and the persistence of Westcentric structures of information and culture in international society'.

116 This is not to say that we should ignore international comparative experience, rather that we should not misconstrue its import, not ignore relevant contextual differences. I have myself written on the Latin American experience. K. Asmal, 'Coping With the Past: The Latin American Experience' (1994) 10 *UNISA Latin America Report* 22.

derail redistribution of power and resources. Therefore we insisted upon an amnesty arrangement, but also refused to grant amnesty without fact-finding. We coupled forgiveness with truth, insisting on full disclosure of past misdeeds. In the end, our truth commission recognised the legitimacy of the struggle against apartheid and also recognised the utter illegitimacy of apartheid and the various self-serving justifications that it peddled in favour of itself (for instance, that the apartheid regime was a bulwark in the fight against "communism"). Our third path towards transitional justice validated the decades-long consensus within the international community on the nature and status of apartheid.

Correspondingly, these developments within South Africa, must be placed in an international perspective. The lessons of crime and punishment within domestic systems have influenced and been influenced by developments at the international level. In making peace and minimising war we must, as in so many other arenas, think local and act global. In this way we may at long last awake from what Yeats calls the "twenty centuries of stony sleep/vexed to nightmare by a rocking cradle." In this way, we can perhaps teach ourselves to hope again for optimism unbroken by cynicism. No longer, then, need idealism cower in nihilism's shadow, nor in the false virtue of naivete. And then, only then, might we perhaps with Seamus Heaney hope for one of those rare historical moments "when hope and history rhyme."

[19]

Youth Development Circles

JOHN BRAITHWAITE

ABSTRACT *Restorative justice circles or conferences have shown considerable promise in the criminal justice system as a more decent and effective way of dealing with youthful law breaking than punishment. The social movement for restorative justice has a distinctive analysis of the crisis of community and the possibility of community in late modernity. This paper raises the question of whether this approach might fruitfully be applied to the holistic development of the learning potential of the young and the whole range of problems young people encounter—drug abuse, unemployment, homelessness, suicide, among others—in the transition from school to work.*

THE LATE MODERN STRUCTURAL DILEMMA OF HUMAN AND SOCIAL CAPITAL

In the new information economy, it is clear that human capital (the skills of people) and social capital (social skills for interacting with others including dispositions such as trust and trustworthiness) are becoming progressively more important to economic development than physical capital (Dowrick, 1993; Fukuyama, 1995; Latham, 1998). Young people whose human and social capital remains undeveloped are destined for unemployment. Mostly families with high endowments of human and social capital pass those on to their children. There is a strong correlation between parental involvement in the education of their children and academic performance (Finn Report, 1991, p. 151). For children whose families lack endowments of human and social capital, we rely on state-funded education systems to compensate.

Yet we quickly run up against the limits of the capabilities of formal education bureaucracies to make up for deficits which are profoundly informal (especially on the social capital side) [1]. Our objective in this essay is to come up with a new policy solution to this limitation [2]. At the same time, we want to help solve the problem of children from families with high endowments, but where human and social capital development is interrupted by problems like drug addiction, bullying by peers, sexual abuse, depression and suicide.

Our hypothesis is that both the low family endowments problem and the interrupted transmission problem need a more informal yet more systematic solution than the formal education system can provide. Mentoring programmes like 'Big Brothers' and 'Big Sisters' head in the right direction (reducing drug abuse and violence in one eight-site evaluation (Elliott, 1998, p. xviii)). But they are insufficiently social, communal and plural to deal with the kinds of deficits at issue with reducing youth unemployment, drug addiction, delinquency and suicide.

In terms of social structure, we see the problem as one of a late modernity where:

240   *Oxford Review of Education*

(a) nuclear families are isolated from extended families which used to compensate for deficits of nuclear families; and

(b) formal education bureaucracies are too formal to compensate for the social aspects of the deficits that thereby arise—for example, in teaching trust, love, respectfulness.

This structural dilemma of late modernity has crept up on us over the past century. Social historians have shown that early in the 20th century parents much more commonly than today shared child-rearing obligations with extended families, churches and other community networks (Lasch, 1977; Zelizer, 1985). Single parents, who in Western societies are more likely to be black and poor (LaFree, 1998, pp. 147–148), are particularly likely to become 'solo practitioners' of child rearing. Mothers struggling alone to educate their children without support from the village therefore worsen inequalities of race and sex. Remedial policies to spread burdens of informal education and support for children are thus imperative to tackling the inequalities arising from our dual structural dilemma of modernity.

HOW THE EDUCATION SYSTEM CAN LEARN FROM THE CRIMINAL JUSTICE SYSTEM

The direction for a solution to this dual structural problem is captured by the African proverb that it takes a whole village to raise a child. But this of course begs the question raised by the structural problem; we do not live in villages in the West. Recent experience with restorative justice innovation in the criminal justice system has come up with an interesting solution to a similar structural dilemma of crime control. Criminologists know that crime is a result of failures of informal community ordering (Sampson & Laub, 1993; Sampson & Raudenbush, 1999) and of social support for young people (Cullen, 1994). Unfortunately, however, most remedial programmes fail because of the structural impossibility of building village solutions in the city or suburb. Neighbourhood Watch seems like a good idea, but the evidence is that it is not very effective in reducing crime (Sherman *et al.*, 1997). One reason is that most of us do not care enough about our community or are just too busy to turn up to Neighbourhood Watch meetings. They work somewhat better in highly organised middle-class communities— where they are least needed in terms of crime.

A recent innovation that has been quite successful in solving this problem has been the restorative justice or family group conference (as they are called in the Southern hemisphere) or healing circle (as they are more often called in North America). Actually, it is an innovation that picks up ancient village traditions of justice and adapts them to the metropolis. When a young person is arrested, they are asked who are the people they most respect, trust, love. The most common answers are mum and dad, brothers and sisters and grandparents. But often with children who are homeless because they have been sexually abused by parents, parents will not be on the list. Members of a 'street family' (Hagan & McCarthy, 1997) may be on the list here. But there still may be an aunt, brother, or grandparent who is loved by the homeless child. That child may have been stigmatised by most of the teachers at his or her school, but there may be just one staff member who he or she believes has treated her decently. That member of the school staff, the street family and the few members of the extended family who are still respected are then brought together in a conference. The conference sits in a circle with victims of the crime (and supporters of the victim) to discuss the consequences of the crime and what needs to be done to right the wrongs that have been done and to get the young offender's and the victim'sl ives back on track. With a homeless child, it might be agreed that the young offender will go and live in the home of his uncle or his older brother, who will undertake to help him get back into school.

The diversity of supporters for young people in conferences or circles is considerable. There can be elders from an indigenous community, football coaches, ballet teachers, neighbours, or friends who share a hobby. It is this diversity which makes the circle modern and urban. Human beings are social animals. There are almost always other human beings they enjoy interacting with. It is simply not true that most homeless children are alone in the world; they have 'street families' whose company they enjoy. Hagan and McCarthy (1997) found that a majority of their youth living on the streets of Toronto and Vancouver actually referred to their intimates as their 'street family'. Second, human beings find meaning from social identity; there always exist people we identify with or respect. We train circle coordinators who report back that ay oung offender who is totally isolated should try again, to work harder to discover people she likes or respects, even if it means bringing in the one sibling or uncle who is respected from another city. The late modem sense of community is fragmented across space, but itexist s. What the restorative justice circle does is bring that community of care together for the first time in one room. In the quintessentially late modem case, one of the participants may be a friend from cyberspace who the young offender physically meets for the first time. It is wrong to say that these faceless friendships are always artificial and meaningless. Community in the metropolis is in some ways more meaningful than community in the village because it can be based on casting a wide net among a very large group of people to find a few who have very similar interests to our own, such as an interest in the history of Reggae music which would be hard to share in a small English village.

Early evidence is only preliminary, but it is encouraging that these conferences mostly work well in various ways, though we still have much to learn about contexts where they backfire (Braithwaite, 1999). The fact from this literature we want to emphasise here is that when supporters are invited to attend these conferences, they generally come. I do not go to Neighbourhood Watch Meetings, even though I think that would be a public spirited thing to do. But if a young neighbour singled me out as someone they would like to be their supporter at a conference after they had got into trouble with the police, I would attend. Why? The answer is that in the conference case I am honoured to have been nominated by a human being as someone they respect. Second, I am personally touched by their predicament. They are in trouble and they have made a personal appeal to me, so I feel it would be callous to be unwilling to give up my evening for the conference. In short, community fails with Neighbourhood Watch but works with the restorative justice conference because it is an individual-centred communitarianism. This individual-centred communitarianism tugs at the sense of obligation that works in the late modern world of community based on geographically dispersed ties of respect and identification.

To date, the evaluation research evidence is consistent with this conclusion. More than a dozen studies have found participant satisfaction (among offenders, victims and their families) running at over 90% (Braithwaite, 1999, pp. 20–27). Both participant satisfaction and participant perceptions of procedural fairness, effectiveness, respect for rights and equality before the law are higher in conference than in court (Braithwaite, 1999, p. 26). It is premature to conclude whether restorative justice conferences are in fact effective in reducing crime. A number of studies show markedly lower reoffending

242   *Oxford Review of Education*

rates among young offenders who go to conferences compared to those who go to court (Forsythe, 1995; Chan, 1996). Large parts of such differences are likely to be selection effects—less serious cases going to conferences—in studies with inadequate controls. Burford and Pennell's (1998) study of adult family violence conferences has more impressive controls and found substantial reductions for conference compared to control families in 31 problem behaviours ranging from alcohol abuse to violence against wives or children. Most notably, abuse/neglect incidents halved in the year after the family group decision making conference. Other early studies of victim–offender mediation with more adequate controls (or randomisation) and with positive effects on reoffending were conducted by Schneider (1986), Pate (1990), Nugent & Paddock (1995) and Wynne (1996). Umbreit *et al.* (1994) found results that favoured victim–offender mediation, but which did not reach statistical significance. McCold & Wachtel's (1998) findings were mixed at best, discouraging at worst, findings that are hard to interpret because of unsatisfactory assurance that the randomly assigned treatment was delivered. The Restorative Justice Group at the Australian National University is finalising the largest randomised controlled trial of conferences compared to court for juvenile and adult offenders under the leadership of Lawrence Sherman and Heather Strang. An update of the Braithwaite (1999) review has been completed as this article goes to press (Braithwaite, forthcoming). It reports a surge of new studies suggesting that restorative justice does contribute to crime reduction.

Now we will seek to translate to education as an institution our analysis from the sociology of crime about what mobilises community. In doing so, we will also attempt to solve one of the problems of restorative justice circles—that the very act of assembling the community of care on the occasion of a youth being in trouble can stigmatise a young person as a troublemaker.

YOUTH DEVELOPMENT CIRCLES—THE IDEA

The basic idea is to translate the conference/circle from criminal justice into the arena of educational development. Unlike conferencing in the criminal justice system, the idea presented now has not been subjected to any piloting. The main difference is that the circle would be a permanent feature of the young person's life rather than an ad hoc group assembled to deal with a criminal offence. Initially, the circle would be constituted to replace parent–teacher interviews in high schools.

Twice a year from entry to high school at age 12 through to successful placement in a tertiary course or a job (modal age 18), the Youth Development Facilitator (operating from an office in a high school) would convene a meeting of the young person's community of care. This meeting would be called a Youth Development Circle.

The circle would have Core and Casual Members. Core Members would be asked up front to commit, as an obligation of citizenship and care, to try to attend all circles *until the young person is successfully placed in a tertiary course or a job* and to continue to be there for him/her should the young person subsequently request a Circle or get in trouble with the police or the courts. Core members would actually sign a contract to keep meeting and helping the young person until that tertiary or job placement was accomplished.

Core Members would normally include:

- Parents or Guardians
- Brothers and sisters

- One grandparent selected by the young person
- One aunt, uncle or cousin selected by the young person
- A 'buddy', an older child from the school selected by the young person
- A pastoral adult carer from the school selected by the young person (normally, but not necessarily, a teacher)
- A neighbour, sporting coach, parent of a friend or any other adult member of the community selected by the young person as a mentor

Casual Members could include:

- Current teachers of the young person
- Current girlfriend or boyfriend
- Closest mates nominated by the young person
- Professionals brought in by the facilitator or parents (e.g. drug counsellor, employer from an industry in which the young person would eventually like to work)
- The victim of an act of bullying or delinquency and victim supporters

The Circle would commence with the facilitator introducing new members and reading the young person's six-month and long-term life goals as defined by him or her at the last meeting (six months ago). The young person would then be invited to summarise how he/she had got on with the six-month objectives and in what ways his/her life goals had changed in that period. In good circles, this would be followed by a series of celebratory speeches around the circle about what had been accomplished and the efforts that had been made. The crucial skill of the facilitator would be to elicit affirmation for accomplishment and offers of help (as opposed to criticism) when there was a failure of accomplishment. Gathering together for the ritual is all the communal signalling needed to show that accomplishment matters; personal criticism on top of this is only likely to foster rejection of the value of accomplishment. Indeed, through the ritual interpretation of poor accomplishment as a communal failure to give a young person the help they need, young people are less likely to interpret poor performance as reason for rejection by those they initially identify with. Rejection of the rejectors and devaluing accomplishment is less likely when there is a community of care who share the burden to build accomplishment come what may—unconditional support.

Normally, expert adults relevant to the six-month life goals would then be invited to comment (the mathematics teacher on a mathematics improvement goal; the school counsellor on improving relationships). Members of the Circle who had undertaken to provide agreed help towards those goals would be asked to report on whether they had managed to deliver it (Auntie Pat reporting whether they had managed to get together for an hour a week to help with maths homework).

In light of this discussion, the young person would be asked his/her thoughts on goals for the next six months and others would be invited to comment on this topic.

The facilitator would then ask the young person first, then all other participants, if they saw any other challenges in the young person's life where care and support might be needed. Whether new goals were needed to respond to these challenges would be discussed.

If no one else raised it, the facilitator would ask the young person and then his/her peers: 'Do your friends and other kids at school help you to achieve your goals or do they sometimes tempt you to do the wrong thing?' Responses to this are discussed by everyone and suggestions for action might be raised.

The facilitator then announces a tea break during which relevant sub-groups (e.g. the nucelar family, the young person's mates) might meet together informally to

244   *Oxford Review of Education*

discuss a plan of action to propose to the Circle. Everyone is asked to think during the break about whether any new objectives or plans should be considered after the break.

The Circle reconvenes to discuss these issues and ends with the young person reading out his/her new goals and the names of members who have agreed in some way to provide help or support towards them. An adult member should be nominated as responsible for ensuring specific and important things be done on time. The facilitator checks that these adult members are happy to take on these obligations. The meeting is closed with thanks to the participants for their care and citizenship.

Over the years, the emphasis on the Circle would shift from educational and relationship challenges to the challenge of securing employment. With young people who were not doing well at school, special efforts would be made by the Core Members of the Circle to bring in Casual Members who might be able to offer work experience, advice on skill training and networking for job search.

A RITUAL OF LOVE

The foregoing makes the Circle seem a dry affair—rather like an expanded parent-teacher interview. For it to change lives, however, it would have to break out of this formal bureaucratic mould to become a ritual of caring in the way good restorative justice circles work. The literature on restorative justice conferences shows that love is central to understanding what makes them succeed. Nathan Harris's (1999) research on Canberra conferences concludes that reintegration (as opposed to stigmatisation) of offenders is critical to success. The attitude item with the highest loading on the reintegration factor in a factor analysis of offender attitudes toward the conference was 'During the conference did people suggest they loved you regardless of what you did?' In court cases, this item had the lowest loading on the reintegration factor of all the reintegration items. In short, the feeling by the offender that they were in receipt of unconditional love seems acrucial ingredient for the success of circles. And so, we hypothesise, with the Youth Development Circle.

The key ingredient for social capital formation that neither good education systems nor dysfunctional families can adequately supply is love. In conditions of modernity, even functional families lack sufficient ritual occasions to communicate how deeply they care about the child and how much they admire her efforts to develop her capacities. The rituals we do have—weddings, funerals, graduation, bar mitzvahs—are too few in the life of moderns. Village life had various low-key rituals around the campfire to compensate for this. Moderns must create new rituals of love and care that are meaningful in amodern setting and that can transmit modern endowments for success in life. This is the idea of holistic Youth Development Circles.

THEORY OF WHY YOUTH DEVELOPMENT CIRCLES MIGHT SUCCEED

There is a lot of failure in existing programmes to deal with youth problems such as poor school performance, hatred of the school as an institution, truancy, bullying, drop-out, drug abuse, delinquency, suicide, homelessness and unemployment. They fail because they approach young people as isolated individuals. Youth development circles would not aspire to treat isolated individuals targeted because of their problems (and thereby stigmatising them as individuals). They would seek to *help young people develop* in the context of their communities of care. The help would not stigmatise as it would be provided universally to young people in a school, not just to the problem students. The young people themselves would be empowered with a lot of say over who those supporters would be. Circles would be amo ve to find something better than seeking to solve educational problems by one-on-one encounters with the school counsellor, drug problems by individual encounters with rehabilitation services, employment by one-on-one interviews at job placement services, youth suicide by public funding of psychiatrists. Certainly, one of the aspirations of circles would be to embed choices to opt for such rehabilitative services in networks of support that build commitment to make them work. But the aspiration is bigger than that.

Cultures of disadvantage are grounded in failures of families and peers with whom young people are most strongly bonded to value and nurture learning. Regular out-of-school help with things as simple as reading stories improves literacy. The accumulated evidence of the discipline of criminology is that social support is one of the strongest predictors of crime prevention (Cullen, 1994). The research on bullying in schools shows that it can be halved by restorative whole-school approaches grounded in utilising the social bonds that operate across asc hool (Olweus, 1993). The evidence from studies of successful job searches is that one-on-one job placement services are less important than access to personal networks of knowledgable people who care enough about the unemployed person to help them with leads, contacts and introductions (Granovetter, 1974). Informal networking seem to be no less the stuff of getting professional, technical and managerial jobs than of blue collar jobs (Granovetter, 1973, p. 1371). Crucial elements of social capital, such as trust and trustworthiness, are learnt in trusting relationships. Yamagishi and Yamagishi'swo nderful Japanese programme of trust research shows that trust builds social intelligence, that you have to learn to take the risk of trusting others to learn how to make wise judgements about who is trustworthy (Yamagishi, 2000). It is this kind of social intelligence that makes young people employable. Human and social capital, in short, are constituted by informal circles of social support. The theory of Youth Development Circles is that an institutional infrastructure would be created to foster the emergence of this informal support, that this institutionalisation would also build a citizenship obligation to participate in circles and that the circles would lend ritual power to informal support. Gathering in the Circle creates a sense of an occasion where it is appropriate to raise certain things, to articulate certain emotions of concern or admiration. Heimer and Straffen (1995) have shown that in contexts where those with power are dependent on people who are normally stigmatised, social regulation of those people is inf act highly reintegrative. In their study, hospital staff from intensive care wards treated young black single mothers highly reintegratively—because they were dependent on those young mothers to hang in with their unhealthy babies and take them off the hospital'shand s. The Australian convict colony treated convicts in a highly reintegrative rather than stigmatising way because there was a labour shortage which meant the colony was dependent on convict labour (Braithwaite, 2001). As a result of this reintegration, the convict colony became a low-crime society in the 19th century. The Youth Development Circle is an attempt to lock people into asimi larly reintegrative institutional dynamic. The only way for the citizens in the circle to end the obligations to attend meetings and offer practical help to the young person is to get them into a steady job or a tertiary institution. Stigmatising them, giving up on them, will be seen in the circle as likely to delay that release.

246   *Oxford Review of Education*

ENRICHING CIVIL SOCIETY

Circles might help educate all of our children for democracy itself. Democratic deliberation is learnt, but our society does not teach it to the young. Being a beneficiary of care, of cooperative problem-solving when one is young, may be the best way to learn to become caring, dutiful democratic citizens as adults. Such citizens who are creative in co-operative deliberation not only build strong democracies but are also able workforces which attract investment (see Putnam, 1993). The hidden curriculum of Youth Development Circles would therefore be giving the young the literacy to live in civil society, learning to listen, to accommodate the perspectives of others in setting their own goals. Democracy cannot flourish without citizens who are educated for excellence in governing their own lives (Barber, 1992). Youth Development Circles are in sum an idea for deliberative education that democratises education as it serves as an education for democracy.

If a programme of Research and Development of the idea showed that Youth Development Circles did meet some of its aspirations in a major way, it would create a case for a new tripartite view of obligations of citizenship:

1. A citizenship obligation to be the primary supporter of the education and development of any child one parents.
2. A citizenship obligation to be a secondary supporter of more than one child beyond one's own children until infirmity excuses us.
3. An obligation of the state to assign a facilitator to ensure that no child misses the benefits of the obligations in 1 and 2.

These are different from the mostly disrespected obligations to attend Parents and Citizens' Association meetings and bake cakes for them. They are obligations to come along to help aparticu lar child whom they love, to whom they have a professional obligation or who has nominated them as someone the child respects. The citizenship obligation to be a supporter of at least one child should not expire with retirement, only with infirmity. The special wisdom that comes with age incurs a special obligation to spend time with the young for passing on that wisdom to a new generation. As elders have lost their seat at the informal rituals of the campfire, respect for elders has been one of the most unfortunate casualties of modernity. Respect for the elders is the missing cement of modern civil society. Old people feel it and for this reason have enormous untapped reserves of willingness to serve the young.

At the other end of the age spectrum, older buddies of the child are especially important. Buddy selection should be driven by a combination of the child's preference for another she identifies with and by the objective of matching children with weak endowments with buddies having the strongest endowments. This is a strength of weak ties argument (Granovetter, 1973). The child with a network low in human and social capital is given a bridge into the social capital of the network of the buddy with wonderful endowments. For the highly endowed buddy, who has few problems at school, a central issue in her own circle becomes setting objectives about helping her younger buddy to succeed—learning to lead, learning to be a builder of civil society. Endowed children would be taught in the circle how to mobilise their own networks to help less endowed buddies—partly through observing how adult leaders mobilise networks to help *them*. The key idea of the circle is that generational help begets help as a dynamic in civil society.

THINKING ABOUT R & D ON YOUTH DEVELOPMENT CIRCLES

In a sense R & D has already been under way since 1991 as restorative justice circles rather like these have been operating in Queensland schools to deal more narrowly with delinquency and behaviour problems (Cameron & Thornborne, 2000). The preliminary evidence is most encouraging (Braithwaite, 1999).

The first priority with R&D more specifically focused on Youth Development Circles would be disadvantaged high schools. Success there could lead on to pilots in primary schools and high schools that are not disadvantaged. Preliminary trials should be qualitative and process oriented. Experimentation would be needed with different ways of running Circles, different invitation lists, different kinds of follow-up, different kinds of training for facilitators. Evaluation measures would have to be piloted.

Then perhaps 10–20 volunteer pilot schools might learn how to manage Youth Development Circles for at least 50 students. An independent review committee might then report to government on whether the preliminary R & D to that point was sufficiently encouraging to proceed with random assignment of say 2000 Year 8 students, 1000 to Youth Development Circles, 1000 to traditional parent-teacher interviews. Each school would then be able to compare at least 50 Circle students with 50 students who continue with traditional parent-teacher interviews. Randomisation would ensure that the two groups were identical in all respects except the Circle intervention.

Data would be collected from these 2000 students (with informed consent from students and parents) annually on:

- School marks
- Self-reported enjoyment of school and learning
- Truancy
- Bullying and victimisation by bullies
- School-reported behaviour problems
- Drop-out
- Employment after drop-out
- Strength of family bonds
- Homelessness
- Self-reported drug use
- Self-reported suicide proneness and depression that predicts actual suicide and attempted suicide (though statistical power may not be sufficient in the latter case even over 10 years for 2000 cases)
- Self-reported delinquency
- Police-recorded delinquency

The process of monitoring these outcomes should continue until evidence of failure or success is clear. Clear failure can be revealed quite quickly under this methodology. Clear success on unemployment reduction would require ade cade of follow-up for 12-year-olds.

At any point during this decade, it might be decided that the accumulated weight of the evidence was sufficient to resource the program beyond the experimental schools. In the first instance, these might be volunteer schools invited to innovate on improving the successful experimental protocol.

248   *Oxford Review of Education*

WHY THE COST OF YOUTH DEVELOPMENT CIRCLES MIGHT BE SELF-LIQUIDATING

Youth Development Circles would be costly. The biggest costs would be born privately by the citizens who gave time to the Circles, to being mentors to young people, to helping them find jobs, to helping them with their science experiments. A cadre of Youth Development Facilitators would also be a substantial burden on the public purse. The off-setting saving on both fronts from replacing parent-teacher interviews would be modest.

However, the offsetting economic benefits of having a more employable workforce, a more socially skilled and committed workforce, might be massive in comparison. The most obvious benefits are with those children who have cost the criminal justice and youth welfare system over a million pounds by the time they are teenagers by virtue of their delinquency and drug abuse. As a universal programme Circles would seek to give problem-free children the social support to set themselves ever-higher goals for excellence, to discover that it might not be uncool after all to be a 'try-hard'. The hope is for enhanced economic performance by nurturing innovation and accomplishment at the top of the curve as well.

The intangible benefits of job creation through acquiring more innovative business leaders with enhanced social intelligence and educational accomplishment acquired as a result of Circles would be impossible to measure, except through the crude proxy of how wealthy these individuals are ten years on. However, the reduced levels of crime, drug abuse and unemployment among 1000 experimental children compared to 1000 control children over 10 years of follow-up could be readily costed and measured against the cost of running the Circles for those 1000 children.

CULTURAL PLURALISM IN IMPLEMENTATION

Obviously there would be great cultural variation in the appropriate ways of implementing Youth Development Circles. One of the depressing things about working on new approaches to tackling unemployment through education or nurturing capital investment in some other way is that they invariably seem more feasible in rich nations than in the poorest nations where investment is most needed. The institutional innovation therefore becomes another way the gap is widened between rich and poor nations. Youth Development Circles are a rare case where the reverse may be true. We have assumed the worst in our analysis—that there exists no village that can be mobilised as a resource to raise a child. But of course in the poorest of nations there are still villages. Creative institutional design might link human and social capital development to persisting extra-familial networks. These networks might be harnessed as an underexploited comparative advantage of pre-modern societies in modern conditions of capital formation.

I will use Bali as a brief case study for two reasons. First, some readers will be familiar with the culture because it is a tourist destination. Second, it is an extreme case of the comparative advantage I have in mind since modernisation came so late to Bali. Due to its lack of good ports, the Dutch did not bother colonising the southern half of the island until 1906. In Bali *every* citizen is a member of a banjar, the traditional social hub of village life. This has been true since at least AD 914 (Eiseman, 1990, p. 72). The banjar is both a physical meeting place and a social organisation for cooperative work groups, education, Hindu religious instruction[3], family and community health planning, management and conservation of the environment and various other cooperative efforts in a village. But even in the large city of Denpasar everyone belongs to a banjar. Indeed Eiseman (1990, p. 88) reports that banjars do such a good job of both adult and child literacy training that there are some banjars in Denpasar without a single illiterate member.

That said, things are far from rosy in Bali, especially with the collapse of the tourist industry in the wake of the Indonesian instability since 1997. While banjar-level commitment to basic education in literacy and Hindu teaching is high, motivating high levels of formal education, constant innovation to find more efficient practices to traditional economic activities (in agriculture for example) often is not the stuff of banjar enthusiasm. Yet surely if the Indonesian state wants to enthuse the populace of Bali about encouraging their children into higher levels of educational accomplishment, into a learning-innovation culture, then the banjar stands ready as the vehicle for accomplishing that. In the Bali context, banjars could graft Youth Development Circles as a banjar institution, and this might give them more clout in human and social capital formation than could ever be hoped for in Western cities.

CONCLUSION

Youth Development Circles are a policy idea to address the dual structural problem of human/social capital formation in late modernity. This is that (a) intergenerational ties that compensated for human and social capital deficits of the nuclear family have unravelled and that (b) formal education bureaucracies cannot compensate for such deficits when they are informal, when they are about love and dependent on intimate circuits of endowment-building beyond the school. This is best accomplished by bringing into a circle around the young person a combination of those she most loves and those she most identifies with—in the hope that the latter will in time come to count among those she loves and those who most encourage her to strive for her goals. It is a hope for a world where funerals become rituals that honour us not only for the care we have extended to our children, but also for the love and help we have granted to children in circles, children we have embraced into our own family, friendship and economic networks, particularly during old age. The idea is to multiply the meaning of care and intimacy in a life through better institutional sharing of the burden of parents during their period of peak load by asking peers and older citizens to work harder at passing on their wisdom during the periods when their burdens of care are lowest. In turn, if Circles succeed in extending ripples of love, we might hope that when children blossom into young adults some might share some of the burdens of care for the old folk who have shown love to them. At both ends, this might help relieve the inequitable burdens of care currently born by post-motherhood women.

The programme we are proposing would not be cheap. Problems such as youth crime and drug abuse involve a staggering cost to the community and there is encouraging evidence now from meta-analyses that educational development may have a significant impact on these problems (Pearson & Lipton, 1999). Moreover, Youth Development Circles are a type of programme that is amenable to random assignment of a sufficiently large number of cases to assess readily measurable costs (such as salaries) and benefits (such as crime reduction) with impressive statistical power. Hence, a government bold enough to spend an eight-figure sum on a decade of R&D would be in a position to ascertain with a high degree of confidence whether my hypothesis that benefits would

250   *Oxford Review of Education*

far exceed costs is wrong. The magnitude of the policy objective of upgrading human and social capital might justify the boldness of the experimentation proposed.

ACKNOWLEDGEMENTS

My thanks to Brenda Morrison for helpful comments on this paper.

NOTES

[1]   One alternative kind of program that seeks to confront this challenge is the Responsible Citizenship Program in Canberra schools. It invites parents and supporters of children to participate in a process that makes conflict resolution an explicit part of the school curriculum. The program's hidden curriculum is building responsible citizenship (see Morrison, forthcoming). Another is the Lewisham Primary School connect project in Sydney (Blood, 1999).
[2]   And in doing so we do not seek to devalue existing approaches to building school–community, professional–public partnerships for problem solving, such as those mentioned in the last footnote.
[3]   Non-Hindu banjar members are excused from these aspects of banjar obligations.

REFERENCES

BARBER, B.R. (1992) *An Aristocracy of Everyone: the politics of education and future of America* (New York, Oxford University Press).
BLOOD,P. (1999) *Good Beginnings: Lewisham Primary School Connect Project* (Sydney, Lewisham Primary School).
BRAITHWAITE, J. (1999) Restorative justice: assessing optimistic and pessimistic accounts, in: M. TONRY (Ed.) *Crime and Justice: a review of research*, Vol. 25, pp. 1–127.
BRAITHWAITE, J. (2001) Crime in a Convict Republic, *The Modern Law Review*, 64, 1, pp. 11–50.
BRAITHWAITE, J. (forthcoming) *Restorative Justice and Responsive Regulation* (New York, Oxford University Press).
BURFORD, G. & PENNELL, J. (1998) *Family Group Decision Making Project: outcome report Volume I.* (Newfoundland, St. John's; Memorial University).
CAMERON,R . & THORNBORNE,M . (2000) Restorative justice and school discipline— mutually exclusive?, in: H. STRANG & J. BRAITHWAITE (Eds) *Restorative Justice and Civil Society*.
CHAN, WAI YIN (1996) Family conferences in the juvenile justice process: survey on the impact of family conferencing on juvenile offenders and their families, *Subordinate Courts Statistics and Planning Unit Research Bulletin*, February (Singapore).
CULLEN, F.T. (1994) Social support as an organizing concept fo criminology: Presidential address to the Academy of Criminal Justice Sciences, *Justice Quarterly*, 11, 4, pp. 527–59.
DOWRICK, S. (1993) New theory and evidence on economic growth and thir implications for Australian policy, *Economic Analysis and Policy*, 23, 2, pp. 105–121.
EISEMAN, F.B. (1990) *Bali: Sekala and Niskala, Volume II* (Singapore, Periplus Editions).

ELLIOTT, D.S. (1998) *Blueprints for Violence Prevention* (Boulder, Institute of Behavioral Science, University of Colorado).

FINN REPORT (1991) *Young People's Participation in Post-compulsory Education and Training* (Canberra, Australian Government Publication Service) p. 151.

FORSYTHE, L. (1995) An analysis of juvenile apprehension characteristics and reapprehension rates, in: *A New Approach to Juvenile Justice: An Evaluation of Family Conferencing in Wagga Wagga*, edited by David Moore, with Lubica Forsythe and Terry O'Connell, A Report to the Criminology Research Council (Wagga Wagga, Charles Sturt University).

FUKUYAMA, FRANCIS (1995) Trust: the social virtues and the creation of prosperity (New York, Free Press).

GRANOVETTER, M .S. (1973) The strength of weak ties, *American Journal of Sociology*, 78, pp. 1360–1380.

GRANOVETTER, M.S. (1974) *Getting a Job: a study of contacts and careers* Cambridge, Mass.; Harvard University Press).

HAGAN, J. & MCCARTHY, B. (1997) *Mean Streets: youth crime and homelessness* (Cambridge, Cambridge University Press).

HARRIS, N. (1999) Shame and Shaming: An Empirical Analysis. PhD dissertation, Law Program, Australian National University, Canberra.

HEIMER, C.A. & STRAFFEN, L.R. (1995) Interdependence and reintegrative social control: labeling and reforming 'inappropriate' parents in neonatal intensive care units, *American Sociological Review*, 60, pp. 635–54.

LAFREE, G . (1998) *Losing Legitimacy: street crime and the decline of social institutions in America* (Boulder, Co., Westview Press).

LASCH, C. (1977) *Haven in a Heartless World* (New York, Basic Books).

LATHAM, M. (1998) *Civilising Global Capital: new thinking for Australian labor* (St. Leonards, Australia, Allen and Unwin).

MCCOLD, P. & WACHTEL, B. (1998) *Restorative Policing Experiment: the Bethlehem Pennsylvania Police Family Group Conferencing Project* (Pipersville, PA, Community Service Foundation).

MORRISON, B.E. (forthcoming) From Bullying to Responsible Citizenship: a restorative approach to building safe school communities (Melbourne, Australian Council for Educational Research).

NUGENT, W.R. & PADDOCK, J.B. (1995) The effect of victim-offender mediation on severity of reoffense, *Mediation Quarterly*, 12, 4, pp. 353–67.

OLWEUS, D. (1993) Annotation: bullying at school: basic facts and effects of a school based intervention program, *Journal of Child Psychology and Psychiatry*, 35, pp. 1171–90.

PATE, K. (1990) Victim-offender restitution programs in Canada, In: B. GALAWAY & J. HUDSON, *Criminal Justice Restitution and Reconciliation* (New York, Willow Tree Press).

PEARSON, F.S. & LIPTON, D.S. (1999) "The Effectiveness of Educational and Vocational programs: CDATE Meta-Analyses", Presentation to the American Society of Criminology Meeting, New York.

PUTNAM, R.D. (1993) *Making Democracy Work: civic traditions in modern Italy* (Princeton, NJ, Princeton University Press).

SAMPSON, R .J. & LAUB, J.H. (1993) *Crime in the Making: pathways and turning points through life* (Cambridge, Ma., Harvard University Press).

252   *Oxford Review of Education*

SAMPSON, R. & RAUDENBUSH, S.W. (1999) Systematic social observation of public spaces: a new look at disorder in urban neighbourhoods, *American Journal of Sociology*, 105, pp. 603–651.

SCHNEIDER, A. (1996) Restitution and recidivism rates of juvenile offenders: results from four experimental studies, *Criminology*, 24, pp. 533–52.

SHERMAN, L., GOTTFREDSON, D., MACKENZIE, D., ECK, J., REUTER, P. & BUSHWAY, S. (1997) *Preventing Crime: what works, what doesn't, what's promising: a report to the United States Congress*, (Washington, D.C., National Institute of Justice).

UMBREIT, M., WITH COATES, R. & KALANJ, B. (1994) *Victim Meets Offender: the impact of restorative justice and mediation*, (Monsey, New York, Criminal Justice Press).

WYNNE, J. (1996) Leeds Mediation and Reparation Service: ten years experience with victim-offender mediation, in: GALAWAY B. & HUDSON J. *Restorative Justice: International Perspectives*, (Monsey, NY, Criminal Justice Press).

YAMAGISHI, T. (2000) Trust as a form of social intelligence, in: K. COOK (Ed.), *Trust in Society*, New York, Russel Sage).

ZELIZER, V. (1993) *Pricing the Priceless Child*, (New York, Basic Books).

Correspondence: Professor John Braithwaite, Law Program, Research School of Social Sciences, The Australian National University, Canberra, ACT 0200, Australia.

[20]

Punishment and the changing face of the governance

CLIFFORD SHEARING

University of Toronto and University of the Western Cape, South Africa

Abstract

The article explores the implication of shifts in the way in which security and justice are being conceived. It argues that the emergence of a logic of risk is refiguring the way in which punishment is being used as a tactic of governance.

Key Words

crime · punishment · regulation · security

INTRODUCTION

This article will consider the implications of shifts in the governance of security for the use of punishment as a regulatory strategy. I use governance in the Foucaultian sense to mean intentional 'efforts to guide and direct the conduct of others' (Simon, 1997: 174; see, for example, Foucault 1982: 220). By the governance of security I refer simply to efforts intended to create spaces within which people can live, work and play safely. My focus is on efforts to ensure that bodies are not hurt and that goods are not misappropriated. My concern is narrower than either criminal justice or social security.

In using the phrase 'the governance of security', rather than the more established term 'policing', I am distancing myself from conventional ways of thinking about security. I do so in order to bring into view features and developments within the regulation of security that the language of 'criminal justice' tends to elide.

In the analysis to follow, I will attempt, in the words of Ulrich Beck, to: 'move the future which is just beginning to take shape into view against a still dominant past' (1992: 9). I will do this by reciting three emblematic stories that illustrate contrasting ways of thinking about the regulation of security. The first parable expresses a 'backward-looking' (Packer, 1968) approach to security (and justice) that focuses attention on violent punishment as a device for expiating the harm and pain the violations of security have created. The second parable expresses a 'forward-looking' orientation that directs attention away from the past towards the promotion of security in the future.

The third, which will be presented later in the article, will be used to present an alternative to the preoccupation with the past presented within the first story.

PARABLES

My first parable is a wonderful Kantian tale[1] by a great storyteller, and a fellow southern African, Doris Lessing (1991 [1987]: 9–10).

> There was once a highly respected and prosperous farmer ... in the old Southern Rhodesia, now Zimbabwe, where [Lessing] grew up ... The farmer ... decided to import a very special bull from Scotland ... He cost £10,000 ... [I]t was a very large sum for the farmer ... A special home was made for him ... He had his own keeper, a black boy of about twelve. All went well; it was clear the bull would soon become the father of a satisfactory number of calves ... Then he suddenly and quite inexplicably killed his keeper, the black boy.

> Something like a court of justice was held. The boy's relatives demanded, and got, compensation. But that was not the end of it. The farmer decided that the bull must be killed. When this became known, a great many people went to him and pleaded for the magnificent beast's life. After all, it was in the nature of bulls to suddenly go berserk, everyone knew that. The herd boy had been warned, and he must have been careless. Obviously, it would never happen again ... to waste all that power, potential, and not to mention money – what for?

> 'The bull has killed, the bull is a murderer, and he must be punished. An eye for an eye, a tooth for a tooth,' said the inexorable farmer, and the bull was duly executed by firing squad and buried.

> [In commenting on this series of events, Lessing notes, that] what [the farmer] had done – this act of condemning an animal to death for wrong-doing – went back into the far past of mankind, so far back we don't know where it began, but certainly it was when man hardly knew how to differentiate between humans and beasts.

> [Lessing goes on to note how] tactful suggestions [not to execute the bull] from friends or from other farmers were simply dismissed with: 'I know how to tell right from wrong, thank you very much.'

My second story expresses a very different way of thinking about the governance of security, one in which the moral concerns that dominated the first story are replaced with more instrumental and pragmatic ones.

> A large steel company in Canada was losing portable power tools – drills, saws, sanders, and the like – because of employee theft. The Chief Executive Officer (CEO) was concerned about the size of the loss and what it was doing to the company's profits. So he called in his Director of Security and asked him to come up with a solution to this problem. Like many directors of security in the mid-1980s, this person was an ex-police officer who had taken up work in private security as a second career. He had changed his institutional location but had not changed his way of thinking – he still thought and acted like a police officer. This mind-set was reflected in his response to the CEO's request. At their next appointment, he presented a plan to the CEO. He proposed that the company hire undercover officers who would spy on the workers and discover who was stealing power tools. On an appointed day workers would be searched as they were leaving the plant and the evidence collected, in conjunction with the evidence collected during the undercover work, would be used to provide direction and justification for

searching workers' homes. Based on the evidence collected, charges would be laid and the offending workers would appear in court and be sentenced and then punished for their thefts. After presenting his proposal, the Director sat back to bask in the glow of his CEO's praise. To his surprise, and then dismay, he found that the CEO was not happy with the plan at all. Instead he looked at the Director and asked him if he was crazy. From the plan, he said, it was clear to him that the Director had no understanding of the community within which he worked and what its values were. To make his point the CEO drew out the implications of the Director's proposal for the company. What was being suggested, the CEO noted, was that the company should hire undercover agents and then pay for the Director and others in the security department to use the evidence the agents had collected to help the police lay charges. At the conclusion of the court process the company would lose the workers charged either because they would be imprisoned or he would be obliged to fire them. These workers, the CEO pointed out, were people who the company had spent a lot of money training. As the company would now be short staffed it would have to spend money advertising for new employees and then train the ones hired. These new employees, he pointed out, were undoubtedly going to be just as likely to steal from the company as the ones who had left. The whole process would likely reduce morale within the company and this would probably have an effect on productivity. This would likely also harden attitudes within the union and that this would make the forthcoming salary negotiations more difficult than they would otherwise have been. The net result of the Director's 'solution' was that the company would lose a lot more money. Whatever the costs of the tool losses this was likely to be doubled or tripled as a consequence of the actions the Director was proposing. The CEO turned to the Director and said that in fact he knew how he could save a lot of money – he could fire the Director. Before deciding to do so, however, he was prepared to give the Director a week to come up with an alternative proposal. He suggested that the Director recognize that the company was in the business of making, not losing, money.

This shook the Director up and the prospect of imminent unemployment concentrated his mind. As he reflected on the situation he began to think that perhaps the employees who were removing tools from the plant were not bad people after all – they were perhaps simply parents, wives and husbands who had repairs to do on their homes, toys to build, and so on. They needed tools and the company had tools. The problem is that they did not know how to ask the company to borrow them so they just took them. Moreover, once they had taken them they did not know how to bring them back. This line of thinking radically changed the way he saw things and new solutions came to mind. By the time his appointment with the CEO came around he had a new proposal. He proposed that the company do nothing whatsoever about the tools that had been taken – what was gone, was gone. However, the company should do something about what happened from then onwards. What they should do, he suggested, is open a tool library that would enable employees to take tools home in the evenings and on the weekends and then bring them back. This time the CEO smiled a big broad smile and the Director found that his next paycheque was a little bigger than his previous one. Our Director had imagined an alternative to the established way of doing security.

TWO MORALITIES

Both these stories are concerned with the governance of security. However, each story gives expression to a different mentality with a different sense of morality and justice (Ewald, 1991). The first, while it takes place on a farm rather than in a court room, illustrates a denunciatory, retributive mode of thought that has been central to criminal justice within Anglo-American societies – a way of thinking that, as Lessing suggests in her own analysis, has proved to be remarkably resilient. Lessing's farmer's focus was on the past and what might be done to undo the harm that had taken place. He felt that while the material things that had taken place might possibly go some way to compensate the family of the boy for their loss, there was a moral dimension to what had happened that extended beyond this. More was required. A symbolic, societal order had been violated that needed to be put right. A 'mystical balance' – a moral equilibrium symbolized by the scales of justice – had been upset that had to be corrected (Zehr, 1990: 74). Until this correction was accomplished, neither he, nor the others would be able to 'go on' with their lives in a normal way. Something extraordinary had happened that needed an extraordinary symbolic response before the ordinary state of affairs could be recovered and ordinary life continued. Justice had to be done. This required a sacrifice that would expiate the wrong – the bull had to be killed. The scales upset by the extraordinary had to be levelled before things could be normalized. This 'reasoning springs from a moral vision of the world' (Ewald, 1991: 202) in which 'justice' and what it required was independent of, and a precondition for, the governance of security. Within this way of thinking utilitarian purposes (and the moral sensibilities associated with them) are admissible only to the extent that they can be integrated with denunciatory and expiatory ones.

Herein lies a source, and perhaps even *the* source, of the centrality of punishment to criminal justice. The tight coupling of a retributive morality and instrumental concerns that underlies Lessing's farmer's motivations is possible in practice because punishment can be utilized to provide for both the regulation of the past and of the future. Punishment, and the violence that so often accompanies it, has been central to criminal justice because it can be used symbolically to expiate the past and prevent future wrongdoing. Punishment, and the pain associated with it, provides for the simultaneous accomplishment of these goals.

The mentality that infuses the second story is quite different. In this story, punishment is not accorded any special privilege. Our CEO is deeply sceptical of the claim that the wrongs of the past must be symbolically corrected before one can 'go on'. For him the past should be left to take care of itself. It needs no rectifying. There is no problem of 'going on'. This future-focused logic, like the logic of insurance, 'proposes a quite different idea of justice' (Ewald, 1991). One acknowledges the past and understands how it was produced so that one can turn one's back on it and create a different future – tools were being stolen, what was required was to reduce the likelihood of this happening in the future. It was the future, and only the future that concerned him. Efforts devoted to reordering the past made no sense to him. Indeed, he viewed a concern with expiation and denunciation as counter-productive – it would make the future worse not better. Rather than allowing one to go on, by providing for closure, they keep the past alive, maintained its grip on the present, and thus, on the future. His response to the logic and morality of retribution that pervades criminal justice was not that it should be improved but that it should be abandoned.

In summary, what distinguishes the mentalities that infuse each of our stories is the priority they give to the problems of the past and to the future. For Lessing's farmer, it is the past and its symbolic order that must, in the final analysis, be determinant. For our CEO, it is 'colonisation of the future' (Giddens, 1991: 111), and the morality this entailed, that should carry the day.

Although our farmer's views about which ordering problem should have priority have been central to the governance of security within Anglo-American societies, this emphasis is increasingly being questioned and contested (see Marinos, 2000). It is to this challenge and the search for alternatives that I now turn.

RISK-FOCUSED SECURITY

Recently, Ulrich Beck (1992) has argued that our contemporary social context is fundamentally different from the one that was dominant only a few decades ago – he terms this context the 'risk society'. Beck in developing this argument, observes that: 'Just as modernization dissolved the structure of feudal society in the nineteenth century and produced the industrial society, modernization today is dissolving industrial society and another modernity is coming into being' (1992: 10). An implication of Beck's argument is that an essential difference between yesterday's world and today's risk society is that yesterday we could, and did, act on the assumption that if things went wrong we would be able to remedy them. If we did not have the knowledge, or the capacity, to do so at the moment this was something that future generations would be able to resolve. This way of being is no longer viable. Modernization has created conditions that have put our collective future, indeed the possibility that we will have a future at all, at risk. We are creating problems that neither us, or our offspring, may be able to solve. We cannot, and increasingly do not, assume that the problems humanity is creating will be ones it can resolve. We can no longer assume that the future will be 'OK'. The point of Beck's argument is nicely captured by Giddens when he writes that it: 'is not that day-to-day life is inherently more risky than was the case in prior eras. It is rather that, in conditions of modernity . . . thinking in terms of risk and risk assessment is a more or less ever-present exercise . . .' (1991: 123– 4).

This concern with risk is giving rise to a new mode of living. Instead of going ahead, doing things, and then coping with the problems this might create, when they arise, we now seek to anticipate problems and avoid them. An obvious example of this risk-based way of thinking is the way in which we seek to anticipate and avoid the possibility of a nuclear accident occurring. With such an accident and other similar potential problems, we do not adopt an attitude in which we are willing to risk the problem occurring knowing that we will be able to cope with it when and if it does.

As a consequence, while it is certainly true that a concern with risk is as old as humanity itself, we are today organizing our lives around risk and the development of risk reduction strategies to an unprecedented extent, and so a qualitative rather than a simply quantitative shift has occurred. We live in a risk society in which risk technologies have acquired a new priority. Associated with this is a new risk mentality. This new mentality promotes a concern with the discovery and application of new and innovative ways of coping with the present in ways that will ensure that we will be able to enjoy a future.

Beck (1992), in developing his arguments for the emergence of a risk society, develops somewhat different, but compatible arguments. He argues that there has been a fundamental shift in the central problem of modern society from one of wealth production to risk management. As human beings have sought to respond to the 'dictatorship of scarcity' they have created a new set of problems – 'the sources of wealth are "polluted" by growing "hazardous side effects"' (1992: 20). While these problems are not new their nature and extent makes them qualitatively different. Beck summarizes his argument in his definition of risk:

> Risk may be defined as a systematic way of dealing with hazards and insecurities induced and introduced by modernization itself. Risks, as opposed to old dangers, are consequences that relate to the threatening forces of modernization and to its globalization of doubt. (1992: 21)

Whether one accepts either Giddens' or Beck's account of the reasons for the contemporary concern with risk, their contention that we live in a society in which risk and its management occupies a central place in human affairs is persuasive. This concern with risk, and the emergence of strategies and associated institutions for coping with them, is being felt across the many and varied arenas of governance. One of these is security, where risk-focused modes of governing are emerging.

Seen from the perspective of this analysis, what our CEO was advocating was a risk-based approach to security that argues that his company can no longer afford the luxury of a mode of management that focuses attention on the past. The message of our CEO to his Security Director was: 'Hey, your insistence that we fix the past is going to put us out of business, and thereby deny us a future, so get going and make sure we as a company do what is required to secure a future for ourselves.'

There is nothing 'soft' about this risk-focused approach to the governance of security. It is not designed to make things easier or better for people who cause problems. Neither is it 'hard'. Rather it seeks to move away from this way of thinking about security entirely. Its concern is not what risk reduction will mean for individual offenders or victims. Instead, the whole victim–offender dichotomy is eclipsed. Its focus is on populations and opportunities (see Ewald's (1991: 206) discussion of insurance).

At this point, it is useful to shift gears and turn to Foucault's thoughts on the 'art of government'. Foucault, working from very different premises, and within a very different theoretical framework from Giddens and Beck, draws attention to a similar shift in governance. He identifies a shift to an art of governance, which he refers to as 'governmentality' (which he uses to reference both the idea of mentalities of governance generally and a particular way of thinking about governance). He describes this particular mentality of governance as a way of governing that seeks 'the right disposition of things arranged so as to lead to a convenient end' (1991: 93). He elaborates on this idea of the governing things as follows:

> The things which in this sense government is to be concerned are in fact men, but men in their relations, their links, their imbrication with those other things which are wealth, resources, means of subsistence, the territory with its specific qualities, climate, irrigation, fertility, etc.: men in their relation to that other kind of things, customs, habits, ways of acting and thinking, etc., lastly, men in their relation to that other kind of things, accidents and misfortunes such as famine, epidemics, death, etc. (1991: 93)

Law within this governmentality promotes a disposition of things.

> [I]t is a question not of imposing law on men, but of disposing things: that is to say, of employing tactics rather than laws, and even laws themselves as tactics – to arrange things in such a way that, through a certain number of means such and such ends may be achieved. (1991: 95)

Within this mentality law becomes a device or procedure for accomplishing a way of doing things that will promote security.

Our CEO sought to respond to risk, as Beck has outlined it, by employing a governmentality that sought to provide for a distribution of things that would minimize hazards and insecurities. Seen in this light what our CEO was insisting upon was a government of things. The logic he encouraged his Security Director to embrace was one that looked to the most appropriate way of arranging things so that the end of security, understood as loss prevention, would be realized. In recognition of this focus on 'things' Ronald Clarke (1995) has termed this way of governing security a situational approach. This situational focus is not simply a future-oriented strategy. The focus within this approach is not on persons per se but on modifying the situations within which they act to encourage behaviour that is consistent with the end of security. The world is conceived as an assemblage of sites to be modified to encourage more appropriate action from people whose natures are accepted as given. Persons and their propensities are accepted as they stand. Attention is not only directed away from a concern with the past but from future-oriented strategies that seek to rehabilitate people.

As O'Malley notes, this way of governing security is not:

> concerned with the meaningful activities of individuals, involving intentions, motivations, understandings, guilt, fault, etc. . . . Instead, its focus is on the distribution and effects of behaviours – in the sense of 'external' physical dispositions rather than 'internal' states . . . [I]t seeks to develop ways of manipulating risk bearing behaviours in order to increase security. (1998: xii)

Within this risk-logic (see Feeley and Simon's (1994) discussion of 'actuarial logic' as a form of risk-thinking), punishment no longer has the privileged status it has hitherto enjoyed as a device that can be employed to simultaneously remedy the past and colonize a future. What makes punishment a useful governing strategy is not the pain it causes but its utility as a way of compelling a particular distribution of things. It has no special priority. It is simply one possible device among many for disposing of things to promote the realization of security. Within this logic, violence, as a source of risk reduction, is attractive only to the extent that it incapacitates (or deters). Within the morality of a risk-logic, its attractiveness as a source of denunciation and expiation disappears.

As deterrence (both specific and general) is now viewed with increasing suspicion because of the difficulty of ensuring certainty of detection (a problem that has been recognized since Bentham), what remains is the value imprisonment holds as a source of incapacitation. However, within this mentality imprisonment ceases to be viewed as punishment and becomes instead a vehicle for keeping dangerous people in a situation in which their potential to harm others is minimized. One does not imprison to be just (as is the case within a retributive logic) – one imprisons because prisons provide an existing, and hence convenient, space within which to keep dangerous people out of harm's way.

Prison, as Feeley and Simon (1994: 174–5) suggest, becomes explicitly a place for warehousing troublesome things. Within this framework, the focus of prison reform becomes to reshape them so that they can cost-effectively meet an incapacitative objective. In

Ontario, Canada for example, the Government has decided that the best way to do this is to close down small prisons designed to promote rehabilitation and replace them with mega-prisons whose principal official purpose will be to warehouse potentially dangerous bodies.

While this shift in thinking and language is beginning to become increasingly evident within the political and policy arenas of state governments, it has long been established within arenas of private governance. Here, the terms policing and police have been replaced by 'security' (both as a noun and a verb) and crime has been replaced by a variety of context-specific terms, the most common of which is 'loss' (in recognition of this Simon, 1997, has suggested that we distinguish between 'governing through crime' and 'governing through security'). This, as the argument to this point suggests, is not just a matter of semantics. It denotes a different way of constructing and thinking about people as things in relation to things. Crime mobilizes a framework that brings to the fore questions of intention and blame. Loss collapses what crime distinguishes. For example, it refuses to distinguish between events such as theft and accidental rain damage by claiming that, from the vantage point of the 'bottom line', they both come, as one security manager put it, 'straight out of profit'.

This difference is critical in identifying and understanding shifts in the use of punishment as an ordering mechanism. What was critical about our CEO was that he was not operating within a state context. His milieu was what one might think of as a 'corporate community' – a private domain or setting set apart from an encompassing social whole. He did not take his point of reference to be society as a whole. He acted within a community context. He saw the world as fractured rather than as one piece (Rose, 1996). There are several implications of this that are worth noting.

The first is the comfort our CEO quite obviously felt with the mentality of governing through risk. This resonated with the culture of management and the logic of the market-place with which he was already familiar. He simply brought his normal problem-solving repertoire and implicit 'business morality' to bear on the problem of security. His security problem was simply another economic problem to be addressed by identifying and mobilizing the appropriate resources. He was, through his training as a business person, already familiar with the idea of promoting 'the proper distribution of things' to achieve a desired end. His complaint about his Director of Security was that he was operating within a logic of criminal justice with its emphasis on denunciation that he felt had no place within his business world. What he required of him was that he stop thinking like a police person and start thinking like a business person.

A second implication is that our CEO was not constrained by a whole set of existing strategies, institutions and practices for doing security that had an affinity with a different mentality. He was not constrained by a series of 'social' technologies. He was thus in a very different position to someone wishing to promote a risk-logic within criminal justice. Consequently, he had relatively little cultural or institutional resistance to overcome. He was able to work from a comparatively clean slate. His situation was thus very different to that of most police managers who typically work within cultural and institutional contexts oriented to goals of ordering that give primacy to punishment as a device for their accomplishment.

Third, our CEO, unlike those who operate within other non-state domains (for example, volunteer organizations), had access to something akin to a tax base that he could draw on to govern security. He had resources to deploy.

It is these and related factors that have enabled persons operating in a variety of corporate settings to govern in the manner advocated by our CEO. A central feature of governance within these contexts is a mentality of risk reduction. While corporate domains are central to the complex network of governance that has emerged alongside state governments, these 'private governments' and the 'bubbles of governance' they create are not limited to business settings narrowly conceived. There are wide ranges of what might be called 'contractual communities' that now pervade Anglo-American societies. These include such spaces as communities of library users, the residential communities that North Americans' term 'gated communities', communities of shoppers at malls as well as virtual communities such as the communities of credit card holders and Internet users. Together, these communities, or arenas of governance, form a complex and expanding archipelago of private governments that together establish what we might term an emerging 'neo-feudalism'.[2]

One of the features of this new feudalism is that the contracts that establish these arenas of governance are, in part, contracts that set out such things as the proper expectations (rights) and responsibilities (duties) of community members. A ubiquitous example is the contract that persons enter into as library users. Most libraries today require, as part of this contract, that members agree to submit themselves to electronic scanning as they enter and leave the book collection. Similar contracts are required if one wishes to fly. At the Toronto airport, this contract is quite explicit. As one enters the area restricted to passengers, one faces a sign that reads: 'You are not required to submit either your bags or your person to a search if you do not wish to board an aircraft.'

In our contemporary world, we move around this archipelago of governance by moving from one contractual community to another. As we do, we move from one bubble of governance to another. Each of these bubbles has its own mode of governance and its own rules (under the umbrella of, and made possible through, state law) that set out the conditions of 'citizenship' or, perhaps more accurately, 'denizenship' in these new spaces of governance.[3]

The logic of risk governance dominates these contractual spaces.[4] Within them, the governance of security tends to take place in the manner advocated by our CEO. Here, the traditional view of punishment as a source of the pain that denunciation and deterrence require has increasingly given way to risk-based strategies. The strategies of governance within this archipelago are very different from those advocated by Lessing's farmer. They are worlds apart. Within the world of our CEO, the established notions of justice have little meaning. Here, punishment is not a central practice of governance. Where violence is deployed this is typically not because of its denunciatory potential but because of its usefulness in governing security (Rigakos, 1999).

These contractual spaces are, of course, not the only spaces in which people live their lives. While some people spend more time within these spaces than others do (almost everyone spends part of their time in them), the poor spend most of their time outside these bubbles. A risk-logic has developed both inside and outside these neo-feudal bubbles of governance. What differentiates them is the extent to which this logic has taken hold of thinking and the way in which it has done so.

RISK AND THE STATE

The logic of risk has, over the last decade or two, begun to penetrate the spaces and institutions of the state in ways that are fundamentally refiguring criminal justice. Two features of these developments are significant for the argument being developed here. First, it is important to recognize that a renewed risk emphasis – risk has always been a feature of state policing especially with respect to what used to be thought of as the 'dangerous classes' – within criminal justice has not led to an abandonment of other ways of thinking about and regulating security. Rather, these ways of being have been, and are being, moulded and adapted to fit within a risk-focused mentality. Habits of mind and action that were developed within the context of a logic of denunciation and deterrence are acquiring new meanings and functions under the influence of a logic of risk – the use of prisons as warehouses to incapacitate people, noted above, provides one example. As Feeley and Simon note:

> Possibly, the clearest indication of actuarial justice is found in the new theory of incapacitation, which has become the predominant model of punishment. Incapacitation promises to reduce the effects of crime in society not by altering either offender or social context, but by rearranging the distribution of offenders in society. If the prison can do nothing else, incapacitation theory holds, it can detain offenders for a time and thus delay their resumption of criminal activity in society. (1994: 174)

The second point to note is how the rebirth of private governments that has accompanied the emergence of a risk logic has enabled the development of elaborate networks of security institutions that include both state and non-state resources (Johnston, 1992, 2000). This possibility has permitted agencies within the state to graft risk strategies located within non-state spheres of governance onto their own endeavours. As Bayley and I have argued (1996: 588), the central feature of community policing is the attempt by the police to build partnerships and networks that position the police and non-state entities as 'co-producers of public safety'. In exploring this development, Ericson and Haggerty (1997) have recently identified the many ways in which state police have organized themselves as brokers who operate the knowledge conduits that networked policing requires.

In developing these partnerships, states typically seek to take advantage of the logic and institutions of non-state sites of governance and to direct their operations in a manner that enables them to 'rule at a distance' (Rose and Miller, 1992). In the networks of security that these partnerships have established – in which the state seeks to maintain control of the 'steering' of governance while encouraging others to accept responsibility for the 'rowing' (Osborne and Gaebler, 1993) – the pattern that has emerged is one in which state agents seek to co-ordinate the available regulatory resources while preserving states' claims to a monopoly of violence. There are now many examples of this strategy within the policing arena. Perhaps the most ubiquitous are neighbourhood watch and safe house schemes in which citizens are encouraged to become the eyes and ears of the police and to call upon them when a coercive response is required to preserve order.

What is being encouraged through these developments is a division of labour in which the state remains a key source of security through its access to violence, while non-state resources are mobilized to establish security networks that operate according to risk management principles. Among the clearest indicators of this is the difference between the security strategies employed within the new feudal domains that the emergence of 'mass private property' has established – for instance the security practices within places like Disney World – and the way in which poor neighbourhoods are policed through the use of target hardening strategies by police agencies and by private security agencies contracted to state agencies (Rigakos, 1999).

One possible consequence of this emerging risk framework one would expect to find is changes in the legal framework within which security operates to permit the application of risk strategies by the state and its partners. Some evidence of this exists, for instance in the United States, in recent court decisions that permit the use of coercive resources within a risk framework. Simon and Feeley draw attention to this when they write that:

> [g]overnment action against criminal activity, even when mixed with traditional punitive functions, is increasingly subject to a different constitutional standard because instead of emphasizing the goals of public justice, it emphasizes the goals of risk management. It is preventative rather than responsive. It seeks not to punish but to exclude those with criminal proclivities. It is directed not at a general public norm but at security within a specialized and functionally defined area (1994: 185).

Of course, states and their agents must frequently contend with the fact that other participants of the networks that they are part of and seek to manage may, and often do, view things differently. These others frequently seek to mobilize networks, including state agents, to do their bidding. The result is that security networks have become sites of contest as participants with different aims seek to mobilize the resources available to promote their objectives. Thus, for example, one finds a host of private governments calling the police only when it suits them and doing so in ways that will fit them into a framework of risk reduction even though the police themselves might be operating within a punitive stance of moral ordering. This is evident, for instance, in the ordering of financial markets by private regulators where although the objective is very clearly the instrumental ordering of the future the law is often invoked to initiate prosecutions when this is viewed as beneficial from the perspective of risk reduction (Addario et al., 1990). This incidentally provides another example of the way in which institutions that operate within a justice framework co-ordinate their activities with institutions that operate within a security-logic (O'Malley, 1992; Simon, 1997).

RETRIBUTION AND RISK

Where states remain either exclusive participants in providing security or are able to shape security networks in accord with their ends, the problem of finding redress for past wrongs tends to be given greater weight than is the case in non-state spheres of governance. Where police have taken charge of a case, they remain likely, if the evidence permits, to follow a retributive logic and to set in motion processes that will give this logic concrete expression. Accordingly, while our CEO might have little difficulty insisting that attention be focused exclusively on the future, this proves to be more difficult within the context of state institutions, where, as the term 'criminal justice' reminds us, a concern with ' doing justice' (where justice is understood in expiatory and retributive terms) remains a priority. To the extent that this is true, and participants are operating within what Zehr (1990) calls the 'retributive paradigm', a tension arises between the dictates of a risk logic, as it gains influence, and the requirements of criminal justice. Although corporate victims, like the shareholders our CEO represents, may have little interest in seeing retributive justice done because they have not been directly involved in the harm that took place, this is less true of individual victims. These victims, who continue to mobilize the criminal justice processes through reports to the police of wrongdoing, are more emotionally involved and less sanguine about the idea of leaving the past to take care of itself. For them, the problem of responding to the past is more pressing. Their concerns and feelings tend to be closer to those of Lessing's farmer than they are to those of our CEO.

In recognition of this, a significant movement has emerged under the rubric of 'restorative justice' which seeks to establish a way of doing justice that will challenge, and it is hoped eventually replace, the conception of justice that lies at the heart of the retributive paradigm. This shift has its roots, like the risk shift, within the world of business in the institutions and practices of tort law and the development of mediation as a mechanism for dispute resolution (Auerbach, 1983: 95–7).[5] Restorative justice seeks to extend the logic that has informed mediation beyond the settlement of business disputes to the resolution of individual conflicts that have traditionally been addressed within a retributive paradigm. It seeks to find ways of responding to the anger and hurt of victims in a manner that does not lead to the punishment, stigmatization and exclusion that have characterized the operations of criminal justice. This rejection of the retributive paradigm resonates with the concerns of our CEO and the morality embedded within them. The difference is that restorative justice proposes a response that acknowledges the importance of symbolically reordering the past.

RESTORATIVE JUSTICE
Once again, a story, this time from John Braithwaite, articulates the essential features of the nature of, and the argument for, restorative justice.

> [Imagine that a teenager is arrested for robbery. Braithwaite calls him Sam. Instead of sending him to court the arresting officer] refers Sam to a facilitator who convenes a restorative justice conference. When the facilitator asks about his parents, Sam says he is homeless. His parents abused him and he hates them. Sam refuses to cooperate with a conference[6] if they attend. After going through various obvious possibilities the facilitator concludes that there is enough of a positive connection between Sam, his Uncle George, his older sister and his hockey coach to have them attend a conference. So, they and the robbery victim and her daughter are invited to a conference. [They all attend and] sit on chairs in a circle. The facilitator starts by intro-ducing everyone and reminding Sam that while he has admitted to the robbery, he can change his plea at any time during the conference and have the matter heard by a court. Sam is asked to explain what happened in his own words. He mumbles that he needed money to survive, saw the [woman] knocked her over and ran off with her purse. Uncle George is asked what he thinks of this. He says that Sam used to be a good kid. But that Sam had gone off the rails. He had let his parents down so badly that they would not even come today. 'And now you have

done this to this poor lady. I never thought you would stoop to violence,' continues Uncle George, building into an angry tirade against the boy. The hockey coach also says he is surprised that Sam could do something as terrible as this. Sam was always a troublemaker at school. But he could see a kinder side in Sam that left him shocked about the violence. The sister is invited to speak, but the facilitator moves to the victim when Sam's sister seems too emotional to speak.

The victim explains how much trouble she had to cancel the credit cards in the purse, how she had no money for the shopping she needed to do that day. Her daughter explains that the most important consequence of the crime was that her mother was now afraid to go out on her own. In particular, she is afraid that Sam is stalking her, waiting to rob her again. Sam sneers at this and seems callous throughout. His sister starts to sob. Concerned about how distressed she is, the facilitator calls a brief adjournment so she can comfort her, with help from Uncle George. During the break, the sister reveals that she understands what Sam has been through. She says she was abused by their parents as well. Uncle George has never heard of this, is shocked, and not sure that he believes it.

When the conference convenes, Sam's sister speaks to him with love and strength. Looking straight into his eyes, the first gaze he could not avoid in the conference, she says that she knows exactly what he has been through with their parents. No details are spoken. But the victim seems to understand what is spoken of by the knowing communication between sister and brother. Tears rush down the old woman's cheeks and over a trembling mouth.

It is the sister's love that penetrates Sam's callous exterior. From then on he is emotionally engaged with the conference. He says he is sorry about what the victim has lost. He would like to pay it back, but he has no money or job. He assures the victim he is not stalking her. She readily accepts this now and when questioned by the facilitator says now she thinks she will feel safe walking out alone. She wants her money back but says it will help her if they can talk about what to do to help Sam find a home and a job. Sam's sister says he can come and live in her house for a while. The hockey coach says he has some casual work that needs to be done, enough to pay Sam's debt to the victim and a bit more. If Sam does a good job, he will write him a reference for applications for permanent jobs. When the conference breaks up, the victim hugs Sam and tearfully wishes him good luck. He apologises again. Uncle George quietly slips a hundred dollars to Sam's sister to defray the extra costs of having Sam in the house, says he will be there for both of them if they need him.

Sam has a rocky life punctuated with several periods of unemployment. A year later he has to go through another conference after he steals a bicycle. But he finds work when he can, mostly stays out of trouble and lives to mourn at the funerals of Uncle George and his sister. The victim gets her money back and enjoys taking long walks alone. Both she and her daughter say that they feel enriched as a result of the conference, [they] have a little more grace in their lives. (1996: 3–4)

Restorative justice, as Braithwaite's story exemplifies, promotes a conception of justice that seeks to restore relationships without a resort to exclusion and the other costs that our CEO found so problematic. While the advocates of restorative justice do not tend to draw attention to its compatibility with the use of a risk-logic in colonizing the future, this is one of its consequences. The logic of restorative justice fits easily with that of risk.

Restorative justice seeks to refigure the ordering of security through processes that shift the meaning of events from one of contesting and 'disputing selves' to one in which the contestants are restored to the status of 'non-disputing selves' who are once again in

PUNISHMENT AND SOCIETY 3(2)

a position to get on with the business of living together (Pavlich, 1996). What is significant about this approach to justice is that, unlike the conception constructed within the retributive paradigm, it fits more easily with the aims and premises of a risk-based approach to security.

What the emerging techniques of restorative justice provide is a 'moral vision' that fits with, and reinforces, the instrumental logic of risk security. This provides opportunities for the development of a symbolic, past-oriented approach that is compatible with the instrumental, future-oriented logic of risk management. This link, although central to many of the programmes of restorative justice that have emerged, is often overshadowed by the attention given, by their advocates, to shaming as a device for doing justice. Consequently, the opportunities to integrate explicitly the restorative and risk-logics often are not taken. However, what is evident in most of these programmes is that in practice the outcomes that result typically include the development of community-based surveillance networks that mobilize local resources to monitor and control the future behaviour of the wrongdoer. This is particularly evident in the variety of forms of 'community service' that wrongdoers contract to undertake as part of the mediation process. A central feature of such service is often that it places the risky person under the surveillance of both state and non-state persons who contract to assist in preventing a reoccurrence of wrongdoing.

One of the reviewers asked whether I would 'speculate some as to why citizens who are privately involved with the kind of private social control oriented towards prevention and actuarial justice nonetheless retain a commitment to retributive justice'. The argument the article develops is that people are most comfortable with regulatory strategies that simultaneously provide for both 'behavioural and symbolic ordering' (Addario, 1990). It is precisely because punishment accomplishes this that it has been so resilient. The article suggests that an integration of risk-based and restorative strategies might provide a basis for establishing a more explicit coupling of behavioural and symbolic ordering strategies than is typically the case in the mentality exemplified by our CEO. Marinos (2000) presents attitude survey and interview data that suggest that both judges and citizens are, at present, more comfortable applying a risked-based logic to property offences but prefer punishment, because of its denunciatory and retributive features, for violent offences. The question this article poses is whether this might be changed.

The reviewer just cited goes on to note that:

> actuarial justice seems to spurn the kind of individualized requalification and emotional work emphasized by restorative justice. Is it really likely that criminal justice institutions can institutionalize both? Can restorative justice provide a source of public satisfaction that tends to be missing from actuarial justice?

My hunch is that it may well be possible to 'institutionalize both'. However, I share the reviewer's scepticism about whether this can be done within the institutions of criminal justice. In my view, the integration that I am suggesting might be possible will require innovations that I suspect are most likely to be discovered outside of criminal justice (for a discussion of some of these possibilities see Braithwaite, 2000).

Ewald (1991) in considering whether the 'moral vision' of 'judicial reasoning' can be integrated with the 'insurer's calculation' suggests that this will require a rethinking of 'justice'. In making this suggestion, Ewald challenges the idea that insurance is a purely factual rather than a moral logic. Insurance, he argues, 'makes it possible to dream of a contractual justice where an order established by conventions will take the place of natural order' (1991: 207). In rethinking justice in ways that permit an integration of past and future-focused strategies of governance, restorative justice offers a promising starting point.

CONCLUSION

I have argued that a risk-logic has emerged that is reshaping the governance of security within both state and non-state terrains. Existing institutions and habitual practices are shaping this risk-logic. This is particularly apparent within the state sphere where the institutional forms and practices that developed in association with a retributive logic have operated to shape the manner in which a risk mentality is realized.

In examining this shift in governance, I have explored its relationship to established concepts and practices of justice. I argued that justice, understood within the context of the reordering of the past, was much less of a concern within non-state arenas, where corporate victims are central, than it was within the state sphere where individual victimization is more significant. Within non-state governance of security, an instrumental approach, that implicitly calls forth a different sense of justice, tends to predominate. Within this instrumental focus, a moral framework, while present, tends to remain in the background. This contrasts with the situation within the public realm. Within this sphere not only is justice a central question in the ordering of security, but the retributive paradigm that tends to predominate does not fit well with the way of thinking advocated by a risk mentality. This tension is being lessened where the mentality and practice of restorative justice is taking hold within criminal justice. What is not yet clear is how these developments will shape the way in which risk is conceived and understood as it is integrated with other mentalities.[7]

Each of these developments has implications for the use of punishment within the governance of security. In both a risk-oriented mentality of security and a restorative conception of justice, punishment loses its privileged status as a strategy to be deployed in the ordering of security. This does not mean that it has been eclipsed as a strategy, but rather that it is considered as one means among others to be used in the governance of security. Further, in both these mentalities, the mechanisms of coercion within criminal justice come to be seen less as a device for inflicting pain and more as a set of resources to be considered in reducing risk.

If the mentalities identified in this article continue to gain ground, this will have very significant implications for the way in which punishment is used and justified within the governance of security. Just how the tensions between different paradigms for thinking about and doing security and justice will be worked out will depend on the outcomes of the many experiments that are taking place around the world in both public and private arenas. The patterns of ordering that we will live with in the future will be shaped through practice rather than philosophical discourses which will, like Hegel's (1836) 'owl of Minerva', take flight only after the new practices are themselves beginning to shift yet again.

My hope is that as we explore these new practices that we will do so in ways that give voice to the knowledge and concerns of the poor and the marginalized as well as the rich and the powerful.

Acknowledgement

I would like to thank David Garland and the three anonymous reviewers for their very helpful comments and suggestions. I am grateful to Sebastian Scheerer for drawing to my attention the significance of distinguishing between citizens and denizens.

Notes

1 See Kant's (1996: 474–5) discussion of the 'law of retribution' and the fable of an island whose residents 'decided to separate and disperse throughout the world' but insist nonetheless on executing the 'last murderer remaining in prison' before doing so.
2 I use this term in a limited sense to draw attention to the emergence of domains of mass private property that are 'gated' in a variety of ways.
3 I am grateful to Sebastian Scheerer for drawing to my attention the significance of distinguishing between citizens and denizens.
4 This is not true of all such spaces. As one reviewer pointed out private schools and certain social clubs adhere to past-oriented strategies. This raises questions as to what determines differences between these contractual spaces. One obvious suggestion is that spaces in which a profit ethic dominates will be more future-oriented. This in turn raises questions about whether all business spaces will be inclined to adopt a future-oriented strategy. For instance is this true of a Japanese business environment?
5 One of the best known forms of restorative justice, family group conferencing, has its direct roots in Maori culture.
6 A conference is a gathering to which the persons affected by the offender's actions and persons significant to him, most importantly his family, are invited to consider his actions and the effects they have had.
7 Ewald's discussion of the play that exists between a mentality and the practices that give it expression is instructive:

> Insurance institutions are not the application of a technology of risk; they are one of its applications. . . . Insurance technology and actuarial science did not fall from the mathematical skies to incarnate themselves in institutions. They were built up gradually out of multiple practices which they reflected and rationalized, practices of which they were more effects than causes, and it would be wrong to imagine that they have now assumed a definite shape. Existing in economic, moral conjunctures which continually alter, the practices of insurance is always reshaping its techniques. (1991: 198)

References

Addario, Susan, Mary Condon, Clifford Shearing and Philip Stenning (1990) 'Controlling interests: Two conceptions of ordering financial markets', in Martin L. Friedland (ed.) *Securing compliance: Seven case studies*, pp. 88–119. Toronto: University of Toronto Press.
Bayley, David and Clifford Shearing (1996) 'The future of policing', *Law and Society Review* 30(4): 585–606.

Beck, Ulrich (1992) *Risk society: Toward a new modernity*. London: Sage.

Braithwaite, John (1996) 'Restorative justice and a better future', Dorothy J. Killam Memorial Lecture, Dalhousie University, October (manscript).

Braithwaite, John (2000) 'The new regulatory state and the transformation of criminology', *British Journal of Criminology* 40: 222–38.

Clarke, R. (1995) 'Situational crime prevention', in M. Tonry and D. Farrington (eds) *Building a safer society: Strategic approaches to crime prevention*, Vol. 19, pp. 91–150. Chicago, IL: University of Chicago Press.

Ericson, Richard and Kevin Haggerty (1997) *Policing the risk society*. Toronto: University of Toronto Press.

Ewald, Francois (1991) 'Insurance and risk', in G. Burchell, C. Gordon and P. Miller (eds) *The Foucault effect: Studies in governmentality*, pp. 197–210. Chicago, IL: University of Chicago Press.

Feeley, Malcolm and Jonathan Simon (1994) 'Actuarial justice: The emerging new criminal law', in David Nelken (ed.) *The future of criminology*, pp. 173–200. London: Sage.

Foucault, Michel (1982) 'The subject and power', in Hubert L. Dreyfus and Paul Rabinow (eds) *Michel Foucault: Beyond structuralism and hermeneutics*, pp. 208–28. Chicago, IL: University of Chicago Press.

Foucault, Michel (1991) *The Foucault effect: Studies in governmentality*. Ed. Graham Burchell, Colin Gorden and Peter Miller. Chicago, IL: University of Chicago Press.

Giddens, Anthony (1991) *Modernity and self-identity: Self and society in the late modern age*. Oxford: Polity.

Hegel, Georg (1836) *Philosophy of right*. London: George Bell & Sons.

Johnston, Les (1992) *The rebirth of private policing*. London: Routledge.

Johnston, Les (2000) *Policing Britain: Risk, security and governance*. London: Longman.

Kant, Immanuel (1996) *Practical philosophy*. Trans. and ed. Mary J. Gregor. Cambridge: Cambridge University Press.

Lessing, Doris (1991 [1987]) *Prisons we choose to live inside*. Concord, Canada: Anansi.

Marinos, Voula (2000) 'The multiple dimensions of punishment: "Intermediate" sanctions & interchangeability with imprisonment', unpublished Doctoral Dissertation, Centre of Criminology, University of Toronto.

O'Malley, Pat (1992) 'Risk, power and crime prevention', *Economy and Society* 21(3): 252–75.

O'Malley, Pat (1998) 'Introduction', in Pat O'Malley (ed.) *Crime and the risk society*, pp. xi–xxv. Aldershot: Ashgate.

Osborne, David and Ted Gaebler (1993) *Reinventing government*. New York: Plume.

Packer, Herbert (1968) *The limits of the criminal sanction*. Stanford, CA: Stanford University Press.

Pavlich, George (1996) 'The power of community mediation: Government and the formation of self-identity', *Law and Society Review* 30(4): 707–33.

Rigakos, George (1999) 'The new parapolice: Risk markets and commodified social control', unpublished Doctoral Dissertation, York University, Canada.

Rose, Nikolas (1996) 'The death of the social: Refiguring the territory of government', *Economy and Society* 25(3): 327–56.

Rose, N. and P. Miller (1992) 'Political power beyond the state: Problematics of government', *British Journal of Sociology* 43(2): 173–205.

PUNISHMENT AND SOCIETY 3(2)

Simon, Jonathan (1997) 'Governing through crime', in Lawrence M. Friedman and George Fisher (eds) *The crime connection: Essays in criminal justice*, pp. 171–89. Boulder, CO: Westview Press.
Zehr, Howard (1990) *Changing lenses*. Waterloo, Ontario: Herald Press.

CLIFFORD SHEARING is a Professor of Sociology and Criminology at the University of Toronto. He is also a Professor in the School of Government at the University of the Western Cape.

Name Index